Women's Rights

Women's Rights

A *Human Rights Quarterly* Reader

Edited by Bert B. Lockwood

The Johns Hopkins University Press
Baltimore

The Johns Hopkins University Press
2715 North Charles Street
Baltimore, Maryland 21218-4363
www.press.jhu.edu

Library of Congress Control Number: 2005937240

ISBN 0-8018-8373-3 (hardcover : alk. paper)
ISBN 0-8018-8374-1 (paperback : alk. paper)

A catalog record for this book is available from the British Library.

Contents

Introduction

As I begin my twenty-fifth year as editor of the *Human Rights Quarterly*, the Johns Hopkins University Press is issuing the first *Human Rights Quarterly* reader. These readers will bring together articles previously published in *HRQ* on particular topics. We have chosen as the first reader one devoted to the subject of women's human rights. This decision reflects the growing number of courses devoted to this subject and the recognition that *HRQ* has played a cardinal role in publishing scholarship on the topic. Many teachers and activists have urged us to publish such a volume, and I am pleased that the present volume will be of value to their important work.

The purpose of this introduction is to acquaint the reader with the rich array of articles we have pulled together. Space limitations have prohibited us from including in this collection all of the *HRQ* articles on the subject of women's human rights, and forthcoming issues of *HRQ* will also include contributions to this literature. The articles appear as they were first published, and authors have not been asked to revise or update the selections. The articles have been grouped into five sections: History and Perspectives; Religion, Culture, and Women's Human Rights; Violence and Women; Economic Rights; and Reproductive Rights.

In the first part, "History and Perspectives," Arvonne Fraser frames the discussion with a review of six centuries of women struggling internationally for basic human rights. She counsels that much of this history has yet to be written, particularly in the non-Western world. She underscores the importance of an historical account because it is from such efforts that role models and traditions are created. Education is key, and knowledge is the platform for asserting rights to equal citizenship and independence. Fraser charts the drive in contemporary times to the achievement of the UN Convention on the Elimination of All Forms of Discrimination Against Women (CEDAW)—a treaty that weaves together all the ideas discussed during five centuries of debate and that places strong emphasis upon the concept of equality in family matters. It would be errant to assume that the treaty is simply the result of an inevitable march towards women's equality; Fraser's account underscores the importance of concerted activism and struggle—a struggle playing out prominently today across the globe.

Political scientists Margaret Keck and Kathryn Sikkink authored an influential book, *Activists beyond Borders: Advocacy Networks in International Politics* (Cornell University Press, 1998). Chapter 5 in that book, "Transnational Networks on Violence against Women," recounts a dramatic description by Susana Chiarotti, one of the founding coordinators of Indeso-

Mujer in Argentina, of when the issue of violence against women began to crystallize internationally. Someone returning from a meeting in California brought her group Charlotte Bunch's *Human Rights Quarterly* article, "Women's Rights as Human Rights." Chiarotti was the only one in her group that read English, so she read the article, finding in it a new approach to human rights, and a new approach to violence as well. She translated it for other members of her group, telling them, "this is the key to end our isolation." Bunch's powerful and influential article is included as the second reading in this collection.

Professor Gayle Binion explores the ways human rights might be understood if the experiences of women were the foundation for theorizing and enforcement. While there is no singular feminist perspective, Binion posits that if one worked from the life experiences common to most women, the human rights principles that emerged would not necessarily be the universe of human rights commonly understood by liberal nation states. To those states, the classic human rights case is the political activist imprisoned for speech critical of his government. Forms of oppression that do not comfortably fit within a bill of rights framework rarely are recognized in international understandings or in national asylum laws. Such oppression would include issues relating to marriage, procreation, labor, property ownership, sexual repression, and other manifestations of unequal citizenship that are routinely viewed as private, nongovernmental, and reflective of cultural differences.

Law professors Hilary Charlesworth and Christine Chinkin critique the international law doctrine of *jus cogens,* norms deemed so fundamental that nations are not permitted to derogate from them. They assert that the doctrine is not properly universal, as its development has privileged the experiences of men over those of women. Drawing upon Carol Gilligan's findings that boys and girls reason in different ways from early childhood, the authors apply the distinction to *jus cogens.* Whereas girls tend to reason in a contextual and concrete manner, boys reason in a more formal and abstract way. Language used to describe *jus cogens,* such as "guarding the most fundamental and highly valued interests of international society," "expression of a conviction, accepted in all parts of the world community, which touches upon the conscience of all nations," and "the higher interest of the whole international community," reflect masculine modes of thinking, according to the authors. The privileged status of its norms is reserved for a very limited, male-centered category—one that may not be shared by women or supported by women's life experiences.

Fundamental norms designed to protect individuals ought to be truly universal in application as well as rhetoric. They should operate to protect both men and women from those harms they are most likely to suffer. Taking women's experiences into account in the development of *jus cogens* will require a fundamental rethinking of every aspect of the doctrine.

The last chapter in this section is Professor Eva Brems' "Enemies or Allies? Feminism and Cultural Relativism as Dissident Voices in Human Rights Discourse." Brems considers the antagonisms, and the similarities, between feminism and cultural relativism—two of the most vigorous and visible critiques of the dominant human rights discourse. On many issues, feminists and cultural relativists have found themselves on diametrically opposed sides. The manifest successes of feminist views inside the human rights system have sometimes been at the expense of cultural relativist views. Brems argues against such antagonism, asserting that the sides seem close enough to allow for building a bridge between their two strands of thought. Instead of wasting part of their creative potential in opposing each other, feminists and cultural relativists could join forces and combine their insights into a constructive critique of the dominant human rights discourse.

Feminists argue that human rights are not what they claim to be; rather, they are a product of the dominant male half of the world, framed in that language and reflecting male needs and aspirations. Today's "universal human rights," feminists argue, overlook women. Cultural relativists also assert that human rights are not what they claim to be. They argue that human rights are a product of the dominant Western world, and framed in language reflecting Western needs and aspirations. According to cultural relativists, today's "universal human rights" are still foreign to non-Westerners, and their argument aims at the rejection of the inclusion of non-Western peoples in the international human rights protection system.

The core of the cultural relativist critique is made up of a "difference" argument, as is feminism. Feminists look at human rights through a gender lens, whereas cultural relativists use the cultural perspective. They clash on issues when their particular perspectives lead to opposite claims and priorities between gender and culture have to be made. For example, to the outsider's eyes certain cultural practices carried out in non-Western cultures might harm or disadvantage women, but these practices are sometimes justified or compensated for by cultural relativists under the wider cultural context.

Neither feminism nor cultural relativism originate in the human rights sphere, but feminists have enjoyed more credibility in the international human rights community than cultural relativists. Part of the explanation for this may be that feminism has been predominantly Western, and therefore more familiar to the dominant Western forces in the international human rights community, and thus viewed as less threatening. Furthermore, cultural relativism also has been employed as a smokescreen by dictatorial regimes to cover up human rights violations.

Even though their strategies differ (feminist critique is offensive whereas cultural relativist critique is defensive), both share several concerns in the critique of human rights. They both agree that human rights should be, as they were intended to be, the rights of all human beings regardless of factors such as gender or culture. The inclusion of all human beings is precisely what the human rights concept is about. However, both sides make clear that universality is not synonymous with uniformity. Real inclusion of all human beings requires attentiveness to their differences.

Part II of this book deals with religion, culture, and women's human rights. Professor Janet Afary explores the state of human rights of Middle Eastern/Muslim women in a selection of North African, Central Asian, and Middle Eastern countries. She contrasts the present state of oppression with the emerging legal reforms and initiatives of a new generation of women's rights activists in these countries. These activists are building new institutions in their homelands despite numerous obstacles and great personal and political risks.

Professor Uche Ewelukwa's chapter, "Post-Colonialism, Gender, Customary Injustice: Widows in African Societies," brings to light the often dire plight of African widows due to customary practices and laws. She focuses particularly on Nigeria and on the tension between customary laws and practices on the one hand, and emerging rights of women on the other. She argues that some customary laws and practices can no longer be justified in a changing Africa. African widows often have no real choices to exercise, and what are often offered as choices have the effect of perpetuating the domination of widows by the male relatives of their deceased husbands. Options such as accepting her husband's brother as a husband, returning to her natal group, or residing with married children do not significantly advance the cause of widows. Ewelukwa calls for a change in the traditional treatment of widows and for the amendment of discriminatory customary laws and practices so that they accord with evolving international human rights standards on equality and nondiscrimination.

Kamala Visweswaran examines recent critiques in feminist theory to explore how gender-based asylum cases and human rights reporting on South Asia rely upon the most static and patriarchal understandings of culture to establish a basis for intervention or advocacy. She argues that while cultural practices indeed reflect upon women's status for gender-based asylum cases, the emphasis may be more effectively placed upon a particular political system's denial of women's rights, or upon the interface between culture and the political system, rather than upon culture itself.

Part III focuses upon the subject of violence and women. It begins with Professor Ustinia Dolgopol's article on the "comfort women"—the estimated 150,000–200,000 women who were coerced into sexual slavery by the Japanese military during World War II. The history of the comfort women is the story of voices being denied and suppressed. When this issue was initially raised, the Japanese government denied that "comfort stations" had been officially sanctioned. The status of women in Japan and elsewhere enabled such actions to be undertaken with impunity. In most countries making up the Allied forces, rape convictions were difficult to secure, and women were often blamed for having brought rape upon themselves. This prevailing attitude resulted in the forced silencing of comfort women, leading to years of emotional and psychological suffering.

Despite the knowledge of what happened to these women, the Allied forces and their respective governments remained silent, thereby compounding the harm. It has taken enormous courage for the women to tell their stories and to provide details of their experiences. One of the most dramatic moments during the 1993 Vienna World Conference on Human Rights was the testimony of comfort women at the Women's Tribunal at the NGO proceedings. However, little is known about what happened to the thousands of women at the close of the war, as only a few hundred of them have ever come forward.

Dolgopol argues that the Allies Forces should accept some responsibility for reparations, due to their failure to address the crimes perpetrated by the Japanese against the comfort women. Silence can be a form of aiding and abetting, and the Allies' silence has contributed to the ongoing suffering of these women. It is the responsibility of all of us to ensure that due recognition is given to human rights violations committed against women, and to take steps to prevent their continuation.

In "Women, War, and Rape: Challenges Facing the International Tribunal for the Former Yugoslavia," Catherine Niarchos reviews the history of rape in war and the manner in which international law has dealt with this subject. Although evidence of rape was presented at Nuremberg, the resulting convictions did not specifically deal with rape. Writing at the beginning of the Yugoslav War Crimes Tribunal, Niarchos powerfully builds the case for specifically including prosecution for rape, and urges the Tribunal to recognize the opportunity to treat rape as the gender-motivated crime of violence that it is.

Todd Salzman's chapter also deals with sexual assaults during the Bosnia-Herzegovina war that is the subject of the International War Crimes Tribunal in the Hague. During this conflict an estimated 20,000 women endured sexual assaults in the form of torture and rape. Although these atrocities were committed by all sides of the warring factions, by far the greatest number of assaults were committed by the Serbs against Muslim women, though Catholic Croats were targeted as well. While in past conflicts rape was considered an inevitable byproduct of war, and thus was largely ignored when it came to punishing the perpetrators, the Bosnian conflict brought the practice of rape with genocidal intent to a new level, causing an outcry among the international community. Evidence suggests that these violations were not random acts carried out by a few dissident soldiers. Rather, this was an assault against the female gender, and violating the female body and its reproductive capabilities was used as a weapon of war. Serbian political and military leaders systematically planned and strategically executed this policy of ethnic cleansing or genocide, with the support of the Serbian and Bosnian Serb armies and paramilitary groups, to create a "Greater Serbia": a religiously, culturally, and linguistically homogenous Serbian nation.

The chapter examines two main issues. First, it investigates the Serbs' systematic use of rape camps with the specific intent of impregnating their victims, along with the cultural, political, and religious foundations that supported this usurpation of the female body. Second, the chapter examines the "secondary victimization" of these women through stigmatization by religious community and the insensitivity of the media, in addition to well-meaning humanitarian groups.

Professor Charli Carpenter also examines the question of genocidal rape during the ethnic conflict in the former Yugoslavia, but in a strikingly different fashion. She unpacks the feminist legal argument of rape as genocide and demonstrates how that "victory" actually resulted in overlooking another significant class of victims. Because of the moral opprobrium encompassing genocide, a premium was placed on characterizing the Serbian policy of the forced impregnation of Bosnian Muslim women and the resulting births as genocide. To fit within the definition of genocide, the consequence of a policy must be the destruction, in whole or in part, of a group. Ironically, this entailed that feminists accept the Serbian argument that the children born of the rape by Serbian soldiers of Bosnian Muslim women take the identity of the father. This legal discourse was framed to identify the children with the perpetrators of the genocide, rather than with the victims. The unfortunate result was that the plight of war-rape orphans escaped notice.

The chapter brings to light the situation of war-rape orphans, and explains the legal framework in which to assess their plight and to suggest redress. It asks the questions: Does international law govern child victims of the ethnic violence in the former Yugoslavia? If so, who are the perpetrators? What form of redress is necessary or appropriate? What specific rights are violated, if any, when a child is forcibly and intentionally conceived in a context that precludes her from acceptance by her family, identity with a community, or access to resources?

The current prevailing international law framework is capable of supplying only partial answers to these questions, due to the inadequacy of international law to address children's rights in general. Even within the narrow scope of available approaches to children's rights in international law, articulating the rights of these particular children constitutes a unique challenge because it complicates several of the givens in international legal theory, including the concept of genocide itself.

Thankfully, international law finally recognizes genocidal rape as one of the most horrendous acts imaginable. However, the current understanding of forced impregnation as genocide is arguably too limited in scope. While, strictly speaking, forced impregnation and forced maternity are crimes solely against rape victims, defining rape as genocide fuses this violation of women's rights with ethnic genocide—a complex manipulation of identity and group cohesion that involves many affirmative acts beyond that of the rape and conception itself.

To reverse the trends of failing to account for the children in this "forced impregnation" definition of crime against women and of identifying the child of these rapes with the perpetrators, Carpenter attempts to situate war-rape orphans in the existing framework of the Geneva and Genocide Conventions, allowing them to emerge as victims of human rights abuses and war crimes. It may be necessary to develop new ways of conceptualizing crimes against children in armed conflict if we accept that children born of genocidal rape are also its victims. The very inadequacy of existing legal and theoretical approaches may prove the biggest barrier to addressing and redressing children's human rights in genocidal conflicts.

Anthropologist Sally Engle Merry, in "Rights Talk and the Experience of Law: Implementing Women's Human Rights to Protection from Violence," considers how a woman can come to understand her problems in terms of rights. This is a critical problem for the battered women's movement as well as for other human rights movements that rely on rights awareness to encourage victims to seek help from the law. The adoption of a rights consciousness requires experiences with the legal system that confirm that subjectivity. Rights-defined selves emerge from supportive encounters with police, prosecutors, judges, and probation officers. This empirical study shows how victims of violence against women come to take on rights consciousness.

In "Used, Abused, Arrested, and Deported: Extending Immigration Benefits to Protect the Victims of Trafficking and to Secure the Prosecution of Traffickers," Professor Dina Haynes examines the problem of human trafficking. Organized crime rings exploit 700,000 to 4 million new victims of human trafficking each year, typically luring them across borders where they are more vulnerable to abuse. Trafficking in Southeastern Europe is a relatively new phenomenon, fuelled by the dissolution of the former Soviet Union as well as the presence of international peacekeepers who have sometimes exacerbated the problem. The two main anti-trafficking models emphasize either the prosecution of the trafficker or the protection of the victim, but neither adequately addresses immigration options that could serve to protect the victim and provide better evidence with which to prosecute the traffickers for their crimes.

The fourth part of this book considers economic rights and women. Professor Clair Apodaca's chapter, "Measuring Women's Economic and Social Rights Achievement," notes that in recent years, empirical research in the field of human rights predominantly focused upon civil and political rights. Economic and social rights, due to the lack of sufficiently valid and reliable measures, have received far less scholarly attention. Similarly, although women's rights have been the focus of scholarly concern, scant consideration has been paid to empirical, cross-national studies on women's economic and social rights. The primary purpose of this chapter is the building of an index with which to measure and evaluate women's equitable realization of their economic and social rights.

The CEDAW Committee noted the importance, and relative absence, of disaggregated and precise indicators on the situation of women. The Committee remarked that statistical information is absolutely necessary to understand the situation of women in each of the states that are party to the treaty. The Committee's General Recommendation No. 9 requests that states make every effort to collect and provide appropriate data on the situation of women. Sex-differentiated data is extremely useful in assessing compliance with provisions in both CEDAW and the Economic and Social Covenant that mandate nondiscrimination and equality of treatment between men and women.

The studies cited in this chapter show that geographical regions determine, in large part, gender inequality and the attainment of economic and social rights. The question of why geographic region should significantly affect women's human rights, however, is not answered. Cultural factors also appear to be very important in explaining variations in the realization of women's human rights. Each region of the world has specific shortcomings.

The relationship between the economic development of a country and women's status is likewise important. The findings lead to the conclusion that economic development increases women's realization of their economic and social rights. Women benefit from the economic development of their country, because their share of the economic pie enlarges. Statistical information is essential to furthering our understanding and assessment of the life situation of women, and of furthering governmental compliance with nondiscrimination and equality of treatment treaty provisions.

The second chapter in this section is Bharati Sadasivam's "The Impact of Structural Adjustment on Women: A Governance and Human Rights Agenda." It is now well established that structural adjustment and stabilization policies (SAPs) undertaken in developing countries receiving condition-based loans from the World Bank and the International Monetary Fund

(IMF) have exacerbated conditions of poverty and deprivation for large sections of the population. It has also been shown that these macroeconomic policies are not class-neutral or gender-neutral, even though they are presented in language that appears to be so. In reality they have a male bias, and they do not affect all sections of the population equally.

Specialized UN agencies have pointed to the increasing human and economic inequalities caused by market-driven growth, and stressed the need to protect the vulnerable—women in particular—from marginalization. There is now a vast and growing volume of literature that not only shows how the gender bias in neoclassical economic theory renders the effects of SAPs on women invisible in any standard measures of policy evaluation, but that also provides empirical evidence of the heavy transitional costs of adjustment on women.

Extreme poverty affects women differently and often more severely than men. Although not uniformly the case, it is clear that women are the shock absorbers of adjustment efforts, at immense cost to their own well-being. It is widely documented that adjustment policies tend to leave large segments of the poor poorer in the short run. It therefore follows that women, who form the great majority of the world's one billion absolute poor, are overwhelmingly affected by these policies. The author argues that the disproportionate cost of adjustment borne by women violates their rights to development guaranteed in international conventions, and makes SAPs unsustainable in the long run.

As powerful development actors deciding the fate of millions, the World Bank and the IMF have governance obligations. Institutions such as these cannot entirely escape their share of responsibility even though, according to international law, the fulfillment of human rights obligations is primarily the responsibility of individual state governments that have accepted these obligations.

The differential impact of structural adjustment on women has come to the attention of those who design and implement economic reform programs. The goal of gender advocacy is to transform economic policymaking so that the human rights dimensions of SAPs are considered in the design stage of the programs, and not as a postscript. Through sustained feminist scholarship and unflagging activism, women's advocates have gained the authority and credibility to influence UN documents—and thereby some national governments and international financial institutions—to reflect gender and poverty concerns in economic policymaking.

Professors Rebecca Cook and Bernard Dickens lead off Part V, "Reproductive Rights," with their chapter "Human Rights Dynamics of Abortion Law Reform." The legal approach to abortion is evolving from criminal prohibition toward accommodation as a life preserving and health preserving option, particularly in light of data concerning maternal mortality and morbidity. The modern momentum for liberalization results from international adoption of the concept of reproductive health, and wider recognition that access to safe and dignified health care is a major human right. Respect for women's reproductive self-determination legitimizes abortion as a choice when family planning services have failed, have been inaccessible, or have been denied due to rape. Recognition of women's rights of equal citizenship with men requires that their choices for self-determination be respected legally, not criminalized.

Professor Siobhán Mullally provides a case study of this subject in her chapter "Debating Reproductive Rights in Ireland." While women's reproductive autonomy has gained limited recognition at the international level, this recognition has been difficult to secure, and remains contentious. Mullally examines the struggle for reproductive autonomy within the context of the abortion debate in Ireland, where reproductive rights particularly and women's rights generally often have been portrayed as hostile to cultural and national sovereignty. The entanglement of religious and nationalist principles with the struggle for reproductive autonomy in Ireland demonstrates the ways in which gender identities and roles are given greater or lesser weight depending on their "fit" with state interests and the ongoing process of nation-building. Lost within these negotiations and compromises is a recognition of the universal legitimacy of women's human rights claims.

Carmel Shalev looks at the interaction between China and the expert committee set up under CEDAW over China's one-child population policy. In "China to CEDAW: An Update on Population Policy" the author notes that China's population policy had raised questions in prior CEDAW committee proceedings, and that there continues to be concern, particularly over coercion employed in the implementation of this policy. Coercive measures are targeted primarily at women, and include both economic sanctions and physical violence. These measures continue to be utilized by local officials in violation of women's rights, and these violations are condoned by the Chinese government through its failure to take any action against the wrongdoers.

Even though information on violations of human rights in China is largely anecdotal due to restrictions on freedom of press and freedom of association, the anecdotes point to a consistent pattern of official actions that constitute violations of China's treaty obligation. CEDAW's concerns about China's birth control policy include: the resulting imbalance in the sex ratio; the increase in bride-selling and trafficking of women because of the shortage of marriageable women; harmful rural practices associated with son preference, such as sex-selective abortions, female infanticide, and the abandonment and nonregistration of female babies; forced reproductive interventions (sometimes performed by unskilled workers under unhygienic conditions), and the resulting discriminatory effect on women's mental and physical health; the lack of women's autonomous right to decide freely and responsibly the number and spacing of her children; the administrative sanctions that result from this population policy; the fact that contraception and family planning is overwhelmingly made the women's responsibility (only 14 percent of men use contraceptives, and in 1992, 95 percent of all sterilizations were tubal ligations, despite the fact that this is a far more complicated, intrusive, and expensive procedure than vasectomy); and concern over the fact that officially nonexistent, unregistered girls are not entitled to education, health care, or other social benefits.

The CEDAW Committee had informed the Chinese government that it should make clear that coercive and violent measures are prohibited, and that it should enforce such prohibitions through fair legal procedures that sanction officials acting in excess of their authority. Rights of due process, whether legal or administrative, are key to respect for human dignity. Shalev notes that the human rights notion of autonomy, human dignity, and privacy in making decisions on intimate matters, such as reproduction and sexuality, free of state interference, is foreign to Chinese culture.

It is our belief that the articles collected in this volume offer the reader a cornucopia of the best literature on women's human rights, and we invite you to continue to follow future developments in forthcoming issues of *Human Rights Quarterly.*

PART I

History and Perspectives

Chapter 1

Becoming Human: The Origins and Development of Women's Human Rights

Arvonne S. Fraser

I. INTRODUCTION

When the Taliban took power in Afghanistan in 1994, one of its first edicts removed girls from school, forbade women from employment outside the home, and required women to wear garments totally covering themselves when they appeared in public. This measure was a clear abrogation of the principles set forth in the Universal Declaration of Human Rights[1] and the Convention on the Elimination of All Forms of Discrimination Against Women.[2] It struck at the most basic of women's human rights, depriving them of economic, physical, and intellectual independence, and overturned what women internationally had been struggling to achieve for more than five centuries.

As John Stuart Mill argued in 1869 in his essay, *The Subjection of Women,*[3] the question is whether women must be forced to follow what is perceived as their "natural vocation," i.e. home and family—often called the private sphere—or whether, in private and public life, they are seen as the equal partners of men.[4] While the division of spheres, based on sex and known as patriarchy, may have been justified as a necessary division of labor in the early evolution of the human species, the system long ago out-lived its functionality and has been challenged by women, and a few men, since, at least, the fifteenth century.

---

1. Universal Declaration of Human Rights, *adopted* 10 Dec. 1948, G.A. Res. 217A (III), U.N. GAOR, 3d Sess. (Resolutions, part 1), at 71, U.N. Doc. A/810 (1948), *reprinted in* 43 Am. J. Int'l L. Supp. 127 (1949) [hereinafter UDHR].
2. Convention on the Elimination of All Forms of Discrimination Against Women, *adopted* 18 Dec. 1979, G.A. Res. 34/180, U.N. GAOR, 34th Sess., Supp. No. 46, U.N. Doc. A/34/46 (1980) (*entered into force* 3 Sept. 1981), *reprinted in* 19 I.L.M. 33 (1980) [hereinafter CEDAW].
3. John Stuart Mill, The Subjection of Women (M.I.T. Press 1970) (1869).
4. *See id.*

This article will trace the evolution of thought and activism over the centuries aimed at defining women's human rights and implementing the idea that women and men are equal members of society. Three caveats are necessary. First, because women's history has been deliberately ignored over the centuries as a means of keeping women subordinate, and is only now beginning to be recaptured, this is primarily a Northern story until the twentieth century. Second, because of this ignorance,[5] any argument that the struggle to attain rights for women is only a Northern or Western effort is without foundation. Simply not enough available records exist detailing women's struggles or achievements in the Southern or Eastern sections of the world. The few records available to Northern writers attest that women in other parts of the world were not content with their status. Third, the oft-heard argument that feminism (read the struggle for women's equality) is a struggle pursued primarily by elite women is simply another example of the traditional demeaning of women. History is replete with examples of male leaders who are not branded with this same charge, even though much of history is about elite men.

In addition, it is hoped that this article, and the current activism on behalf of women's human rights, will stimulate historians and human rights activists to delve more deeply into the history of women's human rights throughout the world and further develop this neglected half of history. Such historical research would be a contribution to promoting women's human rights because it is from history, whether written or oral, that role models and traditions are created.

As historian Gerda Lerner has written:

> [T]he fact that women were denied knowledge of the existence of Women's History decisively and negatively affected their intellectual development as a group. Women who did not know that others like them had made intellectual contributions to knowledge and to creative thought were overwhelmed by the sense of their own inferiority or, conversely, the sense of the dangers of their daring to be different. . . . Every thinking woman had to argue with the 'great man' in her head, instead of being strengthened and encouraged by her foremothers.[6]

II.   EXECUTIVE SUMMARY

The original contributors to women's human rights were those who first taught women to read and, thus, to explore the world outside the home and immediate community. The idea of women's human rights is often cited as

---

5. The term ignorance is used here in its original sense, that of something being unknown.
6. GERDA LERNER, THE CREATION OF FEMINIST CONSCIOUSNESS: FROM THE MIDDLE AGES TO EIGHTEEN-SEVENTY 12 (1993).

beginning in 1792 with Mary Wollstonecraft's book, *Vindication of the Rights of Women*,[7] published in response to promulgation of the natural-rights-of-man theory. Recent historical research, however, has revealed a much longer gestation period, beginning at least in the early fifteenth century with publication of *Le Livre de la Cité des Dames* [*The Book of the City of Ladies*] by Christine de Pizan,[8] which stimulated what French feminists call the *querelle des femmes* (translation: debate about women), a debate that continues to the present.[9]

This long debate has been broad and wide-ranging because human life has so many facets. Much of the debate has involved the traditional demeaning of women: a common, often subconscious, technique of one group seeking to maintain power over another. Demeaning an individual or group over time results in stereotyping and the denial of recognition of that group's accomplishments or contributions to society. As the demeaning becomes customary, discrimination results, establishing a rationale for differential treatment of groups and the individuals within the particular group. With discrimination, the less powerful are deprived of their history, their self-confidence, and, eventually, their legal ability to function as full citizens or members of the larger group. The great irony is that women have been charged with—and have often found security in—maintaining customs and tradition, thus, institutionalizing the discrimination against them through the education and socialization of children.

Breaking tradition, defying custom, and overcoming discrimination requires courage and leadership. Leaders bent on effecting change must develop a new vision of the world, articulate the problems of the status quo and a new theory of social and political order, and, over time, mobilize a critical mass of supporters who share the new vision and new articulation of the problems. For women, taking leadership was a double-edged problem, a contradiction in terms. For most women, especially before safe and effective birth control was available, marriage, home, and family were their means of economic survival and social acceptance. Girls were groomed for marriage, for reproduction and nurturance of the human species. While lauded in the abstract, and often romanticized, marriage and reproduction also have been demeaned throughout history. As Menander said two or three centuries before the birth of Christ: "Marriage, if one will face the truth, is an evil, but a necessary evil."[10]

---

7. Mary Wollstonecraft, Vindication of the Rights of Women (Source Book Press 1971) (1792).
8. Christine de Pizan, The Book of the City of Ladies (Earl Jeffrey Richards trans., Persea Books 1982) (1405).
9. Joan Kelly, Women, History and Theory 65–66 (1984).
10. John Bartlett, Bartlett's Familiar Quotations 651 (9th ed. 1901) (quoting an unindentified fragment).

As the Taliban so clearly understands, the prerequisites for development and implementation of women's human rights are: education; the means and ability to make a living beyond childbearing, homemaking, and caring for families; freedom of movement; and a measure of respect as individual human beings, not prisoners of their sex.

Education involves the ability to receive, create, and disseminate knowledge. Knowledge is power, the foundation of intellectual and political development. It is gained through experience, education, and association with knowledgeable others. Expanded literacy among women allowed those who could not escape the confines of home to learn about the outside world and, through writing, to recount their experiences and express their ideas. Freedom to move in public and to travel independently, even within a limited area, allows both for gaining more experience and for exchanging experiences with others, increasing both knowledge and education. It took centuries for women to gain the right to education and the opportunity to find employment outside the home; it was only after women were afforded these opportunities that they could communicate their experiences inside and outside the home. The resulting education offered new opportunities for women, such as the ability, for sexually active women, to limit childbearing.

The beginning of women's education began with literacy. As literacy rates increased, women began to articulate their view of the world. Many wrote anonymously at first in order to have their work accepted for publication. The Industrial Revolution and the concomitant advances in science and technology contributed immensely to women's emancipation. Not only did more women find employment outside the home, but travel and communication became easier and cheaper. A major breakthrough was the development of safe, effective, and legal means of birth control. The fact that distribution of birth control information and devices was illegal in most countries until the early twentieth century, and that the term "family planning" became a substitute for birth control, is additional testimony to the dilemma Mill identified—that men have believed that they must control women in order for them to engage in their natural vocation, that of bearing and raising children and maintaining homes.

Along with advances in health, sanitation, and medicine, an increasing number of women began living beyond their childbearing years and more children survived. Men's fear that women would not reproduce lessened, and the ability of women to participate in economic and political life increased.

By the time the United Nations was formed in the mid-twentieth century, internationally, a critical mass of women had been educated, were employed outside the home, and had obtained enough legal and social freedom to participate in public life, even at the international level. Numerous international women's organizations had fifty years of experience behind them. As a result of lobbying by these organizations, and with support from female delegates, the phrase "equal rights of men and women" was inserted in the UN Charter.[11] When the Universal Declaration of Human Rights (UDHR) was drafted, the term "everyone" rather than the personal pronoun "his" was used in most, but not all, of its articles.[12] When the Commission on Human Rights failed to recognize women's aspirations adequately, women delegates and the nongovernmental organizations (NGOs) supporting them were politically powerful and astute enough to obtain a freestanding Commission on the Status of Women (CSW).[13] By 1979, the CSW, with the support of women delegates and NGOs and a new wave of feminism underway, had drafted and successfully lobbied the adoption of the Convention on the Elimination of All Forms of Discrimination Against Women.[14]

The Convention wove together all the ideas discussed during the preceding five centuries of debate and placed a strong emphasis on the concept of equality in family matters. The Convention covered civil and political rights as well as economic and social rights, and, in 1980, with the requisite number of ratifications obtained, the Convention became the international women's human rights treaty.[15] At the 1993 world conference on human rights, NGOs, focused on women's human rights, brought the previously hidden issue of violence against women to international attention. "Women's rights are human rights" became the cry. Although the debate, begun in 1405, continues, and the Taliban's edict illustrates that women's position in society can deteriorate, there is now worldwide recognition that the term "women's human rights" is not a redundancy.

The drive to define women's human rights and eliminate discrimination against them can be seen as part of the worldwide democratization effort. The question now is whether women will exercise their political muscle sufficiently at national, local, and international levels to assure universal implementation of the women's human rights treaty. This depends on whether women, in partnership with men, can effectively rationalize the relationships between the private and public spheres—between work, family, and public life. An important related question is whether women in all countries will redeem their history and use it to validate and support their struggle for equality and justice, or whether, as in the past, new women's movements

---

11. U.N. CHARTER pmbl., signed 26 June 1945, 59 Stat. 1031, T.S. No. 993, 3 Bevans 1153 (*entered into force* 24 Oct. 1945).
12. *See generally* UDHR, *supra* note 1.
13. *See generally* ARVONNE S. FRASER, LOOKING TO THE FUTURE: EQUAL PARTNERSHIP BETWEEN MEN AND WOMEN IN THE 21ST CENTURY (1983).
14. CEDAW, *supra* note 2.
15. *Id.*

will have to be organized every few generations to account for the lack of women's history and the shortcomings in traditional education and socialization of girls.

III.   THE ORIGINS: DEFINING THE ISSUES

In 1405, Christine de Pizan's book, *Le Livre de la Cité des Dames*,[16] was published, partially in response to Giovanni Boccaccio's earlier book, *Concerning Famous Women*,[17] that described exceptional women of history who had acquired "manly spirit" and other male attributes such as "keen intelligence . . . and remarkable fortitude"[18] and who dared to undertake difficult deeds. Boccaccio believed the histories of these women should be recorded just as the histories of male leaders were recorded.[19] De Pizan, a widow supporting her family by writing, responded to Boccaccio and other male writers of her day, not only by creating her own list of important women of the past, but also by encouraging women of all classes to look to their own experience and resist being limited and demeaned by men.[20] De Pizan argued for women's right to be educated, to be able to live and work independently, to participate in public life, and be masters of their own fate. One of the leading intellectuals of her day, her extensive published works demonstrate that she was an astute political observer as well as a theorist.[21]

Feminist historian Gerda Lerner credits de Pizan with the first deliberate effort of raising women's consciousness, but laments the fact that, although numerous women later published lists of famous women, few used de Pizan as a reference—an example of how the lack of knowledge of women's history impedes intellectual development.[22] Joan Kelly, another feminist historian, argues that de Pizan opened the *querelle des femmes,* or debate about women, by establishing the basic postulates of feminism.[23] (Feminism is used throughout this article in its original meaning: the theory of, and the struggle for, equality for women.) Kelly also asserts that de Pizan and her European successors focused on what is now called "gender"—the concept that the opposition to women is not simply biologically based but culturally based as well.

---

16. DE PIZAN, *supra* note 8.
17. GIOVANNI BOCCACCIO, CONCERNING FAMOUS WOMEN (Guido A. Guarino trans., Rutgers University Press 1963) (1361).
18. Guido A. Guarino, *Introduction* to CONCERNING FAMOUS WOMEN, *supra* note 17, at xxxviii.
19. *See generally id.*
20. The term "demeaned" was used frequently before the word "discrimination" was popularized.
21. Marina Warner, *Foreword* to DE PIZAN, *supra* note 8.
22. LERNER, *supra* note 6, at 261.
23. KELLY, *supra* note 9, at 65–66.

   Four points are important about de Pizan and her work. The first is obvious but merits restatement: she could not have written her book if she had been illiterate. Like many who followed her, she used the printed word and publication of her ideas to describe the situation of women. She not only contributed to the historical record, she analyzed life from a women's perspective, basing her conclusions not only on her own life, but also on the lives of her predecessors. The ability to gain and disseminate knowledge, to record history, and to express new ideas and life experiences in printed form is, as noted above, a prerequisite for challenging social and political norms. De Pizan used her education and experiences to think, which Wollstonecraft would later argue was a necessity for girls. The ability to analyze one's circumstances and derive wisdom from that analysis is an important intellectual exercise, especially when the individual, her group, and her work are demeaned by the wider world.

   Second, de Pizan directly challenged the confinement of women to the private sphere of home and family. She placed herself in the public sphere and demonstrated that women could provide for themselves economically, as many women, particularly widows, had done before her.

   Third, de Pizan began a tradition of women writing for publication not only to express their ideas, but to offer economic support for themselves and their families. Finally, she understood that history, whether oral or written, is a political tool used to maintain power, to reinforce the dominant culture, and to record actions that affect the public sphere. History is not merely a record of leadership; it provides role models. As Cicero said, history provides guidance in daily life.

   De Pizan understood that denying a group its history and suppressing its record of leadership results in disempowerment of the group. She knew that the record of actions by those who challenge existing power structures is often deliberately suppressed and, unless that group is successful and becomes a new political force, the history is lost. History, as a record of male leadership, has been used, perhaps subconsciously, to reinforce the idea that women are insignificant and subordinate and, therefore, belong to the private sphere. Especially in societies where literacy is low and women's organizations are apolitical, male-dominated history and tradition maintain the existing social and political order. De Pizan and many of her successors have been omitted from recorded history, thus, prolonging the struggle for women to achieve their human rights.

IV.   THE DRIVE FOR EDUCATION AND INDEPENDENCE

Throughout the sixteenth and seventeenth centuries, increasing numbers of girls, primarily in royal and wealthy families, were educated. More and more women began writing for publication, although often anonymously for fear of being seen as "intruding" on the public sphere. During the seventeenth century, numerous women writers, including Marie de Gournay of France, in her *Egalité des hommes et des femmes*,[24] argued for the education of girls and women, citing its lack as a major cause of women's inferior status.[25] In 1659, Anna Maria von Schurman's *The Learned Maid or Whether a Maid May Be a Scholar*[26] appeared in English translation, echoing de Gournay. In 1670, Aphra Behn, said to be the first English woman to make her living by writing, had her play, *The Forc'd Marriage, or the Jealous Bridegroom*,[27] performed in London. While satirizing male behavior, Behn argued in her play for women's education and responded to public criticism of lack of knowledge of Greek and Latin by noting that Shakespeare had not known the languages either. She was one of the first—and still too rare—feminists who used humor and public entertainment to make her point. A generation later, in 1694, Englishwoman Mary Astell, in *A Serious Proposal to the Ladies*,[28] called for institutions of higher learning for women.

De Gournay, Behn, Astell, and others, some still unknown in history, followed in de Pizan's tradition by using their own experiences and skills to expose the folly of women's position in society and to dramatize male condemnation of any deviation from that norm. Behn, a popular, seventeenth-century, English playwright who argued for a woman's right to choose to marry or to remain single, was publicly scorned and her work ignored after her death. At least one historian of the intellectual progress of women, Dale Spender, makes the point that discrimination and sexual harassment are new in name only.[29] Demeaning women took a virulent form in print and in person, not only of women of achievement, but of all women.[30]

Spender argues that it was Astell who defined patriarchy and its attributes by attacking marriage as an institution that served to keep women subordinate. Astell was succeeded in this attack by Lady Mary Wortley Montagu. Spender credits Lady Montagu with being the first English woman to directly enter the political arena by publishing a periodical entitled *The Nonsense of Common Sense*.[31] It is assumed she was also the author of a

---

24. Marie Le Jars de Gournay, Egalité des hommes et des femmes [Equality of Men and Women] (Librairie Droz 1993) (1641).
25. *See id.*
26. Anna Maria von Schurman, The Learned Maid; or, Whether a Maid May Be a Scholar (n.p. 1659).
27. Aphra Behn, The Forc'd Marriage, or the Jealous Bridegroom (1671), *microformed on* Early English Books, 1641–1700; 446:1 (Univ. Microfilms).
28. Mary Astell, A Serious Proposal to the Ladies, for the Advancement of Their True and Greatest Interest, Parts I & II (Patricia Springborg ed., Pickering & Chatto 1997) (1694 & 1697).
29. *See* Dale Spender, Women of Ideas (and What Men Have Done to Them) (1982).
30. *See id.*
31. Lady Mary Wortley Montagu, The Nonsense of Common Sense, 1737–1738 (Robert Halsband ed., 1947).

series signed "Sophia, a Person of Quality." In the series and in her *Letters*, published a year after her death in 1762, Lady Montagu introduced numerous topics attributed to later feminists, including the rights to education and construction of knowledge based on their own experiences; she also discussed the legal and social constraints of marriage and the influence of custom and its confusion with nature.[32]

During the eighteenth century, educated women who argued for women's intellectual equality and promoted expanded educational opportunities for women became known as "bluestockings." Englishwoman Hannah More and others throughout Europe not only argued for women's and girls' education, but also organized women to establish schools. Even the more conservative women argued that education of girls was important because it meant that they would be better wives and mothers.

Organizing women to promote girls' education became socially acceptable, as did writing for publication. As Anne Hutchinson's experience in the colony of Massachusetts dramatically demonstrated, however, organizing for more political purposes was dangerous. In 1637, Hutchinson was charged with heresy for daring to question the religious/political authorities of the colony. Though Hutchinson left no personal written record, the proceedings of her trial for heresy were published.[33] Hutchinson and her husband had emigrated from England as members of a dissident religious community. A midwife and lay medical practitioner, she organized a series of women's meetings in her home where she expressed the belief that individuals had the right to determine their own beliefs, to read the Bible and talk directly to God, and to not be subject to the explications and interpretations of religious authorities. This open assertion of freedom of conscience and of speech was anathema to the colony's religious and political leaders who asserted that only they had the right to interpret God's word. Hutchinson and her merchant husband also hosted discussions in their home about the decisions of the political leaders on business matters in the colony.

Interestingly, at trial, Hutchinson was allowed to testify on her own behalf, a practice that was later abolished in many jurisdictions, leaving representation of women to their husbands or other male relatives. During her trial, Hutchinson refused to be demeaned. She held her own in intellectual

---

32. *See generally* 3 A History of Women in the West: Renaissance and Enlightenment Paradoxes (Georges Duby & Michelle Perrot general eds., Natalie Zemon Davis & Arlette Farge eds., 1993); Ellen Moers, Literary Women (1976); Bonnie S. Anderson & Judith P. Zinsser, A History of Their Own: Women in Europe from Prehistory to the Present (1988); Lerner, *supra* note 6, at 205–6.

33. *See* Amy Schrager Lang, Prophetic Woman: Anne Hutchinson and the Problem of Dissent in the Literature of New England (1987). *See also* Selma R. Williams, Divine Rebel: The Life of Anne Marbury Hutchinson (1981).

sparring with Governor John Winthrop, who served as both judge and prosecutor. Her hosting meetings was considered "a thing not tolerable nor comely in the sight of God nor fitting for [her] sex."[34] Hutchinson was excommunicated for troubling the church and for drawing people away from the church.[35] Although she and her family were banished from the colony and moved to Rhode Island, her assertion of her human rights became legendary. American school children, at least those of the author's generation and earlier, in their study of early American history learned about Anne Hutchinson as a champion of religious freedom.

V. WOLLSTONECRAFT AND THE RIGHTS OF WOMEN

By 1792, when Wollstonecraft published *A Vindication of the Rights of Women,*[36] she only reiterated what numerous women, and a few men, before her had already written. Wollstonecraft had previously written *Thoughts on the Education of Daughters,*[37] as well as an autobiographical novel entitled *Mary*[38] based on her own experiences as the daughter of a violent father and as a governess and teacher. In her *Thoughts on the Education of Daughters,* Wollstonecraft urged that girls be taught to think and their curiosity stimulated, revolutionary ideas for her time. She also responded to Edmund Burke's *Reflections on the French Revolution*[39] with her own pamphlet entitled *Vindication of the Rights of Men,*[40] in which she ridiculed his oversight of poverty in England, an issue that other female writers would discuss in the nineteenth century. Drawing attention to other less powerful groups and analogizing their situations to those of women was a path numerous leaders would later follow.

As a political commentator and translator working for Joseph Johnson and his *Analytical Review,* Wollstonecraft was familiar with the intellectual currents of Europe and was a friend of the American revolutionary writer, Thomas Paine. She was undoubtedly familiar with the work of Frenchwomen

---

34. WILLIAMS, *supra* note 33, at 149 (quoting Governor Winthrop's opening statement against Hutchinson at her trial).
35. *See generally id.* at 180 (citing *A Report of the Trial of Mrs. Anne Hutchinson Before the Church in Boston, 1638,* 4 MASS. HIST. SOC'Y (2d ser. 1889)).
36. WOLLSTONECRAFT, *supra* note 7.
37. MARY WOLLSTONECRAFT, THOUGHTS ON EDUCATION OF DAUGHTERS: WITH REFLECTIONS ON FEMALE CONDUCT IN THE MORE IMPORTANT DUTIES OF LIFE (Microfilm Corp. of America 1980) (1787).
38. MARY WOLLSTONECRAFT, MARY (Janet Todd ed., N.Y.U. Press 1992) (1788).
39. EDMUND BURKE, REFLECTIONS OF THE FRENCH REVOLUTION AND OTHER ESSAYS (E.P. Dutton & Co. 1920).
40. MARY WOLLSTONECRAFT, VINDICATION OF THE RIGHTS OF MEN (1791), *reprinted in* ELEANOR FLEXNER, MARY WOLLSTONECRAFT: A BIOGRAPHY (1972).

Madame de Genlis, who promoted girls' education, and that of Olympe de Gouges, a well-known pamphleteer on behalf of women's political rights and equality in law. Whether she knew of Condorcet's *Sur l'admission des femmes au droit de la Cite,*[41] published in 1790, or of German legal scholar von Hippel's revised views on women that called for political, educational, and professional rights for women is unknown, but both von Hippel and Wollstonecraft acknowledged Englishwoman Catharine Macaulay's earlier work on women's education.[42] A well-known English historian and an early bluestocking, Macaulay was a correspondent of George Washington and an advocate of the American experiment. Her reputation as a historian was tarnished when her *Letters,* in which she bemoaned women's lack of political rights and particularly the lack of married women's legal rights, were published.[43] Both Wollstonecraft and Macaulay lived their beliefs by undertaking unconventional marriages or choosing not to marry at all. Yet, while Wollstonecraft's reputation among feminists survived, Macaulay's did not— despite Wollstonecraft's acknowledgment of her debt to her.

Feminist historians argue that what distinguishes Wollstonecraft is that she was the first to put her theories in the context of a broader liberationist, modern human rights theory. In addition, she wrote in a more modern style, defining and describing women's limitations in public and private life in short, declarative sentences full of fury at both men and women. Wollstonecraft seems to ask female readers, "Have you no integrity, no sense of self?" as she regales against their coquetry and submissiveness to men and their general irresponsibility toward themselves, their children, and society.

Another Wollstonecraft contribution was her emphasis on women's health, promoting exercise of body and mind. Her predecessors made similar arguments for women's education, against the legal disabilities of marriage, and against women's lack of participation in politics, but only Wollstonecraft argued that women should be more active physically and more knowledgeable about health, anatomy, and medicine. She also was a precursor to the discussion of violence against women. In this area, she was almost two centuries ahead of her time: "The being who patiently endures injustice, and silently bears insults, will soon become unjust, or unable to discern right from wrong. . . . Nature never dictated such insincerity;—and,

---

41. JEAN-ANTOINE-NICOLAS DE CARITAT CONDORCET, THE FIRST ESSAY ON THE POLITICAL RIGHTS OF WOMEN: A TRANSLATION OF CONDORCET'S ESSAY "SUR L'ADMISSION DES FEMMES AU DROIT DE CITE" (Alice Drysdale Vickery trans., Garden City Press 1912) (1787).
42. *See* SUSAN GROAG BELL & KAREN M. OFFEN, WOMEN, THE FAMILY AND FREEDOM: THE DEBATE IN DOCUMENTS 97–118 (1983).
43. ANDERSON & ZINSSER, *supra* note 32, at 345, 352.

though prudence of this sort be termed a virtue, morality becomes vague when any part is supposed to rest on falsehood."[44]

Although Wollstonecraft agreed with Rousseau on his rights-of-man theory, his views on women incensed her. Hobbes and Locke had argued that the rights-of-man theory encompassed woman. Rousseau, on the other hand, followed the traditional, paternalistic line of thought: "In the family, it is clear, for several reasons which lie in its very nature, that the father ought to command."[45] Later, in his book, *Emile*, he forcefully asserted the common view that woman's purpose in life was to serve and entertain men. Wollstonecraft devoted an entire chapter to Rousseau's idea that the

> education of women should be always relative to . . . men. To please, to be useful to [them], . . . to educate [them] when young, and take care of [them] when grown up, to advise, to console [them], to render [their] lives easy and agreeable: these are the duties of women at all times.[46]

Wollstonecraft dismissed Rousseau's views as nonsense while strongly criticizing women who taught their daughters, and practiced obedience to, such views.

Meanwhile, in America, Abigail Adams was expressing similar ideas. A respectable married woman and wife of an early president of the United States, Adams is portrayed indulgently by historians for her "don't forget the ladies" letter to husband John while he was off helping draft the new country's constitution.

> Do not put such unlimited power in the hands of the husbands. Remember all men would be tyrants if they could. If particular care and attention is not paid to the ladies we are determine [sic] to foment a rebellion, and will not hold ourselves bound by any law in which we have had no voice, or representation.[47]

These are distinctly personal political sentiments based on women's experience. What most historians ignore is that this letter was only one example of her outspoken irritation at the legal constraints on women.

In other letters, Adams lamented the fact that, although she managed the farm and other family enterprises while her husband was off on political ventures, she could not make contracts or sell any of their property without

---

44. WOLLSTONECRAFT, *supra* note 7, at 105.
45. JEAN-JACQUES ROUSSEAU, *A Discourse on Political Economy, in* THE SOCIAL CONTRACT AND DISCOURSES (G.D.H. Cole trans., 1913), *reprinted in part in* HISTORY OF IDEAS ON WOMAN: A SOURCE BOOK 117, 119 (Rosemary Agonito ed., 1977) [hereinafter HISTORY OF IDEAS ON WOMAN].
46. WOLLSTONECRAFT, *supra* note 7, at 101 (citing 3 JEAN-JACQUES ROUSSEAU, EMILIUS (A TREATISE OF EDUCATION) 181 (1768)).
47. *See* ALICE ROSSI, THE FEMINIST PAPERS: FROM ADAMS TO DE BEAUVOIR 10–11 (1973); SALLY SMITH BOOTH, WOMEN OF '76, at 89 (1973).

his signature. Adams was also concerned about women's education, lamenting her own lack thereof, and inquiring about Macaulay in correspondence with an English cousin.[48]

The pleas of Abigail Adams and other women did not move male political leaders. Women were not considered citizens in the new US Constitution. On the European continent, the Allgemeines Landrecht of 1794 and the Napoleonic legal code of 1804 declared married women legally subordinate.[49] Yet, in 1808, Charles Fourier of France, whom some have called the inventor of feminism, asserted:

> As a general thesis: Social progress and historic changes occur by virtue of the progress of women toward liberty, and decadence of the social order occurs as the result of a decrease in the liberty of women. . . . [T]he extension of women's privileges is the general principle for all social progress.[50]

Fourier's ideas found few adherents. In 1832, the English Reform Act, in extending voting rights, limited those rights to "male persons."[51]

However, by the end of the eighteenth century, strong feminist arguments were being made on both sides of the Atlantic, although no major social or political women's organization existed to promote feminist views except that of education. Before organizing for political purposes, women articulated their experience and ideas through written publications, and only gradually broke the tradition that good women did not address public audiences. A new political movement, the abolition of slavery, gave women experience in organizing and moved them into the political arena and onto public platforms.

VI. MARRIAGE AND CHILDREN

While women's rights in the public arena received some attention, it was discrimination in the private sphere that was the more compelling issue. In the 1830s, the Caroline Norton case in England captured public attention.[52] A member of the well-placed Sheridan family, Caroline married George Norton, a lawyer and member of Parliament, only to find that he was a brutal drunk who expected her earnings to support the new family. A writer and magazine editor whose income, under law, belonged to her husband,

---

48. Phyllis Lee Levin, Abigail Adams: A Biography (1987).
49. Bell & Offen, *supra* note 42, at 37–41.
50. *Id.* at 41.
51. English Reform Act of 1832, 2 & 3 Will., ch. 45.
52. *See generally* Margaret Forster, Significant Sisters: The Grassroots of Active Feminism 1839–1939, at 15–52 (1984).

Norton refused to be quiet, as women of her time were expected to do, about her frequent beatings at his hands. Abjuring feminism and using her social contacts, Caroline Norton argued for justice in marriage, putting her case before the public when the couple separated and her husband filed for divorce and took the children. The case generated immense publicity because of the Nortons' social standing. Like all other English women, she could neither legally appear in court nor be represented. A jury disallowed the divorce and, under law, Norton's husband retained custody of the children. This drove Caroline to a study of English law and cases similar to hers. She not only wrote and distributed a pamphlet, *The Separation of Mother and Child by the Law of Custody of Infants Considered*,[53] in 1837 to Members of Parliament and to the public, but she also got the attention of a young barrister interested in child custody cases. As a result, in 1839, Parliament passed an infant custody reform bill allowing children under seven years of age to remain with their mother if she was of good character and the Lord Chancellor agreed.

This, however, was not the end of the matter for Caroline. George next sued for access to her trust monies and other inheritances to pay his debts. She contracted with him, assuring him an allowance if he gave her a legal separation, forgetting that as a woman she had no legal right to contract. Although she was allowed in court as a witness this time, she lost the case. Again, her response was to go public, achieving immense notoriety. In 1854, she published *English Laws for Women in the 19th Century*.[54] In a private letter, Norton, while disavowing feminism, admitted that she was seen "as a cross 'between a barn actress and a Mary Wollstonecraft.'"[55] At this point, an avowed feminist, Barbara Leigh-Smith (a.k.a. Barbara Bodichon), brought out her own pamphlet on women and the law in England and circulated a women's petition drive for reform of the laws regarding married women, obtaining more than twenty thousand signatures.

In 1857, the British Parliament passed an omnibus bill that allowed wives to directly inherit and bequeath property; permitted a wife who had been deserted by her husband to keep her earnings; empowered courts to direct payments for separate maintenance; and gave a separated wife the right to sue, be sued, and make contracts.[56] Only in 1882, with the Married

---

53. *See id.*
54. *See id.* at 46.
55. *See id.*
56. *See, e.g., id.* at 47, 48, 51; BELL AND OFFEN, *supra* note 42, at 22 (highlighting the Divorce Act of 1857, the Married Women's Property Act of 1870, and its successor act of 1882, three acts that changed the legal position of married women in England); 4 A HISTORY OF WOMEN IN THE WEST: EMERGING FEMINISM FROM REVOLUTION TO WORLD WAR 97–113 (Georges Duby & Michelle Perrot general eds., Genevieve Fraisse & Michelle Perrot eds., 1993).

Women's Property Act,[57] did married women achieve the same rights as unmarried women.

Almost as if to prove the point that women—and especially married women—had little power either in the public sphere or in the home, it took a distinguished Englishman and member of Parliament, John Stuart Mill, to put the question of marriage on the international map. His 1869 essay, *The Subjection of Women*,[58] drew tremendous attention in England and was almost immediately translated and distributed throughout Europe and the United States. Susan Bell and Karen Offen, in *Women, the Family and Freedom: The Debate in Documents,* argue that Mill's essay "forced thinkers to grapple with fundamental issues of political and social theory."[59] Mill argued that men took contradictory positions by believing that women's "natural vocation" is that of wife and mother, while also believing that women must be forced or controlled in order that they engage in this natural vocation. If natural, why was force necessary? Mill thought too many men were afraid of equality in marriage. In that case, he argued, men should never have allowed women "to receive a literary education. Women who read, much more women who write, are, in the existing constitution of things, a contradiction and a disturbing element. . . ."[60]

In his essay, Mill argued that marriage should be thought of as a voluntary association, a contract between equals similar to any business partnership. The partners could be assumed to settle issues of control amicably, each taking those responsibilities at which they were most efficient to perform. He also argued that it was in the interests of children and of society that equal rights within the family be the basis of marriage, otherwise, the family would become

> a school of despotism [when it ought to be] the real school of the virtues of freedom. . . . The moral regeneration of mankind will only really commence, when the most fundamental of the social relations is placed under the rule of equal justice, and when human beings learn to cultivate their strongest sympathy with an equal in rights and in cultivation.[61]

Mill's arguments were exactly what an incipient international women's movement needed. Bell and Offen point out that Mill's essay, and the ferment it caused, were significant in mobilizing women to push for legal, economic, educational, and political rights in virtually every country in

---

57. Married Women's Property Act of 1882, 45 & 46 Vict., ch. 75.
58. *See* MILL, *supra* note 3.
59. BELL & OFFEN, *supra* note 42, at 392.
60. MILL, *supra* note 3, *reprinted in part in* HISTORY OF IDEAS ON WOMAN, *supra* note 45, at 225, 243.
61. BELL & OFFEN, *supra* note 42, 398–99.

Europe.[62] Yet, it was not until 1923 that English women gained equal rights in divorce, and it took fifty more years, until 1973, before Parliament allowed English mothers to have legal custody of children equally with fathers.

VII. THE CONTRIBUTION OF NINETEENTH-CENTURY WOMEN WRITERS

Denied direct access to the world of politics by custom—it was unseemly for women to speak in public—and subordinate under law, many English, French, and American women took to writing literature and political commentary as a means of intruding on the public sphere and, not incidentally, like de Pizan and Wollstonecraft, as a means of economic independence. During the nineteenth century, numerous women writers became noted literary figures, often using the novel to express political sentiments. According to Ellen Moers in *Literary Women,* these writers gave voice, directly and indirectly, to the feelings and aspirations of women.[63] They pitted the conservative, traditional woman against the feminist through literature and indirectly encouraged feminist views in many of their readers. As Wollstonecraft before them, they became spokeswomen for the underprivileged, whether slaves, factory workers, the poor, or women.

Jane Austen and Charlotte Brontë are now the best known novelists of this period, but Fanny Burney of England and Madame de Stael of France were among the early popular writers who described the world from a woman's perspective. Much more famous and widely read during this time was a novel not about women, but about slavery. Harriet Beecher Stowe's *Uncle Tom's Cabin* brought her to international attention.[64] The millions of copies sold not only helped her family survive economically, but contributed to the US Civil War and a change in public policy. What is not mentioned by most literary historians is that novelist George Eliot not only portrayed girls' lives as stifling, but she also was so moved by Harriet Beecher Stowe's portrayal of slavery that she confessed in a letter to Stowe that she "felt urged to treat Jews with such sympathy and understanding as my nature and knowledge could attain to,"[65] which resulted in her novel, *Daniel Deronda.*[66]

---

62. *Id.* at 362.
63. *Id.* at 28.
64. Harriett Beecher Stowe, Uncle Tom's Cabin, or Life Among the Lowly (Macmillan Publ'g Co. 1994) (1852).
65. Moers, *supra* note 32, at 39 (quoting Eliot).
66. George Eliot, Daniel Deronda (Penguin Books 1986) (1876).

Mrs. Gaskell's *Mary Barton*,[67] published in 1848, is, according to Moers, the earliest, most notable novel about factory workers, although it was not the first written by a woman on this subject.[68] That distinction belongs to the aforementioned Caroline Norton, who, left in penury by her dissolute and violent husband, published *A Voice from the Factories* in 1836 and *The Child of the Islands* on child labor in 1845.[69]

Another English writer of this period was Harriet Martineau, well-known for her writings on political economy and one of many European female writers to tour the United States and write—along with Francis Wright and Frances Trollope, Anthony Trollope's mother—about conditions in the United States. During the 1820s and 1830s, Francis Wright became notorious for espousing women's and workers' rights, anti-slavery sentiments, free thought, and public education for both girls and boys. An intimate of General Lafayette of France, Wright's personal life and radical ideas made her *persona non grata,* like many other women before and after her whose non-traditional personal lives have been denigrated in an attempt to lessen the impact of their ideas on the public mind. One of the things that interested Wright, as it did de Tocqueville in his *Democracy in America*,[70] was the position of American women as pragmatic, thinking beings, who knew, or learned, how to organize—a requirement for survival on the frontier.

Another woman, also writing under a man's name, was George Sand of France who achieved international fame, not only for the proletarian political views expressed in her numerous novels, but also for her life of political activism and defiance of social mores. Sand is often remembered as a woman who dressed in men's clothing in order to move more freely around Paris. Widely recognized as the Muse of the 1848 Revolution, she lived out her beliefs. Defying convention, she separated from and divorced her husband; lived with a series of notable men without marriage; demanded custody of her children, inheritance, and property; earned her living by writing while expressing revolutionary thoughts; and became a role model—albeit, a highly controversial one—for women as well as men. She also became one of her generation's most popular and prolific writers, gaining praise from peers such as Dostoyevsky, Turgenev, Henry James, Walt Whitman, and, not incidentally, John Stuart Mill.[71]

Perhaps as important, in terms of women's human rights, as the writings and ideas of the noted women is the interaction between the writers and

---

67. Elizabeth Cleghorn Gaskell, Mary Barton: A Tale of Manchester Life (Oxford Univ. Press 1987) (1848).
68. Moers, *supra* note 32, at 23.
69. *See id.* at 23.
70. Alexis de Tocqueville, Democracy in America (J.P. Mayer & Max Lerner eds. & George Lawrence trans., Harper & Row 1966) (1838).
71. Joseph Barry, Infamous Woman: The Life of George Sand at xiv (1978).

female activists. In today's parlance, this would be called "networking across international borders." Sand was beleagured at times by visitors. Margaret Fuller, American journalist and author of *Woman in the Nineteenth Century*,[72] enroute to Italy to cover its independence movement, was only one of many who called upon Sand. By this time, more women were traveling internationally. Flora Tristan, Sand's contemporary, went to Peru in an attempt to claim her father's inheritance, and then came home to write *Peregrinations d'une paria 1833–34*, followed by *Promenades de Londres* in 1840, and later, in 1846, *L'Emancipation de la Femme ou la testament de la Paria*.[73]

Networking among women who had attracted public attention was taking place, not only across international boundaries, but within borders, too. According to Moers,

> George Eliot knew Barbara Leigh-Smith (founder of the Association for Promoting the Employment of Women); Mrs. Gaskell knew Bessie Parkes; and Charlotte Brontë knew Mary Taylor (early settler and businesswoman of New Zealand), who wrote home . . . denouncing the author of *Shirley* as "coward" and "traitor" for the hesitant ambivalence [Miss Taylor] sensed in Charlotte Brontë's attitude toward work for women.[74]

Ernestine Rose is a prime example of the networking that took place between European and American women who became women's rights activists. Rose, like many others, became interested and active in a variety of progressive movements and the object of a great deal of publicity in her day. Born in Poland, she escaped an arranged marriage and, in court, defended her inheritance claim. She later emigrated to Germany, where she supported herself by selling her own invention, a household deodorant; moved to Paris during the 1830 revolution; and subsequently moved to England, where she became associated with Robert Owen and other reformers. By 1840, she and her English husband moved to the United States where Rose lobbied for passage of a married women's property act in New York. The legislative act allowed women to hold property in their own names and be legal guardians of their children. A forceful orator and leader in the numerous state and national women's rights conventions held in the eastern United States between 1850 and the onset of the US Civil War, Rose kept in touch with European women working on women's rights issues. She often used the term "human rights" in her speeches and in at least one instance sponsored a resolution stating that "by human rights we mean natural rights."[75]

---

72. Margaret Fuller, Woman in the 19th Century (Univ. of S.C. Press 1980) (1845).
73. *See* Moers, *supra* note 32, at 20–22. *See also id.* at 316–17 (for a list of Flora Tristan's publications).
74. *Id.* at 19.
75. Yuri Suhl, Ernestine L. Rose and the Battle for Human Rights 149 (1959).

Women leaders on both sides of the Atlantic were not deterred by resistance to their ideas. At the 1853 New York City Women's Rights Convention, Lucretia Mott, discussed later, introduced Mathilde Francesca Anneke, editor of *Die Frauenzeitung,* who fled Germany when her husband was tried for treason after supporting the 1848 revolutionary movement. Rose was Anneke's translator, although translation services were not needed when an unruly mob entered the hall and brought the meeting to a halt—not an uncommon event for women's rights meetings. Before the meeting was disrupted, however, the convention had adopted a resolution that stated that their movement was "not of America only" and had formed a committee to communicate with women of "Great Britain and the Continent of Europe." Rose, who was made a member of the committee, was also active in peace, free-thought, and social reform movements and kept in touch with European feminists, reading letters and other communications from them at other women's rights conventions.[76]

Although little of women's writings or their leadership in Eastern and Southern nations during the nineteenth century was common knowledge in the Western world, in 1905, "Sultana's Dream," a patently feminist story, was published in the *Indian Ladies Magazine* by Rokeya Sakhawat Hossain.[77] It described, in good humor, a world in which men's and women's positions were reversed and noted the lack of women's education and the strictures of the veil.[78]

VIII. ORGANIZING FOR POLITICAL ACTION—FROM ANTI-SLAVERY TO WOMEN'S RIGHTS

While Europe produced most of the writers who depicted women's experiences, organizing for political purposes was the major contribution of American women to the development of women's human rights. Organizing, as pointed out by de Tocqueville, was a necessity in America. Pioneers in a new land had to organize to survive, especially those who settled the northern sections of the United States where the winters are severe. It was the abolition of slavery—and later the civil rights movement—that provided the impetus for US women to organize to eliminate discrimination and promote women's rights just as the French and American revolutions had contributed to Wollstonecraft's and Abigail Adams' thinking.

---

76. *Id.* at 145–48.
77. Rokeya Sakhawat Hossain, Sultana's Dream and Selections from The Secluded Ones (Roushan Jahan ed. & trans., Feminist Press 1988) (1905 & 1928–1930).
78. *See id.*

Two sisters from the slave-owning South of the United States turned their experiences with slavery first into anti-slavery advocacy and then to advocacy for women's rights. Sarah Grimké, daughter of a leading South Carolina judge and political activist, became deeply frustrated by her family's refusal to allow her to study law with her brother. She had hated slavery from childhood when she was severely reprimanded for secretly teaching her own slave servant/companion to read, an illegal act. Refusing marriage and the traditional life of a Southern lady, she moved to Philadelphia after her father's death and later was joined by her younger sister Angelina. Both found a measure of personal freedom in Quaker society, but soon found even the Quakers and male abolitionists too conservative. As agents for the American Anti-Slavery Society, they were placed in charge of organizing women. Later, Angelina's 1836 anti-slavery pamphlet, *An Appeal to the Christian Women of the South*,[79] brought her to national attention. Angelina frequently spoke in public on the abolition of slavery and was often heckled by unruly mobs—at one such speech, a mob burned the new Philadelphia hall in which she spoke to the ground.

According to Lerner, "the Grimké sisters [came] to represent in the public mind the fusion of abolition and woman's rights . . . [and] precipitated an ideological crisis among reformers."[80] Like Anne Hutchinson before them, Sarah and Angelina refused to be demeaned by religious leaders who resented their interference with doctrine, their organizing of women parishioners, and their daring to speak to audiences of both sexes. Sarah Grimké's incisive *Letters on the Equality of the Sexes*,[81] issued in response to a Pastoral Letter to Congregational Churches, referred to Cotton Mather and witchcraft, a reference to Hutchinson's fate; demanded equality in education and equal pay for equal work; and drew analogies between women's lives and those of the slaves. An intellectual far ahead of her time, Sarah Grimké used language in an essay on marriage similar to that used in the 1993 world conference on human rights: "Human rights are *not* based upon sex, color, capacity or condition. They are universal, inalienable and eternal, and none but despots will deny to woman that supreme sovereignty over her own person and conduct which Law concedes to man."[82]

Action at the 1840 World Anti-Slavery Conference in London spurred two women to organize. Lucretia Mott, a Pennsylvania Quaker, who reput-

---

79. Angelina E. Grimké, An Appeal to the Christian Women of the South (Arno Press 1969) (1836). *See generally* Gerda Lerner, The Grimké Sisters from South Carolina (1967).
80. *See* Lerner, *supra* note 79, at 183.
81. Sarah M. Grimké, Letters on the Equality of the Sexes and Other Essays (Elizabeth Ann Bartlett ed., Yale Univ. Press 1988).
82. Sarah M. Grimké, *Marriage, reprinted in part in* Gerda Lerner, The Female Experience: An American Documentary 89, 89 (1977).

edly kept a copy of Wollstonecraft's book in the foot of her babies' cradle, was an organizer of the Philadelphia Female Anti-Slavery Society, consisting of black and white members. Mott, with her husband, attended the 1840 World Anti-Slavery Conference in London, as did newly-married Elizabeth Cady Stanton. Upon reaching London, they discovered they were barred from participating in the conference despite all their anti-slavery organizing at home—women at the World Anti-Slavery Conference were only allowed to listen from behind a balcony curtain. Although some male delegates—not including Mrs. Stanton's new husband—argued in favor of women's participation, the ban remained.

This manifest discrimination in a cause dedicated to freeing individuals from bondage shocked Mott and Stanton into action. Earlier, Mott, as a school teacher, had unavailingly protested against male and female pay differentials, while Stanton had complained to her father, a lawyer and judge, about women's legal subordination. While in London, the younger Stanton, a rebel by nature, found Mott "a suitable female role model and a willing mentor."[83] Mott told Stanton "of Mary Wollstonecraft, her social theories, and her demands of equality for women."[84] In London, the two women decided to organize a women's rights meeting when they returned to America. It took eight years before their idea came to fruition. Family duties, abolition activities, Stanton's child-bearing, and limited means of travel constrained both women, although they remained in correspondence. In 1848, when Mott was visiting upstate New York, Stanton and Mott called their now-historic Seneca Falls meeting.

By 1848, a strong foundation of thought and advocacy for women's rights had been built, but it had not won public favor. Most of the principles that would appear a hundred years later in the Universal Declaration and the Women's Convention—the rights to education; to employment outside the home with wages paid directly to the woman; to custody of their children; to hold and inherit property; to contract and be represented in court; and to participate in the world of public affairs—already had been espoused. What was required was to put these concepts in a theoretical framework. The framework, in addition to demanding the right to vote, organizing women, and giving women a different vision of the world, was Stanton's contribution. She had spent the eight years between meeting Mott and calling the 1848 convention reading and studying while raising her children.

In the Declaration of Sentiments that Stanton wrote for the 1848 meeting, she expressed strong resentment of the fact that, throughout history,

---

83. Elisabeth Griffith, In Her Own Right: The Life of Elizabeth Cady Stanton 38 (1984).
84. *Id.* at 38 (quoting Stanton).

men had established "an absolute tyranny" over women.[85] Women were required to abide by laws they had no hand in making, and were thereby deprived, viewed "if married, in the eye of the law, [as] civilly dead."[86] Stanton wrote that, without rights to property or to the wages they earned, women become "morally irresponsible in marriage, can be chastised by the husband, are discriminated against in the laws of divorce and, if single and the owner of property, taxed to support a government which recognizes her only when her property can be made profitable [for the government]...."[87] Kept from most profitable employments and professions such as law and medicine, she is paid low wages, when employed, and denied good education, with colleges not open to her. Thus, her confidence is destroyed, her self-respect lessened, and she is subject to a different code of morals, all of which, Stanton continued, made her willing to lead a dependent and abject life, depriving her of her citizenship. She concluded with a prophecy and call to action: "We shall employ agents, circulate tracts, petition the State and National legislatures, and endeavor to enlist the pulpit and the press in our behalf [and] hope this Convention will be followed by a series of Conventions embracing every party of the country."[88]

The resolutions adopted at this historic meeting echoed sentiments expressed by earlier feminists and were reminiscent of Olympe de Gouges' 1791 Declaration of the Rights of Woman and Citizen.[89] Whether Stanton, a well-read intellectual, knew of de Gouges' work is unclear. What is known is that the 1848 meeting was attended by many of the nation's leading reformers—black and white—and received extensive, primarily negative, publicity.

Although her resolution on women's suffrage—the only resolution not passed unanimously—has attracted the most attention from historians, feminist and non-feminist alike, its significance is sometimes over-estimated. "The right to vote is an empty right if power within the home resides in the male," Marsha Freeman of the International Women's Rights Action Watch correctly asserts.[90] In its time, however, the call for the right to vote was for the legal right to participate in the public sphere. Suffrage was the metaphor for equality in public life, for full citizenship. Public discussion of the husband's right to chastise or beat his wife, perhaps, had greater contemporary impact, although it was not discussed widely, or used as an organizing tool, until the late twentieth century when violence against women became an

---

85. Mari Jo & Paul Buhle, The Concise History of Woman Suffrage 94 (1978) (reprinting Stanton's Declaration of Sentiments *in toto*).
86. *See id.*
87. *See id.* at 95.
88. *Id.*
89. Bell & Offen, *supra* note 42, at 98, 104–09.
90. Comments in a conversation with the author.

international organizing effort and united women of all classes and nationalities.

What was important in 1848, and is still important today, is the full legal
and *de facto* capacity of women to act as free, independent, equally
empowered citizens in both the private and public spheres. It was this 1848
call to action on all fronts—public and private—that spurred women's
organizing nationally, and then internationally, and ultimately led, not only
to women achieving the right to vote, but to their increasing political activity. A widely publicized series of state and national women's rights conventions, interrupted by the Civil War, gathered converts to every issue in the
Declaration and, after intense organizational efforts, ultimately led to
American women finally achieving the vote in 1920.[91] These early conventions could be called a first wave of organized consciousness-raising
because they brought a wide range of women's issues to public attention
and spurred individuals and groups of women to action on many fronts.

Another important step was the struggle of women to enter acknowledged professions such as law, medicine, and science. Among the most
notable early trail-blazers were Elizabeth Blackwell of the United States and
Florence Nightingale of England, who both broke barriers for women in
medicine. Blackwell is recognized for her fight to enter medical school and
become the first certified female doctor, while Nightingale is remembered
not only for her pioneering efforts in modern nursing, but also for her
research and advocacy in the field of public health. In the same period,
women also broke the college entrance barrier. Lucy Stone, the first
American woman to attend college, is known for her leadership in the suffrage movement as well as her insistence on keeping her own name upon
marriage and her strong advocacy of education of girls and women.

The resistance to women's participation in public life as professionals in
the United States is illustrated by an 1870 decision of the State of Illinois'
Supreme Court refusing Myra Bradwell admission to the bar on the grounds
that

> God designed the sexes to occupy different spheres of action, and that it
> belonged to men to make, apply and execute the laws. . . . This step, if taken by
> us, would mean that . . . every civil office in this State may be filled by women
> . . . governors, judges and sheriffs. This we are not yet prepared to hold.[92]

However, in 1874, the Illinois legislature passed legislation preventing discrimination in bar admissions on the basis of sex,[93] and in 1879, the US

---

91. U.S. Const. amend. XIX.
92. Eleanor Flexner, Century of Struggle: The Woman's Rights Movement in the United States
   120–21 (1974).
93. *See id.* at 121.

Supreme Court allowed Belva Lockwood to appear before it.[94] In spite of
these victories, it took until 1973, when the US Congress adopted Title IX
of the Education Amendments,[95] which, among other things, was designed
to eliminate discrimination against women in education, to open US law
schools to more than a small quota of women, and to encourage schoolgirls
to participate in sports.

IX.   ORGANIZING INTERNATIONALLY

Women's organizing was not limited to the United States, nor were women's
suffrage leaders the only leaders organizing women for political action.
Although the Women's Christian Temperance Union (WCTU) is remembered, often jokingly, for its crusade against the evils of alcohol, its primary
emphasis, under the leadership of Frances Willard, was local political action
in the name of motherhood and home. Willard's "do everything" policy for
local WCTU units encouraged women to improve their communities. Many
units established kindergartens, libraries, and other community institutions.
This local activity brought new recruits to the suffrage movement. Later,
Willard formed an international WCTU with units in other countries, including Japan.[96]

In March 1888, forty years after the Seneca Falls meeting, an
International Council of Women meeting, organized by Stanton and her
friend and colleague, Susan B. Anthony, was held in Washington, DC.
Anthony had been active in the temperance movement and proved herself
to be the consummate organizer, while Stanton was a theoretical politician.
The International Council of Women meeting was cosponsored by the
WCTU. In addition to delegates from England, France, Norway, Finland,
Denmark, India, and Canada, representatives from over fifty US women's
organizations attended.[97] This meeting was not the first international organ-
ization of women; by 1888, Marie Goegg of Switzerland had formed an
International Association of Women, an International Women's Rights
Conference had been held in Paris, and the World Young Women's Christian
Association (WYWCA) and the World WCTU had been formed. In the early
part of the twentieth century, the International Conference of Socialist
Women was formed under the leadership of Clara Zetkin. This group pro-
posed what later became International Women's Day. Also, in Russia,

---

94. *Id.*
95. 20 U.S.C. § 1681 et seq.
96. Ruth Bordin, Frances Willard: A Biography (1986).
97. Griffith, *supra* note 83, at 193.

Alexandra Kollantai, who concentrated on organizing employed women, built upon and defined the feminist movement.[98]

With headquarters in Zurich, the International Council of Women promoted the formation of national councils to work on social and economic questions. Although Anthony and Willard were extremely pleased that more conservative women were joining the women's rights movement, Stanton and others had a broader, more liberal or progressive vision. By this time, Stanton was spending more and more time in Europe, primarily England and France. Although suffrage remained a primary issue for her, in perhaps the most significant speech of her life, made before the US Senate Committee on Woman Suffrage, she called on women to be self-reliant, independent beings whose birthright was "self-sovereignty."[99] At the age of seventy-six, Stanton argued the essential basis for women's human rights, the sovereignty of the individual:

> No matter how much women prefer to lean, to be protected and supported, nor how much men prefer to have them do so, they must make the voyage of life alone. . . . The strongest reason why we ask for woman a voice in the government under which she lives; in the religion she is asked to believe; equality in social life, where she is the chief factor; a place in the trades and professions, where she may earn her bread, is because of her birthright to self-sovereignty; because, as an individual, she must rely on herself.[100]

Achieving that birthright required organizing internationally. Women's suffrage, at the end of the nineteenth century and the beginning of the twentieth, like the violence against women issue at the end of the twentieth century, became the most visible issue in the feminist movement. Less visible were other issues supported by a variety of women's organizations, ranging from those concentrating on meeting short-term social welfare needs to the more political organizations that were demanding the right to vote.

In 1902, delegates from ten countries—the United States, England, Russia, Norway, Germany, Sweden, Turkey, Australia, Chile, and Canada—attended an International Woman Suffrage Conference held in Washington, DC as part of the National American Women Suffrage Association's annual convention.[101] By this time, New Zealand and Australia had given women

---

98. See Margaret E. Galey, *Forerunners in Women's Quest for Partnership, in* WOMEN, POLITICS, AND THE UNITED NATIONS 1 (Anne Winslow ed., 1995); RICHARD STITES, THE WOMEN'S LIBERATION MOVEMENT IN RUSSIA (1978).

99. GRIFFITH, *supra* note 83, at 203, 204.

100. *Id.* at 203 (indicating that the full text of the speech, The Solitude of Self, can be found in THE HISTORY OF WOMAN SUFFRAGE 189–91 (AYER CO. 1985) (Elizabeth Cady Stanton et al. eds., 1881)).

101. See ARNOLD WHITTICK, WOMAN INTO CITIZEN 22, 31 (1979).

the vote.[102] In 1904, meeting in Berlin, women active in national suffrage campaigns formed the International Woman Suffrage Alliance (IWSA) and elected as president Carrie Chapman Catt, a second-generation US suffragist whose talent was organization. Although suffrage was its original focus, the group understood the importance of setting end goals and developing means to achieve them. Suffrage was a means, not an end. Effecting changes in law and policy required lobbying formal political bodies, garnering political support, and continually educating both women and men about women's concerns.

The principles on which IWSA was established were precursors to ideas that would later find their way into the Convention:

1. That men and women are born equally free and independent members of the human race; equally endowed with intelligence and ability, and equally entitled to the free exercise of their individual rights and liberty.

2. That the natural relation of the sexes is that of interdependence and cooperation, and that the repression of the rights and liberty of one sex inevitably works injury to the other. . . .

3. That in all lands, those laws, creeds, and customs which have tended to restrict women to a position of dependence; to discourage their education; to impede the development of their natural gifts, and to subordinate their individuality, have been based on false theories, and have produced an artificial and unjust relation of the sexes. . . .

4. That self-government in the home and the State is the inalienable right of every normal adult, and the refusal of this right to women has resulted in social, legal, and economic injustice to them, and has also intensified the existing economic disturbances throughout the world.

5. That governments which impose taxes and laws upon their women citizens without giving them the right of consent or dissent . . . exercise a tyranny inconsistent with just government.

6. That the ballot is the only legal and permanent means of defending the rights to the "life, liberty and pursuit of happiness" pronounced inalienable by the American Declaration of Independence, and accepted as inalienable by all civilised nations. In any representative form of government, therefore, women should be vested with all political rights and privileges of electors.[103]

---

102. *See id.* at 32.
103. *Id.* at 31–32.

These principles clearly harken back to Wollstonecraft and the rights-of-man theory. The reference to the home is significant as are the terms "laws, creeds, and customs." These women were out to revolutionize relations between men and women and were determined that women should be full citizens. They had no intention of remaining subordinate and knew that marriage and the home were among the legal, as well as customary, means of maintaining women's subordination. In short, they were taking on the responsibilities of citizenship before they were legally equal citizens, concentrating on civil and political, as well as economic and social, rights.

By 1904, when these principles were adopted at their Berlin conference, increasing numbers of women were employed outside the home as clerks and secretaries in offices and in industrial production. By the 1913 conference in Budapest, where twenty-four countries were represented, IWSA board members had traveled to all continents to survey the status of women. During the conference, the Alliance decided to admit to membership women from countries where suffrage was an impossible or impractical idea, but where a "woman's movement" was either necessary or underway. The Alliance also adopted its first non-suffrage resolution on the problem of "white slave traffic" (trafficking in women).[104] Interest in the "white slavery" issue continued and would occupy the minds of CSW members, eventually finding its way into the Women's Convention in the article on prostitution as well as in the section on marriage and family law requiring consent to marriage.[105]

The Alliance was neither the first nor the only organization to address this issue. In Britain, Harriet Martineau had written on the subject in 1862, and Josephine Butler, president of the North of England Council for the Higher Education of Women from 1868 to 1873, was asked by male doc-

---

104. See id. at 60. The Alliance was not the only organization that developed an interest in ending white slave traffic (trafficking in women). Following World War I, the Union Française pour le Suffrage des Femmes invited women from Allied countries to help lobby against trafficking in women at the Paris Peace Conference. See id. at 70–71. Resolutions on "the moral, political and educational aspects of women's life" were presented to various commissions of the League of Nations. Id. at 71. The resolutions on moral status included the following objectives:

    1. "To suppress the sale of women and children."

    2. "To respect and apply the principle of woman's liberty to dispose of herself in marriage."

    3. "To suppress the traffic in women, girls, and children of both sexes, and its corollary, the licensed house of ill fame."

Id. See also NATALIE KAUFMAN HEVENER, INTERNATIONAL LAW AND THE STATUS OF WOMEN 10–12, 78–102 (1983) (providing cites for international conventions relating to trafficking in women).

105. CEDAW, supra note 2, arts. 6, 16.

tors to lead opposition to the cruel provisions regarding prostitutes in England's Contagious Diseases Act.[106] Under this legislation, prostitutes and women suspected of prostitution were required to submit to medical examinations for venereal disease to protect the health of soldiers and sailors.[107]

During World War I, women's participation in the paid labor force increased exponentially, and, because the war prevented travel and diverted organized women to the war effort, most international women's activities ceased. However, in 1915, an International Congress of Women was held at the Hague in an effort to promote peace among the warring nations. Jane Addams of Hull House in Chicago, notable for her work in urban reform and a supporter of the suffrage movement, was chosen as president of the Hague conference. In 1919, the International League for Peace and Freedom was organized, reflecting many women's concerns for peace.[108] When the 1919 Paris Peace Conference was called, a French women's suffrage union invited a small group of feminist activists to Paris to discuss women's participation in the peace process. The group proposed to Wilson and Clemenceau that women's interests be heard at the peace conference and that women be allowed to participate as both delegates and employees of the League of Nations. The first to hear the group's views was the labor commission, before which the women proposed a forty-four hour work week, a minimum wage, and equal pay for women. Another presentation to the Commission of the League of Nations covered women's education, suffrage, trafficking in women, and improvement in marriage laws.[109]

As a result of this lobbying, the League's Charter included provisions that League positions be open equally to women and men and workers have fair and humane employment conditions; also, the Charter mentioned the issue of trafficking in women and children.[110] Later IWSA members urged the British War Office to send women police to Germany to assure that German girls were not abused by the occupying troops.

All of the postwar activity resulted in the IWSA adopting a charter of women's rights at its 1920 conference that covered, in order of priority, political rights, personal rights, domestic rights, educational and economic

---

106. Forster, *supra* note 52, at 169–71.
107. *Id.*
108. *See* 1 Notable American Women, 1607–1950, at 20 (Edward T. James ed., 1971) (providing section on Addams).
109. *See* Whittick, *supra* note 101, at 70–71.
110. *See id.* at 72 (stating that

> Article 7(3) of the Covenant states that "all positions under or in connection with the League, including the secretariat, shall be open equally to men and women"; while Article 23(a) is concerned "with fair and humane conditions of labour for men, women and children" and 23(c) with "the supervision over the execution of agreements with regard to the traffic in women and children.").

rights, and moral rights.[111] Political rights included, not only suffrage, but equal recognition in legislative and administrative bodies, both nationally and internationally. Personal rights covered protection under laws against slavery and rights of married women to retain or change their nationality. Domestic rights revolved around marriage, with a married woman having the right to "the use and disposal of her own earnings and property, and that she should not be under the tutelage of her husband.... [T]he married mother should have the same rights over her children as the father."[112] Domestic rights also supported the concept that, as widows, women should be accorded guardianship of their children and "the right to maintenance by the State...."[113] The final section stated that "a child born out of wedlock... should have the same right to maintenance and education from the father... as a legitimate child, and that an unmarried mother, during the period when she is incapacitated, should... have the right of being maintained by the father of her child."[114] The new charter of women's rights called for "no special regulations for women's work, different from regulations for men, ... [and] that laws relative to women as mothers should be so framed as not to handicap them in their economic position...."[115] This was a harbinger of the argument over the protection of women workers that would continue into the 1980s.

All of the provisions would eventually find their way into CSW resolutions and into the Women's Convention, though it would take over fifty years of advocacy and lengthy discussions within the CSW and the United Nations. Resolutions at the 1920 IWSA Geneva conference also called for an annual League of Nations women's conference and attention to the problems of venereal disease and prostitution.[116] By this time, twenty-five countries had granted women suffrage, but forward-looking women were already beyond suffrage, and onto a broader women's agenda. Too many historians, male and female alike, have overlooked the broader agenda.

X. BIRTH CONTROL, FAMILY PLANNING, AND WOMEN'S HEALTH

What was not the subject of resolutions at the 1920 IWSA conference was birth control, which was presumably an issue too hot to handle publicly, though, it can be assumed, it was certainly discussed in private conversa-

---

111. *See id.* at 75–76 (reprinting the charter).
112. *Id.* at 75.
113. *Id.*
114. *Id.*
115. *Id.* at 76.
116. *See id.*

tions at the convention. Birth control is at the very heart of male/female relationships, and of any society's future, and few other facets of life have the same emotional depth, as John Stuart Mill and others understood so well. Safe and effective birth control and related information, including information on abortion, threatens a system as old as human life. Just as suffrage was a metaphor for women's equality in public life, birth control meant a measure of equality in private life for sexually active women.

Because of the deep emotions wrought by the issue of birth control and the few radicals, such as Emma Goldman, who publicly discussed birth control, it is understandable why birth control was not an issue on the 1920 IWSA agenda. It would take courage, leadership, time, and a great deal of organizing before birth control would become legal and its use widespread. As with so many other new issues, it was the radicals, those who first dare to speak out on an issue, who put this new issue into the realm of public discourse. Radicals serve an important political function. They make those who follow them, including traditional organizations that may take up the new cause, look more respectable. However, too often, it is the traditional groups that are recorded in history for accomplishments in a particular area or on a specific issue, when it was the radicals who first brought the matter to public attention.

Europeans led the way in developing birth control devices and making the discussion and promotion of their use legal. Although the condom is thought to have originated in Egypt centuries ago, it was only named in the seventeenth century for an English doctor who provided sheaths made from sheep organs to members of the court of King Charles II of England as protection against venereal disease. In nineteenth-century England, Annie Besant and Charles Bradlaugh won a landmark case involving the right to write, publish, and discuss birth control publicly.[117] Later, in the 1880s, the diaphragm was developed in Germany. Information about it and its use spread quickly, although not without strong opposition.

In 1873, the US Congress passed the Comstock Act,[118] which equated birth control information to pornography and made it illegal to mail, transport, or import into the United States any kind of birth control devices or information. However, the dissemination of information with such importance to women could not be stopped. Emma Goldman, a Russian-born US immigrant and sometimes midwife, who was active in the labor movement, took up the cause. A brilliant lecturer, she was unafraid to speak about the issue, arguing that women had to free themselves from within, not simply

---

117. *See* Margaret Sanger, Margaret Sanger: An Autobiography 127–28 (1938). *See also* 13 Birth Control Rev. 106 (1929) (for information on Besant).

118. 20 U.S.C. § 1462.

through suffrage.[119] It was in the labor movement that Margaret Sanger, the preeminent name associated with the US birth control movement, met Goldman, who opened Sanger's mind to the impact birth control could have on women.[120] The fact that Goldman also preached "free love"—love and sexual intercourse without marriage—made her, and, in many ways, the birth control movement, anathema to many.[121] In 1916, Goldman, called "Red Emma" by much of the press, was arrested for lecturing on birth control in New York City and spent fifteen days in jail as a consequence.[122]

Sanger's main concern was women's health and sexuality. She felt passionately that women, especially poor women, needed birth control information and devices for their own health and for that of their children. She had watched her mother die of tuberculosis after bearing eleven children, not uncommon for the time. As a nurse-midwife and labor movement activist, Sanger saw too many poor women at the mercy of their sexuality. In 1912, she began writing a series of articles on female sexuality and on venereal disease in a socialist weekly, but soon became distressed at the reaction of male labor leaders who did not share her passion.

After traveling to Europe with her first husband and learning more about birth control, Sanger returned to the United States in 1914 and, later that year, published a small magazine called "The Woman Rebel" in which she "intended to challenge Comstock's prohibition of information about sexuality and contraception."[123] That same year, Goldman was doing a lecture tour around the United States and sold Sanger's magazine on her tour.[124] Prohibited by law from using the mails to distribute her magazine, it being considered too radical even by left-wingers, Sanger distributed it herself around New York.[125] In August of that year, she was arrested for writing and distributing her magazine. Instead of preparing for trial, though, she wrote a pamphlet called *Family Limitation*[126] with specific birth control information and then escaped to Europe, where she met and became the lover of Havelock Ellis. In England, Sanger lectured before the Fabian Society and became acquainted with the ideas of Olive Schreiner, the South African

---

119. *See* Ellen Chesler, Woman of Valor: Margaret Sanger and the Birth Control Movement in America 85–86 (1992).

120. *See* Notable American Women: The Modern Period: A Biographical Dictionary 623–27 (Barbara Sicherman et al. eds., 1980).

121. *See* Marian J. Morton, Emma Goldman and the American Left: "Nowhere at Home" (1992).

122. *See generally* Candace Falk, Love, Anarchy and Emma Goldman (1984); Morton, *supra* note 121; 2 Notable American Women: A Biographical Dictionary 57–59 (E.T. James et al. eds., 1971).

123. Chesler, *supra* note 119, at 97.

124. *See* Falk, *supra* note 122, at 221–22.

125. *See* Chesler, *supra* note 119, at 99.

126. Margaret Sanger, Family Limitation (5th ed. rev'd, n.d.) (1914), *microformed on* History of Women, Reel 962, No. 9989 (Research Publications).

novelist and activist, and Ellen Key of Sweden, both of whom promoted birth control and women's liberation, although neither were active suffragists.

After visiting England and the Netherlands to learn more about contraception, Sanger opened a birth control advice center in New York that was promptly closed by the police. Despite her radical beginnings, the generation of enormous publicity regarding her activities eventually attracted wealthy women and medical doctors to her cause. Sanger and her supporters smuggled diaphragms into the United States, successfully challenged the Comstock Act and other restrictive laws in court, and established the American Birth Control League, the predecessor of Planned Parenthood Federation of America. Sanger later became involved in the international birth control movement and lived to see the US Supreme Court, in *Griswold vs. Connecticut*,[127] uphold contraception for married couples.

Sanger was by no means alone in the campaign for birth control rights and recognition of women's health issues. In the Dominican Republic, Evangelina Rodriguez, an African/Dominican, became that country's first woman doctor after obtaining her medical degree in Paris in 1909. Upon returning to her native country, she combined a medical career with feminist activism, including assistance to poor children, support of women's suffrage, and promotion of birth control. In Sweden, Elise Otteson-Jensen founded the Swedish Association for Sex Education, promoted family planning, and later worked with Sanger on an international birth control conference. In Egypt, educator Zahia Marzouk helped organize a conference on population issues sponsored by the Egyptian medical association. At the conference, she defied tradition by delivering her own paper on the population issue at a time when women were prevented from speaking in public. Twehida Ben Sheik, a Tunisian woman, went to medical school in Paris and later started a family planning clinic in a Tunisian hospital and worked to make abortion legal in that country.[128] As Perdita Huston has noted in her book, *Motherhood by Choice*,[129] these pioneers in the birth control movement came from a variety of backgrounds, but, "[r]egardless of their social standing, they were insulted and threatened for speaking out, for mentioning human sexuality and advocating the right to voluntary motherhood. . . . [T]hey were an easy target for those who opposed change or women's rights. Theirs was a constant struggle to maintain honour and courage."[130]

Each of these women followed the pattern of earlier feminists by becoming educated, defying tradition, organizing and informing their com-

---

127. Griswold v. Connecticut, 381 U.S. 479 (1965).
128. *See* Perdita Huston, Motherhood by Choice: Pioneers in Women's Health and Family Planning 95–106 (1992).
129. *Id.*
130. *Id.* at 4.

munities, and speaking out publicly. In short, they exercised leadership in the public sphere, helping to put women's health and reproductive issues on the international agenda. Between 1929 and 1935, the All India Women's Conference took up the birth control issue and, in 1935, "went on record in support of artificial contraception, making it the largest group in the world to have done so at the time."[131] In 1940, Eleanor Roosevelt, soon to be chair of the Human Rights Commission, declared herself publicly in favor of birth control. In spite of these gains, however, there were still setbacks. As late as 1959, US President Eisenhower rejected the Draper report that addressed the necessity of population planning in foreign aid. It took Helvi Sipilä of Finland and other strong minded CSW delegates, including those from India, to put birth control on the UN agenda in the 1960s under the rubric of family planning. Still today, however, the abortion issue raises strong objections in many quarters.

XI. THE UNITED NATIONS AND ITS COMMISSION ON THE STATUS OF WOMEN

By the time the United Nations was formed in 1945, women were deeply involved in the public sphere, primarily in nongovernmental organizations, but a number of countries had women among their delegations. The suffrage movement had been successful in thirty-one countries. Women's participation in the paid labor force during both world wars had been massive and never returned to prewar levels. Employed women in Europe and the United States had organized and were part of the international labor movement. The number of women's organizations had increased; these organizations advocated issues ranging from study and self-improvement to social welfare to suffrage, and many employed a variety of measures to draw attention to the causes.[132] Women from many countries also had gained extensive expe-

---

131. CHESLER, *supra* note 119, at 357.
132. In the United States, a women's club movement, primarily dedicated to self-education and social welfare, had expanded across the country. *See* THEODORA PENNY MARTIN, THE SOUND OF OUR OWN VOICES: WOMEN'S STUDY CLUBS, 1860–1910 (1987); ANNE FIROR SCOTT, NATURAL ALLIES: WOMEN'S ASSOCIATIONS IN AMERICAN HISTORY (1991). Social reformers such as Jane Addams, of Hull House in Chicago, had invented social work; Addams later became a force in urban affairs. *See* ALLEN F. DAVIS, AMERICAN HEROINE: THE LIFE AND LEGEND OF JANE ADDAMS (1973); JANE ADDAMS, JANE ADDAMS: A CENTENNIAL READER (1960); JANE ADDAMS, TWENTY YEARS AT HULL-HOUSE (1914). US suffrage leaders ranged from the organizationally minded Susan B. Anthony and Carrie Chapman Catt to the more militant Alice Paul, all of whom were also active internationally. A similar range could be found in England, including the militant Pankhursts. *See* ELLEN CAROL DUBOIS, FEMINISM AND SUFFRAGE: THE EMERGENCE OF AN INDEPENDENT WOMEN'S MOVEMENT IN AMERICA 1848–1869 (1978); CARRIE CHAPMAN CATT & NETTIE ROGERS SHULER, WOMAN SUFFRAGE AND POLITICS: THE INNER STORY OF THE SUFFRAGE MOVEMENT (1970); INEZ HAYES GILLMORE, STORY OF ALICE PAUL AND THE NATIONAL WOMAN'S PARTY (1977); ANTONIA RAEBURN, THE SUFFRAGETTE VIEW (1976) (providing information on Pankhurst).

rience in lobbying government officials locally, nationally, and even internationally. The International Federation of Working Women (IFWW), for example, had lobbied the International Labor Organization (ILO) and achieved adoption of the 1919 conventions on maternity protection and night work for women.[133] An area where the women's organizations had not been successful, however, was in convincing the League of Nations, the predecessor to the United Nations, to take up the question of the nationality of married women.

The work of women's organizations internationally came to fruition with the establishment of the United Nations.[134] Led by South American delegates, notably women from Brazil, Mexico, and the Dominican Republic, and with support from Indian and North American NGOs, the linkage between women's rights and human rights was effectively made in the UN Charter in its introduction and in four separate articles.[135] The equal rights of men and women clause in the UN Charter established a legal basis for the international struggle to affirm women's human rights.

Although only eleven of the fifty-one nations represented in the 1946 UN General Assembly had women on their delegations, with the support of women's NGOs, women made their presence known. Early in 1946, Marie-Helen LeFaucheux of France introduced an agenda item on the participation of women in UN conferences, which was adopted.[136] Brazil proposed establishing a status of women commission, but the proposal was strongly opposed by the US delegate, Virginia Gildersleeve, a founder of the International Federation of University Women. She argued the US position that such a commission would be discriminatory and that the human rights commission was able to deal with women's questions.

Minerva Bernadino of the Dominican Republic suggested that a committee of the Commission on Human Rights be established to work on women's rights. The New Zealand chair of the Economic and Social Council (ECOSOC) Organization Committee took up the suggestion, and, soon thereafter, a Human Rights Sub-Commission on the Status of Women was established. Eleanor Roosevelt, the widow of President Franklin Roosevelt, who was named chair of the Human Rights Commission, is commonly reputed to be the impetus for the establishment of the CSW. This is an his-

133. *See generally* HEVENER, *supra* note 104, at 119, 67–77 (discussing the maternity convention and night work convention respectively).
134. Margaret E. Galey, *Women Find a Place, in* WOMEN, POLITICS, AND THE UNITED NATIONS, *supra* note 98, at 11.
135. Four women signed the UN Charter in 1945, among them Minerva Bernardino of the Dominican Republic.
136. *Declaration on the Participation of Women in the Work of the United Nations: Report of the General Committee to the General Assembly,* U.N. GAOR, 1st Sess., 29th plen. mtg., No. 30, at 527–35, U.N. Doc. A/46 (1946).

torical error. She actually shared the US/Gildersleeve view that the Human Rights Commission and its Sub-Commission on Women could be trusted to deal effectively with women's issues. She had, however, been a signatory, along with Jean McKenzie of New Zealand, Evdokia Uralova of the Soviet Union, and Ellen Wilkinson of Britain, to an "Open Letter to the Women of the World" calling on women to take a more active role in politics and government.[137]

Mrs. Roosevelt's position against a separate women's commission was not sustained. Within a year, the Sub-Commission became a free standing commission, the current Commission on the Status of Women (CSW). Support for a full commission was led by the chair and vice-chair of the Sub-Commission as well as Bodil Begtrup of Denmark, Minerva Bernadino of the Dominican Republic, and Marie-Helen LeFaucheux of France. Bernardino had chaired the Inter-American Commission on Women; Begtrup had been active with the League of Nations on women's issues; and LeFaucheux had been a part of the French resistance movement.[138] These women knew how to organize and strategize, and they realized that a full commission was the only sure way to get their recommendations on women's rights directly to ECOSOC and the General Assembly.

The Sub-Commission had proposed "four immediate tasks.... (1) the creation of a [UN] Secretariat office headed by a competent woman; (2) the conclusion of the worldwide survey of laws on women [originated under the League of Nations]; (3) the promotion of equal educational opportunity; and (4) a [world] women's conference."[139] Dropping the idea of a world conference, the women succeeded in obtaining Roosevelt's support, and, on 21 June 1946, ECOSOC authorized a free standing Commission on the Status of Women and requested the Commission report back in 1947.[140]

The purpose of the full commission was to promote women's rights in all fields of human endeavor. The object was

> to elevate the equal rights and human rights status of women, irrespective of nationality, race, language, or religion, in order to achieve equality with men in all fields of human enterprise and to eliminate all discrimination against women in statutory law, legal maxims or rules, or in interpretations of customary law.[141]

Meanwhile, the UDHR was being drafted, and it is not without interest that the Council of Women and the YWCA were among the twenty-two

---

137. See GALEY, *supra* note 134, at 11–12.
138. Interview with Margaret E. Galey (23 June 1997).
139. GALEY, *supra* note 134, at 13.
140. See *id.* at 14.
141. Margaret E. Galey, *Promoting Nondiscrimination Against Women: The UN Commission on the Status of Women*, 23 INT'L STUD. Q. 276 (1979).

NGOs who urged the United Nations to draft such a declaration. Commission members and female delegates were concerned that terms such as the "rights of man" would not be interpreted to specifically include women. Bodil Begtrup, CSW Chair, stated in one meeting that the drafting of the UDHR "was of fundamental importance for women," and pointed out that because "sex equality was a right which had been acquired but recently, it would be necessary to emphasize it explicitly in certain Articles."[142] Later, she suggested the term "human beings" be substituted for the word "men."[143] Five days later, on 12 December, the wording about women was still an issue. Mrs. Mehta of India objected to the words "all men" and "brothers" fearing that "they might be interpreted to exclude women, and were out of date."[144] The working group drafting the Declaration adopted the idea of a footnote to Article 1 indicating that the word men referred to all human beings.[145] This legislative history clearly shows that the subject was debated and that the women in the drafting group made their point known. Ultimately, the ungendered term "everyone" was used extensively in the UDHR.

The CSW reflected the work on women's rights that had gone on before in the United Nations and earlier within various international bodies and women's organizations. By 1951, as a result of a Commission initiative, the ILO adopted the Convention and Recommendation Concerning Equal Remuneration for Men and Women Workers for Work of Equal Value[146] and later issued recommendations on women's right to employment opportunities, pensions, retirement, and social insurance.[147] By 1952, the CSW succeeded in having the Convention on Political Rights of Women[148] adopted—a direct result of the suffrage movement. Reflecting centuries of concern about the position of women in marriage, the Convention on the Nationality of Married Women was drafted and adopted by the General

---

142. *Working Group on the Declaration of Human Rights, Summary Record of the Second Meeting,* U.N. ESCOR, Comm'n on Hum. Rts., 2d Sess., U.N. Doc. E/CN.4/AC.2/SR.2 (1947). *See also* Johannes Morsink, *Women's Rights in the Universal Declaration,* 13 Hum. Rts. Q. 229 (1991).
143. *See* Morsink, *supra* note 142, at 234.
144. *Working Group on the Declaration of Human Rights, Summary Report of the Thirty-fourth Meeting,* U.N. ESCOR, Comm'n on Hum. Rts., 2d Sess., at 4, U.N. Doc. E/CN.4/AC.2/SR.34 (1947). *See* Morsink, *supra* note 142, at 234.
145. *See id.*
146. Convention Concerning Equal Remuneration for Men and Women Workers for Work of Equal Value (ILO No. C100), *adopted* 29 June 1951 (*entered into force* 23 May 1953); Recommendation Concerning Equal Remuneration for Men and Women Workers for Work of Equal Value (ILO No. R90), *adopted* 29 June 1951.
147. *See* Hevener, *supra* note 104.
148. Convention on the Political Rights of Women, *opened for signature* 31 Mar. 1953, 27 U.S.T. 1909, T.I.A.S. No. 8289, 193 U.N.T.S. 135 (*entered into force* 7 July 1954) (*entered into force for U.S.* 7 July 1976).

Assembly in 1957,[149] supplementing Article 15 of the UDHR. In 1962, the Commission's Convention on the Consent to Marriage, Minimum Age for Marriage and the Registration of Marriages was adopted.[150] CSW also worked with UNESCO on an equal education convention, adopted in 1960,[151] and promulgated recommendations on political and civic education, women's right to inherit property, a contentious issue that would surface again and again, and to equal treatment before the law.[152]

XII. A DECLARATION ON ELIMINATING DISCRIMINATION AGAINST WOMEN

Although the British Federation of Business and Professional Women had suggested to UN General Assembly President Spaak in 1946 that a UN convention on discrimination against women would be in order, it was not until 1963 that the first, tentative steps toward such a convention were undertaken.[153] In that year, a series of events put a new focus on women in the United Nations. A General Assembly resolution was adopted, introduced by developing and Soviet-bloc countries, calling for the CSW to draft a declaration on eliminating discrimination against women.[154] The resolution invited member states and "appropriate non-governmental organizations" to submit comments and proposals on principles that might be included in such a declaration.[155] Also, 1963 was the first year that the CSW formally considered birth control, albeit under the guise of the term "family planning,"[156] and agreed to study the issue. Helvi Sipilä of Finland, a longtime Commission member, was appointed Special Rapporteur on the question of family planning and subsequently produced a landmark work entitled *Study on the Interrelationship of the Status of Women and Family Planning.*[157] Sipilä was typical of many CSW members—she was a professional woman

---

149. Convention on the Nationality of Married Women, *done* 20 Feb. 1957, 309 U.N.T.S. 65 (*entered into force* 11 Aug. 1958).
150. Convention on the Consent to Marriage, Minimum Age for Marriage and the Registration of Marriages, *opened for signature* 10 Dec. 1962, 521 U.N.T.S. 231 (*entered into force* 9 Dec. 1964).
151. *See* HEVENER, *supra* note 104, at 165–76.
152. *See* GALEY, *supra* note 141, at 278.
153. *See* GALEY, *supra* note 134, at 12.
154. *Draft Declaration on the Elimination of Discrimination Against Women*, G.A. Res. 1921 (XVIII), U.N. GAOR, 18th Sess., 1274th plen. mtg., ¶ 1, 1963 U.N.Y.B. 357, U.N. Doc. A/5606 (1963).
155. *Id.* ¶ 2.
156. The two are quite different: birth control refers to the means the individual takes to prevent contraception, while family planning connotes a couple's decision-making.
157. *See* U.N. Doc. E/CN.6/575, at 5, Addendum.

who brought her long experience in the nongovernmental world to the UN system. Before working with the United Nations, Sipilä served as president of the Finnish Girl Guides and the International Federation of Women Lawyers; as a lawyer her primary interest had been family law.

Also in 1963, a new UN Report on the World Social Situation, dealing with housing, population, health, nutrition, education, and social services[158]—all traditional concerns of women—was before ECOSOC. The year also marked the fifteenth anniversary of the Universal Declaration of Human Rights and saw the Human Rights Commission complete a series of regional seminars on the status of women in family law.[159] In the same year, the General Assembly adopted an ECOSOC resolution on women in development, which had originally been submitted by Chile and cosponsored by numerous other delegations.[160] The resolution reflected the contents of the World Report and the new emphasis within the United Nations on development. The resolution called on all UN member states, specialized agencies, and nongovernmental organizations to appoint women "to bodies responsible for the preparation of national development plans" and drew attention to the "importance of training women so as to enable them to participate fully in all phases of . . . national development programmes. . . ."[161]

During the discussion of these resolutions, the CSW was congratulated for its work on the legal status of women and essentially told to consider economic and social development as well. The question became one of priorities: were programmatic efforts to improve women's current circumstances the priority, or was changing laws and policies to improve women's long-term legal and political capacity more important? Within the CSW and ECOSOC, some European and developing country representatives tended to favor the more programmatic, social welfare approach, while others took the more legalistic approach. This division continues to the present. The more simplistic want to know what women want, and the answer is both, and everything, as Frances Willard advised the WCTU years before. The ultimate desire, then and now, is for women to be considered human, a diverse, multifaceted group with both common and conflicting interests.

---

158. *See UN Report on the World Social Situation*, U.N. Doc. E/CN.5/375 Add. 1 & Add. 2 (1963).

159. *See Report of the Third Committee on the Report of the Economic and Social Council*, U.N. GAOR 3d Comm., 18th Sess., 1274th plen. mtg., Agenda Item 12, U.N. Doc. A/5606 (1963) [hereinafter *Report of the Third Committee*]; U.N. GAOR, 18th Sess., Supp. No. 15, U.N. Doc. A/5515 (1963).

160. *Participation of Women in National, Social and Economic Development*, G.A. Res. 1920 (XVIII), U.N. GAOR, 18th Sess., 1274th plen. mtg., 1963 U.N.Y.B. 357, U.N. Doc. A/5606 (1963) [hereinafter G.A. Res. 1920]. *See also Report of the Third Committee*, *supra* note 159, at 2 (stressing "the importance of ensuring greater participation of women in national, social and economic development").

161. G.A. Res. 1920, *supra* note 160, at ¶¶ 1, 2.

Although CSW members were representatives of governments, most also had experience in national or international women's organizations, and, unlike the mainstream human rights organizations, the CSW never reflected strong distinctions between political and civil rights and economic and social rights. Women's experiences tending home and family and as participants in the economic, social, and cultural life of their communities blurred these distinctions. Also, the basic rights to education, employment, and health fall under the economic and social rights rubric.

Against this background, work on a declaration eliminating discrimination against women began. By 1965, thirty governments, fifteen women's NGOs, and four UN specialized agencies had submitted comments on the proposed declaration.[162] Not surprisingly, education was a high priority among the submissions, as was the view that marriage and family law, reinforced by tradition and custom, was at the heart of much discrimination. Interestingly, Afghanistan's reply at that time stated that eliminating discrimination required the "combating of traditions, customs and usages which thwart the advancement of women"[163] and noted that this would require an intensive public education campaign. The idea that public opinion had to be changed was reiterated by numerous governments and NGOs. Afghanistan also suggested that "amends must be made to women by granting them certain privileges,"[164] which suggestion was a precursor of the idea of affirmative action, later called "temporary special measures" by the United Nations.

The same point was also made in the International Social Democratic Women's comments that concentrated on employment rights. There was strong support from Eastern Europe and the Soviet bloc for the declaration with suggestions that the problems of mothers, including employed and unmarried mothers, be taken into account, a clear indication that Alexandra Kollanti's influence survived. St. Joan's Alliance, and international Catholic women's organization, suggested that resolutions adopted at their 1964 Antwerp meeting covering inheritance, ritual operations (a very early reference to female genital mutilation), and equal pay be considered for inclusion in the declaration. Other replies mentioned penal code reform, and many referred back to the UDHR, indicating that numerous respondents understood that women's rights were human rights.[165]

---

162. *See UN Commission on the Status of Women: Report of the Eighteenth Session,* U.N. ESCOR, Comm'n on the Status of Women, 39th Sess., Supp. No. 7, Agenda Item No. 53, at 16, U.N. Doc. E/4025-E/CN.6/422 (1965) [hereinafter *Report of the Eighteenth Session*].

163. U.N. ESCOR, Comm'n on the Status of Women, 39th Sess., U.N. Doc. E/CN.6/426, at 5 (1964) (on Afghanistan).

164. *Id.*

165. *See Report of the Third Committee, supra* note 159.

With these comments, a draft declaration submitted by Poland, and working papers submitted by Ghana and the Mexican delegate, CSW chair Maria Lavalle Urbina, the CSW began drafting a declaration at its 1965 meeting in Teheran. A drafting committee brought forward an eleven-article text that began with a definition and condemnation of discrimination, covered virtually all the areas mentioned in the responses submitted, and concluded with an article calling on women's organizations to educate the public about the declaration's principles.[166] This draft was sent out for comments, an exercise in public education as well as a test of political sentiment. At the 1966 CSW session, the major debate concerned protection of women workers. Many argued that protection perpetuated and reinforced discrimination, while others took the more conventional view that women needed protection because of their maternal function.

When the CSW draft of a declaration came before ECOSOC's Third Committee, an article calling for the abolition of discriminatory customs and traditions and raising the issue of protection of women workers created a furor. Some Third Committee delegates had suggested women be protected from "arduous work." NGOs responded with vehemence that protecting women from arduous work was ridiculous because women worldwide did such work. Nursing, tea picking, child care, and household work were arduous, they insisted, and customary family law simply reinforced women's subordinate status. By the end of their 1967 session, after some astute political maneuvering, the Commission unanimously adopted its draft and, with the support of women delegates to ECOSOC's Third Committee, an eleven-article Declaration was adopted by the General Assembly on 7 November 1967.[167] It covered the issues women had been working on for centuries.

Meanwhile, a second wave of an openly feminist international women's movement was becoming evident in the late 1960s. Small, informal consciousness-raising groups, public demonstrations on a variety of issues, and the exchange of information via informal newsletters and privately published studies and reports characterized this movement on local and national levels. It was essentially an underground movement with primarily negative and disparaging media attention. The emphasis of the new movement was on examining the pervasiveness of sex discrimination at all levels

---

166. *Report on the Eighteenth Session, supra* note 162 at 22, art. 12 (calling on women's organizations to launch a wide-spread educational campaign).
167. *Declaration on the Elimination of Discrimination Against Women,* G.A. Res. 2263 (XXII), U.N. GAOR, 22d Sess., 1497th plen. mtg., Vol. 1, at 35–37, 1967 U.N.Y.B. 521, U.N. Doc. A/6880 (1967). *See also* Arvonne S. Fraser, *The Convention on the Elimination of All Forms of Discrimination Against Women (The Women's Convention), in* WOMEN, POLITICS, AND THE UNITED NATIONS, *supra* note 98, at 77.

of society and strategizing as to the most effective means to overcome it. *Ad hoc* caucuses were organized within professional organizations to examine discrimination within the professions and academia. Integrating women into all facets of public life and at higher levels became one theme of the movement, but, first, the age-old concerns about women's education, health, birth control and abortion, and employment discrimination were analyzed by small groups and gradually brought to public attention. Within the United States, during the 1970s, the new feminists and main line, or traditional, women's organizations collaborated to have the US Congress pass numerous new antidiscrimination laws, including Title IX of the Education Amendments,[168] which required all educational institutions receiving federal funds to eliminate discrimination against women and girls. This eventually brought about exponential increases in the numbers of women studying law, medicine, and science and initiated more sports and physical education programs for girls. All of the activity drew increased media attention. Although often demeaning, the attention was still useful in raising consciousness and expectations among women, not only in the United States, but in the United Nations as well. Like all political and social movements, publicity about the feminist movement attracted attention, motivated people to ponder their own situation and make comparisons, and inevitably resulted in increased numbers joining the movement. As a learned sociologist friend once said, political movements are like snowballs rolling downhill, they gather momentum, get bigger. While the new US feminist groups paid no attention to CSW and little to international affairs in the early 1970s, traditional NGOs who lobbied the Commission were influenced by this new movement, and, with the increased dominance of the US press, the new movement gave momentum to, and reinforced, CSW's work.

Following the UN custom of moving from a declaration to a convention, the Polish CSW delegate proposed the move shortly after the Declaration was adopted in 1967. Yet, it was 1972 before the Commission had a Secretary-General's report on the existing status of women's conventions, their relationships to the Declaration, and responses from governments on the idea of a convention. Also, in 1972, the UN General Assembly approved what had been a dream of some female delegates when the United Nations was formed—the holding of a world women's conference.[169] Moreover, 1975 was designated as International Women's Year.[170] Mexico

---

168. 20 U.S.C. § 1681 et seq.
169. *See International Women's Year,* G.A. Res. 3010 (XXVII), U.N. GAOR, 27th Sess., 2113th plen. mtg., 1972 U.N.Y.B. 454, U.N. Doc. A/8928 (1972); *Conference of the International Women's Year,* G.A. Res. 3276 (XXIX), U.N. GAOR, 29th Sess., 2311th plen. mtg., addendum, 1974 U.N.Y.B. 657, U.N. Doc. A/9829/Add.1 (1974).
170. *Id.*

City was selected as the site for the Conference and Helvi Sipilä, a CSW representative since 1960, was chosen as Assistant Secretary General for Social Development and Humanitarian Affairs in charge of the year and the Conference. Equality, development, and peace were selected as the themes of the Conference—a clear, if unacknowledged, tribute to the 1926 Conference of the International Alliance of Women, which had first used the term "woman's movement" and asserted that the goals of this movement were "Equality, International Understanding and Peace."[171]

Sipilä set to work, traveling the globe, urging governments to support the Conference and to set up "national machineries," the UN term for women's bureaux or commissions. Sipilä also understood that a symbol of the year was needed, one that transcended language barriers. The instantly popular result still symbolizes the international women's movement—a stylized dove, representing peace, with the women's and equality signs embedded in the body of the dove.

Preparations for International Women's Year dominated CSW's agenda, but a special working group, appointed at the suggestion of the Soviet Union, Tunisia, and the United Kingdom and composed of experienced CSW workers, was created to begin work on a possible convention. The Philippines' delegate presented a draft text, noting that it implied no commitment on the part of the Philippine government. CSW leaders from the Dominican Republic, Hungary, and Egypt became the working group's officers. Taking up the Philippines' delegate's strategy of drafting with no commitment from their governments, the group decided not to attribute positions taken on specific articles or language to a particular delegate, thus allowing free discussion among the members. This created what later feminist historians called a "free space" for UN women who believed a legally binding convention was the desired goal.[172]

XIII. THE WORLD WOMEN'S CONFERENCES

The 1975 International Women's Year Conference attracted five thousand representatives, from all branches of the new women's movement, to Mexico City, and to the NGO Tribune held in conjunction with the official UN Conference. In both the Tribune and the governmental Conference, contentious divisions between developing and industrialized countries surfaced and were energetically reported by the world's media. Developing

---

171. WHITTICK, *supra* note 101, at 92.
172. *See* SARA M. EVANS & HARRY C. BOYTE, FREE SPACES: THE SOURCES OF DEMOCRATIC CHANGE IN AMERICA at vii (1986) (discussing the definition of the "free spaces" idea).

country representatives argued development would bring equality; new feminists from industrialized countries vehemently opposed that idea, citing innumerable areas of discrimination in their countries. The atmosphere in Mexico City appeared more tense than it actually was, fed not only by the media, but also by many male delegates who thought the whole idea of a world women's conference was unnecessary, but who used it to test the political waters on such questions as development, the new international economic order (NIEO), and the influence of colonialism on developing countries, many of them newly independent. Soviet and American delegates sparred over Cold War issues in the plenary sessions, while in the drafting committee meetings for the World Plan of Action, women came together around common interests.[173]

A new international women's movement was in the making. In some countries, the formation of in-country women's commissions or the "national machineries" Sipilä had encouraged followed a strong feminist approach. In others, new, avowedly feminist NGOs were formed. In all countries, the symbol adopted by CSW for International Women's Year became visible.[174] These events and the symbol served to bring women together at local and national levels around common concerns and to raise awareness about sex discrimination and equality, as well as women's place in the development process.

The World Plan of Action adopted at the Conference gave credit in its introduction to the work of CSW and to the numerous women's rights conventions already adopted. The Plan noted that the promotion and protection of human rights for all was one of the fundamental principles of the UN Charter and that "[h]istory has attested to the active role which women played ... in accelerating the material and spiritual progress of peoples."[175] It predicted that, "in our times, women's role will increasingly emerge as a powerful revolutionary social force."[176] An overly optimistic fourteen-point list of five-year minimum goals was set forth, including:

> (a) Marked increase in literacy and civic education of women ... ;
>
> . . .
>
> (g) Encouragement of a greater participation of women in policy-making ... ;

---

173. *See* Arvonne S. Fraser, The U.N. Decade for Women: Documents and Dialogue 17–54 (1987).
174. The author of this article, then US Agency for International Development coordinator of the Office of Women in Development, received reports from mission directors that noted that they saw the symbol posted across remote corners of the developing world.
175. United Nations, Report of the World Conference of the International Women's Year (Mexico City, 19 June–2 July 1975), ¶ 6, U.N. Sales No. E.76.IV.1 (1976), *reprinted in* Women and World Development 185–218 (Irene Tinker & Michele Bo Bramsen eds., 1976) [hereinafter World Plan of Action].
176. *Id.*

(h)   Increased provision for . . . health education and services . . . ;
(i)   Provision for parity in the exercise of civil, social and political rights such as those pertaining to marriage, citizenship and commerce;
(j)   Recognition of the economic value of women's work in the home in domestic food production and marketing and voluntary activities . . . ;

       . . .

(l)   The promotion of women's organizations. . . ;
(m)   The development of modern rural technology . . . to help reduce the heavy work load of women . . . ; [and]
(n)   The establishment of interdisciplinary and multisectoral machinery within the government for accelerating the achievement of equal opportunities for women and their full integration into national life.[177]

The Plan called for the "active involvement of non-governmental women's organizations [to achieve] the goals of the ten year World Plan of Action."[178] In the global action section, the Plan called on the United Nations to proclaim 1975 to 1985 the UN Decade for Women; also, it called for the drafting and adoption of a convention on eliminating discrimination against women.[179] In another section, the Plan stated that the theory and practice of inequality begins in the family and called for more equal sharing of family responsibilities between men and women.[180] Without the latter, the Plan stated, women could not be fully integrated in society or achieve equal rights. Also, without more data and information on women, development could not proceed.

The United Nations and women's organizations around the world responded to the outpouring of interest generated by the IWY Conference. The Decade was established by the UN General Assembly with the sub-themes of education, employment, and health, the three issues that women leaders and women's organizations had been discussing for centuries. During the Decade, there was an explosive growth in the number, style, and content of women's organizations. Many were not organizations in the precise meaning of that term, but informal groups operating often on an *ad hoc,* as needed basis. New international organizations were also formed. One of the most notable was the International Women's Tribune Center, devoted to exchanging information worldwide and concentrating on providing readily accessible information to women in developing countries.

---

177. *Id.* ¶ 46.
178. *Id.* ¶ 48.
179. *See id.* Paragraph 182 of the World Plan of Action calls for proclaiming the decade; paragraph 198 calls for high priority to be given to the preparation and adoption of the convention on the elimination of discrimination against women, with effective procedures for implementation. *Id.* ¶¶ 182, 198.
180. *Id.* ¶ 16.

Although its emphasis was on development and on rural women, women's rights were not ignored.

The resurgence of a second-wave women's movement was believed to be concentrated in the United States and Europe—and the majority of the 1975 NGO Tribune's participants were from the industrialized countries—but, by 1976, there was enough activity to warrant and support three international publications: WIN NEWS, established in 1975; *Isis*, a magazine published by a new collective based in Geneva; and the International Women's Tribune Center's newsletters focusing on developing country women's activities. The Tribune Center's materials were distinguished by simple graphics and easy to read content aimed at women with low level reading skills. WIN NEWS emphasized UN activities, while *Isis* emphasized the more radical new women's groups in developing countries and Europe.[181] WIN NEWS and *Isis* represented the two different wings of the new movement: *Isis*, the "liberationists" who wanted to free women from traditional constraints of all kinds, and WIN NEWS, the "legalists" who aimed to change law and policy to guarantee more equality for women.

Also, by the mid-1970s, foreign aid donor nations had responded to the new international women's movement and UN development initiatives by establishing women in development (WID) offices. Ester Boserup's landmark book, *Women in Economic Development*, published in 1969, had persuasively documented the role women played in agricultural production in developing nations.[182] Although the expressed purpose of these WID programs was to assist the male-dominated donor agencies in integrating women as both beneficiaries and agents of economic development, the momentum of the new feminist movements in industrialized countries and the World Women's Conferences influenced how WID funds were allocated. Data collection and income-generating projects were given high priority by most donors, but some, such as Swedish SIDA, supported the new women's bureaux in developing countries while others supported legal literacy and other projects devised by indigenous organizations. In terms of women's human rights, the support of legal literacy programs, including an early one in Nepal, was extremely important.

Among many of the WID officers in donor countries, a primarily long-term, albeit unadvertised, objective was improving the status of women within their own agencies and within developing countries. Leaders of women's groups, researchers and new networks were identified and supported in both developing and industrialized countries. Family planning

---

181. In 1975 the editor of WIN NEWS had published a 300-page International Directory of Women's Development Organizations beginning with the Afghan Women's Society and ending with the World Feminist Commission.
182. ESTER BOSERUP, WOMAN'S ROLE IN ECONOMIC DEVELOPMENT (1970).

organizations, most notably International Planned Parenthood Federation (IPPF), also identified and trained women leaders through their projects in developing countries; IPPF was noted as being one of the most effective NGOs focusing on the CSW.

Before the 1980 Mid-Decade conference, an international consortium of WID offices was established under the OECD/DAC umbrella. Primarily a research, data, and information exchange mechanism, one result of the consortium was that millions of dollars were allocated by the donor nations to support the 1980 UN World Women's Conference held in Copenhagen, Denmark. Funds went not only to support the UN Conference and the parallel NGO Forum, but to support NGO workshops, tremendous numbers of publications, and the attendance of hundreds of developing country participants. While the media focused on the Israeli-Palestinian and other political confrontations at the Copenhagen Conference, the emphasis in the NGO Forum was on networking among women and the importance of women's organizations.

Unnoticed by the media was the solidarity among women in recognizing discrimination even across lines of intense political disparities. Males headed virtually every government delegation, even in the preparatory conferences. Interested primarily in the political issues and protecting their country's point of view, they left their chairs to female delegation members unless a political issue was on the agenda; then the blue suits, white shirts, and ties would emerge *en masse* into the meeting hall. Women would turn around and look at each other knowingly as they relinquished their seats. Finally, in one preparatory meeting when the men emerged from the outer hall, a swell of spontaneous laughter greeted them. By 1985, many women led delegations and the political officers were more discreet.

The Copenhagen Programme of Action,[183] while building on the Mexico City Plan, moved economic considerations to the fore. However, it emphasized that development was not only economic, but covered political, social, and cultural realms as well and that economic development projects often disadvantaged women, depriving them of their traditional forms of livelihood.[184] For the first time, as a result of WID studies, attention was directed to female-headed households, although the term "women who alone are responsible for families" was used, after considerable debate, because some delegations insisted only men could head households.

---

183. *Report of the World Conference of the United Nations Decade for Women: Equality, Development and Peace, Copenhagen, Denmark, July 14–30, 1980,* U.N. Doc. A/CONF.94/35 [hereinafter *Copenhagen Programme of Action*].

184. For more on the Copenhagen conference, including the NGO Forum, see FRASER, *supra* note 173; Jane S. Jaquette, *Losing the Battle/Winning the War: International Politics, Women's Issues, and the 1980 Mid-Decade Conference, in* WOMEN, POLITICS, AND THE UNITED NATIONS, *supra* note 98, at 45.

Extended debate was also had over the Programme's historical perspective section on the "roots of inequality." Western industrialized countries argued that the cause of inequality was the division of labor between men and women—justified by many on the basis of a woman's distinct child-bearing function; developing countries argued that "mass poverty" resulting from colonialism and unjust international economic relations was the cause, while the Soviet bloc argued that the predominant economic analyses of labor and capital (capitalism, that is) ignored women's work as producers and reproducers. Consensus was reached that discrimination was the result, no matter what view of history was taken. The Programme of Action stated that, while women were half the population of the world, they performed two-thirds of the world's work while only receiving one-tenth of world income and owning less than 1 percent of world property.[185]

XIV.   FROM DECLARATION TO CONVENTION TO WOMEN'S HUMAN RIGHTS TREATY

Following the IWY Conference and establishment of the UN Decade for Women, the CSW undertook a three-part program: drafting the Convention; monitoring the status of women, including women in development efforts; and preparing for the second and third world conferences. In 1976, CSW took up the draft convention prepared by the special working group with the objective of having a convention ready for the 1980 Conference in Copenhagen. Articles on access to health services, including family planning, and on rural women were added, the latter clearly a product of women in development efforts. Articles 15 and 16, with very specific provisions for equality under the law and in marriage, were very contentious because they conflicted with national legal systems. The implementation article also proved difficult: should CSW or an expert group be the implementation monitoring body?[186]

In early December 1979, the Third Committee took up the proposed convention. Time was running out if the convention was to be ready for signatures at the 1980 World Conference. The Swedish proposal for a monitoring body of twenty-three experts which would report to the UN General

---

185. *Copenhagen Programme of Action, supra* note 183, ¶¶ 10–16.
186. For a fuller discussion of the drafting and adoption of the Convention, see Fraser, *supra* note 167. *See also Report of the Working Group of the Whole on the Drafting of the Convention on the Elimination of Discrimination Against Women,* U.N. GAOR, U.N. Doc. A/C.3/34/14 (1979); *Note by the Secretary-General,* U.N. GAOR, 34th Sess., U.N. Doc. A/34/60 (1979); U.N. GAOR, 34th Sess., Agenda Item 75, U.N. Doc. A/34/PV.107 (1979).

Assembly through ECOSOC was finally adopted.[187] Then, Mexico proposed giving governments another year to consider such a formidable document. In an astute parliamentary move, the Netherlands delegate succeeded in convincing the committee that the Mexican proposal was not germane. The convention would not be delayed. On 19 December 1979, the General Assembly adopted the Convention on the Elimination of All Forms of Discrimination Against Women,[188] but not without strong debate on the political preamble, on paragraph 2 of Article 9 on the right of women to convey nationality to their children, and on Article 16 on marriage and family law.[189] The ideas John Stuart Mill had described in 1869 were still alive and well in a number of countries.

During the opening ceremony of the 1980 Conference, the Convention was presented to national governments for signature. Fifty-seven nations signed the document, and, by December 1981, the convention had acquired the twenty ratifications necessary to give the Convention force as a treaty. The result was a momentous victory, but most of the newer women's groups were now concentrating on women in development or single issues, such as health care or employment, and other programmatic efforts to improve women's current circumstances—on the whole, the Convention received little attention.

By 1985, when the Third World Women's Conference was held in Nairobi, Kenya, the twenty-three member expert Committee on the Elimination of Discrimination Against Women (CEDAW), which was to receive reports from governments on Convention implementation, had begun its work, albeit rather slowly.[190] The Nairobi Conference, with its approximately fifteen thousand attendees at the NGO Forum held on the University of Nairobi campus, demonstrated to the world through extensive media coverage that the new international women's movement was extremely diverse. Again, WID offices and international donor agencies were joined by national and international foundations in providing support for the conference, yet thousands of women still paid their own way. Attendees ranged from fresh-eyed recruits to sophisticated scholars to parliamentarians. The 1,200 Forum workshops on a wide array of topics reflected the diversity of women and their interests.[191] One multinational group mounted a workshop series on the

---

187. For details on the Swedish Proposal, see U.N. GAOR 3d Comm., at 10–15, U.N. Doc. A/C.3/34/14 (1979). For discussion of the Convention in the Third Committee, see *Report of the Third Committee,* U.N. GAOR, 34th Sess., Annexes, Agenda Item 75, at 1–10, U.N. Doc. A/34/830. For final debate and adoption in the General Assembly, see U.N. GAOR, 34th Sess., 107th plen. mtg., Agenda Item 75, at 1991–1999 (1979).
188. *See* CEDAW, *supra* note 2.
189. *See generally* Fraser, *supra* note 167.
190. *See* 1 United Nations, The Work of CEDAW: Reports of the Committee on the Elimination of Discrimination Against Women, 1982–1985 (1989).
191. For the first time, a number of reports on the NGO conference were published. *FORUM*

Convention. As with most NGO workshops, a standing-room-only crowd gathered each day to learn about the Convention, exchange information, and report on ratification efforts in their own countries. Out of this workshop series, a group called the International Women's Rights Action Watch (IWRAW) was formed to publicize and monitor the Convention and its implementation.

During the NGO Forum, the violence against women issue finally came out of the world's closet and forced itself into the public attention. Innumerable workshops on the topic were held and thousands of publications distributed. Crowds gathered daily at the Peace Tent on the Nairobi campus to discuss the links between violence in the home, violence in society, and violence between nations. The Forward Looking Strategies (FLS) document, adopted by the UN Conference in Nairobi, called for constitutional and legal reform in accordance with the Convention and for equality in social and political participation.[192] In the peace section, the violence against women issue warranted two long paragraphs and was referenced numerous times in other sections. As in the Mexico City and Copenhagen documents, education was the priority. In the FLS, it was called "the basis for the full promotion and improvement of the status of women" and the "basic tool that should be given to women in order to fulfill their role as full members of society."[193] Christine de Pizan had said the same thing centuries earlier, but by 1985, education was not merely about literacy; it encompassed concern about scholarships, stereotyped curricula, access to the highest levels of education, vocational training, and political and legal education.

XV. WOMEN'S RIGHTS AS HUMAN RIGHTS

In the twenty-year period from 1975 to 1995, masses of women moved from portraying themselves as victims at the mercy of male rulers in the private and public sectors to taking leadership roles in demanding their human rights. The three World Conferences allowed an ever-growing mass of activist women to exchange experiences across national boundaries and

---

'85: Final Report, Nairobi, Kenya was commissioned by the NGO Planning Group for the Forum while Images of Nairobi and Caroline Pezzullo's For the Record . . . Forum '85 were both published by the International Women's Tribune Center in 1986. See also FRASER, supra note 173, at 199.

192. This document was officially known as the United Nations Report of the World Conference to Review and Appraise the Achievements of the United Nations Decade for Women: Equality, Development and Peace, Nairobi, 15–26 July 1985, U.N. Doc. A/CONF.116/27/Rev.1, U.N. Sales No. E.85.IV.10 (1986). It was subtitled The Nairobi Forward-Looking Strategies for the Advancement of Women.

193. Id. ¶ 163.

form new international networks around common interests. The electronic and print media as well as governments responded. Women gradually became a new political constituency.

Although IWRAW, through its quarterly newsletter, *Women's Watch*, and other publications focusing on the Convention and the work of CEDAW, tried to draw international attention to the Convention, the majority of women's organizations continued to focus on their more particular issues. It was the violence against women issue, especially domestic violence, that finally drew wide international attention to the idea that women's rights are human rights. The issue transcended race, class and cultures, and united women worldwide in a common cause. It dramatically illustrated women's subordinate position as no other issue had. Activity around the violence issue at local and national levels brought thousands of new recruits into the international movement and moved increasing numbers of women into the political arena.

Although the women's convention did not address violence specifically, in its 1989 session, the CEDAW adopted General Recommendation No. 12,[194] describing how violence against women was covered by the Convention. At its 1992 session, CEDAW expanded on this in General Recommendation No. 19,[195] which stated that gender-based violence is discrimination; that such discrimination violates women's human rights; that the Convention covers both public and private acts; and that governments should take legal and other measures to prevent such violence and, in reporting under the Convention, indicate the measures taken.[196] Earlier, the Asian and Pacific Development Centre in Kuala Lumpur had introduced the violence issue in a book on women's health, and, in 1986, the UN Division for the Advancement of Women convened an expert group to identify implementation measures for the FLS section on violence against women.[197] During the late 1980s and early 1990s, women's organizations, govern-

194. *Report of the Committee on the Elimination of Discrimination Against Women: General Recommendation No. 12, Violence Against Women (8th Sess. 1989), adopted* 3 Mar. 1989, U.N. GAOR, 44th Sess., Supp. No. 38, ¶¶ 7–9, 24, U.N. Doc. A/44/38 (1990), *reprinted in Compilation of General Comments and General Recommendations Adopted by the Human Rights Treaty-bodies,* at 78, U.N. Doc. HRI/GEN/I/Rev.1 (1994) [hereinafter *Compilation of General Recommendations*].

195. *Report of the Committee on the Elimination of Discrimination Against Women: General Recommendation No. 19, Violence Against Women (11th Sess. 1992), adopted* 30 Jan. 1992, U.N. GAOR, 47th Sess., Supp. No. 38, U.N. Doc. A/47/38 (1993), *reprinted in Compilation of General Recommendations, supra* note 194, at 84.

196. *See* U.N. Doc. CEDAW/1992/L.1/Add.15 (1992). *See also* International Women's Rights Action Watch, *Report on CEDAW Session 11,* Aug. 1992, *available from* International Women's Rights Action Watch <http://www.igc.org/iwraw/publications/list/> (visited 19 July 1999).

197. This expert group meeting was only one result of ECOSOC Resolution 1984/14 of 24 May 1984 on violence against women that allowed the Branch for the Advancement of

ments, and the United Nations produced well-researched publications on the issue that were widely distributed.[198] Local and national organizations did the same. The United Nations' *Violence Against Women in the Family*[199] is one of the most comprehensive of these publications. It pointed out the obvious, that violence within the home "has long existed . . . hidden by family privacy, guilt and embarrassment and, to a certain extent, traditional customs and culture."[200]

While some organizations, especially local ones, concentrated on treating the victims of such violence, others worked to bring the issue to public attention. The momentum behind the issue made women's human rights the most dramatic agenda item at the 1993 World Conference on Human Rights held in Vienna, Austria. Virtually every government at the Conference felt compelled to give at least lip service to the violence issue and to women's human rights. The parallel NGO Forum was inundated with materials and activists on both the violence issue and on women's human rights generally. Highlighting the issue, a dramatic tribunal, organized by the Global Campaign for Women's Human Rights, was carried live on TV monitors throughout the conference hall. As a result, the Vienna Declaration and Programme of Action contained an extensive section on women's human rights with additional references throughout the document.[201] It declared that "[t]he human rights of women and of the girl-child are an inalienable, integral and indivisible part of universal human rights . . ." and that women's human rights "should form an integral part of the United Nations human rights activities."[202] Traditional human rights groups that had long concentrated on human rights abrogations by governments against their citizens began to accept the fact that violations of rights by citizens against each other were equally valid human rights abrogations. The private and public spheres began to merge in human rights theory and practice.

The 1995 UN World Conference on Women held in Beijing, China and the regional preparatory meetings for that Conference reaffirmed the conclusions of the Vienna Conference and put women's human rights even more firmly on the world agenda. Among the critical areas of concern for

---

Women to expand work on the subject. *Violence in the Family,* E.S.C. Res. 1984/14, U.N. ESCOR, 19 plen. mtg. (1984).

198. *See, e.g.,* WOMEN'S WATCH (the quarterly newsletter of the International Women's Rights Action Watch) (for a sampling of these publications).

199. U.N. CENTRE FOR SOCIAL DEVELOPMENT AND HUMANITARIAN AFFAIRS, VIOLENCE AGAINST WOMEN IN THE FAMILY, U.N. Doc. ST/CSDHA/2, U.N. Sales No. E.89.IV.5 (1989).

200. *Id.* at 3.

201. Vienna Declaration and Programme of Action, U.N. GAOR, World Conf. on Hum. Rts., 48th Sess., 22d plen. mtg., U.N. Doc. A/CONF.157/24 (1993), *reprinted in* 32 I.L.M. 1661 (1993).

202. *Id.* ¶ 18.

that Conference were, in order of priority: the burden of poverty on women; unequal access to education and training; health care; violence against women; the problems of armed conflict; the economic inequalities; inequality of power and decision-making; insufficient mechanisms to promote the advancement of women; lack of respect and protection of women's human rights; stereotyping of women and inequality in communications, especially the media; and the environment.[203] Discrimination against and violations of the rights of the girl-child was added at the behest of African women who, at their 1995 regional preparatory meeting in Senegal and also at their 1985 Arusha conference, argued what Wollstonecraft and de Pizan had articulated centuries earlier: if attention is not paid to girls and their education, and if girls are not thought of as equal potential citizens, the situation of women will never change. This was a recognition of history and a determination not to repeat it.

XVI.   CONCLUSIONS

The history of the drive for women's human rights indicates that only when women are literate, when they can articulate their view of life in publications and before audiences, when they can organize and demand equality, when girls are educated and socialized to think of themselves as citizens as well as wives and mothers, and when men take more responsibility for child and home care, can women be full and equal citizens and able to enjoy human rights.

The question of shared responsibility for, and the valuing of, the care of children and the home goes to the heart of the implementation of the women's human rights. The Taliban edicts are only an extreme example of the resistance to this idea. Resistance is found even among educated women who accept the double burden of being wholly or partially responsible for both the economic support and physical care of children and the home. Numerous articles in the Convention on the Elimination of All Forms of Discrimination Against Women deal with this problem. Article 5 seeks to eliminate stereotyped roles for men and women and to ensure that family education teaches that both men and women share a common role in raising children.[204] Article 10, dealing with education, reiterates the same

---

203. *Fourth World Conference on Women: Action for Equality, Development, and Peace, Beijing Declaration and Platform for Action, adopted* 15 Sept. 1995, U.N. GAOR, ch. III, ¶¶ 41–44, U.N. Doc. A/CONF.177/20 (1995), *reprinted in* Report of the Fourth World Conference on Women (1995) (recommended to the UN General Assembly by the Committee on the Status of Women on 7 Oct. 1995).
204. CEDAW, *supra* note 2, art. 5.

idea.[205] Article 11 calls for maternity leave and "social services to enable parents to combine family obligations with work responsibilities. . . ."[206]

As John Stuart Mill put it in 1869, marriage should be thought of as a partnership, a partnership of equals analogous to a business partnership, and the family not "a school of despotism," but "the real school of the virtues of freedom."[207] Article 16 of the Women's Convention lays out the legal framework for such a partnership,[208] but the legal and *de facto* situations vary because of age-old customs and traditions. Over the centuries, tremendous progress has been made in defining, demanding, and implementing women's human rights. Women have moved from the private sphere of home and family into the public sphere as citizens and workers.

In many respects and in many countries, women are now considered equal humans, legally if not socially or economically. Yet, reconciling family obligations with political and economic responsibilities remains a challenge for most women of the world. It is a formidable problem in the most industrialized nations and in the poorest families of all nations. The challenge for the twenty-first century is to find ways to reconcile these responsibilities so that women can exercise their human rights and become full citizens in all respects. It may take a new wave of an international women's movement to accomplish this task.

Meanwhile, however, the Women's Convention, now popularly called the women's human rights treaty, has been ratified or acceded to by 163 nations[209] and has become a formidable weapon in the struggle for worldwide implementation of women's human rights. Women's groups around the world are using the principles set forth in the Convention to promote women's rights observance through court cases; as the basis for advocacy in changing national laws and policies; and for highlighting abrogations of women's human rights before international committees. Increasing numbers of women's organizations are developing "shadow reports" on implementation of the treaty in countries coming up for review by the CEDAW Committee, which, in turn, is becoming more aggressive in challenging governments on conformance with the treaty. Christine de Pizan would be delighted to know that Mary Robinson of Ireland is now the United Nations High Commissioner for Human Rights, but early nineteenth-century women

---

205. *Id.* art. 10.
206. *Id.* art. 11.
207. Bell & Offen, *supra* note 42, at 398.
208. CEDAW, *supra* note 2, art. 16.
209. *See Committee on Elimination of Discrimination Against Women To Hold Twenty-First Session at Headquarters,* U.N. Press Release WOM/1125, 4 June 1999, at 4. Sadly, the United States is not one of the ratifying countries. Although Presidents Carter and Clinton both submitted the treaty for ratification to the US Senate, the Senate has yet to act, and US women's organizations have not made ratification a priority item.

writers such as Jane Austen would also recognize the fear that compels Gulf women to write anonymously or to use pseudonyms.[210] Although women's rights are now recognized as human rights, recognition does not mean implementation. Much work still needs to be done to achieve human rights for all.

---

210. *See* WOMEN'S WATCH, Dec. 1998, at 3.

Chapter 2

Women's Rights as Human Rights: Toward a Re-Vision of Human Rights

Charlotte Bunch

Significant numbers of the world's population are routinely subject to torture, starvation, terrorism, humiliation, mutilation, and even murder simply because they are female. Crimes such as these against any group other than women would be recognized as a civil and political emergency as well as a gross violation of the victims' humanity. Yet, despite a clear record of deaths and demonstrable abuse, women's rights are not commonly classified as human rights. This is problematic both theoretically and practically, because it has grave consequences for the way society views and treats the fundamental issues of women's lives. This paper questions why women's rights and human rights are viewed as distinct, looks at the policy implications of this schism, and discusses different approaches to changing it.

Women's human rights are violated in a variety of ways. Of course, women sometimes suffer abuses such as political repression that are similar to abuses suffered by men. In these situations, female victims are often invisible, because the dominant image of the political actor in our world is male. However, many violations of women's human rights are distinctly connected to being female—that is, women are discriminated against and abused on the basis of gender. Women also experience sexual abuse in situations where their other human rights are being violated, as political prisoners or members of persecuted ethnic groups, for example. In this paper I address those abuses in which gender is a primary or related factor because gender-related abuse has been most neglected and offers the greatest challenge to the field of human rights today.

The concept of human rights is one of the few moral visions ascribed to internationally. Although its scope is not universally agreed upon, it strikes deep chords of response among many. Promotion of human rights is a widely accepted goal and thus provides a useful framework for seeking redress of gender abuse. Further it is one of the few concepts that speaks to the need for transnational activism and concern about the lives of people globally. The

Universal Declaration of Human Rights,[1] adopted in 1948, symbolizes this world vision and defines human rights broadly. While not much is said about women, Article 2 entitles all to "the rights and freedoms set forth in this Declaration, without distinction of any kind, such as race, colour, sex, language, religion, political or other opinion, national or social origin, property, birth or other status." Eleanor Roosevelt and the Latin American women who fought for the inclusion of sex in the Declaration and for its passage clearly intended that it would address the problem of women's subordination.[2]

Since 1948 the world community has continuously debated varying interpretations of human rights in response to global developments. Little of this discussion, however, has addressed questions of gender, and only recently have significant challenges been made to a vision of human rights which excludes much of women's experiences. The concept of human rights, like all vibrant visions, is not static or the property of any one group; rather, its meaning expands as people reconceive of their needs and hopes in relation to it. In this spirit, feminists redefine human rights abuses to include the degradation and violation of women. The specific experiences of women must be added to traditional approaches to human rights in order to make women more visible and to transform the concept and practice of human rights in our culture so that it takes better account of women's lives.

In the next part of this article, I will explore both the importance and the difficulty of connecting women's rights to human rights, and then I will outline four basic approaches that have been used in the effort to make this connection.

I. BEYOND RHETORIC: POLITICAL IMPLICATIONS

Few governments exhibit more than token commitment to women's equality as a basic human right in domestic or foreign policy. No government determines its policies toward other countries on the basis of their treatment of women, even when some aid and trade decisions are said to be based on a country's human rights record. Among nongovernmental organizations, women are rarely a priority, and Human Rights Day programs on 10 December seldom include discussion of issues like violence against women or reproductive rights. When it is suggested that governments and human

---

1. Universal Declaration of Human Rights, adopted 10 December 1948, G.A. Res. 217A(III), U.N. Doc. A/810 (1948).
2. Blanche Wiesen Cook, "Eleanor Roosevelt and Human Rights: The Battle for Peace and Planetary Decency," Edward P. Crapol, ed. Women and American Foreign Policy: Lobbyists, Critics, and Insiders (New York: Greenwood Press, 1987), 98–118; Georgina Ashworth, "Of Violence and Violation: Women and Human Rights," Change Thinkbook II (London, 1986).

rights organizations should respond to women's rights as concerns that deserve such attention, a number of excuses are offered for why this cannot be done. The responses tend to follow one or more of these lines: (1) sex discrimination is too trivial, or not as important, or will come after larger issues of survival that require more serious attention; (2) abuse of women, while regrettable, is a cultural, private, or individual issue and not a political matter requiring state action; (3) while appropriate for other action, women's rights are not human rights per se; or (4) when the abuse of women is recognized, it is considered inevitable or so pervasive that any consideration of it is futile or will overwhelm other human rights questions. It is important to challenge these responses.

The narrow definition of human rights, recognized by many in the West as solely a matter of state violation of civil and political liberties, impedes consideration of women's rights. In the United States the concept has been further limited by some who have used it as a weapon in the cold war almost exclusively to challenge human rights abuses perpetrated in communist countries. Even then, many abuses that affected women, such as forced pregnancy in Romania, were ignored.

Some important aspects of women's rights do fit into a civil liberties framework, but much of the abuse against women is part of a larger socioeconomic web that entraps women, making them vulnerable to abuses which cannot be delineated as exclusively political or solely caused by states. The inclusion of "second generation" or socioeconomic human rights to food, shelter, and work—which are clearly delineated as part of the Universal Declaration of Human Rights—is vital to addressing women's concerns fully. Further, the assumption that states are not responsible for most violations of women's rights ignores the fact that such abuses, although committed perhaps by private citizens, are often condoned or even sanctioned by states. I will return to the question of state responsibility after responding to other instances of resistance to women's rights as human rights.

The most insidious myth about women's rights is that they are trivial or secondary to the concerns of life and death. Nothing could be farther from the truth: sexism kills. There is increasing documentation of the many ways in which being female is life-threatening. The following are a few examples:

— Before birth: Amniocentesis is used for sex selection leading to the abortion of more female fetuses at rates as high as 99 percent in Bombay, India; in China and India, the two most populous nations, more males than females are born even though natural birth ratios would produce more females.[3]

---

3. Vibhuti Patel, *In Search of Our Bodies: A Feminist Look at Women, Health and Reproduction in India* (Shakti, Bombay, 1987); Lori Heise, "International Dimensions of Violence Against Women," *Response*, vol. 12, no. 1 (1989): 3.

—   During childhood: The World Health Organization reports that in
    many countries, girls are fed less, breast fed for shorter periods of
    time, taken to doctors less frequently, and die or are physically and
    mentally maimed by malnutrition at higher rates than boys.[4]
—   In adulthood: The denial of women's rights to control their bodies
    in reproduction threatens women's lives, especially where this is
    combined with poverty and poor health services. In Latin America,
    complications from illegal abortions are the leading cause of death
    for women between the ages of fifteen and thirty-nine.[5]

Sex discrimination kills women daily. When combined with race, class,
and other forms of oppression, it constitutes a deadly denial of women's
right to life and liberty on a large scale throughout the world. The most
pervasive violation of females is violence against women in all its manifestations, from wife battery, incest, and rape, to dowry deaths,[6] genital mutilation,[7] and female sexual slavery. These abuses occur in every country
and are found in the home and in the workplace, on streets, on campuses,
and in prisons and refugee camps. They cross class, race, age, and national
lines; and at the same time, the forms this violence takes often reinforce
other oppressions such as racism, "able-bodyism," and imperialism. Case
in point: in order to feed their families, poor women in brothels around
US military bases in places like the Philippines bear the burden of sexual,
racial, and national imperialism in repeated and often brutal violation of
their bodies.

Even a short review of random statistics reveals that the extent of violence against women globally is staggering:

—   In the United States, battery is the leading cause of injury to adult
    women, and a rape is committed every six minutes.[8]

---

4. Sundari Ravindran, *Health Implications of Sex Discrimination in Childhood* (Geneva:
   World Health Organization, 1986). These problems and proposed social programs to
   counter them in India are discussed in detail in "Gender Violence: Gender Discrimination
   Between Boy and Girl in Parental Family," paper published by CHETNA (Child Health
   Education Training and Nutrition Awareness), Ahmedabad, 1989.
5. Debbie Taylor, ed., *Women: A World Report, A New Internationalist Book* (Oxford: Oxford
   University Press, 1985), 10. See Joni Seager and Ann Olson, eds., *Women In The World:
   An International Atlas* (London: Pluto Press, 1986) for more statistics on the effects of sex
   discrimination.
6. Frequently a husband will disguise the death of a bride as suicide or an accident in order
   to collect the marriage settlement paid him by the bride's parents. Although dowry is now
   illegal in many countries, official records for 1987 showed 1,786 dowry deaths in India
   alone. See Heise, note 3 above, 5.
7. For an in-depth examination of the practice of female circumcision see Alison T. Slack.
   "Female Circumcision: A Critical Appraisal," *Human Rights Quarterly* 10 (1988): 439.
8. C. Everett Koop, M.D., "Violence Against Women: A Global Problem," presentation by the
   Surgeon General of the U.S., Public Health Service, Washington D.C., 1989.

— In Peru, 70 percent of all crimes reported to police involve women who are beaten by their partners; and in Lima (a city of seven million people), 168,970 rapes were reported in 1987 alone.[9]
— In India, eight out of ten wives are victims of violence, either domestic battery, dowry-related abuse, or, among the least fortunate, murder.[10]
— In France, 95 percent of the victims of violence are women; 51 percent at the hands of a spouse or lover. Similar statistics from places as diverse as Bangladesh, Canada, Kenya, and Thailand demonstrate that more than 50 percent of female homicides were committed by family members.[11]

Where recorded, domestic battery figures range from 40 percent to 80 percent of women beaten, usually repeatedly, indicating that the home is the most dangerous place for women and frequently the site of cruelty and torture. As the Carol Stuart murder in Boston demonstrated, sexist and racist attitudes in the United States often cover up the real threat to women; a woman is murdered in Massachusetts by a husband or lover every 22 days.[12]

Such numbers do not reflect the full extent of the problem of violence against women, much of which remains hidden. Yet rather than receiving recognition as a major world conflict, this violence is accepted as normal or even dismissed as an individual or cultural matter. Georgina Ashworth notes that:

> The greatest restriction of liberty, dignity and movement, and at the same time, direct violation of the person is the threat and realisation of violence.... However violence against the female sex, on a scale which far exceeds the list of Amnesty International victims, is tolerated publicly; indeed some acts of violation are not crimes in law, others are legitimized in custom or court opinion, and most are blamed on the victims themselves.[13]

Violence against women is a touchstone that illustrates the limited concept of human rights and highlights the political nature of the abuse of women. As Lori Heise states: "This is not random violence.... [T]he risk factor is being female."[14] Victims are chosen because of their gender. The

---

9. Ana Maria Portugal, "Cronica de Una Violacion Provocada?", *Fempress* especial "Contraviolencia," Santiago, 1988; Seager and Olson, note 5 above, 37.
10. Ashworth, note 2 above, 9.
11. "Violence Against Women in the Family," Centre for Social Development and Humanitarian Affairs, United Nations Office at Vienna, 1989.
12. Bella English, "Stereotypes Led Us Astray," *The Boston Globe*, 5 Jan. 1990, 17, col. 3. See also the statistics in Women's International Network News, 1989; United Nations Office, note 11 above; Ashworth, note 2 above; Heise, note 3 above; and *Fempress*, note 9 above.
13. Ashworth, note 2 above, 8.
14. Heise, note 3 above, 3.

message is domination: stay in your place or be afraid. Contrary to the argument that such violence is only personal or cultural, it is profoundly political. It results from the structural relationships of power, domination, and privilege between men and women in society. Violence against women is central to maintaining those political relations at home, at work, and in all public spheres.

Failure to see the oppression of women as political also results in the exclusion of sex discrimination and violence against women from the human rights agenda. Female subordination runs so deep that it is still viewed as inevitable or natural, rather than seen as a politically constructed reality maintained by patriarchal interests, ideology, and institutions. But I do not believe that male violation of women is inevitable or natural. Such a belief requires a narrow and pessimistic view of men. If violence and domination are understood as a politically constructed reality, it is possible to imagine deconstructing that system and building more just interactions between the sexes.

The physical territory of this political struggle over what constitutes women's human rights is women's bodies. The importance of control over women can be seen in the intensity of resistance to laws and social changes that put control of women's bodies in women's hands: reproductive rights, freedom of sexuality whether heterosexual or lesbian, laws that criminalize rape in marriage, etc. Denial of reproductive rights and homophobia are also political means of maintaining control over women and perpetuating sex roles and thus have human rights implications. The physical abuse of women is a reminder of this territorial domination and is sometimes accompanied by other forms of human rights abuse such as slavery (forced prostitution), sexual terrorism (rape), imprisonment (confinement to the home), and torture (systematic battery). Some cases are extreme, such as the women in Thailand who died in a brothel fire because they were chained to their beds. Most situations are more ordinary like denying women decent education or jobs which leaves them prey to abusive marriages, exploitative work, and prostitution.

This raises once again the question of the state's responsibility for protecting women's human rights. Feminists have shown how the distinction between private and public abuse is a dichotomy often used to justify female subordination in the home. Governments regulate many matters in the family and individual spheres. For example, human rights activists pressure states to prevent slavery or racial discrimination and segregation even when these are conducted by nongovernmental forces in private or proclaimed as cultural traditions as they have been in both the southern United States and in South Africa. The real questions are: (1) who decides what are legitimate human rights; and (2) when should the state become involved and for what purposes. Riane Eisler argues that:

the issue is what types of private acts are and are not protected by the right to privacy and/or the principle of family autonomy. Even more specifically, the issue is whether violations of human rights within the family such as genital mutilation, wife beating, and other forms of violence designed to maintain patriarchal control should be within the purview of human rights theory and action. . . . [T]he underlying problem for human rights theory, as for most other fields of theory, is that the yardstick that has been developed for defining and measuring human rights has been based on the male as the norm.[15]

The human rights community must move beyond its male defined norms in order to respond to the brutal and systematic violation of women globally. This does not mean that every human rights group must alter the focus of its work. However it does require examining patriarchal biases and acknowledging the rights of women as human rights. Governments must seek to end the politically and culturally constructed war on women rather than continue to perpetuate it. Every state has the responsibility to intervene in the abuse of women's rights within its borders and to end its collusion with the forces that perpetrate such violations in other countries.

II. TOWARD ACTION: PRACTICAL APPROACHES

The classification of human rights is more than just a semantics problem because it has practical policy consequences. Human rights are still considered to be more important than women's rights. The distinction perpetuates the idea that the rights of women are of a lesser order than the "rights of man," and, as Eisler describes it, "serves to justify practices that do not accord women full and equal status."[16] In the United Nations, the Human Rights Commission has more power to hear and investigate cases than the Commission on the Status of Women, more staff and budget, and better mechanisms for implementing its findings. Thus it makes a difference in what can be done if a case is deemed a violation of women's rights and not of human rights.[17]

The determination of refugee status illustrates how the definition of human rights affects people's lives. The Dutch Refugee Association, in its pioneering efforts to convince other nations to recognize sexual persecution

---

15. Riane Eisler, "Human Rights: Toward an Integrated Theory for Action," *Human Rights Quarterly* 9 (1987): 297. See also Alida Brill, *Nobody's Business: The Paradoxes of Privacy* (New York: Addison-Wesley, 1990).
16. Eisler, note 15 above, 291.
17. Sandra Coliver, "United Nations Machineries on Women's Rights: How Might They Better Help Women Whose Rights Are Being Violated?" in Ellen L. Lutz, Hurst Hannum, and Kathryn J. Burke, eds., *New Directions in Human Rights* (Philadelphia: Univ. of Penn. Press, 1989).

and violence against women as justifications for granting refugee status, found that some European governments would take sexual persecution into account as an aspect of other forms of political repression, but none would make it the grounds for refugee status per se.[18] The implications of such a distinction are clear when examining a situation like that of the Bangladeshi women, who having been raped during the Pakistan-Bangladesh war, subsequently faced death at the hands of male relatives to preserve "family honor." Western powers professed outrage but did not offer asylum to these victims of human rights abuse.

I have observed four basic approaches to linking women's rights to human rights. These approaches are presented separately here in order to identify each more clearly. In practice, these approaches often overlap, and while each raises questions about the others, I see them as complementary. These approaches can be applied to many issues, but I will illustrate them primarily in terms of how they address violence against women in order to show the implications of their differences on a concrete issue.

1. *Women's Rights as Political and Civil Rights.* Taking women's specific needs into consideration as part of the already recognized "first generation" political and civil liberties is the first approach. This involves both raising the visibility of women who suffer general human rights violations as well as calling attention to particular abuses women encounter because they are female. Thus, issues of violence against women are raised when they connect to other forms of violation such as the sexual torture of women political prisoners in South America.[19] Groups like the Women's Task Force of Amnesty International have taken this approach in pushing for Amnesty to launch a campaign on behalf of women political prisoners which would address the sexual abuse and rape of women in custody, their lack of maternal care in detention, and the resulting human rights abuse of their children.

   Documenting the problems of women refugees and developing responsive policies are other illustrations of this approach. Women and children make up more than 80 percent of those in refugee camps, yet few refugee policies are specifically shaped to meet the needs of these vulnerable populations who face consid-

---

18. Marijke Meyer, "Oppression of Women and Refugee Status," unpublished report to NGO Forum, Nairobi, Kenya, 1985 and "Sexual Violence Against Women Refugees," Ministry of Social Affairs and Labour, The Netherlands, June 1984.
19. Ximena Bunster describes this in Chile and Argentina in "The Torture of Women Political Prisoners: A Case Study in Female Sexual Slavery," in Kathleen Barry, Charlotte Bunch, and Shirley Castley, eds., *International Feminism: Networking Against Female Sexual Slavery* (New York: IWTC, 1984).

erable sexual abuse. For example, in one camp where men were allocated the community's rations, some gave food to women and their children in exchange for sex. Revealing this abuse led to new policies that allocated food directly to the women.[20]

The political and civil rights approach is a useful starting point for many human rights groups; by considering women's experiences, these groups can expand their efforts in areas where they are already working. This approach also raises contradictions that reveal the limits of a narrow civil liberties view. One contradiction is to define rape as a human rights abuse only when it occurs in state custody but not on the streets or in the home. Another is to say that a violation of the right to free speech occurs when someone is jailed for defending gay rights, but not when someone is jailed or even tortured and killed for homosexuality. Thus while this approach of adding women and stirring them into existing first generation human rights categories is useful, it is not enough by itself.

2. *Women's Rights as Socioeconomic Rights.* The second approach includes the particular plight of women with regard to "second generation" human rights such as the rights to food, shelter, health care, and employment. This is an approach favored by those who see the dominant Western human rights tradition and international law as too individualistic and identify women's oppression as primarily economic.

This tendency has its origins among socialists and labor activists who have long argued that political human rights are meaningless to many without economic rights as well. It focuses on the primacy of the need to end women's economic subordination as the key to other issues including women's vulnerability to violence. This particular focus has led to work on issues like women's right to organize as workers and opposition to violence in the workplace, especially in situations like the free trade zones which have targeted women as cheap, nonorganized labor. Another focus of this approach has been highlighting the feminization of poverty or what might better be called the increasing impoverishment of females. Poverty has not become strictly female, but females now comprise a higher percentage of the poor.

Looking at women's rights in the context of socioeconomic development is another example of this approach. Third world peoples have called for an understanding of socioeconomic develop-

---

20. Report given by Margaret Groarke at Women's Panel, Amnesty International New York Regional Meeting, 24 Feb. 1990.

ment as a human rights issue. Within this demand, some have sought to integrate women's rights into development and have examined women's specific needs in relation to areas like land ownership or access to credit. Among those working on women in development, there is growing interest in violence against women as both a health and development issue. If violence is seen as having negative consequences for social productivity, it may get more attention. This type of narrow economic measure, however, should not determine whether such violence is seen as a human rights concern. Violence as a development issue is linked to the need to understand development not just as an economic issue but also as a question of empowerment and human growth.

One of the limitations of this second approach has been its tendency to reduce women's needs to the economic sphere which implies that women's rights will follow automatically with third world development, which may involve socialism. This has not proven to be the case. Many working from this approach are no longer trying to add women into either the Western capitalist or socialist development models, but rather seek a transformative development process that links women's political, economic, and cultural empowerment.

3.   *Women's Rights and the Law.* The creation of new legal mechanisms to counter sex discrimination characterizes the third approach to women's rights as human rights. These efforts seek to make existing legal and political institutions work for women and to expand the state's responsibility for the violation of women's human rights. National and local laws which address sex discrimination and violence against women are examples of this approach. These measures allow women to fight for their rights within the legal system. The primary international illustration is the Convention on the Elimination of All Forms of Discrimination Against Women.[21]

The Convention has been described as "essentially an international bill of rights for women and a framework for women's participation in the development process ... [which] spells out internationally accepted principles and standards for achieving equality between women and men."[22] Adopted by the UN General

---

21. Convention on the Elimination of All Forms of Discrimination Against Women, G.A. Res. 34/180, U.N. Doc. A/Res/34/180 (1980).
22. International Women's Rights Action Watch, "The Convention on the Elimination of All Forms of Discrimination Against Women" (Minneapolis: Humphrey Institute of Public Affairs, 1988), 1.

Assembly in 1979, the Convention has been ratified or acceded to by 104 countries as of January 1990. In theory these countries are obligated to pursue policies in accordance with it and to report on their compliance to the Committee on the Elimination of Discrimination Against Women (CEDAW).

While the Convention addresses many issues of sex discrimination, one of its shortcomings is failure to directly address the question of violence against women. CEDAW passed a resolution at its eighth session in Vienna in 1989 expressing concern that this issue be on its agenda and instructing states to include in their periodic reports information about statistics, legislation, and support services in this area.[23] The Commonwealth Secretariat in its manual on the reporting process for the Convention also interprets the issue of violence against women as "clearly fundamental to the spirit of the Convention," especially in Article 5 which calls for the modification of social and cultural patterns, sex roles, and stereotyping that are based on the idea of the inferiority or the superiority of either sex.[24]

The Convention outlines a clear human rights agenda for women which, if accepted by governments, would mark an enormous step forward. It also carries the limitations of all such international documents in that there is little power to demand its implementation. Within the United Nations, it is not generally regarded as a convention with teeth, as illustrated by the difficulty that CEDAW has had in getting countries to report on compliance with its provisions. Further, it is still treated by governments and most nongovernmental organizations as a document dealing with women's (read "secondary") rights, not human rights. Nevertheless, it is a useful statement of principles endorsed by the United Nations around which women can organize to achieve legal and political change in their regions.

4. *Feminist Transformation of Human Rights.* Transforming the human rights concept from a feminist perspective, so that it will take greater account of women's lives, is the fourth approach. This approach relates women's rights and human rights, looking first at the violations of women's lives and then asking how the human rights concept can change to be more responsive to women. For

---

23. CEDAW Newsletter, 3rd Issue (13 Apr. 1989), 2 (summary of U.N. Report on the Eighth Session, U.N. Doc. A/44/38, 14 April 1989).
24. Commonwealth Secretariat, "The Convention on the Elimination of All Forms of Discrimination Against Women: The Reporting Process—A Manual for Commonwealth Jurisdictions," London, 1989.

example, the GABRIELA women's coalition in the Philippines simply stated that "Women's Rights are Human Rights" in launching a campaign last year. As Ninotchka Rosca explained, coalition members saw that "human rights are not reducible to a question of legal and due process. . . . In the case of women, human rights are affected by the entire society's traditional perception of what is proper or not proper for women."[25] Similarly, a panel at the 1990 International Women's Rights Action Watch conference asserted that "Violence Against Women is a Human Rights Issue." While work in the three previous approaches is often done from a feminist perspective, this last view is the most distinctly feminist with its woman-centered stance and its refusal to wait for permission from some authority to determine what is or is not a human rights issue.

This transformative approach can be taken toward any issue, but those working from this approach have tended to focus most on abuses that arise specifically out of gender, such as reproductive rights, female sexual slavery, violence against women, and "family crimes" like forced marriage, compulsory heterosexuality, and female mutilation. These are also the issues most often dismissed as not really human rights questions. This is therefore the most hotly contested area and requires that barriers be broken down between public and private, state and nongovernmental responsibilities.

Those working to transform the human rights vision from this perspective can draw on the work of others who have expanded the understanding of human rights previously. For example, two decades ago there was no concept of "disappearances" as a human rights abuse. However, the women of the Plaza de Mayo in Argentina did not wait for an official declaration but stood up to demand state accountability for these crimes. In so doing, they helped to create a context for expanding the concept of responsibility for deaths at the hands of paramilitary or right-wing death squads which, even if not carried out by the state, were allowed by it to happen. Another example is the developing concept that civil rights violations include "hate crimes," violence that is racially motivated or directed against homosexuals, Jews, or other minority groups. Many accept that states have an obligation to work to prevent such human rights abuses, and getting violence against women seen as a hate crime is being pursued by some.

The practical applications of transforming the human rights concept from feminist perspectives need to be explored further. The danger in pursuing only this approach is the tendency to become isolated from and competitive with other human rights groups because they have been so reluctant

---

25. Speech given by Ninotchka Rosca at Amnesty International New York Regional Conference, 24 Feb. 1990, 2.

to address gender violence and discrimination. Yet most women experience abuse on the grounds of sex, race, class, nation, age, sexual preference, and politics as interrelated, and little benefit comes from separating them as competing claims. The human rights community need not abandon other issues but should incorporate gender perspectives into them and see how these expand the terms of their work. By recognizing issues like violence against women as human rights concerns, human rights scholars and activists do not have to take these up as their primary tasks. However, they do have to stop gate-keeping and guarding their prerogative to determine what is considered a "legitimate" human rights issue.

As mentioned before, these four approaches are overlapping and many strategies for change involve elements of more than one. All of these approaches contain aspects of what is necessary to achieve women's rights. At a time when dualist ways of thinking and views of competing economic systems are in question, the creative task is to look for ways to connect these approaches and to see how we can go beyond exclusive views of what people need in their lives. In the words of an early feminist group, we need bread and roses, too. Women want food and liberty and the possibility of living lives of dignity free from domination and violence. In this struggle, the recognition of women's rights as human rights can play an important role.

Chapter 3

Human Rights: A Feminist Perspective

Gayle Binion

I. FEMINISM AND LAW IN CONTEXT

Perhaps the most profound intellectual stimulant to jurisprudence in the past
generation has been the development of feminist approaches to the study of
law. Whereas a decade ago, significant obstacles were encountered in the
process of accessing this literature,[1] by the mid-1980s feminism became as
deeply rooted in legal scholarship as it had earlier become in several of the
humanities and social sciences. The myriad questions asked and approaches
employed under the feminist rubric have generated a dialogue that raises
fundamental questions about the nature of law: whom the system(s) serves,
the social conditions it both reflects and impacts, and the possibilities for its
transformation.

 Virtually all areas of law have felt feminism's influence. Although those
of most immediate material concern to women, such as family law, employment discrimination, and reproductive rights, were the first to be analyzed
from feminist perspectives,[2] other less obviously gendered subjects, such
as torts, criminal law, and constitutional law, have similarly been viewed
through feminist eyes.[3] Interwoven with these doctrinal analyses have been

---

1. Standard reference sources and indexes in law did not have *feminism* as a category until
   just a few years ago. While women and the law has been a category for at least the past
   twenty years, this did not capture the breadth of the feminist enterprise that had already
   grown in the field. Consequently, the vehicles necessary to build a self-referential and
   communicative dialogue were nonexistent during the most formative years of the enterprise.
2. *See, e.g.*, Martha A. Fineman, The Illusion of Equality: The Rhetoric and Reality of Divorce Reform
   (1991); Lenore J. Weitzman, The Divorce Revolution: The Unexpected Social and Economic
   Consequences for Women and Children in America (1985); Katharine T. Bartlett & Carol B.
   Stack, *Joint Custody, Feminism and the Dependency Dilemma*, 2 Berkeley Women's L.J. 9
   (1986); Herma H. Kay, *Equality and Difference: The Case of Pregnancy*, 1 Berkeley Women's
   L.J. 1 (1985); Christine A. Littleton, *Reconstructing Sexual Equality*, 75 Cal. L. Rev. 1279
   (1987).
3. *See, e.g.*, Leslie Bender, *A Lawyer's Primer on Feminist Theory and Tort*, 38 J. of Legal Educ.
   3 (1988); Kenneth Karst, *Woman's Constitution*, 1984 Duke L.J. 447; Robin West,

perhaps the most challenging critiques which address the law as an inherently gendered *system* and suggest that its processes and principles resonate with only male experience.[4]

Feminist developments in law did not, of course, occur in intellectual isolation. As is commonly the case in sociopolitical scholarly movements, law-oriented insights about the role and function of gender as a socially constructed and constructive variable drew heavily upon the research and literature in the fields of psychology and sociology. Landmark works like Gilligan's *In A Different Voice*,[5] Chodorow's *The Reproduction of Mothering*,[6] and Epstein's *Deceptive Distinctions*[7] addressed not only the status of women within (US) society, but attempted to explain the underpinnings of this "different" life experience. The application of insights such as these and myriad others of the 1970s and 1980s provided important foundations for feminist theorizing in law.[8]

II.   FEMINIST STUDIES AND JURISPRUDENCE: THE FOCUS OF CONCERN

Feminist jurisprudence has certain defining characteristics that are shared with feminist studies generally. These include a focus on women's experience, especially the disempowerment that has been ubiquitous. In a world in which women perform two-thirds of the hourly labor and receive 10 percent of the income and hold barely 1 percent of the property,[9] disempow-

---

Jurisprudence and Gender, 55 U. CHI. L. REV. 1 (1988); Elizabeth Schneider, *The Dialectic of Rights and Politics: Perspectives from the Women's Movement*, 61 N.Y.U.L. REV. 589 (1986); Gayle Binion, *Toward a Feminist Regrounding of Constitutional Law*, 72 SOC. SCI. Q. 207 (1991); Suzanna Sherry, *Civic Virtue and the Feminine Voice in Constitutional Adjudication*, 72 VA. L. REV. 543 (1986). The literature to which I refer herein is all English language, including largely American, British, Australian, and Canadian theorists.

4. *See, e.g.,* CATHARINE A. MACKINNON, FEMINISM UNMODIFIED: DISCOURSES ON LIFE AND LAW (1987). CAROL SMART, FEMINISM AND THE POWER OF LAW (1989); Katharine T. Bartlett, *Feminist Legal Methods*, 103 HARV. L. REV. 829 (1990).

5. CAROL GILLIGAN, IN A DIFFERENT VOICE: PSYCHOLOGICAL THEORY AND WOMEN'S DEVELOPMENT (1982).

6. NANCY CHODOROW, THE REPRODUCTION OF MOTHERING: PSYCHOANALYSIS AND THE SOCIOLOGY OF GENDER (1978).

7. CYNTHIA F. EPSTEIN, DECEPTIVE DISTINCTIONS: SEX, GENDER, AND THE SOCIAL ORDER (1988).

8. Two caveats are important here. First is that the views of the sources of feminist theorizing in law were and are very diverse. For example, while Gilligan clearly addressed perceived differences in how men and women conceptualize moral issues and dilemmas and Chodorow sought to explain identity and empathy as reflective of gender-based rearing patterns, Epstein cautioned against making too much of "difference" and suggested that what men and women have in common far outdistances perceived gender-distinctive characteristics. The second, and related, caveat is that the theorizing in law, while influenced by developments in the social sciences and humanities, is not entirely derivative. A legal scholarship of feminism took root in the 1970s and has flourished as a cross-fertilized but also independent enterprise.

9. UNITED NATIONS, THE WORLD'S WOMEN 1970–1990: TRENDS AND STATISTICS at 30 (1991). It might

erment is clearly economic. In a world in which women are more than 51 percent of the population, fewer than 5 percent of the heads of government, and fewer than 10 percent of the (lower house) parliamentarians,[10] disempowerment is clearly political. In a world in which it is acceptable, *inter alia*, for women to be raped by their husbands; for female detainees to be raped by the police; for women to be educated at half the level and literacy of men; for women to have no access to birth control or abortion; and for women to have no unilateral freedom of movement domestically or internationally, disempowerment is clearly social. To these indicia of societal inequity might also be added the practices of dowry murder, the aborting of female fetuses, the murder of female babies, and nationality laws that are male determinative.[11] The breadth and depth of the critical problems addressed in feminist studies suggest that the undertaking need demonstrate no further that there are academically worthy questions to be asked about gendered economic, political, and social systems. Feminist jurisprudence, which includes a broad field of theorizing, asks questions about where *the law* fits within women's experience, what is its role in perpetuating these gendered systems, and how might law be a vehicle for change.

III.   FEMINIST STUDIES: METHODOLOGY AND ORIENTATION

Feminist studies have more in common than the subject they study; there are a variety of other relatively common features. Feminist analysis tends to be *contextual, experiential,* and *inductive.* Whereas much social theory is hierarchical, abstract, and deductive, the feminist starting point is from *actual human experience* and the implications of that experience. In a significant sense, it is more anthropological than philosophical,[12] and it is marked by

---

also be noted that in the United States women are fewer than 1 percent of the CEOs of the 500 largest corporations.

10. UNITED NATIONS OFFICE AT VIENNA CENTRE FOR SOCIAL DEVELOPMENT AND HUMANITARIAN AFFAIRS, WOMEN IN POLITICS AND DECISION-MAKING IN THE LATE TWENTIETH CENTURY at 10, 58 (1992).

11. For analyses of these issues, see, e.g., Melissa Spatz, *A "Lesser" Crime: A Comparative Study of Legal Defenses for Men Who Kill Their Wives,* 24 COLUM. J.L. & SOC. PROBS. 597 (1991); Lisa C. Stratton, *Note: The Right to Have Rights,* 77 MINN. L. REV. 195 (1992); Gráinne De Búrca, *Fundamental Human Rights and the Reach of EC Law,* 13 OXFORD J. LEGAL STUD. 283 (1993).

12. I do not mean to suggest that feminist studies is therefore difficult or impossible in philosophy. Quite the contrary, in these respects, feminists have written some of the most provocative philosophical work in recent years, work which challenges the presumptions of the field. *See, e.g.,* NANCY C.M. HARTSOCK, MONEY, SEX AND POWER: TOWARD A FEMINIST HISTORICAL MATERIALISM (1983); BEYOND SELF-INTEREST (Mansbridge ed., 1990); SUSAN M. OKIN, JUSTICE, GENDER AND THE FAMILY (1989); CAROLE PATEMAN, THE SEXUAL CONTRACT (1988) (all extrapolating from actual experience).

what Bartlett calls "practical reasoning."[13] Because real life experience is the source and the focus of the theorizing and incorporating the *diversity* of women's lives is highly valued, grand theory is largely eschewed, and absolutes are distinctly suspect.[14] This renders feminist theorizing necessarily *self-consciously limited, tentative, and provisional.*[15] A final unifying feature of feminist theory is that it is inextricably intertwined with contemporaneous social, political, and economic movements. In the law this is an especially prominent feature of the scholarship that has paralleled, influenced, and been influenced by, the movements for legal equality of women since the late 1960s. The interactive realms of scholar and political activist, often practiced but rarely openly respected in some quarters of academia, form, in the world of feminism, a natural liaison. While to some such interaction raises questions about the "objectivity" of the scholarship, to many feminists the larger question is whether the failure to engage the application of scholarship suggests an absence of responsibility.[16]

IV. HUMAN RIGHTS IN FEMINIST RELIEF

Feminist jurisprudence provides very substantial challenges to human rights law as it is institutionally understood. These include both fundamental questions about the processes by which human rights are defined, adjudicated, and enforced, as well as questions about the substance of what is thereby "protected." And, while the focus of analysis is on women's experience, a feminist approach might have immediate implications for the rights of all disempowered peoples and raise questions about social organization generally. If it were necessary to offer one word to capture the essence of feminist jurisprudence, in general and in its significance for human rights analysis, it is *inclusion*. The enterprise critiques the experience of women as persons *excluded* from legal protection and from proportionate political and economic power.

　　Feminist critics of legal institutions question whether these institutions are capable of protecting women. Legal institutions are viewed as hierar-

---

13. Bartlett, *supra* note 4, at 887.
14. In a very stimulating analysis, Smart, *supra* note 4, at 68, 71, has suggested that these features of feminist jurisprudence have rendered the law—which is hierarchical and which values grand theorizing and deductive analysis—an inhospitable environment for women.
15. *See,* Bartlett, *supra* note 4, at 857.
16. It must be noted of course that this debate about the appropriateness of involvement in the practical consequences of one's academic work is limited almost exclusively to only some of the social sciences. In academic medicine, as in business and law schools, as well as, for example, in departments of archeology, music, dance, theater, or engineering, to be involved in such activity is mainstream and expected.

chical, adversarial, exclusionary, and unlikely to respect claims made by women.[17] In apparently stark contrast, exponents of the protection of human rights argue that human rights *must* be seen as a *legal* phenomenon. If principles of justice are not *legalized*, then they are subject to the unilateral control of nation states, and their abuse can be subjected to nothing more than the *ad hoc* expression of moral outrage by those who disagree with the challenged behavior. While the domestic or international codification of policy, like conventional or common law, provides no guarantee that the law will be respected, human rights advocates maintain nevertheless that "law" is a critically important arrow in their quiver. Even in situations in which litigation is either impossible or impractical, this view rests on the assumption that most states do not even want to *appear* to be in violation of international law.[18] Despite the widely held view that all international law is simply international politics, being able to portray a claim as having the backing of "law" removes the dialogue from the realm of being nothing more than self-interested negotiation. A feminist analysis, in contrast, might well argue from experience that human rights law has been a miserable failure in protecting peoples from oppression.

Despite this immediately apparent conflict over whether law is important in the protection of human rights, in a sense, the feminist concern and the classic human rights perspective may not be in fundamental disagreement over the question of *reliance* on law. This is because the major concern expressed by feminist critics of legal institutions, preeminently by Carole Smart, is that *litigation as a process* does not serve women.[19] Human rights advocates also know only too well that litigation is an extremely limited tool in this endeavor.[20] Thus, while women's experience would suggest that reliance on courts, judges, and lawyers to transform society is folly, feminists and traditional human rights activists are both able to appreciate, and

---

17. *See e.g.,* CATHARINE A. MACKINNON, SEXUAL HARASSMENT OF WORKING WOMEN: A CASE OF SEX DISCRIMINATION (1979); Ann C. Scales, *The Emergence of Feminist Jurisprudence: An Essay,* 95 YALE L.J. 1373 (1986); Smart, *supra* note 4. I might have added overwhelmingly "male," but this is not true in all societies. While in the United States and Great Britain women are fewer than 10 percent of the judiciary, in continental countries and Scandinavia this is not the case.

18. Leslie J. Calman, *Are Women's Rights "Human Rights" in* WOMEN IN INT'L DEV., at 12 (Michigan State Univ. Working Paper No. 146, 1987).

19. I do not read Smart's critique, *supra* note 4, as necessarily condemnatory of public policy per se.

20. While the European Court of Justice and the European Court of Human Rights, as well as other similar regional international bodies, have developed some significant human rights law, albeit far more readily for men than for women (*see,* Marie Provine, The Human Rights of Women: A Feminist Analysis (on file with the author); Rebecca J. Cook, *International Human Rights Law Concerning Women: Case Notes and Comments,* 23 VAND. J. TRANSNAT'L L. 779 (1990)), the minimal volume of output, as well as the classic limitations of states as defendants or, in the case of the International Court of Justice, states as litigants, has rendered the "litigation" process of minimal significance in protecting human rights.

perhaps agree, that developing *law as principle and rule* is not an enterprise to be jettisoned. The points of disagreement that are far more fundamental reflect on the political power that is represented in the process of defining these "legal" rights, the limitations on "rights" analysis, and the life experience that should underlie the substantive principles of human rights law to which the world ought to be committed. Where human rights advocates spar with the governmental powers-that-be largely over how they are treating political dissidents, feminist critics maintain that the diameter of the circle of *inclusion* in the realm of human rights law is entirely too narrow.

V.   WORKING FROM "WOMEN'S EXPERIENCE"

In an attempt to visualize how human rights would be understood if women's experience were the foundation for such policymaking, Charlotte Bunch has asked what is basic to women's view of their humanity.[21] While this endeavor of defining human rights from the experience of women is a first step to integrating women into the process of operationalizing and protecting human rights, the outcomes are not entirely women-specific. As suggested above, a feminist perspective on human rights has implications for *all* human rights, not just those of women. For example, if because of women's experience with respect to reproductive policy and nonenforcement of rape laws, such a perspective highly values bodily integrity, this has application as well to issues such as capital punishment and military conscription, governmental practices with which women as a group have not been significantly associated. Similarly, if a feminist perspective is especially sensitive to hierarchy and inequity of power, the implications for all people at the bottom of the social order is significant. Having perhaps the broadest implications for human rights theory and practice is the feminist challenge to the assumption that only government ought to be accountable for human rights violations. If, in women's experience, deprivations of (traditionally understood *principles* of) human rights come most predictably from the nongovernmental sphere, it would then be asked whether men's rights are not similarly most often threatened by actors and conditions that are not necessarily clothed with officialdom.

In sum, feminist approaches lead us to ask particular questions and to challenge certain institutional arrangements, suggesting pragmatic and inductive methodologies in seeking answers. The consequences of this analysis and the alternative visions of society that it engenders might be quite profound and ultimately as relevant to men as to women.

---

21. Charlotte Bunch, *Organizing for Women's Human Rights Globally, in* Ours by Right: Women's Rights as Human Rights 141 (Joanna Kerr ed., 1993) [hereinafter Ours by Right].

VI.   CHALLENGING THE PUBLIC-PRIVATE DISTINCTION

Perhaps no question is more immediately and regularly addressed in a feminist critique of human rights theory than is the assumption of the separate worlds of the "public" and "private," a distinction that roughly corresponds to the governmental and the nongovernmental in contemporary parlance. This dichotomy is largely a product of classical western liberal thought[22] in which, *inter alia,* John Locke sought to deny the legitimacy of the divine right of kings without challenging patriarchal familial structure. To dispute the analogy employed by royalty between their authority over society and the father's authority over the family, Locke argued that the two spheres were separate and distinct. Whereas patriarchal authority was deemed to be divine, political power was deemed to emanate from the governed. The consequences for women of this dichotomous perspective are fundamental and profound. A separate spheres approach has relegated women to the home, away from the political institutions that make policy[23] and away from a substantial role as well in other "public" institutions that determine the nature and quality of life in a community.[24] The Lockean separate spheres approach has also rendered women subject to the control of patriarchal familial authorities—fathers, brothers, and husbands—with the understanding that familial matters are "private" and, therefore, beyond the scope of governmental authority and intervention. Physical and sexual abuse of wives and children, ubiquitous throughout the world, has, consequently, faced little formal challenge within a two-spheres understanding of the social order.[25]

Overcoming the international institutionalization of the public-private dichotomy is one of feminism's greatest hurdles in creating an *inclusionary* approach to human rights and in incorporating the diverse everyday life experiences of women into its models.[26] Feminists find little political sup-

---

22. Nancy Kim has suggested that it is western liberal thought that has treated the "public" as "political" and the "private" as "cultural." Nancy Kim, *Toward a Feminist Theory of Human Rights: Straddling the Fence between Western Imperialism and Uncritical Absolutism,* 25 COLUM. HUM. RTS. L. REV. 49, 66–74 (1993).

23. Carole Pateman's brilliant analysis of *The Sexual Contract, supra,* note 12, demonstrates that in liberal theory women are not parties to the social contract. They are brought into the contract much the way slaves are.

24. One of the many great fallacies associated with the "two-spheres" approach to societal structure is the assumption that there are *only* two spheres: government and family. This approach draws attention away from other loci of great power and potential oppression in society, away from what some social scientists call "mediating institutions." These would include, *inter alia,* corporations, religious organizations, educational institutions, cultural and public interest organizations.

25. Human rights concerns aside, despite overwhelming evidence of the negative social consequences of child abuse, Sweden's outlawing of spanking continues to draw derisive commentary. Similarly, women who accuse their fathers of incest are assumed to be "suffering" from "false memory syndrome."

26. *See* Adelaide H. Villmoare, *Women, Differences and Rights as Practices: An Interpretative*

port for their movement to scale the presumptive wall between state and family and to implicate parties other than the government for human rights violations. Whether it is the malnutrition and mortality of female children, spousal rape, beatings and murder, or the institution of *purdah* (in which women are essentially imprisoned in their homes), the world's actors are not inclined to see these allegedly nongovernmentally perpetrated sexual inequities as human rights issues.[27] While women collectively can argue that *their* experience of oppressive power that denies them moral autonomy, human dignity, and physical security occurs more readily in the home than in the town jail, there appears to be little support outside of the feminist movement for broadening human rights principles to include a wider locus of abuse and a wider range of abusers. There are numerous explanations for this inability to see human rights in broader relief and for the reluctance to model the notion of the international citizen upon the lives of women.

First, perhaps ironically, is the interest of the state in retaining its pre-eminence in the international world. While it is of questionable notoriety to be viewed as the *only* source of violations of fundamental principles of justice and freedom, states might, nevertheless, value the autonomy over their citizenry that this stance implies. By being seen as uniquely oppressive, they simultaneously retain a hegemony over their people and insulate institutions allegedly *beyond* their control from external purview.

Second, the state might promote the dichotomization of public and private to maintain a chasm between the two out of a concern that much can be learned about the political world from an understanding of familial life, and these insights might be destabilizing to the system. Okin and Pateman have both suggested that attention to the patriarchal power structures in family life might heighten citizens' understanding of the hierarchical power that controls the political system.[28] Ironically, whereas Locke, not inclined to challenge paternal authority, saw the conceptual cojoining of state and family as reinforcing political autocracy, feminists, who do challenge familial patriarchy, see the association of the two as having precisely the opposite impact.

It might be argued that the state is not the only powerful actor that wants to limit the reach of human rights to only the "public" domain. The pressure to do so might come as well from the "private" realm. Religious institutions and corporations, for example, have much to gain in the preservation of

---

Essay and a Proposal, 25 Law & Soc. Rev. 385 (1991) (discussing the importance of everyday life experience in the operationalization of a feminist view of rights).

27. *See* Hilary Charlesworth & Christine Chinkin, *The Gender of Jus Cogens,* 15 Hum. Rts. Q. 63, 72–73 (1993) (suggesting that, despite the right to life and freedom from torture that are incorporated within *jus cogens* in international human rights law, *jus cogens* ignores the spheres in which these rights of women are most often jeopardized).

28. Pateman, *supra* note 12; Okin, *supra* note 12, at 110–33.

their autonomy from the illusion of invisibility that the two-spheres theory provides. If human rights concerns are focused solely on the state because of a theory of the insulation of the family as "private," the false illusion of a dual-institution society is reinforced. Exceptionally powerful bodies beyond the familial patriarchy thereby escape scrutiny. Employers (of women and men) who pay unconscionably low wages for work under inhumane conditions would be unlikely to want international human rights law brought to bear against them. Religious orders with gender, race, or caste disqualification policies would similarly not welcome such attention. Under the two-spheres theory of society these institutions do not exist, and their practices are effectively shielded from international human rights review. Were women's experience the focus of human rights law, attention to the non-governmental sphere would be heightened, and patterns of social organization and practices that are exploitative, not just of women and not just by familial patriarchs, but also by other powerful bodies, would be brought into bold relief.[29]

The denial of the existence of a "private" realm of human rights violations is not limited to those with an apparent vested interest in the status quo. Human rights theorists, such as Alston, not uncommonly fear the dilution of human rights principles if the realms are expanded beyond the traditional.[30] Activist friends of human rights, such as Amnesty International, slow to view women as victims of denials of human rights, have held firm in their view that government must be seen as the perpetrator of the violations in order for their organization to act.[31] Prominent feminist theorists often have argued for only a very circumscribed realm of *private* human rights abuses.[32] The standard Anglo-American Bill of Rights view of government as the uniquely powerful potential evil-doer is as endemic in the tra-

---

29. As a related matter, some states and, no doubt, many nonstate interests oppose the International Covenant on Economic, Social and Cultural Rights because of its *material* quality, guaranteeing, *inter alia,* an adequate standard of living, free compulsory primary education, and paid childbearing leave for women. The last provision is one of the reasons why the United States, the only industrial democracy *not* to provide paid maternity leave, has not yet ratified the treaty, which has been in effect since 1976.

30. Philip Alston, *Conjuring up New Human Rights: A Proposal for Quality Control,* 78 Am. J. Int'l L. 607 (1984).

31. See Amnesty International Publications, Women in the Front Line (1991), which clearly states throughout the introductory section that Amnesty International's mandate is to free prisoners of conscience and that its only focus is on state action. It was only in 1989 that Human Rights Watch, an organization with a self-consciously broader mandate than Amnesty International, first set up a Women's Rights Project. See Dorothy Q. Thomas, *Holding Governments Accountable by Public Pressure, in* Ours by Right, *supra* note 21, at 83.

32. For example, Dorothy Q. Thomas & Michele E. Beasley, *Domestic Violence as a Human Rights Issue,* 15 Hum. Rts. Q. 36, 43 (1993), while arguing for the inclusion of such violence within the purview of human rights concerns, would do so only where it could be demonstrated that the state's nonenforcement of its laws against violence was genderbased and, therefore, an *official* act of sex discrimination.

ditional human rights nongovernmental (NGO) community as it is among governments themselves.

VII. PUBLIC-PRIVATE DICHOTOMY: A FALSE DICHOTOMY?

In contrast to the dual-spheres perspective and international respect for familial autonomy, reiterated in the International Covenant on Economic, Social and Cultural Rights, ecofeminist Riane Eisler has observed that "the principle of noninterference with 'family autonomy' is in actuality nowhere fully accepted. On the contrary, a universally established principle is that family relations are subject to both legal regulation and outside scrutiny."[33] Therein lies the major conceptional difficulty with the two-spheres approach to society and to human rights policy. To the extent that the family, or for that matter any societal institution, is separate or autonomous from government, it is *at the sufferance of the state.* Governments world-wide have not endowed "family" with any significant degree of autonomy. The framework for family is everywhere within a collective policy arena. Rules about who may marry, at what age, and with what rights and duties are made by the state (or its functional equivalent). Rules governing divorce, child custody, and inheritance are likewise a matter of "public policy." It is thus unpersuasive to suggest that human rights abuses within family life are *sui generis.* Battery, rape, imprisonment, intimidation from voting, and mur-der are not different from the crimes that they appear to be just because they are perpetrated by a family member.[34]

To the extent that these acts are ignored by the state, there is a failure of official responsibility, not an inability to police the environment. In a femi-nist analysis, the state's choice to overlook such criminal acts is as abusive of human rights as a refusal to interfere with slave trade. Documenting the state's *responsibility* for the perpetuation of such systems of abuse is an easy undertaking, but a feminist analysis would go a significant step further. While the state's failure to act makes *it* legally liable, the abusers are them-selves also directly guilty of a denial of human rights.[35] The assumption that

---

33. Riane Eisler, *Human Rights: Toward an Integrated Theory for Action,* 9 Hum. Rts. Q. 287, 293 (1987).
34. It should be noted, of course, that while imprisonment and intimidation of a voter are rec-ognized human rights problems because of their close connection to the liberal model of the free citizen, rape and battery, common *dehumanizing* experiences of women, are not so defined by the international community, unless directly linked to political acts of the state, such as war. *See* Anna H. Phelan, *The Latest Political Weapon in Haiti: Military Rapes of Women and Girls,* L.A. Times, 5 June 1994, at M4; *see also Rape was Weapon of Serbs, U.N. Says,* N.Y. Times, 20 Oct. 1993, at A1.
35. This approach to human rights, holding the private perpetrator directly responsible, is one of the most difficult reforms to initiate within a system bent on the nation state as defen-

the private *person,* like the *familial milieu,* is outside the purview of human rights law is regularly challenged within feminist jurisprudence.

To argue that family is distinct and "private" also ignores its powerful influence in socializing its members, especially the next generation. Bunch and Okin have noted that the patterns of behavior observed and experienced within the family seriously affect whether, and the way in which, its members function in the "public" world. These include such issues as whether the family encourages democratic participatory values[36] and whether its members are encouraged and supported in their desire to become involved in the political processes of the state.[37] Given the commitment of international human rights policies to *political democracy,*[38] attention to the institution of the family is not only ethically appropriate but also empirically sound. The United Nations seems to be aware of the family as the laboratory of democracy; its declaration of 1994 as the Year of the Family sports the slogan, "Building the smallest democracy at the heart of society."[39]

In sum, the notion that the family is uniquely separable from the larger society and from the human rights issues therein generated is indeed questionable. But again, to reiterate a thematic concern, it is not family alone that needs to be added to government as a potential locus of abuse; it is the proposition that women's experience draws immediate attention to the instruments of repression and disempowerment that exist due to imbalances in power. This mode of analysis, while targeting family structures as perhaps the most ubiquitous source of "unofficial" abuse, is also not necessarily *sui generis.* Similar analyses are then invited with respect to the power of employers, religious and educational institutions, corporate policymakers, etc. and the various ways in which they are capable of locking people into forms of deprivation and degradation equal in severity and often kind to those for which we regularly condemn governments.

---

dant. There are, however, models of human rights that emerge from the Treaty of Rome and European court decisions, which do include "private," albeit nonfamilial, defendants.

36. Okin, *supra* note 12.

37. Bunch has argued that family life is a key factor in determining whether women will be able to be involved in the public life of the community. The lack of spousal support for this activity, the fear of violence or abandonment, all function to keep women from involvement in the "public" world of policy making, the world in which, *inter alia,* decisions are made which define and enforce principles of rights. Bunch, *supra* note 21, at 142.

38. What is especially interesting about international law is that, despite a world in which open democratic politics exist in only a minority of societies, the conventions are all premised on the principle that this is not only the norm, but is essential. *See, e.g.,* the Universal Declaration of Human Rights, *signed* 10 Dec. 1948, G.A. Res. 217A (III), U.N. Doc. A/810, at 71 (1948); the International Covenant on Political and Civil Rights, *adopted* 16 Dec. 1966, G.A. Res. 2200 (XXI), 21 U.N. GAOR Supp. (No. 16), at 52, U.N. Doc. A/6316 (1966); and the International Covenant on Economic, Social and Cultural Rights, *adopted* 16 Dec. 1966, G.A. Res. 2200 (XXI), 21 U.N. GAOR Supp. (No. 16), at 49, U.N. Doc. A/6316 (1966).

39. Bunch, *supra* note 21, at 142.

VIII.   THE QUESTION OF "CULTURE"

Closely associated with the public-private distinction, in which the international order largely immunizes from its purview nongovernmental sources of human rights abuses, is the question of *culture*. In a nutshell, the ongoing debate in this arena is whether human rights values are *universal* or whether *cultural relativism* legitimately is factored into international human rights policies. While some have made significant strides in deconstructing the dichotomy and suggesting the ways in which the gap might be bridged in part,[40] feminist scholars have asked why *culture* appears to be a defense only in regard to gender roles and to the governmental and nongovernmental denials of fundamental rights to women. As Hélie-Lucas points out, while such practices as maiming and corporal punishment regularly elicit international voices of outrage, genital mutilation of women is attributed to "culture."[41] Freeman notes that, under principles of "custom," in many societies women are deprived of custody of their children, left destitute by divorce, or killed by their husbands who face no sanctions for this act.[42] One also must wonder why racially based slavery and apartheid are so roundly condemned despite their entrenchment in *culture,* while women who live under *purdah*—the denial of the right to vote, travel, work, drive, own property, or control their own fertility—are seen as voluntary participants in their "cultures." Ironically, highlighted within the Convention on the Elimination of All Forms of Discrimination Against Women (CEDAW) is an obligation assumed by governments to "take on" cultural traditions, familial and otherwise, and to rid their societies of sexism.[43] It is significant that this provision has been the subject of few "reservations" by signatory states.[44] Perhaps this simply indicates that expressions of principle, even within presumptively binding conventions, might be largely irrelevant to the actual experience of the disempowered.[45]

---

40. See in this regard, Annie Bunting, *Theorizing Women's Cultural Diversity in Feminist International Human Rights Strategies,* 20 J.L. & Soc'y 6 (1993); Kim, *supra* note 22; Alison D. Renteln, *The Concept of Human Rights,* 83 Anthropos 343 (1988); *A Cross-Cultural Approach to Validating International Human Rights: The Case of Retribution Tied to Proportionality, in* Human Rights: Theory and Measurement 7 (David L. Cingranelli ed., 1988).
41. Marie-Aimeé Hélie-Lucas, *Women Living Under Muslim Laws, in* Ours by Right, *supra* note 21, at 61. One might add to Hélie-Lucas' examples of international concern about human rights within the context of alleged cultural difference the recent flogging in Singapore of an American teenager convicted of vandalism.
42. Marsha A. Freeman, *Women, Development and Justice: Using the International Convention on Women's Rights, in* Ours by Right, *supra* note 21, at 100.
43. Convention on the Elimination of All Forms of Discrimination against Women, *adopted* 18 Dec. 1979, art. 5, G.A. Res. 34/180, U.N. GAOR, 34th Sess., Supp. (No. 46), U.N. Doc. A/34/46 (1979).
44. Freeman, *supra* note 42.
45. This phenomenon reminds me of a discussion with a feminist activist in Nepal who com-

The manifesto of the UN-sponsored convention on human rights which met in June 1993 in Vienna, while expressing "respect" for cultural and religious diversity, strongly reaffirmed the principle of the universality of human rights as well as the impossibility of divorcing political rights from economic and social rights. There is little doubt that the significant feminist presence at this meeting, a presence which captured worldwide media attention, was largely responsible for this commitment to principles of universality and unity of rights. This represented, I would argue, not western cultural hegemony, as is often maintained by the ruling elites in nondemocratic, nonegalitarian societies,[46] but rather, a reflection of the experience of women worldwide who very distinctly understand the close interweaving of the various forms of political, economic, and social disempowerment.

Despite women's concerns about respecting cultural diversity, including the diversity of women within societies, women's experience, as it is now being documented in Barbara Nelson and Najma Chowdhury's ambitious study of women in forty-three countries, reflects four unifying themes and concerns. These include eradicating male violence; developing equalizing strategies with respect to education, financial resources, etc.; pursuit of reproductive rights including access to birth control, abortion, infertility services, and maternal and child health care; and effecting political and legal change to the advantage of women.[47] The facts and conditions of cultural diversity among societies cannot, from a feminist perspective, justify a failure to rectify the conditions in which women live worldwide. Women's experience demonstrates one of the ramifications of arguing from "culture"; to argue from culture is to prove too much. All social order, values, and power can be understood as culture. The decision that is thus made covertly, and should be made overtly, is which manifestations of "culture," whether unique to one society or ubiquitous worldwide, are unacceptable to the human family. That is the decision that has been made with respect to slavery since the nineteenth century and should be similarly applied to the conditions of disempowerment under which women live. Women's organizations, products of indigenous experience, wherever not forcefully silenced, argue for more equitable social, economic, and political systems, for an end to patriarchy. Cultural relativists misunderstand or betray their

---

mented that her government "signs everything; does nothing." See discussion below on feminism's concern with actual experience and the consequences of behavior which may be counterposed to expressions of principle.

46. Indeed, western states, including the United States, often fight the failure to distinguish rights that are "political" from those which are "economic and social." While the United States has recently ratified the International Covenant on Civil and Political Rights (in 1992), it has yet to act on the International Covenant on Economic, Social and Cultural Rights, which opened for signature nearly thirty years ago (in 1966).

47. WOMEN AND POLITICS WORLDWIDE (Barbara J. Nelson & Najma Chowdhury eds., 1994).

own credo when they dismiss gender issues as "cultural." To do so is to argue that only men create and sustain culture. Freeman has suggested the development of a principle of *prisoner of culture* that, consistent with CEDAW, would acknowledge that "custom and culture . . . should be respected as a living expression of community norms [,] but must not be allowed to be used as a rationale for denial of human rights."[48] Until women's experience is incorporated within the purview of human rights analysis, it is folly to dismiss it as simply a product of culture.[49]

IX.   SOME MODEST PROPOSALS

A feminist approach to human rights thus asks questions not generally addressed within human rights dialogues, questions generated by the experience of women. That there have been some steps forward in furthering the agenda of women's rights through a human rights model is clear in recent years. CEDAW has been passed and ratified by 121 states. NGOs, such as Amnesty International and Human Rights Watch, have finally set up committees to study and publicize abuses against women. Women's organizations are active all over the world both as domestic and international forces,

---

48. Freeman, *supra* note 42, at 101.
49. It is also important to emphasize that, despite variations among societies as to the nature and extent of the disempowerment, the disempowerment of women is everywhere. It is not a useful activity to create hierarchies of "blame" in which one can simply cite the worst cases, while overlooking the usual. In this respect Hélie-Lucas argues that the common practice of attacking Islam as women's major problem may be misguided. Hélie-Lucas, *supra* note 41, at 52–56. While she documents the very serious setbacks to women's rights in many Islamic countries during the 1980s, she also notes that Islamic societies vary greatly as to their practices and traditions in which, for example, glaring differences exist between the neighboring countries of Algeria and Tunisia (*Id.*), and female genital mutilation, while practiced by Muslims, Christians, and others in Africa, is unknown in Muslim cultures elsewhere. *Id.* at 53. Implicit in her argument is that politics, not religion *per se,* explains the ways in which religion can be used as a source of women's oppression. *See e.g., Id.* at 53. She further suggests that some of the practices now common in Islamic countries, such as the mandatory adoption of a husband's surname, were products of colonialization. *Id.* at 54. Cook echoes the theme by demonstrating that the European human rights courts have upheld western European policies of requiring women to change their surnames to those of their husbands, as well as policies restricting women's rights to custody of their children, to abortion, and to national identity. Cook, *supra* note 20. *See also* Stratton, *supra* note 11; Elizabeth Spalin, *Abortion, Speech and the European Community,* 1992 J. Soc. Welfare & Fam. L. 17 (1992). The practical problems associated with "targeting" a particular source of oppression are also formidable. An attempt within the United Nations less than one decade ago to investigate human rights abuses of women within Islamic countries was precipitously cut off by the General Assembly. Thus, experience suggests not only that Islam is hardly unique in its controls over women—controls often not very different from those in Christian, Hindu, Jewish, or Buddhist societies—but that targeting a particular cluster of societies may be impossible as a matter of strategy, at least within existing international fora.

despite the ostracism and threats to their safety that this might entail. In 1992 women's groups submitted 150,000 signatures from 115 countries demanding that women's rights be on the agenda at the 1993 Human Rights Convention in Vienna.[50] At a more microcosmic level, since 1989, the US government has included within its annual "country reports" data on violence against women.[51] But the status of women has not improved because *actual policy* has not been altered with respect to, *inter alia,* nationality policies, the franchise, economic disenfranchisement, illiteracy, or violence. And debates rage over how best to address social change.

While the formalistic front of written documents and political procedures does not seem especially utile, there are good reasons for making certain that these flanks are not abandoned. If for no other reason than that of symbolic importance, it is critical that CEDAW enforcement processes be raised to those attached by the United Nations to other human rights protocols.[52] It is similarly important that principles governing asylum be revised by nations to recognize women as a social group subject to persecution and that nongovernmental actors and issues of violence be "legalized."[53] Despite serious feminist concerns about formalism, about statism, and about the function of law in general, because women do not set the agenda and are not in the position to design their arenas, the legal front and the diplomatic front cannot be eschewed. This does not mean, however, that their engagement cannot be reconceptualized and a new approach to human rights incorporated.

X.   A RESPONSIBILITY MODEL

One of the most interesting aspects of the debates within feminist jurisprudence is the question of whether rights analysis, domestically or internationally, is useful. Gilligan first highlighted this question effectively in her findings that (US) women were more prone to see themselves within a web of community to which they had responsibilities, rather than in contradistinction to a society against which they had rights; the latter was a

---

50. Bunch, *supra* note 21, at 147. In the longer view, it may turn out that this event, this very successful worldwide organizing effort, will constitute a watershed in the international women's rights movement, and that the multiple strategies used successfully and the liaisons formed will have unexpected consequences.
51. Thomas, *supra* note 31, at 84.
52. *See, e.g.,* Kim, *supra* note 22, at 82.
53. *See, e.g.,* Charlotte Bunch, *Women's Rights as Human Rights: Toward a Re-Vision of Human Rights,* 12 Hum. Rts. Q. 486 (1990); Rebecca J. Cook, *Women's International Human Rights Law: The Way Forward,* 15 Hum. Rts. Q. 230 (1993); M. Forde, *Non-Governmental Interferences With Human Rights,* 56 Brit. Y.B. Int'l L. 253 (1985).

more characteristic male model.[54] Feminist legal theorists have wondered whether the dichotomous and adversarial character of "rights" is not alien to women's experience.[55] If this approach of "responsibility" were applied to the human rights arena, it might be significant in allowing a broader and more open range of action with respect to human rights issues. Key elements of such an approach would be a concern with *impact* rather than *intent* by powerful social actors, governmental and otherwise. It would similarly reconceptualize human rights as human *needs* and would measure the acceptability of the status quo by the extent to which human needs are being met. The goal would be to effect change and not to "blame." These ideas are not entirely new; if one scans international "human rights" documents of the past half century there is much language that speaks to "rights" in the kind of positivistic and material language that not only transcends the politically procedural, but also transcends the nation state[56] in addressing human needs. Most critically, one would challenge the traditional methodology of human rights which catalogues the abuses committed by "guilty governments." In its place one would ask a very different question: to wit, what are the conditions of human freedom, dignity, health, and safety that are fundamental to an experientially meaningful theory of "rights?" The purpose thereof would be to pursue the avenues necessary to further this state of affairs. Identifying the source or causes of the deprivations would thus become second-order and for the purpose of designing strategies for change, not for ensuring that it is *government* that is the perpetrator.

If human rights were subjected to these suggested conceptualizations, decisions on policy would be made that place a priority on meeting the needs of the disempowered.[57] Working from any of the existing, and generally beautifully crafted, human rights documents,[58] one would ask in each situation about each allegation of denial of human rights: Does this fit the model of a legitimate human needs concern? How can this state of affairs be rectified or improved? Absent would be the questions of "governmental involvement," of "guilt," and of "tradition." This approach would therefore alter debates on strategies by asking very different questions and making outcome, *actual experience,* the major focus. It would simultaneously rec-

---

54. GILLIGAN, *supra* note 5, at 54.
55. *See, e.g.,* Sherry, *supra* note 3, at 582, 604; Schneider, *supra* note 3, at 593–97.
56. One is regularly reminded that the UN Charter itself speaks to a covenant among "peoples," not states.
57. The vast majority of human rights principles are in fact already oriented to protecting the (politically, socially, and economically) disempowered. Capitalist principles such as the rights of property holders, while extremely well protected by the existing world order, are distinctly second-order within twentieth-century human rights discourse.
58. For example, CEDAW, the International Covenant on Civil and Political Rights, or the International Covenant on Economic, Social and Cultural Rights.

ognize that not all "abuses" of human rights *are* by design; that, for example, the failure of poor nations to provide health care might reflect only on their poverty. At the same time, under the proposed model, the *need* for that health care to be provided would not be vitiated by the absence of a malevolent offender. While it might be only that one begins to think more in terms of positive incentives to change and a worldwide responsibility for the human condition than in terms of punishment and shame for offenders, it also might be that women's needs for social reordering will fare better under a model of this type. This is a voice that has been largely relegated to the realm of "charity" and "relief work," not politics, and not human rights politics. Research suggests that this might be substantially the female voice.

Chapter 4

The Gender of *Jus Cogens*

Hilary Charlesworth and Christine Chinkin

I. INTRODUCTION: THE DOCTRINE OF *JUS COGENS*

The modern international law doctrine of *jus cogens* asserts the existence of fundamental legal norms from which no derogation is permitted.[1] It imports notions of universally applicable norms into the international legal process. The status of norms of *jus cogens* as general international law, Onuf and Birney argue, "is not a logical necessity so much as a compelling psychological association of normative superiority with universality."[2] A formal, procedural definition of the international law concept of the *jus cogens* is found in the Vienna Convention on the Law of Treaties.[3] Article 53 states that:

> [A] peremptory norm of general international law is a norm accepted and recognized by the international community of States as a whole as a norm from which no derogation is permitted and which can be modified only by a subsequent norm of general international law having the same character.[4]

Such a category of principles has had an uneasy existence in international law as "peremptory" norms do not fit well with the traditional view

---

1. *Jus cogens* norms have also been recognized in many domestic legal systems. *See* Eric Suy, *The Concept of Jus Cogens in Public International Law,* in 2 *The Concept of Jus Cogens in International Law* 17, 18–22 (Carnegie Endowment for International Peace, 1967); J. Sztucki, *Jus Cogens and the Vienna Convention on the law of Treaties* 6–11 (1972). On the existence of the doctrine of *jus cogens* in international law before the 1969 Vienna Convention, *see* Alfred von Verdross, *Forbidden Treaties in International Law,* 31 Am. J. Int'l L. 571 (1937); Egon Schwelb, *Some Aspects of International Jus Cogens as Formulated by the International Law Commission,* 61 Am. J. Int'l L. 946, 948–60 (1967); *International Law Commission Report 1982,* at 132, U.N. Doc. A/37/10 (1982); Lauri Hannikainen, *Peremptory Norms (Jus Cogens) in International Law* chs. 1, 2 (1988).
2. N.G. Onuf & Richard K. Birney, *Peremptory Norms of International Law: Their Source, Function and Future,* 4 Denver J. Int'l L. & Pol'y 187, 190 (1974).
3. Vienna Convention on the Law of Treaties, 1155 U.N.T.S. 331, 63 Am. J. Int'l L. 875, 891 (1969).
4. Article 53 purports to define the notion of *jus cogens* only for the law of treaties within the Vienna Convention itself, but is generally regarded as having wider significance. *See also,*

of international law as a consensual order. If the basis of international law, whether customary or conventional, is the agreement of states, how can states be bound by a category of principles to which they may have not freely consented? On what basis can peremptory norms be distinguished from other rules of international law? Thus Prosper Weil has criticized the theory of *jus cogens* both for forcing states "to accept the supernormativity of rules they were perhaps not even prepared to recognize as ordinary norms"[5] and for generally weakening the unity of the international legal system by introducing notions of relative normativity.[6] As Martii Koskenniemi points out, however, the actual terms of Article 53 contain two distinct strains, non-consensualist ("descending") and consensualist ("ascending"): "*jus cogens* doctrine shows itself as a compromise. . . . [P]eremptory norms bind irrespective of consent . . . but what those norms are is determined by consent."[7]

Article 53, together with Article 64 which provides that treaties conflicting with new peremptory norms of international law become void, was one of the most contentious provisions at the Vienna Conference. Much of the support for the inclusion of the concept of *jus cogens* in the Vienna Convention came from socialist and third world states which saw it as some protection from the unmitigated operation of the principle of *pacta sunt servanda.*[8] Some Western nations were particularly critical of the inclusion of this provision on grounds of its challenge to the principle of state sover-

---

Vienna Convention on the Law of Treaties between States and International Organizations or between International Organizations 1986, art. 53, 25 I.L.M. 572 (1986). Apart to guarantee women equal protection of the law and make elimination of sex discrimination and violence against women a clear national priority. *See* Helsinki Watch, *Hidden Victims: Women in Post-Communist Poland,* Vol. IV, Issue 5 (12 Mar. 1992). from these provisions, explicit references to *jus cogens* in other treaties are rare. *See also,* International Law Commission, *Draft Articles on State Responsibility,* arts. 18(2), 29(1), 33(2), 2 Y.B. Int'l L. Comm'n 30 (1980).

5. Prosper Weil, *Towards Relative Normativity in International Law,* 77 Am. J. Int'l L. 413, 427 (1983). *See also,* Georg Schwarzenberger, *International Jus Cogens,* 43 Texas L. Rev. 455 (1965).

6. Weil, *supra* note 5, at 423–30. Compare W. Riphagen, *From Soft Law to Jus Cogens and Back,* 17 Victoria U. Wellington. L. Rev. 81, 92 (1987) (arguing that relationship between "soft" international law, "hard" international law, and principles of *jus cogens* is not hierarchical, and that "soft" law and principles of *jus cogens* are more accurately seen as closely connected "entry points" to the legal system).

7. Martii Koskenniemi, *From Apology to Utopia* 283 (1989). An example of the operation of the "compromise" *jus cogens* doctrine is the prohibition on apartheid. Although the chief practitioner of apartheid, South Africa, never "consented" to its prohibition, the principle is widely accepted as universally binding as *jus cogens. See* Ted L. Stein, *The Approach of the Different Drummer: The Principle of the Persistent Objector in International Law,* 26 Harv. Int'l L.J. 457, 482 (1985).

8. John H. Spencer, *Review of the Tenth and Eleventh Sessions of the Asian-African Legal Consultative Committee, held in 1969 and 1970,* 67 Am. J. Int'l L. 180, 181 (1973); Richard D. Kearney, *The Future Law of Treaties,* 4 Int'l Lawyer 823, 830 (1970); Robert Rosenstock, *Peremptory Norms—Maybe Even Less Metaphysical and Worrisome,* 5 Denver J. Int'l L. & Pol'y 167, 169 (1975).

eignty, its vagueness, the problem of definition of *jus cogens* norms, and the lack of state practice to support it.[9]

Defenders of the notion of *jus cogens* often explain its basis as the collective international, rather than the individual national, good.[10] On this analysis, principles of *jus cogens* play a similar role in the international legal system to that played by constitutional guarantees of rights in domestic legal systems. Thus states, as national political majorities, accept the limitation of their freedom of choice "in order to reap the rewards of acting in ways that would elude them under pressures of the moment."[11] Among those jurists who accept the category of *jus cogens,* however, continuing controversy remains over what norms qualify as principles of *jus cogens.*

Our concern in this article is neither with the debates over the validity of the doctrine of *jus cogens* in international law nor with particular candidates for *jus cogens* status. Rather, we are interested in the structure of the concept detailed by international law scholars. We argue that the concept of the *jus cogens* is not a properly universal one as its development has privileged the experiences of men over those of women, and it has provided a protection to men that is not accorded to women.

II.   THE FUNCTION OF *JUS COGENS* IN INTERNATIONAL LAW

The clearest operation of the doctrine of *jus cogens* in international law is set out in the Vienna Convention on the Law of Treaties: "A treaty is void if, at the time of its conclusion, it conflicts with a peremptory norm of general international law."[12] The freedom of states to enter into treaties is thus limited by fundamental values of the international community. Despite fears

---

9. Hannikainen, *supra* note 1, at 172–73; Richard D. Kearney & Robert E. Dalton, *The Treaty on Treaties,* 64 Am. J. Int'l L. 495, 535–38 (1970); I.M. Sinclair, *Vienna Conference on the Law of Treaties,* 19 Int'l & Comp. L.Q. 47, 66–69 (1970).

10. *E.g.,* Hannikainen, *supra* note 1, at 1–2. Hannikainen writes that " 'the international community of States as a whole' . . . is entitled to assume in extremely urgent cases, to protect the overriding interests and values of the community itself and to ensure the functioning of the international legal order, the authority to require one or a few dissenting States to observe a customary norm of general international law as a peremptory customary norm." *Id.* at 241.

11. Laurence H. Tribe, *American Constitutional Law* 10 (1978). *See* Jonathan I. Charney, *The Persistent Objector Rule and the Development of Customary International Law,* 56 Brit Y.B. Int'l L. 1, 19–20 (19??).

12. Vienna Convention on the Law of Treaties, *supra* note 3, art. 53. *See also id.* art. 64 (providing that if a new peremptory norm of general international law emerges, any existing treaty which is in conflict with it becomes void and terminates); art. 66 (allowing submission of disputes concerning the application or interpretation of arts. 53 or 64 to the International Court of Justice); art. 71 (setting out the consequences of nullity on the grounds of *jus cogens*).

that the inclusion of this provision would subvert the principle of *pacta sunt servanda* and act to destabilize the certainty provided by treaty commitments, *jus cogens* doctrine has been only rarely invoked in this context.[13] It thus has had little practical impact upon the operation of treaties, although it may possibly exert some restraining influence on the conclusion of treaties.

Inconsistent principles of customary international law cannot stand alongside *jus cogens*.[14] Some jurists have argued that all states have a legal interest, and consequently standing, to complain in international fora about violations of the *jus cogens* by another state.[15] Allusions to *jus cogens*-type norms and their procedural and substantive implications in the jurisprudence of the International Court of Justice, however, have been occasional and ambiguous.[16]

Much of the importance of the *jus cogens* doctrine lies not in its practical application but in its symbolic significance in the international legal process. It assumes that decisions with respect to normative priorities can be made and that certain norms can be deemed to be of fundamental significance. It thus incorporates notions of universality and superiority into international law.[17] These attributes are emphasized in the language used in describing the doctrine: *jus cogens* is presented as "guarding the most fundamental and highly-valued interests of international society";[18] as an "expression of a conviction, accepted in all parts of the world com-

---

13. It has been argued that the Treaty of Guarantee of August 16, 1960, between Cyprus, on the one hand, and Greece, Turkey and the United Kingdom on the other, violated the *jus cogens* norm prohibiting the threat or use of force by reserving the right for the Guarantee powers to take action to reestablish the state of affairs created by the Treaty, and that United Nations resolutions on the issue implicitly acknowledge this. Schwelb, *supra* note 1, at 952–53. On assertions of invalidity of the 1979 Camp David agreements on the basis of conflict with norms of *jus cogens*, see Giorgio Gaja, *Jus Cogens Beyond the Vienna Convention*, 172 Recueil Des Cours 271, 282 (1981). For other examples see Gordon Christenson, *Jus Cogens: Guarding Interests Fundamental to International Society*, 28 Va. J. Int'l L. 585, 607 (1988). The Portuguese application against Australia in the International Court of Justice (Application Instituting Proceedings, filed in the Registry of the Court February 22 1991) obliquely raises *jus cogens* issues in the context of the bilateral Timor Gap Treaty between Indonesia and Australia. 29 I.L.M. 469 (1990).
14. Ian Brownlie, *Principles of Public International Law* 514–15 (4th ed. 1990). *See also,* Jordan Paust, *The Reality of Jus Cogens*, 7 Conn. J. Int'l L. 81, 84 (1991).
15. *E.g.,* Hannikainen, *supra* note 1, at 725–26; Oscar Schachter, *General Course in International Law,* 178 Recueil Des Cours 182–84 (1982).
16. *See, e.g., Barcelona Traction,* 1970 I.C.J. 321, 325 (sep. op. Judge Ammoun); *Namibia* (Advisory Opinion), 1971 I.C.J. 72–75 (sep. op. Judge Ammoun); *US Diplomatic and Consular Staff in Tehran* 1980 I.C.J. 30–31, 40–41, 44–45; *Military and Paramilitary Activities in and Against Nicaragua,* 1986 I.C.J. 14, 100–01. (All discussed in Hannikainen, *supra* note 1, at 192–94.)
17. *See generally,* Onuf & Birney, *supra* note 2.
18. Christenson, *supra* note 13, at 587.

munity, which touches the deeper conscience of all nations;"[19] as fulfilling "the higher interest of the whole international community."[20] Indeed, Suy describes *jus cogens* as the foundation of international society without which the entire edifice would crumble.[21]

In the international legal literature on *jus cogens,* the use of symbolic language to express fundamental concepts is accompanied by abstraction. Writers are generally reluctant to go beyond the abstract assertion of principle to determine the operation and impact of any such norms. A tension thus exists between the weighty linguistic symbolism employed to explain the indispensable nature of *jus cogens* norms and the very abstract and inconclusive nature of their formulation. Some writers have argued that the doctrinal discussion of *jus cogens* has no echo at all in state practice.[22]

The search for universal, abstract, hierarchical standards is often associated with masculine modes of thinking. Carol Gilligan, for example, has contended that different ways of reasoning are inculcated in girls and boys from an early age. Girls tend to reason in a contextual and concrete manner; boys in a more formal and abstract way.[23] Most systems of knowledge prize the "masculine" forms of reasoning. The very abstract and formal development of the *jus cogens* doctrine indicates its gendered origins. What is more important, however, is that the privileged status of its norms is reserved for a very limited, male centered, category. *Jus cogens* norms reflect a male perspective of what is fundamental to international society that may not be shared by women or supported by women's experience of life. Thus the fundamental aspirations attributed to communities are male and the assumptions of the scheme of world order assumed by the notion of *jus cogens* are essentially male. Women are relegated to the periphery of communal values.

Our aim here is not to challenge the powerful symbolic significance of *jus cogens* but to argue that the symbolism is itself totally skewed and gendered. In doing so we propose a much richer content for the concept of *jus*

---

19. Ulrich Scheuner, *Conflict of Treaty Provisions with a Peremptory Norm of General International Law and its Consequences,* 27 Zeitschrift Fur Auslandisches Offentliches Recht und Volkerrecht 520, 524 (1967).
20. Alfred Verdross, *Jus Dispositivum and Jus Cogens in International Law,* 60 Am. J. Int'l L. 55, 58 (1966).
21. Suy, *supra* note 1, at 18. Similarly, the West German Federal Constitutional Court referred to *jus cogens* as "indispensable to the existence of the law of nations as an international legal order." *Cited in* Christenson, *supra* note 13, at 592.
22. *See, e.g.,* Sztucki, *supra* note 1, at 93–94 ("[I]n the light of international practice, the question whether the concept of *jus cogens* has been 'codified' or 'progressively developed' in the [Vienna] Convention, may be answered only in the sense that there has been nothing to codify."); David Kennedy, *The Sources of International Law,* 2 Am. U. J. Int'l L. & Pol'y 1, 18 (1987).
23. Carol Gilligan, *In a Different Voice: Psychological Theory and Women's Development* 25–51 (1982). For a discussion of this characteristic in the context of traditional interna-

cogens; if women's lives contributed to the designation of international fundamental values, the category would be transformed in a radical way. Our focus will be the category of human rights often designated as norms of *jus cogens.*[24]

III.   HUMAN RIGHTS AS NORMS OF *JUS COGENS*

The "most essential"[25] human rights are considered part of the *jus cogens.* For example, the American Law Institute's Revised Restatement of Foreign Relations Law lists as violations of *jus cogens* the practice or condoning of genocide, slave trade, murder/disappearances, torture, prolonged arbitrary detention or systematic racial discrimination.[26] This list has been described as "a particularly striking instance of assuming American values are synonymous with those reflected in international law."[27] At a deeper level, Simma and Alston argue that "it must be asked whether any theory of human rights law which singles out race but not gender discrimination, which condemns arbitrary imprisonment but not death by starvation, and which finds no place for a right of access to primary health care is not flawed in terms both of the theory of human rights and of United Nations doctrine."[28]

The development of human rights law has challenged the primacy of the state in international law and given individuals a significant legal status. It has, however, developed in an unbalanced and partial manner and promises much more to men than to women. This phenomenon is partly due to male domination of all international human rights fora,[29] which itself

---

tional relations theory, *see,* J. Ann Tickner, *Hans Morgenthau's Principles of Political Realism: A Feminist Reformulation,* 17 Millenium: J. Int'l Stud. 429, 433 (1988).

24. Although many asserted norms of *jus cogens* are drawn from the international law of human rights, *jus cogens* is usually defined as more extensive. For example, the International Law Commission's Special Rapporteur, Sir Humphrey Waldock, proposed three categories of *jus cogens* norms: those prohibiting the threat or use of force in contravention of the principles of the United Nations Charter; international crimes so characterized by international law; and acts or omissions whose suppression is required by international law. Sir Humphrey Waldock, *Second Report on the Law of Treaties,* 2 Y.B. Int'l L. Comm'n 56–59, U.N. Doc. A/CN.4/156 and Add. 1–3 (1963). *See also,* Roberto Ago, Recueil Des Cours 320, 324 (1971); Scheuner, *supra* note 19, at 526–67.

25. Scheuner, *supra* note 19, at 526.

26. *Restatement (Third) of the Foreign Relations Law of the United States,* § 702 (1987). *Compare,* Marjorie M. Whiteman, *Jus Cogens in International Law, With a Projected List,* 7 Ga. J. Int'l & Comp. L. 609, 625–26 (1977).

27. Bruno Simma & Philip Alston, *The Sources of Human Rights Law: Custom, Jus Cogens & General Principles,* 12 Aust. Y.B. Int'l L. 82, 94 (1992).

28. *Id.* at 95.

29. For example, within the United Nations, apart from the Committee on the Elimination of all Forms of Discrimination Against Women (whose 18 members are all women), there are

fashions the substance of human rights law in accordance with male values. At a deeper level, it replicates the development of international law generally.

A.   The Gender Bias of Human Rights Law

International law assumes, and reinforces, a number of dichotomies between public and private spheres of action.[30] One is the distinction drawn between international ("public") concerns and those within the domestic ("private") jurisdiction of states. Within the category of international concerns there is a further public/private distinction drawn. International law is almost exclusively addressed to the public, or official, activities of states, which are not held responsible for the "private" activities of their nationals or those within their jurisdiction. The concept of imputability used in the law of state responsibility is a device to deem apparently "private" acts "public" ones. This more basic dichotomy has significant implications for women. Women's lives are generally conducted within the sphere deemed outside the scope of international law, indeed also often outside the ambit of "private" (national) law.[31]

Although human rights law is often regarded as a radical development in international law because of its challenge to that discipline's traditional public/private dichotomy between states and individuals, it has retained the deeper, gendered, public/private distinction. In the major human rights treaties, rights are defined according to what men fear will happen to them, those harms against which they seek guarantees. The primacy traditionally given to civil and political rights by Western international lawyers and philosophers is directed towards protection for men within their public life—their relationship with government. The same importance has not been generally accorded to economic and social rights which affect life in the private sphere, the world of women, although these rights are addressed to states. This is not to assert that when women are victims of violations of the civil and political rights they are not accorded the same protection,[32] but that these are not the harms from which women most need protection.

---

a total of 13 women out of 90 "independent experts" on specialist human rights committees. *See* Hilary Charlesworth, Christine Chinkin & Shelley Wright, *Feminist Approaches to International Law*, 85 Am. J. Int'l 613, 624 n.67 (1991).

30. For a fuller discussion, see *id.* at 625–28.

31. As Professor O'Donovan has pointed out, however, the "private" sphere associated with women is in fact often tightly controlled by legal regulation of taxation, health, education and welfare. Katherine O'Donovan, *Sexual Divisions in Law* 7–8 (1985).

32. Indeed Article 3 of the International Covenant on Civil and Political Rights states they will be accorded equal treatment with men. International Covenant on Civil and Political

All the violations of human rights typically included in catalogues of *jus cogens* norms are of undoubted seriousness; genocide, slavery, murder, disappearances, torture, prolonged arbitrary detention, and systematic racial discrimination. The silences of the list, however, indicate that women's experiences have not directly contributed to it. For example, although race discrimination consistently appears in *jus cogens* inventories, discrimination on the basis of sex does not.[33] And yet sex discrimination is an even more widespread injustice, affecting the lives of more than half the world's population. While a prohibition on sex discrimination, as racial discrimination, is included in every general human rights convention and is the subject of a specialized binding instrument, sexual equality has not been allocated the status of a fundamental and basic tenet of a communal world order.

Of course women as well as men suffer from the violation of the traditional canon of *jus cogens* norms. However the manner in which the norms have been constructed obscures the most pervasive harms done to women. One example of this is the "most important of all human rights",[34] the right to life set out in Article 6 of the Civil and Political Covenant[35] which forms part of customary international law.[36] The right is concerned with the arbitrary deprivation of life through public action.[37] Important as it is, the protection from arbitrary deprivation of life or liberty through public actions does not address the ways in which being a woman is in itself life-threatening and the special ways in which women need legal protection to be able to enjoy their right to life. Professor Brownlie has pointed to the

---

Rights, *adopted* 16 Dec. 1966, *entered into force* 23 Mar. 1976, G.A. Res. 2200 (XXI), 21 U.N. GAOR Supp. (No. 16), at 52, U.N. Doc. A/6316, 999 U.N.T.S. 171 (1966).

33. Compare Brownlie, *supra* note 14, at 513 n.29 (stating that principle of non-discrimination as to sex "must have the same *[jus cogens]* status" as principle of racial non-discrimination). *See also* Hannikainen, *supra* note 1, at 482.

34. Yoram Dinstein, *The Right to Life, Physical Integrity and Liberty,* in *The International Bill of Rights: The Covenant on Civil and Political Rights* 114 (L. Henkin ed., 1981).

35. *See also* Universal Declaration on Human Rights, *signed* 10 Dec. 1948, G.A. Res. 217A (III), art. 3, U.N. Doc. A/810, at 71 (1948); European Convention for the Protection of Human Rights and Fundamental Freedoms, 213 U.N.T.S. 221, art. 2 (1950).

36. Dinstein, *supra* note 34, at 115.

37. There is debate among various commentators as to how narrowly the right should be construed. Fawcett has suggested that the right to life entails protection only from the acts of government agents. J.E.S. Fawcett, *The Application of the European Convention on Human Rights* 30–31 (1969). Dinstein notes that it may be argued under Article 6 that "the state must at least exercise due diligence to prevent the intentional deprivation of the life of one individual by another." He seems however to confine the obligation to take active precautions against loss of life only in cases of riots, mob action, or incitement against minority groups. Dinstein, *supra* note 34, at 119. Ramcharan argues for a still wider interpretation of the right to life, "plac[ing] a duty on the part of each government to pursue policies which are designed to ensure access to the means of survival for every individual within its country." B.G. Ramcharan, *The Concept and Dimensions of the Rights to Life,* in *The Rights to Life in International Law* 1, 6 (B.G. Ramcharan ed., 1985). The examples of

need for empirical, rather than purely abstract, studies on which to base assertions of rights.[38] Such an approach highlights the inadequacy of the formulation of the international legal right to life.

A number of recent studies show that being a woman may be hazardous even from before birth due to the practice in some areas of aborting female fetuses because of the strong social and economic pressure to have sons.[39] Immediately after birth womanhood is also dangerous in some societies because of the higher incidence of female infanticide. During childhood in many communities girls are breast-fed for shorter periods and later fed less so that girls suffer the physical and mental effects of malnutrition at higher rates than boys.[40] Indeed in most of Asia and North Africa, women suffer great discrimination in basic nutrition and health care leading to a disproportionate number of female deaths.[41] The well-documented phenomenon of the "feminization" of poverty in both the developing and developed world causes women to have a much lower quality of life than men.[42]

Violence against women is endemic in all states; indeed international lawyers could observe that this is one of those rare areas where there is genuinely consistent and uniform state practice. An International Tribunal on Crimes Against Women, held in Brussels in 1976, heard evidence from women across the world on the continued oppression of women and the commission of acts of violence against them.[43] Battery is the major cause of injury to adult women in the United States, where a rape occurs every six minutes.[44] In Peru, 70 percent of all crimes reported to police involve women as victims.[45] In India, 80 percent of wives are victims of violence, domestic abuse, dowry abuse or murder.[46] In 1985, in Austria, domestic vio-

---

major modern threats to the right to life offered by Ramcharan, however, do not encompass violence outside the "public" sphere. *Id.* at 7–8.

38. Ian Brownlie, *The Rights of Peoples in Modern International Law,* in *The Rights of Peoples* 1, 16 (J. Crawford ed., 1988).

39. United Nations, *The World's Women, 1970–1990: Trends and Statistics* 1 n.2 (1991); Charlotte Bunch, *Women's Rights as Human Rights: Towards a Re-Vision of Human Rights,* 12 Hum. Rts. Q. 486, 488–89 n.3 (1990).

40. Bunch, *supra* note 39, at 489; United Nations, *supra* note 39, at 59.

41. Amartya Sen, *More Than 100 Million Women Are Missing,* N.Y. Rev. Books, 30 Dec. 1990, at 61.

42. *See, e.g., Women are Poorer,* 27 (3) U.N. Chronicle 47 (1990).

43. *Crimes Against Women: The Proceedings of the International Tribunal* (D. Russell ed., 1984). Richard Falk has pointed out the importance of such grass roots initiatives in contributing to the normative order on the international level (without referring to this Tribunal). Richard Falk, *The Rights of Peoples (In Particular Indigenous Peoples),* in *The Rights of Peoples* 17, 27–29 (J. Crawford ed., 1988). *Compare* Crawford, *The Rights of Peoples: Some Conclusions,* in *id.* at 159, 174–75.

44. Bunch, *supra* note 39, at 490.

45. *Id.*

46. *Id.*

lence against the wife was given as a factor in the breakdown of marriage in 59 percent of 1,500 divorce cases.[47] In Australia, a recent survey indicated that one in five men believed it acceptable for men to beat their wives;[48] while surveys by the Papua New Guinea Law Reform Commission found that up to 67 percent of wives had suffered marital violence.[49]

The United Nations system has not ignored the issue of violence against women. For example, the United Nations Commission on the Status of Women has noted its great concern on this matter and the Economic and Social Council has adopted resolutions condemning it.[50] The General Assembly itself has supported concerted, multidisciplinary action within and outside the United Nations to combat violence against women and has advocated special measures to ensure that national systems of justice respond to such actions.[51] A United Nations report on violence against women observes that "[v]iolence against women in the family has . . . been recognized as a priority area of international and national action. . . . All the research evidence that is available suggests that violence against women in the home is a universal problem, occurring across all cultures and in all countries."[52] But although the empirical evidence of violence against women is strong, it has not been reflected in the development of international law. The doctrine of *jus cogens,* with its claim to reflect central, fundamental aspirations of the international community, has not responded at all to massive evidence of injustice and aggression against women.

The great level of documented violence against women around the world is unaddressed by the international legal notion of the right to life because that legal system is focussed on "public" actions by the state. A similar myopia can be detected also in the international prohibition on torture.[53] A central feature of the international legal definition of torture is that it takes place in the public realm: it must be "inflicted by or at the instigation of or with the consent or acquiescence of a public official or other person acting in an official capacity."[54] Although many women are victims of

---

47. United Nations, *supra* note 39, at 19.
48. Australian Government, Office of the Status of Women, *Community Attitudes Towards Domestic Violence in Australia* 2 (1988).
49. United Nations, *Violence Against Women in the Family* 20 (1989).
50. U.N. E.S.C. Res. 1982/22, 1984/14.
51. G.A. Res. 40/36 (1985), *cited in* United Nations, *supra* note 49, at 4.
52. United Nations, *supra* note 49, at 4.
53. A more detailed analysis of the international law prohibition on torture from a feminist perspective is contained in Charlesworth, Chinkin & Wright, *supra* note 29, at 628–29.
54. United Nations Convention against Torture and Other Cruel, Inhuman or Degrading Treatment or Punishment, G.A. Res. 39/46 (Dec. 10, 1984), art. 1(1), *draft reprinted in* 23 I.L.M. 1027 (1984), *substantive changes noted in* 24 I.L.M. 535 (1985), *also reprinted in Human Rights: A Compilation of International Instruments,* at 212, U.N. Doc. ST/HR/1/ Rev.3 (1988).

torture in this "public" sense,[55] by far the greatest violence against women occurs in the "private" nongovernmental sphere.

Violence against women is not only internationally widespread, but most of it occurs within the private sphere of home, hearth and family.[56] In the face of such evidence, many scholars now have moved from an analysis of domestic violence based on the external causes of such violence to a structural explanation of the universal subordination of women: "wife beating is not just a personal abnormality, but rather has its roots in the very structuring of society and the family; that in the cultural norms and in the sexist organization of society."[57]

Violence against, and oppression of, women is therefore never a purely "private" issue. As Charlotte Bunch noted, it is caused by "the structural relationships of power, domination and privilege between men and women in society. Violence against women is central to maintaining those political relations at home, at work and in all public spheres."[58] These structures are supported by the patriarchal hierarchy of the nation state. To hold states accountable for "private" acts of violence or oppression against women, however, challenges the traditional rules of state responsibility.[59] The concept of imputability proposed by the International Law Commission in its draft articles on state responsibility does not encompass the maintenance of a legal and social system in which violence or discrimination against women is endemic and where such actions are trivialized or discounted.[60] It could be argued that, given the extent of the evidence of violence against women, failure to improve legal protection for women and to impose sanctions against perpetrators of violence against women should engage state responsibility.[61]

The problematic structure of traditionally asserted *jus cogens* norms is also shown in the more controversial "collective" right to self-determination.[62] The right allows "all peoples" to "freely determine their political sta-

---

55. *See, e.g.,* Amnesty International, *Women in the Front Line: Human Rights Violations Against Women* (1991).
56. United Nations, *supra* note 49, at 18–20.
57. *Quoted in id.* at 30.
58. Bunch, *supra* note 39, at 491.
59. *See* Gordon Christenson, *Attributing Acts of Omission to the State,* 12 Mich. J. Int'l L. 312 (1991).
60. The International Law Commission's controversial definition of an international crime in Draft Article 19 (3)(c), *supra* note 4, is also significantly limited in its coverage: it refers to a "serious breach on a widespread scale of an international obligation of essential importance for safeguarding the human being, such as those prohibiting slavery, genocide, apartheid."
61. *See* Americas Watch, *Criminal Injustice: Violence Against Women in Brazil* (1991).
62. This norm is not accepted by all commentators as within the *jus cogens,* but has considerable support for this status. *See* Brownlie, *supra* note 14, at 513.

tus and freely pursue their economic, social and cultural development."[63] Yet the oppression of women within groups claiming the right of self-determination has never been considered relevant to the validity of their claim or to the form self-determination should take.[64] An example of this is the firm United States support for the Afghani resistance movement after the 1979 Soviet invasion without any apparent concern for the very low status of women within traditional Afghani society.[65] Another is the immediate and powerful United Nations response after Iraq's 1990 invasion of Kuwait. None of the plans for the liberation or reconstruction of Kuwait were concerned with that state's denial of political rights to women. Although some international pressure was brought to bear on the Kuwaiti government during and after the invasion to institute a more democratic system, the concern did not focus on the political repression of women and was quickly dropped.

The operation of the public/private distinction in international human rights law operates to the detriment of women. In a sense, the doctrine of *jus cogens* adds a further public/private dimension to international law as *jus cogens* norms are those which are central to the functioning of the entire international community and are thus "public" in contrast to the "private" or less fundamental human rights canon. In this way, women's lives are treated as being within a doubly private sphere, far from the concerns of the international legal order.

B.   A Feminist Rethinking of *Jus Cogens*

In the context of human rights, what can a feminist contribution to the jurisprudence of *jus cogens* be? For example, should we seek to define a "fourth generation" of women's human rights? Such a development could lead to segregation and marginalization of exclusively women's rights and would be unlikely to be accepted as *jus cogens*. It has been argued that the central task of feminist theory in international relations is to understand the world from the perspective of the socially subjugated.[66] One method of doing this in international law is to challenge the gendered dichotomy between public and private worlds and to reshape doctrines based on it. For example, existing human rights law can be redefined to transcend the dis-

---

63. International Covenant on Civil and Political Rights, *supra* note 32, at 1.
64. *See* Christine Chinkin, *A Gendered Perspective to the Use of Force in International Law,* 12 Aust. Y.B. Int'l L. 279 (1992); Charlesworth, Chinkin & Wright, *supra* note 29, at 642–43.
65. *See* Charlesworth, Chinkin & Wright, *supra* note 29, at 642–43.
66. Sarah Brown, *Feminism, International Theory, and International Relations of Gender Inequality,* 17 Millenium: J. Int'l Stud. 461, 472 (1988).

tinction between public and private spheres and truly take into account women's lives as well as men's.[67] Considerations of gender should be fundamental to an analysis of international human rights law.[68]

Feminist rethinking of *jus cogens* would also give prominence to a range of other human rights; the right to sexual equality, to food, to reproductive freedom, to be free from fear of violence and oppression, and to peace. It is significant that these proposals include examples from what has been described as the third generation of human rights, which includes claimants to rights that have been attacked as not sufficiently rigorously proved, and as confusing policy goals with law-making under existing international law.[69] This categorization of rights to which women would attach special value might be criticized as reducing the quality and coherence of international law as a whole.[70] Such criticism underlines the dissonance between women's experiences and international legal principles generally. In the particular context of the concept of *jus cogens,* which has an explicitly promotional and aspirational character, it should be possible for even traditional international legal theory to accommodate rights that are fundamental to the existence and dignity of half the world's population. Professor Riphagen's nonhierarchical analysis of *jus cogens*[71] accommodates the inclusion of these rights even more readily.

IV. CONCLUSION

Fundamental norms designed to protect individuals should be truly universal in application as well as rhetoric, and operate to protect both men and women from those harms they are in fact most likely to suffer. They should be genuine human rights, not male rights. The very human rights principles that are most frequently designated as *jus cogens* do not in fact operate equally upon men and women. They are gendered and not therefore of uni-

---

67. For example, in the context of the right to life, the wide terms of the Human Rights Committee's General Comment on Article 6 of the International Covenant on Civil and Political Rights could be exploited to argue for the prevention of domestic violence as an aspect of this right. *See* U.N. Doc. CCPR/C/21/Rev.1 (1989), at 4–6 (1989). *See also* General Recommendation No. 19 of the Committee on the Elimination of Discrimination Against Women, U.N. Doc. CEDAW/C/1992/L.I/Add.15 (1992), which describes gender based violence as a form of discrimination against women.
68. Interesting work already exists in this area. For example, on the prohibition on apartheid, see Cheryl L. Poinsette, *Black Women under Apartheid: An Introduction,* 8 Harv. Women's L.J. 93 (1985); Penny Andrews, *The Legal Underpinnings of Gender Oppression in Apartheid South Africa,* 3 Aust. J.L. & Soc'y 92 (1986).
69. *See, e.g.,* Brownlie, *supra* note 38, at 16.
70. *Id.* at 15.
71. *See supra* note 6.

versal validity. Further, the choices that are typically made of the relevant norms and the interpretation of what harms they are designed to prevent reflect male choices which frequently bear no relevance to women's lives. On the other hand, the violations that women do most need guarantees against do not receive this same protection or symbolic labelling. The priorities asserted are male-oriented and are given a masculine interpretation. Taking women's experiences into account in the development of *jus cogens* norms will require a fundamental rethinking of every aspect of the doctrine.

It has been argued that the "New World Order" promised as a positive and progressive development from the realignment of the superpowers and the apparent renaissance of the United Nations in fact continues the same priorities as the old world order.[72] The gendered nature of the international legal order is not yet on the agenda in the discussions of any truly new world order. Without full analysis of the values incorporated in *jus cogens* norms or the impact of their application, further work to make them effective in a new international legal order will in fact only continue the male orientation of international law.

---

72. *See, e.g.,* Philip Alston, *Human Rights in the New World Order: Discouraging Conclusions from the Gulf Crisis,* in *Whose New World Order: What Role for the United Nations?* 85 (M. Bustelo & P. Alston eds., 1991).

Chapter 5

Enemies or Allies? Feminism and Cultural Relativism as Dissident Voices in Human Rights Discourse

Eva Brems

I. INTRODUCTION

In recent years, feminism and cultural relativism have been among the most vigorous and the most visible critiques of dominant human rights discourse. On many issues feminists and cultural relativists have found themselves taking diametrically opposed sides. The manifest successes of feminist views inside the human rights system have sometimes been at the expense of cultural relativist views. This paper argues against such an antagonism. An analysis of both the feminist and the cultural relativist positions will uncover parallels and similarities in their respective claims. There seems to be enough common ground to allow for building a bridge between the two strands of thought. Instead of wasting part of their creative potential in opposing each other, feminists and cultural relativists could join forces and combine their insights into a constructive critique.

In Parts II and III of this article the feminist and the cultural relativist critiques of human rights are summarized separately. In Parts IV and V, the two critiques are compared and contrasted. This confrontation usually takes the form of a sharp conflict, which is illustrated in Part IV by means of the recent UN world conferences. Part V reduces the dimensions of the conflict by pointing at parallels and similarities between the two critiques. In Part VI, a constructive approach to the remaining differences between the cultural relativist and the feminist human rights views is advanced.

II. THE FEMINIST CRITIQUE OF HUMAN RIGHTS

Human rights are not what they claim to be, feminists say. They are a product of the dominant male half of the world, framed in their language, reflecting their needs and aspirations. Whereas the "rights of man" as originally conceived by the great liberal thinkers were not intended to include women, today's "universal human rights" still overlook them as a matter of fact. The feminist critique of human rights thus basically argues for the inclusion of women in the human rights protection system. Feminists of all strands[1] advance various means to realize this aim.

A.   Liberal Feminists

Most at ease in the present human rights system are the "liberal feminists."[2] Their major concern, equal treatment of men and women, underlies the nondiscrimination provisions of most human rights treaties.[3] Liberal feminists stay within the existing human rights framework, using its language and logic to argue for an increased concern for women's needs. Karen Engle distinguishes between doctrinalists and institutionalists.[4] The first concentrate on bringing situations where they consider women's rights to be violated under the protection of specific existing human rights provisions. The latter

---

1. The subdivision of feminist thought in different strands used here is one that is frequently encountered. However, like most of reality, feminism resists strict categorization. It is self-evident that the thought of one author may contain elements of different strands, and that my use of these categories here should not be interpreted as an attempt to "box" anyone.

2. *See* Mary Becker et al., Cases and Materials on Feminist Jurisprudence: Taking Women Seriously 17–26 (1994) (discussing the history and characteristics of liberal feminism).

3. *See, e.g.,* International Covenant on Civil and Political Rights, art. 26, *adopted* 16 Dec. 1966, 999 U.N.T.S. 171 (*entered into force* 23 Mar. 1976), G.A. Res. 2200 (XXI), 21 U.N. GAOR Supp. (No. 16) at 52, U.N. Doc. A/6316 (1966) [hereinafter ICCPR]; European Convention for the Protection of Human Rights and Fundamental Freedoms, art. 14, *opened for signature* 4 Nov. 1950, Eur. T.S. No. 5, 213 U.N.T.S. 221 (*entered into force* 3 Sept. 1953); American Convention on Human Rights, art. 24, *opened for signature* 22 Nov. 1969, O.A.S.T.S. No. 36, *reprinted in* 9 I.L.M. 673 (1970) (*entered into force* 18 Jul. 1978).

4. Karen Engle, *International Human Rights and Feminism: When Discourses Meet,* 13 Mich. J. Int'l L. 517 (1992). Engle examines Kay Boulware-Miller, Alison T. Slack, Abdullahi An-Na'im, Rebecca J. Cook, Deborah Maine, and Yougindra Khushalani as examples of the doctrinalist approach. *See* Kay Boulware-Miller, *Female Circumcision: Challenges to the Practice as a Human Rights Violation,* 8 Harv. Women's L.J. 155 (1985); Alison T. Slack, *Female Circumcision: A Critical Appraisal,* 10 Hum. Rts. Q. 437 (1988); Abdullahi An-Na'im, *The Rights of Women and International Law in the Muslim Context,* 9 Whittier L. Rev. 491 (1987); Rebecca J. Cook & Deborah Maine, *Spousal Veto Over Family Planning Services,* 77 Am. J. Pub. Health 339 (1987); Yougindra Khushalani, Dignity and Honour of Women as Basic and Fundamental Human Rights (1982).

   Engle ranks Margaret E. Galey, Laura Reanda, and Noreen Burrows among the institutionalists. *See* Margaret E. Galey, *International Enforcement of Women's Rights,* 6 Hum. Rts. Q. 463 (1984); Laura Reanda, *Human Rights and Women's Rights: The United Nations Approach,* Hum. Rts. Q., Spring 1981, at 11; Noreen Burrows, *International Law and Human Rights: The Case of Women's Rights, in* Human Rights: From Rhetoric to Reality 80, 89–96 (Tom Campbell et al. eds., 1986).

focus on improving the present institutional structure for the enforcement of the human rights of women.

In the eyes of many feminists today, a liberal "add woman and stir" approach does not go far enough. Cultural feminists as well as radical feminists are convinced that a real inclusion of women in the human rights system requires a transformation of that system.[5] The human rights concept must get rid of the "maleness" with which its concepts and structure are imbued.

B. Cultural Feminists

Cultural feminists[6] are the antipodes of liberal feminists in that they stress women's difference from men rather than equality of the sexes. Real equality, as opposed to formal equality, takes this difference into account and values it. Various measures are proposed for the introduction of the female difference approach into the human rights system.

The most obvious difference between the sexes is the biological one. Woman's comparative physical weakness makes her more vulnerable to acts of violence, including sexual violence. Her childbearing and lactating capacities place her in a unique situation and are the presumable biological bases of her widespread role as a child-rearer. This often goes together with a concentration of activities and responsibilities in the home and less involvement in public life. In addition, woman's psychological structure is often argued to be different from man's. Her relational and nonconflictual orientation is especially stressed,[7] and usually some relationship between this and her different biological and cultural factors is claimed.

In its most radical form, this critique rejects law itself as a patriarchal institution because of its abstract, adversarial character.[8] Most feminists, however, consider that the usefulness of law as a strategy outweighs its disadvantages.[9] A reorientation of human rights towards the concrete is advo-

---

5. Such proposed transformations include a focus on human needs instead of human rights, revising the catalog of human rights, breaching the public/private dichotomy, and upgrading social and economic rights and collective rights. *See* discussion *infra* Parts II.B & III.D.
6. *See* Robin West, *Jurisprudence and Gender*, 55 U. Chi. L. Rev. 1 (1988) (discussing cultural feminism and its relation to radical feminism).
7. *See* Carol Gilligan, In A Different Voice: Psychological Theory and Women's Development (1982).
8. John Hardwig, *Should Women Think in Terms of Rights?*, 94 Ethics 441 (1984).
9. Gayle Binion, *Human Rights: A Feminist Perspective*, 17 Hum. Rts. Q. 509, 524 (1995) ("Despite serious feminist concerns about formalism, about statism, and about the function of law in general . . . the legal front and the diplomatic front cannot be eschewed.").

cated, such as a "responsibility model" centered around human needs.[10] Such proposals build upon the existing human rights framework and never reject it as such. However, the catalog of human rights has to be revised in light of woman's differences. This implies the recognition of new rights, such as reproductive rights or sexual autonomy rights, and the "recharacterization"[11] or "particularization"[12] of existing rights. It is this effort of bringing gender-specific violations under the human rights umbrella which is often referred to by the slogan "women's rights are human rights."[13]

A crucial aid in this undertaking is the breaching of the public/private dichotomy. Indeed, while human rights were "designed to regulate the relations between men and the state,"[14] women's oppression is largely situated in a private context: in practices and traditions living in society or in the home itself. The feminist battlecry "the personal is the political" translates in the human rights context into an argument in favor of the horizontal effect or *Drittwirkung* of human rights.[15] In response to this claim, the drafters of the Convention on the Elimination of All Forms of Discrimination Against Women[16] extended the definition of discrimination in Article 1 to "the political, economic, social, cultural, civil or any other field."[17]

Public/private is not the only dichotomy cultural feminists expose as an artificial male construct. Identifying the political sphere as male and the socioeconomic sphere as more central to women's advancement, feminists object to the general priority accorded civil and political rights and the second rate status of social and economic rights. The rights they advance as priorities (for instance, the rights to food, clothing, shelter, work, health, and education) belong to this second category.[18]

---

10. *Id.* at 525.
11. *See* Rebecca J. Cook, *Women's International Human Rights Law: The Way Forward, in* HUMAN RIGHTS OF WOMEN: NATIONAL AND INTERNATIONAL PERSPECTIVES 3, 10 (Rebecca J. Cook ed., 1994) [hereinafter HUMAN RIGHTS OF WOMEN].
12. Burrows, *supra* note 4, at 81.
13. *See* Andrew Byrnes, *Women, Feminism and International Human Rights Law—Methodological Myopia, Fundamental Flaws or Meaningful Marginalisation? Some Current Issues,* 12 AUSTRL. Y.B. INT'L L. 215 (1988–1989) (distinguishing "women's rights [as human rights]" from "women's human rights," the latter term applying to human rights violations which are not gender specific).
14. Burrows, *supra* note 4, at 81.
15. *See also* Riane Eisler, *Human Rights: Toward an Integrated Theory for Action,* 9 HUM. RTS. Q. 287 (1987); Celina Romany, *Women as Aliens: A Feminist Critique of the Public/Private Distinction in International Human Rights Law,* 6 HARV. HUM. RTS. J. 87 (1993).
16. Convention on the Elimination of All Forms of Discrimination Against Women, *adopted* 18 Dec. 1979, G.A. Res. 34/180, 34 U.N. GAOR Supp. (No. 46) at 193, U.N. Doc. A/34/36 (1980), *reprinted in* 19 I.L.M. 33 (1980) (*entered into force* 3 Sept. 1981) [hereinafter CEDAW].
17. *Id.* art. 1.
18. *See* Fran P. Hosken, *Toward a Definition of Women's Human Rights,* HUM. RTS. Q., Spring 1981, at 2–10; Charlotte Bunch, *Women's Rights as Human Rights: Toward a Re-Vision*

As foreign to the female world view as the aforementioned abstract dichotomies, cultural feminists claim, is the liberal concept of the autonomous individual underlying human rights. The underlying rationale is that instead of identifying themselves solely as autonomous individuals, women are more oriented toward the family and other groups or communities than men are. In order to take this relational or "connected" nature into account, a concretization and contextualization of human rights, as well as attention to the "third generation" of collective human rights, is necessary.[19]

C. Radical Feminists

Radical feminists maintain that all theories based on equality or difference make the same mistake of using a "male yardstick." They warn against valuing differences which are a product of a patriarchal society which needs to be dismantled.[20] The key "givens" are male dominance and female subordination, the central locus of which is the sexual sphere.[21] The fact that many women do not perceive their lives in this way is explained by a theory of "false consciousness."[22]

Although radical feminists are stringent in their critique of law and rights as instruments for the perpetuation of male dominance,[23] research for this paper did not uncover any explicit rejection of human rights as such. Rather, like the cultural feminists, they recognize the strategic worth of human rights.[24] From a completely different perspective, radical feminists come to some of the same conclusions as cultural feminists with regard to human rights. The public/private and other dichotomies have to be broken down because they are a cover-up for the maintenance of male domi-

---

of Human Rights, 12 Hum. Rts. Q. 488 (1990); Barbara Stark, Nurturing Rights: An Essay on Women, Peace, and International Human Rights, 13 Mich. J. Int'l L. 144 (1991); Joanna Kerr, The Context and the Goal, in Ours By Right: Women's Rights as Human Rights 3, 4–5 (Joanna Kerr ed., 1993); cf. Adetoun O. Ilumoka, African Women's Economic, Social, and Cultural Rights: Toward a Relevant Theory and Practice in Human Rights of Women, in Human Rights of Women, supra note 11, at 307, 307–325.

19. Hilary Charlesworth, What are "Women's International Human Rights"?, in Human Rights of Women, supra note 11, at 58, 75.

20. See Catharine A. MacKinnon, Difference and Dominance: On Sex Discrimination, in Feminism Unmodified: Discourses on Life and Law 32 (1987).

21. See Catharine A. MacKinnon, The Art of the Impossible, in Feminism Unmodified: Discourses on Life and Law, id. at 5–7.

22. See Becker et al., supra note 2, at 59 (defining false consciousness as "the notion that women sometimes act against their own self interest because they have internalized—as part of their consciousness—male norms and standards").

23. See, e.g., Catharine A. MacKinnon, Toward a Feminist Theory of the State 237–39 (1989).

24. See Charlesworth, supra note 19, at 61; see also Helen Bequaert Holmes & Susan Rae Peterson, Rights Over One's Own Body: A Woman-Affirming Health Care Policy, Hum. Rts. Q., Spring 1981, at 71.

nance in the spheres that are subsequently kept outside human rights scrutiny.[25] The creation of new "women's human rights" and the recharacterization of existing rights are two means advocated to identify instances of women's subordination and of violence against women as human rights violations.[26]

D. Feminist Methodology and Conclusions

A general feature of feminism which offers some interesting perspectives for human rights theory is its methodology. Feminist analysis is described as *"contextual, experiential, and inductive."*[27] Feminists take actual women's experiences as a starting point and place those in their full contexts. They prefer a complex "insider" viewpoint to a simplified and abstract outsider viewpoint.[28] The complexity of this approach has sometimes led to justified accusations of essentialism,[29] where the universality of women's experiences was taken for granted. Yet if this error is avoided, feminist inquiry's well-proven methodology, with its constructive radical potential, can be extremely valuable for human rights theory.[30]

Remarkable in this short overview of the feminist critique of human rights is the finding that human rights as such are never rejected. All strands of feminist critique aim at the inclusion of women in the human rights system.[31]

III. THE CULTURAL RELATIVIST CRITIQUE OF HUMAN RIGHTS

Human rights are not what they claim to be, cultural relativists say. Human rights are a product of the dominant Western parts of the world, framed in their language, reflecting their needs and aspirations. Whereas the "rights of man" as originally conceived by the great liberal thinkers were not intended to include slaves and indigenous inhabitants of the colonies, today's "universal human rights" are still foreign to non-Westerners as a matter of fact.

---

25. *See* Hilary Charlesworth et al., *Feminist Approaches to International Law,* 85 Am. J. Int'l L. 613, 629 (1991).
26. *See* Bunch, *supra* note 18, at 486–98; Charlesworth, *supra* note 19, at 71–76.
27. Binion, *supra* note 9, at 512 (emphasis in original).
28. Julie Mertus & Pamela Goldberg, *A Perspective on Women and International Human Rights After the Vienna Declaration: The Inside/Outside Construct,* 26 N.Y.U. J. Int'l L. & Pol. 201 (1994).
29. *See, e.g.,* Angela P. Harris, *Race Essentialism in Feminist Legal Theory,* 42 Stan. L. Rev. 581 (1990).
30. *See* Byrnes, *supra* note 13, at 206.
31. *See* Binion, *supra* note 9, at 513.

From these premises, cultural relativists derive their argumentation, which is basically aimed at the rejection of the inclusion of non-Western people in the international human rights protection system.[32] The essence of the cultural relativist position on human rights can thus be framed in a way that shows the parallel with the feminist position. In the same way, the different strands of feminism that were examined in the previous section have parallels in the different strands of cultural relativism.

A.   "Liberal Culturalists"

Some advocates for respect for non-Western cultures try to bring protection for cultural rights, including minority rights and rights of indigenous peoples, under the existing human rights provisions or to improve human rights institutions in order to further their claims. These could be called "liberal culturalists" and, in an analogy to liberal feminists, be described as doctrinalists and institutionalists, respectively. However, such activists are not generally labelled "cultural relativists." That name is reserved for those who attack the human rights system from their culturalist position. See the discussion in Part III.C.

B.   Dominance Theorists

Critiques of a Western dominance in the human rights concept sometimes use a "dominance theory" that can be seen as parallel to the radical feminist argument. The locus of Western dominance and non-Western suppression is, in the first place, the economic sphere. In this view, human rights are used in the foreign policy of Western states as instruments of neocolonialism[33] and of economic competition.[34] This position, which has been called the "conspiracy theory,"[35] has a predominantly political and eco-

---

32. It is a fact that the cultural relativist critique of human rights is often abused by those in power to object to the international scrutiny of the human rights situations in their countries. However, a sincere cultural relativism exists as well, and with good reason. It is this sincere form of the critique that I wish to engage in this paper. Due to the negative connotation of the term "cultural relativism," several authors, including Keba Mbaye and Makau wa Mutua, explicitly state that they are not cultural relativists. If I have treated them as such in the present paper, it is because I do not limit the term "cultural relativism" to the radical rejection of human rights.
33. *See* Shashi Tharoor, *The Universality of Human Rights and their Relevance to Developing Countries,* 59 Nordic J. Int'l L. 142 (1990).
34. Bilahari Kausikan, *Asia's Different Standard,* 92 Foreign Pol'y 24, 27–28 (1993).
35. Fernando R. Tesón, *International Human Rights and Cultural Relativism,* 25 Va. J. Int'l L. 896 (1985), *referring to* 2 Karl Popper, The Open Society and its Enemies 94 (1966).

nomic, rather than cultural, character. Yet it is generally carried a step further, arguing that Western imperialism also contains a moral component, because Westerners impose their values on the rest of the world through their insistence on human rights.[36] Thus the argument becomes part of the cultural relativist critique of human rights.

C.   Cultural Relativists

The core of the cultural relativist critique, however, is made up of a "difference" argument, in the style of cultural feminism. Typically, in a first step it is shown how human rights historically and conceptually reflect Western values.[37] In the next step, some particularities of a non-Western culture[38] are highlighted and contrasted with those Western concepts. The conclusion from these premises is to reject human rights.

Different levels of rejection can be distinguished.[39] At the most radical level, human rights are rejected in their totality as foreign to and incompatible with a particular non-Western culture. Although this is the most pure and consistent cultural relativist stance, it is the one least frequently encountered.[40]

More often, cultural relativists either reject specific rights, or reject the specific content or interpretation of those rights. For instance, members of a certain culture might object to freedom of religion. Or while not objecting to the right as such, they might object to its encompassing the freedom to change one's religion, either in its formulation (as permitted under Article 18 of the Universal Declaration of Human Rights[41]) or through interpretation.

---

36. *See, e.g.,* Adamantia Pollis & Peter Schwab, *Human Rights: a Western Construct with Limited Applicability, in* HUMAN RIGHTS: CULTURAL AND IDEOLOGICAL PERSPECTIVES 1 (Adamantia Pollis & Peter Schwab eds., 1979).

37. *See, e.g.,* Josiah A. M. Cobbah, *African Values and the Human Rights Debate: An African Perspective,* 9 HUM. RTS. Q. 309 (1987).

38. A variation of this scheme occurs when the argument is centered around ideological instead of cultural opposition. This form usually comes from communist countries.

39. *See also* Jack Donnelly, *Cultural Relativism and Universal Human Rights,* 6 HUM. RTS. Q. 400, 400–01 (1984) (making similar subdivisions); Douglas Lee Donoho, *Relativism Versus Universalism in Human Rights: The Search for Meaningful Standards,* 27 STAN. J. INT'L L. 345 (1991) (making similar subdivisions).

40. Rejection of human rights as understood by the West is rather widespread in conservative Muslim circles. However, these authors do not reject the concept of human rights as such. Rather, they put forward an alternative set of human rights, based on Islamic sources. *See* Heiner Bielefeldt, *Muslim Voices in the Human Rights Debate,* 17 HUM. RTS. Q. 587, 601–06 (1995).

41. Universal Declaration of Human Rights, art. 18, *adopted* 10 Dec. 1948, G.A. Res. 217A (III), 3 U.N. GAOR (Resolutions, part 1) at 71, U.N. Doc. A/810 (1948), *reprinted in* 43 AM. J. INT'L L. SUPP. 127 (1949).

Finally, on an even more detailed level, cultural relativists might accept a right with all its components and with its general interpretation, but reject the classification of a particular cultural practice as a violation of that right. For instance, in a culture where female circumcision is practiced, the prohibition of torture and cruel, inhuman, or degrading treatment (prohibited under Article 5 of the Universal Declaration of Human Rights and Article 7 of the International Covenant on Civil and Political Rights[42]) may be completely accepted while the classification of female circumcision as such treatment is rejected.

At closer view, only the first, most radical, attitude aims at the exclusion of non-Western cultures from the human rights system. The other, more moderate stances can be translated into claims of inclusion into the system, conditional on its transformation in such a way as to accommodate cultural differences.

One final exclusionist approach deserves mention. Sometimes the cultural relativist argument consists of presenting an alternative system of human rights, or more correctly, an alternative system for the achievement of social justice or the protection of human dignity, as a valid substitute for international human rights.[43] Depending on how much of the international human rights concept is incorporated into the description of the alternative system, this argument comes down to either a total or a partial rejection of human rights. It is, however, a rather problematic position. If the human rights system is simply criticized on one ground or another, it can react to the criticism and a constructive dialogue is at least possible. But if the concept of human rights is appropriated by the critics and given a different content, this results in a deadlock, because the underlying conflict is denied and no opening for dialogue is provided. These critics do not discuss how their claims could be answered by a transformation of the human rights system. Their argument is truly one of exclusion.

D. Criticisms and Demands for Transformation

What are the concrete criticisms that cultural relativists address to the human rights system? Cultural relativists invariably describe human rights as a product of Western liberalism. Some aspects are described as crucial to

---

42. *Id.* art. 5; ICCPR, *supra* note 3.
43. *See* Rhoda E. Howard, *Cultural Absolutism and the Nostalgia for Community,* 15 HUM. RTS. Q. 315 (1993) (giving the name "cultural absolutism" to the idea that all systems of social justice are human rights systems); *see also* Jack Donnelly, *Human Rights and Human Dignity: An Analytic Critique of Non-Western Conceptions of Human Rights,* 76 AM. POL. SCIENCE REV. 303 (1982) (providing a particularly vehement critique of those who equate human dignity with human rights).

the human rights concept, and at the same time as through and through Western. This statement is often accompanied by a historical overview of the origin of human rights and of the Western values in question.[44] The aspects of human rights most often attacked as Western are its individualism, its abstractness, and the concept of rights itself.

From nearly every non-Western culture comes the argument that its members do not define themselves in the first place as autonomous individuals, but instead experience themselves as having an "ascribed status" as members of a larger group or community, such as family, tribe, class, nation, or other group.[45] The use of abstract concepts and categories in human rights is argued to be the product of Western rationality, not shared by non-Westerners. They are convinced it is important to place all matters in their cultural context and to examine them at a concrete level.[46] One axiom of cultural relativism is the statement that judgments of behavior or of situations do not make sense outside the culture in which they take place.[47] The concept of rights itself is argued to be characteristic of a society that thinks in terms of atomized individuals and abstract ideas. Many non-Westerners are wary of the adversarialism inherent in rights talk. Rather than rights, they stress obligations and reciprocal responsibilities. Conflict solu-

---

44. *See, e.g.,* Cobbah, *supra* note 37; James C. Hsiung, *Human Rights in an East Asian Perspective, in* HUMAN RIGHTS IN EAST ASIA, A CULTURAL PERSPECTIVE 1 (1985); Ziyad Motala, *Human Rights in Africa: A Cultural, Ideological, and Legal Examination,* 12 HASTINGS INT'L & COMP. L. REV. 373, 383 (1989); Raimundo Panikkar, *La notion des droits de l'homme est-ell un concept occidental?,* 120 DIOGÈNE 87 (1982); S.S. Rama Rao Pappu, *Human Rights and Human Obligations: An East-West Perspective,* 8 PHIL. & SOC. ACTION 15 (1982); Prakash Sinha, *Human Rights: A Non-Western Viewpoint,* 67 ARCHIV FÜR RECHTS—UND SOZIALPHILOSOPHIE 76 (1981).

45. *See* Claude Ake, *The African Context of Human Rights,* 32 AFRICA TODAY 5, 5 (1987); Cobbah, *supra* note 37; *see also* Louis Henkin, *The Human Rights Idea in Contemporary China: A Comparative Perspective in Human Rights, in* CONTEMPORARY CHINA 7, 21–22 (1986); RHODA E. HOWARD, HUMAN RIGHTS IN COMMONWEALTH AFRICA 19 (1986); Hsiung, *supra* note 44; Christopher C. Joyner & John C. Dettling, *Bridging the Cultural Chasm: Cultural Relativism and the Future of International Law,* 20 CAL. W. INT'L L.J. 286 (1990); Piotr Kowalski, *The Problems of Cultural Relativism and the Universalism of the International Bill of Human Rights, in* 4 STUD. IN THE THEORY & PHIL. OF L. 91, 95 (1988); Makau wa Mutua, *The Banjul Charter and the African Cultural Fingerprint: An Evaluation of the Language of Duties,* 35 VA. J. INT'L L. 339, 339–80 (1995); Panikkar, *supra* note 44; Abdul Aziz Said, *Human Rights in Islamic Perspectives, in* HUMAN RIGHTS: CULTURAL AND IDEOLOGICAL PERSPECTIVES 86 (Adamantia Pollis & Peter Schwab eds., 1979); Sinha, *supra* note 44; Raymond Verdier, *Problématique des droits de l'homme dans les droits traditionnels d'Afrique noire,* 5 DROIT ET CULTURES 97 (1983); Harro von Senger, *Chinese Culture and Human Rights, in* HUMAN RIGHTS AND CULTURAL DIVERSITY 281, 295, 304 (W. Schmale ed., 1993).

46. This theme is implicit in most of the cultural relativist texts already cited in this discussion, and explicit in Ake. *See* Ake, *supra* note 45.

47. *See* MELVILLE HERSKOVITS, MAN AND HIS WORKS 61, 63 (Alfred A. Knopf, Inc. 1964) (1948) (summarizing the principle of cultural relativism as: "Judgements are based on experience, and experience is interpreted by each individual in terms of his own enculturation.").

tion is sought by consensual, cooperative means rather than through legalism and antagonism.[48]

In terms of demands for transformation of the human rights system, the communitarian critique suggests that greater attention should be paid to collective rights,[49] and to placing limitations on individual rights in favor of communal interests. One way of constructing such limitations is to center them around the concepts of obligations and responsibilities.[50] To the extent that the cultural relativist critique is opposed to legalism in human rights, it could support a status quo. As it is now, the international community, lacking the proper institutions for universal legal enforcement, tries to enforce human rights mainly through political pressure and embarrassment in the eyes of the public. Considering that the existing power imbalances in the international community get free play in this system, while they might be more contained in a more legalistic system, it may be wiser for the non-Western world to parallel the feminist solution—i.e., to set aside their cultural objections to "rightism" and play the rights game as a strategy to further their other claims inside the human rights system.

The demand for concretization and contextualization of human rights leads first of all to a focus on their realizations.[51] Also, this demand forms the basis of a "human needs" approach, in which the indivisibility of all human rights is used to frame the argument in favor of flexibility in the prioritizations made in human rights. Generally this results in an attack on the imbalance between civil and political rights on the one hand and social, economic, and cultural rights on the other. Non-Western countries are often third world countries, where it is argued either that economic progress has to be attained as a first priority or that the right to development trumps all other rights.[52]

Finally, a recurring argument derives from the idea that there is a core and a periphery in human rights. The core is essential and universal, while the periphery should permit cultural variations. When this core/periphery model is applied to the catalogue of human rights, it argues for a reduction

---

48. *See* Ake, *supra* note 45, at 5; Cobbah, *supra* note 37; Radhika Coomaraswamy, *To Bellow like a Cow: Women, Ethnicity, and the Discourse of Rights, in* HUMAN RIGHTS OF WOMEN, *supra* note 11, at 39; Henkin, *supra* note 45; HOWARD, *supra* note 45, at 20; Hsiung, *supra* note 44; Panikkar, *supra* note 44; Pappu, *supra* note 44; Sinha, *supra* note 44; von Senger, *supra* note 45, at 301, 305.
49. *See* Ake, *supra* note 45, at 9; Norbert Rouland, *La tradition juridique africaine et la réception des déclarations occidentales des droits de l'homme,* 26 DROIT ET CULTURES 197, 216 (1993); von Senger, *supra* note 45, at 308–09.
50. Mutua, *supra* note 45.
51. *See* Ake, *supra* note 45, at 10–11.
52. *See* Ake, *supra* note 45, at 5; Kausikan, *supra* note 34; Kowalski, *supra* note 45; von Senger, *supra* note 45, at 308–09.

of the list of universal human rights to those not contested anywhere, leaving the rest optional—so that human rights lists vary according to culture.[53]
The core/periphery model can also be applied to each right individually and
used to argue for the succinct formulation of the essence of what is to be
protected within each right, thus leaving room for contextual variation in the
interpretation and application of the right within each culture.[54]

Remarkable in this short overview of the cultural relativist critique of
human rights is the finding that while the critique seems at first sight aimed
at the exclusion of non-Western cultures, closer analysis reveals that this
holds true for only a minority of cultural relativists.[55]

IV. FEMINISM AND CULTURAL RELATIVISM IN CONFLICT

Feminists look at human rights through a gender lens, and cultural relativists
use the cultural perspective. They clash on issues where their perspectives
lead to opposite claims and priorities have to be made. Such issues arise
either when a culture prescribes certain manners in which women should
behave or be treated, or when feminists state that women's advancement
requires certain cultural attitudes.

Compared to cultural relativists, feminists enjoy a lot more credibility in
the international human rights community. In recent years, women's rights
have been advancing rapidly from the margin to the forefront of human
rights concern. In this process, a feminist attack on cultural relativism was
inevitable. Culture and religion are regarded with suspicion by feminists, as
spheres of male dominance and female suppression.[56] A central feminist
demand is the breaching of the public/private dichotomy, so that human
rights are extended to relations between private persons. Culture thus cannot enjoy immunity from human rights scrutiny on the ground that it does
not involve the relationship between the state and its citizens. Moreover,
one of the spheres that gets priority attention in the feminist human rights
campaign, the family, is the sphere in which most cultural traditions are
preserved. This is partly a result of the colonial experience of many non-
Western countries, where the colonizer introduced the distinction between

---

53. Sinha, *supra* note 44, at 89–90; *cf.* Kishore Mahbubani, Deputy Secretary of the Ministry
    of Foreign Affairs of the Republic of Singapore, *quoted in* Christina M. Cerna, *Universality
    of Human Rights and Cultural Diversity: Implementation of Human Rights in Different
    Socio-Cultural Contexts*, 16 Hum. Rts. Q. 741, 745 (1994).
54. *See* Keba Mbaye, Les droits de l'homme en Afrique 50 (1992); Tharoor, *supra* note 33, at 152.
55. An explicit option to stay within the human rights system is found in Kausikan, *supra* note
    34, at 39; *see also* Panikkar, *supra* note 44, at 110.
56. *See* Charlesworth, *supra* note 19, at 74.

a public and a private sphere, imposing his laws on the public sphere, but leaving the private sphere to be governed largely by indigenous rules.[57]

A. Harmful Cultural Practices

In the clash between cultural relativists and feminists, most attention goes to so-called "harmful cultural practices." This term indicates practices particular to certain (non-Western) cultures which, to the outsider's eye, harm or disadvantage women, but which are meaningful to certain participants in those cultures. In these situations, either the culture's insiders perceive no harm or disadvantage, or if the harm or disadvantage is recognized, it is justified or compensated for in the wider cultural context. The criticized practices include widow burning in India (sati), prenatal sex selection and female infanticide resulting from a preference for a son, child marriage, arranged or forced marriage, polygamy, seclusion and veiling, and food taboos for women. But the lion's share of feminist outrage concerns the practice of female circumcision, which has been described as "barbaric torture and mutilation" designed to perpetuate male ownership over women[58] and as "deeply linked to the denigration of women as inferior beings."[59]

The vehemence of this reaction illustrates the deafness of an absolutist position to the arguments of the other side. Feminists refuse to accept cultural objections to universal women's rights, because through their lens they see the culture from which those practices emanate as male created and male dominated.[60] At the same time they refuse to see the culturally determined character of their own position,[61] arguing that the universality of male dominance[62] is a sufficient basis for the universality of women's rights. Thus, they have no qualms about using cultural imperialism in their battle against

---

57. For example, the British colonial rulers in India retained the family laws applicable to different parts of the population (Hindus, Muslims, and Parsis) on the basis of their religion. Today family laws in India are still divided along religious lines. Indian feminists consider this a major obstacle to women's rights in their country. See Kirti Singh, *Obstacles to Women's Rights in India, in* HUMAN RIGHTS OF WOMEN, *supra* note 11, at 375.
58. Eisler, *supra* note 15, at 295, 296.
59. Joan Fitzpatrick, *The Use of International Human Rights Norms to Combat Violence Against Women, in* HUMAN RIGHTS OF WOMEN, *supra* note 11, at 532, 541.
60. Reza Afshari, *An Essay on Islamic Cultural Relativism in the Discourse of Human Rights,* 16 HUM. RTS. Q. 235, 256 (1994); Nancy Kim, *Toward a Feminist Theory of Human Rights: Straddling the Fence Between Western Imperialism and Uncritical Absolutism,* 25 COLUM. HUM. RTS. L. REV. 49, 90 (1993).
61. *See* Coomaraswamy, *supra* note 48, at 40 (arguing that assumptions about the female personality that accompany the discourse on women's rights are not universal).
62. *See* Michelle Zimbalist Rosaldo, *Woman, Culture, and Society: A Theoretical Overview, in* WOMAN, CULTURE AND SOCIETY 17 (Michelle Zimbalist Rosaldo & Louise Lamphere eds., 1974); Charlesworth, *supra* note 19, at 62.

male imperialism.[63] Cultural relativism in its absolutist form makes an analogous reasoning: the communal right to practice and maintain a culture comes first, and the objection from the women's rights perspective is not given serious consideration on the ground that these are a Western construct.[64] Clearly, absolutist positions in the debate between feminism and cultural relativism lead to paradox and deadlock.

B. Acceptance (Dominance) of Feminist Theory

In light of the ongoing battle between feminists and cultural relativists, it is not surprising to see that the acceptance of feminism inside the international human rights discourse is accompanied by a rejection of cultural relativism. The apparent irreconcilability of the two views is of course not the only factor that explains this evolution. There is, for instance, the possibility that feminism, being predominantly Western and therefore familiar to the dominant Western forces in the international community, may be seen as less threatening than cultural relativism. The fear of cultural relativism is explained and partly justified by the fact that the name cultural relativism is often abused by dictatorial governments, who use this to cover up their human rights violations. In international fora, the interlocutors are by definition government representatives, which does not enhance the credibility of their claims in this respect. In addition, the form in which the arguments are presented may equally play a role. The "inclusion" claim made by feminists looks a lot less threatening and is therefore more likely to get a constructive response than the "exclusion" claim made by cultural relativists. Finally, it may be remarked that the international feminist movement is a lot more unified and organized than the cultural relativist movement, if such exists at all.

C. Feminist Successes in Recent UN Conferences

The force of the international feminist movement became clear during the world conferences organized in the last few years by the United Nations in Vienna, Cairo and Beijing, which to different degrees became battlefields of the conflict between feminists and cultural relativists.

---

63. *See* Hope Lewis, *Between Irua and "Female Genital Mutilation": Feminist Human Rights Discourse and the Cultural Divide,* 8 HARV. HUM. RTS. J. 23 (1995).
64. *See* Asma Mohamed Abdel Halim, *Challenges to the Application of International Women's Human Rights in the Sudan, in* HUMAN RIGHTS OF WOMEN, *supra* note 11, at 397, 411.

1. UN World Conference on Human Rights in Vienna

Both feminists and cultural relativists seized the opportunity of the 1993 UN World Conference on Human Rights in Vienna[65] (Vienna Conference) to try to push their claims to the forefront. The cultural relativist move came from the governments of one region, Asia. At Asia's regional preparatory meeting for the Vienna Conference, a "Bangkok Declaration"[66] was adopted, which included the statement that "while human rights are universal in nature they must be considered in the context of a dynamic and evolving process of international norm-setting, bearing in mind the significance of national and regional particularities and various historical, cultural and religious back-grounds."[67] This highly alarmed the Western governments, who interpreted it as an attempt to undermine the entire international human rights system. In response, they became determined to resist any concession to the cultural relativist current.[68]

Feminists evidently organized primarily on a governmental level. A huge lobbying operation was set up[69] with a petition circulating in 120 countries and in women's caucuses, carrying the feminist message to the regional meetings and the UN preparatory meetings held prior to the Vienna Conference. There were two goals. The first goal was the integration of women's concerns in all human rights issues. The second goal was the recognition of violence against women as a human rights violation.

In the final document of the Vienna Conference,[70] the universality of human rights was repeatedly stressed[71] and cultural relativism rendered harmless in a reversal of the controversial Bangkok statement: "While the significance of national and regional particularities and various historical,

---

65. Vienna Declaration and Programme of Action, *adopted by* The World Conference on Human Rights, 2 June 1993, U.N. Doc. A/Conf.157/24 (Part I), at 29 (13 Oct. 1993) [hereinafter Vienna Declaration].
66. Final Declaration of the Regional Meeting for Asia of the World Conference on Human Rights, *adopted* 7 Apr. 1993, U.N. Doc. A/Conf.157/ASRM/8-A/Conf.157/PC/59 (1993) [hereinafter Bangkok Declaration].
67. *Id.* at 3 § 8.
68. For instance, at the interregional meeting organized by the Council of Europe in advance of the World Conference on Human Rights, the affirmation of the universality of human rights was advanced as the first among six proposals for action. *See Conclusions by the General Rapporteur, Mary Robinson, President of Ireland, in* HUMAN RIGHTS AT THE DAWN OF THE 21ST CENTURY: PROCEEDINGS, INTERREGIONAL MEETING ORGANIZED BY THE COUNCIL OF EUROPE IN ADVANCE OF THE WORLD CONFERENCE ON HUMAN RIGHTS 115, 117 (1993).
69. *Women's Rights as Human Rights: an international lobbying success story,* HUM. RTS. TRIB., June 1993, at 29 [hereinafter *Women's Rights Lobbying Success*]; Wendy Parker & Pauline Comeau, *Women Succeed in Vienna Where Others Fail,* HUM. RTS. TRIB., Nov. 1993, at 22.
70. Vienna Declaration, *supra* note 65.
71. "The universal nature of these rights and freedoms is beyond question." *Id.* at 4 ¶ 1. "All human rights are universal, indivisible and interdependent and interrelated." *Id.* at 5 ¶ 5. *See also id.* at 11 ¶ 32; *id.* at 12 ¶ 37.

cultural and religious backgrounds must be borne in mind, it is the duty of States, regardless of their political, economic and cultural systems, to promote and protect all human rights and fundamental freedoms."[72] Commentators considered this reaffirmation of the universality of human rights as "perhaps the most significant success of the World Conference."[73]

With cultural relativism thus "defeated," feminists had reasons to feel victorious. The Vienna Declaration and Programme of Action[74] contains several articles explicitly dealing with women's human rights. It was proclaimed that "[t]he human rights of women and of the girl-child are an inalienable, integral and indivisible part of universal human rights."[75] In addition, the integration of the human rights of women into the mainstream of the UN system was mentioned as a concern,[76] as was the elimination of violence against women in public and in private life.[77] Feminists labelled this result a "milestone"[78] and an "extraordinary success."[79]

The conflict between feminism and cultural relativism was envisaged, but not solved in the ambiguous wording of the paragraph on violence against women in the Programme of Action, which stresses the importance of "the eradication of any conflicts which may arise between the rights of women and the harmful effects of certain traditional or customary practices, cultural prejudices and religious extremism."[80] With regard to children a firmer position is taken: states are urged to "remove customs and practices which discriminate against and cause harm to the girl child."[81]

2.   1994 International Conference on Population and Development in Cairo

Although the 1994 International Conference on Population and Development[82] in Cairo dealt explicitly neither with women, nor with human rights, its Programme of Action[83] contains some references to these themes. Again,

---

72. *Id.* at 5 ¶ 5.
73. Cerna, *supra* note 53, at 742.
74. Vienna Declaration, *supra* note 65.
75. *Id.* at 7 ¶ 18.
76. *Id.; see also id.* at 18 ¶ 37.
77. *Id.* at 7 ¶ 18; *id.* at 19 ¶ 38.
78. Mertus & Goldberg, *supra* note 28, at 202.
79. Donna J. Sullivan, *Women's Human Rights and the 1993 World Conference on Human Rights,* 88 Am. J. Int'l L. 152 (1994).
80. Vienna Declaration, *supra* note 65, at 19 ¶ 38.
81. *Id.* at 21 ¶ 49.
82. *Report of the International Conference on Population and Development,* Cairo 1994, U.N. Doc. A/Conf.171/13 (18 Oct. 1994) [hereinafter *Cairo Conference Report*].
83. Programme of Action of the International Conference on Population and Development, Cairo 1994, *adopted* 13 Sept. 1994, U.N. Doc. A/Conf.171/13.Annex (18 Oct. 1994) [hereinafter Cairo Programme of Action].

feminist concerns seem to have been integrated throughout the conference. One of the fifteen guiding principles of the Cairo Programme of Action states that "[a]dvancing gender equality and equity and the empowerment of women, and the elimination of all kinds of violence against women, and ensuring women's ability to control their own fertility, are cornerstones of population and development-related programmes."[84] The balance of this principle reiterates paragraph 18(1) of the Vienna Declaration and Programme of Action.[85]

Cultural relativists could interpret the recognition that "various forms of the family exist in different social, cultural, legal and political systems"[86] as a concession to their claims. However, it is improbable that this is how it was intended, especially since there is a Western interest in assuring that situations such as the single parent family are covered by the definition. As for "harmful cultural practices," forced marriages and child marriages are referred to implicitly by insisting on the "free and full consent of the intending spouses . . . [and a] minimum age at marriage."[87] Female circumcision is condemned at several instances.[88]

3. 1995 World Conference on Women in Beijing

During the 1995 World Conference on Women in Beijing, the conflict between feminism and cultural relativism moved to the forefront. The main issue in this respect was whether the expression "equity," as a description of the desired relationship between men and women, was acceptable as an alternative to the expression "equality." In Cairo, the juxtaposition of both concepts had been accepted, where one of the objectives was stated to be the "achieve[ment of] equality and equity based on harmonious partnership between men and women."[89] But in Beijing, the West rallied around the goal of firmly closing all doors to cultural relativism. They managed to delete all mention of "equity" in the final text.

The Beijing Platform for Action reaffirms the universality of human rights, including the human rights of women.[90] In harmony with the Cairo Programme of Action, the Beijing Platform for Action also explicitly adopts

---

84. *Id.* princ. 4.

85. Vienna Declaration, *supra* note 65, ¶ 18(1).

86. *Cairo Conference Report, supra* note 82, § 5.1; *see also* Cairo Programme of Action, *supra* note 83, princ. 9.

87. *Cairo Conference Report, supra* note 82, § 4.21.

88. *See id.* §§ 4.22, 7.6.

89. *Id.* § 4.3(a).

90. Beijing Declaration and Platform for Action, *adopted* 15 Sept. 1995, Fourth World Conference on Women: Action for Equality, Development and Peace, ¶ ¶ 9, 213, *reprinted in* Meiklejohn Civil Liberties Institute, Beijing Declaration and Platform for Action: Advance Unedited Draft (1996). *See also id.* ¶ ¶ 211, 212.

the principles of paragraphs 5 and 18(1) of the Vienna Declaration and Programme of Action.[91] However, the Beijing Platform adds a reference to "the significance of and full respect for various religious and ethical values, cultural backgrounds and philosophical convictions of individuals and their communities"[92] made in the text. Nevertheless, the eradication of "harmful cultural practices," with a special emphasis on female circumcision, is called for in the global framework,[93] as well as in the chapters on health,[94] on violence against women,[95] and on the girl child.[96] It is also stated that governments should refrain from invoking any custom, tradition or religious consideration to avoid their obligations with respect to the elimination of violence against women.[97] Custom is also pointed at as a factor contributing to discrimination against women in areas outside the "harmful cultural practices" context, for instance with regard to ownership of land[98] and access to education.[99] In addition, the Platform for Action includes a warning against religious extremism, which may have a negative impact on women[100] as well as a recommendation to take steps so that religion is not a basis for discrimination against girls.[101]

It should be added that Cairo's recognition of various forms of the family is reiterated in the Beijing Platform for Action[102] and that a few other mentions of respect for cultural diversity are made in specific contexts.[103] Nevertheless, the 1995 World Conference on Women provides a telling illustration of the simultaneity of the rise of feminism and the rejection of cultural relativism in the international community.

V.   PARALLELS AND SIMILARITIES

Neither feminism nor cultural relativism originated in the human rights sphere. Both are strong movements, each with its own history and dynamics, which in many respects makes it impossible to compare them. But when they become critiques of human rights, feminism and cultural relativism make parallel claims.

---

91. *Id.* ¶ 2.
92. *Id.* ¶ 9.
93. *Id.* ¶ 40.
94. *Id.* ¶ 108(a).
95. *Id.* ¶ ¶ 114(a), 119, 125(i), (k).
96. *Id.* ¶ ¶ 225, 232(g), (h), 283(d), 274(f), 276(b).
97. *Id.* ¶ 125(a).
98. *Id.* ¶ 158.
99. *Id.* ¶ 71.
100. *Id.* ¶ 25.
101. *Id.* ¶ 276(d).
102. *Id.* ¶ 30.
103. *See also id.* ¶ ¶ 85(p), 107(c), 242(d).

Both start from a finding that the liberal concept of human rights was developed by the dominant group, excluding the group whose perspective they defend, making this conception of human rights inadequate for their group.

Their strategies do differ. The feminist critique is offensive: it accuses human rights of not being universal because they exclude women's concerns. The cultural relativist critique is defensive: it rejects the universality of human rights because they exclude the concerns of non-Western cultures.

But each critique wants the same thing: changes in the human rights system so as to incorporate either a gender perspective or a perspective of cultural diversity. Each wants to make the "human" in "human rights" a little less abstract by returning its gender or its culture. They agree that human rights should be, as they were intended to be, the rights of all human beings regardless of elements such as gender or culture. However, in order to achieve this intended gender neutrality or culture neutrality, human rights must be neither gender blind nor culture blind. Because if neutrality comes down to blindness, human rights will further privilege the privileged and further disempower the disempowered, which is not what they are designed to do. This partial reconcretization or recontextualization of human rights is what Keba Mbaye names "la spécificité,"[104] in English specificity or particularity.

Because feminism and cultural relativism each concentrate on one specificity, each faced the same danger of ignoring all other particularities and so becoming absolutist or essentialist. And because the commonality of gender is the basis for feminists to organize, just like the commonality of culture is the basis for cultural relativists to organize, the tendency to reduce everything to this common element is natural. It increases a movement's internal coherence as well as the power of its arguments. Yet it is not excusable, because this results in a repetition, albeit in a different form, of the very problem the critique reacted against, and so causes a loss of a lot of its constructive potential. Inside the feminist movement, the danger of essentialism has been identified as inherent especially to cultural and radical feminism[105] and is being addressed. While feminists still want to make women's "different voice" heard, they recognize that this voice is composed of many different voices, because women vary across class, race, age, wealth, sexual orientation, and culture.[106]

Building on this anti-essentialist strand of feminism, some authors argue for reducing the tension between feminism and cultural relativism through

---

104. MBAYE, *supra* note 54, at 41.
105. *See* Kim, *supra* note 60, at 99–101.
106. *See* Catherine Harries, *Daughters of our peoples: International Feminism Meets Ugandan Law and Custom*, 25 COLUM. HUM. RTS. L. REV. 493, 509 n.55 (1994) (making reference to challenges of essentialist feminism).

changes in the feminist ideology. For instance, African feminists argue for a broader conception of feminism, one which would recognize on the one hand the African historical experience of imperialism combined with patriarchy, and on the other hand, the contemporary divergent cultural contexts within which feminism must be situated. They call for a "multiple consciousness [that] acknowledges competing claims about what constitutes the self and the community in which it is embedded."[107] Annie Bunting argues for an "asymmetrical anti-essentialism," which tolerates essentialist arguments only as a self-consciously employed strategy in the hands of non-Western women, so that through their contribution feminism can get rid of its stereotypical views of other cultures.[108] If feminism can thus manage to pursue its insistence on specificity even inside the concepts of "woman" and "man," it would indeed take an important step toward bridging the gap with cultural relativism.

It would become even more promising if cultural relativism were to make a parallel move by recognizing that "culture" is neither fixed nor monolithic. Nobody is in a position to determine what is the essence of a particular culture, just like nobody is in a position to determine what is the essence of a particular gender. Linked to the problem of essentialism is the practice of rejecting "inauthentic voices." Attempting to create the "essential woman" or the "essential African" or Asian or whatever, leads not only to ignoring the differences inside those categories, but also to an artificial isolation from their opposite, which is perceived as the enemy. In reality though, women and men, Westerners and non-Westerners frequently interact and reciprocally influence each other. Just like internal variations, this intertwinedness with the enemy is a part of reality that essentialists refuse to take into account. Women who feel happy in their "subordinate" roles are ascribed "false consciousness." Their views are not taken seriously by many feminists because they are considered to be the product of enculturation in the despised patriarchal society. Likewise, members of non-Western cultures who abandon part of their cultural heritage are often put aside by cultural relativists as "non-authentic" and "Westernized."

If part of reality is ignored by feminists and cultural relativists alike, the results of their activism can at best benefit only part of the people whose interests they pretend to represent. While the sacrifice of the other part may be acceptable from the viewpoint of feminist revolution or of cultural conservatism, it is not acceptable from the viewpoint of human rights. The argument in favor of increased specificity of human rights precisely aims at improving their reach, at making human rights meaningful for the greatest possible number of people.

---

107. *Id.* at 511–12.
108. Annie Bunting, *Theorizing Women's Cultural Diversity in Feminist International Human Rights Strategies*, 20 J.L. & Soc'y 6, 11–13 (1993).

Keeping in mind this warning against the risk of essentialism inherent in both feminism and cultural relativism, consider the positive side of the demand for specificity by examining the parallels in the transformatory claims that feminists and cultural relativists address to the human rights system. In both currents, it is recognized that a consistent insistence on specificity would lead to a rejection of the concepts of "law" and "rights." Yet after formulating their rights critique, both feminists and cultural relativists decide to rehabilitate the concepts for tactical reasons.

Feminists have been very successful in translating their concerns into rights, arguing both for the recognition of new rights and the reinterpretation of existing rights. Cultural relativists, although less successful, similarly aim at a "domestication"[109] of human rights. But with regard to new rights, cultural relativists are somewhat limited by the negative framing of their demand, which leads them to focus on the rejection rather than the affirmation of rights. However, in the current international context, where a lot of attention goes to cultural minorities, an approach through the right to respect for one's culture could be very fruitful. While both feminists and cultural relativists are willing to pursue their goals through the tough game of law, they consider the "softer" legal methods to be most consistent with their specificity. Thus they prefer decision-making as well as dispute resolution through negotiation and consensus rather than adversarial means.[110]

A striking commonality of feminists and cultural relativists is their substitution of the abstract individual with a situated, connected self.[111] While it is only logical that feminists look at women as a group and that cultural relativists focus on cultural groups, it is remarkable that the "groupness" aspect of their specificity claims goes beyond that. Being a member of a group such as a family or a local community is argued to be particularly significant for women as well as for non-Westerners. However, while cultural relativists see this aspect only in a positive light, feminists also point at groups as the locus of oppression. Although they share the cultural relativists' concern with collective rights, feminists therefore add the necessity of breaching the immunity of private groups to human rights scrutiny.

Another striking parallel between feminist and cultural relativist human rights critiques is their rejection of the prioritization of civil and political

---

109. Ake, *supra* note 45, at 9.
110. *See* Charlesworth et al., *supra* note 25, at 616–17 (noting this parallel). *See also* Isabelle R. Gunning, *Arrogant Perception, World-travelling and Multicultural Feminism: The Case of Female Genital Surgeries,* 23 Colum. Hum. Rts. L. Rev. 189, 189–248 (1991– 1992) (noting that the lack of a strong enforcement mechanism in the international human rights system is a strength rather than a weakness in light of the need for a capacity for cultural sensitivity).
111. Sandra Harding, *quoted in* Charlesworth et al., *supra* note 25, at 617; *cf.* V. Spike Peterson, *Whose Rights? A Critique of the "Givens" in Human Rights Discourse,* 15 Alternatives 303 (1990).

rights.[112] The social and economic spheres are argued to be of particular importance to women as well as to non-Western people. Civil and political rights are by no means rejected, but a different balance is argued for, one in which social and economic rights would have equal importance. Both on the feminist[113] and on the cultural relativist side, the insistence on social and economic rights is sometimes the result of a "human needs" approach. Such an approach, which starts from the concrete needs of real women or real non-Western people, also expresses a final important common characteristic of the feminist and cultural relativist critiques of human rights: the bend away from abstract categorization toward attention for the concrete contextualized human being.[114]

VI. TOWARD A CONSTRUCTIVE APPROACH TO THE REMAINING DIFFERENCES

The parallels and commonalities between the feminist and cultural relativist critique of human rights uncovered in the previous section show that the conflict between those two currents is not as profound as it often seems. A lot depends in this respect on the internal dynamics of each critique, and specifically on their capacity to avoid essentialism. However, conflicts between the perceived rights of women and the perceived rights of culture will continue to arise. In order to prevent or solve these, many authors urge for efforts to be made inside particular cultures. They want to change the customs or traditions that are seen as human rights violations. Proposed methods include consciousness raising,[115] reinterpretation of religious laws,[116] and selecting the "positive aspects" of a culture.[117]

Efforts to integrate human rights in all cultures are indeed crucial. The effectiveness of human rights depends to a large extent on their being alive

---

112. Bunting, *supra* note 108, at 10; *cf.* J. Oloka-Onyango & Sylvia Tamale, *"The Personal is Political," or Why Women's Rights are Indeed Human Rights: An African Perspective on International Feminism,* 17 Hum. Rts. Q. 691, 711–12 (1995).
113. Binion, *supra* note 9, at 524–26.
114. Peterson, *supra* note 111 (referring to parallel critiques of human rights by feminists and cultural relativists).
115. *See, e.g.,* Halim, *supra* note 64, at 419; Florence Butegwa, *Using the African Charter on Human and People's Rights to Secure Women's Access to Land in Africa, in* Human Rights of Women, *supra* note 11, at 495, 509–11; Jennifer Jewett, *The Recommendations of the International Conference on Population and Development: The Possibility of the Empowerment of Women in Egypt,* 29 Cornell Int'l L.J. 191 (1996).
116. *See* An-Na'im, *supra* note 4; Abdullahi Ahmed An-Na'im, *State Responsibility Under International Human Rights Law to Change Religious and Customary Laws, in* Human Rights of Women, *supra* note 11, at 167.
117. Ronald Thandabantu Nhlapo, *International Protection of Human Rights and the Family: African Variations on a Common Theme,* 3 Int'l J.L. & Fam. 1, 17 (1989).

in civil society and public opinion.[118] Human rights should fit within the categories in which people think; they should be obvious to everybody, and they should not contradict other obviousnesses. However, this ideal of truly universal human rights will not be brought about by working from within cultures alone. The human rights system will have to make some accommodations as well. At present, cultural objections to particular human rights clauses too often lead to reservations to treaties or declarations or simply to non-enforcement. If the system could be relied upon to be sensitive to cultural diversity, this problematic situation might end.

A.   Introduce Concreteness into Human Rights

It is beyond the scope of the present paper to elaborate in detail how the human rights system can accommodate cultural variations. Yet from the comparative analysis of the cultural relativist and the feminist critiques to the system a few guidelines emerge. The first concerns the need to be wary of excessive abstractness. If an idea is, like human rights, intended to be meaningful all over the world, it has to take into account the heterogeneity of the world's people. Therefore a measure of concreteness, specificity, or particularity has to be incorporated into the human rights concept. That human rights are valid for all humans does not imply that these humans have to remain abstract. Rather on the contrary: if human rights are modelled to fit abstract humans, there is bound to be a fitting problem when they are confronted with real persons.

The need for a contextualized concept of the person has been elaborated by many contemporary theorists. Michael Sandel, for instance, criticizes liberalism for its unrealistic conception of an "unencumbered self" which denies the possibility that any roles, commitments, or community memberships could be constitutive of the self.[119] Anti-essentialist feminism is developing an interesting "insider" methodology to approach conflicts of culture and women's rights. An influential theory in this respect is Seyla Benhabib's "interactive universalism."[120] This concept wants to avoid both the substitutionalist error of elevating the experiences of a specific group to the "human" norm and the relativistic paralysis of endorsing all pluralities and differences as morally and politically valid. It criticizes the "generalized

---

118. Coomaraswamy, *supra* note 48, at 39.
119. Michael J. Sandel, *The Procedural Republic and the Unencumbered Self*, 12 POL. THEORY 81, 81 (1984).
120. Seyla Benhabib, *The Generalized and the Concrete Other: The Kohlberg-Gilligan Controversy and Feminist Theory, in* FEMINISM AS CRITIQUE 77 (Seyla Benhabib & Drucilla Cornell eds., 1987).

other" by taking the standpoint of the "concrete other," "an individual with a concrete history, identity and affective-emotional constitution."

B. Frame Conflicts in Legal Terms

It has been argued that the legal context and particularly litigation is very suitable for the application of the theory of "interactive universalism."[121] Indeed, the law is perpetually concerned with the tension between the abstract (the rule) and the concrete (the facts of a case). The need for, and feasibility of, a relational, contextualized approach to rights within the legal system has been convincingly demonstrated by Martha Minow in her wonderful work *Making All the Difference.*[122] Therefore, the second guideline for broaching the opposition between feminism and cultural relativism is that conflicts can be substantially deflated if they are framed in legal terms. This option for human rights-as-law may conflict with the argument that both women and non-Western people feel uncomfortable about using legal methods. However, neither feminists nor cultural relativists eventually reject law as such, probably because they realize that the alternative is human rights-as-politics, where power differentials play an important role. What does the conflict between women's human rights and cultural relativism look like in legal jargon?

1.   Conflict between rights

A first possibility is to view it as a conflict between rights. On the one hand there are "women's human rights," on the other "cultural" or "religious" rights. Women's human rights are laid down in several texts, the principle one being the Convention on the Elimination of All Forms of Discrimination Against Women.[123] In addition, rights to religion and culture are found in Articles 18 and 27 of the International Covenant on Civil and Political Rights[124] and in Article 15 of the International Covenant on Economic, Social and Cultural Rights.[125] If opposing claims can each be framed in terms of a right, and if those rights have equal validity as a matter of princi-

---

121. Nitya Duclos, *Lessons of Difference: Feminist Theory on Cultural Diversity,* 38 Buff. L. Rev. 325, 375–80 (1990).
122. Martha Minow, Making All the Difference (1990).
123. CEDAW, *supra* note 16.
124. ICCPR, *supra* note 3.
125. International Covenant on Economic, Social and Cultural Rights, art. 15, *adopted* 16 Dec. 1966, 993 U.N.T.S. 3 (*entered into force* 3 Jan. 1976), G.A. Res. 2200 (XXI), 21 U.N. GAOR Supp. (No. 16) at 49, U.N. Doc. A/6316 (1966).

ple, a constructive approach is possible. This was convincingly demonstrated by Donna Sullivan, who elaborated a framework for the resolution of conflicts between gender equality and religious freedom.[126]

In the present state of international law, however, cultural rights do not have the same status as religious rights. Freedom of religion is one of the oldest human rights. It is classified among the civil and political rights, which enjoy *de facto* priority status inside the human rights system. Its respect is regularly enforced by national as well as international bodies. In contrast, cultural rights are considered to be "second generation rights," a category that is usually not given enforceable status. And even within the second generation, cultural rights receive less attention than social rights, and are formulated a lot more succinctly.[127]

Religious rights are generally intended to protect the unique character of a variety of religions. Cultural identity, however, seems to be protected only in the contexts of protection of minorities and protection of the rights of indigenous peoples. A general right "to protect custom and practices that sustain a particular culture's unique identity"[128] does not exist as yet. The disparity between the status of religious and cultural rights creates an awkward situation from the cultural relativist point of view. Most, if not all religious practices can be termed cultural. Yet those cultural practices that are religious are met with much higher respect than those that are not. In real life, the line between religious culture and other culture is often hard to draw. For instance, should the official doctrine of a religion or the people's perception of what their religion requires be decisive? As long as cultural rights do not have an equal status with women's rights, it is impossible to dissolve the opposition between feminism and cultural relativism through a framework based on conflicts of rights.

2. *Rights and grounds for limiting those rights*

Another way of framing the problem in legal terms, is by viewing one interest as a right, and the other as an acceptable ground for limitation of that right. That rights can be subject to limitations is an accepted feature of the international human rights system. Article 29 (2) of the Universal Declaration of Human Rights stipulates that:

---

126. Donna J. Sullivan, *Gender Equality and Religious Freedom: Toward a Framework for Conflict Resolution,* 24 N.Y.U. J. INT'L L. & POL. 795 (1992).
127. *Cf.* International Covenant on Economic, Social and Cultural Rights, *supra* note 125, art. 15 ¶ 1(a) (proclaiming the right "to take part in cultural life"). Judging from the rest of Article 15, the framers did not intend to protect cultural identities, but rather the participation in art, science, etc. *See id.*
128. *See* Joyner & Dettling, *supra* note 45, at 290 (pleading for the formulation of such a right).

In the exercise of his rights and freedoms, everyone shall be subject only to such limitations as are determined by law solely for the purpose of securing due recognition and respect for the rights and freedoms of others and of meeting the just requirements of morality, public order and the general welfare in a democratic society.[129]

Similar limitation clauses accompany several rights in the International Covenant on Civil and Political Rights[130] and in the European Convention for the Protection of Human Rights and Fundamental Freedoms.[131] The enumerated interests do not automatically trump the rights in question; rather, limitations have to be provided by law and pass a proportionality test. Through this test the controlling body aims at striking a fair balance between the demands of the general interest of the community and the requirements of the protection of the individual's fundamental rights. It could be possible to frame "gender equality" as a community interest in the name of which the "right to practice one's culture" could be limited. Yet given the present status of that right in the human rights system, this solution looks rather farfetched. But what about the opposite, culture as a community interest that justifies limitations of women's rights if a proportionality test is satisfied? Several problems appear. For one, formulations of women's rights are not usually accompanied by limitation clauses. Another obstacle is the requirement in all limitation clauses that the measure limiting the right be provided by law. While some cultural traditions are part of "customary law," it is clear that many others are not "provided by law," even in the widest sense of the word.

3.   Interpretation

Then how can the law deal with the feminist-culturalist conflict? The smoothest way seems to be through interpretation. The interpretative enterprise is the meeting place of the concrete and the abstract. Human rights language is necessarily general. This permits the judge to take into account all kinds of particularities of the situation brought before him or her, including the cultural context and the human rights view of the people concerned. The same situation may be a human rights violation in one cultural context and not in another. If an invariable core of meaning of each right is respected, such a margin of cultural variability is by no means a revolutionary concept. The acceptability of various cultural interpretations has already been agreed upon with regard to some concepts, such as that of "family." Also, one of the

---

129. Universal Declaration of Human Rights, *supra* note 41, art. 29(2).
130. ICCPR, *supra* note 3.
131. European Convention for the Protection of Human Rights and Fundamental Freedoms, *supra* note 3.

functions of the "margin of appreciation" doctrine in the case law of the European Court of Human Rights is to permit a different balancing of interests in different cultural contexts.[132] An obstacle to the approach of cultural variation in interpretation, however, is the fact that sometimes the formulation of a right in an international document already contains a certain culturally specific interpretation.[133]

C. The Individual as the Starting Point

The third guideline for handling conflicts between feminism and cultural relativism is to take as a starting point the individual. Not the liberal concept of an abstract individual which is rejected by cultural relativists and feminists alike, but a contextualized individual, who conforms to our "specificity" guideline. To abandon the individual in favor of an approach through group rights would, however, deny the feminist concern about the oppressiveness of groups. If the viewpoint of the group is taken, there is a risk of essentialism, because it becomes difficult to take internal differences and evolutions inside the group into account. Group rights are not the only way to express the "connectedness" or "embeddedness" of human beings in terms of human rights. Individual rights can have an important communal aspect. This is clear for family rights, religious rights, and associational rights. But also, if a certain way of speaking is characteristic for a particular community a communal dimension may be integrated into the freedom of speech. And some cultural or communal aspects of someone's way of life may be brought under the right to privacy.[134]

Many other examples could be given, but the main point is that introducing specificity in an individual rights approach makes it possible to value a concrete person's communal ties, not those that the dominant forces inside the community would like to attribute to him or her. Each individual should have the right to practice his or her culture and traditions, but likewise, each individual should have the right to reject them, for instance

---

132. Eva Brems, *The Margin of Appreciation Doctrine in the Case-Law of the European Court of Human Rights*, 56 ZEITSCHRIFT FÜR AUSLÄNDISCHES ÖFFENTLICHES RECHT UND VÖLKERRECHT 240 (1996).
133. Pieter van Dijk, *A Common Standard of Achievement: About Universal Validity and Uniform Interpretation of International Human Rights Norms*, 13 NETH. Q. HUM. RTS. 105, 117 (1995) (citing Article 16, paragraph 2 of the Universal Declaration of Human Rights to illustrate this point in reference to marriage). *See also* Universal Declaration of Human Rights, *supra* note 41, art. 16 ¶ 2 ("Marriage shall be entered into only with the free and full consent of the intending spouses.").
134. *E.g.*, Buckley v. United Kingdom, 19 Eur. H.R. Rep. C.D. 20, ¶ 65 (1995) (gypsy who was prevented from living with her family in her caravans, on her land, claimed that this treatment interfered with her rights regarding family life, private life, and home).

because he or she has been influenced by contact with another culture or with international feminism. These influences are as much a part of reality as traditional culture is. The international human rights system should defend this "opt-out" possibility[135] and take up responsibility for the women who use it.[136]

VII. CONCLUSION

Feminists and cultural relativists criticize the dominant human rights discourse from very different angles and backgrounds. They are certainly not natural allies, yet they have some points of critique in common. That finding is significant. Maybe there really are some faults in the international human rights system. Maybe something should be done to mitigate the ruling conception of abstract individualism and to balance the different categories of rights.

What makes both critiques even more convincing is the fact that essentially they come down to demands for inclusion of substantial groups of the world community in the human rights system. Inclusion of all human beings is precisely what the "human rights" concept is all about. It is central to the ideal of universality. What both the feminist and cultural relativist critiques of human rights make clear is that universality is not synonymous with uniformity. Real inclusion of all human beings requires attentiveness to their specificities.

Even though they do not seem much aware of it, cultural relativists and feminists share several concerns in their critique of human rights. These are important concerns. For instance, both critiques state that human rights should improve the lives of real people, taking account of their needs as well as of their contexts and particularities. In addition, both critiques share the concern that all human rights are indivisible, which means that social and economic rights and collective rights should not be less important than civil and political rights. If human rights were to aim at these goals, not only women and non-Western cultures, but all humans would benefit from it.

---

135. HOWARD, *supra* note 45, at 198; Katherine Brennan, *The Influence of Cultural Relativism on International Human Rights Law: Female Circumcision as a Case Study,* 7 L. & INEQ. J., July 1989, at 367, 398.

136. If Western countries seriously believe that particular cultural practices violate women's human rights, the minimum these countries should do is accord refugee status to women fleeing such practices. *Cf.* Pauline Comeau, *Woman fleeing Islamic edicts allowed to stay in Canada,* HUM. RTS. TRIB., Winter 1993, at 19 (illustrating the rare exception to the thesis that Western states' commitment to human rights stops where the states feel that their own policies are somehow threatened by the demands of human rights).

If cultural relativists and feminists stopped wasting their breath and energy on issues on which they are opposed and focused instead on issues they have in common, they could develop a powerful constructive human rights critique. Since cultural relativists enjoy little or no credit on the international human rights scene, they have everything to gain from such an alliance. Feminists also have an interest in maximizing the constructive critical potential of their critique. Feminists must be aware that their present rise to the forefront of human rights discourse is partly as a result of the efforts from the dominant West to exclude other currents from that forefront, such as cultural relativism and the broader movement for social and economic rights.[137] It has been noted that "the previous U.S. government raised women's rights or violence against women to avoid its obligations around socio-economic rights, and rights to development."[138] Similarly, in Vienna, where women's human rights were the big success story, social and economic rights were rather neglected. This means that very likely, the advance of feminist concerns in human rights will stop where the overlap with these other critiques starts: at the point where Western states start to feel threatened, because they can no longer be certain to respect all the demands of human rights without having to adapt their behavior. Given that human rights were most certainly not designed to make states feel comfortable, but rather the opposite, a coalition designed to force these "difficult issues" to the forefront may indeed be necessary.

---

137. *Cf.* Craig Scott, *The Interdependence and Permeability of Human Rights Norms: Towards a Partial Fusion of the International Covenants on Human Rights*, 27 Osgoode Hall L.J. 769 (1989); Rolf Künnemann, *A Coherent Approach to Human Rights*, 17 Hum. Rts. Q. 323 (1995).
138. *Women's Rights Lobbying Success, supra* note 69, at 30.

PART II

Religion, Culture, and Women's Human Rights

Chapter 6

The Human Rights of Middle Eastern and Muslim Women: A Project for the Twenty-first Century

Janet Afary

I. INTRODUCTION

In her widely read novel, *The Handmaid's Tale*,[1] Margaret Atwood took the futuristic nightmares of George Orwell's *1984* and Aldous Huxley's *Brave New World* one step further by imagining a misogynist state that was ruled by fundamentalist men. The new state of Gilead, located in Boston, Massachusetts, denied women jobs and education, persecuted homosexuals, banned other religious sects, and moved "undesirable" populations to colonies. Women were turned against women through domination and indoctrination, the state controlled women's sexuality, and reproduction became an instrument of terror. Atwood wrote her novel in 1986, perhaps a literary response to both the Iranian Revolution of 1979, which brought an Islamic Republic to power, and the growth of Christian fundamentalist organizations in the United States. Yet despite this foreboding novel, in the last decade threads of her vision have become a reality in Europe, the Middle East, and most egregiously, Afghanistan.

Historians might call the turn of the twenty-first century "The Era of the Gender Wars." The word "war" is not only used as a euphemism for intellectual and political debates, but also as a reference to the bloody carnage that persists over who gets to control the women's minds and bodies in the new millennium. By definition, a war has both victories and losses, and these ongoing gender wars in the Middle East/Muslim world are no exception. The growth of Islamist movements worldwide and the rise of new nationalisms after the fall of the Soviet Union unleashed new atrocities

---

1. MARGARET ATWOOD, THE HANDMAID'S TALE (1986).

aimed at women. At the same time, Middle Eastern/Muslim women reached new milestones in the 1990s by placing women's human rights, women's centers, and feminist scholarship on the political agenda.

This report will attempt to present both sides of the ongoing struggle. First, it will examine the dismal state of human rights of Middle Eastern/Muslim women in a selection of North African, Central Asian, and Middle Eastern countries, situations attesting to a vision not unlike Atwood's. The article then turns to some of the legal reforms and attempts made by a new generation of women's rights activists; women who are building new institutions in their homelands despite numerous obstacles and great personal and political risk. Finally, this article concludes with a discussion of Shirin Ebadi, an Iranian judge, author, staunch women's rights activist, and the 2003 winner of the Nobel Peace Prize. Her award has generated a great deal of excitement among Iranian advocates of women's rights as an optimistic omen for the next decade, an omen that alludes to an increased level of world attention and significant improvement for human rights and Middle Eastern women.

II. HUMAN RIGHTS AND WOMEN'S RIGHTS

The 1990s opened with the war in the former Yugoslavia, leaving behind the carnage of Bosnian and Croatian women. After Serbian nationalists besieged Sarajevo close to 10 percent of the Bosnian Muslim female population, or nearly 100,000 women, were raped. Over 60 percent became pregnant as a consequence of this systematic rape, and by 1993 over 35,000 babies were born as a result of rapes in concentration and death camps.[2] After the war, and as the decade dragged on, trafficking in women reached epidemic proportions.[3] Throughout Bosnia and Herzegovina women are to this day held in debt bondage in brothels. They are forced to provide free sexual services to local police who sometimes participate in the trafficking as owners and employees of clubs, or as middlemen who provide false documents. Even some members of the International Police Task Force (UN Police) have been charged with visiting brothels as clients.[4]

The world once again watched in horror when a similar scenario was

---

2. *Bosnian Feminists Shatter Myth About War* an interview with Diana Kapidzic & Aida Daidzic, representatives of women refugees from Bosnia, *in* BOSNIA-HERZEGOVINA: ACHILLES HEEL OF WESTERN "CIVILIZATION" (Chicago: News and Letters, 1996).

3. Human Rights Watch, *Hopes Betrayed: Trafficking of Women and Girls to Post-Conflict Bosnia and Herzegovina for Forced Prostitution,* 14 HUMAN RIGHTS WATCH PUBLICATIONS 9, 11 (2002), *available at* www.hrw.org/reports/2002/bosnia/Bosnia1102.pdf.

4. *Id.*

repeated in 1999, this time aimed at the Muslim Albanian women of Kosovo, as well as other women of the former Yugoslavia.[5] Rape and various forms of sexual violence were used as weapons of war and instruments of systematic ethnic cleansing. Rapes were not isolated acts of individuals; they were weapons "to terrorize the civilian population, extort money from families, and force the population to flee their homes."[6] The purpose of rape by the Serbian and Yugoslav forces was to force the ethnic Albanian Muslims out of Kosovo. According to Human Rights Watch, the perpetrators were the Serbian special police in blue uniforms, the Yugoslav army soldiers in green, and especially the Serbian paramilitaries, bearded men who carried long knives. Rape often took place in the presence of military officers and with their acquiescence.[7]

Sandwiched in between these two European atrocities was the genocidal episode of the Taliban in Afghanistan (1997–2001).[8] The Taliban (and before them the Mujhidin of the United Front) sexually assaulted and abducted women on a large scale during the years of conflict. Under the Taliban, women of all social classes and ethnicities were targeted, though the most systematic violations were aimed at the minority Hazara and Tajik women.[9]

Under the Taliban regime, severe restrictions were placed on the liberty and basic freedoms of all women, thereby practically erasing them from public life.[10] The Taliban banned women's employment (in most sectors), closed girls' schools, and forbade women from appearing in public without supervision by a close male relative.[11] All had to wear the burka, a restrictive, head-to-toe covering, instead of the lighter veil that had become more common in the urban centers in the last few decades. The religious police, the Ministry for the Promotion of Virtue and the Prevention of Vice (modeled after similar institutions in Saudi Arabia and Iran), ruthlessly enforced these laws. Women were severely beaten for showing their wrists, hands, or ankles. They were even tormented for begging on the streets.[12]

---

5. HUMAN RIGHTS WATCH, FEDERAL REPUBLIC OF YUGOSLAVIA: KOSOVO-RAPE AS A WEAPON OF "ETHNIC CLEANSING" (2000), *available at* www.hrw.org/reports/2000/fry/index.htm#TopOfPage.

6. *Id.*

7. *Id.*

8. Human Rights Watch, *Afghanistan: Humanity Denied,* 13 HUMAN RIGHTS WATCH PUBLICATIONS 5, 2 (2001), *available at* www.hrw.org/reports/2001/afghan3/. *See also* Valentine M. Moghadam, *Women, the Taliban, and the Politics of Public Space in Afghanistan, in* SEPTEMBER 11, 2001: FEMINIST PERSPECTIVES 260 (Susan Hawthorne & Bronwyn Winter eds., 2002).

9. Human Rights Watch Afghanistan, *supra* note 8, at 8.

10. *Id.*

11. *Id.* at 2.

12. *Id.*

These actions took place at a time when Kabul alone had forty thousand war widows.[13] Prostitution, while legally banned, became rampant, and the Taliban leaders, the same men who had forced female doctors out of the medical profession, routinely frequented the houses of prostitution.[14] Many of these restrictions are still imposed on women in Kuwait and Saudi Arabia, as well as several other nations with which the international community maintains routine political and economic ties.

While not reaching the level of denial of women's rights found in Bosnia, Kosovo, or Afghanistan, the spread of Islamist movements, and in some cases the increase in poverty and war in parts of Africa, Central Eurasia, South Asia, and the Middle East, has led to a loss of rights and benefits for women in a number of other countries.

A. Kuwait

In Kuwait, despite the active participation of women in education and employment and their impressive leadership role in various institutions, little effort has been made to modify the numerous forms of institutional discrimination against women. In 1999, the ruler of Kuwait, Sheikh Jabar AlSalah attempted to give women the right to vote, but his decree was vetoed by a majority of the legislators.[15] Women are denied equal inheritance rights and have limited rights in marriage and divorce.[16] The penal code reduces or eliminates punishment of men in so-called "honor crimes." Men who kill female relatives in "honor crimes" serve a maximum of three years.[17] A woman is never free to make a marriage decision on her own.[18] Between the ages of fifteen and twenty-five a guardian can prohibit her from marrying. Even after a divorce or being widowed, when a woman can choose her spouse, she still needs a guardian to contract her marriage.[19] Additionally, a husband has a unilateral and unconditional right to divorce his wife, a right his wife does not enjoy. A man who kidnaps a woman may be excused from all punishments if the guardian of the woman consents to the marriage.[20]

---

13. *Id.*
14. *Id.*
15. Ilene R. Prusher, *Kuwaiti Women Seek Right to Vote,* Christian Science Monitor, 8 Aug. 2000, *available at* www.csmonitor.com.
16. Press Release, Human Rights Watch, New Report Charges Serious Discrimination (25 Oct. 2000) *available at* www.hrw.org/press/2000/10/ku102500.htm.
17. *Id.*
18. Human Rights Watch, *Kuwait: Promises Betrayed—Denial of Rights of Bidun, Women, and Freedom of Expression* (2000), *available at* www.hrw.org/reports/2000/kuwait/.
19. *Id.*
20. *Id.*

In sum, Kuwaiti women face severe discrimination in both their public and private lives. Women can not pass their nationality to their spouse or children.[21] Women are banned from voting and many public positions, including serving as judges. Many of these restrictions, including men's guardianship over women, repudiation, "honor killings," and lack of citizenship rights, are also enforced in other countries of the region.[22]

B. Nigeria

In Nigeria, the Shariat law was instituted in twelve northern states in the late 1990s with dire repercussions for women. In the northern state of Zamfara, which has declared itself an Islamic state, Safiya Hussaini Tungar-Tudu was recently sentenced to death by stoning for having non-marital sex. In February 2002, as a result of intense international pressure, her sentence was commuted to seventy-five lashes.[23] Additionally, another woman named Amina Lawal was sentenced to death for committing adultery, as she had given birth to a child without a husband. Again, in September 2003, as a result of national and international pressure, the verdict was overturned.[24] Safiya and Amina's cases show how the more lenient sexual mores of the village community are being replaced with a harsh and unprecedented and intolerant reading of Malaki Islamic law. Indeed, the judges were able to set aside Amina's sentence by returning to a more traditional reading of Malaki laws and showing that her adultery was not proved beyond doubt.[25] The men who had sex with Safiya and Amina were set free by the court for lack of sufficient evidence.[26]

C. Pakistan

Despite the impressive leadership role of Pakistani women and the work of the feminist organization Sherktgah, which is affiliated with the international network, Women Living Under Muslim Law, violence against

---

21. *Id.*
22. *Id.*
23. *Nigerian Spared Death by Stoning,* BBC News World Edition, 25 Sept. 2003, *available at* www.news.bbc.co.uk/1/hi/world/africa/3137890.
24. *Id.*; Press Release, Human Rights Watch, Nigeria: Woman Sentenced to Death Under Sharia (23 Oct. 2001) *available at* www.hrw.org/press/2001/10/nigeria1023.
25. Somini Sengupta, *Facing Death for Adultery, Nigerian Woman is Acquitted,* N.Y. Times, 26 Sept. 2003, at A3.
26. Press Release, Human Rights Watch, Nigeria: Woman Sentenced to Death Under Sharia, *supra* note 24; *Nigerian Spared Death by Stoning, supra* note 23.

women continues in significant numbers in Pakistan.[27] In a one hundred page report on Pakistan, Human Rights Watch documented a "virtual epidemic of crimes of violence against women, including domestic violence rates as high as 90 percent, at least eight reported rapes every twenty-four hours nationwide, and an alarming rise in so-called honor killings."[28]

Furthermore, the Organization of Islamic Clerics of Pakistan demanded the expulsion of all Western-financed nongovernmental organizations (NGOs), and the closing of all women's centers and organizations. They claimed that several NGOs in Pakistan "propagate obscenity, immoral behavior, and Christianity to please their Western donors."[29] The Organization also urged Pakistani women to shun such groups and to regard them as centers of prostitution. The Islamic Clerics of Pakistan further encouraged its members to kidnap members of women's organizations, keep them locked away at home, or force them into marriage to pious Muslims.[30]

D.   Saudi Arabia

In Saudi Arabia, women "face pervasive discrimination, ranging from strictly enforced gender segregation in public places—including schools, universities, and the workplace—to unequal legal status with men in matters relating to marriage, divorce, and child custody."[31] Women are restricted in their movements, are not permitted to drive, and do not have the right to transmit their nationality to their children.[32] The religious police, known as the Office for the Propagation of Virtue and the Prevention of Vice, which is funded by the government, abuses women who do not conform to the traditional restrictive dress code, or appear in public with men who are not related to them.[33]

Saudi Arabia does not have a constitutionally elected parliament.[34] The consultative parliament, which has 120 members, serves as an advisory body to the government. There are no women on this council.[35] There are

---

27. XIII NEWSHEET, Jan. 2002 (on file with the author). Newsheet is a publication of Sherkatgah (an organization in Lahore, Pakistan) and is affiliated with the international network of Women Living Under Muslim Law (WLUML).
28. *See* Press Release, Human Rights Watch, Pakistan: Women Face Their Own Crisis (19 Oct. 1999) *available at* www.hrw.org/press/1999/oct/pakpr.htm.
29. XIII NEWSHEET, *supra* note 27.
30. *Id.*
31. Human Rights Watch, *Human Rights in Saudi Arabia: A Deafening Silence,* HUMAN RIGHTS WATCH BACKGROUNDER 4 (2001), *available at* www.hrw.org/backgrounder/mena/saudi/.
32. *Id.*
33. *Id.*
34. *See* U.S. Department of State, *Background Note: Saudi Arabia* (Nov. 2001), *available at* www.state.gov/r/pa/ei/bgn/3584.
35. Human Rights Watch, *Human Rights in Saudi Arabia: A Deafening Silence, supra* note 31, at 4.

also no women's rights organizations in Saudi Arabia.[36] Saudi Arabia has ratified the 2000 Convention on the Elimination of All Forms of Discrimination against Women, but no changes in the treatment of women have appeared as a result. Prince Naif, the Interior Minister, was quoted in January 2001, to the effect that any public discussion on women's rights was simply "out of the question." In April 2001, he maintained that lifting the ban on women's driving was impossible.[37]

E. Sudan

In Sudan, the governor of the state of Khartoum issued a ban in September 2000 that prevented women from "working in public places where they come into direct contact with men."[38] Under the rubric of respecting the "honor of women," the law bars women from working in bars, restaurants, and gas stations, as well as cafeterias, and anywhere in the service sector. The ban apparently was a reaction to the news that the Shell Oil Company had started employing women in service stations. The law requires employers to fire all their women employees. Many Sudanese activists fear that, in the tradition of the Taliban in Afghanistan, "the decree is a prelude to removing women from all fields" of work outside the home.[39] The law has resulted in a particularly sad reality for Sudanese women, as "after years of civil war, many women are the sole providers for their families."[40] International monitoring organizations, including Human Rights Watch, have "called on all employers, including foreign companies whose female employees will be affected by this law, to privately and publicly protest the ban."[41]

F. Syria

In Syria, following Bashar al-Asad's assumption of the office of the presidency in July 2000, there were some hopes that the country's human rights record might improve.[42] Six hundred political prisoners were released, and for the first time in over thirty-five years a privately-owned newspaper was

---

36. *Id.* at 4–5.
37. *Id.* at 5.
38. Press Release, Human Rights Watch, Sudan Blasted on Women's Ban (8 Sept. 2000) *available at* www.hrw.org/press/2000/09/sudan908.
39. *Id.*
40. *Id.*
41. *Id.*
42. Memorandum from Human Rights Watch on Syria's Compliance with the International Covenant on Civil and Political Rights, to the United Nations Human Rights Committee, *available at* www.hrw.org/press/2001/04/syriam–0405.

allowed to publish.[43] Pro-democracy advocates and civic forums encouraged by these reforms began to appear. Unfortunately, in February 2001, the government began to "clamp down" on all such activities, dimming the hopes for increased women's rights in Syria.[44]

Syrian law grants women the same formal legal and political rights as men, but the personal status law and the penal code retain major forms of discrimination.[45] An adult woman cannot marry without the permission of a male guardian.[46] The minimum age for girls is seventeen, but the judge can allow marriage of a minor girl of thirteen if the father consents.[47] Muslim women may not marry non-Muslims, a right that is available to Muslim men.[48] A wife has to obey her husband and may not work outside the home without his permission.[49] Men retain the right to marry four wives simultaneously and to divorce their wives by repudiation.[50] In some cases, however, women can sue for divorce in court due to irreconcilable differences or marital discord if all attempts at reconciliation fail.[51] As in most Muslim countries, marital rape is not even recognized as an issue. "Honor killings" continue in Syria and a man who kills his wife or sister for committing adultery is exempt from any legal penalty.[52]

G.   Uzbekistan

In Uzbekistan, despite claims by the government that women enjoy broad human rights protection, Human Rights Watch reports that women are doubly victimized, both by their husbands and by the state.[53] In the post-Soviet era, the average marriage age for girls has declined.[54] Likewise, women's educational attainment has dropped. In 1991, about 40 percent of students in higher education were girls; by 1997, that figure had dropped to 37 percent.[55] Many officials openly express the sentiment that higher educa-

---

43. *Id.*
44. *Id.*
45. *See* the Personal Status Law No. 34, discussed in Memorandum on Syria's Compliance, *supra* note 42, *available at* www.hrw.org/press/2001/04/syriam–0405.
46. *Id.* art. 21.
47. *Id.* art. 18.2.
48. *Id.* art. 48.2.
49. *Id.* art. 73–74.
50. *Id.* art. 17.
51. *Id.* art. 105–15.
52. *Id.* art. 548.
53. Human Rights Watch, *Uzbekistan: Sacrificing Women to Save the Family?*, 13 HUMAN RIGHTS WATCH PUBLICATIONS 4, 3 (2001), *available at* www.hrw.org/reports/2001/uzbekistan/uzbek0701.pdf.
54. *Id.* at 9.
55. *Id.* at 10.

tion should be limited to men.[56] Instead of protecting women from domestic violence, the government of Uzbekistan routinely pressures women to stay in violent marriages and prevents them from having access to divorce.[57] In a fifty-seven-page report based on interviews with victims of domestic violence, women's rights activists, lawyers, judges, police, doctors, and government officials, at the national, province, district, village, and local community levels, Human Rights Watch showed that state policies actually prevent women from recourse against spousal abuse.[58] Officials rarely prosecute husbands who beat their wives and try to reconcile couples without any concern for the women's safety.[59]

III. WOMEN FIGHT BACK: NEW POLITICAL AND LEGAL REFORMS, NEW FEMINIST INSTITUTIONS

It is important to note, however, that the rights of women have not been curtailed everywhere in the Middle East and Muslim world in the last two decades. As specifically discussed below, in Tunisia, Malaysia, Indonesia, Israel, Jordan, and Iraq, women have maintained most of the rights they obtained in the 1970s and in some areas extended them. Most of the countries in this category, are, however, controlled by secular authoritarian rulers that makes the future of these reforms highly questionable were there to be a change in government.

In Tunisia, a full-fledged Ministry of Women, Family, and Children's Affairs was established in September 2002. In addition, polygamy was abolished and a woman's right to divorce was legalized.[60] Additionally, a campaign to end the practice of veiling has been underway in the last decade. A new form of multicultural education has been introduced in both high schools and universities. Sexist and chauvinistic comments regarding women and people of non-Muslim faiths were removed from school texts, and new required courses on the Universal Declaration of Human Rights and democracy were developed.[61]

In Malaysia, the current anti-discrimination laws are being further amended to give women equal constitutional rights. Discrimination based

---

56. *Id.*
57. *Id.* at 3.
58. *Id.*
59. *Id.*
60. Press Release, United Nations Committee on Elimination of Discrimination Against Women, Committee Experts Commend Tunisia's "Great Strides Forward" in Promoting Equality Between Women, Men (14 June 2002) *available at* www.un.org/News/Press/docs/2002/wom1348.doc.
61. Susan Sachs, *In One Muslim Land, an Effort to Enforce Lessons of Tolerance,* N.Y. Times, 16 Dec 2001, § 4, at 4.

on religion, race, ethnicity, and sex will be prohibited. A women's office at the ministerial level was created. The head of the central bank, the Attorney General, and the Solicitor General are all women.[62]

The 1990s also witnessed the proliferation and growth of a new feminist scholarship on Muslim women in a variety of fields, such as Anthropology, History, Sociology, Political Science, and Literature. At the same time, through grassroots initiatives, a number of shelters for abused women, hotlines, and women's centers have been established in the region. In Iran, Israel, Turkey, Egypt, and Jordan, activist women routinely held meetings, conferences, and even public demonstrations. In these countries, there is a feeling that the fundamentalist movements (Muslim and Jewish) might have reached their peak especially after 11 September 2001. In a number of countries, women have formed think tanks seeking cultural, social, and political change. Many women's rights organizations publish journals. *Newsheet* in Pakistan, *Al-Raida* in Lebanon, *Zanan, Jense-i Dovvom, Hoquq-i Zan* in Iran, and *Nogo* in Israel stand at the forefront of the women's movement in their respective nations and report on feminist activities around the globe. Despite this progress, it seems we often move two steps forward and one step back in most areas of the region, especially with regard to institutions and regulations that control women's sexuality.

A.   Algeria

Algeria continues its decade-old bloody battle against the Islamic Salvation Front (FIS) in which over 150,000 have died.[63] The FIS regards political independence from France as only phase one of the struggle against colonialism and calls for the rejection of all "foreign" cultural influences. In this retrograde discourse, it is a woman's "religious duty" to cater to her husband and children.[64] At the same time foreign customs that fit the patriarchal mold were introduced, such as the practice of temporary marriage (mut'a), which is mainly a Shi'ite Iranian practice.[65] Sexual slavery of women became routine in the 1990s as Islamist vigilantes killed, burned, raped, and looted villages then selected and kidnapped the most attractive women for themselves.[66]

---

62. XIII Newsheet, *supra* note 27.
63. Eric Goldstein, *While the West Backs Algeria's Rulers, the People Suffer,* Int'l Herald Trib., 12 Jan. 2002, *available at* www.hrw.org/editorials/2002/algeria_011202.
64. *See* Marnia Lazreg, *Citizenship and Gender in Algeria, in* Gender and Citizenship in the Middle East 58, 66 (Suad Joseph ed., 2000).
65. *Id.* at 67.
66. *Id.* at 67–68.

Simultaneously, the political liberalization of the last several years has brought a multiparty system and a freer press. A number of women's associations have been formed, though most are attached to the male-controlled political parties, especially the Reassemblement pour la Culture et la Democratie (RCD) and the Front des Forces Socialistes (FFS).[67] Algerian feminists formed independent and audacious organizations in the 1990s, in their valiant battle against the FIS. They were rewarded in the summer of 2002 with five cabinet posts—an unprecedented number—including two that went to outspoken feminists.[68]

Two major demands in the current struggle for greater democracy are the recognition of one of the Kabyle-Berber dialects as the official language of Algeria and the abolition of the Family Code.[69] The Kabyle-Berber dialects, and not Arabic are native dialects of many North Africans. The recognition of one of these dialects would be particularly helpful to women as it would make print media available to them in their native language. The abolition of the Family Code would eradicate many retrogressive gender practices that have been legalized through this code.

B.   Bangladesh

In Bangladesh, where orthodox Muslim clerics issued a fatwa (a religious edict) that called for the death of feminist author and medical doctor Taslima Nasrin a few years ago, new laws were passed that increase punishment for crimes against women, including rape, kidnapping, and the throwing of acid on women's faces. The high court has declared that fatwas are illegal and has asked the parliament to enact appropriate laws in this regard.[70]

C.   Egypt

In Egypt, parliament voted to give women a traditional Islamic right known as *khol'* divorce. This is the right of a woman to divorce her husband. In return, she has to give up all the money, property, and gifts she has received, and also relinquish her right to alimony. Still, feminists support the law and the Al-Azhar University in Cairo, the oldest institution for Islamic teaching

---

67. *Id.* at 68–69.
68. *See* Valentine M. Moghadam, *Engendering Citizenship, Feminizing Civil Society: The Case of the Middle East and North Africa,* 25 Women & Pol. 63–89 (2003).
69. *Id.*
70. XIII Newsheet, *supra* note 27.

in the world, supported the decision by the parliament.[71] At the same time, however, some of the ulama (Muslim clerics) and the state embarked on an unsuccessful campaign against two secular and progressive intellectuals. In July 2001 the Egyptian courts dismissed a case against Nawal al-Saadawi, an Egyptian feminist author and medical doctor. The religious authorities had been calling for the automatic divorce of Saadawi from her husband because of her feminist activities, on the grounds that she had renounced Islam, something she denies vehemently. Similarly, the sociologist Saad al-Din Ibrahim was jailed twice in 2001–2003 by the Egyptian government for discussing electoral fraud, for speaking of the persecutions of the Coptic minority, and for criticism of President Hosni Mubarak.[72]

In addition, the Egyptian women's movement has recently made a number of new efforts, such as income generating projects and small loans for women, workshops that promote legal awareness of existing laws, and a Female Genital Mutilation Task Force. Feminists are also fighting for a woman's right to travel abroad without her husband's permission. Research on the hitherto taboo issue of violence against women has begun. Seminars and workshops on gender training, on NGOs, and on women's media are offered. Both the Islamists and the government continue to accuse women of links to imperialism and of receiving funds for carrying out a Western agenda and spying. The irony is that the Egyptian government is the largest recipient of US aid after Israel.[73]

D.   Iran

As a result of retrogressive laws introduced in 1979 after the Islamic Revolution, Iranian women still face significant legal discrimination in marriage, divorce, child custody, dress, and in their ability to travel freely even though Iran has signed various international agreements on human rights.[74] After the election of President Khatami in 1997, some degree of liberalization took place. The strongest supporters of Khatami were university students and women. Initially, Khatami was successful in relaxing some of the requirements imposed on women and also allowed for a greater freedom of the press. In the years that followed, however, Khatami proved to be less effective and his reform measures were routinely subverted by the more

---

71. *Id.*
72. For details of both cases *see* Janet Afary, *Special Supplement on the Association for Middle East Women's Studies*, 32 INT'L FEDERATION FOR RESEARCH IN WOMEN'S HISTORY (Fall 2001).
73. Nadje S. Ali, *Women's Organizations in Egypt,* AL-RAIDA No. 90–91, at 10–14 (Summer/Fall 2000).
74. For human rights of Iranian women *see generally,* REZA AFSHARI, HUMAN RIGHTS IN IRAN: THE ABUSE OF CULTURAL RELATIVISM (2001); ELIZABETH MAYER, ISLAM AND HUMAN RIGHTS (1995).

conservative religious leader Ali Khameneh'i and the clerical establishment.[75] Nevertheless, Iranian women have made dramatic progress in educational attainment.[76] The birth rate has dropped to a rate comparable to
many European countries.[77]

In 2001, about 60 percent of those who were accepted at universities
were women. Women were elected to the provincial councils, constituting
11 percent, and for the first time several advocates of women's rights were
elected to the parliament. Iran's parliament finally granted unmarried
women the right to apply for a scholarship to study abroad. In August 2002,
the parliament voted to give women an equal right to divorce, but the highly
conservative Council of Guardian has repeatedly vetoed the measure.[78]
According to Zahra Bonyanian, of the Women's Participation Center, a new
hotline to address domestic violence was recently set up in Tehran.
Women's Studies as an academic discipline has been officially adopted by
Iran's universities and a new feminist library was recently established in
Tehran. In 2002 the national entrance exams for colleges and universities
included the field of Women's Studies. In 2003 four colleges and universi-
ties, including Tehran University, accepted students in this major.[79]

E.   Israel

In Israel, women (Jewish and Arab) do have a number of rights with regard
to education, employment, and participation in the political process. Some
51 percent of Jewish women and 18 percent of Arab women participate in
the paid labor force. Still, with few exceptions, women are under-repre-
sented in their respective communities. Throughout Israel's history only one
woman, Golda Meir, has become premier and six have become cabinet
ministers. In 1999, a total of fourteen women (12.5 percent) were elected to
the Knesset, including one Israeli-Arab woman, the largest number ever. The
most impressive statistic is in the judiciary where 40 percent of the judges
are women. On the Supreme Court 15 percent of the judges are women.[80]
No Israeli-Arab woman has ever held the position of judge. As in many
Muslim countries, the orthodox rabbinical authorities control Israeli family

---

75. *See generally* Press Release, Human Rights Watch, Iran Blocks Overseas Education for
    Women: Reform Effort to Give Broader Rights to Women Scuttled (26 Jan. 2001), *avail-
    able at* www.hrw.org/press/2001/01/iran0123.
76. Afshari, *supra* note 74, at 256.
77. *See generally* Jim Muir, *Condoms Help Check Iran's Birth Rate*, BBC World News, 24 Apr.
    2002.
78. Parvin Ardalan, *Majaraha-yi Ta'sis-i Reshteh-yi Motale'at-i Zanan,* 81 Zanan 36–39 (2001);
    XIII Newsheet, *supra* note 27.
79. XIII Newsheet, *supra* note 27.
80. *Id.*

law. Jewish men may refuse to grant their wives divorce and are protected by the rabbis. For years, Israeli women have demonstrated on behalf of the "chained women" or the *agunot,* women who cannot remarry. The orthodox community considers a second marriage of such a woman and any children born of such a marriage to be illegitimate.[81]

In the last decade the peace process has been the main issue around which feminists have organized. But the second most important issue has been violence against women. A recent study concluded that 20 percent of Israeli female soldiers were sexually harassed during the mandatory military service.[82] Israeli feminists have set up a host of shelters, hotlines, centers for rape victims, and have demanded greater accountability by the police and more public awareness. In response, the government has taken some modest steps. For the first time Yitzhak Mordechai, a former defense transportation minister in the government of Sharon, was charged with and convicted of sexual violence against two women employees.[83] Women's groups called the event an important step toward combating sexual harassment, which they say is rampant in Israel.[84]

F. Jordan

Statistics show that Jordanian women have made remarkable advances. The literacy rate for women is 83.9 percent. Sixty-seven percent of women (and 65 percent of men) have some secondary education.[85] Women hold 6 percent of top government positions. Life expectancy for women is seventy years.[86] Jordan has a large number of women's centers, associations, and professional clubs. The country hosts one of the offices of the international organization Sisterhood Is Global and Jordanian universities offer courses on women's and gender studies.[87] Other legal reforms are gradually being implemented. In the 1990s it was estimated that twenty-five to thirty women died every year in so-called honor killings.[88] In 1999, women and human rights activists gathered 13,000 signatures calling for an end to the current legal sanctioning of honor killings. In 2001 the Jordanian gov-

---

81. *Id.*
82. *20% of Female Soldiers Report Sexual Harassment,* Haaretz, 2 June 2003.
83. Deborah Sontag, *Israeli Official is Found Guilty of Sex Charge,* N.Y. Times, 22 Mar. 2001, at A4.
84. *Id.*
85. Al-Raida 106 (Winter 2003).
86. *Id.*
87. Abir Handun, *Women Centers in Jordan,* Al-Raida No. 90–91, *supra* note 73, at 15–19.
88. Press Release, Human Rights Watch, Jordanian Parliament Supports Impunity for Honor Killings (27 Jan. 2000) *available at* www.hrw.org/press/2000/01/jord0127.

ernment canceled Article 340 of the Personal Code which had acquitted the men who had committed this crime. New revisions to the personal status law also raised the legal age of marriage to eighteen for both men and women.[89]

G. Lebanon

In Lebanon, the struggle for greater representation of women in decision-making positions and the reform of the Personal Status Law are on the agenda. There are nineteen religious sects in Lebanon, each with its own personal status code on issues such as marriage, divorce, custody, and inheritance. At the forefront of the movement is the Institute for Women's Studies in the Arab World (established in 1973), which is located at the American University in Beirut and is the oldest such institute in the region. The institute offers a variety of courses related to women's issues and plans to offer a minor in Gender Studies. The Institute's publication, the English language *al-Raida*, is one of the most sophisticated feminist journals in the entire region. Each issue focuses on a special theme and includes articles, conference reports, book reviews, interviews, and art news.[90]

H.   Morocco

At the First International Conference of the Arab Human Rights Movement in Casablanca in April 1999, it was noted that the general human rights situation in Morocco had witnessed "relative progress in the last decade, due to the efforts of the Moroccan and international human rights organizations."[91] The Casablanca Declaration signed at the convention agreed to a ten-point action plan. The document specifically singled out the suffering of Arab women, which had occurred as a result of the growth of the Islamist movement in the region, and "called upon women and human rights NGOs . . . to challenge the culture of discrimination, and to adopt courageous stances in exposing the practice of hiding behind religion to legitimize the subordination of women."[92] As in Algeria, an important debate on the status of the Berber language is taking place in Morocco. This debate will inevitably have

---

89. For more information *see* the website of the Jordan Ministry of Foreign Affairs, *available at* www.mfa.gov.jo/map_map.php.
90. Interview, Mona Khalif, Editor, *Al-Raida*, Bellagio, Italy (Aug. 2001).
91. The Casablanca Declaration of the Arab Human Rights Movement, *adopted* 23–25 Apr. 1999, First International Conference of the Arab Human Rights Movement, *reprinted in* Middle East & Islamic Studies Collection *available at* www.library.cornell.edu.
92. *Id.*

gender implications, since gender lines are directly tied to language choice. Arabic is the language of politics and hence the "male sphere." Berber and French are the languages used by women; Berber is the language used in the family, but most urban women are educated in French.[93]

Morocco is also the scene of a major debate over revision of the Personal Code. The new revisions would raise the minimum age of marriage for girls to eighteen, require a judge's authorization for polygamy, give women equal rights concerning divorce and community property, and permit divorced mothers who remarry to ask for custody of their children. In the year 2000, over 400,000 people took to the streets, with half supporting the measure and the other half opposing it. In October 2003, King Mohamed VI approved the measure which is expected to be ratified by the Moroccan parliament.[94]

I. Palestinian Territory

Palestinian women have been in the difficult position of presenting a feminist agenda in the midst of a nationalist movement, especially since the Islamist tendencies of Hamas and Islamic Jihad have become more dominant. Nevertheless Bir Zeit University has set up a Women's Studies Institute in both Bir Zeit and in Jerusalem that has challenged the male-dominated character of the nationalist movement and questioned the phenomenon of early marriage during the Intifada. The Institute tries to bring greater awareness to issues such as violence against women and has developed an academic research program on women and gender issues, offering a master's degree in Gender, Law, and Development.[95]

J. Turkey

Turkey remains one of the most liberal Muslim nations on women's rights, with Malaysia, Tunisia, and Indonesia not far behind. In November 2001, advocates of women's rights reformed the Civil Code, primarily through public campaigns. The new changes benefit women educationally and economically. The supremacy of men in marriage was legally terminated and

---

93. Fatima Sadiqi, unpublished paper presented at Bellagio, Italy (Aug. 2001); Feminist Movement: Origin and Orientation (Fatima Sadiqi ed., Fez: Centre d'Etudes et de Recherches sur la Femme, 2000).

94. Stephanie Irvine, *Morocco Women Win Rights,* BBC News, UK Edition, 11 Oct. 2003, *available at* news.bbc.co.uk/1/hi/world/africa/3183576.

95. Eileen Kuttab, Recounts, al-Raida No. 90–91, *supra* note 73, at 20–22.

men and women were declared equal in marriage. The law scrapped the traditional right of a man to unilateral divorce. The marriage age of girls was raised to eighteen. Children born out of wedlock were granted equal inheritance rights. Single parents may now adopt children. The most original and controversial sections of the Reform Law were its provisions for community property, fifty-fifty split in the case of divorce. Eventually, the conservative and nationalist as well as religious elements in the parliament accepted the new law. A last minute controversy limited its validity to property acquired after January 2003. Women's groups plan to fight this amendment.[96]

In 2001, under pressure from the Islamist Rifah party, certain restrictions with regard to sexuality were imposed anew. The Turkish government reinstituted virginity tests for girls studying medicine in high schools. Turkish Women's and Human Rights Organizations were outraged at the government for resurrecting the practice and Human Rights Watch called on the Prime Minister Bulent Ecevit to rescind this new regulation. In February 2002, the Turkish government finally rescinded the law when five female students tried to kill themselves by taking rat poison instead of undergoing the humiliating vaginal exam.[97]

III. HOPE FOR THE FUTURE?

The list of Middle Eastern and Muslim countries with Women's Studies centers and programs continues to grow and includes among others: the Women's Studies and Research Center at the University of Aden and University of San'a in Yemen, the Institute for Gender and Women's Studies at the American University in Cairo, Egypt, the Afhad University for Women in Sudan, among others.

Even in some of the Arab countries of the Persian Gulf, where traditional gender relations have been hard to change, a new day may be dawning. In Qatar, women can now participate in municipal elections and in Bahrain they voted in the 2002 elections.[98] In Saudi Arabia, in November 2001, the government agreed to issue identity cards to women and to gradually discontinue the practice of issuing family cards under the names of male heads of household.[99] The ID cards will include a photograph of the unveiled woman, but the minister of the interior insisted that the new system "in no

---

96. XIII Newsheet, *supra* note 27.
97. *Turkey Scraps Virginity Tests,* BBC World News, 28 Feb. 2002, *available at* news.bbc.co.uk/1/hi/world/europe/1845784.
98. al-Raida 96, 122 (Winter 2003).
99. Human Rights Watch, *Human Rights in Saudi Arabia: A Deafening Silence, supra* note 31, at 5.

way means an end to women's modesty or to exposing them to unveiling, anything shameful, or any violation of Islamic law."[100] Even in this highly patriarchal country, there is a movement to establish a Women's Studies Program, to be housed in the King Abdulaziz Foundation for Research and Archives in Riyadh.[101]

In Atwood's novel the central character Offred[102] eventually finds the courage to rebel against her sexual enslavement through remembering her mother's feminist heritage and joining a resistance movement. It remains to be seen if the social, political, and cultural emancipation of Middle East/Muslim women will be accomplished in our time. The turn of the twenty-first century has been a highly contradictory one for advocates of women's rights. Alongside the brutal and misogynistic nationalist and Islamist movements that have tried to push women's rights back, there has developed a remarkable and courageous feminist movement, one that attempts to undo the outdated notion that feminism is a Western or "imported" phenomena or that it is irrelevant to Middle Eastern and Muslim women. Instead, through journals, women's centers, and academic publications new indigenous expressions of feminism are gradually and painstakingly constructed, articulated, and disseminated.

We witnessed this new spirit in Afghanistan as women celebrated the defeat of the Taliban and began the very difficult task of claiming their rights, especially in the sphere of education. In Iran, Shirin Ebadi, this year's winner of the Nobel Peace Prize, is one of the best representatives of this generation.[103] Ebadi, who is a practicing Muslim, is also a staunch advocate of the separation of religion and state. Ebadi was appointed Iran's first woman judge before the 1979 revolution, but after the revolution she was removed from her post and demoted to the position of a clerk in the new religious courts. Gradually, Ebadi and her colleague Mehrangiz Kar were able to practice law again. They distinguished themselves by taking up the cases of abused women and children as well political dissidents. Ebadi, who is the author of eleven books, has defended the rights of women against divorce. She has also worked to give women custody of their children and compensation after divorce. Ebadi was the first lawyer to investigate the murder of the famous dissident couple, Dariush and Parvaneh Foruhar. Her efforts led to the creation of the Committee for the Defense of the Rights of the Victims of Serial Murders in Iran. In 1999, when government assailants violently attacked student protesters and several students were killed during the ram-

---

100. *Id.*
101. Personal e-mail from Eleanor Doumato, Saudi Arabia, Fall 2002 (on file with author).
102. ATWOOD, *supra* note 1.
103. *Iranian Lawyer and Professor Wins Nobel Peace Prize,* THE CHRONICLE OF HIGHER EDUCATION, 10 Oct. 2003, *available at* chronicle.com/free/2003/10/2003101005n.

page at Tehran University, Ebadi took up the case of the jailed students, an act that landed her in solitary confinement for a few months.[104]

After the announcement of the award and her return to Iran, over 200,000 Iranians jubilantly greeted her in the airport and showered her with white flowers. In her first news conference, Ebadi announced that she would take up the case of Zahra Kazemi, a Canadian-Iranian journalist who was murdered in prison while reporting on Tehran's prisons for international news agencies. Ebadi has also publicly called for the release of all political prisoners. Ebadi remains a harbinger of positive change for human rights in Iran, announcing "I am proclaiming the Iranian people's message of peace and friendship to the world. We are a peace loving people. We hate violence. We condemn terror. We are not hostile toward other religions."[105]

Despite the ongoing human rights atrocities in the Middle East/Muslim world, positive changes are continually being made. Perhaps those Western scholars and observers who essentialize the women (and men) of the Middle East and the Muslim world should expand the definition of feminism and human rights to encompass the voices of Muslim feminists such as Shirin Ebadi and Mehrangiz Kar. Not every misogynistic interpretation of religion is "authentic" and "indigenous," just as not every liberal and progressive reading is "Western" and "foreign" influenced and therefore "inauthentic." This type of labeling has been the tactic of the Islamist movements in their effort to gain power. It is now being challenged by some intellectuals and women's rights activists of the region, individuals whose voices need to be heard more often.

---

104. Keith B. Richburg, *Peace Prize is Awarded to Iranian: Rights Activist is First Muslim Woman to Win*, Wash. Post Foreign Service, 11 Oct. 2003, *available at* www.washington-post.com.
105. *Id.*

Chapter 7

Post-Colonialism, Gender, Customary Injustice: Widows in African Societies

Uche U. Ewelukwa[1]

> Pure and undefiled religion before God and the Father is this: to visit orphans and widows in their trouble.
>
> James 1:27

> When a man dies, the surviving wife is subjected to dehumanizing funeral rites. Every hair on her head is cleanly shaven; she is allowed the minimum of clothing just enough to cover her nakedness; she is made to sleep on the bare floor and to eat with broken plates. She is confined to the recesses of an inner chamber forbidden to see the light of day for some period prescribed by custom. The woman dare not complain. She will rather count herself lucky that she was not buried along with her husband.[2]
>
> Mr. Justice Chukwudifu Oputa
Former Judge of the Nigerian Supreme Court

---

1. This article is based on the author's personal experiences as a woman born and raised in Nigeria, as well as on information gathered during a six-week human rights monitoring mission to Nigeria. The author interviewed more than sixty widows in different parts of Southern Nigeria. Most women spoke on condition of anonymity, so the names used in this paper have been changed to protect them. This article is intended only as an introduction to an issue deserving more extensive study. Clearly many more widows will have to be interviewed to get a broader picture of the varied experiences of widows in Africa. The male viewpoint, to the extent that the author feels it important, is largely absent. The author hopes that future research will more thoroughly address the issues of widows' empowerment and strategies for change. By drawing comparisons across national borders, the author is uncovering how widows in different African societies are attempting to overcome the structural, institutional, and legal barriers that confront them. The article does not undertake a detailed analysis of the effectiveness of the international human rights regime in addressing the plight of women in diverse cultures. The reason for this is that a detailed critique of the international human rights system from African women's viewpoint forms the subject of another paper the author is currently working on.

   Initial research for this paper was conducted in 1994. Informal discussions with various individuals in Nigeria, many of whom provided anecdotal evidence, confirm that the situation remains the same in 2000. For more on the topic see Uche U. Ewelukwa, *Caught Between Tradition, The Courts and Survival: Widows in Contemporary African Societies,* in WOMEN'S RIGHTS ARE HUMAN RIGHTS: CULTURAL AND SOCIOECONOMIC REALITIES IN AFRICA AND THE AFRICAN DIASPORA (Nnaemeka Obioma ed., forthcoming 2002).

2. Chukwudifu Oputa, *Women and Children as Disempowered Groups, in* WOMEN AND CHILDREN UNDER NIGERIAN LAW 1, 9 (Awa U. Kalu & Yemi Osinbajo eds., 1989).

I. INTRODUCTION

Agnes was only twenty when her husband died, leaving her with three children, the youngest of whom was only two weeks old. More than fourteen years after his death, Agnes is still fighting to recover parts of his estate currently controlled by her sister-in-law. A lawsuit she filed in 1988 is still pending and Agnes is uncertain as to when and how the case will finally resolve. Meanwhile, she has had to support herself and her three children without any help from her in-laws, the village community, or the state. Agnes is able to maintain the lawsuit because she bore two sons for her husband. Had she been childless or had she had only female children, her story would have been very different.[3]

Beatrice's husband died intestate in 1991, six years after their marriage. Immediately after his burial, Beatrice's in-laws summoned her to a family meeting and accused her of killing her husband. They forcibly took away her two small children, ordered Beatrice, five months pregnant at the time, to move out of her matrimonial home without her belongings, and told her that she could return after having the baby to swear an oath that she did not kill her husband. Only if they found her innocent would her belongings be released to her. Four years after her husband's death, Beatrice is still very frightened and confused. While she has contemplated legal action, she is afraid of losing the support of her own family, who has advised her to remain quiet. Moreover, she cannot afford the cost of a lawsuit on her meager salary.[4]

When Zina's husband died ten years ago, she had to observe certain mandatory mourning rituals which have left her permanently incapacitated. She was prohibited from leaving town during the mourning period, her hair was shaved, and she was confined to a small, thatched outdoor hut for thirty days. The customary law forbade her from entering her home during these thirty days. Because this occurred during the rainy season and her palm leaf hut leaked, rain fell on her during most of the time she was outside. Zina has since developed rheumatism which she traces to her thirty-day ordeal in the rain.[5]

These are not isolated accounts of the experiences of widows in Nigeria.

---

3. Interview with Agnes (not her real name), in Enugu, 16 July 1994. Agnes married her husband under the customary and statutory law of the country when she was sixteen.
4. Beatrice's in-laws returned her children to her after about six months, largely because they were both girls and the in-laws considered them too burdensome to maintain. However, Beatrice has not recovered any of her or her husband's personal property. Her position is particularly precarious because she has no male child, and under the customary law a man's estate is inherited by his sons or his nearest surviving male relative. *See generally,* Martin C. Okany, Nigerian Law of Property ch. 29 (1986).
5. Interview with Zina (not her real name), in Illah, Delta (formerly Benue) State, 13 July 1994.

Throughout much of Southern Nigeria,[6] widows undergo harrowing and humiliating treatment following the death of their husbands.[7] Nigerian women who lose their husbands are not given the chance to grieve privately but are routinely subjected to painful, dehumanizing public treatment as a result of the continued application of patently discriminatory laws and practices. Men who lose their wives are usually not subjected to similar practices. In the limited cases where certain rules are prescribed for men, choice of observance is often left to their discretion. By contrast, recalcitrant widows face punishments ranging from fines to excommunication and even banishment.[8]

Despite the obvious injustice Nigerian widows suffer, there is no consensus in Nigeria on the importance of the customary legal rules relating to widows, on the need for change, and on the larger question of the proper place of customary law in the changing Nigerian society.[9] Yet practices which hitherto have been taken as settled and widely accepted are now unraveling in the face of the changing socioeconomic conditions in Nigeria. Rather than offer protection to widows, received common law[10] and statutory laws in the country perpetuate the discrimination against them[11] by fail-

---

6. Northern Nigeria is predominantly Muslim and has a somewhat different practice with regard to widows. The author understands that generally a widow can inherit part of her husband's property. *See* OKANY, *supra* note 4, at 712. He states with respect to succession under Islamic law:

> The rules of distribution are as follows: on the death of the man intestate, his widow is entitled to one-quarter of the estate. But if there are children or grandchildren, her share will be reduced to one-eighth. Where there is a plurality of wives, they share the one-quarter or one-eighth equally between them.

Id.

7. The experiences of Nigerian widows range from disinheritance and forceful deprivation of property to the mandatory observance of some rituals.
8. Excommunication generally involves a total isolation of the widow by the village community though she is still allowed to remain in the village. An order might exist prohibiting people from associating with her. She may not be able to buy or sell to anyone. With banishment, however, the widow is literally driven out of the village. For a widow who has children, parents, and other relatives living in the village, the cost of banishment can be great indeed. In one case where a widow refused to fulfill all the burial requirements, she was warned not to return to the village. Though the author did not speak with the widow in question, she was reliably informed by another widow from the same town, that the widow has since not returned to this town, at least publicly. The few times she has gone back, she has done so under the cover of darkness. She knows the full implication of her being found and realizes that she returns at great risk to her person.
9. This assertion is the author's own conclusion after extensive discussion with women, men, and traditional rulers in Nigeria, as well as from the types of cases appearing before the courts. *See generally* MARTIN CHANOCK, LAW, CUSTOM, AND SOCIAL ORDER: THE COLONIAL EXPERIENCE IN MALAWI AND ZAMBIA (1985).
10. "Received common law" is used to mean the common law passed on by the United Kingdom during the Colonial Era.
11. Convention on the Elimination of All Forms of Discrimination Against Women, *adopted*

ing to prescribe positive laws to protect their interests and prescribing rules which reinforce traditional notions of women as inferior objects. Moreover, inconsistencies, contradictions, and confusion inherent in the Nigerian legal system, a product of Nigeria's colonial past, jeopardize the position of women generally and prevent a meaningful resolution to the problem of widows.[12]

Sadly, Nigerian widows are not alone in their plight. In other parts of Africa, widows are accorded second class status and are generally denied adequate legal protection. African customary law generally does not recognize the right of a widow to inherit her husband's property and, most often, views a widow as her husband's property. Recent decisions in Kenya and Zimbabwe illustrate this point. In *Murisa v. Murisa*,[13] for example, the Supreme Court of Zimbabwe unanimously overruled a decision of the magistrate court that a widow could inherit her deceased husband's estate.[14] According to the Supreme Court, "The question of law that arises can be formulated fairly simply in these terms: Does our customary law recognize the right of a widow to be appointed heir to her deceased husband's estate ad intestato?"[15] The reply was an emphatic "No."[16] Moreover, in *Otieno v. Ougo*

---

18 Dec. 1979, G.A. Res. 34/180, U.N. GAOR, 34th Sess., Supp. No. 46, art 1, U.N. Doc. A/34/46 (1980) (*entered into force* 3 Sept. 1981), 1249 U.N.T.S. 13, *reprinted in* 19 I.L.M. 33 (1980) (hereinafter referred to as CEDAW) defines discrimination against women as "any distinction, exclusion or restriction made on the basis of sex which has the effect or purpose of impairing or nullifying the recognition, enjoyment or exercise by women, irrespective of their marital status, on the basis of equality of men and women, of human rights and fundamental freedoms in the political, economic, social, cultural, civil or any other field."

While there is no single source for the international law on non-discrimination, Anne Bayefsky summarizes the content of the concept of equality and non-discrimination under international law to include: (i) the idea that a distinction is discriminatory if it has no objective and reasonable justification or if there is not a reasonable relationship of proportionality between the aim and the means employed to attain it; (ii) that traditional outlooks or local prejudice will not count as reasonable justification for differential treatment; (iii) that preferences may still be discriminatory if they have the effect of impairing equality; (iv) that non-discrimination applies to all state action regardless of whether such action is itself required by international law; (v) that positive state action is sometimes required by the state in order to fulfill its duty to respect equality; and (vi) that positive state action may extend to protecting individuals from impediments of equality imposed by private parties. *See* Anne F. Bayefsky, *The Principle of Equality or Non-Discrimination in International Law*, II Hum. Rts. L. J. 1, 34 (1990).

12. *Murisa v. Murisa*, (1) Zimbabwe L. Rep. 167 (S) 1992.
13. *Id.*
14. *See id.* Furthermore, the court held the provisions of the Legal Age of Majority Act (1982) which conferred majority status on African women who had been perpetual minors under customary law, inapplicable to widows. *Id.* at 169.
15. *Id.* at 169.
16. It was immaterial to the court that the deceased had previously dissociated himself entirely from his tribal origins and did not follow Luo customs, and that the plaintiff was

& *Anor*,[17] the Kenyan Court of Appeal denied a widow the right to bury her husband, holding that under the Luo law to which the deceased was subject, a wife had no right to bury her husband.[18] The simplistic approach adopted by courts in Africa in interpreting and analyzing questions of women's rights and entitlements unfortunately denies and/or ignores the deep and multifaceted structural, economic, and social changes that have been taking place in the continent since the onset of colonialism. These changes make formal resort to customary law unrealistic at best.

The social and legal structures of many African countries today are the result of at least three superimposed cultural stratifications: the traditional and pre-industrial phase; the colonial experience; and the post colonial economic, social, and political structure. Thus, a continued wholesale application of precolonial cultural practices is unrealistic at best, and works great injustice to a majority of the African women, whose voices are usually not represented in national policy debates today. Though family patterns have changed, customary laws of the past are still applied. While it may be that an emerging nuclear family pattern in Africa "does not stem from the evolution of pre-existing family structures but from the forced integration of traditional societies into capitalist economy,"[19] the fact is that these largely irreversible changes must be accepted. The problem lies in the blind idealization of the past.[20] Unfortunately, "the idealized version of the extended

---

acting as the personal representative of the deceased. According to the court, "At present there is no way in which an African citizen of Kenya can divest himself of the association with the tribe of his father if the customs of the tribe are patrilineal." See *Virginia Edith Wamboi Otieno v. Joash Ochieng Ougo & Omola Siranga* (Civil Appeal No. 31 of 1987), EUGENE COTRAN, KENYA CUSTOMARY LAW 331 (1987).

The above case follows a line of cases in which the Kenyan Courts have emphatically denied widows any say in decisions regarding the burial of their husbands. In a 1981 case on the same issue, Judge Gachuhi of the Kenyan High Court, reiterated and upheld customary law rules regarding burial, explaining:

> In the past, customarily, the responsibility for the burial fell on the eldest son or in his absence on the brothers of the deceased. . . . In those days even when dead bodies were being thrown to hyenas, as this court has been informed, women took no part. I have also been told that even in the present days, women do not take part except carrying flowers. That being so, there is no cause for the widow having a tug of war over the body of the deceased.

See *Carmelina Ngami Mburu v. Marv Nduta, Hellen Amoka & Medical Officer of Health Nairobi* (Civil Suit No. 3209 of 1981). *See also James Apeli & Enoka Olasi v. Prisca Buluka* (Civil Appeal No. 12 of 1979).

17. See *Otieno v. Ougo & Siranga, supra* note 16.
18. The court also held that under this Luo, custom, "she has no right to bury her husband and she does not become the head of the family upon the death of her husband." The court held this custom was not immoral or repugnant to natural justice. *See* COTRAN, *supra* note 16, at 343.
19. MARIA ROSA CUTRUFELLI, WOMEN OF AFRICA: ROOTS OF OPPRESSION 13 (1983).
20. *Id.* at 13.

family . . . is *inconsistent* with the reality of present-day Africa. The extended family is not a static unit, but a dynamic entity modified by individuals to suit their changing circumstances."[21] Many African societies are committed to the ideal of the extended family, much like nineteenth-century American society deified the nuclear family.[22]

Studying the position of widows in Africa very potently highlights the tensions and contradictions in the newly emerging states in the continent. Tensions exist between tradition and modernity; between individual autonomy and group solidarity; and between individual rights and duties. There are tensions in the varied and often conflicting justifications for given customary law or practice; and more recently, tensions in the new development trends in the Third World. The fact that the rights and interests of a widow often conflict sharply with those of other family members, such as the wives and other children of a deceased husband, casts doubt on the rights paradigm as the easy solution to the problems of women in the Third World. The study of widows reveals the painful position of women as both the defenders and the victims of culture. This position reveals their agency in perpetuating practices dehumanizing to them and in overturning entrenched customary and religious practices. More importantly, the paradoxical position of women calls for a deep introspection into how we perceive, understand, and ultimately ascribe value to practices embedded in cultures outside our own. Perhaps an understanding of the minds and lives of these "other" women would lead to more meaningful public dialogues, resulting in more constructive approaches to improving women's rights in the Third World. Finally, a study of the plight of widows reveals how actions, omissions, and decisions in the international arena, particularly in the global economic order, impact the lives of rural women in the Third World.

---

21. MARIANNE JENSEN & KARIN POULSEN, HUMAN RIGHTS AND CULTURAL CHANGE 9 (1993).
22. On the history of reform against family violence in the United States, Elizabeth Pleck notes that:

> The single most consistent barrier to reform against domestic violence has been the Family Ideal—that is, unrelated but nonetheless distinct ideas about family privacy, conjugal and parental rights, and family stability. In this ideal, with origins possibly extending into antiquity, the "family" consists of a two-parent household with minor children. Other constellations, such as a mother and her children, were seen not as a family but a deviation from it.

See ELIZABETH PLECK, DOMESTIC TYRANNY 7 (1987).

Despite the move towards the nuclear family structure, the emphasis in most of Africa remains the extended family in which the authority resides with the family elders. *See generally,* ALICE ARMSTRONG ET AL., UNCOVERING REALITY: EXCAVATING WOMEN'S RIGHTS IN AFRICAN FAMILY LAW 6 (1992). The authors note, for example, that "the dominant family form in Africa (even to-day) is the so-called extended family." *Id.* What is evident is the willingness of women to endure hardship in the interest of the family. Much that goes on within the family is still shrouded in secrecy and shielded from general public scrutiny.

This article examines the position of widows under Nigerian law, focusing particularly on the tension between customary laws and practices on the one hand, and emerging rights of women on the other. It argues that some customary laws and practices can no longer be justified in the changing face of Africa of today.[23] If they existed at all,[24] customary laws and practices may

---

23. Much of the personal laws in precolonial Africa flowed from the then existing kinship and family structure in which the extended family had primacy. Efforts were made to keep property within the family. Thus, in patrilineal societies inheritance followed a male line of descent. A man's property was usually inherited by his sons or, in the absence of sons, by the nearest surviving male relatives for and on behalf of all the beneficiaries of the estate. Yet even then variations existed. Thus, in some societies which were not necessarily matrilineal, women could inherit immovable properties and sometimes were given priority over the men.

    In an attempt to make sense of the traditional rules of inheritance, Julie Stewart argues that:

    > Such a process of inheritance may still be satisfactory where the family organization conforms to strictly traditional customary pattern. In such situations the family may still operate from the mutual support basis and if this is the case it would, particularly with a small estate, be unwise to disturb this arrangement.

    See Julie Stewart, *Some Points to Ponder Arising from the White Paper on Marriage and Inheritance in Zimbabwe*, 5 Legal Forum 27 (1993); Julie Stewart, *Coping with the Muddle: Choices of Law in Intestate Succession in Post-Independence Zimbabwe*, 2 Legal Forum 14 (1990). It is, however, difficult to summarily conclude that such a system may have once been satisfactory without adequate information about how women reacted and objected to the system.

24. Chanock, *supra* note 9, at 4. One of the ongoing debates in Africa centers on the validity or authenticity of the customary laws as they exist today. Many believe that the existing customary laws are, in large part, mere constructs of the colonial powers in collusion with some local chiefs. At the onset of colonialism and with resulting instability and power imbalance, a struggle ensued as different interest groups reacted to reassert themselves or create new space for themselves in the new colonial structure. While the politics of the struggle were cast in the rhetoric of morality, kinship, and public good, the underlying agenda was an acute struggle for power and control in a fast transforming environment. Chanock, offers an excellent account of the colonial experience in Malawi and Zambia. He notes generally that:

    > The law was the cutting edge of colonialism, an instrument of the power of an alien state and part of the process of coercion. And it also came to be a new way of conceptualizing relationships and powers and a weapon within African communities which were undergoing basic economic changes, many of which were interpreted and fought over by those involved in moral terms. The customary law, far from being a survival, was created by these changes and conflicts.

    Id.

    What might be grasped from this "legal history" is how people worked to exercise both actual and moral control over the processes that were reshaping their world. It must also become clear that it is only by failing to integrate the study of customary law with the huge transformation in the relations of production in colonial Africa that one can possibly continue to hold notions of its survival and continuity.

    Id. at 12.

have been reasonable and sustainable in years past. Despite the profound changes evident in most African societies,[25] customary laws which are largely artificial constructs of men in positions of power, have lagged behind and are reluctant to change with the changing times. As Welshman Ncube argues, there is no patriotism in reasserting customary laws which are largely false and, in their constructed form, highly oppressive.[26] Rather "our concern should be to remake our laws in such a way that they are fair, just and reasonable."[27]

Contrary to the assertion by Betty Potash that African "widows in most societies have choices and exercise them,"[28] this article argues that African

---

See LANDEG WHITE, MAGOMERO: PORTRAIT OF AN AFRICAN VILLAGE 180 (1987). White's historical account of events in a village in the southern region of Malawi between 1878 and the present also provides a vivid illustration of how rules and customs were reinterpreted and overturned during the colonial period and particularly, the impact of these changes on women. According to him:

> [W]ith the introduction of indirect rule, some of the chiefs of the Shire Highlands, carefully vetted and poorly paid, were incorporated into the lower ranks of the colonial bureaucracy. But there was an unconscious irony in the term "native authority." The "native customs" they were responsible for administering represented a codification by colonial officials of the powers the chiefs claimed they had wielded in the years before their defeat in the 1890s. Nothing illustrated this more clearly than the effects of the new structures on the women whose interpretation of custom was very different.

Id.

25. Changes are evident in almost every sector of the society but particularly in the transformation of the rural societies, in the breakdown of traditional social structures, and in the change in family patterns. *See generally,* ARMSTRONG, *supra* note 22. *See also,* G.K. Nukunya, *The Family and Social Change in* COLONIALISM AND CHANGE: ESSAYS PRESENTED TO LUCY MAIR 163 (Maxwell Owusu ed., 1975). With respect to the family several changes are evident: the move from polygamy to monogamy, from extended family network to the modern nuclear family, from close-knit traditional kinship network with emphasis on land, to a dispersed, highly individualistic, urban focus. JENSEN & POULSEN, *supra* note 21, note a twofold deterioration of the traditional support network of the extended family system: "a tendency for the extended family to *break up,* not least in the urban areas," and "a tendency—even where extended families persist—for kinship loyalties to change, and for customary norms dictating rights and duties to become *reinterpreted and manipulated* to the disbenefit of women." *Id.* at 9.

26. According to Ncube,

> [M]ost of what is today held out as "our" customary law is a "construction" of the colonial judiciary in complicity with some elders of the African society, who redesigned most of what is today presented as customary law so as to increase male authority and control over women and children, to compensate for the loss of their political and social power to the colonial state."

See Welshman Ncube, *The White Paper on Marriage and Inheritance in Zimbabwe: An Exercise in Superfluity and Mischief,* 5 LEGAL FORUM, 10, 12 (1993). [Hereinafter referred to as *White Paper.*]

27. *Id.* at 12.
28. Betty Potash, *Widows in Africa: An Introduction,* in WIDOWS IN AFRICAN SOCIETIES: CHOICES AND

widows have no real choices to exercise. What are offered as choices have often had the effect of perpetuating the domination of widows by further subjecting their interests to the decisions of some male relatives. Thus options such as accepting her husband's brother as a husband, returning to her natal group, or residing with married children do not significantly advance the cause of widows, but rather serve to numb societal sensitivity to their plight.[29]

This article calls for a change in the traditional treatment of widows and for the amendment of discriminatory customary laws and practices in accordance with evolving international human rights standards on equality and non-discrimination. Given the number of women affected, their age, and their relative importance to the economy of African states, there exists an urgent need for meaningful reform. This article is divided into four parts. Part II briefly examines the life experiences and treatment of widows. Part III analyzes local laws, both customary and statutory, affecting the rights of widows in Nigeria. Part IV examines legal action by widows and critically evaluates judicial pronouncements on their rights. Part V focuses on the politics of reform in Nigeria and examines recent changes in the customary

---

CONSTRAINTS 4 (Betty Potash ed., 1986). Potash believes that the treatment widows suffer is from the complex influence of the structural-functionalism paradigm which "stresses the rights of kin groups in marriage and tends to treat widows as passive pawns." *Id.* at 2. She asserts, for instance, that "the widow who remains in her husband's community generally does so because of the structure of the property rights, because of ties to children, or because she finds other advantages in remaining." *Id.* at 4.

The author believes that widows are greatly constrained by social, economic, and political structures in their societies. Usually, widows make decisions not because of any perceived advantages, but because they are often the only options available. For instance, while a widow may decide to remain in her husband's home because of ties to children, such decisions are fundamentally influenced by rules which, for instance, deny her access and custody to her children otherwise. Structural barriers operating against widows in traditional African societies have regrettably been transferred to and entrenched in the modern state apparatus on the continent thus perpetuating their domination.

29. Defenders of the status quo mischievously point to a few lucky widows to prove their point that "our" widows are well cared for. Yet throughout Nigeria, instances of neglected widows abound. No effort has been made to determine what exactly widows want. The paternalistic attitude which prevails obscures the basic truth that widows are regarded as objects who live at the mercy of relatives. This does not deny the fact that there are indeed some widows who see nothing wrong with their situation, who reject any change, who benefit from, and readily embrace the options currently available to them. The problem lies, however, in the absence of real choice for the growing number of widows who reject some or most of the cultural expectations on them and who demand a more equitable and humane regime. The arguments of the idealist traditionalists also obscure the glaring inequalities in opportunities and real income experienced by a greater percentage of African women and the socioeconomic barriers that undermine women's attempt to take control of their lives. Indeed, the idea and nature of women's agency under oppression in the African context is a complex one.

laws affecting women's rights in the country, including efforts by newly emerging nongovernmental organizations and other grassroots initiatives by women. The obstacles to change as well as recent gains in the fight for a recognition of the rights of widows will also be examined. The article concludes in Part VI with an examination of alternative solutions to the plight of widows. Attempts are made throughout the paper to analyze and draw lessons from recent developments in other countries in Africa.

II.   THE EXPERIENCES OF WIDOWS IN NIGERIA

The experiences of Nigerian widows generally fall into two broad categories: disinheritance and deprivation of property and the mandatory observance of prescribed burial rituals.[30] Customary law, however, varies from one ethnic group to another, from state to state, and most often from one town to another.

A.   Disinheritance and Derivation of Property

To understand customary law rules of inheritance, one must understand family structure in precolonial agrarian society in Sub-Saharan Africa with its emphasis on kinship network and lineage under the guidance or leadership of a man. Usually the male heir who had a duty to support the deceased's beneficiaries inherited the property.[31] Customary laws on immovable property reflected an entrenched desire to retain property within the family for all times—families in which women generally held subordinate positions.[32] As

---

30. The most common practice that the author encountered in the course of her interviews is that of looting the personal and matrimonial property of a widow immediately after the husband dies, even before any burial arrangements are made. A number of widows recount their experience of returning from their husband's deathbed in the hospital to find their house cleared of all their belongings by in-laws. Interviews conducted in Southern Nigeria, 1–30 July 1994. In many cases, properties are removed on the pretext of safekeeping, the truth is that in-laws, aware of an impending death and believing themselves to be the rightful heirs, remove these properties to prevent widows from getting them. Though such acts can clearly constitute the offense of stealing, police are reluctant to intervene in a matter which they regard as a purely "domestic affair." The author rarely encountered examples in which the police arrested anyone in connection with an alleged looting of a deceased's property by his relatives. Moreover, a widow faced with the death of a loved one is usually too distraught to think of filing charges with the police. In many cases she does not have the precise information demanded by the police such as the exact names of the suspected looters.

31. *See generally,* E.I. Nwogugu, Family Law in Nigeria ch. 15 (1990) (discusses intestate succession under customary law).

32. Under this system, immovable property is normally inalienable either inter vivos or by

a general rule, widows have no right of inheritance in their husband's estate but are rather treated as objects to be inherited by the heir to the estate.[33] Some widows lose both their personal property and jointly acquired matrimonial property on the death of their husbands as these are generally considered part of a man's estate.[34] Childless widows and widows with only female children are in worse situations and oftentimes face expulsion from their matrimonial home on the death of their spouse.[35]

Testamentary disposition of property, while affording hope to some widows, provides no real or lasting relief to a vast majority of Nigerian women. The belief that the making of wills hastens the death of a testator makes wills an unpopular mode for the disposition of property. A woman who persuades her husband to make a will is suspected of plotting his death and is in danger of being accused of murder in the event of her husband's death.[36] The sudden appearance of someone claiming to be a child of a deceased hus-

---

will. The ordinary member of the family regards the alienation of such property as an outrage against native law and custom and an act likely to entail serious misfortune. This is particularly so with a sale of family property. The houses and farmland left by a deceased ancestor becomes after his death the family property for the members of his family. G.B.A. COKER, FAMILY PROPERTY AMONG THE YORUBAS 39 (1966).

33. Coker notes of the prevailing customary law, "the wives of a man constitute part of his immovable property; and the fact that they continue to be attached to the family even after his death demonstrates clearly that they are part of his immovable property. They are, of course, a type of property that could only be *inherited* by the male members of the family! As opposed to movable property, however, they could not be subject of bequests wills, nor can they be given away out of the family when the property of the deceased is distributed *post mortem.*" COKER, *supra* note 32, at 39.

34. Because the girl child is also disinherited under most African customary rules of inheritance, women suffer double deprivation inheriting neither from their fathers nor from their husbands. Few exceptions to the rule of female disinheritance exist. For example, among the Yorubas in Western Nigeria, the rule is that all the children of the deceased share equally in the estate regardless of sex. *See Salami v. Salami,* WESTERN NIGERIA L. REV. 10 (1957).

35. Interview with Dinah (not her real name), in Asaba, Delta State, 14 July 1994. Dinah had three girls with her husband and was seven months pregnant with the fourth child when her husband died in 1985. Immediately after his burial, she was ordered by her brother-in-law to pack her belongings and leave the family. Dinah left and has since not returned leaving behind all of her husband's property and even jointly acquired properties. Because she had only girls, Dinah believes she has no standing to challenge her brother-in-law who, under the customary law, is the rightful heir to her husband's estate. *Id.*

With respect to the Yoruba ethnic group in Nigeria, Coker notes that "[a] widow who has no issue is not entitled to any portion of the husband's property. According to strict native law and custom she could be taken to wife by any of the other junior male members of the family; but it is usually considered imprudent to take to wife a woman more or less incapable of child-bearing." *See* COKER, *supra* note 32, at 43.

36. Interviews in Port Harcourt, Rivers State, 25 July 1994. Out of eight women interviewed, only two said their husbands had left a will. No empirical study done. The basic point is

band often carries significant consequences for a widow and her children, as such a child can divest a widow of any possessory interest she may have in a husband's property. In some cases the rights of such a person have triumphed over those of the legitimate children of the deceased—for instance, where the latter are all female children and the illegitimate child is male. Perhaps the most humiliating aspect of it all is the surprise that is sprung on a grieving widow who discovers only at the burial of her husband that not only did he have children outside the marriage, but that these children may have better standing than she and her children.[37] To punish a widow, in-laws have often gone to great lengths to discover an illegitimate child of a deceased.[38]

The position of widows is complicated by the unfair property regimes which prevail in most parts of Africa. The law makes very little distinction between a widow's prenuptial property, jointly acquired property of the marriage, and the individual property of the husband.[39]

---

that generally, making of wills under statutory law is still very unpopular. In both instances, the husband left a vast proportion of the estate to the wife. Testamentary disposition of property does not, however, remedy the inherent discrimination against women in the various customary law rules of inheritance.

37. The primary issue is not about legitimacy or illegitimacy, but about the fairness of depriving a woman her interest in her husband's property, especially given the fact that such properties may have been acquired through a joint effort. Often the so-called illegitimate child may not really be a child but a grown adult scheming, with the full cooperation of in-laws, to deprive a widow of what is rightfully hers.

Given the lack of appropriate technology for paternity tests, there is a chance that this person may not really be a child of the deceased, but whatever the family decides stands. When the illegitimate child is male, he can acquire right of inheritance to the entire estate where a widow is childless or has only female children. Even if the widow has male children, this person can be named heir over and above the widow's younger children. In the final analysis, this is a case of two competing interests: those of a widow and those of a child or children the deceased husband had outside marriage. It is doubtful whether an easy equitable solution can be found that will satisfy both sides.

38. An otherwise illegitimate child acknowledged as a child of a deceased by his family can have as much right to a share in the deceased estate as his legal children. In a developing country like Nigeria with its largely rural, illiterate population, access to modern medical science in proving paternity is still rare. In most cases, the determination of paternity by in-laws is final and rarely subject to challenge by a widow.

In *Okon v. The Administrator General (Cross River State) & Ekput,* 6 Nig. Wkly. L. Rep. 473 (1992), a widow learned of the existence of a child of the deceased husband only during the funeral write-up of the husband. The in-laws asserted, and the court accepted, that the said child was indeed a child of the deceased. Moreover, the court in denying her letters of administration over her husband's estate, considered her attitude towards this child decisive. *Id.*

39. By "individual property" the author refers to property acquired by a man through his own effort as opposed to family, clan, tribal or communal property which he may have inherited from his ancestors and which he is expected to pass on to future generations.

Loss of property is often not the only deprivation widows suffer. Widows also stand the chance of losing their children, particularly if they are male children.[40] In Agnes' case, her three children, the last of which was two weeks old when her husband died, were taken from her immediately after her husband's burial.[41]

B.   Widowhood, Burial, and Mourning Rituals

Burial and mourning rituals imposed on widows inflict different kinds of losses—the loss of personal dignity, the loss of health, and sometimes, the loss of life. To show respect for the dead, customary law often prescribes rules and rites to be observed by surviving close relatives, particularly the wives, husbands, daughters, and sons of a deceased person. In practice however, widows suffer disproportionately on the death of their mate. Because a woman is deemed to belong to her husband, she is expected to respect and serve him even in death—a respect displayed by the meek observance of prescribed rituals. While the former practice of burying a wife along with her husband has disappeared, most women are still made to undergo various humiliating burial rituals.

These practices are inhumane and degrading because they inflict pain and anguish on widows, because widows often cannot opt out of these

---

40. Under most customary law operating in Nigeria, children are deemed to belong to a man's family. See NWOGUGU, *supra* note 31, at 341. He states, "under most systems of customary law in Nigeria, the father has an absolute right to the custody of his legitimate or legitimated children." *Id.* Though modern statutory law decides custody on the basis of the best interest of the child, what is surprising is that many people still operate as though these laws were non-existent. Thus, the Matrimonial Causes Act provides that in custody proceedings, " . . . the court shall regard the interest of (the) children as the paramount consideration." The Matrimonial Causes Act, 1970, No. 18 of 1970, § 71(1). Thus as between a man and his wife, custody would invariably go to the man. Children could, however, be allowed to remain with their mother while they are still in infancy. Under the modern statutory law of marriages, the best interest of the child is theoretically the guiding consideration in determining custody. *Id.* § 71 (1). It further provides that "in proceedings with respect to the custody, guardianship, welfare, advancement or education of children of a marriage the court shall regard the interest of those children as the paramount consideration." *Id.*
41. According to Agnes:

About twenty-eight days after the burial, my sister-in-law called me and said, "we are taking our children from now on. When your people have finalized the burial, you should go with them." They took my two boys first . . . and later came and took the girl. I was still in school then and nearly committed suicide.

Her in-laws told her that since she was still so young and not financially independent, they were in a better position to care for the children. Yet implicit in the sister-in-law's statement is the idea that Agnes was an unwelcome intruder while her children belonged to the family and should be left behind. *See* Interview, *supra* note 3.

practices, because they provide perfect opportunities for in-laws to "settle scores" with women at a time when they are most vulnerable, and because in many cases the perpetuation of these practices have resulted in illness, permanent incapacitation and even death.[42] Because customary law does not prescribe similar rituals for men, the burial rituals reinforce the notion of women as the property of men and their families.

While burial rituals are varied and differ from one town to another, they have generally included varying degrees of isolation and confinement, restricted freedom of movement and association, and hair shaving.[43] In one town in the Delta State of Nigeria, for instance, after an initial seven-day (fourteen days for a titled man) confinement, a subsequent thirty-day confinement in a tiny outdoor hut is mandatory for widows.[44] They are obliged to stay in the hut and are forbidden, under threat of sanctions, from entering their homes during this period.[45] Public outings and activities are generally forbidden for the widow during prescribed mourning periods.[46]

Many of the African women affected by these practices are rural women whose livelihoods depend primarily on farming and trading activities. Laws prohibiting public outings by widows strike at a woman's basic need for survival and are based on very false assumptions about the existence of a strong family support for widows.[47]

---

42. Author's conclusions and personal observation. Death is however very rare and when it occurs is an indirect consequence of the funeral ordeal. No study has however been done to determine the effect of the widowhood ordeal on the long-term health of widows.

43. Periods of confinement both before and after the burial varies from one town to another and usually range from about one month to two years.

44. These huts, specially built for the purposes of the burial, are made from palm leaves and are traditionally very small in size, about 6ft. × 6ft. × 5ft. The widows usually cannot stand erect inside the hut and sleep in a bent shape because of the size of the hut. Interview with Mrs. Yoma (not her real name), in Delta State, 14 July 1994. The author did not see any such hut.

45. Exposure to rain, cold, insects, and dangerous animals are commonplace. Not even in times of serious emergencies are widows permitted to go into their homes. Interview with Mrs. Roseline in Illah, Delta State, 13–14 July 1994 (general account of women interviewed in this town).

46. Restrictions vary but generally extends to farming activities, economic (marketing) activities, and general social functions.

47. In practice, such support is largely absent. Most of a widow's period of confinement is spent in idleness and extreme loneliness. While these practices may have worked in the past when, given the existence of a large agricultural family, a widow was sure of company and was provided for. Today this is not the case. After the real burial, most people actually disperse to the urban cities where they live, thus, leaving the widow alone in the village. (Author's personal knowledge as one who has witnessed many burials in Eastern Nigeria.) For childless widows and widows without relatives, this can be a very traumatic period. Some widows interviewed continued their business as petty traders during this period and overcame restrictions on their freedom of movement by selling their wares through their children. (General account of women, also author's observation over the years.)

Some groups still observe other practices such as wife inheritance (or levirate marriage),[48] though widows are increasingly given the option to refuse. An inverse relationship exists between the degree of a widow's economic independence and her willingness to accept a levirate marriage. Given the burial rituals widows are made to undergo, a majority of the widows interviewed said they turned down the offer for a marriage, choosing rather to suffer the economic hardship involved. In most localities, this practice has been totally abandoned. Moreover, widows now appear to have a greater say in whether or not to accept such arrangements.

Perhaps the greatest objection to the treatment of widows lies in the different, almost special, treatment accorded men who lose their wives.[49] While widowers may be expected to shave their hair, abstain from public and social functions, and avoid sexual relations during the mourning period, no real sanction is imposed on the defaulting widowers. At most, a man may suffer from social scorn and loss of public opinion.[50] Differences also exist in the inheritance rights of widowers *vis-à-vis* those of the widows. While theoretically, pre-nuptial and personal properties of a woman are inherited by her children, in practice most of a woman's property vests in the husband upon her death.[51] With the concept of joint ownership of matrimonial property unknown under most African marriage laws, a woman and all that she owns is generally deemed to belong to her husband. Ncube observes:

---

48. The death of a husband does not automatically terminate a marriage under most customary laws in Africa. As a result, avenues are made for continuing a marriage even after the death of the man either for the widow's own protection or as a means of making use of her reproductive capacity to produce more children for the lineage. Such avenues include the levirate marriage and widow's inheritance. Under the levirate system, "another man from the deceased's family may be appointed to stand in the footprints of the dead man and discharge in relation to the widow and her children, all the functions of a husband and father, on behalf of his dead relative." Under the system of widow's inheritance, however, the widow's marriage to the dead husband is assumed to have been terminated by his death and the new man "acquires rights in the marriage as if the widow had remarried." ARMSTRONG, *supra* note 22, at 3–4; *see also* COTRAN, *supra* note 16, at 186–87.

49. Because society generally assumes that men are the principal breadwinners, rules about physical confinement are greatly relaxed. Most widows the author interviewed smiled and were surprised when asked of the customary expectations on widowers. Since men own their wives, some widows thought it strange that men should be expected to observe any such rituals. Author's impression.

50. According to one traditional ruler in a town in Eastern Nigeria, "if a wife dies, the man is confined in the house for a month but the men break the rules. It cannot be an abomination if he breaks the rule but people can talk. There are no sanctions. Maybe sanction by shunning. It becomes an abomination if he impregnates another woman during that mourning period." Interview 19 July 1994.

51. With respect to a married woman's estate, Nigerian law distinguishes between her immovable ante-nuptial property, immovable property acquired during marriage and her movable property. In Eastern Nigeria, "the general principle is that a woman's ante-nuptial property—excepting those things she took with her to her husband's place—

Under customary law, all meaningful property is owned and controlled by the husband. Women are often, if not always, reduced to the status of property-less dependents who have to submit to the will of their husbands in order to survive. The customary law on matrimonial property perceives a married woman as an unpaid servant of her husband. She works for him, looks after his family, acquires and preserves property for him.[52]

C.   Choices, Constraints, and Agency

What choices exist for widows and to what extent are widows willing victims of the various customary rules and practices affecting them? At the risk of alienation, banishment, torture, loss of children and much more, a widow may attempt to defy prevailing customs. While the educated, urban women may have the option of escaping to the city and thereby avoiding the harsh demands of the custom, such option does not exist for the majority of the African women who reside in rural areas and who depend on their farms for survival. In the context of post-colonial Africa, "mechanisms of power and dominance make it hard for women to challenge male strategies and 'authentic' interpretations of culture. This may be the case for educated and well-to-do women; their demands for rights are within boundaries of what is attainable."[53] Legal and administrative barriers to justice also diminish the real options available to widows. Particularly for the rural women far removed from the modern centers of power, legal recourse does not exist as a viable option. Unfortunately, the traditional methods of conflict resolution which emphasized compromise and reconciliation and which operated through the family network are proving inadequate today.[54]

---

belongs to her father's family." *See* Nwakama Okoro, The Customary Law of Succession in Eastern Nigeria, 135 (1966). Immovable property acquired after marriage is inherited in the following order: her sons of that marriage; her husband; and her husband's successor who may be his son by another wife. Finally, her daughters inherit her movable property (usually referred to as "feminine property," comprising such household items as cooking utensils and dresses). *Id.* at 136–37.

52. Welshman Ncube, Family Law in Zimbabwe 170–171 (1989). This customary law rule holds good in most African states. As a judge in Zimbabwe observed, "property acquired during a marriage becomes the husband's property whether acquired by him or his wife." *Id.* at 170. *See, e.g.,* Coker, *supra* note 32.

53. Jensen & Poulsen, *supra* note 21, at 15. In practice, the option of escaping to the city, offers no real relief to a widow because by the banishment, the widow is deprived of her freedom of association, and of assembly, her right to privacy, and freedom to found a family. Given the cost involved, most women, regardless of their class or educational background, accede to the demands of the custom.

54. Under the traditional system, "the method of *conflict resolution* is not to identify guilty party but to reestablish the relationship to everyone's satisfaction, thus ensuring the cohesiveness of the extended family and safeguarding the rights and welfare of the individual in the communal context." Jensen & Poulsen, *supra* note 21, at 9. *But see* Chanock, *supra*

Deprived of ownership interests in real properties, options available to a widow include: marrying elsewhere, accepting her husband's heir as husband, returning to her natal group, limited temporary rights in her husband's family, durable (life-interest) rights in her husband's property, living with grown children, or exercising ownership rights in the name of grown male children.[55] The fact that widows desperately explore, exploit, and maximize these options may be more a reflection of their need to survive than an indication of their free-willed exercise of meaningful choices. A widow's life is therefore invariably dependent on the decisions of others, particularly decisions of men either in her husband's community or in her own natal community. Within these boundaries, widows attempt to create space for themselves. Factors such as beauty and physical fitness, acquisition of useful skills and knowledge, age and life-cycle state, as well as individual personality, also affect the ultimate fate of the widow. A widow with grown male children or rich, supportive, and influential brothers, may indeed not present the picture of a weak, helpless, and poor woman.[56]

---

note 9, at 7–8 (questioning the extent to which the images of precolonial African justice system are myths constructed as much by the white anthropologists as by Africans).

Today, such a system often works against the interest of women. Most widows express a feeling of utter helplessness at their plight. (General observation.) Where a widow's properties are taken by the in-laws, to whom does she turn? How can the family be expected to be impartial under the circumstances? Growing legal action by women which pits them against their husband's family may be a reflection of their deep seated dissatisfaction with the system. It cannot, however, be denied that where legal recourse is nonexistent, slow, or ineffective, women are sometimes better off under the informal, traditional conflict resolution mechanism than they would have been under the more formal, adversarial judicial procedure.

55. See Potash, *supra* note 28. Several factors influence the decisions of widows and the options they choose to exercise. This would include: the age of the widow, the widow's claims on natal group, the age and sex of her children, and whether children have acquired interest in their father's property. Where a widow is, for instance, a junior wife in a polygamous home and conditions become extremely harsh, she may choose to reside with grown children, if she has any. Where such a woman is still young and childless or has only young female children, she may decide to return to her natal group if conditions are better there. Invariably, much depends on a widow's relationship with her in-laws. When in-laws are nice and sympathetic, some widows have remained in their husband's home and continued to manage his estate for herself and for her children.

Most of the widows the author spoke with or knows personally have remained in their husband's home even after their death and are living independent, though very poor, lives. The option of returning to natal group is one which most widows interviewed do not consider unless conditions become extremely bad or the widow is actually chased away by her in-laws. Particularly for the women in many parts of Eastern Nigeria where women are denied inheritance rights in their father's estate, return to natal group is not an attractive option.

56. Indeed some widows interviewed said they did not have any problems either with the existing customary laws or with their in-laws. One woman whose husband left, by will, virtually all of his property told the author that she has never had any problem with her

A disturbing paradox exists in the fact that African women, in their roles as mothers, sisters, and daughters, have been the prime agents for the perpetuation and enforcement of gruesome widowhood practices. Women have often been most resistant to any change that might lighten the customary expectations placed on widows. Women in Ibo society, in their role as the daughters of the lineage (the Umu Ada) comprise a formidable group who ensure the strict observance of the customary burial rituals by widows.[57]

It is disturbing that while as wives and potential wives, women condemn the customary prescriptions for widows; the same women in their roles as sisters and daughters support these practices. Given this paradox, an analysis of the agency of African women in the maintenance of customary practices that subordinate them becomes extremely difficult. It could be argued that African women generally are all victims of long-standing myths and ideologies artificially constructed and continually employed to maintain them in subordinated positions.[58] A study of various traditional practices which may be harmful to women demands a more than superficial understanding of why women succumb to, yield to, accept, or otherwise support these practices. The experiences of widows in Nigeria suggest several reasons for this phenomenon, including, a belief in the cultural and social significance of the practice; ignorance of other possibilities; superstition; lack of choice; sense of duty to the family and community; and even love for their husbands.

D.   Rationales for Africa's Widowhood Practices

Customary rules of inheritance, emphasizing the male descent, are sometimes justified by the need to keep family property within the family.[59]

---

in-laws; nor has anyone attempted to deprive her of her property; and that she was quite happy with the existing customary law. Interview with Mrs. S [name withheld], in Port Harcourt, Rivers State, 25 July 1994.

57. See, *infra,* Section V on the politics of reform. Note that this is a general observation as some women did not think any change was desirable. This is the author's personal knowledge as one who is also a daughter of a lineage.

58. The issue of female circumcision presents a similar paradox in the sense that, while women are clearly the real and intended victims of this practice, the active monitoring and enforcement by women has sustained this practice. *See generally,* NAHID TOUBIA, FEMALE GENITAL MUTILATION: A CALL FOR GLOBAL ACTION 29 (1983). She notes that: "Traditionally, the role of the circumciser is an inherited one, performed by the female laypeople. (Some men have performed FGM, but this is rare.)" *Id.*

59. By "family property," the author refers to properties which have been in the family for centuries and passed on from one generation to another. A man who inherits such property from the father is obliged, under most African customary laws, to pass it to his sons and thus retain it in the family. *See* NWOGUGU, *supra* note 31, at ch. 16 (discusses the

Clement Masongo, for instance, argues that "the sole reason for excluding females from the male line of succession was, and still is, the need to retain the family regenerative property within the extended family, where it is administered by a member of the extended family for the benefits of a deceased's dependents at customary law."[60] According to Masongo:

> Women, when they get married, leave their parental home to join that of their husbands and more often than not adopt the surnames of their husbands (relinquishing their father's surnames). . . . Because of the effects of marriage on the status of African females, there is no way females can reasonably be expected to effectively exercise control [of] their fathers' "house" for the benefit of its members.[61]

The need to keep property within the family, however, serves only as a cover for an entrenched customary distrust of women and a general perception of women as perpetual minors.[62] The justification advanced by Masongo, even if accepted, does not explain why women are also excluded from inheriting even those properties which do not form part of the family holdings.

It also fails to explain why single, divorced, widowed women, or women who have disavowed any interest in marrying or changing their name are nonetheless excluded from a share in family property. Surely, if the sole concern was with the ability of a married woman to exercise control over her father's house, as Masongo asserts, the exclusion of females from the line of succession would have been limited to married women only. The fact that sale of family property is an ever increasing phenomenon in many African societies also vitiates the argument for retaining such properties within the family and creates an environment for a reconsideration of some earlier customs and practices prejudicial to the interest of women. If a man can, subject to satisfaction of customary requirements, sell a piece of family property to an outsider, it becomes preposterous to argue against female inheritance simply because a daughter or wife may take the property outside the family.

Rather than offer justification for the treatment of widows, others have simply questioned critics' assertions that the various widowhood practices actually work hardship on women. They argue, for instance, that the rules

---

extended family and rights of individual members in family property). He cannot by testamentary disposition, divest himself and his family of such property. *Id.*

60. Clement Masongo, *Chihowa v. Mangwende S-84–87: A Critique*, 5 Legal Forum 2, 55, 56 (1993) (a critique of the Supreme Court of Zimbabwe's decision recognizing the right of daughters to inherit properties on the same footing as the sons).

61. *Id.* at 56.

62. According to this perception, women are incapable of managing real property and must themselves be managed and controlled by some male relative. Moreover, the entrenched belief is that a woman is most likely to pass on such property to a male lover.

providing for male inheritance to the exclusion of women were established to guarantee the proper maintenance for widows and to ensure they were not exploited by "wicked" men.[63] Properties were therefore conferred on men who were then expected to take care of the widow. Such paternalistic attitudes are however unnecessary today and, unfortunately, create the environment for the actual exploitation of the very women the custom claims to protect. Stories of unjust enrichment by male relatives to the detriment of widows and their children abound throughout Africa.

While such a process of inheritance may still be satisfactory where the family organization conforms to strictly traditional customary patterns, it is out of touch with existing realities in most African states. Today, with ever increasing urban migration and improved transportation systems, male heirs may reside thousands of miles away from the traditional homestead and may generally ignore their duties to the deceased's wife and children. Customary law imposes on widows difficult conditions which, if breached, are used as pretext for cutting off support. Because the jurisdiction of local rulers do not extend beyond their small locality, such an heir can conveniently avoid his obligations without fear of sanctions. He may of course be shunned and his behavior condemned by the village community, but of what relief is that to a starving widow and her children?[64]

Burial and mourning rituals are justified on several grounds including the need to pay due respect to the dead, protect widows from the attacks of evil spirits, and even encourage the living toward good deeds.[65] Some have

---

63. Author's personal knowledge.
64. Perhaps the greatest problem of the customary rules of succession lies in the fact that no meaningful system exists today to check any potential abuse. It is a system which depends so much on the goodwill of men, yet as Jensen and Poulsen note, due to the changing conditions in Africa, "traditional obligations towards all members of the extended family are being replaced by considerations of an individualistic nature favoring only the closest kin." See JENSEN & POULSEN, supra note 21, at 9–10.
65. It is hard to imagine how these burial rituals encourage the living towards good deeds, but so thought justices of the Kenyan Court of Appeal. According to the court:

> The evidence on "magenga" the shaving hair "tero buru" and other rites shows that the practices are innocent and are meant to underscore the deep loss to the clan, to distinguish the particular deceased from the other deceased who are not as prominent, and no doubt, the ceremony is intended to encourage members of a clan to aim high by doing good deeds to the community.

See Otieno v. Ougo & Siranga, supra note 16, at 343.

It has also been argued that the whole burial rituals were designed with the protection of the widow in mind. Because in the olden days it was believed that a widow was vulnerable to attack from evil forces, her physical confinement and close monitoring by relatives are said to have been specially designed for her protection. The same has also been used to explain the need for river and forest baths, a cleansing bath signifying the breaking of ties with the dead. Thus according to one traditional ruler, "these customs were never designed to humiliate women or treat them harshly. They were rather devised to

suggested that economic motivations could also account for why women choose to undergo these rituals. In some localities, a feast is held in honor of a woman who successfully concludes the burial rituals.[66] While respect for the dead is an admirable objective, the burial rituals as practiced in many parts of Nigeria serve no purpose other than to humiliate.[67] The rituals also serve as a deterrence to women generally. The common practice is to suspect the wife whenever a husband dies. The reasoning is that a woman, knowing what she will undergo if her husband dies, will think twice before maltreating or killing him or even antagonizing her in-laws. It would therefore appear that many of these burial rituals operate to induce desired social behavior in women.

One traditional ruler honestly observes the suffering widows undergo:

> If you search for the reasons you find cases when it is necessary for women to go through them and other times,—"when it is not necessary. All wives are not the same." Some love their husbands and others may have caused their husband's death. This was in the olden days. In our time things are different. We want to change it. But some wives deserve the punishment.[68]

Embedded in this observation is the traditional distrust of women in Africa and the idea that women deserve to be punished for breaches of what is usually a gendered definition of acceptable social behaviors. The above observation also underscores growing tensions in many African societies today between the need for change and the desire to retain traditional forms of social control, particularly as they apply to women and children. Tension is also felt between the quest of African states to be perceived as modern and an equal desire to maintain social, economic, and political structures that serve the interests of the dominant groups.

---

protect women. In the olden days, once it was dark, it was believed that the spirit world came to hurt people especially a woman in mourning." Interview with local chief, Asaba, Delta State, 14 July 1994. If they exist to protect widows, one wonders why widows are given no option to refuse to undergo such practices and why defiant widows are punished.

66. No one has however investigated to find out what these women would rather have. In the absence of real alternatives, most women have no choice but to make the most of existing customary rules—hence their participation in such ceremonies. Most women interviewed described their mourning experiences as something they would rather not go through again hence their decision not to remarry. These women's response would support the conclusion that, whatever incentives widows' are offered are insignificant compared to the pain and humiliation they endure.

67. This explains why widows were in the past buried alive alongside their dead husbands and why widows are given no choice in the matter. It also explains the wide disparity in the cultural expectations on men and women. Why is a dead man more important than a dead woman and hence worthy of more respect? Why is the wife particularly singled out to show the respect needed by the dead?

68. Interview with *Igwe* of Abagana, traditional ruler, in Mbaukwu, Anambra State, 16 July 1994.

A step toward gender equality would begin with a recognition of the autonomy and independence of women and a re-examination of the rationales for the various widowhood practices in light of changing economic, social, and political circumstances. The solution must include an abolition of those practices considered inhuman and degrading burial rituals, and a recognition of the rights of widows to inherit those properties falling outside the class of family property.[69]

III. THE LEGAL CONTEXT OF WIDOWS' RIGHTS IN NIGERIA

The problem of widows in Nigeria is rooted in several factors. They include: an inequitable property regime; the general acceptance of polygamy; and the absence of any equitable means for protecting the respective interests of the different wives of a man; loopholes in the administration of estate laws which allow virtually any third party to contest a widow's right to administer her husband's estate; insensitivity and even hostility on the part of the police, the administration, and the judiciary; the absence of any law specifically addressing the problems of widows; and the general unpopularity of wills, coupled with the absence of effective means for enforcing wills.

Fundamental contradiction inherent in the Nigerian legal system—the coexistence of modern, statutory laws with traditional customary laws and practices—has created a complex and confusing legal regime under which women generally are denied adequate legal protection. Today, both systems of law, together with English common law, form an integral part of the Nigerian legal system. One scholar identifies six sources of Nigerian Law: (i) local laws and customs; (ii) English Common Law, the doctrines of equity and Statutes of General Application; (iii) local legislation; (iv) law reports; (v) textbooks on Nigerian law; and (vi) judicial precedents.[70]

---

69. Modern statutory law in Nigeria currently recognizes the right of a man or woman to divest his/her properties at will. Thus a man can by will vest certain real properties to his daughters and wife. Unfortunately, where a man dies intestate, the same property are usually distributed according to customary laws which generally exclude women. See generally, Nwogugu, supra note 31, at ch. 4 (discusses succession under the general law in Nigeria).

70. See Taslim O. Elias, The Nigerian Legal System 12 (2d ed., 1963). Section 45 of the Interpretation Act, Cap. 89 of 1958, Laws of Nigeria provides that "the common law of England and the doctrines of equity, together with the statutes of general application that were in force in England on the 1st day of January, 1900, shall be in force...." See also The High Court Law of Eastern Nigeria, Cap. 61, Laws of Eastern Nigeria, 1963, § 14 & 28. Under these general provisions such English statutes as the Wills Act 1837 and the Married Women Property Act 1882 operate as laws in Nigeria and do affect the rights of widows in the country. English statutes in force in England on 1 January 1900 are applicable in Nigeria, subsequent repeal or amendment in England notwithstanding. See Young v. Abina, 6 W. Afr. Ct. App. 180 (1940). In Western Nigeria and Bendel States, the

Not surprisingly, many of the problems which are faced today in much of Africa "are the products of trying to piece together, in a hasty fashion, not only the different legal systems but also fundamentally different conceptions of society and the family."[71] Balancing the monogamous family system with the polygamous system; the nuclear family structure with the extended; and the growing individuality and autonomy of persons with the strong kinship network of the not so distant past, poses no small problem to African poli-cymakers today.[72] In Nigeria, the result is that despite constitutional provi-sions espousing the principles of equality and nondiscrimination, patently discriminatory customary laws and outdated English common law[73] still form part of Nigerian law and are routinely upheld by the courts.

---

wholesale application of English law is no longer the case. By the Laws of England (Application) Law (Cap. 60), only selected pre-1900 and post-1900 English statutes were reenacted into regional laws. *See* G.O. Ezejiofor, *Sources of Nigerian Law, in* INTRODUCTION TO NIGERIAN LAW 7 (C.O. Okonkwo ed., 1980).

Section 19(1) of the Supreme Court Ordinance, 1914 provides: "Nothing in this Ordinance shall deprive the Supreme Court of the Right to observe and enforce the obser-vance, or shall deprive any person of the benefit of any Native Law and Custom. . . ." Past decisions of the Nigerian courts support the view that the courts have a duty, subject to certain requirements, to enforce native laws and customs. *See, e.g., Eshugbaye Eleko v. Government of Nigeria*, App. Cases 662 (1930); *Oke Lanipekun Laoe & Ors. v. Amao Oyetunde*, App. Cases 170 (1944). In the latter case, in an appeal from the West African Court of Appeal to the Privy Council in England, Lord Wright, who delivered the opinion of the court, stated: "The courts which have been established by the British Government have a duty of enforcing these native customs, so far as they are not barbarous, as part of the laws of the land." *Id.* at 172–73.

71. Stewart, *Coping with the Muddle, supra* note 23, at 27.
72. Many African governments, unsure of the proper path, are reluctant to engage in mean-ingful reform, particularly in those areas where women's rights are at issue, preferring to allow for extreme decentralization in matters of family or personal law. Author's con-clusion.
73. The Nigerian legal system has for the most part retained the old common law doctrine on marital property without the corresponding legislative changes that have since occurred in England. Underlying this common law relating to marital property is the doc-trine of marital unity which subsumes the identity of the woman into that of her husband, the two now becoming one upon marriage. Thus according to Blackstone, "the very being or legal existence of the woman is suspended during the marriage, or at least is incorporated and consolidated into that of the husband; under whose wing, protection and cover, she performs everything." SIR WILLIAM BLACKSTONE, COMMENTARIES ON THE LAWS OF ENGLAND IN FOUR BOOKS 387 (Thomas Cooley ed., 4th ed., 1899) *cited in* NORMA BASCH, IN THE EYES OF THE LAW 48–49 (1982).

Thus, in many respects, the common law position on a woman's right to marital property closely resembles the customary law position in most African states given that under both systems, a married woman assumes a subservient position in relation to her husband. Under customary law, a husband, having paid the prescribed dowry, was assumed to own the wife. The common law rule on the position of women achieved a similar purpose. As Basch concludes:

The doctrine of marital unity not only mandated the wife's subservience to her hus-band, but it also held the distinction of obliterating her legal identity. At common law

The Nigerian Constitution provides for the right to personal liberty, equal treatment, and nondiscrimination.[74] In the same vein however, the Constitution protects and preserves Nigerian cultures without stipulating clear principles for resolving internal conflict that may arise in the pursuit of what many believe to be mutually exclusive goals. In its statement of Fundamental Objectives and Directive Principles of State Policy, the 1979 Constitution expressly provides that "the State shall protect and enhance Nigerian culture"[75] and that "every citizen shall have equality of rights, obligations and opportunities before the law."[76] Article 245 created the Customary Courts of Appeal of the States.[77] The Customary Court of Appeal is vested with appellate and supervisory power in civil proceedings involving questions of customary law.[78] A judge of the Customary Court of Appeal of a state is appointed by the governor of the state on the advice of the State Judicial Commission.[79]

The 1989 Constitution replaced Section 20 of the 1979 Constitution with the stipulation that "the State shall protect, preserve and promote the Nigerian cultures which enhances human dignity and are consistent with the fundamental objectives as provided in this chapter."[80] Though an improvement over the 1979 Constitution, these provisions have had no beneficial effect for women for several reasons. First, the 1989 Constitution

---

a wife was a nonentity in most situations; her husband subsumed her legal personality. The law created an equation in which one plus one equaled one by erasing the female one.

Id. at 17.

74. *See, e.g.,* Constitution of Nigeria, art. 39(1) (1979), provides that no citizen shall on the basis of sex:

be subjected either expressly by, or in the practical application of, any law in force in Nigeria or any administrative action of the government to disabilities or restrictions to which citizens of Nigeria of other . . . sex . . . are not made subject to.

The Constitution further guarantees the right to freedom of movement (art. 38), the right to personal liberty (art. 32), the right to human dignity (art. 31), and the right to life (art. 30). *See also* Constitution of the Federal Republic of Nigeria (Enactment) Act, CAP. 62, 1979. Similar provisions exist in the 1999 Constitution: Article 41 (right to freedom of movement); Article 34 (right to dignity of human person); and Article 33 (right to life).

Similary, the Constitution of Nigeria, arts, 41, 33, 34 (1989) provides for the right to freedom from discrimination, the right to dignity of human person, and the right to personal liberty.

75. Nigerian Const., art. 20 (1979).
76. *Id.* art. 17 (2)(a).
77. *See id.* art. 245.
78. *See id.* art. 247.
79. *See id.* art. 246 (2).
80. Nigerian Const., art. 21 (1989).

never went into force and hence is a dead document. Moreover, Section 21 appears in the non-justiciable section of the Constitution and arguably cannot be taken to have conferred substantive rights on anyone.[81]

The simultaneous application of differing systems of law and the fragmented and largely unwritten nature of African customary laws are problems which African widows must contend with in their search for fairness and justice. Nigerian customary law is largely unwritten and, most often, depends on the recollection of male elders presumed to have special knowledge of the customs and practices of their people. Only in a few instances are provisions made for a written declaration of customary law on specific issues.[82] An intractable problem in post-colonial Africa, therefore, is what the author calls the tension between protected rights and preserved cultures. An unpredictable, vague, largely inconsistent, and highly discretionary legal regime is the result. In the absence of codification or harmonization,[83] the Nigerian courts have held that customary law is a matter of evidence to be

---

81. See Nigerian Const., § 21, art. 1(1) (1979), provides that the 1979 Constitution "is supreme and its provisions shall have binding force on all authorities and persons throughout the Federal Republic of Nigeria." Article 1(3) of the Constitution provides: "if any other law is inconsistent with the provisions of the Constitution, this Constitution shall prevail, and that other law shall to the extent of the inconsistency be void." Id. art. 1(3).

Hopefully in the future a duly drafted Constitution will grapple with the fundamental question of the role and place of customary law in a changing, highly pluralistic society such as Nigeria. Until then, much depends on the whims and caprices of lawmakers, the judiciary, and law enforcement personnel.

82. Under the Native Authority Ordinance, Cap. 140 of 1948 (now repealed), § 78 of the local Government Law, Cap. 68, Laws of Western Nigeria, as well as the Native Authority Law, § 48 Cap. 77, Laws of Northern Nigeria, local authorities have power, or, when instructed by the governor, a duty, "to make a declaration, either of what it considers the customary rule on a particular topic within its area to be, or any modification which it regards as desirable." See Ezejiofor, supra note 70, at 42. For more recent enactments from the different states, see Local Government Law 1976, § 60, Laws of Anambra State; Local Government Law, § 48, Laws of Kano State (1977).

Regional laws also provide for the use of adoptive by-laws to make pronouncement on what the customary law in a given area is. The Minister of Local Government is empowered to frame model by-laws upon subjects regulated by customary law. Upon the adoption of the by-laws by the Local Government Council, such laws form part of the customary law of the area displacing any existing custom upon the same topic. See also Western Nigeria, Local Government Law, § 83 (Cap. 68); Eastern Nigeria, Local Government Law, § 90 (Cap. 97).

83. The question of codification and harmonization of customary law is one which has plagued most African states since the independence era. In favor of codification and harmonization is the argument of certainty and uniformity, advocates of customary law argue equally strongly that if customary law is a living law, codification would stunt its development and eventually stifle any modernization. Non-codification then is in the interest of women, since it keeps the debate open and allows for eventual changes in the law.

decided on the facts presented before the court in each particular case unless judicial notice has been taken of it.[84]

The test of the validity of a customary law in Nigeria is the repugnancy test, an old English concept imported into Africa during the colonial period. A custom is valid if it is not "repugnant to natural justice, equity and good conscience."[85] Nigerian courts are yet to develop concrete, equitable standards to guide their interpretation in applying this test. Much is therefore left to the individual judges.[86] The standard of "natural justice, equity, and good conscience" is at best vague and at worst, reflects the views of the dominant powers in the society. During the colonial rule, it reflected the views of the white colonial officials. Today in Nigeria, it reflects the views of the male dominated judiciary. Prior to independence, judgment depended much on

---

84. A given custom is prima facie valid until the courts rule otherwise. *See Romaine v. Romaine* 4 Nig. Wkly. L. Rep. 650 (1992); *Adeniyl v. Fabiyi* 5 Nig. Wkly. L. Rep. 489 (1993); *Kimdey & Ors v. Military Governor of Gongola State* 2 Nig. Wkly. L. Rep. (pt. 77) 445 (1988).

Section 58 of the Nigeria Evidence Act Cap. 62, Laws of the Federation of Nigeria and Lagos (1958) provides four levels of evidence in the proof of customary law: options of native chiefs; opinions of other persons having special knowledge of native law and customs; and any book or manuscript recognized by natives as a legal authority.

The burden of proving the existence of a custom is on the one alleging it. *See also Onwuchekwa v. Onwuchekwa* 5 Nig. Wkly L. Rep. 739 (a court of appeal decision) (1991); *Abiodun v. Erimolokun* I Sup. Ct. Nig. L. Rep. 377 (1961). Formal proof is not required, however, when judicial notice has been taken of a particular custom. A custom qualifies for judicial notice "only if it has been so often proved, pronounced upon and acted upon by a court of Superior or co-ordinate jurisdiction in the same area to such an extent that it can be said that it has acquired notoriety." Nnaemeka-Agu J.S.C., *Romaine v. Romaine* 650, 669; *see also, Agidigbi v. Agidigbi* 2 Nig. Wkly. L. Rep. 98 (1992).

85. *See* Supreme Court Ordinance, § 19(1), No. 4 of 1876; Supreme Court Ordinance, § 19(1) 1914, provides that:

> nothing in this Ordinance shall deprive the Supreme Court of the right to observe and enforce the observance, or shall deprive any person the benefit of any Native Law and Custom, such law or custom not being repugnant to natural justice, equity and good conscience, nor incompatible either directly or indirectly with any law for the time being in force.

See also The High Court of Lagos Act, § 27(1) (Cap. 80); Eastern Nigeria High Court Law, § 20(1) (Cap. 61); Western Nigeria High Court Law, § 12(1) (Cap. 80); Northern Nigeria High Court Law, § 34(1) (Cap. 49); the Nigerian Evidence Act, 1958, § 14(3).

Customary courts are also enjoined to apply the repugnancy test in their determination of the validity of a given customary law. *See also* Customary Court Law, Cap. 31, Laws of Western Region; Customary Courts (No. 2) Edict, No. 29 of 1966, Laws of Eastern Nigeria; Native Court Law, Cap. 78, Laws of Northern Region.

86. *See, e.g., Onwuchekwa v. Onwuchekwa, supra* note 84, at 739 ("the repugnancy doctrine as basis of determining the validity of customary law, is one troublesome area in our jurisprudence. And the trend of the decisions paint the troublesome picture, some of which are in irreconcilable camps.").

European standards of fairness and good conscience. It can be argued that in post-colonial Nigeria, the test should be changed to reflect values evident in modern constitutions democratically passed and accepted and should reflect evolving human rights standards as reflected in major international human rights treaties.[87]

To the extent that the courts have adopted any standards to guide their application of the repugnancy tests, these standards are vague and, in their practical application, impose undue burden on women. First, according to the courts, the test of repugnancy must be interpreted in the context of Nigerian jurisprudence which includes the totality of Nigerian customary laws.[88] Second, the courts insist that in reviewing a given customary law, they are not allowed to pick and choose but must examine the totality of the law.[89] Because this binds the court to either wholly accept or totally reject a given custom, it effectively discourages potential legal challenges as one is forced to challenge entire practices, some aspects of which may be acceptable or beneficial to women. Most women are in favor of some widowhood rituals, but reject those aspects of the custom that inflict pain and hardship on them.[90] The rule effectively discourages potential legal challenges by women because it has the effect of pitting women against the custom and the larger society as women come to be perceived as destroyers of custom.

---

87. *See, e.g.,* International Covenant on Civil and Political Rights, *adopted* 16 Dec. 1966, G.A. Res. 2200 (XXI), U.N. GAOR, 21st Sess., Supp. No. 16, U.N. Doc. A/6316 (1966), 999 U.N.T.S. 171 *(entered into force* 23 Mar. 1976); International Covenant on Economic, Social and Cultural Rights, *adopted* 16 Dec. 1966, G.A. Res. 2200 (XXI), U.N. GAOR, 21st Sess., Supp. No. 16, U.N. Doc. A/6316 (1966), 993 U.N.T.S. 3 *(entered into force* 3 Jan. 1976); CEDAW, *supra* note 11.

88. *See Rufai v. Igbira Native Authority,* N. NIG. L. REP. 178 (1957); *Onwuchekwa v. Onwuchekwa, supra* note 84, at 739. It is still not clear if the Nigerian courts will interpret the repugnancy clause in light of international human rights instruments to which Nigeria is a party. Though the African Charter on Human and Peoples' Rights, *adopted* 27 June 1981, O.A.U. Doc. CAB/LEG/67/3 Rev. 5 *(entered into force* 21 Oct. 1986), *reprinted in* 21 I.L.M. 58 (1982), now form part of Nigerian law, the courts have yet to interpret customary laws in light of the Charter. The African Charter forms part of the Nigeria law by virtue of the African Charter on Human and Peoples' Rights (Ratifications and Enforcement) Act, Cap. 19 (1983).

89. *See Onwuchekwa v. Onwuchekwa, supra* note 84, at 752. Thus, though a given custom or practice might appear unjust, the courts may hold differently after considering the totality of the custom giving rise to the questionable custom. According to Justice Tobi:

> In the application of the doctrine, a court must look at the total package of the customary law involved and not a watered down version of it or a tutored version. In the application of the doctrine, the court is not allowed to pick and choose certain aspects of the customary law and leave other aspects.

> *Id.*

90. Based both on conversations with women in the course of my research and in broader discussion with women in Nigeria. The general sense of the author was that a total absence of burial ritual is considered something of an abnormality by most people.

Finally, according to the courts, the burden of proving repugnancy is on the plaintiff.[91] The overall effect then of the repugnancy test has been the preservation of discriminatory customary practices.

A. Legal Rights, Privileges, and Disabilities of Widows

Nigerian law recognizes both monogamous and polygamous marriage systems. Each creates different legal rights and expectations for women and has serious implications for the property rights of a widow.[92] Generally, women who contract monogamous, statutory marriages enjoy greater formal protection and have their property rights determined by a wide range of statutory laws.[93] By contrast, widows who contract potentially polygamous,

---

91. *Onwuchekwa v. Onwuchekwa, supra* note 84, at 753. A woman's allegation that a custom which denied her interest in a jointly acquired property and which deemed her and her money as a property of her husband was repugnant to natural justice, failed. Despite the provisions of the Nigerian constitution on equality before the law and freedom from discrimination, the Court of Appeal held that she had not sufficiently proved that the custom in question was "repugnant to natural justice, equity, and good conscience." *Id.*

92. The Interpretation Act of 1964 defined monogamous marriage as the "voluntary union of one man and one woman to the exclusion of all others during the continuance of the marriage." These are registered marriages and may include some Christian marriages. Statutory marriages can be celebrated either in a licensed place of worship or in the Registrar's office. Monogamous marriages in Nigeria are regulated by a variety of statutes including the Marriage Act of 1914, the Marriage Act, Cap. 115, 1958 Laws of the Federation of Nigeria and Lagos (Marriage Act of 1958), and the Matrimonial Causes Decree 1970.

A "Christian marriage" per se, which is a marriage celebrated in accordance with the beliefs of a given church, imposes no legal duty per se on the parties under the Marriage Act. A statutory marriage celebrated in a licensed church however carries all the rights, duties, and obligations stipulated in the Nigerian Marriage Act. *See* ALFRED B. KASUMU & JESWALD W. SALACUSE, NIGERIAN FAMILY LAW 66–67 (1966).

A polygamous marriage, by contrast, is the voluntary union of one man with one or more wives and is governed by customary law and by Islamic law. Such marriages can be polygamous or potentially polygamous. The determinant factor is not the number of wives a man currently has but whether he could marry more wives under the nature of marriage contracted. Marriage Act of 1958, § 35 which establishes the monogamous marriages, for example, provides: "nothing in this Act contained shall affect the validity of any marriage contracted under or in accordance with any native law and custom or in any manner apply to marriages so contracted." *Id.* at 18.

93. *See, e.g.*, Marriage Act of 1914 & 1958, the Marriage (Amendment) Act, No. 14 of 1971 (Marriage Act of 1971), the Matrimonial Causes Decree 1970, and some provisions of the 1979 Nigerian Constitution. Other federal statutes affecting the legal rights of such widows include: The Matrimonial Causes Act, No. 18 of 1970; The Matrimonial Causes (Amendment) Act, No. 2 of 1975; Marriage (Validation) Decree, No. 46 of 1971; Legitimacy Act, 1929, Cap. 103, Laws of the Federation of Nigeria, 1958. Regional and state adaptation of these laws exist and include: the Legitimacy Law, 1929, Cap. 76, Laws of Eastern Nigeria, 1963; Administration-General Law, Cap. 4, Laws of Eastern Nigeria, No. 17, 1961; Administration of Estate Laws, 1959, Cap. 1, Laws of Western Region

customary law marriages, are not similarly protected, but have their legal rights determined exclusively under customary law.[94] In practice widows enjoy little legal protection regardless of the nature of marriage contracted.

The general unpopularity of wills and statutory restrictions on the nature of property disposable by will further exposes widows to abuse.[95] Wills, however, cannot cure the discriminatory nature of customary laws with respect to widows' inheritance. Generally the Nigerian will prohibits the disposal by will of any property which under customary law cannot be affected by testamentary disposition.[96]

In the absence of proof of a will, the presumption is that the deceased died intestate and the general law on intestacy will apply. In the case of intestacy, all the husband's property would, under local native law and custom, devolve on those entitled. In Eastern Nigeria, this is provided for by Section 36 of the Marriage Act which provides that in the event of a man's death:

> The personal property of such intestate and also any real property of which such intestate might have disposed [of] by will, shall be distributed in accordance with the provisions of the laws of England relating to the distribution of

---

1959; Legitimacy Law, 1929, Cap. 62, Laws of Western Nigeria, 1959; Married Women's Property Law, 1958, Cap. 76, Laws of Western Nigeria, 1959; the Succession Law Edict, 1987, Laws of Anambra State; Administration of Estate Law, Cap. 2, Laws of Bendel State, 1976; Married Women Property Law, Cap. 98, Laws of Bendel State, 1976; Administration of Estates Law, Cap. 2, Laws of Lagos State, 1973.

94. The general level of illiteracy prevailing in much of Africa, combined with the fact that a significant percentage of the women are rural dwellers uninformed about changes in the law mean that a significant percentage of these women still contract customary law and hence enjoy no protection under the formal statutory laws. Besides, oftentimes a woman may not even have the choice as to which type of marriage to contract. On illiteracy, the United Nations *Human Development Report 1997* puts Sub-Saharan Africa's adult literacy rate at 44.4 percent (female) and 64.3 percent (male); the combined primary, secondary, and tertiary gross enrollment ratio is 38.4 percent (female) and 46.6 percent (male). *See* UNITED NATIONS DEV. PROG., HUMAN DEVELOPMENT REPORT 1997, at 224 (1997) (UNDP).

95. *See, e.g.,* Wills Law of Bendel State, § 3(1) provides for the power to make wills, "subject to any customary law relating thereto." *See also Oke v. Oke* 3 SC 1 (1974) (holding that the effect of § 3(1) is that a testator cannot devise an undivided or unpartitioned allotment of family property by will since this is contrary to customary law); *Agidigbi v. Agidigbi, supra* note 84, at 98 (holding that the phrase, "subject to any customary law relating thereto," is not a qualification on the testator's capacity to make a will but a qualification of the subject matter of the property disposed of or intended to be disposed of). For Nigerian wills law, see generally The Wills Act, 1837 and The Wills Amendment Act, 1852 (English statutes of general application); Wills Law, Cap. 133, Laws of Western Nigeria 1959; Wills Law, Laws of Lagos State, 1973; Wills Law, Cap. 172, Laws of Bendel State, 1976.

96. See laws cited in *supra* 95; *see also* NWOGUGU, *supra* note 31, at ch. 14. For instance, referring to the Wills Law, Cap. 133, Laws of Western Nigeria, 1959, he notes, "... by § 3(1) of the Wills Law, real property which cannot be effected by testamentary disposition under the applicable customary law, cannot be disposed by will." *Id.* at 379.

personal estates of the intestates, any customary law to the contrary notwithstanding.[97]

The applicable English law is the English Statutes of Distribution 1670 and 1685, which provide that when a man dies leaving behind a widow and his children, the wife is entitled to one-third of his personal estate. When there is no child, the widow is entitled to one half of the whole estate. Real property devolves according to the English Common Law applicable in Nigeria, and women generally have no right of inheritance in real property.[98] The estate law operative in the western and midwestern region attempts to place women on equal footing with men by prescribing the same rule for men and women. The law is gender neutral and makes no distinction between real and personal property of a deceased:

> [w]here any person who is subject to customary law contracts a marriage in accordance with the provisions of the Marriage Ordinance and such person dies intestate after the commencement of this law leaving a widow or husband or any issue of such marriage, any property of which the said intestate might have disposed by will shall be distributed in accordance with the provisions of this law, any customary law to the contrary notwithstanding.[99]

---

97. The Marriage Act of 1915, § 36(b). Originally passed for the colony of Lagos, the Act was extended to all the states in Eastern Nigeria by virtue of a Supreme Court decision in *Administrator-General v. Egbuna* 18 Nig. L. Rep. 1 (1945). The Act is therefore applicable in Rivers, Cross-Rivers, Imo, Abia, Enugu, and Anambra States of Nigeria. By virtue of the Act, rules governing the administration of estate in England before 1900 will apply. This includes, the English Statutes of Distribution of 1670 and 1685, but not the English Administration of Estates Act, 1925 and 1952.

98. The Common Law in force in Nigeria, is that in force in England before 1900. Changes in English law including recent legislation and judicial decisions affecting the property rights unfortunately do not form part of the Nigerian legal system unless incorporated by local legislation. The Administration of Estate Act, 1925 & 1952 Laws of England that has changed the common law position on property rights of married women is, as a result, inapplicable in most parts of the country. Only in Western Nigeria, has the Administration of Estate Law, 1959 of the region been modeled after the 1925 Act of England.

Common Law widows were entitled to a dower which is a life interest in a third of the real estate of her husband. On intestacy, real property devolves on the eldest son—the heir at law. Bash explains that at common law, the curtesy, the husband's interest in his wife's realty was considerably greater than the dower, that is the wife's corresponding interest in her husband's realty. However, while a husband could exceed the provisions of the dower by substituting a settlement in lieu of a dower in his will, he could not exclude his wife from her dower right. *See* Basch, *supra* note 73, at 53. The Act also excludes real property, the succession of which cannot by customary law be affected by testamentary disposition. Such property descends in accordance with customary law which most often does not recognize the rights of women to own properties.

99. The Administration of Estates Law, 1959, §49 (5), Cap. 1, Laws of Western Region. The law is modeled after the English Administration of Estate Act, 1925 and the English Intestate Estate Act, 1952. This law applies in all the western states in Nigeria including

Where the intestate leaves a husband or wife but no issue, parent, brother, or sister of the whole blood, the law provides that "the residuary estate shall be held in trust for the surviving husband or wife absolutely."[100] Where, however, the deceased is survived by a spouse and an issue, the surviving spouse will take the personal chattels absolutely and will, in addition, receive one-third of the residuary estate.[101]

In practice, the overall effect of these laws is far from satisfactory. The laws unsuccessfully attempt to protect the rights of widows who contract statutory law marriages while retaining aspects of customary law on succession which perpetuate gender inequalities. Even though these laws are expressly stated to apply "any customary law to the contrary notwithstanding," none of the administration of estate laws apply to real property, the succession to which cannot by customary law be affected by testamentary disposition.[102] When this exclusionary clause catches all of a man's property, a widow is left without any protection whatsoever. Apparently estate laws do not attempt to place women on an equal footing with men and appear to have been intended as a middle ground in the tension between customary rules on inheritance and growing rights of women. Moreover, new laws still reflect the deep seated cultural biases against women.[103] What is more, in the day to day application of these laws, widows have experienced a disregard of even the minimal protection accorded them.

A Nigerian judge, writing with regard to the position of women under the customary law of succession, rightly cautions that:

Lagos, Ogun, Ondo Oyo, Bendel, and Delta States. The individual states have also reenacted the provisions of the law as state laws.

100. The Administration of Estates Law, 1959, Western Region of Nigeria, § 49(1)(i); *see also* Nwogugu, *supra* note 31, at 388.

101. *Id.* § 49(ii).

102. The Administration of Estates Law, 1959, *supra* note 100, § 49(5)(b) provides that "any real property the succession to which cannot by customary law be affected by testamentary disposition shall descend in accordance with customary law anything herein to the contrary notwithstanding." *See also* Marriage Act of 1958, *supra* note 92, § 36(1)(b); Nwogugu, *supra* note 31, at 388–90.

103. Succession Law Edict, § 1987; Laws of Anambra State, for example, provides:

> If the intestate leaves a husband or wife but no children, parent or brothers or sisters of the whole blood, the residuary estate shall be held in trust for the surviving spouse absolutely. However, where the surviving spouse is a wife, and the intestate leaves brothers or sisters of the half blood, the wife's interest will be for her life or until she marries whichever first occurs. Thereafter, the residue of her interest shall go to the intestate's brothers and sisters absolutely in equal shares.

> *See* Nwogugu, *supra* note 31, at 393.

> The law in effect reinforces the customary law in most parts of Eastern Nigeria that deny wives ownership interest in the estate of a deceased husband. Women who contract statutory marriages are, under this law, in no better position than those who marry under customary law.

It is necessary to appreciate that rules and customary law on the subject are unwritten. Our source is mere oral traditional history and testimony of men in leadership of their community. . . . Men played a dominant role in the formulation of customary law and practice. They are the judges and witnesses.[104]

In Western Nigeria, among the Yoruba people, the prevailing rule is that a wife does not inherit a deceased husband's property.[105] Similarly, men generally have no inheritance rights in the estate of their deceased wife.[106] A deceased property is usually inherited by the children in common, and in the absence of children, by relatives.[107] To the extent that neither spouse is entitled to succeed to the property of the other, widows are not disadvantaged. Yet in practice women remain disadvantaged since personal, in-kind contributions of a wife to the estate of her husband are generally ignored in what constitutes his estate.

Among the Bini of Midwestern Nigeria, the prevailing customary law rule is the rule of primogeniture, under which the oldest surviving son of a man inherits his estate.[108] Advocates of this custom argue that "its sole motive is the maintenance of the identity of the family."[109] Justice Ogbobine argues that the custom is just, as it seeks to equip the eldest son with resources necessary for the fulfillment of his customary duties:

If the eldest surviving child is to play his traditional position in the family as the guardian of his younger brothers and sisters, and the custodian of the family shrines . . . then the social structures of the community must be regularized in

---

104. Justice Eke Ozobu, Law of Succession and Land Law, paper delivered at the National Workshop for Magistrates, Area and Customary Judges, 15–26 June 1992.
105. *Suberu v. Sumonu,* 2 F.S.C. 33–35 (1957).
106. See Nwogugu, *supra* note 31, at 400. A woman's property, on intestacy, devolves on her children in common. See also *Johnson v. Macaulay,* 1 Nig. L. Rep. 743 (1961) (Supreme Court).
107. See *Shaibu v. Bakare,* Sup. Ct. 115 (1983), where the Supreme Court reiterated the custom that where a person dies intestate under Yoruba law and custom, his property devolves on his children. The court cited with approval an earlier court decision in *Lewis v. Bankole,* 1 Nig. L. Rep. 81 (1908) (*cited in* The Digest of 9 Supreme Court Cases at 250).

Under the Yoruba customary law, all children of the deceased inherit regardless of their gender though its management is usually under the control of the Dawodu, who is the eldest surviving son of the deceased. See *Adesanya v. Adesanya,* 1 F.S.C. 84 (1956); *see also* Okany, *supra* note 4, at 687. In a 1957 case, *Salami v. Salami,* W. Nig. L. Rep. 10 (1957), the court held that the plaintiff's (a female) right to inherit under Yoruba Customary Law "could not be affected by her absence, minority and sex, and that the Dawodu (i.e., the eldest son) was not entitled to a greater share than the other children." Okany, *supra* note 4, at 690.

Yoruba customary law recognizes two methods of distribution: distribution per stripe, i.e. according to the number of wives or women with children for deceased (Idi-Igi), and distribution per capita, according to the number of the deceased children (Ori-Ojori). See *Akinyele v. Opere* 1 All Nig. L. Rep. 65 (1968).

108. See Okany, *supra* note 4, at 704–07.
109. See R.A.I. Ogbobine, Materials and Cases on Benin Land Law 36 (1978).

order to prevent the imposition of social and family duties on the eldest son without the existence of some proprietary rights with which to meet such obligations.[110]

However, this author argues that the custom exists today to maintain male dominance in a changing society. While the heir is obliged to care for his other siblings and his father's wives, no enforceable rights vest in the intended beneficiaries.[111] Widows are in particularly precarious situations where the legal heir is a son from another wife or an otherwise illegitimate child of the deceased.[112] Despite its discriminatory nature and the hardship visited on widows, the courts have held the custom not repugnant to natural justice, equity, and good conscience.[113]

The author would argue that this custom, however justified, is repugnant to natural justice and good conscience. The fact that a widow, despite her life contribution to a deceased husband's estate may be left destitute and totally disinherited by possibly even a stranger is morally reprehensible. The custom clearly ignores or trivializes a woman's direct and indirect contributions to her husband's estate. Moreover, because the emphasis is on a male heir, the law has a wider reach and would affect childless widows and widows with only female children adversely.[114]

---

110. OGBOBINE, *supra* note 109, at 39.

111. *Id.* at 36. The most important part of a deceased estate is the house he lived in and made his abode prior to his death. The eldest son automatically inherits this house in its entirety.

112. A number of widows interviewed said they were living on a lot given them by their husband's heir who was not their son. While many of them thought it preposterous that the heir should ever send them packing, they readily admitted they were virtually at the mercy of the heir.

113. *See Agidigbi v. Agidigbi, supra* note 84, at 98; *Ogamien v. Ogamien,* NIG. MONTHLY L. REP. 245 (1967); *Idehen v. Idehen,* 6 NIG. WKLY. L. REP. (pt. 198) 382 (1991). According to the then Chief Justice of Nigeria in the 1967 case, *Ogamien,* rejecting the allegation of repugnancy:

> This custom the learned judge dubbed as repugnant to natural justice, equity and good conscience; he refused to be bound by it. As it is not a point material to this appeal we refrain from making comments on this except that we see nothing wrong in this custom. We can only say that it is unknown in some other highly civilised countries of the world.

Id.

Ogbobine argues that the custom is justice as it seeks to equip the eldest son with resources necessary for the fulfillment of his customary duties. According to him:

> If the eldest surviving child is to play his traditional position in the family as the guardian of his younger brothers and sisters, and the custodian of the family shrines . . . then the social structures of the community must be regularised in order to prevent the imposition of social and family duties on the eldest son without the existence of some proprietary rights with which to meet such obligations.

Id. at 39.

114. As Nwogugu noted:

In Eastern Nigeria, while provisions are made for the welfare of the widow, the customary law falls short of according full recognition to widows and is laden with conditions that make widows subject to the whims and caprices of her in-laws.[115] Widows' privileges vary and include: while living in the husband's family, a right to be maintained by the person who inherits her husband's estate; a right to live as a member of the family in her late husband's compound until she remarries or dies; and where she has no son but was given a piece of land or an economic tree by her husband in his lifetime for her exclusive use, a right to continue to enjoy such land or tree until she remarries or dies. But she has no right to sell or make an outright gift of any of them.[116]

What rights widows are allowed they exercise as proxies for their minor sons, always acting under the supervision of a husband's male relative.[117] In contrast, men can and do inherit their wives' properties.[118]

> The duty of the male heir to maintain the widow is often neglected with the result that the male heir takes the benefits without the burden. This may be particularly hard on the widow where she has contributed significantly to the acquisition of the property in question. It has been the case that in some cases, widows are left destitute despite the fact that their husband left substantial estate behind which by customary law is inherited by some male heir who is not her son.

Nwogugu, *supra* note 31, at 408.

115. Privileges are enjoyed "subject to good behavior" as defined by the family. *See* S.N.C. Obi, et al., The Customary Law Manual: A Manual of Customary Laws Obtaining in Anambra and Imo States of Nigeria (Customary Law Manual) (1977). Section 225 (1) of the customary laws obtaining among the Ibos in Eastern Nigeria, for instance, provides: "A widow, even if she has no son, has a right to live as a member of the family in her late husband's compound till she remarries or dies. But the family has power to remove her for persistent bad conduct." *Id.*

116. *See id.* §§ 224–26.

117. According to the Customary Law Manual:

> Where all the children born of the same mother but are too young to take care of the estate, their mother has a right to do so on their behalf, but she does so under the general supervision of the nearest oldest paternal male relatives.

Id.

118. According to one traditional ruler in the country:

> A wife's inheritance depends on the position of her husband. She inherits whatever is her husband's provided she has abided by all the burial rites. She inherits along with the children. Provided that if the man has no male child, she can use them while she is alive. On her death, everything reverts to the family. She inherits under the umbrella of her children. We don't accept joint contribution. What we know is that the property belongs to the man.

Interview, *supra* note 68.

> On a husband's right to inherit the wife's property, the same traditional ruler added, "a man is supposed to inherit his wife's property. Her personal effects go to her daughters. She can pass her property to her children if she likes but if she does not make a will, everything reverts to the man." *Id.*

Customary laws which may have been satisfactory and justified in bygone years of close-knit, agrarian family with strong social expectations and effective societal sanctions are unsuitable in Africa today. Unfortunately, the courts are reluctant to denounce discriminatory customary rules and practices and have routinely upheld laws which by any objective standard would appear to violate even the most minimum standard of natural justice, equity, and good conscience.

IV. TAKING ON THE JUDICIARY: WIDOWS AND THEIR BATTLE FOR JUSTICE

If the widows interviewed for this article are typical, very few widows in Nigeria have attempted to make use of the formal, legal, judicial system.[119] Widows rarely challenge the legality of prevailing customary rules of inheritance or raise the question of discrimination inherent in these rules. On the contrary they have generally employed whatever version of customary law that best suited their case regardless of the overall implication on the rights of women. In other words, the customary laws are often taken as a given and within these boundaries widows attempt to raise arguments best suited for their case. For instance, actions are generally brought not in the widow's name but in the name and on behalf of their male children.[120]

Few have filed complaints with the police and fewer have attempted challenging the constitutionality of oppressive customary rules and practices. The lack of lawsuits could be attributed to several factors. In most cases where action has been brought regarding inheritance, widows have brought such actions on behalf of their minor male children and hence, have the standing under customary law to bring such action. While her action may shock in-laws and villages, it may still be perceived by some as a battle for survival and a personal battle against greedy in-laws—not a challenge to the entire society. On the other hand, by challenging the constitutionality of a given burial ritual, a widow is perceived as rejecting longstanding customary rules and the society at large. Such legal challenges are not viewed as motivated by the need for survival, but as evidence of the negative impacts of westernization. Finally, because the privileges accorded

---

119. Most widows interviewed did not even perceive legal action as an option. Perhaps this is largely a product of a culture which generally frowns at the modern, adversarial legal system inherited from the colonial powers. It is considered almost sacrilegious for a family member to drag another family member to court, yet few still express confidence in the traditional, family-centered, dispute resolution mechanism.

120. See Interview, *supra* note 3. In Agnes' case, her action brought for and on behalf of her children, in effect, challenges the rights of her sister-in-law, as a woman, to manage the family property.

to widows, such as the "right" of maintenance and allotment of residential home, are enjoyed subject to good behavior and a successful completion of the mourning rituals, a widow is constrained from challenging these rules.

Several factors prevent legal action by widows including past court decisions upholding patently discriminatory laws; insensitivity on the part of the police and the courts; the length and cost of potential lawsuits; ignorance; fear and superstition on the part of the widows themselves; and the absence of any meaningful support network.[121] One Nigerian magistrate stated:

> It is very rare to see widows bring case(s) to court. They lack courage and face social ostracism if they do it. . . . Widows normally don't have the money to hire lawyers. If they had free legal services, some of them, with little education, can take action against their in-laws. The state has free legal services but it is limited to criminal cases and not civil cases.[122]

The costs of lawsuits are prohibitive and the length of lawsuits, normally between three and ten years, serve as effective deterrence to widows who in their vulnerable state are preoccupied with the more pressing need for survival. Returning to the widows mentioned earlier, a 1988 suit brought by Agnes calling for an account of her husband's estate currently controlled by her sister-in-law is still pending.[123] The delay has not only affected Agnes' finances but has prolonged her psychological and emotional ordeal.[124] Similarly, Peace has been in court since 1992 when her husband died. According to Peace,

> When people talk about court, you don't know what it means until you are involved. I had thought that maximum, the court case would be over in one year. We are now in the third year and nothing has been done so far. We have not even started the proceedings.[125]

---

121. Interview with Dinah (not her real name), in Delta State, 18 July 1994. Women interviewed frequently cited their fear of repression by in-laws, children's safety, and fear of witchcraft. Dinah whose husband was brutally murdered said she was too afraid to bring a lawsuit. She feared that she would be killed the same way her husband was killed. With three young children to think of, Dinah said she would not contemplate a lawsuit though all property of her husband was completely taken over by her brother-in-law.
122. Interview with Mrs. Otaluka, Snr. Magistrate with the Anambra State Judiciary, Enugu, 17 July 1994.
123. *See* Interview, *supra* note 3.
124. Since 1988 when Agnes decided to bring the lawsuit, she was practically excommunicated by her in-laws and her husband's community at large. With each appearance in court, the animosity against her had grown. According to Agnes, "the decision to sue was ridiculous in our cultural setting. Everyone turned against me in the town. . . . I then decided to join my mother-in-law's name as a party to the suit. This made even the enlightened men to turn against me. Most people stopped talking to me." *Id.*
125. Interview with Peace, in Port Harcourt, 24 July 1994. Unlike most other widows, Peace

The absence of family and societal support, and lack of financial capability are also vital consideration for any widow contemplating a lawsuit. Beatrice's experience exemplifies the dilemma of most African widows, the obstacles in their quest for justice, and the inadequacy of traditional methods for resolving disputes and enforcing legal and social obligations in Africa today. Accused of killing her husband by poisoning and driven out of her matrimonial home in 1992 by her in-laws, Beatrice is still not sure as to what to do. She knows that her situation is precarious because she has no male child. Her application to be granted sole letters of administration over her husband's estate was denied.[126] The financial and social costs of a lawsuit are too high for Beatrice who is barely surviving on a meager salary. Unfortunately, every other potential avenue of recourse has proved inadequate.[127] People such as Beatrice and Peace perceive the police as being very corrupt and dishonest, and the local chiefs are grossly ineffective today.

Underlying the problems of widows is a fundamental structural problem which affects the wider African society—that is, the gradual erosion of traditional structures for conflict resolution and social security without concomitant effort to establish "modern" (western), viable alternatives. Few legal options exist for widows unhappy with their situation. Urban, educated women, widows with grown children, or widows with strong natal group support have been able to take on the system, but even then the ten-

---

was in court defending the terms of her husband's will challenged by the deceased children from previous marriages and past relationships. Under terms of the will her husband had bequeathed about half of his estate to Peace. Because she had no children with the deceased, her position was especially precarious.

Peace's remark is indeed a condemnation of the whole justice system in the country. The ordinary man in Nigeria has lost every faith in the law and in the judicial process. Today, the general belief is that justice can be bought by the highest bidder. An urgent need therefore exists for a meaningful reform of the entire legal system taking into special consideration, the plight of the poor and uneducated.

126. Interview with Beatrice (not her real name), in Enugu State, 15 July 1994. Because her children are all minors, the administrator of estates insisted that one of her brother in-laws be named a co-administrator to the estate. Under different administration of estate laws, an administrator usually determines what should happen to any given estate. *See* Administration of Estates Law, *supra,* note 100, at 66. This is a common administrative policy usually intended to protect the interest of minors but which usually has the opposite effect of placing the property beyond the reach of the children. It would appear that the policy stems from the general distrust of women. It is feared that a spouse might administer the estate and use the money in a manner prejudicial to the interest of the minor beneficiaries to the estate. While the belief may have some basis in a polygamous setting, it is unwarranted in a monogamous setting where a woman has only the interest of her own children to consider.

127. Interview, *Id.* The author was introduced to Beatrice by the president of the local women's organization. While the organization has provided free advisory services to Beatrice and was willing to take her case to court, Beatrice was still reluctant, evidently afraid of repercussions of such a lawsuit on her relationship with her in-laws and her own family.

dency has been for widows to bring action in the name of their male children. Traditional options such as appeal to the local ruler or family elders are ineffective today, buttressing the need for new avenues for protecting the basic rights of the more vulnerable members of the society. Unfortunately, the modern adjudicatory and law enforcement mechanisms in Nigeria remain underdeveloped and ill-equipped to cope with the changing times. The public/private distinction is used as a cover to prevent state involvement in situations threatening the life and welfare of widows.[128]

A. Judicial Interpretation on the Rights and Entitlements of Widows

In their interpretation and application of the laws, the courts have displayed insensitivity to the precarious position of widows. Past decisions of the courts endorsing patently discriminatory laws have discouraged present and future lawsuits by and on behalf of widows. The courts have, in the past, upheld as not repugnant to natural justice, equity or good conscience, customary laws that disinherit female children[129]; that deny widows any meaningful entitlement in the estate of a deceased husband[130]; and that deem a woman, together with all she owns, a property of her husband.[131]

---

128. Interview with Comfort, Abagana, Anambra State, 16 July 1994. Only in cases where gross physical harm occur do the police attempt to intervene. In one case where a widow, Comfort, was seriously beaten by her in-laws for refusal to perform certain traditional burial rites, the police intervened and subsequently brought an assault charge against the offenders.

   According to Comfort:

   I reported to the police on December 27, 1992. The police came and arrested them and took them to the charge office. The case was taken to court on January 1993, charging them with assault. I was well received by the police. Later the Investigation Police Officer (IPO) started changing and dropped most of the charges without giving any reason. The police were very prompt and even took me to the hospital. The case is before a magistrate court.

   Id.

   Constitutional protection against discrimination in Nigeria extends only to acts of state officials. The 1979 Constitution § 39 (2) prohibits discrimination "either expressly by, or in the practical application of, any law in force in Nigeria or any executive or administrative action of the government." It can be argued that customary laws, which provide for most of the treatment meted out to widows, form part of the laws "in force in Nigeria" and thus covered by the constitutional provision against non-discrimination. Yet in practice, the tendency has been to shield both customary and religious laws in the country from judicial scrutiny.

129. *See Ogamien v. Ogamien, supra* note 113; *Idehen v. Idehen, supra* note 113; *Agidigbi v. Agidigbi, supra* note 84.

130. *Nezianya v. Okagbue,* All Nig. L. Rep. 352 (1963).

131. *Onwuchekwa v. Onwuchekwa, supra* note 84, at 739. *See supra,* notes 85–91 and accompanying text.

In *Nezianya v. Okagbue,* the Nigerian Supreme Court held that a widow's possession of her deceased husband's property, however long it is does not make her the owner. The court found that:

> It is abundantly clear that a married woman, after the death of her husband can never under native law and custom be a stranger to her deceased husband's property; and she could not, at any time, acquire a distinct possession of her own to oust the family's rights of ownership over the property.[132]

So entrenched is the rule against inheritance by widows that it has been enforced even in the face of express wishes of the deceased to the contrary. In one such case, a Nigerian lower court judge held that the heir to an estate, a nephew of the deceased, could evict the widow from her matrimonial home for good reasons.[133]

Knowing what constitutes the "deceased husband's property" in Nigeria is crucial to an understanding of the extent of deprivation widows suffer.[134] The plight of widows would be mitigated if a woman's contributions to a

---

132. *Nezianya v. Okagbue, supra* note 130, at 352. The term "family" as used by the court, referred to the deceased male relatives. In *Nezianya,* Mary Menkiti was married to Ephraim Agha in 1895 under the Christian form of marriage. The couple had one daughter. Subsequently, the couple separated and remained so until the death of Ephraim. Mary's attempts to sell some property led to a family dispute with her in-laws challenging her right of alienation. An action in the native court was pending when Mary herself died. In her will, Mary devised the disputed land to her grand-daughters, the plaintiffs in the present action. The grand-daughters lost, since, according to the court's reasoning, Mary had no right to bequeath the property to her and Ephraim's daughter; if they had had a son, no case would have arisen.

133. *See Eze v. Eze,* Suit No. C/S 31–59 *citing* OKORO, *supra* note 51, at 93. In *Eze,* despite the deceased's instruction that his most senior wife, the defendant, should manage his estate and use the revenue derived therefrom to maintain herself and his other wives, the deceased's nephew instituted an action claiming that he was the rightful person to inherit the deceased's estate and asked for a court order to eject the defendant from the compound. The district court entered judgment for him on grounds that a wife cannot under customary law lay claim on her late husband's estate and cannot administer his estate as against male descendants and relatives. Second, that the male relative had the right to expel a wife from her late husband's compound if she committed a breach of custom that would have entitled her husband to divorce her. On appeal, the County Court confirmed the lower court's decision. On further appeal to the magistrate court, the magistrate simply reversed the expulsion order on ground that the conduct alleged against the defendant was not serious enough to warrant the sanction.

    These are decisions of the lower court (Obollo District Court and Nsukka County Court Appeal); it is unclear how a higher court would react. However given the long line of cases from the Supreme Court enforcing patently discriminatory customary laws, a higher court would most likely uphold the decision of the magistrate in *Eze.*

134. *See, e.g., Okon, supra* note 38, (denying a widow's application for a grant of letters of administration over her deceased husband's estate). In *Okon,* the High Court ordered her to surrender all the properties of the deceased husband, including those jointly owned by her, to the Administrator-General, "for the proper administration in the interest of all parties concerned in the estate of the deceased." *Id.* at 483. Though the consequential order of the High Court was eventually dismissed on further appeal, the ruling reflects a gen-

husband's estate could be quantified and severed prior to the administration of such an estate, or if a prima facie presumption of joint contribution existed in her favor. Without such a presumption, the burden of proof of such contributions as imposed by the courts in Nigeria is such that most women are unable to meet it. Courts demand documented evidence of material contributions to the estate. In the 1992 case of *Amadi v. Nwosu*[135] the defendant/appellant challenged her husband's right to sell a jointly owned matrimonial property, contending that she had contributed labor and sand to the building of the property. The High Court, the Court of Appeal, and the Supreme Court all rejected her claim for lack of evidence. According to a justice of the Supreme Court, she "[o]ught to have explained the quality and quantity of her contribution. She also ought to have given details and particulars of the contributions."[136] Given the level of female illiteracy existing in most of Africa, providing the records demanded by the Nigerian courts are not feasible for most widows.

In *Onwuchekwa v Onwuchekwa*,[137] the court ignored the very important question of joint contribution but rather accepted a husband's contention that, under the customary law prevailing in his area, a woman and all that she owns belongs to her husband. In this case, Ada Onwuchekwa (appellant) challenged her husband's (first respondent) rights to sell a piece of property which she alleged was bought and developed by their joint contribution. She asked for a declaration that the property was owned in equal shares, a cancellation of sales, or a declaration that she was entitled to half of the proceeds. Her husband contended that even if the appellant had contributed to the property she was not entitled to half of the estate because under Isikwuato customary law under which they were married, the appellant with her property is owned by her husband.[138]

Change is possible and there are hopeful signs that the courts will change as more women press for reform and as human rights norms become increasingly incorporated into the law. The 1997 decision of the Court of

---

eral failure or reluctance to acknowledge a woman's independent contributions to a deceased husband's estate.

135. *Amadi v. Nwosu,* 5 Nig. Wkly. L. Rep. 273 (1992).

136. *Id.* at 20. Because the appellant had contracted a customary law marriage with her husband, the provisions of the Married Women's Property Act (1881) were held to be inapplicable. The Act is a British Statute of General Application in force in England before 1900 and applicable to Nigeria by virtue of colonial legislation. The Act conferred on married women the capacity to hold and dispose property in their own right. See The Law Reports and the Public General Statute ch. 75 (1882). Prior to the Act, married women were minors under the law. Section 1(1) of the Act provides that a married woman "shall be capable of acquiring, holding, and disposing by will or otherwise, any real or personal property as her separate property, in the same manner as if she were a feme sole, without the intervention of any trustee." *Id.* § 1(1).

137. *Onwuchekwa, supra* note 84, at 752.

138. *Id.*

Appeal (Enugu Division) in *Mojekwu v. Mojekwu*[139] offers much hope to Nigerian women. In *Mojekwu,* the question was whether the "Oli-Ekpe" customary law of inheritancy under which the nephew of a man inherits his property where the man himself has no surviving son or brother was inconsistent with the doctrine of equity. Under the customary law as the Court of Appeal noted, "the Oli-Ekpe inherits the land, the wives of the deceased and if the deceased had daughters, he will give them in marriage. In other words, the Oli-Ekpe inherits the assets and liabilities of the deceased." In a highly celebrated decision, the Court of Appeal found the Oli-Ekpe custom to be inconsistent with equity. The judge who delivered the lead judgment said:

> Is such a custom consistent with equity and fairplay in an egalitarian society such as ours where the civilised sociology does not discriminate against women? Day after day, month after month and year after year, we hear of and read about customs which discriminate against women in this country. They are regarded as inferior to the menfolk. Why should it be so? All human beings— male and female—are born into a free world and are expected to participate freely, without any inhibition on grounds of sex; and that is constitutional. Any form of societal discrimination on grounds of sex, apart from being unconstitutional, is antithesis to a society built on the tenets of democracy which we have freely chosen as a people. We need not travel all the way to Beijing to know that some of our customs, including the Nnewi "Oli-Ekpe" custom relied upon by the appellant are not consistent with our civilised world in which we all live today, including the appellant. . . . On my part, I have no difficulty in holding that the "Oli-Ekpe" custom of Nnewi, is repugnant to natural justice, equity and good conscience.[140]

While this is a remarkable decision that could potentially change the judicial attitude to women's rights questions in Nigeria, the decision is a Court of Appeal decision and does not overrule earlier Supreme Court decisions that have upheld related customary law rules relating to widows and inheritance.

With the exception of few isolated cases therefore, the tendency has been a strong judicial leaning in favor of customary law rules[141] and a

---

139. *See Augustine Nwofor Mojekwu v. Caroline Mgbafor Okechukwu Mojekwu,* 7 NIG. WKLY. L. REP. 283 (1997).

140. *Id.* at 304–05.

141. *See, e.g., Ezejiofor v. Ezejiofor & Ezejiofor,* Suits No. E/53/77 and E/54/77 (unpublished) (case on file with author). In this case, a widow's in-laws attempted to show that she was not a lawful wife of the deceased and was therefore not a beneficiary to his estate. They submitted evidence to show that the deceased had married another wife, and that the widow had divorced the deceased prior to his death by making holes in her water-pot— an act which they said symbolized divorce under customary law. The court rejected their allegations and dismissed their case. According to the trial judge, "A marriage under the Marriage Act cannot be dissolved in a customary way. . . . I do not believe that the defen-

marked unwillingness by the courts to intervene decisively to invalidate customary laws and practices that harm widows.

B.   Administration of an Estate: The Widow's Lot

This section primarily discusses matters of administration on intestacy as it relates to widows under a statutory, monogamous marriage. Where there is a will, the will would most often name an administrator. In the absence of a will, the fundamental question becomes, who has the right to a letter of administration. Under customary law widows usually do not have much right in this regard because under most customary law rules, women are excluded in matters of administration. Under the statutory law, anybody having a beneficial interest in an estate can generally apply for grant of letters of administration over the estate in the absence of a will naming an administrator. Even in those cases where widows have certain statutory rights, the courts have interpreted rules relating to the administration of estates in a manner prejudicial to their interests.

The Nigerian administration of estate laws enjoins the courts to "have regards to the rights and interests of persons interested in the estate."[142] In granting letters of administration, however, the courts have generally denied widows exclusive letters of administration over the estate of a deceased husband and insisted on naming a husband's male relative as a co-administrator of the estate. Widows become victims of the law because anyone, including the mistresses and illegitimate children of the deceased and in-laws can file a claim to prevent her being granted the letters of administration over her husband's estate.[143]

The approach of the courts could be interpreted as a rejection of the monogamous system of marriage in favor of the polygamous system, a practice still predominant in much of Africa.[144] On the other hand, other holdings of the courts could be either calculated efforts to restrict widows'

---

dant made any holes in the pot as sign of divorce or that she ever packed out of her husband's home." *Id.* at 16.

142. The Administration (Real Estate) Law § 3, Cap. 3, for example, provides that:

when a person dies intestate possessed of real estate, the court shall in granting letters of administration, have regard to the rights and interests of persons interested in his real estate, and his heir-at-law if not one of the next of Kin, shall be equally entitled to the grant with the next of kin.

Id.

143. *See Okon, supra* note 38 (caveat filed by the deceased's sister using as a prop someone alleged to be the deceased's child from another woman); *Anowo v. Anowo* 7 Nig. Wkly. L. Rep. 58 (1991) (action brought by someone claiming to be the deceased's "other wife").

144. *See generally* Armstrong, *supra* note 22, at 23–28.

access to their deceased husbands' estates or honest attempts to make sense of the complexities in African societies today. In societies characterized by marked dichotomies between the old and the new, the traditional and the foreign, and the individual and the group, -negotiating the rights and the entitlements of individuals within extremely complex social and family relations presents a very difficult task for even the most impartial judiciary.

In general, the attitudes of the Nigerian courts toward widows have bordered on outright hostility.[145] Their decisions could be deliberate attempts to cling to a fast-disappearing past. Courts appear to rank interests of women as wives last; their primary consideration is usually for the children, however begotten, of a deceased male. This approach may be lauded by children's rights activists who condemn discrimination based on circumstances of one's birth, but the fact that a woman's life savings and property (usually considered her husband's) may be taken by a child of whom she knows nothing is highly problematic.

In *Okon v. Administrator-General* (Rivers State), the High Court ordered a widow to surrender all the properties of her deceased husband, including those jointly owned by her, to the Administrator-General, "for proper administration in the interest of all parties concerned in the estate of the deceased."[146] According to the court:

> The facts proved in the instant case were that the appellant was totally hostile to her husband's relations to the extent that she did not show up at her husband's funeral. Although she admitted that she learnt for the first time from the funeral write up of her late husband that he had a daughter, called Mabel Okon, it was apparent from her attitude towards her husband's family that she would not likely give the girl's case an unbiased consideration if she was made the administrator of the estate.[147]

Similarly in *Anowo v. Anowo,* a widow who had married her husband under the statutory law was effectively prevented from obtaining letters of administration over the deceased husband's estate by an alleged mistress who claimed to have married the deceased under customary law.[148] The

---

145. Ewelukwa, *supra* note 1. Author's own observation based on a review of several cases by the courts.

146. *See, Okon, supra* note 38, at 483. The High Court's order was subsequently dismissed on technical grounds.

147. *Id.* at 486.

148. *Anowo v. Anowo, supra* note 143, at 58. The case may be explained by the fact that the undisputed wife of the deceased did not prove that her marriage to the deceased was a statutory marriage protected by law. The Court of Appeal rejected her claim that she had married her deceased husband in a Catholic church in accordance with the Marriage Act, because she failed to produce a marriage certificate in support of her claim. A marriage under the Marriage Act, as she alleged, would have had the effect of rendering any subsequent marriage between the deceased and the plaintiff null and void. According to the

Court of Appeal awarded judgment to the alleged second wife of the deceased, saying,

> I take note that the defendants did not make any concession as would convey that they were prudently handling the affairs of the estate . . . their attitude amounts to this; "we are the wife and children of the deceased. The plaintiff, a girlfriend of the deceased is an imposter. We are entitled to keep and spend the rents collected." I do not think the lower court should have allowed that attitude to prevail.[149]

The fact that the Nigerian courts should deem a widow's attitude toward in-laws, alleged mistresses, or illegal wives and illegitimate children of the deceased sufficient grounds for denying a widow's application for a grant of letters of administration over her husband's estate is very disturbing.[150] The cases illustrate one of the many problems of African societies in transition: the disconnection between law and reality and the inability or unwillingness of those who interpret the law to deal with changing situations effectively.

V. CONCEPTUALIZING CHANGE, DECONSTRUCTING MYTHS: THE POLITICS OF REFORM

A rejection of the customary rules of inheritance today by the growing women's movement in the continent stems not so much from any intrinsic lack of rationality as from their inability to deal with changing circumstances in Africa. The impact of colonialism, urbanization, globalization, and the emergence of modern states in the continent have produced irreversible social, cultural, and economic changes in the continent which cannot be readily ignored. A major problem that faces policymakers in

---

court, "if the 1st respondent had produced evidence of a marriage under the Act, the appellant would have been unable to maintain any locus standi." *Id.*

149. *Id.* at 58.

150. In an unreported High Court decision, *Orakwue v. Orakwue,* Suit No. E/35M/80 (unpublished) (case on file with author), a widow opposed the grant of letters of administration over her husband's estate to her son and her stepson (husband's son from a first wife) and asked to be named co-administrator to her husband's estate. Her case was rejected on several grounds including her hostility to her in-laws and the fact that under customary law prevailing in her area, Umuoji in Anambra State, she could not, as a woman married under customary law have a prior right of administration over anyone including her son. According to Judge E.O. Araka, "It is my view that the respondent is incapable of seeing any good in others, and is highly cantankerous. Her son, the second appellant does not even talk to her. No court can give her any estate to manage." *Id.* at 7. The *Orakwue* court followed a previous decision of another High Court in *Aileru v. Anibi,* 20 Nɪɢ. L. Rᴇᴘ. 46 (1952), which denied certain widows the letters of administration over their husband's estate because by customary law widows cannot administer their husband's estate and because they were on hostile terms with one another.

Africa today is "how to find a solution to the problems of inheritance in a changing social and economic environment,"[151] and more broadly, how to acknowledge and incorporate the changing needs and entitlements of women, children, and other marginalized groups within the post-colonial framework. Until the policymakers and the larger society are ready to confront the structural changes rapidly occurring in the African continent, the pace of reform will remain very slow, and civil discontent will grow as each group attempts to assert its presence in the new framework.[152]

Complex inheritance issues also arise from the ability of African men to jump from one form of marriage to another:

> Men marry wives under civil law, then add a few more under custom or start the other way around and then marry a wife under general law. Although such combinations and "juggling" of wives may cause complications during the life of the man ... the real problem arises when he dies and the resources of the family have to be allocated among the various competing "groups" within the family.[153]

Serious problems therefore arise when men move from monogamous, statutory marriages to polygamous, customary law marriages or vice versa, an act which clearly constitutes the offense of bigamy under existing laws in most African states.[154] Unfortunately, the offense of bigamy exists only on

---

151. *See* Justice Anthony Gubbay, *Women's Rights,* 1 Legal Forum 9 (Mar. 1989). Gubbay however believes that there is nothing wrong with existing customary rules of inheritance. According to him:

> There is a tendency to decry the customary law as a method for the distribution of a deceased estate. It is not the customary law that is wrong but rather the relatives that abuse it, or the fact that the family has little connection to the customary law.

Id. Yet, in the same breath, the Justice added, "Despite the unsatisfactory state of the law relating to inheritance, there have been some significant changes." *Id.* at 9. Given the high incidence of abuse of existing customary law rules of inheritance, and given their inability to accommodate changing situations, it is clear that continued application of existing customary law in toto can no longer be justified.

152. The contemporary situation in Nigeria may have historical precedent. For instance, Basch attributes reform in New York marital property law in the nineteenth century to the pressing need to adapt law to structural changes in the economy:

> The world of husbands and wives in antebellum New York was far removed from the agricultural world of baron and feme in medieval England. New Yorkers lived amidst an intricate network of speculation, credit, insurance, stocks, and wages which was subject to cycles of boom and bust. ... New institutions engendered new legal questions. Could a married woman own a savings account in her own name? Could she become the beneficiary of her husband's life insurance?

Basch, *supra* note 73, at 39.

153. Stewart, *Some Points to Ponder, supra* note 23, at 28.
154. For laws criminalizing the offense of bigamy in Nigeria, see, The Criminal Code Act, Cap.

paper in most African states. In Nigeria, for instance, with the exception of a single prosecution in the early 1960s, no one has been prosecuted for the offense.[155]

Given the complex relations arising, the courts are inevitably cast into a difficult interest-balancing role. Several interests exist: the interest of the legal wife of a monogamous, statutory union, the interest of the legitimate children of such marriage, the interest of the other "wives" and mistresses of a man who had previously contracted a monogamous marriage, the interest of the various wives in a polygamous, customary law marriage, the interest of the many children born in a polygamous, customary law marriage, and the interest of the illegitimate children of the deceased. Other second-tier interests would include those of the parents, brothers, and sisters of a man. So complex is the web of relationships and interests that may exist with regard to a single estate that several calls have been made for legislation to deal with the problem.

Being preoccupied with "more important" issues of state craft, the fragile Nigerian state has found little time or resources to invest in needed reform. Being inherently patriarchal, a genuine commitment towards improving women's lives on the part of the Nigerian government is found to be lacking. Formal laws, have in the past proved unsuccessful in bringing about desired changes. In the absence of effective enforcement, and given widespread involvement of state officials in the very practices the laws seek to abolish, justice for women has been hard to achieve.

A.   The Politics of Reform

With growing awareness of human rights in Africa, the necessity and legality of previously accepted customary rules and practices are increasingly contested, if not in court, then in general public discourses. A growing women's movement in the continent and improved information network have been effective in galvanizing and strengthening internal struggles for women's rights in many African countries. Despite recent gains in the strug-

---

42; Marriage Act of 1958, Cap. 115. *See also* The Matrimonial Causes Decree, 1970 (condemning bigamy). A popular criticism of these laws is that they are imports from the colonial powers and hence at odds with social practice. The problem though is that only men get to decide what aspects of western ideas and culture to import into Africa.

155. In *Regina v. Princewell*, N. Reg. Nig. L. Rep. 54 (1963), the court held that a person who, being a party to a subsisting potentially polygamous marriage, went through a monogamous marriage ceremony with a third party cannot be convicted under the provisions of the Criminal Code § 370, which makes it a felony to contract a marriage during the subsistence of a valid monogamous marriage. The author's research has not revealed any other prosecutions.

gle by women, a majority of African women remain disadvantaged and yet remain reluctant to take on the entire society by contesting the legality of widely accepted social practices—a problem complicated by the apparent division between African women on the very important question of the place of custom in Africa today. Given that women have been both the victims and perpetrators of the various customary law rules prejudicial to their interest, it must be accepted that an absolute consensus on the subject may never be found.

Regarding the status of widows, a marked variation exists in Nigeria between the views of the older women who, viewing themselves as the custodians of culture, insist on the strict observance of customary widowhood practices and those of the younger, educated, urban women who, seeing little relevance in the maintenance of some of these practices, plead for a relaxation of the rules. Indeed one local women's leader in one of the towns, (who is the eldest woman in her town), saw nothing wrong with the custom as it is. According to her, "I met it as it is. It is good as it is. If the town agrees to change it, I have no objection but I will not be the one to propose change."[156]

An effective reform strategy would require a more concerted effort by the women themselves, a definition of the real issues at stake, of the desired goals and of the best means for achieving these goals. Any attempt to alienate any class of women is bound to yield unfortunate results. It is of utmost importance that the voices of the women most affected by the problem be heard and the campaigns for reform strategized in a manner that best reflects their desires. Rash, uninformed presumptions on the part of the elite African women and western women have often backfired and most often do not address the needs of the rural women.

The task of reforming entrenched customary laws and practices is not one that African women can undertake alone. Societal attitudes must be changed, myths deconstructed, and new ideologies and frames of reference established. This must take place in the context of a commitment towards the removal of structural and institutional barriers that have oppressed

---

156. Interview with Omu, in Illah, Delta State, 13 July 1994. The author found a certain vindictiveness evident in the discourse. Because the older women have gone through some of these cultural requirements, they insist that everyone must also suffer the same fate. In the few cases where local laws have been passed amending some customary practice, women have been known to protest the change. In the words of one traditional ruler,

> There is need for changes. It is the women who are against the women-fold. The Umu Ada has gone through these and want everyone to go through the same. The women do not want change. Often it is women who object to change.

Id. Every woman born into a lineage is referred to as "Nwa Ada" (singular). The totality of the women born to a lineage is referred to as "Umu Adi" (plural). Author's personal knowledge.

African women. A study of social reform in other countries indicates that effective reform demands an integrated societal involvement requiring the participation of a cross-section of the society.[157] Therefore, reformers must challenge at the onset the general apathy with which the problem of widows is met, and address systematic structural and institutional biases against African women.

Finally, reform often comes at a cost. In the case of widows, the cost of abolishing longstanding cultural practices must be taken into account and means sought to protect women from the immediate effects of reform. For instance, reformers may anticipate that a rejection of traditional practices considered harmful to women may also result in a removal, by the society, of other traditional, informal protection accorded to widows.

B. The Indispensable Enemy: The Role of Traditional Rulers in Law Reforms[158]

In localities where serious changes have occurred, they have come about as a result of efforts of local women, sometimes acting with the support of the newly emerging nongovernmental organizations in the country, influences from neighboring localities, and the willingness of traditional rulers and village elders to allow for change.[159] In a number of towns that the author

---

157. Of reform efforts against domestic violence in the United States in the nineteenth century, Pleck notes:

> In all the reform periods, small organizations and dedicated individuals—ministers, millionaires, physicians, temperance activist, and women's liberationists—have made family violence a social issue that demanded public attention. Some have tried to pass legislation against domestic violence; others have founded institutions. . . . All these activists were concerned about alleviating human suffering. Some were directly involved with the victims of the abuse, while for others domestic violence was an abstract, even philosophical issue.

PLECK, *supra* note 22, at 5.

158. Beyond the structures set up by the modern state, for example, such as the legislature, executive, and judiciary, there exists at the grassroots level, chiefs with jurisdiction over clusters of villages or towns. This group of local leaders is what the author refers to as the traditional rulers. Their mandate is often not spelled out in any written form but reflects consensus within a given village or town. Only in recent times are some towns beginning to write up constitutions to guide their local affairs.

159. The author has personally witnessed numerous changes in cultural practices and attitudes towards widows in her home village in Nigeria. These include a relaxation of the requirement for black mourning clothes and an expansion of a widow's personal liberty and freedom of movement. While it was once mandatory that a widow remain in the village for at least one month following the burial of her husband, today the village elders understand that working women residing in towns must return to work or face dismissal. This concession is made for government workers only; women who are private entrepreneurs

investigated, traditional rulers have begun the process of reform. In Abagana and Asaba, towns in Anambra and Delta States respectively, committees have been set up to investigate the plight of widows. In another town, Illah, for instance, the period of a widow's solitary confinement in an outdoor hut was reduced by the villagers from three months to one month, and fresh initiatives exist to reduce it to seven days as is the practice in neighboring towns.[160] The precise mode of decisionmaking in this town is not known to this author. Often, this involves a period of negotiations, and usually a consensus is sought. Other times a final decision is made by the traditional ruler and his ruling cabinet. In Enugwu-Ukwu, a town in Anambra State, the mourning period of seven native weeks (twenty-eight days) has been reduced to three native weeks (twelve days) with further talks by the traditional ruler to have it reduced to seven days.[161] According to the ruler, it would then become an offense for anyone to go beyond the prescribed period. In this town, a committee has been set up to look into issues of burial ceremonies, widowhood, and marriage ceremonies.[162]

In Abua, Rivers State, the mourning period now lasts for only four days and hair shaving is not required. When Mary's husband died in 1994, she was able to move around to greet people but could not go to the burying site. Her hair was not shaved, though her first daughter was required to undergo a river bath accompanied by three women. The entire burial ceremony lasted for only four days. In Cross River State, the practice of shaving a widow's hair has long been discarded as unnecessary and humiliating.[163]

Customs have changed, however, only when a traditional ruler was insistent on change. To some extent therefore, customary law reflects the individual dictates of the traditional ruler and his council of elders. Rules which could be changed overnight have often remained, sustained by various myths and superstitious beliefs. Reform is less of a problem when a

---

or rural dwellers are usually not so lucky. There was a time when a widow had to wear black mourning clothes and black alone, but today white clothing is allowed. What is more, standards governing the quality and texture of the mourning clothes have been relaxed. While widows were once expected to sit and sleep on the floor during the mourning period, now it is not uncommon to find women sitting on chairs and sleeping on mattresses.

What is interesting is that some of these changes occurred without much contestation. Sometimes all that was necessary was one courageous woman to take the first step. It has been the author's experience that women's groups at the village level have also afforded women a forum in which to voice their complaints, challenge accepted norms, and prescribe alternative modes of conduct. The problem is that in a traditional society like the author's village, excessive innovation on the part of a woman can be seen as a sign of her waywardness, something no woman wants to be accused of.

160. Interviews with women and home ruling elders, July 1994.
161. Interview with *Igwe*, Enugwuukwu, 18 July 1994.
162. *Id.*
163. Information gathered in the course of the interview, July 1994.

given local chief is sympathetic to the cause of women and is willing to bring about desired change.

Unfortunately, in most cases the opinions of local rulers can and do often operate as a restraint on reform.[164] Often, a wide public outcry for change is also instrumental in the reform of customary practices. However, in cases where the public is clearly divided, the ruling elders make the decisions. Given the general exclusion of women from traditional decision-making bodies, customary laws have characteristically reflected the male viewpoint.[165] Although much has been said of the democratic principles that prevailed in many precolonial African societies, Nigerian women have for the most part been denied active participation in decisionmaking processes. In the absence of any democratic processes at the village level, local chiefs, free of any state oversight, determine the fate of individuals within their jurisdiction. Herein lies the dilemma of social reformers that while traditional rulers are necessary instruments for reform, they can and do pose the greatest obstacles to reform.

Left to the absolute discretion of local chiefs and in the absence of broad guidelines from the state, meaningful protection of the rights of widows cannot be realized. In matters affecting the fundamental rights of its citizens, the state must intervene decisively to ensure meaningful reforms across the board. Working in conjunction with the various traditional rulers, it is possible for the state to promote rights awareness and initiate meaningful reform without resorting to forceful means which may antagonize and alienate the traditional rulers.

At the formal level, the Nigerian government would appear to have done much to improve the lot of women generally. Governmental efforts have included the organization of national conferences to address the plight of women and children, as well as the passage of laws establishing such bodies as the National Commission on Women.[166] No federal laws, however, address fundamental gender inequalities, confer specific rights on widows, or abolish harmful customary practices. Successive recommendations for change by Nigerian women's groups have also generally been ignored.[167]

---

164. Author's reflection and conclusion.
165. Author's conclusion. Women are increasingly consulted in issues affecting their welfare but the final decision is most often made by the traditional ruler.
166. In 1989, for example, the Federal Ministry of Justice convened a National Conference on Better Protection for Women and Children held at Owerri, 24–26 Oct. 1989 (National Conference) to address the plight of women, including widows. A Decree was also passed in 1989 creating the Better Life for Rural Women Program aimed at eradicating ignorance, poverty, and disease at the rural level. In 1993, the government established the National Commission on Women (NOW).
167. For instance, a Communique issued at the 1989 National Conference on Better Protection for Women and Children recommended that "inhuman widowhood rites and other

C. Conceptualizing Change

Cultures and traditions are not static but change as circumstances and situations change. Customs are made by people and it is people who can change them. They are fashioned to suit prevailing socioeconomic order and it is on this basis that women feel that certain aspects of customary law are simply obsolete and out of step with the situation in Zimbabwe today.[168]

Factors that have proved conducive for change include a strong local women's voice, influences from more progressive neighboring towns, the presence of a strong, "progressive" traditional ruler, and the existence of a general consensus on the need for new laws to meet with changing times.

Reforms which focus less on formal laws and which embrace and involve the larger society would have a more lasting effect. The need to challenge and thereby change entrenched cultural prejudices against women is great in most African countries. As Justice Gubbay notes with respect to Zimbabwe:

> There is still a need for further reform, perhaps not so much of the law but of attitudes towards women. . . . we still find outmoded attitudes by virtue of which women attending the theater or going out for an evening of entertainment are treated as prostitutes and rounded up like errant cattle. . . . And all women must try and re-educate society as to their real position, rights and entitlements.[169]

Past attempts by the Nigerian government to change long-standing customs by means of abrupt legislation have been largely unsuccessful and are lasting reminders of limits of bare legislation to bring about desired social behavior.[170] A lack of meaningful and committed enforcement has pre-

---

customary practices which debase womanhood should be prohibited," and called for the "reform [of the] customary laws on intestacy which patently discriminate against women." Thirteen years after the conference, the Nigerian government has yet to take effective steps towards implementing any aspect of the recommendations. *See* Communique of the National Seminar on Women and Children, arts. 9 & 14.

168. Speech delivered by the Acting Chief Justice Gubbay at the opening ceremony of the Association of Women of Zimbabwe's Annual Conference 1988, Gubbay, *supra* note 151, at 3.

169. *Id.* at 9.

170. Such laws include, the Abolition of the Osu System Law, 1956, Cap. 1: Laws of Eastern Nigeria which attempted to abolish the caste system in Eastern Nigeria; the Limitation of Dowry Law, Cap. 76, Laws of Eastern Nigeria, 1963; and the Age of Marriage Law, 1956, Cap. 6, Laws of Eastern Nigeria, 1963 which fixed the age of marriage at sixteen. The Osu system stigmatizes a person who is a slave or was symbolically sacrificed to an idol or the descendants of such person and makes them subject to social stigma, legal, and social disability. The Abolition of Osu System Law attempted to correct the injustice by abolishing the system. The law made it an offense to discriminate against anyone on the basis of the Osu status and provides that "all persons who were previously

vented the realization of the goals of such legislation.[171] Moreover, radical changes have the propensity to disrupt the actual basis of the society and further distance the civilian population from the state.[172] It may be that Nigerian society is already in such disarray that nothing short of a revolution can correct past injustices and bring about meaningful change in the lives and experiences of women in Nigeria.

It is necessary that the government create a conducive environment for such a change. This would include: paying particular attention to financial, administrative, and procedural barriers women encounter in their search for justice; exposing the abuses that occur at home; and recognizing the treatment of widows as a form of violence against women. Delays in the administration of estates and delays in court proceedings is a major concern which could be addressed by establishing family courts dealing only with family law issues. Special training of legal, judicial, and administrative personnel working for the court is important. The cost of lawsuits could be addressed by expediting legal action and providing free legal services for indigent widows. In this respect, newly emerging women's and human rights groups in Nigeria could be most useful; these groups could help women understand their legal rights and work through the system. Without such moral and financial support, it is unlikely that many widows would attempt to use the new system.

---

regarded as Osu are free from the handicap of that status, and are able to exercise all the rights and privileges of other members of the community." *See* Nwogugu, *supra* note 31, at 4.

Nwogugu notes with regard to the Osu System Law in Nigeria that "despite its altruistic motive, this piece of legislation has failed to alter the attitude of the people in the areas where the Osu system existed." *Id.* at 50.

171. Perhaps legislation to change cultural practices has been unsuccessful because of the reluctance of state officials to enforce these laws. Thus, despite the laws which make it an offense to discriminate on the basis of the Osu status or to marry an under-aged girl, virtually no one has been charged for violating these laws.

172. Stewart, *Coping with the Muddle, supra* note 23, at 14, cautions that:

If the form which any change takes is such as significantly to alter the way in which people view succession and the rights and obligation that flow from it, then it is more than possible that they will simply ignore the formal procedures which should be followed in the distribution of an estate. This will mean that they will revert to the old customary law which could further mean that they lose confidence in the legal system itself, and will thus be beyond state assistance in pursuing their rights.

Id.

Unfortunately, some African states have used this argument to justify their inactivity in the realm of legal reform. Moreover, perhaps African women have already lost faith in the legal system, and Stewart's fears are meaningless to them and serve only to protect or preserve viewpoint.

D. Legal Reform

Legal reforms and judicial decisions in other national jurisdictions in Africa can be drawn on to guide future reforms in Nigeria. In Zimbabwe, for instance, the Deceased Person Family Maintenance Act[173] and the Legal Age of Majority Act, 1982,[174] are laws which have changed the condition of women in the country. In a recent decision, the Supreme Court of Zimbabwe went a step further toward gender equality by recognizing the right of daughters to inherit their father's property on the same footing as sons. In *Chihowa v. Mangwende*,[175] the question arose as to the right of a daughter who is the eldest child of a deceased to be appointed the intestate heiress to the father's estate. The father was survived by a wife, with whom he had no children, and two daughters but no son. Relying on provisions of the Legal Age of Majority Act 1982, the Supreme Court held that "now the eldest daughter of a father who dies intestate can take the lot but not for herself only but for herself and her late father's dependants."[176] According to the court, there is nothing in the wording of subsection (3) of Section 3 of Act 15 of 1982 which remotely suggests that "for the purposes of inheritance, a woman can still be regarded as a minor."[177]

---

173. The Deceased Persons Family Maintenance Act of 1978 as amended by Act 21 of 1987 addresses, to a great extent, the important problems widows face on the death of a spouse: that of maintenance and the looting of property by in-laws. Regarding the question of maintenance, the Act makes provision for a widow to apply for maintenance from the estate of a deceased. Section 7 of the Act enjoins the court making the award to have regard to such factors as: the age of the applicant and the duration of the marriage to the deceased; the contributions made by the applicant to the welfare of the family of the deceased, including any contributions made by looking after the home or caring for the family; and the provisions the applicant might have reasonably expected to receive if the marriage instead of being terminated by decree of divorce had been terminated by a death. The Act is impressive in its attempt to challenge previously accepted societal practices. Much would depend on its effective enforcement.

174. The Legal Age of Majority Act § 3(1)(1982) simply states that "a person shall attain the legal age of majority on attaining eighteen years of age," but is made to apply to any law including customary law. *Id.* §§ 3(1), 3(3). This short piece of legislation has had a wide ranging impact on the Zimbabwean society. The courts in Zimbabwe have relied on it to nullify entrenched customary laws and practices which discriminate against women or seek to treat them as perpetual minors. In *Katekwe v. Muchabiwa* (Supreme Court Judgment No. 87/84), the court held that an African father/guardian has lost the right under customary law to sue for damages for the seduction of a daughter who has attained the age of eighteen years at the time of the seduction.

175. *Chihowa v. Mangwende,* 1 Zimb. L. Rep. 228 (5)(1987).

176. *Id.* While the *Chihowa* decision has no direct bearing on the rights of widows, it is nonetheless a major step towards dismantling gender stereotypes and customary disabilities experienced by women in Africa. In a later case the same court has attempted to narrow its ruling and to limit the idea of a female heir to those situations in which a deceased has no surviving son. In *Vareta v. Vareta,* S-126-90, the court held that in deciding who should be appointed heir to a deceased's estate, "preference should be given in terms of the customary law to the eldest male child of the deceased." *See* Julie Stewart, *Women, Law and Development,* 3 LEGAL FORUM 5 (1991); Masongo, *supra* note 60, at 55.

177. *See* Gubbay, *supra* note 152.

To achieve concrete legal reform, changes must be made in all areas of the law, starting with the Constitution. While this may be perceived as counter-productive in the sense that it would further subject women to the coercive influences of the state, in the African context, national constitutions, though imperfect, have sometimes provided African women with a legal basis for challenging traditional biases against them. Therefore, it is particularly important that the Nigerian Constitution clearly addresses the continuing tension between protected rights and preserved cultures and indicate which is to have priority in the event of a conflict.

The Constitution of the Republic of Uganda, 1995, may serve as a useful guide in this respect. The Constitution declares as part of the national objectives and directive principles of state policy that "cultural and customary values which are consistent with fundamental rights and freedoms, human dignity, democracy, and with the Constitution may be developed and incorporated in aspects of Ugandan life."[178] More emphatically, the Constitution as part of its fundamental rights provision provides that "women shall have the right to affirmative action for the purpose of redressing the imbalances created by history, tradition or custom."[179] Furthermore, "laws, cultures, customs or traditions which are against the dignity, welfare or interest of women or which undermine their status, are prohibited by this Constitution."[180]

At a more general level, the need exists for rules which specifically address the degrading burial practices and create a more humane property regime for widows. Regarding burial rituals, laws abolishing some of the dangerous practices are what is needed.

Such laws will be in line with the Communique of the National Seminar on Women and Children issued in 1989 following the conclusion of the National Conference on Better Protection for Women and Children.[181] The Communique had recommended that "inhumane widowhood rites and other practices which debase womanhood should be prohibited,"[182] and pointed to the "need to reform customary law on intestacy which patently discriminate against women."[183]

Deciding what constitutes "inhuman widowhood rites" would undoubt-

---

178. *See* National Objectives and Directive Principles of State Policy, art. XXIV, Constitution of the Republic of Uganda, 1995.

179. Constitution of the Republic of Uganda § 33 (5), 1995.

180. *Id.* § 33(6). The Uganda Constitution, if taken seriously, will be far reaching in its scope and should offer some hope to women in Uganda. Much will however depend on the willingness and ability of the government to bring about meaningful change.

181. *See* WOMEN AND CHILDREN UNDER NIGERIAN LAW xiii (Awa Kalu & Yemi Osibanjo eds.). The National Conference was held at Owerri 24–26 Oct. 1989.

182. *Id.* at xiv.

183. *Id.*

edly be a subjective decision. Practices such as hair shaving, solitary confinement for extended periods of time, sleeping on bare floors, or under the rain, must be rethought in light of emerging human rights norms including the provisions of the African Charter on Human and People's Rights. This Charter espouses the principles of individual liberty, equality and non-discrimination.[184] The state could work with the Council of Chiefs to change attitudes and challenge the basis for widowhood rites, and the most progressive local rules can bring pressure on their more conservative peers.

To create a more humane property regime for women, a two-tier reform approach could be adopted under which the more manageable issues are dealt with first. At one level would be laws addressing the endemic problem of looting of property by in-laws, the nature of properties to be governed by customary rules of intestacy, and the nature and extent of interest a widow should have in a husband's estate. The looting of a deceased's property should be criminalized by a law along the same lines as Section 8 of the Deceased Property Family Maintenance Act in Zimbabwe. The Zimbabwean Maintenance Act declares "the right of surviving spouse and/or any child of the deceased to remain in occupation of any immovable property that the deceased was ordinarily occupying before his death,"[185] "confirms the right of such persons to use the tools, implements, household goods and effects and vehicles used by the deceased in relation to the immovable property," and makes it a criminal offense punishable by a fine of up to $2000 or two years imprisonment, to act with the intention of depriving the surviving wife or children of the deceased of this right.[186] Critics may view such a law as superfluous given that the Nigerian Criminal Code and indeed the criminal codes of most African states already criminalize stealing which, in effect, is what the looting of a deceased property amounts to. A specific provision declaring state's intent to protect widows in this regard and imposing stiff penalties for violation may, however, send a message to the general public and possibly make the law enforcement officials more willing to intervene in a matter which has characteristically been defined as a "private family matter."

A law creating a prima facie presumption of a wife's contribution in a husband's estate is needed.[187] Stewart suggests "tacit Universal Partnerships" as grounds on which a widow may make a claim on a deceased husband's property. According to her:

---

184. *See* Stewart, *Coping with the Muddle, supra* note 23, at 16.
185. *Id.*
186. *Id.*
187. *See* Zimbabwe's Deceased Family Maintenance Act § 7, at 39 of 1978 as amended by Act 21 of 1987.

It is a fairly common phenomenon that both spouses contribute financially to purchase of a house or other capital items in the estate, yet these are often registered in the name of, or appear to be the property of the husband. If the surviving spouse is able to successfully establish a tacit universal partnership, then even before the distribution of the estate is commenced the surviving spouse will have protected what is theirs by right.[188]

Defining which properties will be governed by customary rules of inheritance will require intense negotiation and progressive change. As a preliminary concession to the traditional viewpoint and as a matter of practical necessity, certain properties should be excluded from any new law recognizing the rights of widows in a husband's estate. This would include assets acquired by way of inheritance, assets acquired in terms of any custom and intended to be held personally in accordance with such custom, and property of sentimental value.

Other jurisdictions have adopted a similar approach. The Ghanian Law Reform Commission considered reforming the rules of intestate succession and invited the public to express views on several proposals, including proposals that a new norm recognizing a widow's inheritance right in a husband's estate, "should solely apply to the property purchased by the intestate. They should not apply to family, clan, tribal or communal property, or to any position in these institutions."[189] Moreover,

> if the deceased leaves a spouse and/or children, then all the family movable property purchased by the deceased, such as a refrigerator, a television set, a radio, furniture, knick-knacks, earthenware, kitchenware, books, etc, all this should go to the surviving spouse and to the children (if any) in absolutely equal parts.[190]

This very modest proposal presumably will be attacked by both radical women's groups and by traditionalists in Nigeria. The position can, however, be defended as a middle ground that takes into account the complexities of African society with its growing urbanization and industrialization on the one hand, and a continuing emphasis on clan and kinship network on the other. A more radical reform Justice Gubbay of Zimbabwe warned, "might alienate the more traditional and conservative elements in the society" and backfire on the very women we are seeking to protect.[191] This proposal must be seen as a first step towards a gradual, incremental recognition of the rights of widows, and hence can be changed over time. Such a proposal is

---

188. Stewart, *Coping with the Muddle, supra* note 23, at 14.
189. *See* CUTRUFELLI, *supra* note 19, at 66.
190. *Id. See generally* provisions of Zimbabwe's Matrimonial Causes Act, 1985 (No. 33 of 1985) §§ 7–11 relating to the division of assets and maintenance in the event of divorce.
191. *See* Gubbay, *supra* note 152, at 8–9.

not meant to be static but must be left open to progressive review in light of changing times.

At another level of the two-tier reform approach, attempts must be made to address the complex but very important question of prioritization in the protection of the widows. Should monogamous marriages enjoy greater protection or should all widows be similarly protected regardless of the nature of marriage? Any reform must be able to address a number of possible marital arrangements. For example, a man may first contract a monogamous statutory marriage and subsequently enter into other customary marriages in a manner clearly constituting the offense of bigamy. Alternatively, he may first contract a customary law marriage and subsequently enter into a statutory marriage with another woman. Finally, he may enter into several polygamous, customary law marriages.

As a guiding principle, any new law must attempt to meet the legitimate expectations of the parties involved. Based on this principle, the final scenario poses the least problem. Thus where all wives of a deceased are similarly situated, having all contracted a potentially polygamous customary marriage, any law recognizing a widow's right to intestate succession should treat all such widows alike.[192] The first two however pose problems of a more serious type. How are the interests of widows married under different systems of law and at different times to one man protected? Up until now, two views have been expressed on the question.

The first view, advanced by Lovemore Madhuku, calls for a uniform marriage law that treats all widows alike, regardless of the nature of marriage each contracted with the husband. This view in effect calls for a marriage regime under which the monogamous marriage system is made inconsequential. Arguing that the law has no business intervening in the "intricacies of love and lovemaking," Madhuku calls for a uniform regime under which all widows are treated equally. According to him, "[T]here are only two extremes available: either outlaw customary law for all purposes (which is unacceptable) or treat widows equally (which is better!)."[193]

Madhuku cited *Mujawo v. Chogugudza,* in which a widow who had contracted a customary marriage with her deceased husband was denied any interest in his estate, the court favoring the second wife who married the deceased under the civil law. According to Madhuku:

---

192. The argument for this is that in the case of lawful polygamous marriages, there are no surprises and hence, there will be no unmet expectations. Having all contracted potentially polygamous marriage, the different women could not have expected to be accorded the status of an only wife. The first wife is taken to have understood that her husband could take more wives and the last wife contracted the marriage knowing the man to have been married before.

193. Lovemore Madhuku, *Government White Paper Again: A Reply to a Reply,* 6 Legal Forum 20, 24 (1994).

Once a woman is validly married according to customary law, which the legal system allows, it is to be unacceptably technical and elitist to describe such a woman as a "mistress." There can be no justification for preferring one married according to civil rites other than the assertion that she has taken the trouble to register her marriage.[194]

The second view, advanced by Ncube, also of the University of Zimbabwe, calls for the preservation of monogamy and thus, a regime under which a wife of a monogamous marriage is protected and ranked in priority over "other wives" of a deceased. According to Ncube, "a marriage is either civil and monogamous or it is customary and potentially polygamous. One cannot have his cake and eat it too."[195] Ncube also calls for a regime that completely denies any form of legal recognition to the system of "mistress wives." According to him, "the average woman who contracts a civil marriage does so under the belief that it is monogamous as provided by law. Surely she is entitled, as long as she remains married to that man, to all the law's protection of the essential character of her marriage."[196] According to Ncube:

> To accept Madhuku's argument would make nonsense of the institution of civil marriage. According to his argument a marriage would be civil and monogamous only to the extent that the husband wishes it to be so. The husband could unilaterally and secretly opt out of its monogamous nature. The wife might then discover, after the death of her husband, that she is not the only recognized widow but that there are several other "widows" with their own children who would be entitled to an inheritance share in the estate. Civil marriages would thereby be reduced to a disreputable hide and seek game with no fixed rules, in which the goal posts constantly change. The logical conclusion of Madhuku's argument would be the acceptance of the ridiculous notion that our law should not recognize the offence of bigamy.[197]

Ncube's suggestion is that all the "mistress wives" be disregarded, but the innocent children involved be allowed to claim maintenance from the deceased's estate.

Ncube's arguments are indeed very compelling. Despite the persistence of polygamy in Africa, the truth is that a growing number of people contract monogamous, statutory marriages with the expectation to avail themselves

---

194. *Id.* at 24. When a man marries under customary law and subsequently contracts a civil law marriage, it would be most unfair and inequitable to disregard the earlier marriage in the favor of the subsequent one simply because the latter was a registered statutory marriage. The important question is what was the legitimate expectation of the two women involved.

195. Ncube, *White Paper, supra* note 26, at 13.

196. *Id.*

197. *Id.*

of legal protection afforded such marriages.[198] In such cases, it is necessary that the law accords them the protection promised. Ncube however envisages only situations where a civil law marriage predates a customary law marriage, which is not always the case.

Taking into consideration the degree to which polygamy exists, there are three options that could be employed:

1.   A concerted effort towards the enforcement of existing laws;
2.   Treat all wives of a deceased alike thus rendering the monogamous marriage system inconsequential; or
3.   Create a complex, dual regime which allows both marriage systems to operate thus reflecting the complexities of post-colonial social structures and arrangements in Africa.

On the latter, Madhuku rightly notes that "the strongest argument against abolishing polygamy remains the submission that it is too intricate a matter for the intervention of the law at this stage."[199]

In many African societies, a wide range of possibilities exist between the old and the new and between individual autonomy and group solidarity. A choice must be made, at least in the short term, between laws which are fair and just, and laws which may not achieve the highest degree of equality or fairness. These laws, nonetheless, minimize conflicts, make for peaceful coexistence and attempt to placate the different competing interests in the society.

Nigerian widows may resort to remedies in the international human rights arena, but to what extent does international law address the needs of women around the world, and more concretely, to what extent does the international regime offer relief to a majority of women in the Third World? At the normative level, the international human rights regime appears to offer some hope. The Convention on the Elimination of All Forms of Discrimination Against Women expressly condemns all forms of discrimination against women and enjoins state parties to "take in all fields, in particular in the political, social, economic and cultural field, all appropriate measures, including legislation, to ensure the full development and advancement of women."[200] Furthermore, CEDAW obliges state parties to take all appropriate measures "to modify the social and cultural patterns of conduct of men and women, with a view to achieving the elimination of

---

198. Author's personal knowledge.
199. Madhuku, *supra* note 193, at 21. In view of the fact that many women today willingly contract polygamous marriage, how can the law intervene? Perhaps the biggest problem posed in the enforcement of bigamy laws is the general lack of registration of marriages. Marriages are simply not registered, making it difficult to trace offenders. With the high level of illiteracy in Africa, a majority of the population is probably not even aware of any legal requirement to register marriages.
200. *See* CEDAW, *supra* note 11, art. 3.

prejudices and customary and all other practices which are based on the idea of the inferiority or the superiority of either of the sexes"[201] and to adopt "temporary special measures aimed at accelerating de facto equality between men and women."[202]

The distinction on the basis of sex in the customary laws on inheritance constitutes discrimination under international law,[203] while the degrading burial rituals arguably come under the rubrics of "harmful traditional practices" already condemned by the Committee on the Elimination of Discrimination Against Women (the Committee).

Translating the normative prescriptions of CEDAW into practical realities for widows would be almost impossible due to fundamental institutional and enforcement problems in the regime. Persuading the Committee to characterize the experiences of widows as a serious violation of human rights may prove to be a difficult task. Moreover, since CEDAW provides no avenue for individual complaints, women could only hope the state report required under CEDAW would make references to their particular plight.[204] Finally, the possibility that their government may have made a reservation, on cultural and religious grounds to key provisions of the Convention is real and remains one of the main obstacles to the realization of women's human rights under the international human rights regime.[205]

VI. CONCLUSION

Widows have continued to suffer in most African societies. The multiplicity of cultures and the gendered nature of existing cultures have prevented effective reform and spirited advocacy for change.

The intractable social and political problems of the African states—the constant change in governments, the lack of democratic processes, and the

---

201. *Id.* art. 5 (a).
202. *Id.* art. 4.
203. *Id.* art. 2.
204. *Id.* art 18 (1), under this article state parties undertake to: "Submit to the Secretary-General of the United Nations, for consideration by the Committee, a report on the legislative, judicial, administrative or other measures which they have adopted to give effect to the provisions of the present Convention."

The Committee is expected only to "make suggestions and general recommendations based on the examination of reports and information received from the State Parties." For more on CEDAW see generally Noreen Burrow, *The 1979 Convention on the Elimination of All Forms of Discrimination Against Women*, 32 Neth. Int'l L. Rev. 419–60 (1985); Andrew Byrnes, *The "Other" Human Rights Treaty Body: The Work of the Committee on the Elimination of Discrimination Against Women*, 14 Yale J. Int'l L. 1 (1989).

205. See generally, Belinda Clark, *The Vienna Convention Reservation Regime and the Convention on Discrimination Against Women*, 85 Am. J. Int'l L. 281 (1991).

absence of women in major decisionmaking bodies have also prevented meaningful discussions on the plight and conditions of women.

Despite the structural barriers to the advancement of women in the continent, much still depends on women themselves and emerging women's human rights organizations. As Gubbay observes:

> Law does not implement itself. Until individuals, and in this case women, seek the remedies and solutions it provides, a law is virtually useless. If women continue to accept passively the old and inequitable ways of distributing estates and do not seek the right to be considered as an heir then the changes in the law have been for nought.[206]

The view of the judge is somewhat echoed by another traditional ruler in Nigeria:

> Women are not as aggressive in the pursuit of change as we would have thought. Maybe it is because of traditional norms that women do not speak out or because they are not really oppressed. Sometime ago men thought of revising the whole thing concerning the burial rites. The men were intent on changing it until women rejected the idea of revision.[207]

Overcoming centuries of myths, superstitious beliefs, and male-shaped ideology is not an easy task. Stewart suggests "vigorous use of a range of complementary remedies."[208] Such remedies could include an increased use of the international human rights mechanisms and perhaps a more aggressive stance by the women themselves. Women activists must first characterize many of the burial rituals imposed on widows as a form of violence against women.

Emerging human rights and women's rights organizations in Nigeria must seek to address factors that have traditionally prevented the contestation of the legality of existing laws by women such as the cost of lawsuits, the absence of support groups, and advisory services and shelters for women. Ideally, human rights organizations, currently located in the big cities, should avail their services to grassroots, rural women by embarking on mass rights awareness education and providing free legal advice. Very few organizations currently engage in such grassroots education and the concept of shelter for abused women is almost unknown in Nigeria. In this respect, emerging women's organizations in the country have much to learn from their counterparts in South Africa.

Women's rights organizers must also attempt to combat the entrenched reluctance or fear of using the legal system thereby placing the system in the hands of the women who need it most. Bringing "test cases" to court would

---

206. *See* Gubbay, *supra* note 152, at 9.
207. Interview, *supra* note 68.
208. Stewart, *Coping with the Muddle, supra* note 23, at 16.

be one way of opening the debate and challenging previously held assumptions about the rights and welfare of widows in the society.

It is also important that women's rights groups question the interpretation of customary laws by those in positions of authority. Surely the time has come for women's voices to be heard on what constitutes customary law. Surely a wiser, more progressive approach would be a careful evaluation of customs with a view to expunging inhuman, degrading, and discriminatory aspects while retaining the rest of the custom.

Nigerian and other African women must learn and draw lessons from women's struggles for gender justice in jurisdictions other than their own. The ongoing struggle for a more equitable property regime in the continent is not unlike that fought in the United States and England in the nineteenth century.

The fight against traditional practices harmful to women form part of a global struggle against violence against women in the private sphere.

The problem of widows in Africa cannot be divorced from the larger problems facing many Third World nations and particularly, the problems of women, children, and other marginalized groups within these nations. The plight of widows in Africa clearly implicates the institutional, public, and private actors in the international scene. The legal and political problems of widows in Nigeria point to the issues of rural underdevelopment; the feminization of rural poverty in the Third World; the invisibility of women within the international economic system; and the secondary position allotted to economic and social rights in the human rights regime.

Until women's work is adequately valued and compensated, until development goals and development models embrace and address the Third World poor, and until access to economic and productive resources are open to women, real changes in the lives of widows will be very slow indeed.

African widows still have a long way to go in the realization of their rights. With increasing changes in the continent, a reformulation of existing rules and customary practices is inevitable. Economically, whole societies suffer as a result of continuing discrimination against widows. Furthermore, with the current source of HIV/AIDS in Sub-Saharan Africa, debates about the rights and entitlements of widows take on new meaning. The caution by Jacques Vignes is therefore very apt:

> Nothing is more dangerous than rites robbed of their significance and surviving in a changing world. Men clutch these empty forms with even a greater determination as they feel that the earth is shifting under their feet. Feeling uncertain about what is now and what is to come, they stubbornly cling to what is left of their past, unaware that they are clinging to mere corpses.[209]

---

209. Jacques Vignes, Sguardo sull Africa (1968) *cited in* Cutrufelli, *supra* note 19, at 72.

Chapter 8

Gendered States: Rethinking Culture as a Site of South Asian Human Rights Work

Kamala Visweswaran

I. INTRODUCTION

Pick up any recent Amnesty International Report for South Asia and the titles are arresting: *Women in Afghanistan: The Violations Continue; Bangladesh: Institutional Failures Protect Alleged Rapists; India: Amnesty International Campaigns Against Rape and Sexual Abuse by Members of the Security Forces in Assam and Manipur; Pakistan: Honor Killings of Girls and Women.*[1] More recently, consider the newspaper headlines on the plight of Afghan women which were so readily generated by the current administration as a justification for going to war in Afghanistan in October 2001. I have drawn the title for this article from the way particular nation-states: Afghanistan, Bangladesh, India, Pakistan, Sri Lanka, often are reduced to a set of cultural practices deemed violent for women in human rights reporting. In this essay, I examine the transparency with which human rights claims are made about South Asia by exploring how the language of universal feminism and human rights recreates patterns of cultural deviance which fall disproportionately upon some nations and geographical areas, and not upon others.

How is culture gendered so that particular countries or nation-states are marked by their crimes against women, so that they assume certain identities, not as democracies or dictatorships, but as bride-burners or honor-killers? In the process, how is it that women become exiled, not from their nations of origin, but from their communities of birth or affiliation? By ask-

---

1. AMNESTY INTERNATIONAL, WOMEN IN AFGHANISTAN: THE VIOLATIONS CONTINUE (June 1997); AMNESTY INTERNATIONAL, BANGLADESH: INSTITUTIONAL FAILURES PROTECT ALLEGED RAPISTS (July 1997); AMNESTY INTERNATIONAL, INDIA: AMNESTY INTERNATIONAL CAMPAIGNS AGAINST RAPE AND SEXUAL ABUSE BY MEMBERS OF THE SECURITY FORCES IN ASSAM AND MANIPUR (Nov. 1998); AMNESTY INTERNATIONAL, PAKISTAN: HONOR KILLINGS OF GIRLS AND WOMEN (Sept. 1999).

ing such questions, the objective is neither to reject nor condemn feminist human rights work (which we urgently need), but rather to explore some of its (unintended) consequences as a mode of subjectification when women's rights are divorced from community or nation-state and relocated in an abstract international realm. Liberal human rights discourses recapitulate a nineteenth century "woman question" when first world human rights activists depict brown women in need of saving from brown men. To paraphrase Gayatri Spivak's famous sentence,[2] I want to address how a current debate in feminist theory: the critique of feminist universalism (or gender essentialism)—the idea that women all share something in common, regardless of race, class, sexuality or national origin—founders when it comes to human rights work in South Asia. This paper examines how culture brings human rights talk on South Asia into crisis.

The critique of gender essentialism, of course, posits that women share nothing in common as women that warrants the attempt to understand women's condition as a universal one. Women become women in ways as complex and diverse as the world's sexual orientations, class, and religious and cultural formations might suggest. If the second wave feminism of Robin Morgan posited a global sisterhood based on shared victimization, and Mary Daly catalogued a list of cultural practices from footbinding to sati as instances of women's universal degradation, feminists like Bernice Johnson Reagon and Chandra Mohanty were quick to assert shared survival as the basis of feminist solidarity and resistance. These writers also have made it clear that claims to the very category of experience reified woman as a universal subject. Yet, most feminist human rights work locates the foundation of feminist internationalism in women's shared experience of oppression, constructing a transnational identity of "woman." With respect to the feminist legal scholarship on human rights, Vasuki Nesiah has written cogently:

> Most feminist human rights theorists posit the experience of the denial of women's human rights across the globe as proof of, and grounds for, an international sisterhood. They emphasise that although women are "one half of humanity," they suffer oppression all over the world. They thus illustrate a gendered gap between rights theory and action. The attraction of the human rights framework is notable. . . . If "woman" could become "a name for a way of being human," then the gap between the rights women have as women, and the rights they should have as humans would be eliminated.[3]

Nesiah warns that this form of feminist universalism masks global structural contradictions in gender oppression—a point to which I return. At this junc-

2. Gayatri Chakravorty Spivak, *Can the Subaltern Speak? in* MARXISM AND THE INTERPRETATION OF CULTURE 297 (Cary Nelson & Lawrence Grossberg eds., 1988). The original phrase is: "White men saving brown women from brown men."

3. Vasuki Nesiah, *Toward a Feminist Internationality: A Critique of U.S. Feminist Legal Scholarship, in* FEMINIST TERRAINS IN LEGAL DOMAINS (Ratna Kapur ed., 1996); *see also* Inderpal

ture it is important to note that there are times when the *critique* of feminist universalism, when it rests upon the axis of cultural differentiation, is indistinguishable from a form of cultural essentialism that uses gender as the logic of articulation. Contemporary human rights discourse on women is one such example, producing the "Female Subjects of Public International Law" through a notion of the "Exotic Other Female."[4] On the one hand, legal instruments such as gender asylum rely upon an understanding of universal rights that give women venues for redress against gender discrimination outside their nation-state of origin. On the other hand, such human rights "instruments" also depend upon the naming of culturally specific practices such as dowry harassment, honor killings, or female genital mutilation (FGM) as a means of validating universal principles of justice, precisely by pointing to how violence against women is culturally constructed, resulting in what philosopher Uma Narayan has called "death by culture."[5]

While most feminist theorists would acknowledge that gender subordination is a feature of all known societies, some, like the political philosopher Susan Okin, assume an implicit scaling for understanding women's rights cross-culturally. Thus, "[i]n many cultures in which women's basic civil rights and liberties are formally assured, discrimination practiced against women and girls within the household not only severely constrains their choices, but also severely threatens their well-being and even their lives."[6] Lest one think Okin might also be referring to women in the United States or Europe, she clarifies, "Western majority cultures, largely at the urging of feminists, have recently made substantial efforts to preclude or limit excuses for brutalizing women"[7]—the presumption here is that other societies have not made similar efforts. A recent article in *The New York Times* on the United Nations Children's Fund (UNICEF) campaign on Violence Against Women also aptly illustrates the point:

> In some countries, even when laws defending the right of men to use violence against women are repealed, the culture that created them continues to exert a tremendous influence over behavior. . . . The situation is worst across a swath of countries stretching from the Mediterranean to the edge of Southeast Asia, especially Pakistan, India and Bangladesh (sic).[8]

Grewal, *Women's Rights as Human Rights: Feminist Practices, Global Feminism, and Human Rights in Transnationality,* 3 Citizenship Stud. 337 (1999).

4. Karen Engle, *The Female Subjects of Public International Law: Human Rights and the Exotic Other Female, in* After Identity: A Reader in Law and Culture 210 (Dan Danielsen & Karen Engle eds., 1995).

5. Uma Narayan, Dis-Locating Cultures: Identities, Traditions, and Third-World Feminism (1997).

6. Susan Okin, *Is Multiculturalism Bad for Women?* in Is Multiculturalism Bad for Women? 22 (Joshua Cohen et al. eds., 1999).

7. *Id.* at 19.

8. Barbara Crossette, *UNICEF Opens a Global Drive on Violence Against Women,* N.Y. Times, 9 Mar. 2000, at A8.

Knowing something of the strength and vibrancy of feminist movements in South Asia—movements that can produce remarkable documents, such as the 1996 apology from Pakistani feminists to Bangladeshi women for the rapes and abductions of the 1971 war[9]—the move to assign particular atrocities to cultural norms rather than political conflict is one that bears scrutiny. Clearly the articulate and outspoken women who organize to change the unjust conditions that affect their lives also find support and sustenance from the cultures that produce them as individuals.[10]

Although this article focuses on one particular legal instrument (political asylum) as it relates to human rights, UN, and newspaper reports, it bypasses a conventional definition of human rights founded in international protocols. My understanding of what constitutes human rights operates not only at the level of international conventions, but includes refugee and immigration law as it operates within particular nation-states, local dispute resolution practices which function largely outside the domain of formal courts, and grassroots activist movements, or what are now called "transnational advocacy networks."[11]

The overall aim is to stage a conflict between the recognition of civil rights or liberties in the national realm and human rights in the international realm, to describe what Michael Hardt and Antonio Negri have called a "juridical formation."[12] Flexible networks of authority/sovereignty and mechanisms of command would establish continuities through the horizontally-linked institutions of the new world order: the International Monetary Fund (IMF) and the World Bank; non-governmental organizations (NGOs) such as Amnesty International and Human Rights Watch; the global health organizations (like Médecins Sans Frontières); as well as the new regional political-economic structures: General Agreement on Tariffs and Trade

---

9. WAF would like to use this opportunity to build public awareness on the issue of state violence and the role of the military in 1971. At the same time there is the need to focus on the systematic violence against women, particularly the mass rapes. While we try to focus the nation's attention towards a period in our history for which we stand ashamed, Women's Action Forum, on its own behalf, would like to apologise to the women of Bangladesh that they became the symbols and targets in the process of dishonoring and humiliating people.

   Women's Action Forum Apologises to Women of Bangladesh, *Women Living Under Muslim Laws*, 14/15 Dossier 7–8 (1996). By one estimate, more than 200,000 Bengali women were raped by West Pakistani soldiers, and some were held in military brothels. Catherine N. Niarchos, *Women, War, and Rape: Challenges Facing the International Tribunal for the Former Yugoslavia*, 17 Hum. Rts. Q. 667 (1995).

10. *See* Sayantani Dasgupta & Shamita Das Dasgupta, *Journeys: Reclaiming South Asian Feminism, in* Our Feet Walk the Sky: Women of the South Asian Diaspora 123 (Women of the South Asian Descent Collective ed., 1993).

11. *Cf.* Margaret Keck & Kathryn Sikkink, Activists Beyond Borders: Advocacy Networks in International Politics (1998).

12. Michael Hardt & Antonio Negri, Empire (2000).

(GATT); the North American Free Trade Agreement (NAFTA); the European Union (EU); the Organization Of African Unity (OAU); and the South Asian Association for Regional Cooperation (SAARC).[13] If we are to locate human rights in the world system, I assert that we need to understand its increasing linkage to structural adjustment policies on the one hand, and as Saskia Sassen urges, the overlap and contradiction between global and national arenas on the other hand. This overlap is not seamless, but rather causes disjunctures and displacements amenable to the analytic cartography this paper also undertakes.

As some analysts have observed, the international community created two distinct legal regimes for the articulation of human rights: the regime of international human rights law to monitor and deter abuse, and the refugee law regime to provide surrogate state protection for those crossing borders.[14] Some have seen these two bodies of law as mutually reinforcing, with refugee law able to absorb Nuremburg human rights jurisprudence,[15] or in the vanguard of affording protection for certain kinds of persecution (sexual orientation asylum) in advance of changes made to international treaties and protocols;[16] while others have seen these bodies of law as more distant from each other, in part because international refugee law is seen to be imbedded in the domestic law of particular countries.[17] The United States for example, is not a party to the 1951 UN Convention Relating to the Status of Refugees, but Congress did pass the Refugee Act of 1980 to bring the United States into compliance with its ratification of the 1967 UN Protocol Relating to the Status of Refugees. Tensions also emerge between international and domestic refugee law however, as when the United States initiated its "expedited removal process" for asylum applicants under the terms of the Illegal Immigration Reform and Immigrant Responsibility Act of 1996, putting domestic policy in conflict with the Refugee Convention's principle of "non-refoulement" imbedded in the 1967 Protocol.[18]

The emergence of gender-based asylum as a category of political asylum is a good example of how international human rights law and refugee

13. *See* Madhavi Basnet, *South Asia's Regional Initiative on Human Rights,* 4 Hum. Rts. Brief 2 (1997).
14. *See* Deborah Anker, *Refugee Law, Gender and the Human Rights Paradigm,* 15 Harv. Hum. Rts. J. 135 (2002).
15. *See* Ryan Goodman, *The Incorporation of International Human Rights Standards into Sexual Orientation Asylum Claims: Cases of Involuntary "Medical" Intervention,* 105 Yale L.J. 255 (1995).
16. *See* Timothy Wei & Margaret Sattherwaite, *Symposium, Shifting Grounds for Asylum: Female Genital Surgery and Sexual Orientation,* 29 Colum. Hum. Rts. L. Rev. 467, 505–06 (1997).
17. Anker, *supra* note 14.
18. *See* Cathleen Caron, *Asylum in the United States: Expedited Removal Process Threatens to Violate International Norms,* 6 Hum. Rts. Brief 2 (1999).

law regimes come into contact in particular regions of the world. Perceived failures in the workings of law internal to South Asian nation-states become the basis for a displacement of women's rights into unenforceable international protocols such as the Convention on the Elimination of All Forms of Discrimination Against Women (CEDAW).[19] This process in turn places pressures upon refugee law to "open up," so that refugee law, as a subset of the immigration laws of particular countries, becomes the means for realizing human rights precisely because most international conventions cannot be enforced.[20] In other words, there is a displacement of women's rights from the national realm to the international, resulting in their reintroduction into another, explicitly national realm, creating simultaneous moments of disarticulation and rearticulation.

II.   THE EMERGENCE OF GENDER-BASED ASYLUM

About 20 percent of the one million immigrants to the United States are political refugees, pointing to displacements at the level of international refugee law and creating a new immigration regime in the United States where human rights discourse becomes the means of defending "illegal immigrants." In the last several years, increasing numbers of gender-based asylum cases have been heard in the United States. Women filing such claims often have been victims of domestic violence, and their immigration status is usually contingent upon their husbands' visas. If the woman's husband is a US citizen or legal permanent resident, the woman can file a "battered spouse waiver" under provisions of the Violence Against Women Act (VAWA) in order to stay in the country. If, however, a woman is unmarried, or her spouse is not a citizen or permanent resident, an asylum claim may be the only thing standing between her and deportation.[21]

In recent years, new forms of political asylum have emerged to contend with issues of sexuality and violations of women's human rights. Though more than half the refugees in the world are women (and 80 percent of all refugees are women and children), gender-based (or gender) asylum is a

---

19. Convention on the Elimination of All Forms of Discrimination Against Women, *adopted* 18 Dec. 1979, G.A. Res. 34/180, U.N. GAOR, 34th Sess., Supp. No. 46, U.N. Doc. A/ 34/46 (1980) (*entered into force* 3 Sept. 1981), 1249 U.N.T.S. 13, *reprinted in* 19 I.L.M. 33 (1980) (hereinafter CEDAW).
20. *See* Anker, *supra* note 14, for a different formulation of this point.
21. Recent changes to the Violence Against Women Act of 1994, 103rd Cong. 2nd sess., 29 Sept. 1994, under the reauthorization of VAWA of 2000, Violence Against Women Act of 2000, 106th Cong. 2nd sess., Rept. 106–891, 20 July 2000, created two new visa categories: the T visa and U visa, which may be granted to women victims of domestic violence regardless of marital status.

recent concept under US immigration law, emerging in part from the difficulties women had in filing successful claims for political asylum. The UN High Commissioner for Refugees, the 1951 Convention Relating to the Status of Refugees, and the 1967 Protocol Relating to the Status of Refugees define refugee as a person with a "well-founded fear of being persecuted for reasons of race, religion, nationality, membership of a particular social group or political opinion."[22] Women who fell out of the first four categories usually sought asylum under "membership in a social group."

Historically, women had little success obtaining political asylum in the United States when facing gender-based persecution arguing under membership in a social group. In the 1980s for example, Salvadoran women who petitioned that rape had been used as a political tool to intimidate them and their families were denied asylum because immigration judges understood rape to be a private act or an expression of random, "spontaneous sexual impulses" committed by individual military officers or guerrillas in their own self interest. In one case, even the chanting of political slogans during a rape did not persuade the judge that the act was public/political in nature.[23] Women were thus unable to prove they had been singled out for rape because of membership in a particular social or political group.

Though rape frequently has been used as a political weapon during times of war and ethnic or communal conflict (most recently in Rwanda and Sierra Leone, but also during the Partition of India in 1947,[24] and the Bangladesh War for Independence in 1971), it has not always been seen as a form of persecution. The mass rapes of Bosnian women by Serbian forces during 1991–1992, and the insistence of the international community that rape be treated as a human rights violation and war crime, has helped to establish it as a form of gender persecution.[25]

Following the 1991 United Nations High Commissioner for Refugees (known now as UNHCR) *Guidelines for the Protection of Refugee Women*

---

22. Convention Relating to the Status of Refugees, art. 1(A)(2), *adopted* 28 July 1951, U.N. Doc. A/CONF.2/108 (1951), 189 U.N.T.S. 150 (*entered into force* 22 April 1954), *reprinted in* 3 WESTON III.G.4; Protocol Relating to the Status of Refugees, *signed* 31 Jan. 1967, 19 U.S.T. 6223, T.I.A.S. No. 6577, 606 U.N.T.S. 267 (*entered into force* 4 Oct. 1967) (*entered into force for U.S.* 1 Nov. 1968).

23. *See* Audrey Macklin, *Refugee Women and the Imperative of Categories,* 17 HUM. RTS. Q. 213 (1995).

24. *See* Purushottam Agarwal et al., *Legitimising Rape as a Political Weapon, in* WOMEN AND THE HINDU RIGHT 29 (Tanika Sarkar & Urvashi Bhutalia eds., 1995); Urvashi Bhutalia, *Muslims and Hindus, Men and Women: Communal Stereotypes and the Partition of India, in id.* at 58.

25. *See* Niarchos, *supra* note 9, at 350; Todd Salzman, *Rape Camps as a Means of Ethnic Cleansing; Religious, Cultural and Ethical Responses to Rape Victims in the Former Yugoslavia,* 20 HUM. RTS. Q. 348 (1998); Judith Gardham & Hilary Charlesworth, *Protection of Women in Armed Conflict,* 22 HUM. RTS. Q. 148 (2000); Christine Strumpen-Darrie, *Rape: A Survey of Current International Jurisprudence,* 7 HUM. RTS. BRIEF 2 (2000).

and the 1992 UNHCR Handbook which holds that circumstances surrounding women's fear of persecution may be "unique to women," Canada,
in March 1993, became the first country to issue "Guidelines on Women
Refugee Claimants fearing gender-related persecution." These guidelines
have been the model for US law on the subject.

A person seeking asylum must establish actual or well-founded fear of
persecution, which hinges on two elements. First, the harm apprehended has
to amount to persecution. The claimant may be the victim of violent crime,
but that does not necessarily count as persecution. Second is the question of
state accountability for the infliction of harm. If the state is unwilling or
unable to control the perpetrators of persecution, a case for asylum can be
made. The March 1995 INS Memorandum on "Considerations for Asylum
Officers Adjudicating Asylum Claims from Women," like the Canadian
guidelines, defines two broad areas of gender persecution which can be
argued under "membership in a particular social group": 1) the persecution
is a type of harm that is specific to the applicant's gender (such as domestic
violence, rape, sexual abuse, genital mutilation, bride burning, infanticide,
forced marriage, forced sterilization or forced abortion), and 2) the persecution is imposed because of the applicant's gender (as in violation of social
norms defining women's roles, or refusal to accept restrictions of women's
rights).[26]

An example of an asylum claim meeting the first criteria for gender
persecution might be that of an Indian Hindu woman who has faced physical or sexual abuse from her husband or in-laws for inability to meet continual dowry demands. Despite the fact that the giving and receiving of
dowry is illegal in India, and recent legislation exists with the intent of making it easier for women to file dowry harassment complaints, dowry harassment in India frequently results in death or severe injury in the form of
"bride burnings." Since the state fails to protect women by enforcing its
own laws, the claimant could plead that her forced return to India would
be life-threatening.

Another example of gender persecution argued under the first criteria
might be the case of a Pakistani woman who has been raped by an outsider
or family member. Under the Hudood Ordinances, a woman must corrob-
orate her complaint with the testimony of four male witnesses. Failure to
prove that sexual contact occurred without her consent makes the woman
herself subject to criminal prosecution for adultery or fornication. False
cases of Hudood offenses may also be registered against women who are
seeking divorce, who choose to marry against their parents' wishes, or who

---

26. Memorandum of the INS, Considerations for Asylum Officers Adjudicating Asylum Claims
    for Women (26 May 1995) (on file with author).

are related to men who are wanted by the authorities for other reasons.[27] Although the UNHCR Guidelines state that the line between discrimination and persecution is unclear, and that a woman seeking refugee status cannot base her claim solely on being subject to laws she objects to, the Hudood Ordinances can be seen as a form of legal discrimination which is persecutory because, though all Pakistani citizens are subject to these laws, they are disproportionately applied to women with more devastating consequences.

An example of an asylum claim filed under the second criteria might be an Afghan Muslim woman who refused to veil in public, although the Taliban interpretation of Islamic law in Afghanistan required women to do so. Since the punishment or social sanctions for a woman who defied this aspect of the law might be severe or life threatening, she could make a case for being awarded gender asylum in this country. In fact, asylum was granted on these grounds for twelve of the nineteen cases I reviewed that were filed by Afghan women in the United States as of August 2000. The Clinton administration opposition to the Taliban regime had resulted in the State Department doubling its resettlement quota for South Asian refugees from 4,000 to 8,000 specifically to allow more Afghan women into the country.[28]

III.   WOMEN AS A SOCIAL GROUP AND "ESSENTIAL" PERSECUTIONS

Although the above three examples of South Asian gender asylum cases establish gender persecution under "membership in social group" in different ways, one of the difficulties with the case law developed around gender asylum is that it tended to naturalize a collapsing of gender with "women" so that all the persecutions faced by women became de facto examples of gender persecution. Rape and domestic violence, harms typically identified with women, also have male victims or may involve same sex partners, but appeared in the law review literature as predominantly heterosexual women's concerns.[29]

---

27. *See* HUMAN RIGHTS WATCH, DOUBLE JEOPARDY: POLICE ABUSE OF WOMEN IN PAKISTAN 47–94 (1992); Macklin, *supra* note 23, at 230.
28. HUMAN RIGHTS WATCH, ANNUAL REPORT (2000). Here one might also note that Iran and Pakistan have absorbed the vast majority of Afghan refugees, yet the asymmetry of the world system means that the refugee-selecting countries of the North where asylum law operates are in a position to formulate both international and national laws while refugee-receiving countries are not; witness US instructions to Pakistan to reopen its borders to Afghan refugees when the bombing of Afghanistan began on 7 October 2001.
29. *See, e.g.,* Patricia Seith, *Escaping Domestic Violence: Asylum as a Means of Protection for Battered Women,* 97 COLUM. L. REV. 1804 (1995). "Since men are generally not persecuted

The narrow understanding of gender in gender asylum cases eventually led to the emergence of a series of "sexual orientation" asylum cases[30] that faltered on the definition of social group used by a number of courts for adjudicating gender asylum cases. This definition came from a 1985 Bureau of Immigration Appeals (BIA) decision, *Matter of Acosta,*[31] which held that a social group consisted of those who 1) share a common, immutable characteristic or 2) share a characteristic that is so fundamental to one's identity of conscience that it ought not be changed. The BIA also named sex as an "immutable characteristic" which was seen as critical for women fearing gender-based persecution, especially for the landmark Fauziya Kasinga FGM case of 1996.[32] Thus, the notion of social group operating in *Acosta* led to a fairly essentialist notion of gender operating in the idea of "gender persecution" which some theorists would also see as a conflation of (biological) sex with (socially constructed) gender.

Although *Acosta's* first definition of social group has been effective for many gay male asylum applicants,[33] the immutability criteria implies a narrow and essentialist definition of sexuality that prevents asylum seekers from defining their sexuality as entirely or partially chosen. The second definition in *Acosta* might similarly require the applicant to prove that sexual orientation is fundamental to his or her identity.[34] In the case of a gay transgender male who dressed effeminately, for example, the court, relying upon a distinction between identity and conduct, found that his membership in a social group was not immutable because he chose to dress in women's clothes, drawing a distinction between identity and conduct.[35] The Ninth Circuit Court of Appeals, however, ruled in favor of Geovanni Hernandez-Montiel's asylum petition, adding a test of voluntary associational member-

---

by means of rape, domestic violence or FGM, biases against (recognizing) such forms of violence exist among adjudicators." *Id.* at 1824.

30. *See* Goodman, *supra* note 15; Wei & Sattherwaite, *supra* note 16. According to one 1997 assessment, the US has accepted over one hundred sexual orientation asylum applications since 1994; the number of successful sexual orientation asylum applications in 1996 was fifty-seven. *See* Tracy J. Davis, *Opening the Doors of Immigration: Sexual Orientation and Asylum in the United States,* 6 Hum. Rts. Brief 3 (1999).

31. 19 I & N. Dec. 211, 233 (BIA 1985), rev'd in part on other grounds by In re Mogharrabi, 19 I & N. Dec. 439 (BIA 1987).

32. *See* Andrea Binder, *Gender and the Membership in a Particular Social Group Category of the 1951 Refugee Convention,* 10 Colum. J. Gender & L. 167, at 179 (2001); In re Fauziya Kasinga, Int. Dec. 3278 (BIA 1996).

33. Interestingly, it has informed the recent House of Lords decision in R. v. Immigration Appeal Tribunal and another, ex parte Shah of 1999; *see* Deborah Anker, *Refugee Status and Violence Against Women in the "Domestic" Sphere: The Non-State Actor Question,* 15 Geo. Immigr. L.J. 391 (2001).

34. *See* Davis, *supra* note 30.

35. This conflict between sexual orientation being seen either as primarily about identity or conduct is also mirrored in other sexual orientation legislation in the US. *See* Sonya Katyal, *Exporting Identity,* 14 Yale J.L. & Feminism 97 (2002).

ship to the immutability and fundamental identity criteria, leading to a more expansive definition of "particular social group."[36]

Before the recent emergence of the more expansive definition of social group, its narrow application of gender also led to the erosion of any standard to hold the state accountable for the persecution of women because they were members of distinct ethnic or religious communities. Early arguments for gender asylum held that "[t]he failure to recognize women as a social group persecuted on account of their gender either ends in the denial of otherwise valid claims, or results in the incorrect tailoring of a claim to fit into one of the other specified groups of persecution."[37] Yet defining women as a "social group" also meant that the specific political conditions tended to be sidelined in favor of emphasizing cultural practices like pardah. For example, while opposition to the Taliban restrictions on Afghan women could be argued under other asylum group categories, many have been decided using "particular social group" criteria. In other words, though the Taliban, which was largely dominated by the Pashthun community, also persecuted Afghan religious and ethnic minorities like the Hazara or Tajik, a Tajik woman was more likely to have asylum granted as an Afghan woman facing "repressive social norms" than as a member of a persecuted religious or ethnic minority.[38]

Here we can see how the need for international intervention might be signaled by how violence against women stood for a community's oppression, but the successful gender asylum application might ignore the role of the state in perpetrating gender violence as part of its strategy for waging ethnic or communal violence, because women were understood to be a part of a social group with immutable characteristics that were all shared regardless of differences of community or culture of origin.

Asylum cases typically have a "state action" component for establishing persecution: the harm has to be inflicted by the government or by persons or organizations the government would normally control. Yet the trend in

---

36. The 1st, 2d, and 7th Circuit Courts of Appeal apply "particular social group" in a way that mirrors *Acosta*. The 8th and 9th Circuit Courts construe "particular social group" to require a "voluntary associational relationship" among members. The 2d Circuit has adopted a variation that includes external perceptions, immutability, and voluntary associations. *See* Davis, *supra* note 30.

37. Anjana Bahl, *Home is Where the Brute Lives: Asylum Law and Gender-Based Claims of Persecution* 4 Cardozo Women's L.J. 33, 58 (1997).

38. Consider, *e.g.,* the case of a Tajik Afghan woman who details extensive violence she faced as a Shia; yet the immigration judge, citing *Kasinga,* emphasized her membership in a social group of women who were badly affected by the Taliban, *available at* www.uchastings.edu/cgrs/summaries/1-50/summary9. There are many other ironies in the processing of Afghan women's asylum applications: a number were granted to women who were members of the communist party or Najibullah government, a shift in the application of asylum to those fleeing from communist regimes from the 1950s through 1980s.

gender asylum cases has been precisely to push for a recognition of harm by non-state actors so that domestic violence has come to be seen as the paradigmatic example of gender specific abuse committed by private actors. It was the combination of serious harm in conjunction with inattention and inaction of the state (or "state failure") that established battering as a systematic discriminatory practice.[39] However, the gap between the law and the state's will to either make or enforce it inevitably was filled by culture. In other words, the state's failure to draft legislation protecting women, or to enforce existing laws protecting women, was often attributed to the force of culture, rather than to inadequate state policy or lack of political will. Despite the routine use of anthropologists to provide evidence of harmful cultural practices in gender asylum cases,[40] cases filed on behalf of Muslim women claiming to hold a political opinion ("feminism" or membership in women's organizations) at odds with state laws,[41] suggest that many South Asian cases might be more ably explained through an analysis of state-level practices, and not by a cultural description of oppression. This would still not answer the question however, of why it is that the preference seems to be to grant gender and sexual orientation asylum cases under the "social group" category, rather than the "political opinion" category, which are more frequently turned down. Does the United States, as a refugee receiving country, have a preference for women asylees who are cultural victims, rather than political dissidents?

IV. CULTURE AND THE PROBLEM OF THE STATE

One of the difficulties with "gender persecution" as a condition of asylum, is that the shift from active state persecution to "state failure to protect" required to understand rape, domestic violence, or FGM as forms of perse-

---

39. *See* Anker, *supra* note 33.
40. *See* Lisa Gilad, *The Problem of Gender-related Persecution: A Challenge of International Protection, in* Engendering Forced Migration: Theory and Practice 334 (Doreen Indra ed., 1999); Sidney Waldon, *Anthropologists as "Expert Witnesses," in id.,* at 343; Charles Piot, Representing Africa in the Kasinga Asylum Case (Duke University 2001) (on file with author).
41. In a 1993 appeal, however, a young Iranian woman who claimed that her feminist beliefs and her unwillingness to veil would put her at risk if she were deported for Iran, was considered ineligible for asylum because, though she was a member of a particular social group (which included supporters of the former Shah), and her feminism qualified as a political opinion, she had not demonstrated that she would be harmed solely because of her gender. Still, the case did show that "an applicant who could demonstrate a well-founded fear of persecution on account of her (or his) beliefs about the role and status of women in society could be eligible for refugee status on account of political opinion." Memorandum of the INS, *supra* note 26, at 11.

cution established a relationship between a "failed state" and patriarchal culture, subjecting the cultures of the South to new forms of surveillance and scrutiny. Asylum cases typically use country reports done by the US State Department or human rights organizations like Amnesty International to help document the persecutions being addressed. Given the heavy traffic between human rights reporting and asylum adjudication, it makes sense to turn to this reporting in more detail.

The title of a recent Human Rights Watch Report, *Crime or Custom? Violence Against Women in Pakistan,* suggests that the possibility exists that violence against women might be the result of state policy rather than social "custom." Yet while the report makes clear that the Islamization of the law was a policy decision undertaken by the Zia regime, it also makes blanket assertions such as "Pakistani women remain . . . second class citizens as a result of . . . social and cultural norms and attitudes" which are all too frequently reproduced in asylum cases.[42] The slippage between government "institutionalized misogyny" and religious/cultural ideas is also illustrated in the following argument on gender persecution by a feminist legal scholar:

> The definition of refugee should be expanded to include those with a well-founded fear of persecution because of their gender. This would protect women from institutionalized misogyny in which the government carries out sanctions, or ignores oppression of or violence against women because they are women. The most notorious example of such persecution is probably Islam with its strict rules regarding the status and behavior of women. However, similar conditions exist in India under the Hindu religion, in Africa under tribal laws, and in Latin America under the tradition of machismo.[43]

In this passage, we can see how government sanctions are conflated with the "strict rules" of Islam, Hinduism, and tribal laws, though all societies have "rules regulating the status and behavior of women." Regional and country-specific differences in the interpretation of Islamic traditions are obliterated, so that Islam is seen to be universally bad for women,[44] with parallels drawn to Indian Hinduism, African tribalism, and Latin American machismo.

Gender asylum cases often straddle the line between communal violence and domestic violence, forcing us to confront the continuities between these forms of violence, and to be attentive to recognizing active state

---

42. HUMAN RIGHTS WATCH, CRIME OR CUSTOM? VIOLENCE AGAINST WOMEN IN PAKISTAN (Aug. 1999), *available at* www.hrw.org/reports/1999/pakistan/Pakhtml-03.htm#P324_45508.
43. *See* Linda Cipriani, *Gender and Persecution: Protecting Women Under International Refugee Law,* 7 GEO. IMMIGR. L.J. 513 (1993).
44. *See* Susan Musarrat Akram, *Orientalism Revisited in Asylum and Refugee Claims,* 12 INT'L J. REFUGEE L. 7 (2000).

persecution of women as members of minority or oppressed communities. This requires a rigorous analysis of state level practices, rather than detailed cultural description. Yet in a review of 120 case summaries through the year 2000 available from the Center for Gender and Refugee Studies, clearly particular countries became associated with particular persecutions: of sixteen cases filed in the last five years concerning genital mutilation, all except four were in West Africa, the majority in Nigeria. Of forty-three cases filed under the category "Repressive Social Norms," twenty or almost half were filed for Afghanistan, while fifteen (almost one third) were filed for Irani women (one each was filed for Pakistan and Nepal). Honor killings, on the other hand, have come to be associated primarily with Jordan and Pakistan.

The thirty-five cases filed under rape/sexual violence were spread out over several countries, as were twenty-five cases categorized as domestic violence cases, with five from South Asia (one Nepal, one India, three Pakistan). Yet most of the successful asylum cases concerning women who had experienced some form of gender-related violence were actually granted on the basis of race, religion, or political opinion and not membership in a social group. In one Indian case, a Sikh woman who was a member of the All India Sikh Student Federation and who was arrested and raped by Indian police, received asylum on the basis of political opinion and religion. Similarly, a Bangladeshi Christian woman and her daughter who had been harassed and raped by Muslim men and whose house had been burned to the ground, were granted asylum on the basis of religious persecution in 1999. Likewise, a Christian Anglo-Pakistani woman married to a Muslim, a Nepalese Christian woman married to a Hindu, and a Tamil Christian Sri Lankan woman married to a Buddhist were all granted asylum based on race and religion.

That a number of these cases involved the communalization of marriage in South Asian plural societies under various forms of religious nationalist regimes is notable. In other words, in a country like Sri Lanka where the Singhalese majority state and Tamil militants have been engaged in long-term violence, inter-caste and interfaith marriages are subject to more cultural pressure and become vulnerable targets of political attack. The same would be true (in different ways) for India and Bangladesh.[45]

In the five cases described above, rape, sexual harassment and/or domestic violence did not constitute the basis for an asylum ruling, membership in a persecuted minority group (Sikhs or Christians) provided the

---

45. In Bangladesh, where one analysis links state-sponsored women's development programs to a backlash against women and to a rise in Islamic fundamentalism, mixed marriages, or non-Muslim marriages are subject to attack. In an explicitly Hindu nationalist state like India, which is hostile to its Sikh, Christian, Muslim, Dalit, and tribal communities, inter-caste and interfaith marriages become vulnerable to criticism and attack.

claim. This strategy appropriately puts the emphasis on state practices or ideology, and not upon culture.

While unprecedented lobbying by feminists at the Vienna World Conference on Human Rights in 1993 resulted in the UN Declaration on the Elimination of Violence Against Women (DEDAW), and the notion that "women's rights are human rights"[46] (the rallying cry of the 1995 Women's Conference in Beijing) seems so commonsensical as to warrant no comment, the call for mainstreaming women's rights into human rights protocols[47] often works to condemn cultural practices without analysis of state-level involvement in those practices. On the face of it, the call for western countries to recognize rape, sexual harassment and/or domestic violence as valid reasons for an asylum claim seems an enabling gesture. Yet a pernicious double-movement is enacted whereby universalist criteria are asserted at the expense of culture (women constitute a social group apart from membership in a culture), at the same time that culture is used as a means to specify the qualitative nature of violence,[48] so that heterogeneity and diversity within communities is downplayed in order to establish evidence of persecution. The notion of culture itself remains strangely one-dimensional and static—a caricature of its worst patriarchal tendencies.[49] Sherene Razack, in her criticism of Canadian gender asylum cases, has noted that the successful asylum seeker must cast herself as a cultural other, "fleeing from a more primitive culture," and Anita Sinha has similarly shown the tendency to grant gender-based asylum in the United States only when a strong "cultural hook" (persecutory practices seen to be cultural in nature) exists for US cases (a phenomenon also true of gay gender asylum cases).[50]

Yet most host states offering surrogate protection can no more protect asylees from rape or domestic violence than can their home states. One feminist legal scholar has suggested that since most states cannot protect peo-

---

46. See WOMEN'S RIGHTS/HUMAN RIGHTS: INTERNATIONAL FEMINIST PERSPECTIVES (Julie Peters & Andrea Wolpers eds., 1995); Radhika Coomaraswamy, *Reinventing International Law: Women's Rights as Human Rights in the International Community, in* DEBATING HUMAN RIGHTS 167 (Peter van Ness ed., 1999).

47. See Anne Gallagher, *Ending the Marginalization: Strategies for Incorporating Women into the United Nations Human Rights System,* 19 HUM. RTS. Q. 283 (1997); Avronne Fraser, *Becoming Human: The Origin and Development of Women's Human Rights,* 21 HUM. RTS. Q. 853 (1999).

48. See Leti Volpp, *Blaming Culture for Bad Behavior,* 12 YALE J. L. & HUMAN. 89 (2000); Volpp, *Feminism Versus Multiculturalism,* 101 COLUM. L. REV. 1181 (2001).

49. Bonnie Honig, *My Culture Made Me Do It, in* IS MULTICULTURALISM BAD FOR WOMEN? *supra* note 6, at 12.

50. Anita Sinha, *Domestic Violence and U.S. Asylum Law: Eliminating the Cultural Hook for Claims Involving Gender-Related Persecution,* 76 N.Y.U. L. REV. 1562 (2001); SHERENE RAZACK, LOOKING WHITE PEOPLE IN THE EYE: RACE AND CULTURE IN COURTROOMS AND CLASSROOMS 88, 92 (1998). *See also* Sonya Katyal, *Exporting Identity,* 14 YALE J. L. & FEMINISM 97 (2002) for an analysis of the *Hernandez-Montiel* sexual-orientation asylum case.

ple from domestic violence, this should become the operating assumption in refugee law, and evidentiary hurdles for claimants seeking to demonstrate failure of state protection should either be lowered or eliminated entirely.[51] The contradictions of South Asian women immigrants who have experienced domestic or sexual violence in the United States (as a continuation of the violence they have experienced in the subcontinent) applying for asylum in the United States are immense. Asylees fleeing domestic violence, rape, or other persecutions in their home country, are often confronted with the same set of harms in the host country through institutionalized sexism, racism, or homophobia. As Saeed Rahman puts it:

> One of the things that I learned during my asylum process, and one that I hope lawyers are aware of, is that the language around asylum applications is rooted in imperialism. The ways in which the asylee and his or her country were constructed, in fact, the entire discourse was at times problematic for me. It is incredibly difficult as a colonized subject not to feel discomfort when colonial language is being produced to describe your country of origin. When lawyers use terms like intolerant, police brutality, Islamic fundamentalism, etc. images of the Third World, underdeveloped folks, backwardness and fanaticism are evoked. . . . However for some asylees this can be a difficult discussion. . . . We are also aware of the ways in which our histories are shaped by the U.S. For instance, in my case, I grew up under a military dictatorship in Pakistan which was strongly supported and maintained by the United States. . . . It would not have worked out to my advantage if I gave an introductory class to my immigration officer on U.S.-Pakistan relations. . . . It needs to be clear that although there are homophobic practices in different parts of the world, the ways in which they are talked about in front of the INS works within a highly problematic framework. . . . It needs to be acknowledged that we do not all come to the table with the same types of negotiating power in determining historical, political and cultural context. It is also important to know that universal human rights do not seem to include the violations that happen in the U.S. It is still legal in certain states to fire, evict and harass queers. . . . Even though there are important laws in this country to fight homophobia, granting asylum does not mean that the same kinds of homophobic practices will not happen here. When standards are placed on other nations, they should be consistently maintained here.[52]

As Rahman's narrative suggests, the deployment of apparently culturally specific descriptions of violence thus does not result in the strategic use of an essentialism one should endorse. A more sound tactic would be to try to distinguish between gender enabling and gender discriminatory practices

---

51. *See* Melanie Randall, *Refugee Law and State Accountability for Violence Against Women: A Comparative Analysis of Legal Approaches to Recognizing Asylum Claims Based on Gender Persecution,* 25 HARV. WOMEN'S L.J. 284 (2002).
52. *See* Wei & Satterthwaite, *supra* note 16, at 517–18.

within South Asian cultures; in this way the emphasis is upon particular values, institutions, or practices within a culture that are patriarchal, so that no one culture or community is characterized as exclusively patriarchal. This distinction recognizes that gender norms within cultures are frequently contested by women themselves, and that cultures also carry feminist traditions of resistance and rebellion. A mischaracterization of women's complex relation to patriarchy elsewhere leads to a misrecognition of patriarchy in the United States, which has profound consequences for feminist movements in this country. The hyper-visibility of culturally constructed violence to women is linked to the continued pervasiveness and invisibility of violence against women in the United States.[53]

The double movement between the universal and the culturally particular in human rights discourse pits women's rights against her community's rights, as if they were separable elements, for the very articulation of the category "women as a social group" depends on splitting women from their cultures. It is in fact the very success of mainstreaming a particular form of feminism into human rights culture that leads Michael Ignatieff to proclaim,

> Human rights is the only universally available moral vernacular that validates the claims of women and children against the oppression they experience in patriarchal and tribal societies; it is the only vernacular that enables dependent persons to perceive themselves as moral agents and to act against practices—arranged marriages, purdah, genital mutilation, domestic slavery and so on, that are ratified by the weight and authority of their cultures.[54]

Yet the critique of gender essentialism also teaches us that a woman's rights are often not separable from her community's rights, so surely moral agency is generated as much through those communities as through the discourse on human rights. This is also literally true in India, where a woman's civil rights are imbedded in the personal laws of her community. That this situation is inherited from colonial times does not make it any less a subject of debate and critique.[55] Indeed this situation is one of the major issues facing the civil rights community in India today.

For countries like India, with long histories of democratic contestation, the current practice of recognizing gender-based persecution as it occurs with regard to membership in a social group based upon religion or ethnicity is probably a better alternative than arguing that domestic violence

---

53. *See* NARAYAN, *supra* note 5.
54. MICHAEL IGNATIEFF, HUMAN RIGHTS AS POLITICS AND IDOLATRY 68 (2002).
55. *See* FLAVIA AGNES, LAW AND GENDER INEQUALITY (1999); FEMINIST TERRAINS IN LEGAL DOMAINS (Ratna Kapur ed., 1996); RATNA KAPUR & BRENDA CROSSMAN, SUBVERSIVE SITES: FEMINIST ENGAGEMENTS WITH LAW IN INDIA (1996); Nivedita Menon, *Rights, Bodies and the Law: Rethinking Feminist Politics of Justice, in* GENDER AND POLITICS IN INDIA (Nivedita Menon ed., 1999); JANAKI NAIR, WOMEN AND LAW IN COLONIAL INDIA (1996); ARCHANA PARASHAR, WOMEN AND FAMILY LAW REFORM (1992).

should be seen as a form of gender-based persecution.[56] The standard used to show that the Indian state is negligent in enforcing its own laws, or that a woman facing harassment cannot reasonably move to another part of the country, rarely takes into account the considerable resources provided by women's groups and lawyers who are working not only to change laws, but to see that they are enforced. In other words, successful US gender asylum cases argued on the basis of domestic violence might have the unintended effect of undermining the civil rights movement and feminist democratic politics in India.[57] Ironically, international law would not have changed without the influence of those feminist movements, and yet the successful application of asylum law in a domestic context must assume that those movements either do not exist, or are too weak to provide protection and sustenance to women victims and survivors who have galvanized those very movements.[58] Why is it that feminist legal scholarship finds its surest footing in portraying South Asian women as victim subjects but is less able to deal with the agency of South Asian feminist theorists and activists?[59] At this moment structures of accountability that operate between women's groups in the United States and South Asia can pose an important challenge to human rights discourse, allowing us to ask about the politics of culture in human rights feminism.[60]

Despite the tremendous and growing influence of transnational feminist movements through mainstream and non-mainstream sites, the language of universal human rights works to recreate patterns of deviance which fall disproportionately upon some nations or geographical areas and not others. In the case of gender asylum, culture or community collapses back upon the

---

56. Here, however, the metonymic identification of women with community is not automatically altered. The rape of women may be seen as THE defining mode of a community's subjection, as in the mass abductions and rapes of women during Partition, or through the detention of Panjabi Sikhs by the Indian state over the last twenty years.

57. *See* David Kennedy, *The International Human Rights Movement: Part of the Problem?*, 3 Eur. Hum. Rts. L. Rev. 245 (2001), for a similar observation.

58. *See* Radha Kumar, A History of Doing (1995); Nandita Shah & Nandita Gandhi, Issues at Stake: Theory and Practice of the Indian Women's Movement (1992); Amrita Basu, The Challenge of Local Feminisms: Women's Movements in Global Perspective (1995); Vasantha & Kalpana Kannabiran, *Looking at Ourselves: The Women's Movement in Hyderabad, in* Feminist Genealogies, Colonial Legacies, Democratic Futures (M. Jacqui Alexander & Chandra Mohanty eds., 1997) for recent accounts of feminist movements in India.

59. *See* Nesiah, *supra* note 3; Mary E. John, Discrepant Dislocations: Feminism, Theory and Postcolonial Histories (1996), for related critiques. Susan Moller Okin, *Feminism, Women's Human Rights, and Cultural Differences, in* Decentering the Center, Philosophy for a Multicultural, Postcolonial and Feminist World (Uma Narayan & Sandra Harding eds., 2000) productively marks the disjuncture between the theoretical critique of gender essentialism by "Third World feminists" and of universalizing tendencies of feminist human rights discourse, but mistakenly holds that the former was confined by its postmodern excesses to the academy while the latter was better realized through the politics of grassroots NGOs.

60. *See* Arati Rao, *The Politics of Gender and Culture in International Human Rights Discourse, in* Women's Rights/Human Rights, *supra* note 46, at 167.

state.[61] Particular states then assume certain identities, not as democracies or dictatorships, but as bride-burners, honor-killers, or genital mutilators. These states are the classic "weak states" of international relations and dependency theory—unable to separate culture from politics, or to muster adequate political will to contain the vicissitudes of culture. The characterizations of such gendered states work to obscure both the pervasiveness of domestic violence in the United States as well as other US human rights violations.

When are nation-states still the legitimate arbiters of women's rights? At what moments should "universal" or international rights instruments be applied? In India and Sri Lanka, for example, it matters that civil wars and ethnic conflict have been endemic to both countries for the past thirty years. It matters that India is a democracy, and that Pakistan and Bangladesh have seen almost as many years of military dictatorship as democratic governance.[62] It matters that Indian gender asylum cases emerge from a complex colonial history that established the personal laws of different communities as sites of non-intervention, and substituted a uniform penal code as a default civil code. It matters that US support of Zia al-Haq in Pakistan, and the mujahideen in Afghanistan undermined the People's Democratic Party of Afghanistan (PDPA), and gave rise to fundamentalist forms of Islam that led to the erosion of women's rights in both Afghanistan and Pakistan.[63] While a recent Human Rights Watch report on Pakistan notes that "the militarization of politics have had a profound impact on the trajectory of women's advancement,"[64] it fails to mention that the notorious Zina Ordinances were brought into law during the US backed Zia regime; a regime that was the beneficiary of millions of dollars of aid in the form of US military contracts. Gender asylum cases in both Pakistan and Afghanistan thus need to be seen as the direct result of US cold war policies of intervention in the region. According to Amnesty International, Afghans are the single largest refugee group in the world.[65] Yet neither the recent Amnesty report *Women in*

---

61. *See* Adamantia Pollis, *Cultural Relativism Revisited: Through a State Prism,* 18 Hum. Rts. Q. 316 (1996). In one of the few attempts to analyze the place of the state in human rights discourse, Pollis criticizes human rights scholars for failing to develop "a conceptual framework within which to analyze whether a state's claims of cultural distinctiveness are consistent with that culture's conceptions of rights, dignity and justice, or whether it is a wanton exercise of power by the elites." *Id.* at 323. While her points are well-taken, they are less relevant for plural societies, which contain a number of cultures. They also illustrate the degree to which culture and state are too frequently collapsed.

62. *See* Hamza Alavi, *The State in Post-Colonial Societies: Pakistan and Bangladesh,* 74 New Left Rev. 1 (July/Aug. 1972).

63. *See* Diana Cammack, *Gender Relief and Politics During the Afghan War, in* Engendering Forced Migration, *supra* note 40, at 94.

64. *See* Human Rights Watch, Crime or Custom, *supra* note 42, § III.

65. *See* Amnesty International, Refugees from Afghanistan: The World's Largest Refugee Group (1999).

Afghanistan: Pawns in Men's Power Struggles[66] or *Pakistan: Honor Killings of Girls and Women*[67] makes mention of the effects of US policy in the region. When these reports specify the myriad ways in which women were made victims, one would never know that women in the People's Democratic Party of Afghanistan fought the political agenda of the mujahideen (who opposed, among other things, universal education for women),[68] or that Pakistani feminists have been organized against both the Islamization of law and its unfair application for almost two decades.[69]

In states where formal legal equality pertains, the problem lies with implementation of the law and enforcement—and that is true in the United States as well. In the United States, 1.3 million people are stalked each year, and yet stalking laws exist on a piecemeal basis, and are difficult to enforce. An "Order of Protection" is only a piece of paper—it cannot stop an enraged partner from perpetrating further violence and harm. Yet no one argues that the difficulty in enforcing these laws is a reason for American women to claim gender asylum in France or India. Culture, then, makes its appearance in gender asylum cases in troubling ways. The problem cannot be solved simply by avoiding the use of cultural stereotypes, as some feminist asylum advocates urge.[70] This approach ignores the ways in which culture itself increasingly is assumed as the grounds for human rights work in general, and gender asylum claims in particular. One must, therefore, insist on marking the asymmetry of the very production of cultural explanation, even as one recognizes that this asymmetry emerges from the interface of the international economy and liberal theory.

The point is not to force a choice between universalistic or relativistic criteria—to my mind, that debate has stalled, and it need not be rehearsed

---

66. Amnesty International, 11 Nov. 1999, AI Index ASA 11/011/1999.

67. Amnesty International, *supra* note 1.

68. *See* Valentine M. Moghadam, Modernizing Women: Gender and Social Change in the Middle East 207 (1993); Valentine M. Moghadam, *Nationalist Agendas and Women's Rights: Conflicts in Afghanistan in the Twentieth Century, in* Feminist Nationalism 75 (Lois A. West ed., 1997).

69. Two exceptions are notable: Human Rights Watch, Crime or Custom, *supra* note 42, mentions the formation of the Women's Action Forum in 1981, as does a September 1999 Amnesty Public Statement. *See* Amnesty International, Pakistan: Afghan Women's Day Protesters Must be Protected (1999). This report also calls for protection of women activists in the Revolutionary Association of Women (RAWA) at International Women's Day protests. For more information on feminist organizing in Pakistan, *see* Khawar Mumtaz, Women of Pakistan: Two Steps Forward: One Step Back (1987); Ayesha Jalal, *The Convenience of Subservience: Women and the State of Pakistan, in* Women, Islam and the State (Deniz Kandiyoti ed., 1991); Shahnaz Rouse, *Gender, Nationalisms and Cultural Identity, in* Embodied Violence (Kumari Jayawardene & Malati de Alwis eds., 1996); Khawar Mumtaz, *Identity Politics and Women: Fundamentalism and Women in Pakistan, in* Identity Politics and Women 228 (Valentine M. Moghadam ed., 1994).

70. *See* Jacqueline Bhabha, *Internationalist Gatekeepers?: The Tension Between Asylum Advocacy and Human Rights,* 15 Harv. Hum. Rts. J. 155 (2002); Anker, *supra* note 14, at 152.

here.[71] I want rather to reinstitute questions of culture and community in South Asian human rights work by moving beyond a universal human rights versus cultural rights dichotomy to examine the antimonies of displacement that emerge from the confrontation of the two as they move unevenly through national and international arenas. The task is to understand at what points the application of universalist criteria forces the emergence of culturalist explanation, and conversely to identify those points at which we mistakenly attribute a cultural explanation when a "universal" one might serve as well.

Consider one example: the South Asian languages of honor and shame have been used to explain why rapes go unreported and women are reluctant to share stories of sexual violence even with close family members. The argument is that intense cultural shame about bringing further dishonor to their families prevents women from talking about rape or sexual violence.[72] This issue has been raised for Sikh women fleeing state violence in the Panjab who are seeking asylum in the United States and have been reluctant to recount their experiences to asylum officers. Yet, domestic and sexual violence specialists know that victims of sexual violence anywhere may feel intense shame and reluctance to talk about what they have experienced. In this instance, something not understood as a universal experience might effectively be applied as one, and the attempt to use culture as a form of explanation is employed as an essentialist tool to make the case for gender asylum.

Given the sensationalized reporting of such cases by the international media, there is both a stereotyping of non-western cultures as oppressive to women, and a presumption that patriarchal norms, discriminatory laws and gender-related violence are not also features of western societies. Yet the observation that "the UN sometimes uses sexist human rights language and does not consistently include a gender perspective in human rights reporting and gender expertise in field visits and operations" as well as the call by

---

71. See, e.g., Alison Dundes Renteln, The Unanswered Challenge of Relativism and the Consequences for Human Rights, 7 Hum. Rts. Q. 514 (1985); Alison Dundes Renteln, Relativism and the Search for Human Rights, 90 Am. Anthropologist 56 (1988); Alison Dundes Renteln, International Human Rights: Universalism Versus Relativism (1990); Ann- Belinda Preis, Human Rights as Culture Practice: An Anthropological Critique, 18 Hum. Rts. Q. 286 (1996); Eva Brems, Enemies or Allies? Feminism and Cultural Relativism as Dissident Voices in Human Rights Discourse, 19 Hum. Rts. Q. 136 (1997); Annette Marfording, Cultural Relativism and the Construction of Culture: An Examination of Japan, 19 Hum. Rts. Q. 431 (1997); Michael J. Perry, Are Human Rights Universal? The Relativist Challenge and Related Matters, 19 Hum. Rts. Q. 461 (1997); John J. Tilley, Cultural Relativism, 22 Hum. Rts. Q. 501 (2000).

72. This issue also has been raised with regard to the Partition of India. See Veena Das, National Honor and Practical Kinship: Of Unwanted Women and Children, in Critical Events 55 (Veena Das ed., 1995); Ritu Menon & Kamla Bhasin, Abducted Women, The State and Questions of Honor: Three Perspectives on the Recovery Operation in Post-Partition India, in Embodied Violence, supra note 69, at 1.

Amnesty International and others for the United Nations "to bring women's human rights from the margins into the mainstream by adopting gender-sensitive language"[73] also has resulted in the highlighting of cultural difference to reinforce stereotypic assumptions in human rights reports. For example, a recent News Release by Amnesty International on the twentieth anniversary of the Women's Convention began with this lead: "Pakistan 1999. Ghazala was set on fire by her brother in the name of honor. Her burned and naked body lay unattended on the street for two hours as nobody wanted to have anything to do with it."[74] The report continues, "Pakistan has ratified the United Nations Convention on the Elimination of all Forms of Discrimination Against Women (Women's Convention). The government is failing to take serious measures to safeguard and protect women's human rights."[75]

Amnesty International also singled Pakistan out for a special report on CEDAW in March 1997, *Pakistan Women's Human Rights Remain a Dead Letter: No Progress Towards the Realization of Women's Rights After the Ratification of the Convention on the Elimination of All Forms of Discrimination Against Women.*[76] Yet the United States is the only state in North America and Europe that is not a signatory to the Women's Convention.[77] All nations of South America have signed. The South Asian countries of India, Pakistan, Bangladesh, Bhutan, Sri Lanka, and Nepal have signed. CEDAW was also the basis of providing for constitutional protections for women's rights in Nepal and Sri Lanka; while feminists in Bangladesh were successful in reducing the number of the country's reservations on CEDAW. India ratified CEDAW in 1993, but also specified reservations on Articles 5(a) relating to cultural and customary practices, and 16 (1) relating to equality in marriage and family relations.[78] It is important to realize however, that these reservations are not necessarily regressive in the sense that the state is refusing to protect women from their communities (though many would argue that this is indeed the case), but can be seen as accountable to the tremendous ferment in the country about the merits of having a uniform civil code versus having reforms generated by women's

---

73. Press Release, Amnesty International, International Women's Day—50 Years of Women's Rights? (6 Mar. 1998).
74. *Id.*
75. *Id.*
76. Amnesty International Special Report (1997).
77. President Carter signed the treaty in 1980, but the US Senate failed to ratify the treaty in 1994 and again in 2002. *See* Lester Munson, *CEDAW: It's Old it Doesn't Work and We Don't Need It,* 10 Hum. Rts. Brief (2003).
78. CEDAW, *supra* note 19. The government of India issued a declaration, stating that it would follow a policy of non-interference in the personal affairs of different communities when implementing these provisions, as well as a reservation:

    With regard to articles 5 (a) and 16 (1) of the Convention on the Elimination of All Forms of Discrimination Against Women, the Government of the Republic of India

rights activists within those communities.[79] In other words, the supposed failure to observe international law—the point at which national sovereignty is either challenged by or exercised through the woman question—may also be the space where democratic civil libertarian politics emerge to hold the nation-state accountable.

CEDAW might eventually become an effective alternative to gender asylum. It calls for UN member states to ratify sixteen articles which pertain to women's social, economic and political rights. Article 19 specifies gender-based violence as a form of discrimination. At this moment, only 165 of 188 member nations have signed. In 1999, the United Nations also established an Optional Protocol to the Women's Convention which would allow women to bring complaints against states that have failed to uphold their commitments to the Women's Convention.[80] Only twenty-eight states have so far signed the Optional Protocol. The Women's Convention also establishes a committee of twenty-three independent experts, which reviews the reports that state parties are required to submit indicating measures taken to implement the Women's Convention.

V.   US DOMESTIC VIOLENCE AS A HUMAN RIGHTS ISSUE

In a recent Human Rights Watch Report on Pakistan, it was estimated that eight women were raped every twenty-four hours, and 70–95 percent of all

---

declares that it shall abide by and ensure these provisions in conformity with its policy of non-interference in the personal affairs of any Community without its initiative and consent.

With regard to article 16 (2) of the Convention on the Elimination of All Forms of Discrimination Against Women, the Government of the Republic of India declares that though in principle it fully supports the principle of compulsory registration of marriages, it is not practical in a vast country like India with its variety of customs, religions and level of literacy.

Reservation:

With regard to article 29 of the Convention on the Elimination of All Forms of Discrimination Against Women, the Government of the Republic of India declares that it does not consider itself bound by paragraph 1 of this article.

Available at www.hri.ca/fortherecord1999/documentation/reservations/cedaw.

79. *See* Flavia Agnes, *Redefining the Agenda of the Women's Movement Within a Secular Framework, in* Women and the Hindu Right, *supra* note 24, at 136; Nivedita Meon, *Women and Citizenship, in* Wages of Freedom 241 (Partha Chatterjee ed., 1998); Rajeshwari Sundar Rajan, *Women Between Community and State: Some Implications of the Uniform Civil Codes Debates in India,* 18 Social Text 5 (2000).

80. CEDAW, *supra* note 19, art. 12; *Elaboration of a Draft Optional Protocol to the Convention on the Elimination of All Forms of Discrimination Against Women, Draft Report of the Open-ended Working Group,* U.N. ESCOR, Comm'n on the Status of Women, 40th Sess., Agenda Item 5, U.N. Doc. E/CN.6/1996/WG/L.1 and Add.1 (1996).

women had experienced domestic or familial violence.[81] Those are rather shocking statistics. Still, the recitation of such statistics also works to obscure certain facts about the United States where:

— As many as four million women are abused by their husbands or live-in partners each year.

— A woman is raped every two minutes (or according to another esti-mate, 1.3 women are raped every minute, resulting in seventy-eight rapes each hour, 1,872 rapes each day, 56,160 rapes each month, and 683,280 rapes each year).[82] Between 1995 and 1996, more than 670,000 women were the victims of rape, attempted rape, or sexual assault. Yet for that same year, it was estimated that only 31 percent of rapes and sexual assault were reported, less than one in every three.[83]

— In 1992, the United States had the world's highest rape rate of the countries that publish such statistics: four times higher than Germany, thirteen times higher than England, and twenty times higher than Japan.[84]

— 31 percent of all rape victims develop Rape-Related Post-Traumatic Stress Disorder (RR-PTSD) at some point during their lifetimes. Based on US census reports, it has been estimated that 1.3 million currently have RR-PTSD, 3.8 million women have had RR-PTSD and roughly 211,000 will develop RR-PTSD each year.[85]

Violence against women has reached epidemic proportions in the United States. Yet, one will never see any of these statistics cited in a Human Rights report.[86] The Human Rights Watch webpage on "Domestic Violence" states that "[u]nremedied domestic violence essentially denies women equality before the law and reinforces their subordinate social status. Men use domestic violence to diminish women's autonomy and sense of self-worth. States that fail to prevent and prosecute domestic violence treat

---

81. HUMAN RIGHTS WATCH, CRIME OR CUSTOM, *supra* note 42, § V.
82. NATIONAL VICTIM CENTER AND CRIME VICTIMS RESEARCH AND TREATMENT CENTER, RAPE IN AMERICA: A REPORT TO THE NATION, 23 Apr. 1992 (on file with author). Another estimate from the FBI, US Dept. of Justice, Uniform Crime Reports 1992, held that a woman was raped every five minutes, resulting in 105,120 rapes per year. Revised estimates from the Bureau of Justice Statistics at the US Dept. of Justice put the number of sexual assaults against women at 500,000 for 1992 and 1993, including 170,000 rapes and 140,000 attempted rapes. These numbers would mean that a woman was sexually assaulted almost every minute for 1992–1993. *See* ASSOC. PRESS, *Survey Questioning Changed, FBI Doubles its Estimates of Rape,* N.Y. TIMES, 17 Aug. 1995, at A18.
83. BUREAU OF JUSTICE STATISTICS, U.S. DEPT. OF JUSTICE, NATIONAL CRIME VICTIMIZATION SURVEY (1997).
84. *Id.*
85. NATIONAL VICTIM CENTER REPORT, *supra* note 82.
86. Though abuses against women in US prisons have been the subject of special investiga-tions.

women as second-class citizens and send a clear message that the violence against them is of no concern to the broader society"[87] and goes on to list fifteen states, including Nepal and Pakistan where domestic violence is a problem.[88] The United States is not mentioned.

Examining the percentage of women who have been physically assaulted by an intimate partner, the rate is 22 percent for the United States (based on a 1993 survey, and remember that one in three rapes go unreported), 26 percent for India (based on a study of six states for 1999), and 47 percent for Bangladesh (based on 1992 study). By one set of estimates, then, the United States and India share much more in common in terms of rates of domestic abuse (certainly a "quality of life" issue) than might be supposed by perusing the United Nations Development Programme Human Development Index in which the United States is ranked second, and India is ranked 134. (Sri Lanka is ranked 97, Pakistan 128, Bangladesh 146, Nepal 151, Bhutan 160, and Afghanistan 170 in 1995.)[89] Attempts to use such measures,[90] or country reports issued by the US State Department[91] to assess the degree to which women in non-western countries possess rights thus deploy a very flawed yardstick. The "woman question," once a marker of colonial and nationalist discourses, now stands literally as a signifier of the neo-liberal economy not only of the extent to which "developing nations" have successfully adopted structural adjustment development policies.

VI. CONCLUSION

In several ways culture brings human rights talk in South Asia into crisis. First, culture is gendered and violently masculinized so that particular countries or nation-states are marked by their crimes against women: to say India is to think dowry deaths, to say Pakistan is to think honor killing, to say Bangladesh is to think of acid-throwing disfigurement. These forms of description do the work of characterizing weak states in a neo-liberal economy, and as the cultural face of globalization both constitute and are constituted by human rights discourses on the region. One has only to

---

87. Human Rights Watch webpage, Domestic Violence, *available at* www.hrw.org/women/domesticviolence.html.

88. Similarly in its webpage for Sexual Violence the lead sentence reads "women everywhere are sexually assaulted, and their primary attackers are granted impunity" but the primary examples on the page are Russia, India, and Pakistan. *Available at* www.hrw.org/women/sexualviolence.html.

89. United Nations Development Program, Human Development Report 155–57, tb. 1 (1995).

90. *See* Clair Apodaca, *Measuring Women's Economic and Social Rights Achievement,* 20 Hum. Rts. Q. 139 (1998).

91. *See* Steven C. Poe et al., *Global Patterns in the Achievement of Women's Human Rights to Equality,* 19 Hum. Rts. Q. 813 (1997).

remember the call for the World Bank to undertake "rights-based development" to actualize this connection.[92] The mainstreaming of human rights norms into multi-lateral lending institutions should give us pause. While the imposition of international human rights norms upon the global South[93] may on the surface be appealing to many, they may also mask the ways in which lending policies exacerbate or even help to create the social divisions implicated in the very human rights violations international lending institutions seek to monitor.

The link between domestic violence and globalization may not appear to be a direct one, but it is possible that human rights discourse works to obfuscate, if not sever that very linkage. As Nesiah reminds us, the universalization of women's oppression in feminist human rights discourse works to mask global structural features.[94]

Feminist scholars have productively established that domestic violence is not a private, familial matter; it cannot be separated from an understanding of public attitudes toward women. In a like vein, violence against women cannot be separated from the violence of the international economy. "In a world in which women perform two-thirds of the hourly labor and receive ten percent of the income and hold barely one percent of the property, disempowerment is clearly economic."[95] It is thus important to understand domestic violence as part of the structural violence wrought by liberalization and structural adjustment policies. Liberalization has impoverished millions, and there are indications that structural adjustment policies have hit women the hardest,[96] with some evidence that women in urban as well as rural areas are working multiple jobs and two to three shifts per day. More work does not mean economic freedom—it means deepening subjection to already entrenched forms of male authority. Just as many theorists are now arguing that economic rights should be considered human rights,[97] so too should domestic violence be understood as a part of the structural violence against women produced by the international economy.

---

92. *See, e.g.,* Korinna Horta, *Rhetoric and Reality: Human Rights and the World Bank,* 15 HARV. HUM. RTS. J. 228 (2002); Dana Clark, *The World Bank and Human Rights: The Need for Greater Accountability,* 15 HARV. HUM. RTS. J. 205 (2002).

93. *See, e.g.,* THE POWER OF HUMAN RIGHTS: INTERNATIONAL NORMS AND DOMESTIC CHANGE 1, 12 (Thomas Risse et al. eds., 1999) which seeks to understand "the conditions under which international human rights norms are internalized in domestic practices" and develops a series of models to understand nation-state "instrumental adaptation to pressures."

94. Nesiah, *supra* note 3, at 18–19.

95. Gayle Binion, *Human Rights: A Feminist Perspective,* 17 HUM. RTS. Q. 509, 511 (1995).

96. *See* Bharati Sadasivam, *The Impact of Structural Adjustment on Women: A Governance and Human Rights Agenda,* 19 HUM. RTS. Q. 630 (1997).

97. *See* Wesley Milner et al., *Security Rights, Subsistence Rights and Liberties: A Theoretical Survey of the Landscape,* 21 HUM. RTS. Q. 403 (1999); Craig Scott, *Reaching Beyond (Without Abandoning) the Category of "Economic, Social and Cultural Rights,"* 21 HUM. RTS. Q. 633 (1999).

Finally, while one might expect the critique of gender essentialism to suggest that women cannot be partitioned from their communities, the discourse on women's human rights forces a separation of women's rights from community rights that reinstates gender as the primary determinant of a women's identity. What does it mean when the language of gender asylum creates the conditions for women's exile not only from her national origin, but from her community of affiliation? Does human-rights feminism, as an instance of a universalizing discourse, re-enact a form of cold-war citizenship with hidden consequences for how we understand the process of claiming rights? What role does the South Asian diaspora play in redefining women's rights on the subcontinent? What are the consequences for the feminist and civil libertarian movements of South Asia when scholars, legal critics and activists in diaspora must resort to human rights "instruments" that inevitably incite talk of negative cultural difference? I cannot claim answers to these questions, but if one remembers that women are not only victims, but also agents with the capacity to effect political change, then the contradictions of gender asylum should teach us to pay more attention to feminist democratic politics in South Asia and how we reflect on the relationship between the movement to end domestic violence in the United States and those movements in South Asia.

I end with two questions. First, what would it mean to understand domestic violence in South Asia and its narrative production, as a product not only of culture, but of state-level policy and the neo-liberal economy? Second, what would it mean to speak of a culture of violence against US women, and to understand domestic violence in the United States as a human rights issue?

PART III

Violence and Women

Chapter 9

Women's Voices, Women's Pain

Ustinia Dolgopol[1]

I. INTRODUCTION

The feminist movement has brought to the forefront the necessity of listening to women's voices and appreciating the distinctive insights of women. For centuries societies dominated by males have failed to document the experiences of women. Often there is a denial of the individuality and separateness of women's experiences.

The history of the comfort women is the story of voices being denied and suppressed. It is also the story of oppression and subjugation. Between 1928 and 1945 approximately 150,000 to 200,000[2] women were taken by the Japanese and used as sex slaves.[3] There is little doubt that the inferior status of women in Japan and elsewhere enabled the Japanese to believe that

1. The author was a member of an investigative mission sent by the International Commission of Jurists to the Philippines, Japan, the Republic of Korea, and the Democratic People's Republic of Korea to interview government officials and victims of military sexual slavery. A preliminary report of the mission has been published by the International Commission of Jurists under the title: *Comfort Women: The Unfinished Ordeal*. Much of the factual material in this paper is based on the work undertaken by the mission. A final report has recently been published under the same title.
2. No definitive figures exist as to the number of women taken. Researchers in the Republic of Korea have suggested that the number is at least 200,000. The report, issued by the government, does not state a figure, urging that more research be done in this area. George Hicks, an independent journalist who has spent eighteen months researching the issues believes the number to be about 135,000. George Hicks, The Comfort Women: Sex Slaves of the Imperial Japanese Army (draft, in personal possession of the author). Won-Loy Chan, an Allied officer who interrogated some comfort women at the end of the war, wrote that no one knew exactly how many women had been taken by the Japanese, but that some estimates range as high as 200,000. It appears that he believed that was the number taken from the Korean peninsula, which suggests that far more might have been taken overall. CHAN, WON-LOY, BURMA—THE UNTOLD STORY.
3. Most often the term "comfort women" has been used, as this is the English translation of the Japanese terminology. The two organizations that were interviewed by the mission preferred the term "military sexual slavery" as they believed this more accurately conveyed the situation of the women.

it was possible to undertake such actions with impunity. This belief was not dispelled by Allied action at the close of the war. Despite their knowledge of what had happened to these women, the Allied Forces and their respective governments remained silent, thereby compounding the harm[4] inflicted on these women. References to the "comfort women" in Allied documents either contorted the women's experiences to make them appear responsible or focused on the Japanese military and the "amenities" provided to it, thereby making the women objects.[5]

Because the voices of the comfort women have been denied for so long, the emphasis of this paper will be on their experiences. In the world of men, labels are ascribed to phenomenon, and analysis is considered all important. However, if the experiences of women are to have an impact on our understanding of our world and our history, it is important that events particular to women be chronicled. Therefore, the following paper will concentrate on the lives of the women. Much of the factual material resulted from an investigative mission sent by the International Commission of Jurists (ICJ) to the Philippines, the Republic of Korea, the Democratic People's Republic of Korea, and Japan to interview the women and government officials. In order to give a "context" to the stories of the women, a brief overview of the events that took place in the Korean peninsula and the Philippines is necessary.

II.   THE HISTORICAL CONTEXT[6]

Relations between Japan and Korea have rarely been free of tension. Over the centuries Japan has tried to control or dominate Manchuria and the

---

4. I have chosen the word "harm" intentionally. See Adrian Howe, *The Problem of Privatised Injuries: Feminist Strategies for Litigation in* AT THE BOUNDARIES OF LAW (Fineman & Thomadsen eds., 1991), for a discussion of how the definition of harm can exclude the experiences of women.

5. By the close of the war the Allied Forces were aware of the existence of the comfort stations. British military documents include interviews of Korean women taken to Burma by the Japanese military. Despite their knowledge of the methods by which the women were taken—by force and deceit—the military officers still referred to the women as "camp followers." The Allied intelligence services described the comfort stations in other documents compiled to detail "amenities in the Japanese armed services." *See* Inter-ministerial Working Group on the Comfort Women Issue, Republic of Korea, *Military Comfort Women under Japanese Colonial Rule,* Interim Report (Seoul, July 1992) [hereinafter Inter-ministerial Working Group].

6. Much of the material in this section is taken from the preliminary report of the mission. *See* Ustinia Dolgopol & Snehal Paranjape, *Comfort Women: The Unfinished Ordeal* (International Commission of Jurists, Geneva, 1993) [hereinafter Preliminary Report]. The final report canvasses some of the same factual materials but gives greater detail on the comfort stations; it also includes new chapters. Ustinia Dolgopol & Snehal Paranjape, *Comfort Women: The Unfinished Ordeal* (International Commission of Jurists, Geneva, 1994) (draft, in personal possession of the author) [hereinafter Final ICJ Report].

Korean peninsula.[7] In recent times the government of Japan has apologized for its aggressive behavior toward the Korean people. Typical is a statement made in January 1992 by the then Prime Minister:

> We must not forget that our two countries have been linked for thousands of years. Regrettably, during much of this time, my country has historically been the aggressor and yours the victim. I take this opportunity to once again express my most heartfelt apologies for the unbearable pain and suffering brought upon you by my country in the past. Especially with the matter of comfort women coming to light, I am filled with pain and remorse.[8]

In 1905 Korea and Japan signed a treaty, making Korea a protectorate of Japan. The Korean Emperor ceded all sovereign power to the Japanese Emperor by treaty in 1910. The treaty stated that, henceforth, Koreans were to be Japanese subjects. Many scholars, Korean and Non-Korean, consider both of these treaties to be void under international law.

What distinguishes the period from 1905 onward in the minds of many Koreans is Japan's attempt to subjugate Korean culture to that of the Japanese and to eliminate the distinctive identity of the Koreans. Through a series of decrees, Japan took control of the system of education, making Japanese the language of instruction and introducing measures for teaching Japanese to adult Koreans. Koreans were also forced to change their names so that they more closely resembled those of the Japanese. For Koreans this was a particularly onerous obligation as names denoted ancestry and clan affiliation; to change their names meant breaking with family tradition and fundamentally affected the way in which family honor could be maintained.[9]

Korea was ruled through a Japanese Governor-General, usually a high-ranking military officer. The police and gendarmerie were controlled by the Japanese and included some Japanese nationals. Local village offices continued to be held by Koreans, but these officials were viewed with suspicion by the Korean people as they were thought to be under the control of the Japanese.

In addition to its control over the political life of the country, Japan assumed control of the economy. Agricultural produce, especially rice, and natural resources were confiscated and sent to Japan. After its invasion of China, Japan began to view the Korean peninsula as a potential source of labor, initially for its factories and ultimately for its military.[10]

---

7. Chong-Sik Lee, Japan and Korea: The Political Dimension (1985).
8. Inter-ministerial Working Group, *supra* note 5.
9. Lee, *supra* note 7, at 7–13.
10. *Id.* at 13–20. *See also* Memorandum in Support of Complaint against the Government of Japan for Damages Subcommittee by the Victims of the Asian-Pacific Theatre of World War II, submitted on 6 Dec. 1991 (Park, Chio-Bong and Thirty-four Others v. The Government of Japan) (English translation in possession of the author) [hereinafter Memorandum of Complaint].

During the 1930s, a supposedly voluntary mobilization program was introduced to marshal the human and material resources of Japan and Korea for the purpose of national defence. Under this program many Koreans were taken to Japan to work in mines, factories, and in agriculture. This program was expanded in 1939. Three years later Japan instituted a program of "collective mobilization." Between 1939 and 1942 somewhere between 258,666 and 294,467 men were conscripted, and an additional 282,000 were mobilized "voluntarily."[11] Given the numbers of people involved, it is difficult to accept that this recruitment of labor took place voluntarily. The strict security measures surrounding the factories suggest that Korean men were not allowed to leave their place of work.[12]

Then, in 1944, Japan began the compulsory mobilization of labor; from 1943 until 1945 somewhere between 502,616 and 858,366 men were forcibly conscripted. During this same period another 481,000 men were "mobilized voluntarily."[13]

Although information about the "mobilization" of women is more difficult to obtain, it appears that they were also regarded as a potential source of labor. In 1937 a program was introduced to encourage the recruitment of Korean women into the labor force. Again this program was nominally voluntary, but the evidence suggests that pressure was put on women to work in factories.[14] In 1941 Japan enacted legislation which stipulated that women between the ages of fourteen and twenty were to participate in the National Labor Service Corps for thirty days or less per year. Two years later the term was extended to sixty days. Subsequently, in 1944 the ages were revised to fourteen and forty-five years of age. Operating in tandem with this was the creation of a "voluntary corp" which had as its purpose the long term mobilization of women, usually for periods ranging from one to two years. Many women were sent to factories, particularly war industries in Korea and Japan.

It is within this context that the taking of women for the comfort stations has to be understood. By the late 1930s Japan was forcibly conscripting both women and men from the Korean peninsula. Such forcible conscription was tantamount to slavery. Given this situation it was inevitable that, when Japan decided to establish comfort stations on a massive scale, Korean women would be taken and forced to submit to sexual slavery in those stations.

---

11. Lee, *supra* note 7, at 13–20. It has been suggested that one of the causes of the decline in Japanese rice imports from Korea during this period of time was the movement of Korean labor from agriculture to industry in order to supply Japanese military needs in China. *See* Alan S. Milward, War, Economy and Society 1939–1945 (1977).

12. Lee, *supra* note 7, at 15–16.

13. *Id.* at 13–20

14. *Id.; see also* Memorandum of Complaint, *supra* note 10.

Another factor that should be borne in mind is the extensive poverty which existed in Korea during this period of time. It was not unusual for young children to leave their families in order to find work in towns and cities. This made them more vulnerable as there were no family members to advise or protect them. Also, it was common practice for families to use their children, particularly girls, to pay off family debts or to obtain immediate cash for housing and food. Most often, girl children were put to work as maids or nannies. Although girl children were sometimes sexually abused, it should not be assumed that this was routine. However, the separation from their families and the powerlessness of this situation made it easier for ruthless "masters" to sell these children to the Japanese. A number of the Korean women interviewed by the ICJ mission were sold in this manner to "recruiters" for the Japanese.

What happened to the Filipino women must also be understood in light of the events which took place in their country. Japan invaded the Philippines in 1942. Immediately prior to the outbreak of the Second World War the United States of America had agreed to release its colonial hold on the country. There was enormous resistance to Japanese rule in most parts of the country; several guerrilla armies were formed in an attempt to dislodge the Japanese. The Japanese retaliated with brutality. The International Military Tribunal for the Far East (hereinafter the Tribunal) described in detail the treatment meted out by the Japanese. The following excerpt from the judgment was in reference to massacres perpetrated in anticipation of Japanese withdrawal from the Philippines; it described a massacre which occurred at the Manila German Club in 1944:

> Japanese soldiers surrounded the club by a barricade of inflammable material then put gasoline over this barricade and ignited it. Thus the fugitives were forced to attempt to escape through the flaming barricade. Most of them were bayoneted and shot by the waiting Japanese soldiers. Some of the women were raped and their infants bayoneted in their arms. After raping the women the Japanese poured gasoline on their hair and ignited it. The breasts of some of the women were cut off by the Japanese soldiers.[15]

The Tribunal noted in its judgment that files captured by the Allies contained explicit instructions for the killing of Filipinos.[16] The Tribunal made it clear that the highest ranking members of the government and the military condoned and endorsed the actions taken by military officers in the field and that the government failed to punish any of those committing such atrocities. Japanese control over the Philippines meant that military personnel felt at liberty to seize Filipinas and use them for their sexual gratification.

---

15. 20 R. J. Pritchard & S. M. Zaide, The Tokyo War Crimes Trial 49, 592 (1981).
16. *Id.* at 49, 693–94.

The military authorized the establishment of comfort stations throughout the Philippines. Because of this complete objectification of women, Japanese soldiers believed it was their right to have women available to them. Thus, soldiers would kidnap women from their villages and take them to nearby military installations. It is apparent that those in command felt able to take women as they wished, even if they had not been given permission to establish a comfort station.

III. THE COMFORT STATIONS

A. Government Responsibility

When the issue of government responsibility was initially raised in Japan, the government denied that the comfort stations had been officially sanctioned by the government of that time. It was suggested that all the comfort stations were set up by "private entrepreneurs." This version of events was not accepted by scholars or activists within Japan. Professor Yoshimi of Chuo University, Japan, spent many hours in the archives of the Ministry of Defence. He uncovered documents establishing conclusively that the Japanese military authorized the establishment of the comfort stations. Further evidence of government involvement has come from former soldiers who were prompted to speak out after the government's denial. As a result of efforts by the women themselves, scholars, and activists the government has been forced to change its position and has now accepted full responsibility.

It appears that a policy favoring the establishment of comfort stations was adopted sometime between 1936 and 1937.[17] During the 1930s Japan invaded China. The behavior of its troops in Shanghai and Nanjing (then referred to as Nanking) led to an international outcry. Worried about its international reputation, the Japanese government and military became concerned by the Chinese reprisals against Japanese soldiers. These concerns apparently prompted the military to consider the establishment of "comfort houses." An entry in the official log of the Ninth Brigade referred to a circular, dated 27 June 1938, which was issued by Naosaburo Okabe, Chief of Staff of the North China Expeditionary Troops. The circular stated that the number of rapes committed by Japanese soldiers was threatening security in

---

17. It appears that "comfort stations" may have existed prior to this, but on a less extensive scale and without such direct involvement from the military. A statement issued by the Japanese government on 4 Aug. 1993 refers to the existence of a comfort station in Shanghai during 1932 and states "it is assumed that comfort stations were in existence since around that time to the end of World War II."

northern China, and that the Chinese were taking revenge. In Okabe's view it was necessary to set up "comfort houses" as soon as possible.[18]

What is not clear from the documents is the nationality of the women being placed in the early comfort stations. It has been suggested that the instructions to create such establishments could only have been carried out this rapidly if the majority of women were Chinese, but there is no conclusive evidence about this point. There have been reports that Chinese women were put into comfort stations in other theaters of war, which would support the view that they were taken to the early comfort houses.[19]

A statement taken from a former soldier, Mr. Kuki Nagatomi, by the ICJ mission supports the view that Chinese women were used in these first comfort stations. Mr. Nagatomi originally went to China as a student, eventually joining the Special Missions Organization, a form of secret service operating within the military. In 1938 he was told by the military to set up a comfort station in the Anching area (located in the region between Shanghai and Nanjing), which he did. A local person was used to establish the comfort house, and the women taken into it were Chinese.

The general acceptance of the use of girls and women for the sexual gratification of the Japanese military meant that Japanese troops felt it was their "right" as soldiers to have women available to them. In the Philippines a number of the women were taken to military barracks, as well as to areas which were not established garrisons. The prevailing ethos in the military allowed the soldiers to feel that they would not be penalized for such actions.

From the available evidence it is clear that the Japanese military condoned the establishment of the comfort stations and, in some cases, was responsible for their construction, furnishing, and day to day management. Some of the comfort stations were "managed" by civilians, but even in these circumstances they were heavily regulated by the military. Documents made available through the United Kingdom Ministry of Defence and the United States Defense Department contained translations of regulations issued by the Japanese military for brothels maintained in southern China and various regions of the Philippines.[20] These regulations were incredibly

---

18. Final ICJ Report, *supra* note 6, at 27.
19. There is no doubt that there were Chinese women in some of the comfort stations. A report prepared by the Supreme Commander of the Allied Powers included translations of regulations issued for the south China area. The report included a chart which enumerated the rates for different nationalities; the chart referred to Japanese, Korean, and Chinese women. Supreme Commander of the Allied Powers, "Amenities in the Japanese Armed Forces," (Nov. 15, 1945). See also Final ICJ Report, *supra* note 6, at 29–37, for greater detail on these regulations.
20. *See* Final ICJ Report, *supra* note 6, at 29–37 (referring to separate regulations issued by the various branches of the Japanese military).

detailed, covering such points as who was to have access, the rates to be charged soldiers, petty officers, and commissioned officers, the hours of operation, and medical examinations of the women. They also included forms for licenses to be issued by the military.[21]

By the 1940s the women were being euphemistically referred to in correspondence as "Special Service Personnel Group." A series of documents which went between the field and Tokyo military headquarters included requests for additional comfort women and referred to "recruiters" heading to Korea to obtain additional women. These documents demonstrated the immense organizational effort put into the operation and control of the comfort stations by the Japanese military. One such communication from Rikichi And, Commander in Taiwan to the Minister-of-War, Hideki Tojo (later one of the main defendants in the Tokyo war crimes trials), requested travel permits for three recruiters chosen to go to Korea to select women for the troops stationed in Borneo. According to the telegraph the request emanated from the troops in the field. An affirmative reply to his request was sent from Tokyo.

The involvement of the Navy in this practice was first made public in 1955 when Minoru Shigermura, a commander in the Japanese Navy, documented a communication from the Naval Affairs Bureau to the Chief of Staff for the South West Pacific. The Bureau detailed the responsibility of the Navy for providing accommodation and furnishings for the comfort women who would be arriving. The communique stated that the comfort houses would be privately operated but supervised by the Navy. The document contained a list of the places to which comfort women would be sent: fifty to Penang, Malaya; forty-five to Macau; forty to Barihappan, on the island of Borneo; thirty to Java, Indonesia; and unspecified numbers to Singapore and Ambong.

The military was extensively involved in the recruitment and transportation of the comfort women as well. A number of the Korean women interviewed stated that members of the Japanese military police were present when they were taken from their families. Sometimes military police would use force to take them; in some instances family members who attempted to stop the kidnapping were killed or seriously injured. In the Philippines women testified to being kidnapped by members of the military.

Evidence gathered by the Allies supported the oral testimony of the women. Allied documents concerning Burma contained an interview with a civilian brothel owner, a Japanese man who had gone to Korea as a restaurateur. The Japanese military suggested that he could earn more money by establishing a brothel for Japanese troops in Burma. Due to declining trade he decided to take up the suggestion and applied for permission to take girls

---

21. *Id.*

from Korea to Burma. His application was made to the local Army head-quarters. The documents he received from the army giving him permission to take girls to Burma also requested all other military units to give him any necessary assistance with respect to transport, rations, and medical care.

After purchasing twenty-two Korean girls,[22] he headed to the port of Pusan where he boarded a ship with ninety other Japanese men undertaking the same venture. He stated that there were a total of 730 Korean girls on the ship. Although on a passenger ship, they received a military escort. They headed to Singapore where they changed vessels and headed to Rangoon. The Army provided free passage for the girls, although the man was required to pay for meals.

Many of the Korean women interviewed by the ICJ mission described being kept at an "inn" with new girls arriving everyday. After several days, they travelled by train to a port city such as Pusan and were placed on passenger ships. Some of the women stated that they were on military ships. In either case the military was heavily involved and was well aware of the reasons for the women's transport from the Korean peninsula.

One of the former soldiers, Mr. Yoshiro Suzuki, provided information on the manner in which the women had been brought to the comfort stations and were forced to remain there. He said that a particular woman whom he visited frequently told him that she had thought she was becoming a nurse with the Japanese military. He indicated that she repeatedly said that she had been deceived; she cried for most of the time that he knew her. Mr. Suzuki also stated that his colleagues told him that they had heard similar stories from the women they visited. Each of these women claimed to have been deceived and wanted to go home. As the women were controlled by the organizers and managers, they would not have been able to go home; also none of them would have had money. Mr. Suzuki believed that the women were afraid of the managers, that they were constantly supervised, and that they were afraid to go out of the comfort house. The managers were responsible for supplying food and clothing. Mr. Suzuki described the women's situation as one of extreme poverty.

B.   Organization of the Comfort Stations

One of the Japanese military police interviewed, Mr. Schiro Ichikawa, was in charge of a comfort house while stationed in Manchuria in 1944.

---

22. In Korea as in Japan at this time poor families sometimes sold their children to pay off debts or to obtain immediate cash for housing or food. Usually there was an agreement concerning the number of years a child would have to stay with the person paying for them. Although girl children were sexually abused, it cannot be said that when families sold a

During his testimony Mr. Ichikawa drew a general outline of a comfort house under his control which showed an entrance area, a small waiting room, and a central corridor with adjoining smaller rooms. He indicated that each of the rooms was approximately four feet by five feet and was furnished with a mat, mattress, and blanket. This particular building was made of brick.

According to his testimony, the house was under the control of the military although there were outside managers: a husband and wife of Korean origin who were stationed there to oversee the women. Mr. Ichikawa was firm in his view that this house and many other houses were under the control of the military. Private houses were more often established within a local restaurant and most often catered specifically to military officers.

All ranks in the military had access to the comfort house under Mr. Ichikawa's control. The fee varied according to the rank of the soldier. Upon arrival a soldier would obtain a permit for entry: those for the rank and file were black, those for non-commissioned officers were blue, and those for officers were red. The military police kept an accurate account of the number of times a soldier visited a comfort house. Given the soldiers' low wages, the officials' suspicions would be raised if a rank and file soldier visited a comfort house more than once or twice a month. Too great a frequency might indicate that the soldier was trafficking in a prohibited substance or was defrauding the local population.

The military police, concerned that soldiers might reveal military secrets to the women, limited the number of visits to prevent relationships developing between a soldier and a comfort woman. Every morning the Korean couple provided to the military police a list of users for each woman and the military police would look to see if one particular soldier was visiting the same woman too often.

Once a week a medical doctor examined each woman to determine whether or not she was suffering from a venereal disease. Mr. Ichikawa emphasized that this was not done for the benefit of the woman but for the benefit of the soldiers. Most of the women were suffering from uritis, an inflammation of the urethra.

He did not know whether any of the women were paid. The managers bought food for the women in the commissary. He does not recall ever seeing a woman making a purchase for herself.

---

child they were aware that they would be used as mistresses or put into houses of prostitution. Sometimes girls were put to work as maids or nannies and were not sexually abused. The witness' testimony relating to his purchases of the girls cannot be assumed to mean that all of the families were aware of what would happen to their children.

Having made this admission, Mr. Ichikawa was frank enough to state that he had availed himself of the service. There were approximately thirty women at this comfort station, all of whom were Korean. It was located in the center of the town, and troops stationed in the general area, as well as those moving through, had access to the comfort station.

Testimony taken during the ICJ mission revealed that the vast majority of the women were held as virtual prisoners. Most of the women interviewed stated that they were not allowed outside of designated areas, such as army garrisons (which most often occurred in the Philippines) or small areas away from the main buildings (which seems to have been the case in China and Burma). In some areas, such as Manila, the military issued specific regulations about the women's freedom of movement. These regulations prohibited the women from going outside of designated areas without permission. The women were only allowed to take walks in specified areas between 8:00 am and 10:00 am; otherwise permission was needed from the officer in charge. Only a few of the women interviewed by the ICJ mission stated that they were allowed to go into a local village or town. It should be recalled that many of the Korean women were held in these comfort stations for as long as nine years. Some of the women were held in complete isolation, not being allowed to speak with one another or with any one else such as cooks or cleaners.

The number of women taken to comfort stations even by the end of the 1930s can only be guessed at, but must have been quite large. A report dated April 1939, prepared by the Twenty-first Army Unit deployed in southern China, stated that there were 850 comfort women under the Unit's immediate control. Another 150 women were under the control of various troops being supervised by the Unit. The report also indicated that comfort houses originally established for officers were being opened to ordinary soldiers.[23] Furthermore, the report furnished evidence of the military's involvement in the control and management of the comfort houses; in particular, it referred to the control and management of the Security Division and head of the Military Police.

The conditions of the women can be gleaned from this report. The Twenty-first Army Unit had approximately 50,000 soldiers. This meant that 1,000 women were being held for the sexual gratification of 50,000 soldiers. Mr. Suzuki was not aware of the number of soldiers that each woman was forced to receive each day, but does remember on Sundays there were long queues of soldiers. He estimated that each woman was forced to receive twenty to thirty soldiers.

---

23. Final ICJ Report, *supra* note 6, at 28.

C.   The Aftermath

Little is known about what happened to the women at the close of the war. Although one would guess that several thousand women should still be alive,[24] only a few hundred have come forward. Many women did not survive; there are accounts of Japanese soldiers killing women because they feared the women would reveal their ordeal or military secrets to the Allies. This is confirmed by the Allied reports referred to above. Women interviewed by the mission said that they witnessed several women commit suicide because they feared the shame that would attach to them if they returned home. Mr. Yoshiro Suzuki described the desertion of the women by Japanese troops. Some of the women taken to China stayed there after the war.

Many of the women would have been suffering from venereal diseases. Several of those we interviewed stated that they sought medical treatment for various forms of venereal disease when they returned to their homeland (Korea) or homes (Philippines). Some of the women felt unable to seek medical assistance and either treated themselves or were treated by their families with herbal medicines. Many have had continuing medical problems because of their infestation with venereal disease. Mr. Suzuki referred to estimates made during the war that between thirty and forty percent of Japanese soldiers were suffering from some form of venereal disease. He suggested that there was not a single woman in any of the comfort houses who enjoyed complete health.

Most of the women interviewed were unable to reveal their experiences to anyone, including members of their immediate families. This forced them to carry alone an enormous emotional and psychological burden. Fear of revealing their shameful secret compelled many women to keep their distance from relatives and friends. The pain of what they endured was evident in their language and the great emotional strain the interviews placed on them. Because of this, the violation of their human rights has to be understood as something more than an act for a defined period of time: it is a violation which continues to affect their lives today.

IV.   THE HIDDEN PAIN

Under the auspices of the International Commission of Jurists, women were interviewed in the Republic of the Philippines, the Republic of Korea, and

---

24. George Hicks has surmised that at least 58,000 women should still be alive. Hicks, *supra* note 2, at 3.

the Democratic People's Republic of Korea. The majority of the women came from economically disadvantaged families and were particularly vulnerable to force and deceit. The tragedy these women endured must be understood in the context of the societies in which they lived. At the time these women were taken by the Japanese, heavy emphasis was placed on chastity. Therefore, the acts of brutality committed against the women went beyond the immediate and horrific suffering of the continual rapes. For the most part, the women were left with a profound sense of shame and considered themselves to be inferior human beings. Their pain and suffering has endured throughout their lifetime.

It has taken enormous courage for the women to tell their stories and to give the details of their experiences. The interviews recalled to them the full horror of what had happened as they virtually relived their experiences. As a woman, I feel deeply indebted to them for giving so much of themselves emotionally and for enabling me to gain greater insight into the history of women.

No greater manifestation of courage could exist than that exhibited by women such as Lola (Grandmother) Rosa, the first Filipina to come forward and tell her story. Many of the Filipinas we interviewed told us that they would not have come forward if they had not heard her speaking on the radio and television. While in Manila, Lola Rosa accompanied the ICJ mission to Fort Santiago, and we witnessed the respect that many Filipinos, young and old, have for her. Her commitment to insuring that this aspect of Filipino and women's history is not lost is admirable. Despite her age she now travels the country to encourage other women to come forward. She has also been to Japan for the Public Hearings organized in December 1992 and is a party to one of the lawsuits filed in Japan seeking compensation from the Japanese government. Her story is not reproduced here as it available from other sources.[25]

Below are excerpts from some of the interviews undertaken during the ICJ mission. Because the women chose individually to come forward, the stories told here may not fit the general pattern of women being taken to and held in comfort houses. This is particularly true in the Philippines where the majority of women interviewed were not held in what might be described as "typical" comfort houses. Many of the women in the Philippines lived in military camps, either in established barracks or in tents with soldiers. One woman lived inside a tunnel. Superficially this pattern appears different

---

25. Those interested can obtain a copy of the text of her interview with the ICJ mission from the ICJ, Geneva, Switzerland, or can write to the Filipina Task Force for Women Drafted into Military Sexual Slavery by Japan and ask for written materials produced by that organization.

from the experience of the Korean women. However, the kidnapping and rape of the Filipinas was also fostered by the general attitude toward women. The availability of the comfort houses, established, controlled, and in many cases operated by the Japanese military, influenced the soldiers to believe that they too were entitled to take women and use their bodies without fear of punishment.

A.   Philippines

1.   Julia Porras, age 64[26]

One day when she was thirteen, she heard her sister who was washing clothes downstairs shout "run." She was surprised and looked out of the window. She saw some Japanese men dressed in camouflage outfits moving in the grass toward their house. She saw her sister running and instinctively jumped out of the window and cut her leg on a tree stump near the house. Because of her wound she was slow to get away and a Japanese soldier caught her by her hair and pulled her to the ground. She began to bow and to shout "I surrender" at which point she was slapped and her mouth and nose began to bleed. The soldier tied her hands with a handkerchief and she was dragged into the woods where two trucks were waiting.

One truck was full of soldiers and the other seemed to be a patrol truck as it only had a few soldiers. She was thrown into the second truck. At this point the soldiers began laughing at her. The truck took her and the soldiers to a tunnel which was full of military equipment including machine guns, rifles, bullets and canned goods as well as some cots to sleep on. Ms. Porras described the space to the interviewer: it would have been approximately seven feet in diameter and ten to twelve feet in length; as to height, the tunnel was just large enough to stand in. When she arrived, there were two other women there.

The first person to come over to her was an officer who she believes had indicated to the other soldiers that they ought to stay away from her. He untied her hands and began to kiss her; at first she thought that he was trying to calm her down because she was so young and then later realized that his actions had sexual overtones. As she attempted to evade his moves he grabbed her and slapped her face. At this point he put his hand under her dress and began to pull down her underwear, pushed her down onto a tarpaulin and pushed her legs apart. As she was attempting to keep her legs closed he continued to beat her all over her legs. The soldier never took his clothes off as he raped her. She continued to shout from the pain. After it

---

26. Preliminary Report, *supra* note 6, at 23–26.

was over she said she was unable to stand and curled up in a corner of the tunnel feeling as if her entire body were in pain. She was bleeding and continued to cry. After the officer raped her she was raped by another four soldiers.

She does not remember how many soldiers she was forced to have intercourse with each day; all she remembers is that each time one soldier was finished she would be forced to wipe herself with a cloth before the next soldier came to her. She was not permitted to speak with the other women in the tunnel and they were placed in separate areas.

The rapes continued on a nightly basis and sometimes occurred during the day. In addition to the soldiers in the tunnel she was sometimes forced to have sex with soldiers patrolling their area. There were fifteen to twenty soldiers in the tunnel on a permanent basis. As with other victims, Ms. Porras described herself as entering into a state of numbness while in the tunnel.

After the American bombardment of the Philippines began the Japanese soldiers ran from the tunnel and she and the other women were able to run away. She headed for her family home and arrived to discover that they had moved to another area; a neighbor went to get her parents for her. While waiting for their return she contemplated suicide, feeling herself to be worthless. When her parents came to her and asked what had happened she was unable to tell them and just cried. She believes that her mother knew although they never spoke about it. It was only when other women began to come forward that she decided to tell her story.

B.   Republic of Korea

1.   Kim Pok Sun[27]

Ms. Kim was born on 20 February 1926, by the lunar calendar. She lived in a remote village with her grandfather, her parents and two siblings both of whom were girls. Her parents were poor farmers. Her parents were divorced when she was twelve years old and she went to live with her paternal uncle.

During 1944 her uncle became concerned about her situation having heard that girls were being kidnapped for "sex slaves." She did not believe that she was at risk of being kidnapped because she was "immature" and "tall and fat." She said that her uncle had tried to convince her to get married but that she had refused a marriage proposal made to her.

Her uncle became increasingly concerned about her welfare and told her she should stay out of sight and remain in the family's attic. She followed her uncle's instructions for approximately two weeks, then believing that the

---

27. *Id.* at 43–47.

atmosphere had calmed down, went out in the yard to have lunch with her cousins. As there was no gate around the family's house it was possible for neighbors and others to see what was happening in the general vicinity of their house.

During lunch a Korean man in a military uniform came in with two Japanese Military Police. The Korean man sat on the ground while she and her cousins finished their lunch and then said to her uncle, "Why do you leave your niece at home, you must send her to Japan for one year in order for her to work. She can earn big money there. And when she returns with the money she can meet a good man and get married." She asked this Korean man how much she would earn per month, how long she would have to stay in Japan and when she would be able to go home. He again repeated that she would stay for one year and said that she could either be paid monthly or have all her money deposited during that period and take it all with her when she left. Her uncle indicated that he was responsible for her as her parents were divorced and that she should get married in Korea and not go to Japan.

At this point the mood of the Korean and the Japanese changed; until that point they had been quite friendly to the family but when her uncle said no, the Japanese stood up and dragged her out of the yard. She asked to be able to take her personal belongings with her and was told that she would not need any clothing or other belongings as they would all be provided for her. She was driven to Kwanju where she was made to stay in an inn with five other girls. No one would tell her what was happening to her. As she understood a little Japanese from her school days, she listened to a conversation between the Japanese and a Mr. Trae, a Korean man. Mr. Trae was told not to say anything to her. During the two days at the inn she spoke to some of the other women; they were from various places on the Korean Peninsula. Some of them were married, others were quite young. The women were guarded constantly. At the end of two days they boarded a train; the Japanese soldier paid for the tickets.

They arrived in Seoul and were put on another train and taken into Inch'ŏn where she was taken to a Japanese military camp. She estimated there were already sixty girls at the camp. The building they were put into had three rooms, each housing twenty girls. Six girls were put into another separate room. She stayed there one night and was examined by a Japanese doctor. The doctor did chest x-rays and four of the six girls were declared to be healthy; two others had consumption and were sent home. After this process a group of twenty girls were put together, and each of them was told that they would have to change their names to a Japanese name. Her Japanese name was Kanani Mosiko. They stayed at this military camp for one week and the only thing that was said to them was that they were all going to Japan. They were given two sets of slacks, two sets of underwear and two t-shirts. They were then put on a ship and sent to Pusan.

From Pusan to Osaka they travelled on a military ship. On arrival at Osaka they were taken to a military camp where she saw forty other girls. She and the other women were put into a plywood building. At this point she again asked Mr. Trae whether she was really going to have a job in a factory. She was told that there were no longer any jobs open in Japan and that they would have to move on to another country. She was then taken by military ship to Saigon with approximately sixty other women. There she was sent to a large military camp where the women were divided into groups of twenty; at this point all of the women realized that they had been deceived and came to understand what was going to happen to them.

Twenty of the women were then sent from the camp in Saigon to Rangoon in Burma. She said that she was told by Mr. Trae that she should put up with the pain of what was going to happen to her for one year and that she should try and endure the mental suffering that she would experience. She was told by Mr. Trae that if she cried and resisted she would be hit and beaten by the Japanese; she therefore decided to resign herself to her fate and consequently was not beaten.

At Rangoon they were placed on a military truck and travelled for about an hour and a half into the mountains, finally arriving at a military base. There they saw a sign indicating the name of the comfort station. The buildings, were run down and, from her description, it appears that they were made of plywood. The building had a central corridor with ten rooms on each side and toilets at one end. The rooms were numbered one to twenty and she was put into room number three with her Japanese name hung on the door. Throughout the night many of the girls cried and she could hear them being hit by the Japanese soldiers because of their crying. The next day they were forced to begin "accepting" Japanese soldiers; on that day they were sent as many soldiers as the number on their room. Apparently, the Japanese soldiers went into the comfort house with tickets which they gave to Mr. Trae. Ms. Kim stated that she asked one of the soldiers for a notebook and kept count of the number of soldiers that she was forced to serve in that book. The maximum number that she was forced to accept in one day was twenty. Although many of the girls were bleeding at the end of their first day the Japanese soldiers continued to rape them and the girls were told by a Japanese doctor that they were not bleeding because of what was happening to them but because they were menstruating. Some of the women were given a rest period of three or four days to recover from the pain.

This comfort house was heavily regulated; there were separate hours for the soldiers, petty officers, and officers. Only officers were allowed to stay overnight. The hours for the soldiers were nine to three, for the petty officers three to seven and the officers from nine to the following morning. Because of the time constraints, many of the soldiers would strip before entering into the room. Because of her fear of venereal disease, Ms. Kim collected used condoms left by the soldiers. It appears that in this comfort station the women were able to refuse soldiers who were not using, or were unwilling to use, condoms. However, some of the soldiers when refused would beat her before leaving.

When the Japanese decided to move the military camp because of the intensity of Allied bombing, Mr. Trae told her and a friend of hers which truck to get onto and advised them to be the last to get onto the truck. However, she and her friend decided not to get on the truck and hid in the darkness; a few minutes later Mr. Trae came back and they decided to make their way through the jungle. They found their way into India and spent five months with an Indian family. When they found out that the air raids had stopped they decided to go to Rangoon in order to go home; on their way to Rangoon the other woman in the party drowned.

She said that while she was in Rangoon she was interviewed by some English soldiers. She relayed her story about being a "sex slave." She is not sure that the soldiers actually believed her, as she developed malaria about this time.

Asked to describe the location of the comfort house, vis-a-vis the military camp, Ms. Kim indicated that there was a perimeter fence around the camp and that the comfort house was immediately outside of that perimeter fence. The rooms in the comfort house were approximately five feet by three feet. It was the only building immediately adjacent to the military camp and was the only building that had women in it. The closest village was approximately one hour away.

She headed back to her home village but was unable to locate any of her family. She has lived alone since that time. She operates a small restaurant which she has done for the past thirty-four years.

As with many of the other women, Ms. Kim has lived an isolated life keeping herself secluded from other people in large part because of her sense of shame about what had happened to her. She said that it was a miracle that she had survived as many of the women in the comfort station died because of the conditions there.

C. Democratic People's Republic of Korea

1.   Ri Po Pu[28]

Ms. Ri was born on 16 March 1921, by the lunar calendar. She grew up in the sub-county of Anju in South Pyonyang Province. Her father was a ser-

---

28. *Id.* at 64–67.

vant on land owned by a Kim Yun Si An; in addition to her father's work, her mother did cooking and washing for the family.

When she was eighteen years old a Korean policeman came to her family to say that he was going to establish a bar in Beijing and that she should come with him because she could earn lots of money. The man was known to the family for whom her parents worked. She went with him to Beijing along with four other women. Those women left the train near the border with China. The bar manager ordered her to play music and sing songs whereupon she responded by saying: "You told me that I was coming here to cook." He was quite angry with her and sent her to the kitchen where she washed vegetables. She was there for a total of three days; several times the manager told her to dance in the bar but she continued to refuse.

On the third day another Japanese man came to the bar; the policeman who had taken her from her village told her to follow the man and that, if she did so, she would be freed and allowed to go home. This was not to be the case as this second Japanese man took her to the comfort station. She does not know the exact location of the comfort station, she indicated that she was so frightened that she didn't pay attention to the direction in which they were heading. When they arrived she was sent into a house which was in the style of military barracks. There were several doors; behind the doors were mats. She had been taken to the military camp in a military vehicle.

The room she was given was very narrow; there was only enough space for one person. She was given two blankets and two pillows. On the first night she was not approached by any soldiers. She stated that when the Japanese man came to the bar he was dressed in civilian clothing, but she later saw him dressed in the uniform of a captain. Apparently there were three other girls in the truck with her but they continued to travel with the Japanese soldiers who were also in the truck; she does not know where they went.

The day after her arrival many soldiers began to come to the house and she was ordered by the manager to change into Japanese clothing. At some point the manager, who was a Japanese man, ordered a soldier to hit her; she did not understand why she was being hit. As she did not fully understand Japanese and the soldiers did not speak Korean there was no real communication between them. Apparently she managed to make it through the first day without being raped, but on the following day a number of soldiers again came to her room. She again resisted, then an officer came to her room and told the soldiers not to touch her.

The following day an officer came and forcibly raped her. When she resisted his efforts she was pushed to the floor and raped. He remained in her room throughout the night. She told him that she wanted to go home, but, as he only spoke Japanese and she only spoke Korean, he did not understand what she was saying to him, responding to her with grunts. The day after this ten soldiers came into her room and violated her. She said that by the end of this she was unconscious.

When asked to describe the location of the comfort station she indicated that the station and the soldiers' barracks were about twenty meters apart, but that both were inside the perimeter fence. She believes that the comfort station was an old store house.

At some point during her ordeal, after she lost consciousness, someone threw cold water on her and she awoke to find that there were still a number of Japanese soldiers outside her room. She decided to make an effort at running away thinking that one way or another she was going to die. She left the house through a rear door where a Chinese man was cooking food. She ran out the door and got about one hundred meters before being shot by a Japanese soldier. One bullet went into her knee and the other went into her groin. The interviewer was shown the scars from these injuries.

She was taken back to the comfort station. Despite the fact that she had been wounded she was forced to accept soldiers. She believes that, as she was new to the comfort station, every soldier wanted to go to her room. She was not given any medicines nor was she given a bandage. She indicated that she tore her clothes and used them as a bandage around the wound which apparently swelled quite profusely. Because of the swelling in her groin area it was impossible for the soldiers to have sex with her so she was carried by five soldiers to a lake and was thrown in. However, she did not land in the deep part of the water and was able to crawl four kilometers to a village called Linjo. At the village she encountered an old man who was selling tea. She begged him for food and also asked him to provide her with Chinese trousers and a jacket, which he did. She disguised herself as a Chinese woman. She then crawled to the train station (as her wound had not received any treatment, it was still quite painful and she was unable to walk). At the train station she met a Korean who asked her what had happened to her but she felt unable to tell him and just said that she had fallen down. He gave her train fare and asked her to carry a parcel with her to Korea. However, because of her wound she was unable to board a train and stayed in the town for about a month. Eventually her wound healed and she was able to walk with two sticks. She arrived in Ch'ŏngjin the following summer while the Japanese were still occupying Korea. They were defeated four months after her arrival.

She felt unable to tell anyone of her experiences as she thought that what had happened to her would disgrace her in the eyes of her fellow citizens. She lived an isolated life devoting herself to her work. However, after watching a television program during which it was stated that the Japanese were unwilling to apologize and had denied military involvement in the running of the comfort stations, she decided to speak out. It was important to her that the younger generation of Koreans learn of this part of their history and about the "crimes" committed by the Japanese. She repeatedly stated that, as a woman, what had happened to her was very disgraceful and emphasized how difficult it was for a Korean woman to speak out. She asserted that she was determined not to die before the government gave an official apology for what had happened. She also stated that she has often been struck with grief by the fact that as a result of what the soldiers had done to her she felt unable to marry and therefore had not been able to have children. She indicated that this was particularly difficult for her in the context of Korean society where it is important to have someone, particularly children, to bury you: "if I die, who will bury me?"

V.   THE CLOSE OF THE WAR AND THE KNOWLEDGE OF THE ALLIES

Although nothing can diminish the responsibility of the Japanese for what was done to these women, the Allies' lack of action in bringing to justice those responsible makes one question the views of Allied military officers. Despite extensive documentation about the conditions under which the women were taken from their homelands and mistreated, little was done to assist the women in their recovery or to make clear that such conduct was unacceptable under rules of international law.

As the Allied Forces moved through the Pacific and into Asia, they found Korean women as far afield as Burma, Manchuria, Borneo, Papua New Guinea, the Rykuku Islands, and the Philippines. These women were interrogated, and reports were filed with the Allied Command. One such report, prepared by the United States Office of War Information, Psychological Warfare Team (attached to the US Army Forces, India-Burma Theatre), described the experiences of twenty women in a camp in Burma. It described how Japanese agents, in recruiting women, had arrived in May 1942 and told Korean girls that they were to be enlisted for service in newly conquered Japanese territories in southeast Asia. They were told that they were being enlisted to give "comfort" to the Japanese soldiers, but the nature of what was expected of them was not detailed in any meaningful way. The girls were left with the impression that they would be rolling bandages, visiting wounded and ill soldiers in hospitals, and generally assisting with cooking, cleaning, and other chores around the camps. Money was offered by the recruiters to either the girls or their families. They were promised a new and more prosperous life in Singapore. When the girls enlisted for service they were given an advance of money. The report described the women as being, for the most part, uneducated and naive.

One of the officers who interrogated these women was Won-loy Chan, a combat intelligence officer on the staff of General Joseph W. Stilwell.

Chan later wrote that most of the Korean women seemed to be daughters of farmers and peasants, although some came from city slums.[29] (This coincides with the impression gained from the interviews of twenty-eight women from the Korean Peninsula by the ICJ mission.) It is clear from his description that he believed most of the women had come to Burma against their will. It was not his impression that they were what the military then referred to as "camp followers." Of the fifty women at the camp, only twenty-one were still there when the Allied troops arrived. It was assumed that many of them died while trying to escape either with the Japanese or after the Japanese had left. (Testimony that Chan took from one brothel manager indicated that some had tried to escape on their own when they realized that Japanese troops were about to flee and that many died either from gunshot wounds from Allied soldiers or through accidents while heading down the Irrawady River or in the jungles of Burma.) There were also reports that Japanese soldiers used the women as human shields while trying to escape from the Allies.

No one has yet explored the motivation of the Allied Forces in not pursuing this issue at the war crimes trials.[30] Some Allied documents categorized the women as "camp followers." It is impossible to understand how the women could have been categorized in this fashion given the knowledge of the Allies.

For the most part, it seems Allied interviews were conducted in order to gain intelligence information; little thought was given to the possibility of bringing this particular atrocity to the attention of the world. Only the Dutch included the use of women in Japanese military brothels in the war crimes trials. Two such trials occurred in what was then called Batavia, now the island of Java. However, both trials concerned the treatment of European women. Nothing was done to bring to light the horrors inflicted on Indonesian women.[31]

One suspects that prevailing attitudes toward women governed the decision-making process. In most of the countries making up the Allied Forces, rape convictions were difficult to secure; women were often blamed for having brought it upon themselves. It is possible that some officers believed it would be better not to pursue these crimes because of the great shame it could bring upon the women. Certainly there were overtones of this attitude in Australian military documents.

However, what occurred was the forced silencing of these women

---

29. CHAN, *supra* note 2.
30. Yuki Tanaka suggests that the Allies did not pursue this matter because their soldiers also raped women. See Yuki Tanaka, "Rape and War: The Japanese Experience." However, the Tokyo War Crimes Judgment is replete with references to single instances of rapes. It is the particular situation of the comfort women which is not addressed.
31. *See* Report of a Study of Dutch Government Documents on the Forced Prostitution of Dutch Women, 24 Jan. 1994 (unofficial translation in the possession of the author).

which led to years of emotional and psychological suffering. Their pain could not be voiced, unlike that of the civilian and military prisoners of war. Although no outward recognition was given to their suffering, people knew that something had happened. Rumors abounded which meant that some women were treated harshly by their own societies.

In this author's view, colonialism and racism played a part in the Allies' lack of action. The decision to prosecute the Axis powers was taken by the Allies in their guise as the "United Nations" (those states that had united against the Axis powers). These countries decided what would and would not be a war crime, gathered the evidence for the prosecution, and determined who would be prosecuted.[32] They also made the decision to prosecute Japan only for those acts that affected their own nationals. This excluded any crime committed against the Korean people as they had been subject to Japanese colonial domination.

The emphasis on nationals also meant that little attention would be given to the local population of those areas still subject to the colonial domination of the Allies, such as Malaysia and Indonesia. The only major exception to this was acts directed against Filipinos. Acts against the Philippines were treated as acts against the United States.

Because of the their failure to address the crimes perpetrated by the Japanese against women in the Asia/Pacific region, the Allies should accept some responsibility for reparation. In saying this I am not attempting to equate their responsibility with that of the Japanese. Nothing can lessen the legal and moral responsibility Japan has to the comfort women.

VI. RECOMMENDATIONS: PRELIMINARY VIEWS

Women have not only begun to identify their harms but have also begun to identify new ways in which harms can be rectified.[33] One aspect of the existing tort system which has come under fire from feminists is the reliance on monetary damages to compensate victims. Some feminist scholars have argued that more should be done to personalize the redress offered to victims, in part so that those committing the harm can understand what they have done to the victims. To some extent the Public Hearing held in Tokyo in December 1992 undertook this function. However, the Public Hearing and the many efforts to educate the Japanese public and to sensitize them to the pain suffered by the women have been undertaken by individuals or

---

32. See Pritchard & Zaide, *supra* note 15; Arnold C. Brackman, The Other Nuremberg: the Untold story of the Tokyo War Crimes Trials (1987).

33. See Lesley Bender, *Changing Values in Tort Law* 25 Tulsa L. J. 759 (1990); *A Lawyer's Primer on Feminist Theory and Tort,* 38 J. Legal Educ. 3 (1988).

groups outside the Japanese government. The sole exception is the final report issued by the government.

On several occasions the government has extended its sincere apologies to the women of the Korean Peninsula and the Philippines through official channels. However, it has not sought personal interviews with the women in their home countries for the purpose of offering an apology.[34] I believe it should do so.[35]

Before going further, I should state that I am not in favor of attempting to bring any form of criminal prosecution against responsible members of the military or the civilian government who may still be alive. Recent trials in Australia, Israel, Canada, and the United States demonstrate the difficulty of proving a case after the lapse of so many years. It is also an incredibly expensive exercise, and I believe that the money would be better spent on individual compensation or group programs such as the establishment of health clinics. (This is a personal view and should in no way be attributed to the other member of the ICJ mission, Snehal Paranjape, or the ICJ itself.) Also, unfortunately, I have not had an opportunity to present this view to the women or the organizations working with them.

Japan must do more than it has done to make full restitution to the women. Although the government has now admitted the involvement of its military authorities in requesting, establishing, and managing the comfort stations, as well as the physical movement of the women, it has not as yet enacted any measures of compensation.[35] This is not a situation of which Japan can be proud.

When defending its position on the compensation issue, Japan has relied upon the existence of various treaties between itself and the Allied Powers and between itself and the governments of the Republic of Korea and the Republic of the Philippines. The author does not accept that those treaties were in any way intended to cover the issues raised by the mass enslavement of women.[36] Furthermore, the issue of Japan making further restitution was explicitly left open by the Treaty of San Francisco. More importantly, however, Japan has chosen to make a distinction between the legal and the moral: it admits moral culpability but denies legal responsibility. It would seem that, having admitted to a moral wrong, Japan would feel compelled to make some form of restitution for that moral wrong. There

---

34. In comparison, the government did interview women for the purpose of finalizing its report.
35. Statement by the Delegation of Japan to the Sub-Commission on Prevention of Discrimination and Protection of Minorities, Aug. 1993 referring to the Japanese government report "Facts on the Issue of Wartime 'Comfort Women.'" (Statement in the personal possession of the author) [hereinafter Statement].
36. See Final ICJ Report, supra note 6 (exploring the legal arguments in connection with this position).

is nothing precluding Japan from setting aside any legal defenses it may have and moving forward of its own volition.

Given Japan's desire to obtain a permanent seat on the Security Council, it would set a precedent in international relations if Japan were to take a moral lead in this area. Other countries such as Germany, the United States, and Canada have on some occasions accepted their responsibility to redress past wrongs. Japan could demonstrate its commitment to the ideals of the Charter of the United Nations by attempting to make restitution. This would send a clear signal to those who continue to perpetrate atrocities that world opinion will demand that they account for their deeds.

The Japanese government, in an interview with the ICJ mission, stated that it would consider possible steps to convey its feelings of compassion. The government representatives refused to elaborate on what might be done. Japan's expression of remorse is hard to accept when it has done so little to compensate for what it has referred to as the "immeasurable pain and incurable physical and psychological wounds"[37] the women suffered. I am not unmindful of the difficulties presented by the potential number of women who may seek compensation and the possibility of the relatives of those who have already died making claims. But these are not insuperable difficulties. The handling of mass tort litigation in several industrialized countries offers ample precedent for procedures which could be established to handle the factual verification of claims. Lawsuits arising in India for violations of human rights also offer examples for the investigation and verification of claims.[38]

It is the personal view of this author that the Parliament of Japan should enact legislation awarding compensation to the women. The lawsuits which have been commenced in Japan may take years to complete,[39] especially as the government has chosen to defend them vigorously. Legislation could overcome any procedural or other hurdles to the women's claims. It would give due recognition to those who have so courageously spoken out before the passage of time ensures their death prior to any resolution.

The government should nominate a sum to be paid to each of the women who have come forward thus far and those who may come forward in the future. Given the passage of time and the enormous emotional strain of coming forward, it is doubtful that the numbers of women seeking compensation would surpass five or six thousand. Thus far fewer than 400 have

---

37. Statement, *supra* note 35, at 4.
38. See Uprenda Baxi, *Social Action Litigation in the Indian Supreme Court,* 29 INT'L COMM'N JURISTS REV. 37 (1982) for a description of some of the Indian cases.
39. The lawyers who met with the ICJ mission indicated it could take up to eight or nine years before all avenues of appeal were exhausted.

come forward from the Philippines, the Republic of Korea, the Democratic People's Republic of Korea, and the Netherlands. Less has been publicized about investigations underway in Indonesia, but it appears that there may be a significant number of women there who will be able to demonstrate that they were held as comfort women. Although some organizations have suggested the sum of $20,000, I believe that this is too little. It in no way reflects the seriousness of the violations of human rights and does not take into account the continuing nature of the harm the women have suffered. A more realistic sum should be negotiated in conjunction with the organizations established to represent the women, and their lawyers. (It may be appropriate to include Japanese lawyers as well as lawyers from the women's countries of origin.) Efforts should be made to support the women in verbalizing their opinions about this matter.

A legislative framework could be created for the determination of claims: lawyers or others chosen by the Japanese government could travel to each country in which women have come forward to establish in a general way the veracity of their claims. It would be unfortunate if Japan attempted to turn each interview into a small-scale trial; it is not necessary to cross examine each of the women, as one might in a civil lawsuit, in order to verify their stories.

In addition to the payments to the individual women, Japan should consider the creation of health clinics and services for the women. As demonstrated in the ICJ report, most of the women continue to suffer physical effects from their ordeal. In addition, many of them bear psychological scars. They require specialized medical care, and this could more easily be made available through the establishment of specialized centers. Again, negotiations about how this might be done should be carried out with the organizations representing the women and with the participation of the women themselves.

The right of the women to compensation and their need for adequate health care override any concern that Japan might attempt to purchase goodwill. There may be reasons why the Japanese government may choose not to pursue these matters on the diplomatic front, but this should not prevent the women from pushing forward their claims. Suggestions from the government that it is time to look to the future and move away from the past are not of assistance to the women. Such statements make it more likely that they will feel isolated and that these crimes will be viewed as something to hide.

Some groups, in their enthusiasm to detail the full extent of the horror, have urged that efforts be made to identify all the women who were put into comfort stations. However, there are issues of privacy involved. Many women have chosen to remain silent. Their reasons for doing so vary, though they appear in many cases to arise out of an unfounded sense of shame (as described most poignantly by the women interviewed during the ICJ mission) and a desire to insure that the lives they have managed to build for themselves are not damaged in any way. Those choices should be respected. To do otherwise is to deny the women autonomy over their lives and would only serve to lower their self esteem, not build it. Similarly, it is not appropriate to identify the families of women who may have perished. Perhaps a more fitting tribute to their suffering would be the establishment of a memorial, something which has been urged by both the Korean Council and the Filipina Task Force. Any such memorial or memorials should be created in consultation with the women.[40]

Finally, it would be appropriate if the countries making up the Allied Forces, in particular the United Kingdom, the United States, and the Netherlands, contributed to the creation of the memorial, as well as to the creation of health clinics. As outlined above, these countries knew of the atrocities perpetrated against the comfort women yet did nothing to prosecute those responsible nor to insure that the world viewed these acts as the heinous crimes that they were. This has contributed to the ongoing suffering of the women. Silence can be a form of aiding and abetting.

It is the responsibility of all of us to ensure that due recognition is given to the nature of these human rights violations committed against women and to begin to take steps to prevent their continuation.

---

40. I do not agree with those who argue that some form of compensation should be paid to the countries from which the women came. I am sympathetic to the arguments raised by some Korean scholars that the taking of so many thousands of women could be viewed as a form of genocide. But it is also the notion of patriotism and the state which, based as it is on male notions of power and hierarchy, led to the commission of such horrendous violations of the human rights of women. This is an opportunity to give recognition to women, and it should not be lost. In saying this I am not ignoring the differences in the individual's relation to her community that exist in countries such as Korea and the Philippines, but the community and its values must sometimes give recognition to a portion of its members and allow the community's values to be shaped by their experiences. It can not be forgotten that many of these women were isolated by their communities and were not given the opportunity to remain full members of the community.

Chapter 10

Women, War, and Rape: Challenges Facing the International Tribunal for the Former Yugoslavia

Catherine N. Niarchos

I. INTRODUCTION

As I began this project, I assumed that I knew little about the subject of rape, let alone rape during war. After research and reflection, however, I realized that all women know a great deal about rape, whether or not we have been its direct victims. Rape haunts the lives of women on a daily basis: it is the stranger approaching on the street; the violent husband or partner at home. More than other crimes, fear of rape leads us, consciously or unconsciously, to restrict our movements and our life choices, or alternatively to prepare for battle armed with mace, tear gas, and our rage. We ask whether it is safe for *women,* thereby accepting a double standard for our personal liberty and security. We learn to adjust from an early age: from fairy tales to the classics, we are conditioned to the fact that we are vulnerable to attack at any time because of our gender.[1] We arrange our lives accordingly; rape is an effective means of social control.

Rape is also a crime of extreme violence. It is an expression of dominance, power, and contempt, a rejection of the woman's right to self-determination, a denial of her being. Rape is not passion or lust gone wrong. It is first and foremost an act of aggression with a sexual manifestation.[2] Rape

---

1. For example, Susan Brownmiller describes *Little Red Riding Hood* as a "parable of rape" in that Red Riding Hood, once attacked by the wolf and finding herself defenseless, compliantly promises never to wander into the forest again. According to Brownmiller, other fairy tales describe similar catastrophes that "seem [ ] to befall only little girls." Susan Brownmiller, Against Our Will: Men, Women and Rape 309–10 (1975). Women fare no better in the classics; in the *Iliad* there is much quarrelling over women, several of whom find themselves abducted as slaves and concubines. *Id.* at 33.

2. Ruth Seifert, *War and Rape: A Preliminary Analysis, in* Mass Rape: The War against Women

is widespread: in the United States, government statistics indicate that a woman is raped every five minutes.[3] In so-called times of peace, rape is just one of many forms of violence suffered by women,[4] a fact that belatedly has led the United Nations to appoint a Special Rapporteur on the subject.[5] There can be no doubt that rape is a human rights violation of the gravest dimension.

The relationship between rape in peace and rape in war, Catharine MacKinnon observes, is what anti-Semitism is to the Holocaust. One is the inevitable result of the other, but the scale of horror is vastly different.[6] As in peacetime, rape has always occurred in war. Since the beginning, it has ranked along with plunder as one of war's "unfortunate byproducts." The inevitability of wartime rape appears to be accepted by political and military leaders[7] and until recently was largely ignored by historians, sociologists, and journalists. If rape has always occurred in war, it has also been defined as a war crime since the earliest codifications of the laws of war. Wartime rape is exploited for its propaganda value, but when the time comes for prosecutions it is often overlooked or folded into a larger category of crimes against civilians. It has yet to be recognized as a crime of gender.

The war in the former Yugoslavia involves savage rape on a horrifying scale. It is rape as torture, mutilation, femicide, and genocide. It is war

---

IN BOSNIA-HERZEGOVINA 54, 55 (Alexandra Stiglmayer ed. & Marion Faber trans., 1994) [hereinafter MASS RAPE].

3. FEDERAL BUREAU OF INVESTIGATION, U.S. DEP'T OF JUSTICE, UNIFORM CRIME REPORTS FOR THE UNITED STATES 1992, at 4 (1992). This statistic, which translates to approximately 105,000 rapes per year, was recently revised. The Bureau of Justice Statistics at the US Department of Justice now estimates that in 1992 and 1993, there were 500,000 sexual assaults annually on women in the United States, including 170,000 rapes and 140,000 attempted rapes. N.Y. TIMES, 17 Aug. 1995, at A18.

4. *See, e.g.,* CRIMES AGAINST WOMEN: PROCEEDINGS OF THE INTERNATIONAL TRIBUNAL 110–74 (Diana E. Russell & Nicole Van de Ven eds., 1976).

5. United Nations, Economic and Social Council, Commission on Human Rights, *Question of Integrating the Rights of Women into the Human Rights Mechanisms of the United Nations and the Elimination of Violence Against Women,* CHR Res. 1994/45, U.N. Doc. E/CN.4/1994/132 (1994). The General Assembly has also issued a declaration condemning violence against women. Declaration on the Elimination of Violence Against Women, G.A. Res. 48/104, U.N. Doc. A/RES/48/104 (1994); *see also* United Nations World Conference on Human Rights, Vienna Declaration and Programme of Action, pt. 1 ¶ 28, pt. 2 ¶ 38, U.N. Doc. A/CONF.157/24 (Part I) (1993) (calling for elimination of violence against women and "effective response" to violations of women's human rights in armed conflicts).

6. Catharine A. MacKinnon, *Rape, Genocide, and Women's Human Rights, in* MASS RAPE, *supra* note 3, at 183, 186–87. Similarly, the International Military Tribunal at Nuremberg recognized that the Holocaust was the inevitable outcome of Nazi doctrines of racial superiority. *United States v. Göring,* 22 TRIAL OF THE MAJOR WAR CRIMINALS BEFORE THE INTERNATIONAL MILITARY TRIBUNAL 411, 491 (1948) [hereinafter TRIAL BEFORE THE IMT]

7. For example, General Patton said that despite best efforts "unquestionably" there would be some raping in war. BROWNMILLER, *supra* note 2, at 31 (quoting GENERAL GEORGE S. PATTON, JR., WAR AS I KNEW IT 23 (1947)).

fought on and through women's bodies. It is rape as a military strategy. It is rape that, at last, has caught the world's attention. As the result of outrage at the atrocities, the International Tribunal for the Prosecution of Persons Responsible for Serious Violations of International Humanitarian Law Committed in the Territory of the Former Yugoslavia Since 1991 (Tribunal) was established in 1993.[8] Unlike the International Military Tribunals in Nuremberg (IMT) and in the Far East (IMTFE), the Tribunal includes in its founding statute an explicit reference to rape,[9] and it has been encouraged to give priority to cases of abuse of women and children.[10] The Tribunal faces many hurdles. In the light of the enormity of its task, one wonders whether it is realistic to hope for justice for the thousands of rape victims. Already, some are skeptical. Others, however, are hopeful that the Tribunal will establish precedent relevant to all women, in times of peace and war. For this Tribunal, like the Nuremberg and Tokyo tribunals, has responsibilities that go beyond everyday judicial process; while it must render justice and fair process to these victims and defendants, it also has a human rights mission that transcends the particular. In his opening statement in *The Medical Case* at Nuremberg, Telford Taylor described the court's responsibilities:

> The mere punishment of the defendants, or even of thousands of others equally guilty, can never redress the terrible injuries which the Nazis visited on these unfortunate peoples. For them it is far more important that these incredible events be established by clear and public proof, so that no one can ever doubt that they were fact and not fable; and that this Court . . . stamp these acts, and the ideas which engendered them as barbarous and criminal. . . .
>
> . . . .

---

8. On 22 February 1993, the Security Council acting under Chapter VII of the United Nations Charter decided to establish the Tribunal. S.C. Res. 808, ¶ 1, U.N. Doc. S/RES/808 (1993). The Tribunal's founding statute was adopted on 25 May 1993. S.C. Res. 827, ¶ 2, U.N. Doc. S/RES/827 (1993), *reprinted in* 32 I.L.M. 1203 (1993). Its rules of procedure and evidence entered into force on 14 March 1994, and have been amended three times on 5 May 1994, 4 October 1994, and 30 January 1995. *International Tribunal for the Prosecution of Persons Responsible for Serious Violations of International Humanitarian Law Committed in the Territory of the Former Yugoslavia Since 1991, Rules of Procedure and Evidence,* U.N. Doc. IT/32/Rev.3 (1995), *reprinted in* 33 I.L.M. 484, amended, 33 I.L.M. 838 (1994), *amended,* 33 I.L.M. 1619 (1994) [hereinafter *Rules of Procedure and Evidence*].

9. United Nations, Security Council, *Report of the Secretary-General Pursuant to ¶ 2 of Security Council Resolution 808 (1993),* Annex, art. 5(g), U.N. Doc. S/25704 (1993), *reprinted in* 32 I.L.M. 1159 (1993) (containing Statute and Secretary-General's commentary) [hereinafter *Statute and Report of the Secretary-General,* respectively]. Control Council Law No. 10, the jurisdictional basis for trials held in Nuremberg between 1946 and 1949, did include a reference to rape, however. 1 Trials of War Criminals Before the Nuermberg Military Tribunals Under Control Council Law No. 10, at xvii, art. II(1)(c) (1949) [hereinafter Trials under CCL 10].

10. United Nations, General Assembly, *Rape and Abuse of Women in the Areas of Armed Conflict in the Former Yugoslavia,* G.A. Res. 48/143, ¶ 10, U.N. Doc. A/48/143 (1993).

It is our deep obligation to all peoples of the world to show why and how these things happened. It is incumbent upon us to set forth with conspicuous clarity the ideas and motives which moved these defendants to treat their fellow men [and women] as less than beasts. The perverse thoughts and distorted concepts which brought about these savageries are not dead. They cannot be killed by force of arms. . . . They must be cut out and exposed. . . .

. . . .

Wherever those doctrines may emerge and prevail, the same terrible consequences will follow.[11]

This Tribunal has similar responsibilities: not only must it punish, but it also must demonstrate, beyond doubt, what the victims have suffered, and expose and condemn the twisted ideas and visions that caused madness to break out in the former Yugoslavia. Rape is just one of the many atrocities suffered by civilians during this war, but it is the peculiar and odious way in which women suffer in all wars. This paper considers rape of civilian women in this conflict and others, the status of rape under international humanitarian law, and the challenges facing the Tribunal in the light of the legacy it has inherited.[12]

II. RAPE IN WAR: "FACT AND NOT FABLE"

A. Legal Discourse

When atrocities are discussed, the tones are usually hushed. The crimes are described as "unspeakable"; there is a reluctance to confront the murderous side of human nature—to accept, in the words of playwright Arthur Miller,

---

11. *United States v. Brandt*, 1 Trials under CCL 10, *supra* note 10, at 27–29. Also of interest is the court's decision, which set forth ten ethical principles concerning medical experiments on human subjects. Telford Taylor, *The Nuremberg War Crimes Trials*, 450 Int'l Conciliation 242, 284–86 (1949). Professor Taylor viewed the trial and judgment as a "signal contribution both to international law and to medical jurisprudence." *Id.* at 286. The trial disclosures led the World Medical Association to modify the Hippocratic oath to prohibit "race, religion, party politics or social standing" from interfering with professional judgment and to require that knowledge not be used contrary to the laws of humanity. *Id.* at 286. It would indeed be fortunate if the Tribunal could make a similar contribution towards ending violence against women.

12. A few words must be said about the scope of the paper. The focus is the treatment of rape at the international level. For the most part, rape prosecutions brought in national military courts are not considered. During the conflict in the former Yugoslavia, men as well as women have been sexually assaulted; however, the situation of male victims raises different issues and is not considered here. "Rape" is used throughout the paper, but much of the discussion applies equally to the related crimes of forced prostitution and forced impregnation. Discrete issues raised by these crimes, however, are not discussed. *See, e.g.*, Anne Tierney Goldstein, Center for Reproductive Law and Policy, Recognizing Forced Impregnation as a War Crime Under International Law (1993). Finally, although the focus is

that "we are very dangerous."[13] Traditional legal discourse tends to play along with the conspiracy: lawyers shun drama, emotion, and "unnecessary" detail. In writing of the former Yugoslavia, the old temptation to censor arises; the crimes have been brutal. However, the bowdlerized version—to state that a certain number of rapes occurred in a particular region—does not express the whole egregious story. A significant part of the tragedy is suppressed; when the endeavor is to establish truth, there is a great disservice to the victims.

Feminist jurisprudence calls for a revised methodology: individual experience and narrative constitute the basis for argument; theory is recast based on experience and experience based on theory.[14] The benefits of this methodology are twofold. First, through the interplay of experience and theory, "the social dimension of individual experience and the individual dimension of social experience" are revealed.[15] Second, when narrative is the basis for argument, reality and perception are more likely to coincide. Thus, in discussing rape the feminist approach requires an exposition of the facts, in all their horrifying and indelicate detail. Only in this way can the full extent of female suffering be conveyed to a male-dominated legal culture.[16] From this vantage point, it becomes apparent just how divorced from reality are legal protections for women in war.

B.   Rape in the Former Yugoslavia

1.   The investigations

In August 1992, following initial reports of atrocities, the United Nations Commission on Human Rights appointed a Special Rapporteur to investigate human rights abuses in the former Yugoslavia.[17] In October 1992, the Security Council established a Commission of Experts to analyze data con-

international humanitarian law, human rights concepts are sprinkled throughout the paper; this is intended as an acknowledgement of the obvious relationship between the two bodies of law. *See* Louise Doswald-Beck & Sylvain Vité, *International Humanitarian Law and Human Rights Law,* 33 Int'l Rev. Red Cross 94 (1993).

13. Arthur Miller, After the Fall 176 (1978).
14. *See* Katharine T. Bartlett, *Feminist Legal Methods,* 103 Harv. L. Rev. 829, 863–67 (1990); Robin L. West, *The Difference in Women's Hedonic Lives: A Phenomenological Critique of Feminist Legal Theory,* 3 Wis. Women's L.J. 81, 90 (1987).
15. Bartlett, *supra* note 15, at 864 (quoting Elizabeth M. Schneider, *The Dialectic of Rights and Politics: Perspectives from the Women's Movement,* 61 N.Y.U. L. Rev. 589, 603 (1986)).
16. *See* West, *supra* note 15, at 85.
17. *Report of the Commission on Human Rights on Its First Special Session,* U.N. ESCOR, Supp. 2A, Comm. Hum. Rts., U.N. Doc. E/1992/22/Add.1/Rev.1, E/CN.4/1992/84/Add.1/Rev.1 (1992) (adopting CHR Res. 1992/S-1/1).

cerning atrocities and to conduct its own investigation.[18] To the extent possible, these two bodies were to avoid duplication of their efforts.

Both the Special Rapporteur and the Commission of Experts relied on information forwarded to them and on-site investigations. In January 1993, the Special Rapporteur sent a team of medical experts to Bosnia and Herzegovina to investigate rape allegations and to file a report.[19] Although rape is also discussed in several of the Special Rapporteur's subsequent reports, the issue was primarily left to the Commission of Experts.[20] In March 1994, the Commission of Experts sent teams of female lawyers and male and female mental health specialists to conduct interviews with victims and witnesses in Croatia and elsewhere, including Slovenia and Austria. A total of 223 people were interviewed. Due to time constraints the teams were unable to meet with all those willing to come forward.[21] Unfortunately, the Commission had insufficient time to evaluate the data because its Final Report was submitted one month after completion of the interviews.[22] The Final Report states, however, that the results of the interviews are consistent with conclusions reached based on earlier data.[23]

In addition to United Nations efforts, human rights organizations, women's groups, and journalists have investigated rape allegations in the former Yugoslavia.[24] Apart from some controversy concerning the number of rapes, there is little disagreement about the facts.

---

18. S.C. Res. 780, U.N. SCOR, 3119th mtg., U.N. Doc. S/RES/780 (1992), *reprinted in* 31 I.L.M. 1476 (1992).
19. United Nations, General Assembly and Security Council, *Report of the Team of Experts on Their Mission to Investigate Allegations of Rape in the Territory of the Former Yugoslavia from 12 to 23 January 1993*, Annex II, U.N. Doc. A/48/92, S/25341 (1993) [hereinafter *Report of Experts*].
20. *See* United Nations, General Assembly, *Rape and Abuse of Women in the Areas of Armed Conflict in the Former Yugoslavia: Report of the Secretary-General*, ¶ 23, U.N. Doc. A/48/858 (1994).
21. United Nations, Security Council, *Final Report of the Commission of Experts Established Pursuant to Security Council Resolution 780 (1992)*, Annex ¶ 241 n.65, U.N. Doc. S/1994/674 (1994) [hereinafter *Final Report*]. The Commission also sent a team of military personnel to conduct a pilot rape study in Sarajevo in June and July of 1993, but the study was "relatively generalized" and not aimed at development of specific cases. *Id.* ¶¶ 238–40.
22. *Id.* ¶ 243. It appears that the delay in sending out the investigative teams was due to an admixture of budgetary problems, bureaucracy, and politics. R.C. Longworth, *Peace vs. Justice; DePaul Professor Fears UN Sabotaged his Inquiry into Yugoslav War Crimes*, Chi. Trib. 2 Sept. 1994, at 1.
23. *Final Report, supra* note 22, ¶ 243.
24. *See, e.g.,* Amnesty Int'l, Bosnia-Herzegovina: Rape and Sexual Abuse by Armed Forces (1993); Human Rights Watch, War Crimes in Bosnia-Herzegovina (1993); International Human Rights Law Group, No Justice, No Peace: Accountability for Rape and Gender-Based Violence in the Former Yugoslavia (1993); Slavenka Drakulic, *Women Hide Behind a Wall of Silence; Mass Rape in Bosnia*, The Nation, 1 Mar. 1993, at 253. Julie A. Mertus, Center for Reproductive Law and Policy, Meeting the Health Needs of Women Survivors of the Balkan Conflict (1993).

2.   The crimes

Rapes are still reported.[25] However, most documented cases occurred between the fall of 1991 and the end of 1993, with a concentration of cases between April and November 1992.[26] Moreover, although rapes of Muslim, Croatian, and Serbian women have been reported, the majority of cases involve rapes of Muslim women from Bosnia and Herzegovina by Serbian men.[27] The perpetrators include soldiers, paramilitary groups, local police, and civilians.[28] The number of rapes is disputed. A delegation from the European Community suggested a figure of 20,000;[29] the Bosnian Ministry of the Interior said 50,000;[30] the Commission of Experts declined to speculate on the number.[31] Although the precise number of victims may never be known, it is important that the scale of the tragedy be ascertained. In this way, the assessment of each individual case will be more meaningful, and the political and social consequences of the crimes can be evaluated.[32]

The rapes that have been documented seem to fall into five patterns.[33] In the first pattern, the rapes are committed before fighting breaks out in a region. Individuals or small groups break into a house belonging to the target ethnic group, terrorize the inhabitants, steal their property, and rape the women. The women might be raped by one man or many; in either case, there is often a gang atmosphere. In one case, a woman was gang raped by eight soldiers in front of her six-year-old sister and five-month-old daughter.[34]

In the second pattern, the rapes occur in conjunction with invasion and capture of towns and villages. When a town or village is captured, the population is assembled and prepared for deportation. Women are raped either in empty houses or in public; again, gang rapes are common.[35] In one case,

---

25. *See e.g.*, Stephen Kinzer, *Bosnian Refugees' Accounts Appear to Verify Atrocities*, N.Y. Times, 17 July 1995, at A1; Chuck Sudetic, *Serb Gang Expels 566 Muslims From Their Homes in Bosnia*, N.Y. Times, 3 Sept. 1994, at A2.
26. *Final Report, supra* note 22, ¶ 237.
27. *Id.* ¶ 251; *Report of Experts, supra* note 20, ¶ 59.
28. *Final Report, supra* note 22, ¶ 236.
29. United Nations, General Assembly and Security Council, *European Community Investigative Mission into the Treatment of Muslim Women in the Former Yugoslavia*, Annex I ¶ 14, U.N. Doc. A/48/92, S/25240 (1993).
30. Aryeh Neier, *Watching Rights; Rapes in Bosnia-Herzegovina*, The Nation, 1 Mar. 1993, at 259.
31. *Final Report, supra* note 22, ¶ 234.
32. *See* Befreier und Befreite: Krieg, Vergewaltigungen, Kinder 46 (Helke Sander & Barbara Johr eds., 1992) [hereinafter Befreier und Befreite]; Neier, *supra* note 31 (expressing concern about "pernicious effect" of overstating number of rapes).
33. *Final Report, supra* note 22, ¶ 244.
34. *Id.* ¶ 245.
35. *See* Alexandra Stiglmayer, *The Rapes in Bosnia-Herzegovina, in* Mass Rape, *supra* note 3, at 82, 93–111.

a victim witnessed the rape of an elderly woman in front of a group of 100 villagers.[36]

In the third pattern, the rapes occur while women are held in detention. After a town or village is cleared, the men are executed or sent to detention camps; the women are sent to separate camps. The Commission of Experts reports: "Soldiers, camp guards, paramilitaries and even civilians may be allowed to enter the camp, pick out women, take them away, rape them and then either kill them or return them to the site."[37] Camp commanders have participated in the rapes.[38] Gang rapes are common, and the rapes/murders are particularly sadistic, involving severe beatings and torture.[39]

In the fourth pattern, the rapes occur in so-called "rape-camps." Some of the camps are large and well organized; others consist of houses or cafes. In this setting, the women are raped frequently, perhaps numerous times each day. They are humiliated, beaten, and some are killed. Some captors say their intention is to impregnate the women, to make "Chetnik babies."[40] In one camp, where as many as 2000 women might have been held, the women were examined by gynecologists. If found to be pregnant, they were segregated, given special privileges, and held until their seventh month when it was too late to obtain an abortion; at that point, they were released.[41]

In the fifth pattern, the women are forced into brothels to sexually entertain soldiers. These women are more often killed than released. In one reported case, a number of women were held in a private house for six months; they were raped every fifteen days when the soldiers returned from the front.[42]

There are certain characteristics common to all the rapes, regardless of the setting. Most of the rapes are gang rapes, or at least involve the participation of other men even if they do not personally assault the victim.[43] Many rapes involve the element of spectacle, occurring in the presence of the victim's family, the local population, or other victims. Many victims have

---

36. *Final Report, supra* note 22, ¶ 246.
37. *Id.* ¶ 247.
38. *Id.*
39. *Id.;* Catharine A. MacKinnon, *Turning Rape into Pornography: Postmodern Genocide, in* Mass Rape, *supra* note 3, at 73, 78–80; Stiglmayer, *supra* 36, at 89–93.
40. The "Chetniks" were Serbian partisans during World War II; the name has been appropriated by Serbs in the current conflict, thus resurrecting a historic conflict with the Croats and Muslims. *See* Andrew Bell-Fialkoff, *A Brief History of Ethnic Cleansing,* Foreign Aff., Summer 1993, at 110, 116–17.
41. *Final Report, supra* note 22, ¶ 248; Stiglmayer, *supra* note 36, at 116–19. The journalist who reported the figure of 2000 detainees expressed some skepticism at the number, but was assured that it was accurate, and even understated. *Id.* at 116.
42. *Final Report, supra* note 22, ¶ 249.
43. *See id.* ¶ ¶ 245–49, 250(c). *See generally,* Stiglmayer, *supra* note 36, at 82–162.

suffered multiple rapes.[44] Many rapes involve sexual torture and sadism: victims have been sexually abused with guns, broken bottles, or truncheons; family members have been forced to assault each other.[45] Some witnesses describe atrocities of a ritualistic nature where, after the rapes, women's breasts are cut off and their stomachs slit open.[46] Other rapes appear to replicate acts portrayed in sadomasochistic material, which survivors say is pervasive in some of the rape camps.[47] Some of the rapes have been video-taped and shown on Serbian television, with the Bosnian or Croatian victims presented as Serbian women and the Serbian attackers as Muslim or Croatian men.[48]

The victims range in age from seven to sixty-five years old, but virgins and young women between thirteen and thirty-five have been targeted.[49] The victims sometimes recognize their attackers as friends, neighbors, and acquaintances from nearby villages.[50] Perhaps in a last showing of faith or incredulity at what has happened, the Bosnian Muslim women say that local Serbian soldiers are less vicious than their colleagues from Serbia.[51] The victims are often threatened with death if they report what has occurred.[52]

For the most part, the rapes are not random acts, but appear to be carried out as deliberate policy. Many of the attackers claim they were ordered to rape, or to ensure that the victims and their families would never want to return to an area.[53] About eighty percent of the rapes occur in custodial settings,[54] a factor that led the Commission of Experts to conclude:

> These patterns strongly suggest that a systematic rape policy existed in certain areas, but it remains to be proven whether such an overall policy existed which was to apply to all non-Serbs. It is clear that some level of organization and group activity was required to carry out many of the alleged rapes.[55]

At several levels, the rapes reflect the policy of "ethnic cleansing":[56] rape is used as a means to terrorize and displace the local population, to force the

---

44. *Final Report, supra* note 22, ¶ 250(a), (c).
45. *Id.* ¶ 250(a), (d).
46. Seifert, *supra* note 3, at 65 (citing report of Croatian journalist, Ines Sabalic).
47. MacKinnon, *supra* note 40, at 77–80.
48. That this was a deliberate act of disinformation became apparent in one case when the videotape failed and the real voices of the victims and perpetrators were heard. *Id.* at 75–76.
49. *Final Report, supra* note 22, ¶ ¶ 230(o), 250(a).
50. *Id.* ¶ 248; Stiglmayer, *supra* note 36, at 92, 98–99, 105.
51. Stiglmayer, *supra* note 36, at 96, 106–07, 120.
52. *Final Report, supra* note 22, ¶ 250(b).
53. *Id.*
54. *Id.* ¶ 236.
55. *Id.* ¶ 253.
56. "Ethnic cleansing" is the Serbian policy of aggression, which aims at ethnic and religious exclusivity in certain regions. *Id.* ¶ 130.

birth of children of mixed "ethnic" descent in the group, and to demoralize and destroy.[57] The rapes are also an expression of misogyny: women are targeted not simply because they are the "enemy" but also because they are women. Gender is essential to the method of assault. As MacKinnon observes, "[x]enophobia and misogyny merge here; ethnic hatred is sexualized; bigotry becomes orgasm."[58]

The rapes have had a devastating impact on the victims. Health care workers describe severe emotional and psychological trauma among the survivors, as well as physical injuries.[59] Many women who became pregnant as a result of rape have obtained abortions; others who were forced to give birth have rejected the infants; and there are rumors that some infants have been killed.[60] Many victims are reluctant to speak of their experience from a sense of shame or fear of rejection by their families.[61] Others express anger, or bewilderment at the hatred directed at them.[62] United Nations organizations and voluntary agencies have attempted to respond to the medical needs of the victims, but it will be many years before the full consequences are known.[63] There have been few studies on wartime rape, and the effects of rape are usually determined by social and cultural context.[64] Organizations working with the victims have had to proceed cautiously. Some women feel exploited by repeated interviewing, and attempted suicides following interviews have been reported.[65]

C.   Rape in Other Armed Conflicts

The mass rape in the former Yugoslavia, and the sinister use of rape as a military strategy, has galvanized the public, as well it should. However, rape in war, or even rape as a weapon of war, is hardly an innovation of this con-

---

57. In addition, rape is also used as a means to boost morale. Serbian commanders have been quoted as saying that rape of Muslim women is "good for raising the fighters' morale." THEODOR MERON, HENRY'S WARS AND SHAKESPEARE'S LAWS: PERSPECTIVES ON THE LAW OF WAR IN THE LATER MIDDLE AGES 112 n.179 (1993) (quoting The Rape of Bosnia, INT'L HERALD TRIB., 8 Dec. 1992, at 4).
58. MacKinnon, supra note 40, at 75.
59. Shana Swiss & Joan E. Giller, Rape as a Crime of War: A Medical Perspective, 270 J. AM. MED. ASS'N 612, 614 (1993).
60. Id. at 614; Daniela Horvath, The Children of the Rapes; Young Victims of "Ethnic Cleansing," WORLD PRESS REV., June 1993, at 11, 12.
61. Swiss & Giller, supra note 60, at 614.
62. See, e.g., Stiglmayer, supra note 36, at 121.
63. United Nations, Economic and Social Council, Commission on Human Rights, Rape and Abuse of Women in the Territory of the Former Yugoslavia: Report of the Secretary-General, U.N. Doc. E/CN.4/1994/5 (1993) (describing response of UN system) [hereinafter Rape and Abuse].
64. Swiss & Giller, supra note 60, at 614.
65. Rape and Abuse, supra note 64, ¶ 13.

flict. In fact, in terms of motive and method, the rapes in the former Yugoslavia mirror the wartime sufferings of women through the centuries. A selective review of the history of women in war demonstrates, with alarming clarity, how little has changed for women caught in the crossfire.

In primitive warfare, women as the propagators of the enemy's soldiers were the objects of direct attack. One scholar writes: "[t]he savage mind could be pictured as logically concluding that the most economic use of his energies in war would be to guarantee that he would not have to face his enemy again. One way to achieve this result was to eliminate the source of future supply."[66] Among the ancient Greeks, Romans, and Hebrews, women were often seized as prize, along with the lands and livestock of the vanquished. The captured women might become wives, servants, slaves, or concubines.[67] The Trojan War, described in the *Iliad*, demonstrated that women could expect rape and enslavement from warfare.[68] The Old Testament reported that Hebrew tribes invading Canaan seized the following spoils of war, in this order, "sheep, cattle, asses, and thirty-two thousand girls who had had no intercourse with a man."[69] The Book of Deuteronomy sanctioned the seizure of women as legitimate booty, although captors were obliged after a period of mourning to marry their stolen treasures.[70] Hugo Grotius, writing in the seventeenth century, described classical admonitions to respect the "chastity of the women and girls," as well as frequent viola-

---

66. Richard S. Hartigan, The Forgotten Victim: A History of the Civilian 17 (1982).
67. Brownmiller, *supra* note 2, at 21, 33; *see* Riane Eisler, The Chalice and the Blade: Our History, Our Future 49 (1987).
68. The following lines, intended to spur the troops for the capture of Troy, are revealing:

    So now let no man hurry to sail for home,
    not yet . . . not till he beds down with a faithful Trojan wife,
    payment in full for the groans and shocks of war
    we have all borne for Helen.

    Homer, The Iliad, bk. 2:420–24, at 111 (Robert Fagles trans., 1990); *see generally*, P. E. Easterling, *Men's xλέος and Women's γόος: Female Voices in the Iliad*, 9 J. Mod. Greek Stud. 145 (1991).

69. Eisler, *supra* note 68, at 49 (citing Numbers 31:32–35).
70. Michael Walzer, Just and Unjust Wars: A Moral Argument with Historical Illustrations 134–35 (1992). The relevant passage of Deuteronomy provides:

    When thou goest forth to battle against thine enemies, and the Lord thy God deliverest them into thy hands, and thou carriest them away captive, and seest among the captives a woman of goodly form, and thou hast a desire unto her, and wouldst take her to thee to wife; then thou shalt bring her home to thy house . . . and she shall . . . bewail her father and mother a full month; and after that thou mayest go in unto her, and be her husband, and she shall be thy wife. And . . . if thou have no delight in her, then thou shalt let her go whither she will; but thou shalt not sell her . . . for money, thou shalt not deal with her as a slave. . . .

    Id. (quoting Deuteronomy 21:10–14).

tions of those admonitions; although Grotius frowned on rape during warfare, he apparently found the practice of seizing women for purposes of
marriage more acceptable.[71]

The ancient perspective of women as spoils of war was consistent with
the legal status of women. Women were regarded as virtual property—
certainly they were without legal capacity—and rape committed by a member of the community was considered an injury to the male estate and to the
community, but not to the woman.[72] Of course, there was no corresponding
obligation to respect your enemy's property, so women were fair game during warfare. In fact, as long as the rape of women was considered a crime
against the male, the rape of enemy women had a salutary military effect.
Susan Brownmiller explains:

> Men of a conquered nation traditionally view the rape of "their women" as the
> ultimate humiliation, a sexual *coup de grace*. . . . In fact, by tradition, men
> appropriate the rape of "their women" as part of their own male anguish of
> defeat. This egocentric view does have a partial validity. Apart from a genuine,
> human concern for wives and daughters near and dear to them, rape by a con-
> queror is compelling evidence of the conquered's status of masculine impo-
> tence. Defense of women has long been a hallmark of masculine pride, as
> possession of women has been a hallmark of masculine success. Rape by a con-
> quering soldier destroys all remaining illusions of power and property for men
> of the defeated side. *The body of a raped woman becomes a ceremonial bat-
> tlefield, a parade ground for the victor's trooping of the colors. The act that is
> played out upon her is a message passed between men—vivid proof of victory
> for one and loss and defeat for the other.*[73]

By the Middle Ages, during the age of chivalry, women had gained
some legal protection, at least on paper. Ordinances of War promulgated
during the Hundred Years War (1337–1453) by Richard II at Durham in
1385 and by Henry V at Mantes in 1419 prohibited rape during war, on
penalty of death.[74] The prohibition was not usually respected, however.[75]
Also, the prohibition did not apply to cities taken by siege, the more com-

71. *See* HUGO GROTIUS, THE LAW OF WAR AND PEACE, bk. III, ch. IV, pt. XIX, at 657 (Francis W.
    Kelsey trans., 1925) (1646).
72. *See* BROWNMILLER, *supra* note 2, at 18; ROGER JUST, WOMEN IN ATHENIAN LAW AND LIFE 68–69
    (1991). In the Greek *polis*, for example, rape was considered a personal outrage to the
    woman's guardian, as well as a threat to the community because the certitude of descent
    could not be guaranteed. Notably, in the *polis*, seduction was punished more severely
    than rape. One possible explanation is that rape caused a less serious injury to the *male*
    than seduction because it was unlikely to alienate the woman's affection for her husband.
    Id. at 68.
73. BROWNMILLER, *supra* note 2, at 38 (emphasis added).
74. MERON, *supra* note 58, at 92. For a discussion of the tradition of chivalry and attitudes
    towards women, see RICHARD BARBER, THE KNIGHT AND CHIVALRY 71–76 (1974).
75. MERON, *supra* note 58, at 111.

mon method of medieval conquest, and so proved hollow.[76] In fact, Theodor Meron observes: "the license to rape was considered a major incentive for the soldier involved in siege warfare."[77] Even Francisco de Vitoria, who opposed rape during siege, conceded that the sacking of cities (presumably including rape) might serve as a "spur to the courage of the troops."[78] Due to this ambivalence about wartime rape as boon or bale, in 1646 Grotius was able to write only that punishment of rape in war was "the law *not* of all nations, but of the better ones."[79] At about this time, the historical association between wartime plunder and rape filtered into the English language: since later Middle English (circa 1350–1450), "rape" has referred to violent seizure or carrying away of property and persons, especially women; the more specific definition of rape as violation appeared in the language slightly later.[80]

In the nineteenth and twentieth centuries, principles developed over centuries concerning immunity of civilians were codified; legal protection for women improved. The influential Lieber Code, promulgated in 1863 as the military code for the Union Army, made rape a capital offense.[81] The Hague and Geneva Conventions provided explicit or implicit protection

---

76. *Id.* at 101–02.
77. *Id.* at 111–12. "The prospect of this free run of his lusts for blood, spoil and women was a major incentive to a soldier to persevere in the rigours which were likely to attend a protracted siege." *Id.* at 102 (quoting M. H. Keen, The Laws of War in the Late Middle Ages 121–22 (1965)).
78. *Id.* at 112 (quoting Franciscus de Victoria, De Indis et de Jure Belle Relectiones 184–85 (Ernest Nys ed. & John P. Bate trans., 1917) (1696)). Gentili, however, believed that rape should be prohibited under all circumstances. *Id.* (quoting Alberico Gentili, De Jure belli Libri Tres 257 (John C. Rolfe trans., 1933) (1594)).
79. Grotius, *supra* note 72, at 657 (emphasis added). Notably, Grotius also appears to accept the ideas that women are property and that rape causes injury to the male. In *The Law of War and Peace,* Grotius wrote:

   Whether rape is contrary to the law of nations.

   I. You may read in many places that the raping of women in time of war is permissible, and in many others that it is not permissible. Those who sanction rape have taken into account only the injury done to the person of another, and have judged that it is not inconsistent with the law of war that everything which belongs to the enemy should be at the disposition of the victor. A better conclusion has been reached by others, who have taken into consideration not only the injury but the unrestrained lust of the act; also, the fact that such acts do not contribute to safety or to punishment, and should consequently not go unpunished in war any more than in peace.

   Id. at 656–57.

80. 2 The Shorter Oxford English Dictionary on Historical Principles 1746–47 (1973). The earlier meaning of rape, as spoliation, is seen in twentieth century examples such as the "Rape of Belgium" in World War I, the "Rape of Nanking" in World War II, and the "Rape of Kuwait" in the last decade.
81. Francis Lieber, *Instructions for the Government of Armies of the United States in the Field, promulgated as* US War Department, Adjutant General's Office, General Orders No. 100, art. 44 (Apr. 1863), *reprinted in* 1 The Law of War: A Documentary History 158, 167 (Leon Friedman ed., 1972) [hereinafter Lieber Code].

against rape.[82] Nevertheless, despite this apparent amnesty, the twentieth century was disastrous for women.

In fact, in the twentieth century, the plight of all civilians worsened significantly.[83] Simply as a matter of probabilities, women were more likely to suffer war's consequences, including rape. In addition, rape, which had always been an effective weapon of war, became more self-consciously so; rape was recognized as a means to demoralize and destroy the enemy. Ruth Seifert writes:

> [A]s tactical objectives, women were of special importance: if the aim is to destroy a culture, they are prime targets because of their cultural position and their importance in the family structure. In "dirty wars" it is not necessarily the conquest of the foreign army, but rather the deconstruction of a culture that can be seen as a central objective of war action. . . . Military history shows that dead and wounded people, civilians especially, constitute the path to military victory.[84]

In World War I, according to Arnold Toynbee's accounts, German soldiers marching into Belgium and France used rape and other atrocities in a deliberate campaign to instill terror in the local population.[85] After the war, a commission created to investigate war crimes enumerated thirty-two crimes, listing rape and forced prostitution as numbers five and six.[86]

In World War II, rape was widespread in Europe and Asia. Before the IMT in Nuremberg, the French and Soviet prosecutors, who were responsible for establishing war crimes and crimes against humanity in Western and Eastern Europe respectively, introduced evidence of rape.[87] A witness called

---

82. Geneva Convention Relative to the Protection of Civilian Persons in Time of War, art. 27, *opened for signature* 12 Aug. 1949, 6 U.S.T. 3516, 3536, 75 U.N.T.S. 287, 306 [hereinafter Geneva Convention IV]; Convention Respecting the Laws and Customs of War on Land, Annex of Regulations, art. 46, 18 Oct. 1907, 36 Stat. 2277, 2306–07, 1 Bevans 631, 651 [hereinafter 1907 Hague Regulations]; Convention with Respect to the Laws and Customs of War on Land, Annex of Regulations, art. 46, 29 July 1899, 32 Stat. 1803, 1822, 1 Bevans 247, 260 [hereinafter 1899 Hague Regulations].

83. In World War I, about 5 percent of those killed were civilians; in World War II, the figure climbed to 48 percent; recently, in some conflicts, such as Lebanon, it is as high as 80 or 90 percent, with women and children a significant majority. Sandra Singer, *The Protection of Children During Armed Conflict Situations*, 26 Int'l Rev. Red Cross 133, 141 (1986); Jeanne Vickers, Women and War 24–25 (1993). The war in the former Yugoslavia is likely to exact an equally bloody toll on the civilian population. *Id.* at 24.

84. Seifert, *supra* note 3, at 62–63.

85. Brownmiller, *supra* note 2, at 41–42.

86. Commission on the Responsibility of the Authors of the War and on Enforcement of Penalties, *Report Presented to the Preliminary Peace Conference*, 29 Mar. 1919, 14 Am. J. Int'l L. 95, 114–15 (1920).

87. Four charges were brought in the trial of the major war criminals before the IMT in Nuremberg: conspiracy, crimes against peace, war crimes, and crimes against humanity. The US prosecution team was responsible for the conspiracy count, the British for crimes against peace, and the French and the Soviets for war crimes and crimes against humanity. Telford Taylor, The Anatomy of the Nuremberg Trials: A Personal Memoir 79–80 (1992).

by the French, Marie Claude Vaillant-Couturier, a member of the French Constituent Assembly, testified about treatment of women prisoners at Auschwitz and Ravensbrück, where she had been held for almost two years. Much of her bone-chilling testimony does not relate to this discussion; however, towards the end of her direct examination, she was asked how the SS guards treated women prisoners. As hers was one of the few female voices heard at Nuremberg, her words are duplicated here:

> Mme. Vaillant-Couturier: At Auschwitz there was a brothel for the SS and also one for the male internees of the staff, who were called "Kapo." Moreover, when the SS needed servants, they were accompanied by the Oberaufseherin, that is, the woman commandant of the camp, to make a choice during the process of disinfection. They would point to a young girl, whom the Oberaufseherin would take out of the ranks. They would look her over and make jokes about her physique; and if she was pretty and they liked her, they would hire her as a maid with the consent of the Oberaufseherin, who would tell her that she was to obey them absolutely no matter what they asked of her.

> M. Dubost [French Prosecutor]: Why did they go during disinfection?

> Mme Vaillant-Couturier: Because during disinfection the women were naked.

> M. Dubost: This system of demoralization and corruption—was it exceptional?

> Mme. Vaillant-Couturier: No, the system was identical in all the camps where I have been. . . . I believe that Auschwitz was one of the harshest; but later I went to Ravensbrück, where there was also a house of ill fame and where recruiting was also carried out among the internees.

> M. Dubost: Then, according to you, everything was done to degrade those women in their own sight?

> Mme. Vaillant-Couturier: Yes.[88]

The French prosecutor went on to describe, through documentary evidence, a reign of terror in France, where rape and other atrocities against the civilian population were committed wantonly or as reprisals for acts of the Maquis, the French resistance group. Although he recited the gruesome details of other atrocities,[89] the prosecutor was restrained when it came to making a record concerning rape.[90]

---

88. 6 Trial before the IMT, *supra* note 7, at 213–14.

89. *See, e.g., id.* at 405–07.

90. Susan Brownmiller observes that the French prosecutor used the "standard censoring mechanism that men employ when dealing with the rape of women." Brownmiller, *supra* note 2, at 56. She points to the following part of the prosecutor's presentation:

> I quote, "The Maquis had evacuated the town several days earlier . . . 54 women or young girls from 13 to 50 years of age were raped by the maddened soldiers."

The Soviet prosecutor was less reticent. He read into the record the notes of V. M. Molotov, People's Commissar for Foreign Affairs in the USSR, which described rape in Soviet territory:

> Women and young girls are vilely outraged in all the occupied areas.
>
> In the Ukrainian village of Borodayevka, in the Dniepropetrovsk region, the fascists violated every one of the women and girls.
>
> In the village of Berezovka, in the region of Smolensk, drunken German soldiers assaulted and carried off all the women and girls between the ages of 16 and 30.
>
> In the city of Smolensk the German Command opened a brothel for officers in one of the hotels into which hundreds of women and girls were driven; they were mercilessly dragged down the street by their arms and hair.
>
> Everywhere the lust-maddened German gangsters break into the houses, they rape the women and girls under the very eyes of their kinfolk and children, jeer at the women they have violated, and then brutally murder their victims.
>
> In the city of Lvov, 32 women working in a garment factory were first violated and then murdered by German storm troopers. Drunken German soldiers dragged the girls and young women of Lvov into Kesciuszko Park, where they savagely raped them. An old priest, V. I. Pomaznew, who, cross in hand, tried to prevent these outrages, was beaten up by the fascists. They tore off his cassock, singed his beard, and bayonetted him to death.
>
> Near the town of Borissov in Bielorussia, 75 women and girls attempting to flee at the approach of the German troops, fell into their hands. The Germans first raped and then savagely murdered 36 of their number. By order of a German officer named Hummer, the soldiers marched L. I. Melchukova, a 16-year-old girl, into the forest, where they raped her. A little later some other women who had also been dragged into the forest saw some boards near the trees and the dying Melchukova nailed to the boards. The Germans had cut off her breasts in the presence of these women, among whom were V. I. Alperenko, and V. H. Bereznikova.
>
> On retreating from the village of Borovka, in the Zvenigorod district of the Moscow region, the fascists forcibly abducted several women, tearing them away from their little children in spite of their protests and prayers.
>
> In the town of Tikhvin in the Leningrad region, a 15-year-old girl named H. Koledetskaya, who had been wounded by shell splinters, was taken to a hospital (a former monastery) where there were wounded German soldiers. Despite her injuries the girl was raped by a group of German soldiers and died as a result of the assault.[91]

> The Tribunal will forgive me if I avoid citing the atrocious details which follow.... A medical certificate from Doctor Nicolaides, who examined the women who were raped in this region—I will pass on.

Id.; 6 Trial before the IMT, *supra* note 7, at 405.

91. Brownmiller, *supra* note 2, at 55–56; 7 Trial Before the IMT, *supra* note 7, at 440, 456–57. In addition, despite the Nazi's 1935 Nuremberg race laws, rape was also used as a

Yet, despite this grisly litany of crimes, "rape" does not appear once in the 179 page judgment of the IMT. It is apparently folded into the general category of "ill treatment of the civilian population."[92]

The Nuremberg tribunal was constituted by the Allies, so for the most part their own crimes escaped scrutiny.[93] One episode of widescale rape, which went unpunished and even unexamined for many years, occurred in Berlin when Soviet soldiers capturing the city in 1945 were reported to have raped more than 110,000 women; less conservative estimates put the figure at over 800,000.[94] A recent study of these events finds particularly astonishing the fact that so little has been written on the subject.[95] Lack of documentation is, however, yet another aspect of women's experience in war. Another relatively unexamined episode occurred in Italy in 1943–1944 when Moroccan soldiers of the French army were apparently given license to rape.[96] Many Italian women who did not take shelter in the mountains were raped. Their story is known because the Italian government later offered them a pension.[97]

Unlike Nuremberg, rape charges were brought against defendants tried before the IMTFE. Evidence was presented concerning widescale atrocities committed by Japanese soldiers against the civilian population of Nanking in December 1937, in what came to be known as the "Rape of Nanking." Rape was widespread; although none of the victims testified in person, evidence was introduced by affidavit and through missionaries who had remained in the city.[98] The IMTFE found:

> There were many cases of rape. Death was a frequent penalty for the slightest resistance on the part of a victim or the members of her family who sought to protect her. Even girls of tender years and old women were raped in large num-

---

weapon in the persecution of the Jews. This description in Susan Brownmiller's book reveals striking similarities to "ethnic cleansing" in the former Yugoslavia:

> When the advancing German Army approached a Polish or a Russian village, the pattern of first-phase violence was almost invariable. Homes were looted, but first and especially the Jewish homes, and Jewish girls were singled out for torture and rape, often in front of their parents. Days, weeks or months later, depending on the timetable, the second, or "serious," phase began: the roundups of the Jewish population, the mass shootings, the herding into ghettos, and the eventual dispatch in boxcars to the concentration camps and the Final Solution.

BROWNMILLER, *supra* note 2, at 49–50.

92. See 22 TRIAL BEFORE THE IMT, *supra* note 7, at 475.
93. Some countries, including the United States, did court martial their own soldiers for rape.
94. BEFREIER UND BEFREITE, *supra* note 33, at 48, 54–55. At the time, the female population of Berlin was 1.4 million. *Id.* at 54.
95. *Id.* at 9–11.
96. WALZER, *supra* note 71, at 133–34.
97. *Id. at 134;* Ignazio Silone; *Reflections on the Welfare State,* 8 DISSENT 185, 189 (1961). The story of these women was at least told through film in De Sica's production *Two Women.*
98. BROWNMILLER, *supra* note 2, at 57–61.

bers throughout the city, and many cases of abnormal and sadistic behavior in connection with these rapings occurred. Many women were killed after the act and their bodies mutilated. Approximately 20,000 cases of rape occurred within the city during the first month of the occupation.[99]

The historical effect of the IMTFE's finding cannot be gainsaid. As Susan Brownmiller wrote, "[h]ad it not been for the Tokyo war-crimes tribunal, who would have believed the full dimensions of the Rape of Nanking?"[100] By way of contrast, the IMTFE did not receive evidence concerning the "comfort women," the Korean, Chinese, Filipina, Indonesian, Burmese, Dutch, and Japanese women who were forced into Japanese military brothels; it was many years before the plight of these women was known or acknowledged by Japanese officials.[101]

One frequent consequence of rape is that the victim is rejected by her spouse or family. This has been the case at least since the classical period, when a husband was required to divorce a wife who had been raped.[102] The reaction stems from the tendency to view the woman as a coconspirator in her own victimization. Even in supposedly more enlightened minds, rape victims are regarded as stigmatized in a way that does not apply to victims of other crimes. The rape victim is cloistered emotionally and cannot speak openly of her assault; she is considered defiled, dishonored, and ruined.[103] Joan Didion writes, "[t]hese quite specifically masculine assumptions . . . tend in general to be self-fulfilling, guiding the victim to define her assault as her protectors do."[104] In patriarchal societies, where female chastity is sacred (an equivalent male standard is rare), the situation is exacerbated. Predominantly Muslim Bangladesh provides an example. In 1971, that country, then East Pakistan, declared its independence. In the ensuing war, in what has been characterized as a deliberate campaign, at least 200,000 Bengali women were raped by West Pakistani soldiers.[105] Some of the women were held in military brothels. Many women were rejected by their husbands and families, despite the government's efforts to restore their positions by declaring them national "heroines."[106]

---

99. 1 The Tokyo Judgment: The International Military Tribunal for the Far East, 29 Apr. 1946–12 Nov. 1948, at 389 (B. V. A. Röling & C. F. Rüter eds., 1977).
100. Brownmiller, *supra* note 2, at 61–62.
101. See David A. Boling, *Mass Rape, Enforced Prostitution, and the Japanese Imperial Army: Japan Eschews International Legal Responsibility?*, 32 Colum. J. Transnat'l L. 533 (1995); Ustinia Dolgopol, *Women's Voices, Women's Pain*, 17 Hum. Rts. Q. 127 (1995); Karen Parker & Jennifer F. Chew, *Compensation for Japan's World War II War-Rape Victims*, 17 Hastings Int'l & Comp. L. Rev. 497 (1994).
102. Just, *supra* note 73, at 70.
103. Joan Didion, *Sentimental Journeys, in* The Best American Essays 1992, at 6, 11 (Susan Sontag ed., 1992).
104. *Id.* at 11.
105. Brownmiller, *supra* note 2, at 78–80.
106. *Id.* at 78.

Rape also played a role in the Vietnam War. It was one of the atrocities committed by US soldiers at My Lai; charges were brought in the resulting courts martial but later dismissed.[107] In testimony at a public forum in Detroit in 1971, 100 veterans testified about atrocities they had witnessed in Vietnam.[108] A number of the veterans testified about humiliation, rape, torture, and mutilation of Vietnamese women by US soldiers;[109] in the words of one veteran, rape of Vietnamese villagers was "pretty SOP," or standard operating procedure.[110] Prostitution, often forced by economic circumstances, was rampant in Vietnam. Here, it was sex for the sake of morale; and, incredibly, to keep the troops content, brothels were organized within military compounds.[111] The situation of Vietnamese women worsened even as they fled their country; thousands of asylum-seeking women were raped, tortured, and killed in the Gulf of Thailand and the South China Sea.[112]

Mass rape in war and the use of rape as a weapon of war are as old as time, and have occurred within the last ten years in El Salvador, Guatemala,[113] Liberia,[114] Kuwait,[115] and the former Yugoslavia. Yet, for the most part, wartime rape has been ignored; history has been just that—His Story. Women were peripheral; their suffering was overlooked or viewed as so pervasive and fundamental to the nature of warfare as not to warrant comment. Rape in the former Yugoslavia speaks to the universality of women's experience in war. Almost every motive for wartime rape is present—rape as

---

107. *Id.* at 105.
108. *Veterans' Testimony on Vietnam—Need for Investigation,* 117 Cong. Rec. 9947–10,055 (1971) (*entering into record,* Winter Soldier Investigation Testimony, Testimony given at Detroit, Michigan, 31 Jan. 1971, 1–2 Feb. 1971—sponsored by Vietnam Veterans Against the War, Inc.).
109. *Id.* at 9950, 9951, 9973, 10,002, 10,005.
110. *Id.* at 9973.
111. *Id.* at 9977.
112. Indeed, all refugee women are particularly vulnerable to rape and other forms of physical assault. *See* Anders B. Johnsson, *The International Protection of Women Refugees: A Summary of Principal Problems and Issues,* 1 Int'l J. Refugee L. 221, 225–28 (1989).
113. *See* Adrianne Aron, Shawn Corne, Anthea Fursland, Barbara Zelwer, *The Gender-Specific Terror of El Salvador and Guatemala: Post-traumatic Stress Disorder in Central American Refugee Women,* 14 Women's Stud. Int'l F. 37 (1991) (discussing issues arising from rape of Salvadoran and Guatemalan women by armed forces).
114. *See* Shana Swiss, Physicians for Human Rights, Liberia: Anguish in a Divided Land 4–5 (1992); Shana Swiss, Physicians for Human Rights, Liberia: Women and Children Gravely Mistreated 5–6 (1991) (women and children raped and tortured in civil war).
115. *See* United Nations, Economic and Social Council, Commission on Human Rights, *Question of the Violation of Human Rights and Fundamental Freedoms in Any Part of the World, with Particular Reference to Colonial and Other Dependent Countries and Territories: Situation of Human Rights in Occupied Kuwait,* ¶¶ 181–84, U.N. Doc. E/CN.4/1992/26 (1992) (Report of Walter Kälin, Special Rapporteur of the Commission on Human Rights). The Special Rapporteur found that Kuwaiti and foreign women were raped by Iraqi soldiers during house searches, at a nurses' hostel, as a method of torture, and that some were abducted for that purpose. He concluded that "rape did not occur as an isolated incident." *Id.*

misogyny, rape to destroy culture and community, rape to instill terror, rape to boost morale, rape as reward, and rape as the messenger of defeat.[116] The only point of distinction is that rape in the former Yugoslavia has been chronicled to an unprecedented degree. Perhaps this fact will prevent rape in this war from becoming what it has been in other wars—the "forgotten war crime."[117]

D.   Militarism, Misogyny, and Rape

As early as the 1930s, feminists began to write of the connection between militarism and misogyny.[118] The threat to women's liberties from *fascist* militarism was clear—the fascist state was autocratic, dominated by a male warrior caste and male violence, and viewed women as useful only for pleasure and procreation—but feminist writers directed their attacks at *liberal* militarism as well.[119] The discussion of militarism as antithetical to women's human rights continues to the present.[120] Indeed, contemporary writers, such as Betty Reardon, believe that the more militarist a society, the more sexist it is likely to be.[121]

In general, the military ethos has been male and vehemently heterosexual. With notable exceptions, past and present, women have not made decisions about wars, women have not fought in wars, women have not even written about wars, and women certainly have not been present to judge war's aftermath. Women are war's victims, often its supporters, and usually its symbolism, but waging war is male territory. In Virginia Woolf's words:

> For though many instincts are held more or less in common by both sexes, to fight has always been the man's habit, not the woman's. Law and practice have developed that difference, whether innate or accidental. Scarcely a human being in the course of history has fallen to a woman's rifle; the vast majority of birds and beasts have been killed by you, not by us.[122]

---

116. See generally, Seifert, *supra* note 3, at 57–66; Stiglmayer, *supra* note 36, at 84.
117. Seifert, *supra* note 3, at 69.
118. Susan Gubar, *"This is My Rifle, This is My Gun": World War II and the Blitz on Women,* in Behind the Lines: Gender and the Two World Wars 227, 227–28 (Margaret R. Higonnet et al. eds., 1987). *See, e.g.,* Virginia Woolf, Three Guineas 53, 102 (Harbinger Books 1963) (1938).
119. Eisler, *supra* note 68, at 182–83. Nazi ideology, for example, limited women to traditional roles—"Kinder, Kirche, Küche" (children, church, kitchen). Gubar, *supra* note 119, at 239.
120. See, e.g., Betty A. Reardon, Sexism and the War System (1985); Ann Scales, *Militarism, Male Dominance and Law: Feminist Jurisprudence as Oxymoron?,* 12 Harv. Women's L.J. 25, 39–44 (1989).
121. Reardon, *supra* note 121, at 14.
122. Woolf, *supra* note 119, at 6. Similarly, Margaret Mead describes warfare as an "invention," which satisfies the needs of men in primitive and not-so-primitive societies:

War is viewed as an initiation to manhood, a license to destroy that has no civilian equivalent; the masculinity of those who choose not to partake is questioned. The military tends to cultivate patriarchal notions of man as protector; it also fosters exaggerated notions of male sexuality and virility. The result of these two male illusions is behavior towards women that oscillates between "extremes of gentility and fury."[123] Although physically absent, women's presence is apparent in a manner unknown in civilian life. Military language and training is saturated with sexual imagery, much of it misogynous;[124] and society more or less accepts the idea that soldiers are permitted a voracious sexual appetite. J. Glenn Gray writes,

> Anyone entering military service for the first time can only be astonished by soldiers' concentration upon the subject of women and, more especially, upon the sexual act. . . .
>
>   . . . .
>
> If we are honest, most of us who were civilian soldiers in recent wars will confess that we spent incomparably more time in the service of Eros during our military careers than ever before or again in our lives.[125]

The linkages between waging war and aggressive sexual behavior are clear: in each case, conquest and submission to force is the *raison d'etre*. Gray comments:

> Observation of others and being honest about our own sensations must convince us that sexual passion in isolation and the lust for battle are closely akin. . . .To be sure, the sexual partner is not actually destroyed in the encounter, merely overthrown. And the psychological aftereffects of sexual lust are different from those of battle lusts. These differences, however, do not alter the fact that the passions have a common source and affect their victims in the same way while they are in their grip. We should not forget, either, that sometimes the consequences are not so different, after all. Sexual lust often leads to murder, and in wartime, particularly, the same person often suffers rape and murder. Both reveal man as a beserker, outside of his humanity, a dangerous beast of prey.[126]

Warfare is just an invention known to the majority of human societies by which they permit their young men either to accumulate prestige or avenge their honor or acquire loot or wives or slaves or grab lands or cattle or appease the blood lust of their gods or the restless souls of the recently dead. *It is just an invention, older and more widespread than the jury system, but none the less an invention.*

Margaret Mead, *False Heroes, in* Women on War 134 (Daniela Gioseffi ed., 1988) (emphasis added).

123. Susan Faludi, *The Naked Citadel,* New Yorker, 5 Sept. 1994, at 62, 70.
124. *Id.* at 70, 72; Carol Cohn, *Sex and Death and the Rational World of Defense Intellectuals, in* Women on War, *supra* note 123, at 86–89; *see* Reardon, *supra* note 121, at 29–30, 53.
125. J. Glenn Gray, The Warriors: Reflections on Men in Battle 61 (1967).
126. *Id.* at 68; *see also* Reardon, *supra* note 121, at 39.

Wartime propaganda reinforces the link between war and sexuality and further objectifies women: the enemy is portrayed as he who will rape and murder "our" women; the war effort is directed at saving "our" mothers, daughters, and wives. At the same time, women are portrayed as unworthy, untrustworthy, even as the enemy: they are seen as "irresponsible in their garrulity" (loose lips sink ships), "sinister in their silence" (the treacherous *femme fatale*), or carriers of venereal diseases.[127] Through such images, soldiers are conditioned to cherish certain women and to have no regard for others.[128] Perpetuation of these stereotypes depends on the absence of women who might challenge them. As one feminist writes, if military success depends on gender stereotypes, "commanders may be right to resist women's military participation."[129]

Just as objectification of the enemy makes it possible for soldiers to kill, so objectification of women, along with the "stylize[d] masculinity"[130] created by the military, can lead to rape. One observer writes:

> That does not mean that every soldier rapes. But it does mean that the construction of the soldier—or to express it differently, the subjective identity that armies make available, by fusing certain cultural ideas of masculinity with a soldier's essence—is more conducive to certain ways of behavior rather than others. For in a stress situation like war, how one reacts depends not only on the specifics of the stressful situation, but beyond that also "on the individual and sociocultural availability of certain coping strategies. Part of coping is also the culturally coded manner of dealing with emotions." Whether or not one reacts violently in a certain situation, then, also depends for example on which alternatives are available for the channeling of feelings in a cultural context (and in various cultures and also in various armies that includes varying ideas of masculinity and femininity).[131]

Even beyond the battlefield, militarism leads to aggression against women. In Croatia, for example, domestic violence against women has increased by nearly 30 percent since the outbreak of war; the violence is especially great after nationalistic television programming.[132] A similar trend was noted in Israel during the Gulf War.[133] The link between militarism and violence against women, in war and in peace, has been recognized by peace

---

127. Gubar, *supra* note 119, at 240.
128. *See* REARDON, *supra* note 121, at 51.
129. Judith Hicks Stiehm, *The Protected, The Protector, The Defender,* 5 WOMEN'S STUD. INT'L F. 365, 372 (1982).
130. Siefert, *supra* note 3, at 60–61.
131. *Id.* at 61 (quoting HANS-GÜNTHER VESTER, EMOTION, GESELLSCHAFT UND KULTUR: GRUNDZÜGE EINER SOZIOLOGISCHEN THEORIE DER EMOTIONEN 144 (1990)).
132. *Id.* at 66.
133. *Id.*

researchers. They argue that the cycle of violence will not end until the system of militarism is dismantled and feminist modes of thought are permitted into the centers of decisionmaking.[134]

III.   RAPE UNDER INTERNATIONAL HUMANITARIAN LAW[135]

Because rape and war have been so inexorably linked over time, the question arises whether rape is a crime under international humanitarian law (IHL). Although the answer is an incontrovertible yes,[136] rape does have an uncertain status under IHL. In conception and enforcement, the prohibition of rape reflects confusion as to whether it is a crime against women or against men and the community, and whether it is persecution based on gender or an inhuman act, like maiming or torture, in which gender is of no relevance. From a feminist perspective, IHL has mischaracterized the crime and has ignored its gender aspects. Rape is regarded not as a violent attack on women but as a challenge to honor (whose honor is not entirely clear), and it has yet to be recognized as an assault motivated by gender, not simply by membership in the enemy camp. In these respects, IHL must be seen as a gender-biased body of law.[137]

A.   Rape as a Crime Against Honor and Dignity

Occasionally, IHL has paid homage to the fact that rape is a crime of violence, but the predominant characterization is that rape is a crime against honor and dignity. The modern history of IHL begins with the Lieber Code; two provisions are relevant. The first provision gives special protection to women, in a provision which by context links women and family relations.[138] The second provision prohibits rape upon penalty of death: in

---

134. *See, e.g.,* BETTY A. REARDON, WOMEN AND PEACE: FEMINIST VISIONS OF GLOBAL SECURITY 68–69 (1993).

135. This section, like the balance of the paper, discusses legal protection of women as members of the civilian population only. Additional provisions of international humanitarian law protect women who take part in hostilities. *See generally,* Françoise Krill, *The Protection of Women in International Humanitarian Law,* 25 INT'L REV. RED CROSS 337 (1985).

136. *See, e.g.,* YOUGINDRA KHUSHALANI, DIGNITY AND HONOUR OF WOMEN AS BASIC AND FUNDAMENTAL HUMAN RIGHTS (1982); Theodor Meron, *Rape as A Crime Under International Humanitarian Law,* 87 AM. J. INT'L L. 424 (1993).

137. *See* Judith Gardam, *A Feminist Analysis of Certain Aspects of International Humanitarian Law,* 12 AUST. Y.B. INT'L L. 265, 267 (1992) (describing IHL as gendered legal regime); Judith Gardam, *Gender and Non-Combatant Immunity,* 3 TRANSNAT'L L. & CONTEMP. PROBS. 345, 358–59 (1993) (women's marginalization evident in attitude of law of war to rape); Brande Stellings, Note, *The Public Harm of Private Violence: Rape, Sex Discrimination and Citizenship,* 28 HARV. C.R.-C.L. L. REV. 185 (1993) (discussing rape as sex discrimination).

this context, rape appears to be recognized as a violent crime.[139] The Lieber Code was not an international document; nevertheless, it influenced the Hague Conventions in many significant respects.[140] Shortly after the Lieber Code was promulgated, international documents adopted the concept of "family honor and rights," which became the basis for the prohibition of rape; the Lieber Code's alternative characterization of rape as a violent crime was abandoned. The 1874 Declaration of Brussels mandated respect for "the honour and rights of the family."[141] Article 46 of the Hague Regulations of 1899 and 1907; which has been construed to prohibit rape,[142] requires respect for "[f]amily honour and rights, the lives of persons, and private property, as well as religious convictions and practice."[143] The Fourth Geneva Convention of 1949 incorporates these concepts in a provision giving women special protection against rape. Article 27 states:

> Protected persons are entitled, in all circumstances, to *respect for their persons, their honour, their family rights, their religious convictions and practices, and their manners and customs.* They shall at all times be humanely treated, and shall be protected especially against all acts of violence or threats thereof and against insults and public curiosity.
>
> *Women shall be especially protected against any attack on their honour, in particular against rape, enforced prostitution, or any form of indecent assault.*[144]

The commentary to the Geneva Convention explains that the second paragraph of Article 27 was intended to denounce widespread abuse during World War II of women and children, including rape, mutilation, and forced

---

138. Article 37 of the Lieber Code provides in part:

> The United States acknowledge and protect, in hostile countries occupied by them, religion and morality; . . . the persons of the inhabitants, especially those of women; and the sacredness of domestic relations. Offenses to the contrary shall be rigorously punished.

Lieber Code, *supra* note 82, art. 37.

139. Article 44 of the Lieber Code provides:

> All wanton violence committed against persons in the invaded country, all destruction of property not commanded by the authorized officer, all robbery, all pillage or sacking, even after taking a place by main force, all rape, wounding, maiming, or killing of such inhabitants, are prohibited under the penalty of death, or such other severe punishment as may seem adequate for the gravity of the offense.

Id. art. 44.

140. KHUSHALANI, *supra* note 137, at 7; TAYLOR, *supra* note 88, at 10.
141. Declaration of Brussels Concerning the Laws and Customs of War, art. 38, 27 Aug. 1874, *in* 1 THE LAW OF WAR: A DOCUMENTARY HISTORY, *supra* note 82, at 194, 200. The rules drafted at the Brussels Conference were not adopted by the nations concerned. *Id.* at 194.
142. KHUSHALANI, *supra* note 137, at 10; Meron, *supra* note 137, at 425.
143. 1907 Hague Regulations, *supra* note 83; 1899 Hague Regulations, *supra* note 83.
144. Geneva Convention IV, *supra* note 83, art. 27, 6 U.S.T. at 3536, 75 U.N.T.S. at 306 (emphasis added).

prostitution.[145] Yet, the commentators also view this paragraph as offering additional protection for "family rights" mentioned in the first paragraph,[146] and they apparently do not see it as integral to the right to physical integrity also covered by the first paragraph.[147] In fact, rape is conspicuously absent from Article 32, which prohibits certain violations of physical integrity "which have shocked the conscience of the world."[148]

Not only does the Geneva Convention overlook the violent nature of rape, but the prohibition of rape is attached to the wrong category of rights. The word "honor" has various meanings: dignity, esteem, allegiance to the good or the right, but concerning women it also means chastity, purity, and good name.[149] As the commentary suggests, it was these interests for which protection was sought:

> The Conference listed as examples certain acts constituting an attack on women's honour, and expressly mentioned rape, enforced prostitution, i.e. *the forcing of a woman into immorality by violence or threats,* and any form of indecent assault. These acts are and remain prohibited in all places and in all circumstances, and women, whatever their nationality, race, religious beliefs, age, marital status or social condition have an *absolute right to respect for their honour and their modesty, in short, for their dignity as women.*[150]

The pitfalls in linking rape and honor are many. First, reality and the woman's true injury are sacrificed: rape begins to look like seduction with "just a little persuading" rather than a massive and brutal assault on the body and psyche.[151] As reports from the former Yugoslavia indicate, violations of honor and modesty are wholly inadequate concepts to express the suffering

---

145. COMMENTARY ON IV GENEVA CONVENTION RELATIVE TO THE PROTECTION OF CIVILIAN PERSONS IN TIME OF WAR 205 (Jean S. Pictet et al. eds., 1958) [hereinafter COMMENTARY ON GENEVA CONVENTION IV].
146. *Id.* at 202.
147. *See id.* at 201. The right to physical integrity is one aspect of the right to respect for the person. *Id.* The Commentary notes that the right to physical integrity is reinforced by two other provisions, but Article 27, ¶ 2 is not one of these. *See id.* Ironically, because Article 27 offers special protection to women only, sexual assaults of men would be considered as a violation of the right to physical integrity, thereby recognizing the violence of the assault when directed at a man, but not at a woman.
148. *Id.* at 201. Article 32 prohibits a state party,

> from taking any measure of such a character as to cause the physical suffering or extermination of protected persons in their hands. This prohibition applies not only to *murder, torture, corporal punishment, mutilation and medical or scientific experiments not necessitated by the medical treatment* of a protected person, but also to *any other measures of brutality* whether applied by civilian or military agents.

> Geneva Convention IV, *supra* note 83, art. 32, 6 U.S.T. at 3538, 75 U.N.T.S. at 308 (emphasis added).

149. 1 THE SHORTER OXFORD ENGLISH DICTIONARY ON HISTORICAL PRINCIPLES 980–81 (1973).
150. COMMENTARY ON GENEVA CONVENTION IV, *supra* note 146, at 206 (emphasis added).
151. Seduction, however, can also be rape when it vitiates consent. *See* SUSAN ESTRICH, REAL RAPE 70 (1987) (describing breadth of seduction as without parallel in criminal law); Ellen

of women raped during war. Second, by presenting honor as the interest to be protected, the injury is defined from society's viewpoint, and the notion that the raped woman is soiled or disgraced is resurrected.[152] Third, on the scale of wartime violence, rape as a mere injury to honor or reputation appears less worthy of prosecution than injuries to the person.

That rape has not been regarded as a serious crime is confirmed by its omission from Article 147, which lists grave breaches under the Geneva Convention.[153] The significance of a grave breach is that it gives rise to universal jurisdiction; also, it is a tacit indication of the perceived gravity of the crime.[154] Although rape appears to fall within the general clauses of Article 147 and the Commentary indicates that the grave breach of "inhuman treatment" includes violations of Article 27,[155] the failure to specify rape is illuminating: among the crimes seen fit to include as grave breaches, and which presumably rated more attention than rape, are forcing a person to serve in the forces of a hostile power and destruction and appropriation of property.[156] Although the International Committee of the Red Cross and the US State Department have recently declared that rape is a grave breach under Article 147,[157] this proposition should not rest on interpretation; an amendment is needed.

The 1977 Protocols to the Geneva Conventions reflect a slightly more enlightened approach. Protocol I, Article 75, entitled "Fundamental Guarantees," prohibits in gender-neutral terms "outrages upon *personal dignity*, in particular humiliating and degrading treatment, enforced prostitution and any form of indecent assault."[158] Protocol II, Article 4 provides similar pro-

---

Rooney, *"A Little More than Persuading": Tess and the Subject of Sexual Violence, in* Rape and Representation 87, 91–94 (Lynn A. Higgins & Brenda R. Silver eds., 1991) (viewing rape and seduction as on continuum).

152. Rhonda Copelon, *Surfacing Gender: Reconceptualizing Crimes against Women in Time of War, in* Mass Rape, *supra* note 3, at 197, 200.
153. Article 147 lists the following crimes as grave breaches:

> wilful killing, torture or inhuman treatment, including biological experiments, wilfully causing great suffering or serious injury to body or health, unlawful deportation or transfer or unlawful confinement of a protected person, compelling a protected person to serve in the forces of a hostile Power, or wilfully depriving a protected person of the rights of fair and regular trial, . . . taking of hostages and extensive destruction and appropriation of property, not justified by military necessity and carried out unlawfully and wantonly.

Geneva Convention IV, *supra* note 83, art. 147, 6 U.S.T. at 3618, 75 U.N.T.S at 388.

154. Copelon, *supra* note 153, at 201.
155. Commentary on Geneva Convention IV, *supra* note 146, at 598.
156. Geneva Convention IV, *supra* note 83, art. 147, 6 U.S.T. at 3618, 75 U.N.T.S. at 388.
157. Meron, *supra* note 137, at 426–27.
158. Protocol Additional to the Geneva Conventions of 12 August 1949, and Relating to the Protection of Victims of International Armed Conflicts (Protocol I), art. 75(2)(b), *opened for signature* 12 Dec. 1977, 1125 U.N.T.S. 3, 37, 16 I.L.M. 1391, 1423 (1977) (emphasis added) [hereinafter Protocol I].

tection, but adds an express reference to rape.[159] Protocol I, Article 76 also provides special protection for women: "[w]omen shall be the object of special respect and shall be protected in particular against rape, forced prostitution and any other form of indecent assault."[160] Still, although dignity is a more germane referent than honor, it does not adequately express the fact that sexual assault is a violent crime; indeed, the Protocols *distinguish* sexual assaults from crimes of violence.[161] That is not to deny that rape is a violation of dignity: the point is that it is also and it is primarily a physical assault. The failure to recognize the violent nature of rape is one reason that it has been assigned a secondary status in IHL.[162]

Another weakness in the laws concerning rape is that, until recently, protection was patchy. Article 27 of the Fourth Geneva Convention applies only to a certain category of women; others are not protected.[163] Also, Article 27 applies to international conflicts only.[164] In noninternational conflicts, women can rely only on Article 3, the so-called "mini-convention" common to the four 1949 Conventions, which does not expressly prohibit rape.[165] The 1977 Protocols remedy these shortcomings to an extent. Protocol I, Article 76 covers *any* woman in the hands of a party to an international conflict, and Protocol II, Article 4 protects women caught in

---

159. Protocol Additional to the Geneva Conventions of 12 August 1949, and Relating to the Protection of Victims of Non-International Armed Conflicts (Protocol II), art. 4(2)(e), *opened for signature* 12 Dec. 1977, 1125 U.N.T.S. 609, 612, 16 I.L.M. 1442, 1444 (1977) [hereinafter Protocol II].

160. Protocol I, *supra* note 159, art. 76(1), 1125 U.N.T.S. at 38, 16 I.L.M. at 1425.

161. Protocol I, Article 75(2)(a) and Protocol II, Article 4(2)(a) condemn "violence to the life, health, or physical or mental well-being of persons," including murder, torture, corporal punishment, or mutilation. Protocol I, *supra* note 159, art. 75(2)(a), 1125 U.N.T.S. at 37, 16 I.L.M. at 1423; Protocol II, *supra* note 160, art. 4(2)(a), 1125 U.N.T.S. at 612, 16 I.L.M. at 1444. "Outrages upon personal dignity" are discussed separately. Protocol I, *supra*, art. 75(2)(b); Protocol II, *supra*, art. 4(2)(e).

162. Copelon, *supra* note 153, at 200–01.

163. Article 27 of the Geneva Convention IV protects only women in the hands of a state party to the conflict of which they are not nationals. Women of the same nationality as their captors, or from neutral or co-belligerent states, or states not parties to the Convention, are not protected. Geneva Convention IV, *supra* note 83, art. 4, 6 U.S.T. at 3520, 75 U.N.T.S. at 290.

164. *Id.* art. 2, 6 U.S.T. at 3518, 75 U.N.T.S. at 288.

165. In pertinent part, Article 3 prohibits the following acts against noncombatants:

> (a) violence to life and person, in particular murder of all kinds, mutilation, cruel treatment and torture;

> . . . .

> (c) outrages upon personal dignity, in particular humiliating and degrading treatment.

Geneva Convention IV, *supra* note 83, art. 3(1), 6 U.S.T. at 3518, 3520, 75 U.N.T.S. at 288, 290.

noninternational armed conflicts.[166] The Protocols have not been widely ratified, however, and are not considered by all to be customary international
law.[167]

B.   Rape as a Crime Against Humanity

Among the crimes prosecuted before the IMT and the IMTFE were crimes
against humanity. The Charter of the IMT at Nuremberg defines crimes
against humanity as follows:

> CRIMES AGAINST HUMANITY: namely, *murder, extermination, enslavement,
> deportation, and other inhumane acts committed against any civilian popula-
> tion*, before or during war, or *persecutions on political, racial or religious
> grounds* in execution of or in connection with any crime within the jurisdiction
> of the Tribunal, whether or not in violation of the domestic law of the country
> where perpetrated.[168]

The definition in the Tokyo Charter is similar.[169] Neither charter mentions
rape.[170] Although the enumerated crimes are not intended as an exhaustive
catalog, and rape clearly falls under "other inhuman acts," prosecution of
mass rape was not a priority of the drafters.[171] Nor was it a priority of the

---

166. COMMENTARY ON THE ADDITIONAL PROTOCOLS OF 8 JUNE 1977 TO THE GENEVA CONVENTIONS OF 12
     AUGUST 1949, at 892 (Yves Sandoz et al. eds., 1987); Krill, *supra* note 136, at 342.
167. For example, in his commentary on the Statute of the Tribunal, the Secretary-General
     omits the Protocols from the body of law he considers to be customary international law.
     See Report of the Secretary-General, supra note 10, ¶ 35. The Commission of Experts
     finds, however, that certain provisions of the Protocols constitute customary international
     law. *Final Report, supra* note 22, ¶¶ 51, 309.
168. Agreement for the Prosecution and Punishment of the Major War Criminals of the
     European Axis, Charter of the International Military Tribunal, art. 6(c), 8 Aug. 1945,
     amended, 6 Oct. 1945, 59 Stat. 1544, 1547, 82 U.N.T.S. 279, 288 [hereinafter
     Nuremberg Charter].
169. The Tokyo Charter refers to persecution on "political or racial" grounds; the reference to
     religious persecution in the Nuremberg Charter is omitted. Charter of the International
     Military Tribunal for the Far East, art. 5(c), 19 Jan. 1946, *amended* 26 Apr. 1946, T.I.A.S.
     No. 1589, at 6, 4 Bevans 20, 23 [hereinafter Tokyo Charter].
170. Rape is also omitted from the list of war crimes in the Nuremberg Charter; the Tokyo
     Charter does not specify particular war crimes. Nuremberg Charter, *supra* note 169, art.
     6(b), 59 Stat. at 1547, 82 U.N.T.S at 288; Tokyo Charter, *supra* note 170, art. 5(b), T.I.A.S.
     No. 1589, at 6, 4 Bevans at 23.
171. The Nuremberg Charter was drafted at the London Conference in 1945; it became the
     basis for trials before the IMT at Nuremberg, and also served as a model for the Tokyo
     Charter. Both the plain language of the crimes against humanity provision and its draft-
     ing history indicate that the crimes were not intended to be exhaustive. *See, e.g.,* ROBERT
     H. JACKSON, REPORT OF THE US REPRESENTATIVE TO THE INTERNATIONAL CONFERENCE ON MILITARY TRIALS,
     LONDON 1945, at 298 (1949) (comment of Soviet delegate that exhaustive list of crimes
     impossible). Also, the drafting history shows that little discussion was devoted to crimes

decisionmakers, at least at Nuremberg. Although evidence of rape was presented, it was not mentioned in the IMT's judgment.[172]

Rape was listed as a crime against humanity in Control Council Law Ten (CCL 10), the enactment that served as the jurisdictional basis for later proceedings in Nuremberg.[173] Even so, it was not prosecuted in any of the twelve subsequent trials. These trials, however, did establish several principles that will affect prosecutions of all crimes against humanity, including rape. The first is that crimes against humanity are committed against a "civilian population": they require proof of government participation in or approval of systematic atrocities or persecution; an isolated case is not sufficient.[174] Thus, rape on a wide scale would be prosecuted as a crime against humanity; a single case would be prosecuted as a war crime. The second principle, suggested but not confirmed by the trials, is that atrocities committed during peacetime also can serve as the basis of liability.[175] This principle has been strengthened by post–World War II human rights conventions, such as the conventions against genocide and torture, which criminalize certain conduct whether committed in times of war or peace.[176] It is accepted by some governments and scholars.[177] Unfortunately, how-

---

against humanity; this is in contrast to crimes against peace, which were debated at length. *See, e.g., id.* at 293–309, 327–38, 375–401, 415–18 (discussing definition of crimes).

172. *See supra* text accompanying note 93. In Tokyo, rape was prosecuted as a war crime and discussed in the judgment. *See supra* text accompanying notes 99–100.

173. Because the Nuremberg Charter and CCL 10 relied on the same two antecedent documents, neither of which mentioned rape, it is possible that the first Nuremberg trial, which had been underway for one month at the time CCL 10 was adopted, was influential. *See* Telford Taylor, Final Report to the Secretary of the Army on the Nuernberg War Crimes Trials Under Control Council Law No. 10, at 8 (1949).

174. In *The Justice* case, the court stated,

We hold that crimes against humanity as defined in C.C. Law 10 must be strictly construed to exclude isolated cases of atrocity or persecution whether committed by private individuals or by governmental authority. As we construe it, that section provides for punishment of crimes committed against German nationals only where there is proof of conscious participation in systematic government organized or approved procedures amounting to atrocities and offenses of the kind specified in the act and committed against populations or amounting to persecutions on political, racial, or religious grounds.

United States v. Altstoetter, 3 Trials Under CCL 10, *supra* note 10, at 982.

175. *See* Taylor, *supra* note 174, at 108–09.

176. Convention Against Torture and Other Cruel, Inhuman or Degrading Treatment or Punishment, art. 2(2), *opened for signature,* 10 Dec. 1984, G.A. Res. 39/46, U.N. Doc. A/RES/39/46, *reprinted in* 23 I.L.M. 1027 (1984), *amended,* 24 I.L.M. 535 (1985); Convention on the Prevention and Punishment of the Crime of Genocide, art. 1, *opened for signature* 9 Dec. 1948, 78 U.N.T.S. 277, 280; *see also* Theodor Meron, *War Crimes in Yugoslavia and the Development of International Law,* 88 Am. J. Int'l. L. 78, 84–85 (1994) (discussing link between crimes against humanity and state of war).

177. Meron, *supra* note 177, at 85–87.

ever, it is unlikely to be addressed by the Tribunal, whose jurisdiction is limited to crimes against humanity "when committed in armed conflict."[178] The third principle is that responsibility is not limited to military personnel; persons occupying key positions, including doctors, lawyers, judges, diplomats, and businesspersons, may also be liable.[179] In the former Yugoslavia, this would mean that the net would be cast widely; certainly medical personnel monitoring forced pregnancies in the "rape camps" could be punished.

C.   Rape as a Crime Against Gender

The Nuremberg trials before the IMT and under CCL 10 established principles of enormous significance; they were idealistic undertakings and a triumph of the rule of law, particularly in view of alternatives proposed at the time.[180] For all of that, it cannot be said that the Nuremberg trials advanced international law concerning wartime rape significantly. Perhaps prosecutions of crimes violating the right to life (murder, reprisals, hostagetaking) were considered more weighty. The more likely explanation is that rape as a *distinct* category of atrocity was not recognized; it was not seen as the particular way in which women suffer in war; it was not seen as persecution based on gender. It may be anachronistic to expect the Nuremberg tribunals to have grasped this concept; after all, it is still considered novel today.[181] By analogy, however, it now would be unthinkable to cast the Holocaust as persecution of civilians, without taking into account the ethnic and religious aspects of the crime; yet, the word "genocide" was coined only during World War II.[182] In the same way, it now would be insensible to fail to recognize rape, in war or in peace, as an extreme form of gender discrimination and as gynocide. Either by amendment to the current conventions or by declaration, IHL should be revised to reflect this concept.[183] Of course, another problem is that those who interpret and apply the law must take wartime rape seriously; because it is pervasive does not mean that it is not preventable or that it should not be condemned in the strongest possible terms.

---

178. *Statute, supra* note 10, art. 5; *see infra* note 206.
179. TAYLOR, *supra* note 174, at 109.
180. Some of the alternatives were execution without trial of the major war criminals, execution or banishment of the German general staff, and reducing Germany to an agrarian society. *See* TAYLOR, *supra* note 88, at 30–31, 107–08.
181. *See* Stellings, *supra* note 138.
182. TAYLOR, *supra* note 88, at 103.
183. A parallel situation exists under asylum law. The UN Convention Relating to the Status of Refugees, 22 Apr. 1954, 189 U.N.T.S. 137, does not mention gender persecution as a ground for asylum, and adjudicators often neglect the gender-related claims of women.

IV. PROSECUTING RAPE BEFORE THE TRIBUNAL

The prospect of rape prosecutions before the Tribunal presents something of a duality. On the one hand, the creation of the Tribunal reflects the best humanitarian intentions. On the other, as far as women's human rights are concerned, the Tribunal begins its task already hampered by a long history of neglect and by legal structures that may be inadequate to redress the situation. Also, there is the risk that the Tribunal, as the product of an international system in which women have been largely invisible, may find itself an improficient or clumsy arbiter of women's suffering.[184] Already the signs are ominous: only two of the eleven judges on the Tribunal are women and the current prosecutor is male, as was his predecessor.[185] Photographs of the Nuremberg trials reveal a sea of male faces—judges, prosecutors, defense attorneys, and defendants; women appear only as support personnel and a handful in the later trials as prosecutors, defense attorneys, and witnesses.[186] Fifty years after Nuremberg, it is reasonable to insist on correction of the gender imbalance and on abandonment of traditional views concerning the professional roles of women, particularly women in law enforcement.[187]

Nancy Kelly, *Gender-Related Persecution: Assessing the Asylum Claims of Women*, 26 CORNELL INT'L L.J. 625, 627 (1993). Recently, however, Canada and the United States have adopted guidelines permitting asylum based on gender persecution. *See* Audrey Macklin, *Refugee Women and the Imperative of Categories*, 17 HUM. RTS. Q. 213, 214 (1995); Ashley Dunn, *U.S. to Accept Asylum Pleas for Sex Abuse*, N.Y. TIMES, 27 May 1995, at A1.

184. *See* Hilary Charlesworth, Christine Chinkin, Shelley Wright, *Feminist Approaches to International Law*, 85 AM. J. INT'L L. 613, 615, 621–25 (1991) (describing international law as gendered and noting absence of women from international organizations).

185. The General Assembly considered twenty-two jurists for eleven judgeships. Only two women were on the list; one from Costa Rica, the other from the United States. United Nations, General Assembly, *Election of Judges of the International Tribunal for the Prosecution of Persons Responsible for Serious Violations of International Humanitarian Law Committed in the Territory of the Former Yugoslavia Since 1991, Curricula Vitae of Candidates Nominated by States Members of the United Nations and Non-Member States Maintaining Permanent Observer Missions at United Nations Headquarters*, U.N. Doc. A/47/1006 (1993). Both women were elected. As for the prosecutor's position, it does not appear that any of the nominees were women, either the first or the second time the position was available. Copelon, *supra* note 153, at 217–18 n.43; Longworth, *supra* note 23; *U.N. Trims List of Candidates for Tribunal on Balkan War Crimes*, N.Y. TIMES, 22 Aug. 1993, at 15.

186. For photographs of the proceedings before the IMT at Nuremberg, *see* TAYLOR, *supra* note 88, pages following 130, 354, and CHARLES W. ALEXANDER, JUSTICE AT NUERMBERG: A PICTORIAL REVIEW OF THE TRIAL OF NAZI WAR CRIMINALS BY THE INTERNATIONAL TRIBUNAL AT NUERMBERG, GERMANY, 1945–6 (1946). For photographs of the subsequent Nuremberg proceedings, see pages following TRIALS UNDER CCL 10, *supra* note 10, vol. I, at 6; vol. II, at 357; vol. IV, at 6, 602; vol. VI, at 7; vol. VII, at 6; vol. IX, at 4; vol. X, at 8; vol. XI, at 762; and vol. XII, at 6. All prosecutors and defense attorneys of record in the first Nuremberg trial were male; a few women worked as prosecutors and defense counsel in the subsequent proceedings. 1 TRIALS UNDER CCL 10, *supra* note 10, at 7.

187. In his commentary to the Statute, the Secretary-General states, "[g]iven the nature of the crimes committed and the sensitivities of victims of rape and sexual assault, due consid-

Still the existence of the Tribunal holds promise. At worst, it would seem that the Tribunal will do what has been done before—to ignore the gender aspects of rape and to treat it as another weapon in a genocidal war. At best, the Tribunal might recognize rape as a violent crime that stands alone because it is part of a universal pattern; it might condemn rape, whether the result of a random act or a deliberate strategy, as gender persecution and a grievous violation of IHL and human rights. In this vein, the ultimate contribution of the Tribunal depends not only on the applicable law and procedure, but also on the human factor—the willingness of women to testify, the commitment to prosecuting rape, and the character and sensitivity of judges and attorneys. These elements are not analyzed readily in advance; however, the framework within which the process will unfold is contained in the statute and rules of the Tribunal.

A. Subject Matter Jurisdiction

The Statute of the Tribunal (Statute)[188] makes no judgment as to whether the conflict in the former Yugoslavia is international or internal. Resolution of this issue will affect the body of humanitarian law that is applied. In terms of rape prosecutions, the applicable law is significant because rules governing internal conflicts are less protective than those governing international conflicts.[189] The Commission of Experts and some scholars believe that the rules pertaining to international conflicts apply—an opinion based on the nature of hostilities, principles of state succession, declarations of the newly independent states, and a series of agreements between the parties.[190] The ultimate determination, however, is for the Tribunal.

The Tribunal's subject matter jurisdiction is set forth in four articles, giving it jurisdiction over grave breaches of the Geneva Conventions of 1949 (Article 2), violations of the laws or customs of war (Article 3), genocide (Article 4), and crimes against humanity (Article 5). Only Article 5 mentions rape specifically, yet each of the four articles is potentially relevant.

---

eration should be given in the appointment of [the prosecutor's] staff to the employment of qualified women." *Report of the Secretary General, supra* note 10, ¶ 88. The US Ambassador to the United Nations, Madeline Albright, echoed these comments when she said: "My Government is also determined to see that women jurists sit on the Tribunal and that women prosecutors bring war criminals to justice." United Nations, Security Council, Provisional Verbatim Record, at 14, U.N. Doc. S/PV.3217 (1993). Of course, the nature of the crimes is not the only reason to insist that women are equally represented on the Tribunal.

188. *Statute, supra* note 10.
189. *See supra* text accompanying notes 165–68.
190. *Final Report, supra* note 22, ¶¶ 42–44, 125 & n.27; James C. O'Brien, *The International Tribunal for Violations of International Humanitarian Law in the Former Yugoslavia,* 87 Am.

Article 2 creates jurisdiction over grave breaches of the Geneva Conventions of 1949.[191] As already noted, rape is not explicitly a grave breach; however, it has been recognized as falling within the definition of one grave breach ("inhuman treatment")[192] and would seem to qualify under two others ("torture" and "wilfully causing great suffering or serious injury to body or health").[193]

Article 3 gives jurisdiction over violations of the laws and customs of war, defined in a nonexhaustive list of crimes drawn from the 1907 Hague Regulations and the Nuremberg Charter.[194] Rape does not appear, presumably because it is perceived as subsumed within Article 2.

Article 4 establishes jurisdiction in cases of genocide; the provisions of this article are drawn from the 1948 Genocide Convention.[195] The policy of "ethnic cleansing" meets the definition of genocide and rape as a tool of "ethnic cleansing" satisfies several subsections of the article.

Article 5 creates jurisdiction over crimes against humanity committed in armed conflicts. The crimes are defined as "murder, extermination, enslavement, deportation, imprisonment, torture, rape, persecutions on political, racial, and religious grounds, and other inhumane acts."[196] Following from CCL 10, rape is listed as a crime against humanity, yet this will be the first time that it has been prosecuted as such.

Articles 6 and 7 pertain to the basis of liability. The Tribunal rejects the concept of organizational liability used at Nuremberg and imposes liability only on natural persons.[197] Under the Statute, individual liability may be imposed on any person who "planned, instigated, ordered, committed or

---

J. INT'L L. 639, 647–48 (1993); see YVES SANDOZ, INTERNATIONAL COMMITTEE OF THE RED CROSS, A CONSIDERATION OF THE IMPLEMENTATION OF INTERNATIONAL HUMANITARIAN LAW AND THE ROLE OF THE INTERNATIONAL COMMITTEE OF THE RED CROSS IN THE FORMER YUGOSLAVIA 4–11 (1993) (describing agreements).

191. Statute, supra note 10, art. 2.
192. See supra text accompanying note 156.
193. Copelon, supra note 153, at 201; see Meron, supra note 137, at 426 (in "certain circumstances" rape rises to level of torture and inhuman treatment). The International Committee of the Red Cross has stated that rape is covered by the grave breach of "wilfully causing great suffering or serious injury to body or health." Id.
194. Statute, supra note 10, art. 3; see Nuremberg Charter, supra note 169, art. 6(b), 59 Stat. at 1547, 82 U.N.T.S. at 288; 1907 Hague Regulations, supra note 83, arts. 23(a), 23(e), 25, 27, 28, 36 Stat. at 2301–03, 1 Bevans at 648–49.
195. Statute, supra note 10, art. 4; Convention on the Prevention and Punishment of the Crime of Genocide, supra note 177.
196. Statute, supra note 10, art. 5.
197. Id. art. 6. At Nuremberg, a number of Nazi organizations were indicted; the theory was that once organizations were declared criminal, members would be liable automatically upon proof of membership. TAYLOR, supra note 88, at 75; Nuremberg Charter, supra note 169, arts. 9–10. The IMT, however, narrowed the scope of liability by requiring proof that persons had joined the organization voluntarily and had knowledge of its criminal pur-

otherwise aided and abetted in the planning, preparation or execution of a crime."[198] Command responsibility may be imposed if a superior "knew or had reason to know" that a subordinate was about to commit a crime or had committed a crime and failed to take reasonable measures to prevent the crime or punish the perpetrator.[199] A claim of superior orders is not recognized as a defense, but may mitigate punishment,[200] and immunity is not extended to heads of state or other government officials.[201] Under these principles of liability, guilt may be assigned to attackers who claim to be acting under orders, to persons who "aid and abet" a rape through taunts or other provocations, and to persons in authority who fail to take action to prevent rape or to punish those responsible.

Overall, the Statute's approach is conservative: presumably to avoid the criticism directed at the Nuremberg proceedings of infidelity to the *nullum crimen sine lege* principle (similar to the *ex post facto* provision in the US Constitution),[202] the statute draws only from sources that are textual and clearly part of customary international law. Although Article 3 is elastic, providing a nonexhaustive list of war crimes, and all articles are subject to interpretation, the Secretary-General's commentary urges the Tribunal to apply only rules of IHL that are "beyond any doubt" part of customary international law.[203] As a result of this cautious drafting style, rape is omitted from both Articles 2 and 3. While rape is undoubtedly a grave breach (Article 2) and a war crime (Article 3), it has been left to the Tribunal to make this declaration, assuming of course it is given an opportunity to do so. In the event that rape prosecutions are not brought under these articles, however, there is the danger that rape will be left with an uncertain status in the laws of war, by virtue of the Tribunal's silence in the light of such egregious facts. It is unfortunate that the drafters did not see fit to list rape under Article 2: it

---

pose or acts, or that they were personally implicated in crimes. 22 TRIAL BEFORE THE IMT, *supra* note 7, at 500. For a discussion of issues arising from organizational liability at Nuremberg and in other contexts, see Jonathan A. Bush, *Nuremberg: The Modern Law of War and its Limitations*, 93 COLUM. L. REV. 2022, 2074–80 (1993) (reviewing TELFORD TAYLOR, THE ANATOMY OF THE NUREMBERG TRIALS: A PERSONAL MEMOIR (1992)).

198. *Statute, supra* note 10, art. 7(1).
199. *Id.* art. 7(3).
200. *Id.* art. 7(4).
201. *Id.* art. 7(2).
202. See TAYLOR, *supra* note 88, at 627–29; M. Cherif Bassiouni, *"Crimes Against Humanity": The Need for a Specialized Convention*, 31 COLUM. J. TRANSNAT'L L. 457, 466–69 (1994) (discussing criticisms directed at Nuremberg on basis of *nullum crimen sine lege*).
203. The Secretary-General identifies the following conventions as sources of customary international law: the four Geneva Conventions of 1949, the 1907 Hague Convention (IV) and Regulations, the Genocide Convention, and the Nuremberg Charter. *Report of the Secretary-General, supra* note 10, ¶ ¶ 34–35. Omission of the 1977 Protocols prompted a rejoinder from the Commission of Experts that certain provisions of Protocol I have become part of customary international law. *Final Report, supra* note 22, ¶ ¶ 51, 53.

would not have been a significant innovation to do so and the omission ultimately might lead to a setback for women.[204]

Genocide (Article 4) and crimes against humanity (Article 5) are likely
to be the focus of the prosecution's efforts concerning rape. Given that the
Genocide Convention applies in times of war and peace and that crimes
against humanity probably have the same scope of application, prosecutions under these articles have the unique potential for producing precedent
relevant to all women, in times of war and peace.[205] This is a contribution to
look forward to. Yet, by focusing on widespread and systematic rape and
rape that constitutes genocide, there is the danger that less calculated rape
will be overlooked. As decisions are made, it is important that the Tribunal
condemn not only systematic rape, but rape per se.

B. Procedure and Evidence

Even in a national system, rape victims are reluctant to report the crime and
testify at trial. Linda Fairstein, a veteran prosecutor of sex offenses,[206]
believes that women's fears about testifying at trial are based on a wish:

> to avoid what they anticipate will be the rigors of seeing their assailant and
> being cross-examined; reliving the terror of their victimization, especially in a
> public courtroom; the humiliation or embarrassment of describing the intimate
> acts forced upon them so violently; being questioned about their personal
> lives.[207]

---

204. While the Statute might have been subject to the charge of illegality if the facts had driven
the law to an unfair degree, it does not appear that the drafters gave sufficient attention
to the facts. Rape, forced prostitution, and other forms of indecent assault are war crimes
under Article 27 of the Fourth Geneva Convention; the commentary to the Convention
indicates that violations of Article 27 also constitute grave breaches. COMMENTARY ON GENEVA
CONVENTION IV, *supra* note 146, at 598. At the time the Statute was drafted, all of these
crimes were known to have taken place in the former Yugoslavia. Yet, none was included
in Articles 2 or 3 of the Statute.

205. By its terms, the Genocide Convention applies in times of war or peace. Convention on
the Prevention and Punishment of the Crime of Genocide, *supra* note 177. In terms of
crimes against humanity, the Tribunal's jurisdiction is limited to crimes committed "in
armed conflict." *Statute, supra* note 10, art. 5. The Secretary-General broadens the potential application of this provision by adding that crimes against humanity can be committed during international or internal conflicts. *Report of the Secretary-General, supra* note
10, ¶ 47; Meron, *supra* note 177, at 87. In addition, the phrase "in armed conflict" is
subject to interpretation; armed conflict can exist independently of a state of war. *Id.* For
decisions of the Tribunal to impact upon women in times of peace, a further step must be
taken, which is to disengage crimes against humanity from any nexus to war.

206. Linda Fairstein has been the director of the Sex Crimes Prosecution Unit in the Manhattan
District Attorney's Office for almost twenty years. The unit was established in 1974 and
was the first of its kind in the United States. LINDA A. FAIRSTEIN, SEXUAL VIOLENCE: OUR WAR
AGAINST RAPE 80, 104–05 (1993).

207. *Id.* at 92.

Describing acts of sexual abuse in a courtroom is difficult, not only because the violation is so personal, but also because rape is still a misunderstood crime. Rape victims are made to feel tainted not only by the acts committed, but also by describing those acts in a public forum. The woman becomes a sexual spectacle; she is "lowered by proving [her] injury. [The man] is not."[208]

The perils will be infinitely greater before the Tribunal. Women victims have been traumatized by the crime, by the war, by the loss of loved ones. They may not have the residual strength to testify or see hope in doing so. They have lost everything; what can a court restore to them? They may have to testify in the distant, unfamiliar setting of The Hague, before the eyes of the international media. In multiple-defendant cases, they may have to testify before several of their assailants. They will fear reprisals, especially because the first indictments will be announced while the conflict is ongoing.[209] Even after peace is restored, they might not be secure from the threat of roving gangs. And, in the one trauma that was preventable, many victims will have to testify before panels of male factfinders.[210] Yet, despite all these grounds for trepidation, there is reason to think women will come forward. In most of the trials, the women will not testify alone; there will be other rape victims, as well as victims of other atrocities. A number of the victims have voiced anger and a wish for revenge, emotions that could be channeled into a desire for justice.[211] Victims of all atrocities have expressed faith in the Tribunal and the hope that prosecutions will go forward.[212]

The Tribunal has enacted Rules of Procedure and Evidence, some of which will ease the burden of testifying and otherwise protect victims and

---

208. Catharine A. MacKinnon, Only Words 66 (1993).

209. By 26 July 1995, the Tribunal had indicted 46 individuals, including Radovan Karadzic, the Bosnian Serb leader, and General Ratko Mladic, commander of the Bosnian Serb military. Marlise Simons, *Conflict in the Balkans: War Crimes; U.N. Tribunal Indicts Bosnian Serb Leader and a Commander*, N.Y. Times, 26 July 1995, at A9.

210. At the trial level, the judges will sit in panels of three; as only two of the eleven judges are female and at any one time five of the judges may be sitting with an appellate panel, most of the trial panels will have two or three male judges. See *Statute, supra* note 10, art. 12.

211. See, e.g., Stiglmayer, *supra* note 36, at 93, 97, 99. For example, one twenty-one-year-old Bosnian woman expressed these confused thoughts about revenge and the need to establish the truth:

> I know I can't join the army. I was thinking about it, but I'm the only one who can help my mother and look out for her later on. . . . If it weren't for her I wouldn't have to think very long about taking up a gun. . . . Maybe I'd be brave because revenge is spurring me on. . . . But since I know I can't take up a gun, I'll at least tell about what they did. These things are really happening. . . . When people know about this maybe someone will help us, help our fighting men so we can prevent it ever happening again, 'cause the women and girls'll be in even more danger if no one helps us.

Id. at 96–97.

212. *Final Report, supra* note 22, ¶ 320.

witnesses in rape prosecutions.[213] One is Rule 96, which includes evidentiary standards and, in effect, a definition of rape; it provides:

In cases of sexual assault:

  (i)   no corroboration of the victim's testimony shall be required;
  (ii)   consent shall not be allowed as a defence if the victim
         (a)   has been subjected to or threatened with or has had reason to
               fear violence, duress, detention or psychological oppression,
               or
         (b)   reasonably believed that if the victim did not submit, another
               might be so subjected, threatened or put in fear;
  (iii) before evidence of the victim's consent is admitted, the accused
         shall satisfy the Trial Chamber *in camera* that the evidence is rele-
         vant and credible;
  (iv)   prior sexual conduct of the victim shall not be admitted in evi-
         dence.[214]

Elimination of a corroboration requirement, inadmissibility of the victim's
sexual history, and defining the crime in terms of the force applied by the
defendant rather than the resistance offered by the victim represent the
modern approach to rape prosecutions.[215] While it was prudent to adopt

---

213. Rules of Procedure and Evidence, *supra* note 9; *see Statute, supra* note 10, art. 22
     (Tribunal shall provide in rules for protection of victims and witnesses).
214. Rules of Procedure and Evidence, *supra* note 9, at Rule 96. Rule 96 has been amended
     twice. Originally, it provided:

     In cases of sexual assault:

       (i)   no corroboration of the victim's testimony shall be required;

       (ii) consent shall not be allowed as a defence;

       (iii) prior sexual conduct of the victim shall not be admitted in evidence.

     Rules of Procedure and Evidence, *supra* note 9, at Rule 96, as adopted 11 Feb. 1994.
     On 5 May 1994, the rule was amended to provide:

     In cases of sexual assault:

       (i)   no corroboration of the victim's testimony shall be required;

       (ii) consent shall not be allowed as a defence if the victim

             (a) has been subjected to or threatened with or had reason to fear violence,
                 duress, detention or psychological oppression, or

             (b) reasonably believed that if she did not submit, another might be so subjected,
                 threatened or put in fear;

       (iii) prior sexual conduct of the victim shall not be admitted in evidence.

     Id., as amended 5 May 1994. Finally, on 30 January 1995, the Rule was revised to its cur-
     rent form.
215. *See* Estrich, *supra* note 152, at 57–59; Rosemarie Tong, Women, Sex, and the Law 96–98,

Rule 96, one must question its relevance in this setting. The rapes that have been documented are characterized by a high level of intimidation and violence; the circumstances are unambiguous, more akin in domestic parlance to "stranger rape" than "simple rape."[216] When the victim has been threatened with a gun, when she has been forced to watch as family members are killed, when she has been beaten or tortured, can anyone in good faith suggest consent based either on circumstances or sexual history?[217]

Three other procedural rules will be relevant in cases of sexual assault: one permits the prosecutor to seek an order preventing disclosure of the identity of a victim or witness during the investigative stage;[218] a second permits deposition evidence in exceptional circumstances, which will spare some victims and witnesses the burden of traveling to The Hague;[219] and the third permits the Tribunal to order measures before or during trial for the privacy and protection of victims and witnesses.[220] This last rule, Rule 75, contemplates measures such as expunging names from the public record, nondisclosure to the public of identifying information, closed sessions, and testimony through closed-circuit television and image- and voice-altering devices. These measures will minimize public exposure and, in the case of testimony by closed-circuit television, will spare the victim the trauma of testifying before her attackers.[221] These measures are to be balanced

---

104–09 (1984). Feminists, however, disagree as to the wisdom of focusing on force as the basis of the crime. *See* Estrich, *supra* note 152, at 80; Catharine A. MacKinnon, Toward A Feminist Theory of the State 178 (1989). Because Rule 96 is the first attempt to codify a definition of rape at an international level, careful study of the rule is required.

216. Estrich, *supra* note 152, at 3–4.

217. Perhaps doubts such as these prompted the most recent revision of Rule 96 on 30 January 1995, which now requires an *in camera* offer of proof before evidence of consent is presented. Interestingly, the other respect in which Rule 96 was revised was to make it gender neutral. Despite the disclaimer in the Rules that the "masculine shall include the feminine, . . . and vice-versa," Rules of Procedure and Evidence, *supra* note 9, Rule 2(B), and consistent use of the masculine pronoun throughout, the prior version of Rule 96, as amended on 5 May 1994, used the feminine pronoun to describe the victim. This word choice reveals the deception in the generic use of the masculine pronoun. When women are *truly* the intended beneficiaries of a rule, the, the feminine is used. See Hilary Charlesworth, Christine Chinkin, & Shelley Wright, *Feminist Approaches to International Law,* 17–20, Conference Paper presented at International Law Weekend, Australian National University, Canberra, Australia, May 1989 (on file with author). Moreover, traditional evidentiary rules requiring corroboration and proof of resistance and permitting evidence of the victim's prior sexual history were designed to counter perceptions of the female as liar and temptress. Tong, *supra* note 216, at 100–04. The use of the feminine in the prior version of Rule 96, even to disavow these beliefs, only reaffirms that such qualities have never been imputed to male victims of sexual assault. Unlike the Rules of Procedure and Evidence, the Statute is written in gender-neutral terms, with occasional lapses into the masculine.

218. Rules of Procedure and Evidence, *supra* note 9, Rule 69.

219. *Id.* Rule 71.

220. *Id.* Rule 75.

221. Rule 75 provides, in part:

against the rights guaranteed to the accused, particularly the rights to cross-examine witnesses, to a public hearing, and to adequate time to prepare a defense.[222] In and of themselves, the measures adequately protect privacy interests of victims and witnesses and do not unreasonably infringe upon the defendant's rights. They are in accordance with steps permitted by the US Supreme Court in cases of sexual assault and child abuse.[223] However, it remains to be seen where, as a matter of discretion, the balance is struck between victim and witness protection and the rights of the accused. Protective measures will necessarily limit public access to information—an interest which is of heightened importance in this proceeding—but the interference will be temporal, requiring the public to wait for an expunged transcript, or insignificant, involving elimination of the names of witnesses or victims.

Finally, the Rules of Procedure and Evidence provide for the creation of a Victims and Witnesses Unit within the Registry, the Tribunal's administrative organ. This unit will recommend protective measures and provide counseling and support, particularly in cases of rape and sexual assault.[224] The unit is to give consideration to the appointment of qualified women.[225] The effectiveness of the Victims and Witnesses Unit will depend on the Tribunal's

---

(B) A Chamber may hold an *in camera* proceeding to determine whether to order:

    (i) measures to prevent disclosure to the public or the media of the identity or whereabouts of a victim or a witness, or of persons related to or associated with him by such means as:

        (a) expunging names and identifying information from the Chamber's public records;

        (b) nondisclosure to the public of any records identifying the victim;

        (c) giving of testimony through image- or voice-altering devices or closed circuit television; and

        (d) assignment of a pseudonym;

    (ii) closed sessions in accordance with Rule 79 [to ensure "safety, security or nondisclosure of the identity of a victim or witness"];

    (iii) appropriate measures to facilitate the testimony of vulnerable victims and witnesses, such as one-way closed circuit television.

(C) A Chamber shall, whenever necessary, control the manner of questioning to avoid harassment or intimidation.

Id.; Rule 79(A)(ii).

222. *Statute, supra* note 10, arts. 21(2), 21(4)(b), 21(4)(e). The rights of the accused are drawn from Article 14 of the International Covenant on Civil and Political Rights, *opened for signature,* 16 Dec. 1966, 999 U.N.T.S. 171 (1967).
223. Special Task Force of the ABA Section of International Law and Practice, Report On the International Tribunal to Adjudicate War Crimes Committed in the Former Yugoslavia 32–34 (1993).
224. Rules of Procedure and Evidence, *supra* note 9, Rule 34(A).
225. *Id.* Rule 34(B).

willingness to defer to its recommendations; however, the unit's counseling function may be undermined because the Rules do not guarantee the confidentiality of the information obtained. In addition, although no specific provision is made, the same considerations prompting creation of the Victims and Witnesses Unit suggest that the prosecutor should also create a special unit, to be staffed primarily by women, for the prosecution of cases of rape and sexual assault. The advantages of such a unit have been demonstrated in a domestic context.[226]

One area of weakness in the rules concerns protection from reprisals because, even if the strongest protective measures are adopted, the witness's identity will be known to the defendant. Reports indicate that one solution will be to recommend individuals for political asylum;[227] the fact that such a step is deemed necessary indicates how much women have to lose by coming forward. Yet, there is also much to be gained. Those women who offer evidence will have the chance, through the catharsis of trial, to contribute to a lasting peace for themselves and for others. For this to happen, the Tribunal must ensure that women can tell their stories in a manner that allows them to preserve their dignity.

V.   CONCLUSION

There can be no doubt that war is an invention of *mankind,* literally.[228] Although warfare, by biology or circumstance, is the male habit, tragic numbers of women are the victims of men's wars. Women's suffering in war is specifically related to gender—women are raped, forced into prostitution, forcibly impregnated. The war in the former Yugoslavia is the most recent episode in a long history; in that war, women have endured what women in all wars endure. Rape in war and rape in peace exist on a vastly different plane, but the connection is clear. In both situations, women are reminded that they are vulnerable, unequal, and exist only by man's good graces.

Rape has been prohibited under IHL through many wars, but the prohibition has been largely ignored or unenforced. This dismal state of affairs results from the interplay of two systems. One is a legal system that tends to overlook or dismiss women's pain; the other is a war system in which rape is an effective weapon. Both systems reveal themselves as male-dominated, with little regard for the rights of women. This is the legacy that the Tribunal

---

226. Fairstein, *supra* note 207, at 81–82, 121.
227. Roger Cohen, *Bosnian Camp Survivors Describe Random Death,* N.Y. Times, 2 Aug. 1994, at Al (Tribunal investigators recommend witness, former Serbian concentration camp guard, for political asylum in United States).
228. *See supra* note 123 and accompanying text.

must overcome. The challenge is great, but the very existence of the Tribunal and its mandate to prosecute rape represent progress. In terms of process and result, the trials will test the commitment of the international system to women's human rights and determine whether women can participate as equals in an international legal system created by men. The trials are an opportunity to redress the enormous suffering of women in war. Women everywhere will be watching and judging the Tribunal's work.

Chapter 11

Rape Camps as a Means of Ethnic Cleansing: Religious, Cultural, and Ethical Responses to Rape Victims in the Former Yugoslavia

Todd A. Salzman

I.   INTRODUCTION

Currently, the International War Crimes Tribunal in The Hague, Netherlands, is trying indicted war criminals in the Bosnia-Herzegovina war. During this conflict an estimated 20,000 women endured sexual assaults in the form of torture and rape.[1] Although these atrocities were committed on all sides of the warring factions, by far the greatest number of assaults were committed by the Serbs[2] against Muslim women, though Catholic Croats were targeted as well.[3] While in past conflicts rape was sometimes considered an inevitable byproduct of war, and thus largely ignored when it came to pun-

---

1. See *Working Paper on the Situation of Systematic Rape, Sexual Slavery and Slavery-Like Practices During Wartime, Including Internal Armed Conflict, Submitted by Ms. Linda Chavez in Accordance with Subcommission Decision 1994/109*, U.N. ESCOR, Comm'n on Hum. Rts., 47th Sess., Agenda Item 16, ¶ 4, U.N. Doc. E/CN.4/Sub.2/1995/38 (1995) [hereinafter *Working Paper*]; M. Cherif Bassiouni & Marcia McCormick, Sexual Violence: An Invisible Weapon of War in the Former Yugoslavia 3 (1996) (distinguishing between rape, sexual assault, and sexual violence).

> *Rape* denotes vaginal, oral, or anal sexual intercourse without the consent of one of the people involved. *Sexual assault* is a broader term, which includes rape and other forced or coerced sexual acts, as well as mutilation of the genitals. *Sexual violence* is the most general term, used to describe any kind of violence carried out through sexual means or by targeting sexuality.

> *Id.*

2. Clearly many Serbs were appalled at the atrocities that took place during the Bosnian war. In this article, "Serbs" refers to those who were politically and militarily responsible for the policy of ethnic cleansing and the atrocities committed against non-Serbs.
3. See Bassiouni & McCormick, *supra* note 1, at 10–11.

ishing the perpetrators, the Bosnian conflict brought the practice of rape with genocidal intent to a new level, causing an outcry among the international community. Evidence suggests that these violations were not random acts carried out by a few dissident soldiers.[4] Rather, this was an assault against the female gender, violating her body and its reproductive capabilities as a "weapon of war." Serbian political and military leaders systematically planned and strategically executed this policy of ethnic cleansing or genocide with the support of the Serbian and Bosnian Serb armies and paramilitary groups to create a "Greater Serbia": a religiously, culturally, and linguistically homogenous Serbian nation.[5] This article will examine two main issues. First, in section two the Serbs' systematic use of rape camps with the specific intent of impregnating their victims is investigated, along with the cultural, political, and religious foundations that support this usurpation of the female body. The third section will then analyze the "secondary victimization" of these women and the various responses implicitly supporting the Serbian practice and objective.

II. THE SERBIAN USURPATION OF THE FEMALE BODY

In a traditionally patriarchal society, the Serbian government, military, and Orthodox church have explicitly formulated a perception of the female gender and its role and function within society. Essentially, the female is reduced to her reproductive capacities in order to fulfill the overall objective of Serbian nationalism by producing more citizens to populate the nation. Limiting womanhood to a single physiological quality in this way proves nondiscriminatory in that not only are Serbian women thus perceived, but non-Serbian women are as well. This attitude has certainly had an impact, conscious or unconscious, on the overall perception and treatment of women, playing a part in the establishment of rape camps and the usurpation of women's bodies to achieve ethnic cleansing.

A.   Serbian Usurpation of the Serbian Female Body

Perhaps the traditional role of the Serbian woman is most clearly depicted by the Mother of the Jugovici, the epic heroine from the Battle of Kosovo in 1389, who, in spite of the death of her nine sons in the battle with the Turks, did not weep.[6] Her courage, self-sacrifice, altruism, and, most of all, her fer-

---

4. *See id.* at 8.
5. *See id.* at 5.
6. *See* Wendy Bracewell, *Mothers of the Nation,* 36 WARREPORT, Sept. 1995, at 28.

tility, have been utilized to inspire and serve as a paradigm for Serbian women and their responsibility as mothers of the nation. According to this twisted reasoning, the necessity of reproduction guarantees Serbian perseverance against Her aggressors and establishes a greater Serbia, "Mother-Homeland." To shirk one's duty of reproduction amounts to antipatriotism and treason. The assertion of a Sarajevo woman who claimed that she planned to "fire off one baby every year to spite the aggressors" reflects the power of this myth and its message.[7] Serbians have waged this propaganda campaign of women's national and social reproductive responsibility on both political and religious fronts with remarkable success, as is evidenced in legislation "encouraging" women's reproductive responsibilities.

1.   Governmental policy and demography

In October 1992, powerful organs in Serbian society published a document entitled "Warning," focusing on demographic issues.[8] Signed by the Serbian ruling party, the Serbian Socialist Party (SPS), the Serbian Academy of Arts and Sciences, and the Serbian Orthodox Church, this document highlighted the imbalance in terms of growth and renewal of various ethnic groups. In particular, "Albanians, Muslims and Romans [sic], with their high birth rate, are beyond rational and human reproduction."[9] The SPS conference adopted this document, and the Serbian Parliament enacted a resolution promoting "population renewal," seeking to stimulate the birth rate in some areas while suppressing it in others.[10] Perhaps it is by no means coincidental that those areas designated for an increase in birth rates were predominantly developed Serbian areas, whereas the suppression of birth rates was encouraged in predominantly undeveloped Albanian and Muslim areas. In fact, statistics in many areas of the Balkans do reveal higher reproduction rates among non-Serbs,[11] but the reasons given for this difference vary depending on the source.

While numerous sociological, cultural, and historical factors may account for the differences in population growth among the different cultural and religious groups, the Serbian government has focused on ideological and naturalist reasons. Ideologically, non-Serbs reproduce as a political strategy to outgrow the Serbian nation. The naturalist reason asserts that non-Serbs are intrinsically primitive in their ethnic reasoning, and will not

---

7. See id.
8. See Zarana Papic, How to Become a "Real" Serbian Woman?, 36 Warreport, Sept. 1995, at 41.
9. Id.
10. See id.
11. See Vatro Murvar, Nation and Religion in Central Europe and the Western Balkans—The Muslims in Bosnia-Hercegovina and Sandžak: A Sociological Analysis (1989).

adjust or adapt to the Serbian mentality.[12] Such political rhetoric instills the fear that the subtle, though very real means of a shift in demography and population growth threatens the Serbian nation and thus promotes a nationalist sentiment. It singles out Serbian women and their responsibility to serve the nation through reproduction to insure population expansion and to provide future soldiers to defend the nation in times of war.[13] Furthermore, governmental legislation supporting reproduction found ecclesiological support from the Serbian Orthodox Church.

2.   *The Serbian Orthodox Church: reproduction
      and religious sanctions*

In December 1994, Patriarch Pavle, leader of the Serbian Orthodox Church, delivered a Christmas message denouncing the "White Plague," that is, the low birth rate among Serbian women.[14] This plague results from infanticide "committed by women who choose not to give birth because of their 'contentment.'"[15] The "disease" can only be cured by making Serbian women want to bear children. Accomplishing this objective mandates religious sanctions to stigmatize a woman for not wanting to procreate, and declare such an attitude to be a threefold sin: against themselves, the Serbian nation, and God himself.[16] The women sin against themselves because "many mothers who did not want more than one child, today bitterly cry and pull their hair in despair over the loss of the only son in the war . . . why did they not give birth to more children and have them as consolation."[17] They sin against the Serbian nation because "in twenty years, the Serbs will, if such a birth-rate remains, become an ethnic minority in their own country."[18] Finally, they sin against God because "when they come to meet God, those mothers who never allowed their children to be born will meet their children who will sadly ask: why did you kill me? Why did you not let me live?"[19] In a passionate plea, Archbishop Pavle appealed to the nationalistic sentiment of Serbian women to willfully reproduce for the betterment of the country. In his speech, Pavle drew certain parallels between women, their bodies, the survival of the nation, and the war effort. By not giving birth to more children, women have placed the survival of the nation in jeopardy. Therefore, Serbian women must heed the battle call and respond by offer-

---

12. *See* Papic, *supra* note 8, at 41.
13. *See* NORMAN CIGAR, GENOCIDE IN BOSNIA: THE POLICY OF "ETHNIC CLEANSING" 78–80 (1995).
14. *See* Papic, *supra* note 8, at 40 (quoting Archbishop Pavle's speech).
15. *Id.*
16. *See id.* at 40–41.
17. *Id.* at 40.
18. *Id.*
19. *Id.*

ing their bodies as incubators, preferably to male children. This attitude is reflected in the frequently cited aphorism that "for every Serbian soldier dead in battle in Slovenia, Serbian mothers must bear 100 more fighters!"[20]

Serbian reproduction then has served two particular objectives: to create more Serbs to further the Serbian nationalist ideology, and to create more soldiers to defend the country. The obvious irony of the nationalistic appeal for Serbian women to reproduce so that their (male) children can die for the country is that it somewhat defeats the purpose of the first objective. This irony notwithstanding, the attitude limits women's potential as human beings to their reproductive faculties; they are a means of attaining the end of a greater Serbia. In a very real sense, Serbian women have served as a "weapon of war" for the military agenda of their own country. This attitude and perception of women and their bodies had much broader implications, however.

B.   Serbian Usurpation of Non-Serbian Women: Rape Camps as a Weapon of War

1.   Serbian propaganda: muslims raping Serbian women

Propaganda has played a major role in conflicts of the twentieth century both to instill feelings of compassion, sympathy, and solidarity among a people and to incite and justify violence toward a real or perceived enemy. Serbia is no exception. As early as 1981, the media reinforced and exploited Serbian nationalism in its depiction of the uprising of the Kosovo Albanians seeking autonomy from Serbia.[21] Though Serbian forces immediately suppressed the uprising, the Serbian people heard of an Albanian genocidal plot against ethnic Serbs involving various atrocities, including mass rapes committed against the local Serbian population in Kosovo.[22]

Even though these accusations were highly exaggerated, they accomplished their objective by stirring nationalistic Serbian feelings, uniting the country in solidarity against Albanians initially and, later, against all non-

---

20. Bracewell, *supra* note 6, at 28.
21. *See* Alexandra Stiglmayer, *The War in the Former Yugoslavia, in* MASS RAPE: THE WAR AGAINST WOMEN IN BOSNIA-HERZEGOVINA 1, 14 (Alexandra Stiglmayer ed., 1994) [hereinafter MASS RAPE].
22. *See* Srdjan Vrcan, *Faith Under Challenge*, 40 WARREPORT, Apr. 1996, at 26. One of the leading papers spreading the alleged persecutions of Serbs in Kosovo was the religious Serbian newspaper Pravoslavlje. In 1982, twenty-one Orthodox priests openly appealed to Serbian political leaders for better protection of the remaining Serbs in Kosovo. This request religiously legitimated these accusations and gave almost unanimous support to the Serbian national political strategy. *See id.*

Serbs, and bringing Slobodan Milosević, the "most zealous advocate of the thesis of the 'genocidal Kosovo Albanians'" into power.[23] Milosević rapidly developed the plan for a greater Serbia through the calculated use and manipulation of the media to foster popular support. In fact, Milosević immediately took over the press and national television.[24] Already having successfully roused national Serbian sentiment against the Albanians, the Serbian propaganda machine went into full force when the Muslims and Croats of Bosnia-Herzegovina declared independence on 3 March 1992.

National television aired what appeared to be Muslims or Croats raping Serbian women when, in actuality, the scenes showed Serbs raping Muslim or Croat women.[25] Roy Gutman, the Pulitzer Prize winning reporter on ethnic cleansing in Bosnia, depicted another case of the blatant use of propaganda to incite the Serbian people when he recounted an interview with Major Milovan Milutinovic.[26] When Gutman met with him, Milutinovic was working on a text, "Lying [sic] Violent hands on the Serbian Woman."[27] This document maintained that Muslims and Croats were committing genocide against the Serbian people.[28] One of the most telling citations from this document deals with the alleged atrocities committed by Muslims against Serbian women:

> By order of the Islamic fundamentalists from Sarajevo, healthy Serbian women from 17 to 40 years of age are being separated out and subjected to special treatment. According to their sick plans going back many years, these women have to be impregnated by orthodox Islamic seeds in order to raise a generation of janissaries [i.e., Turkish military elite composed of Christian youth forced to convert to Islam in the middle ages] on the territories they surely consider to be theirs, the Islamic republic. In other words, a fourfold crime is to be committed against the Serbian woman: to remove her from her own family, to impregnate her by undesirable seeds, to make her bear a stranger and then to take even him away from her.[29]

What Gutman, the UN Security Council, and the world have come to discover is that this is, indeed, an accurate portrayal of what was taking place, with one minor exception: the perpetrators were primarily Serbs, and the victims were primarily Muslim women and children.

---

23. Stiglmayer, *supra* note 21, at 14.
24. *See id.* at 14–15.
25. *See* Catharine A. MacKinnon, *Rape, Genocide, and Women's Human Rights, in* Mass Rape, *supra* note 21, at 183, 190.
26. Roy Gutman, A Witness to Genocide at x (1993).
27. *Id.* at ix.
28. *See id.*
29. *Id.* at x.

2. Ethnic cleansing and genocide

Serbian governmental and military powers appear to have utilized systematic rape as a weapon of war[30] to serve their overall objective of "ethnic cleansing," a euphemism for genocide. According to a Commission of Experts appointed by former UN Secretary General Boutros Boutros-Ghali, the expression "ethnic cleansing" is relatively new.[31] "Considered in the context of the conflicts in the former Yugoslavia, 'ethnic cleansing' means rendering an area ethnically homogenous by using force or intimidation to remove persons of given groups from the area."[32] Ethnic cleansing is accomplished through the use of "concentration camps, torture, sexual violence, mass killings, forced deportations, destruction of private and cultural property, pillage and theft, and the blocking of humanitarian aid."[33]

In 1944, Raphaël Lemkin coined the term genocide, from the Greek word *genos* (race or tribe) and the Latin suffix *cide* (to kill), to depict the Nazi atrocities against the Jews.[34] He described genocide as the destruction of a nation or ethnic group, although not its total extermination.[35] The UN legal definition of genocide likewise reflects this qualification by declaring that genocide is the intent "to destroy, *in whole or in part,* a national, ethnical, racial or religious group, as such."[36] The early formulators of this definition included the phrase "in whole or in part" to emphasize the fact that genocide does not require the aim of killing all the members of a group.[37] Some scholars have argued that the Serbian policy towards Muslims cannot be considered genocide because it was concerned primarily with control over territory rather than inhabitants, and the Serbian "intention was to get rid of the Moslems not to exterminate them."[38] Nevertheless, several acts

---

30. See BASSIOUNI & McCORMICK, *supra* note 1, at 21. While the policy of systematic rape by the Serbian military remains to be proven definitively, there is substantial evidence supporting the existence of such a policy.
31. See *id.* at 7. On 6 October 1992, the UN Security Council adopted Resolution 780 establishing a Commission of Experts to investigate allegations of violations of international humanitarian law in the former Yugoslavia. *Resolution 780 (1992)*, U.N. SCOR, 3119th mtg., U.N. Doc. S/RES/780 (1992).
32. *Final Report of the Commission of Experts Established Pursuant to Security Council Resolution 780 (1992)*, U.N. SCOR, Annex 1, ¶ 129, U.N. Doc. S/1994/674 (1994) [hereinafter *Final Report*].
33. BASSIOUNI & McCORMICK, *supra* note 1, at 5.
34. RAPHAËL LEMKIN, AXIS RULE IN OCCUPIED EUROPE 79–80 (1944).
35. See *id.* at 79.
36. Convention on the Prevention and Punishment of the Crime of Genocide, *adopted* 9 Dec. 1948, 78 U.N.T.S. 277, 280 (*entered into force* 12 Jan. 1951) (*entered into force for U.S.* 23 Feb. 1989) [hereinafter Genocide Convention] (emphasis added).
37. *Final Report, supra* note 32, ¶ 93.
38. ALAIN DESTEXHE, RWANDA AND GENOCIDE IN THE TWENTIETH CENTURY 19 (1994). For a critique of his

committed by the Serbian military constitute genocide as enumerated in Article II of the 1948 Convention on the Prevention and Punishment of the Crime of Genocide.[39] These acts include killing members of another group on the basis of their religion, physical and mental torture, using measures whose aim is to prevent births within the group, and forcibly transferring children from one group to another.[40] Evidence suggests that all of these acts were committed according to a logistically coordinated policy that unequivocally constituted genocide.

In essence, genocide and ethnic cleansing coincided, the goal being the establishment of a greater Serbia—that is, a Serb-inhabited region purged of all non-Serbs throughout Serbia, Bosnia-Herzegovina, and Croatia. Within the Bosnian, Muslim, and Catholic communities, sexual assault and rape served as particularly effective means of achieving this goal.

3. Rape and sexual assault: evidence of a policy

According to Ruth Seifert, "[a] violent invasion into the interior of one's body represents the most severe attack imaginable upon the intimate self and the dignity of a human being: by any measure it is a mark of severe torture."[41] This violent invasion has occurred against the women on all sides of the conflict in Bosnia: Serbs, Croats, and Muslims. What differentiates the Serbian practice of rape and sexual assault from other assaults is that it is a systematic military policy conceived and planned before the outbreak of the war to effect the ethnic cleansing of Muslims from Serbian territory. On the subject of rape and sexual assault, the United Nations Commission of Experts concluded that "the practices of 'ethnic cleansing,' sexual assault and rape have been carried out by some of the parties so systematically that they strongly appear to be the product of a policy."[42] In a follow-up report, the United Nations General Assembly asserted that it was "[c]onvinced that this heinous practice [rape and abuse of women] constitutes a deliberate weapon of war in fulfilling the policy of ethnic cleansing carried out by Serbian forces in Bosnia and Herzegovina, and . . . that the abhorrent policy of ethnic cleansing was a form of genocide."[43] Several factors support this allegation of a Serbian rape policy.

---

position see David Rieff, *An Age of Genocide: The Far-Reaching Lessons of Rwanda,* The New Republic, 29 Jan. 1996, at 27, 34–36.

39. Genocide Convention, *supra* note 36, art. II.
40. *See Final Report, supra* note 32, ¶ 98.
41. Ruth Seifert, *War and Rape: A Preliminary Analysis, in* Mass Rape, *supra* note 21, at 54, 55.
42. *Final Report, supra* note 32, ¶ 313.
43. *Rape and Abuse of Women in the Areas of Armed Conflict in the Former Yugoslavia,* G.A. Res. 49/205, U.N. GAOR, 49th Sess., at 2, U.N. Doc. A/RES/49/205 (1995). *See also Preliminary Report Submitted by the Special Rapporteur on Violence Against Women, its*

a.   The RAM plan

First, and most importantly, documentation exists substantiating the claim of a Serbian military policy to ethnically cleanse Bosnia-Herzegovina, and designating rape as a specific means of attaining this goal. This policy is clearly spelled out in the so-called RAM plan written by Serb army officers around the end of August 1991.[44]

An Italian journalist and the Ljubljana newspaper DELO both confirm the existence of this plan and its policy to target "women, especially adolescents, and . . . children" in order to cause fear and panic among the Muslims and bring about a Muslim retreat from the designated territories.[45] The DELO reports that the Yugoslav National Army (JNA) Psychological Operations Department in Belgrade developed a plan to drive Muslims out of Bosnia based on an analysis of Muslim behavior which "showed that their morale, desire for battle, and will could be crushed more easily by raping women, especially minors and even children, and by killing members of the Muslim nationality inside their religious facilities."[46] Concrete evidence accumulated by various humanitarian organizations, including the United Nations and Human Rights Watch, supports the existence of such a practice. These organizations' reports indicate that the research, planning, and coordination of rape camps was a systematic policy of the Serbian government and military forces with the explicit intention of creating an ethnically pure state.

b.   Official tolerance of rape

In their final report, the Commission of Experts appointed by the United Nations to investigate allegations of rape and sexual assault in the former Yugoslavia speculated that camp commanders had direct control over those who committed rapes within these camps, indicating that the commanders could have halted the practice and punished the perpetrators if they chose.[47] The Commission cited as evidence the fact that during the height of the reported rapes (April to November 1992) the media attention gradually grew

---

Causes and Consequences, Ms. Radhika Coomaraswamy, Submitted in Accordance with Commission on Human Rights Resolution 1994/45, U.N. ESCOR, Comm'n on Hum. Rts., 50th Sess., Agenda Item 11(a), ¶ 268, U.N. Doc. E/CN.4/1995/42 (1995) [hereinafter *Preliminary Report*].

44. *See* BASSIOUNI & MCCORMICK, *supra* note 1, at 21 n.4; *see also* BEVERLY ALLEN, RAPE WARFARE: THE HIDDEN GENOCIDE IN BOSNIA-HERZEGOVINA AND CROATIA 56–60 (1996).

45. ALLEN, *supra* note 44, at 57.

46. BASSIOUNI & MCCORMICK, *supra* note 1, at 21 n.4.

47. *Final Report, supra* note 32, ¶ 253. *See also* BASSIOUNI & MCCORMICK, *supra* note 1, at 21–22.

from a few reports in March 1992 to a high of 535 stories in January 1993 and 529 in February 1993.[48] In the months following these media reports, the number of reported cases dropped dramatically. The correlation between increased media attention and the decrease in reported cases of rape, the Commission speculated, "would indicate that commanders could control the alleged perpetrators if they wanted to. This could lead to the conclusion that there was an overriding policy advocating the use of rape as a method of 'ethnic cleansing,' rather than a policy of omission, tolerating the widespread commission of rape."[49]

c. Patterns of rape and sexual assault

Perhaps the strongest indication of a Serbian systematic policy is reflected in the five patterns of rape documented by the United Nations Commission of Experts.[50] These patterns required logistical coordination, especially within rape camps where rape was used to impregnate Muslim and Catholic Croat women.

---

48. *Final Report, supra* note 32, ¶ 237.
49. *Id.* The Commission's tentative conclusion, however, though it implicates those in authority and points to an official policy of tolerating rape, does not necessarily reflect a decreased number of rapes after international media coverage. One needs only to consider, for example, the rampant spread of AIDS throughout the world, and the relatively sparse media coverage of this disease, to realize that the media by no means provides an accurate representation of what is occurring in reality. Beverly Allen notes that in October 1994, she spoke with Dr. Kozaric-Kovacic who reported that pregnant survivors from rape/death camps continued to arrive in Zagreb and yet there was nothing or next to nothing in the international media acknowledging these events. ALLEN, *supra* note 44, at 156–57 & n.6. The decline in reports of rapes, then, could be a result of the media's loss of infatuation with the topic. It could also be associated with a silencing of the victims by the perpetrators who feared that they would be called to justice as news of an International War Crimes Tribunal spread in early 1993. On 22 February 1993, the UN Security Council established an international tribunal for the prosecution of persons responsible for serious violations of international humanitarian law committed in the territory of the former Yugoslavia since 1991. *Resolution 808 (1993)*, U.N. SCOR, 3175th mtg., at 2, U.N. Doc. S/RES/808 (1993), *cited in* Catherine N. Niarchos, *Women, War, and Rape: Challenges Facing The International Tribunal for the Former Yugoslavia*, 17 HUM. RTS. Q. 651, 651n.9 (1995) [hereinafter *Resolution 808*]. The perpetrators frequently threatened women who were raped that if they told anyone of the incident, either they or their family members would be hunted down and murdered. Thus, a possible interpretation of the decline in rape cases reported by the media is that while the number of rapes did not decrease significantly in conjunction with increased media attention, the tendency for victims to publicly reveal such events decreased because of the perpetrators' threats of reprisal inspired by fear of being called to justice by the War Crimes Tribunal. These are tentative conclusions, the truth of which is difficult to establish.
50. *Final Report, supra* note 32, ¶ 244 ("Five patterns emerge from the reported cases, regardless of the ethnicity of the perpetrators or the victims."). This indicates that all sides utilized rape as a systematic policy. However, in a later paper, Professor Cherif Bassiouni, who chaired the Commission of Experts, emphasizes that the Serbs ran most of the deten-

In the first pattern, sexual violence occurred with looting and intimidation before widespread fighting broke out in a particular region.[51] As ethnic tensions grew, those in control of the local government would encourage paramilitaries, individuals, or gangs of men to initiate a policy of terrorizing local residents. These people would break into homes, steal property, and torture and sexually assault the inhabitants, oftentimes in front of other family members or in public.[52]

The second pattern of sexual violence occurred during fighting. In the process of attacking a town or village, the forces would rape or sexually assault some women in their homes.[53] Once the town was secured, the forces would gather the surviving population and divide them according to sex and age, selecting some women for rape or sexual assaults.[54] The forces then transported the remaining population to detention facilities. The psychological impact of these atrocities is evident. Through fear and intimidation, victims and witnesses would be hesitant to return to the scene of such events.

The third pattern of sexual violence occurred in detention facilities or other sites referred to as refugee "collection centers."[55] After the population had been divided, men of fighting age were either tortured and executed or sent off to work camps while women were generally sent to separate camps. There, soldiers, camp guards, paramilitaries, and civilians raped or sexually assaulted many of the women.[56] Generally, these sexual assaults occurred in one of two ways. The most common practice involved selecting women from crowded rooms, taking them to another location, raping them, and either murdering them or returning them to the collection center. Another, though less frequent practice, entailed raping and sexually assaulting women in front of other detainees, or forcing detainees to rape and assault one another, thus humiliating the victims and instilling terror in the witnesses.[57] In this setting, gang rapes were frequently reported as being accompanied by beatings, torture, and other forms of humiliation.[58]

---

tion camps where sexual violence occurred. BASSIOUNI & McCORMICK, *supra* note 1, at 16. Furthermore, ethnic cleansing to create a "greater Serbia" was a specific political and military objective unique to the Serbs. While all sides may have utilized sexual violence to oppress the enemy, and in particular the women of the enemy, it was the Serbian overall objective which utilized sexual violence as a form of ethnic cleansing that has received the greatest attention and provoked the greatest outcry. *See id.*

51. *Final Report, supra* note 32, ¶ 245.
52. *See id.*
53. *See id.* ¶ 246.
54. *See id.*
55. *See* BASSIOUNI & McCORMICK, *supra* note 1, at 17.
56. *See Final Report, supra* note 32, ¶ 247.
57. *See id.* ¶ 248.
58. *See* BASSIOUNI & McCORMICK, *supra* note 1, at 17–18. In male camps, this public form of

A fourth pattern of sexual violence occurred in rape camps established in buildings such as hotels, schools, restaurants, hospitals, factories, peacetime brothels, or even animal stalls in barns, fenced pens, and auditoriums.[59] No one was exempt from the punishment in these camps. Frequently, the Serbian captors told women that they were trying to impregnate them. In so doing, they would create "Chetnik babies" who would kill Muslims when they grew up. Furthermore, "they repeatedly said their President had ordered them to do this."[60] One woman, detained at a rape camp in the northern Bosnian town of Doboj, reported that women who became pregnant had to remain in the camp for seven or eight months.[61] Gynecologists examined the women and those women found pregnant were segregated from the rest and received meals and other "special privileges."[62] Only after it was too late for these women to get an abortion were they released and usually taken to Serbia.[63] The frequently reported intent of Serbian soldiers to impregnate Muslim and Catholic Croats, the presence of gynecologists to examine the women, and the intentional holding of pregnant women until it was too late to legally or safely procure an abortion all point to a systematic, planned policy to utilize rape and forced impregnation as a form of ethnic cleansing.

A fifth pattern of sexual violence occurred in "bordello" camps.[64] Rather than a form of punishment, women were held in these camps to provide sex for men returning from the front lines. While many of the women in the other camps were eventually exchanged for other civilian prisoners, these women were generally killed.[65]

Through an analysis of these five patterns of rape as well as other data, the Commission detected a number of characteristics indicating an overall Serbian systematic policy including: similar characteristics in the practice of sexual assault and rape in noncontiguous areas; concomitant acts of other international humanitarian law violations; simultaneous military activity; simultaneous activity to displace civilian populations; common characteristics in commissioning rape aimed at maximizing shame and humiliation of the victim, her family, and her community; and the timing of the rapes, with the majority of documented cases occurring from April to November

---

sexual assault took place as well. In one documented instance, a prisoner was forced to bite off the genitals of another. *See id.*

59. *See* ALLEN, *supra* note 44, at 65.
60. *Final Report, supra* note 32, ¶ 248.
61. *See* Alexandra Stiglmayer, *The Rapes in Bosnia-Herzegovina, in* MASS RAPE, *supra* note 21, at 82, 119.
62. *See* Niarchos, *supra* note 49, at 657.
63. *See* Stiglmayer, *supra* note 61, at 118–19.
64. *See Final Report, supra* note 32, ¶ 249.
65. *See id.*

1992.[66] Particularly significant is the large number of rapes, "approximately 600 of the 1,100 documented cases," that occurred in detention camps.[67] "These rapes in detention do not appear to be random, and they indicate at least a policy of encouraging rape supported by the deliberate failure of camp commanders and local authorities to exercise command and control over the personnel under their authority."[68]

4. The genocidal purpose of sexual assault

Beverly Allen rightly points out that although the five patterns of rape delineated by the Commission exemplify various practices of sexual assault, they do not clearly indicate the genocidal nature and purpose of those assaults.[69] Consequently, she labels as "genocidal rape" the Serbian military policy of rape for the purpose of genocide and ethnic cleansing, distinguishing three forms of this policy. First, prior to the arrival of the official Serbian military (Yugoslav Army or Bosnian Serb forces), Serb militias, civilians, or Chetniks would enter a village and terrorize the inhabitants, especially through the use of public rape and sexual assault.[70] Frequently the women recognized their assailants as neighbors, law enforcement personnel, or other members of the community. Recognition seemed an important part of Serbian policy. The persecuted would be less likely to return to their towns and villages if their assailants were local inhabitants rather than from distant territories. Consequently, invading Serbian military personnel would frequently employ local Serbs through force, threats, or psychological pressure to participate in the atrocities.[71] Word of these atrocities would quickly spread throughout the town or village instilling fear in the inhabitants. Subsequently, official Serbian military forces would arrive offering safe passage for the townspeople out of the village if they agreed never to return.[72] In this way, the goal of ethnically cleansing a particular town, village, or region was attained.

---

66. See id. ¶ 252.
67. BASSIOUNI & McCORMICK, supra note 1, at 10. This figure differs from that of the Final Report which states that "out of 514 allegations which are included in the database, 327 occurred in places of detention." Final Report, supra note 32, ¶ 252 n.71. The discrepancy between these numbers is most likely due to the fact that the database in Geneva was not adequate to handle the immense amount of information accumulated by the Commission of Experts (about 65,000 pages of documents and 300 hours of videotape). The information could only be thoroughly processed subsequently when an adequate database was established at DePaul University under the direction of M. Cherif Bassiouni, the Commission's Rapporteur on the "Gathering and Analysis of Facts."
68. Final Report, supra note 32, ¶ 252.
69. ALLEN, supra note 44, at 155–56 & n.7.
70. See id. at vii, 62–63.
71. See Stiglmayer, supra note 61, at 160–61.
72. See ALLEN, supra note 44, at vii, 62.

The second form of genocidal rape occurred in Serb concentration camps where Bosnian-Herzegovinan and Croatian women (and sometimes men)[73] were randomly chosen to be raped. The victim was often murdered after the sexual assault.[74]

The third form of genocidal rape occurred in "rape/death camps." Bosnian-Herzegovinan women were arrested and imprisoned in these camps and systematically raped for an extended period of time by Serb, Bosnian Serb, and Croatian Serb soldiers, Bosnian Serb militias, and Chetniks.[75] Either the women were raped as a form of torture preceding death or with the purpose of forced impregnation. As noted earlier, if a woman became pregnant, she would be held in the concentration camp until it was too late to procure an abortion safely.[76] In cases where the victims were murdered following repeated rapes and sexual assaults, the genocidal intent is obvious. Not so obvious, however, is genocide in the form of forced impregnation. Is not the propagation of a species the antithesis of genocide? How would the forced impregnation of Muslim and Croat women serve the objective of creating a greater Serbia?

5.   Number of forced pregnancies due to rape

Even though the exact number of Bosnian women raped by Serbs and the pregnancies resulting from those acts of violence will probably never be known, in January 1993 the United Nations sent a team of five people to investigate reports of the widespread occurrence of rape and, in particular, the systematic use of rape, especially in Bosnia-Herzegovina, for the goal of ethnic cleansing.[77] Though limited by temporal, personnel, and financial constraints, the team's findings were revealing. The team of experts spent twelve days (12–23 January, 1993) interviewing physicians and reviewing medical records from six major medical centers in Zagreb, Sarajevo, Zenića, and Belgrade. Through their investigations, they identified 119 pregnancies as a result of rape during 1992.[78] Of these pregnant women, eighty-eight received abortions.[79] In Zenića, sixteen women between the ages of seven-

---

73. *See* Bassiouni & McCormick, *supra* note 1, at 17–18.
74. *See* Allen, *supra* note 44, at 63.
75. *See id.*
76. *See* Bassiouni & McCormick, *supra* note 1, at 18.
77. *See id.* at 7–8.
78. *Report on the Situation of Human Rights in the Territory of the Former Yugoslavia Submitted by Mr. Tadeusz Mazowiecki, Special Rapporteur of the Commission on Human Rights, Pursuant to Commission Resolution 1992/S-1/1 of 14 August 1992*, U.N. ESCOR, Comm'n on Hum. Rts., 49th Sess., Agenda Item 27, Annex II, ¶ 9, U.N. Doc. E/CN.4/1993/50 (1993) [hereinafter *Report on the Situation*].
79. *See id.* ¶ ¶ 10–14.

teen and twenty-two were more than twenty weeks pregnant and, therefore, could not receive abortions.[80]

Medical studies estimate that a single act of intercourse results in pregnancy between 1 and 4 percent of the time.[81] Due to the trauma of rape, the lower percentage more accurately reflects these occurrences. Consequently, this suggests that the 119 pregnancies were a result of approximately 11,900 cases of rape.

In analyzing these figures, there are several variables that must be taken into consideration. First, the majority of women were raped more than once, and, in the case of rape/death camps where some women reported being held for several months, women were raped hundreds of times. Such frequency of repeated rapes on an individual would lower the overall total of women raped.

Second, the team of experts only investigated six medical facilities throughout the former Yugoslavia. Countless other hospitals and clinics exist where women could have aborted pregnancies resulting from rape. In addition, many women did not have access to medical facilities and either tried to induce abortion themselves, gave birth to the baby and abandoned it, or acted as if the child belonged to their husbands to avoid the possibility of being ostracized and rejected. Thus, the number of impregnated women is most likely quite higher than the 119 discovered by the investigative team.

Third, even in the hospitals that the team of experts did visit and investigate, the policy of some personnel is not to inquire of women requesting abortions whether or not they had been raped. Indeed, it seems highly probable that women would not admit to being raped even if asked. Some women did not disclose having been raped until after their request for an abortion was denied.[82] In some hospitals in Zagreb, doctors actively shielded rape survivors from public exposure.[83]

Fourth, the investigation took place in the early months of 1992 when the conflict in Bosnia-Herzegovina was only a year old. Some people maintain that such rape camps still existed as late as the spring of 1996. Thus, there are four additional years where women may have become pregnant due to rape.

---

80. See id. ¶ 13 (stating that of the nineteen women, sixteen "were more than 20 weeks pregnant as a result of rape and could not receive abortions."); see also Stiglmayer, supra note 61, at 134–35 (providing contrasting statistics). Stiglmayer asserts that out of the 119 pregnancies, 104 women decided to abort the pregnancy. In her table, she lists nineteen abortions out of nineteen pregnancies in Zenića. Id.

81. See Shana Swiss & Joan E. Giller, Rape as a Crime of War: A Medical Perspective, 270 JAMA 612, 613; see also Report on the Situation, supra note 78; ¶ 3.

82. See Report on the Situation, supra note 78, ¶ 8.

83. See WORLD COUNCIL OF CHURCHES, RAPE OF WOMEN IN WAR: REPORT OF THE ECUMENICAL WOMEN'S TEAM VISIT—ZAGREB (DECEMBER 1992) 9 (1994) [hereinafter WCC REPORT].

The fifth variable to consider is that in 1992 the clinic in Sarajevo that the team of experts visited reported that the number of abortions performed had doubled in September, October, and November (400–500 per month) compared to prewar rates (approximately 200 per month).[84] During this time, the number of patient visits decreased by half.[85] This indicates a phenomenal increase in unwanted pregnancies. One could speculate that rape accounted for this increase. The report warns that such an analysis might not be accurate, however: "While this increase could reflect a rise in pregnancies due to rape, it could also reflect a more general response to economic and social instability created by war."[86] Finally, coercion and intimidation from the fear of ostracism by a woman's family, society, or community, fear of reprisals by their attackers either on themselves or their families and communities, and a sense of futility among the women for any possibility of justice prevented many women from reporting these crimes.

All of these factors combined make it impossible to arrive at any accurate statistics on the number of rapes, the number of rape survivors, and the number of pregnancies that resulted from those rapes. Estimates vary anywhere from 20,000 rape survivors reported by the United Nations Special Rapporteur[87] to as many as 50,000–70,000 reported by the Bosnian government.[88] The Bosnian government estimated that some 35,000 women, primarily Muslim but also Croat, became pregnant from rape.[89] Given medical estimates of the percentage of pregnancies from rape, this would indicate some 3,500,000 incidents! This shocking statistic reveals another shortcoming to obtaining accurate information on the number of rapes and pregnancies resulting from rape; namely, the use of statistics for propaganda to incite the masses. Though the statistics vary, sometimes radically depending on the source, what is undeniable is that the practice of rape, and in particular rape with the intent to impregnate the victim, was both widespread and systematic among the Serbian forces, paramilitary groups,[90] and civilians.

---

84. *See Report on the Situation, supra* note 78, ¶ 16.
85. *See id.*
86. *Id.* ¶ 27.
87. *See Working Paper, supra* note 1, ¶ 4.
88. *See* WCC Report, *supra* note 83, at 9.
89. *See* Allen, *supra* note 44, at 96.
90. These included traditional groups such as "Chetniks," known for their atrocities during WWII, as well as more recent groups such as "Arkan's Tigers" and the "White Eagles." *See* Mujeeb R. Kahn, *From Hegel to Genocide in Bosnia, Some Moral and Philosophical Concerns*, 15 Inst. Muslim Minority Aff. 1, 6 (1994). Kahn points out that, it "is important to note . . . that these professional killers were armed and directed in their 'cleansing operations' directly by the Belgrade government." *Id.*

6.   *Reproduction as genocide?*

Beverly Allen's third form of genocidal rape,[91] rape and forced impregnation, is one of the most heinous crimes targeting the female body. Allen is correct in questioning the Serbian logic that motivates this practice: How can it be that rape, enforced pregnancy, and enforced childbirth equal genocide?[92]

According to Allen, this equation becomes conceivable only if one denies both science and culture.[93] Biologically, the fetus shares an equal amount of genetic material between the non-Serb mother and the Serbian father. Culturally, unless that child is raised by the father within a Serbian community, he or she will assimilate the cultural, ethnic, religious, and national identity of the mother. Allen summarizes: "Serb 'ethnic cleansing' by means of rape, enforced pregnancy, and childbirth is based on the uninformed, hallucinatory fantasy of ultranationalists whose most salient characteristic, after their violence, is their ignorance."[94] We concur with Allen that this mentality, what we label the genetic and cultural patriarchal myth, is indeed ignorant. However, the acceptance of this myth is not limited to Serbs, but is supported by Muslim and Catholic men and women as well. The idea that the male determines a child's ethnic identity is crosscultural and common, though misinformed. No matter how much one argues against such a perspective, a person's (mis)perceptions often dictate both how he perceives reality and his concrete practices, regardless of the facts.

Just as this genetic myth is based on a patriarchal system, so too is the ignorance that it cultivates. In the Balkans, a patriarchal society, the family name passes on through the male, regardless of religion or ethnicity. Even though biologically the child shares an equal amount of genetic material from the male and female, this fact does not overcome the sense that a child born from rape by a Serb will always be considered Serbian. Culturally, where it is recognized that the baby's father is Serbian, if the child is brought up in the Muslim or Catholic culture he or she will oftentimes not be assimilated entirely within that culture given the circumstances of conception.[95] The very practice of rape and impregnation as a form of genocide depends not only upon the perpetrators buying into the genetic and cultural myth, but the victims, their families, and their communities accepting the myth as

---

91. *See* ALLEN, *supra* note 44, at 63; *see supra* text sec. II.B.4.
92. *See* ALLEN, *supra* note 44, at 95.
93. *See id.* at 96–97.
94. *Id.* at 97.
95. *See* Stacy Sullivan, *Born Under a Bad Sign,* NEWSWEEK, 23 Sept. 1996, at 50.

well. As demonstrated by the response of Catholic and Muslim women who refer to their fetuses as "filth" and "that thing," the Serbs are not the only group who accept this myth.[96]

A report by the World Council of Churches (WCC) maintained that

> the use of rape as a weapon of war is perceived as having its roots in patriarchal systems. Destruction and violation of women can be one way of attacking male opponents who regard the women as "theirs" and whose male identity is therefore bound up with protection of "their" women.[97]

From the perpetrator's perspective, or the policy that he follows, the resultant child is considered Serbian, receiving its ethnic identity only from the Serbian father. In fact, many of the raped women interviewed reported that their assailants frequently claimed that they intended to impregnate them so that they would have a Serbian or "Chetnik baby."[98] When asked about reports of the deliberate impregnation of women to create "Serbian babies," a typical response representative of a patriarchal society was that if the biological father was Serb, the child "would always be considered in some way Serb."[99] In this way, Serbian seed becomes implanted and spread through non-Serbian women, even though the resulting baby is only half Serb genetically speaking.

From the victim's perspective, because of the humiliation and terror experienced, and the fact that the perpetrators were often neighbors or people from their community, they do not wish to return to their homeland. Also, many women sustained physical injuries to such an extent through the process of sexual assault, torture, and rape, that they are now unable to conceive. This fulfills one of the UN criteria that defines an act of genocide as one "intended to prevent births within the group."[100] In cases where women did become pregnant, the children may serve as constant reminders of their experiences and prolong the intended trauma of this practice.

Genocide is further accomplished through rejection of the victim by her husband because of the disgrace that the rape brings to him and his family. Often blamed for the rape, the woman faces ostracism from her family and community. Furthermore, those women impregnated as a result of rape are often viewed as tainted and unworthy for reproduction. All these components function to remove non-Serbs from Serbian territories and to break down the very social fabric of non-Serbian cultures. Not only does the prac-

---

96. *Id. See also* Stiglmayer, *supra* note 61, at 137.
97. WCC Report, *supra* note 83, at 22.
98. *See* Stiglmayer, *supra* note 61, at 92, 96, 104, 109, 118–19, 130, 132, 135.
99. WCC Report, *supra* note 83, at 20.
100. Genocide Convention, *supra* note 36, art. 2(d).

tice of rape and rape for impregnation ethnically cleanse Serbian territories, but it functions to kill, in whole or in part, the non-Serb culture and reproductive capabilities once people have fled Serbian territories. The impact of this practice is far-reaching, and its success is based on the unilateral acceptance of a patriarchal system.

III. THE SECONDARY VICTIMIZATION OF RAPE VICTIMS: RELIGIOUS, CULTURAL, AND ETHICAL RESPONSES

The systematic rape of Muslim and Catholic Croat women with the explicit purpose of impregnation to create "Chetnik babies," to effect ethnic cleansing, and to attain a greater Serbia is an atrocious usurpation of the female body as a weapon of war. Perhaps the only atrocity that could compare to this is the treatment, perception, and exploitation of these women if and when their experiences become public knowledge. This section examines the religious and cultural responses to these women, the media's treatment of them, and the failure thus far of the international community to bring the perpetrators to justice. All of these elements have contributed to the secondary victimization of these women, thus prolonging their physical, emotional, and psychological healing processes.

A. Religious Responses

1. Islamic responses

A traditional Muslim aphorism states: "As our women are, so also is our community."[101] Islamic religious culture strongly emphasizes the protection of a woman's dignity and honor. Bosnian Muslims frequently recount the story of Emina, a young Muslim woman who attempted to defend her village against loyalist Serbian Chetniks during World War II. Unable to hold off the advancing Serbs, when she fell into their hands her one request was, "[o]nly leave me my honor; I will forgive you my death."[102] To be raped, humiliated, and defiled was a fate worse than death for this Muslim woman, so high is the virtue of "honor" held within Islam. The point of the story is that a woman's purity in Islam and the Muslim patriarchal culture is not only held sacred, but is seen as an essential element to insure the stability of the

---

101. Azra Zahihic-Kaurin, *The Muslim Woman, in* Mass Rape, *supra* note 21, at 170–71.
102. *Id.* at 173.

society and culture. This is true even though this concept of female honor has come under increasing and justifiable scrutiny.[103] Also relevant is that there is a vast chasm, not always recognized in Islamic sexual ethical mores, between a woman who is violated through rape and a woman who freely engages in a premarital or extramarital sexual relationship. The violation of a woman's honor, as is the case for raped Muslim women in Bosnia, produces various, often contradictory, religious and cultural responses.

First of all, the Koran does not extensively address the issue of rape among Muslims, let alone between Muslims and non-Muslims. This may be a result of its rather explicit view of the social roles of women in Islamic culture and the requirement that men accompany women in public.[104] This being the case, rape is considered to be a relatively infrequent occurrence. When a rape does occur, society generally concludes that, since the woman was unaccompanied by a male guardian (husband, father, brother), she was "on the make" and perhaps looking for a sexual encounter; in such a case, sexual intercourse, even if violent, could be warranted given the woman's violation of religious customs.[105] In the event that a woman accuses a man of rape, the case goes before the religious court. If found guilty, the man faces a penalty of death by stoning or a lengthy jail term. In order to be found guilty, however, four respectable Muslims must have witnessed the event.[106] In the unlikely event of producing such witnesses, the woman must further prove that she has lived an exemplary or chaste life.[107] Even though the Muslim jurists who interpret the Koran address the issue of rape and sanction severe penalties for perpetrators of this crime, prosecution of rapists in Muslim society occurs rather infrequently. More likely, the women will be accessed of *zina*—sex outside marriage including adultery, fornication, and rape—by her assailant and will herself be sent to jail.[108] (This has happened in many rape cases in Pakistan.) This travesty of justice is not unlike the difference between the religious ideals of the Bosnian Muslim community and the actual practices of that community when Muslim women are raped by non-Muslims.

---

103. *See* Niarchos, *supra* note 49, at 672–76; *see also* ANNE TIERNEY GOLDSTEIN, RECOGNIZING FORCED IMPREGNATION AS A WAR CRIME UNDER INTERNATIONAL LAW 20–22 (1993).
104. *See* JAN GOODWIN, PRICE OF HONOR: MUSLIM WOMEN LIFT THE VEIL OF SILENCE ON THE ISLAMIC WORLD 56 (1994). In some conservative areas of Pakistan, the traditional *chador and chardiwari,* "the veil and four walls," is still practiced. According to this custom, a woman should only go out of the house three times in her life: when she is born; when she leaves for her husband's home after marriage; and when she dies and is taken to be buried. *See id.*
105. *See id.*
106. *See id.* at 51.
107. *See Women Jailed for Being Raped,* MARIE CLAIRE, Oct. 1996, at 74, 75.
108. *See* GOODWIN, *supra* note 104, at 51.

In interviews with Bosnian Muslim religious leaders, the WCC reported that leaders have taken measures to insure that victims of rape will be treated compassionately on several accounts.[109] Within the religious community itself, according to Aruna Gnanadason, a member of the WCC commission, religious leaders consider raped women heroines and receive them unconditionally into the communities.[110] Her claim, however, conflicts with reports asserting that raped women are frequently stigmatized and ostracized within these communities. The international community frequently voices its concern that, if her experience becomes public knowledge, a raped woman will be considered an outcast in certain cultures; her husband will abandon her or, in the case of an unmarried woman, she will be unable to marry if she so desires because of the stigma associated with the event. Muslim leaders, however, assured the WCC commission that "young men of the community have been pledged to marry women victims."[111] In the case of impregnation, religious leaders have sympathized with the situation of these women and have condoned abortions up until the 120 day legal limit.[112] For those women held past the limit, or those who chose not to abort, there were offers of adoption by international Muslim communities.[113] The official WCC report substantiated Gnanadason's claim from a religious perspective. It added, however, that practically and culturally speaking, this openness and receptivity is not always evident.[114]

2.   Catholic response

The Croatian Catholic response to victims of rape suffers from similar tensions between religious ideology and cultural practice. In an address by Pope John Paul II to Archbishop Vinko Puljic of Sarajevo, the Pope called for the entire community to "be close to these women who have been so

---

109. WCC Report, *supra* note 83, at 9, 20.
110. Interview by World Council of Churches with Aruna Gnanadason, Geneva, Switzerland (16 July 1996).
111. WCC Report, *supra* note 83, at 9.
112. *See id.* According to the *Hanafi* Jurists' interpretation of the *hadith* (sayings, practices, judgments, and attitudes of Muhammad), ensoulment takes place 120 days after conception. They allow for abortion during this time "only for juridically valid reason[s]." *Abortion, in* 1 The Oxford Encyclopedia of the Modern Islamic World 17, 17–18 (John L. Esposito ed., 1995). *See also* Mirjana Rasevic, *Abortion as a Method of Birth Control,* 31 Yugoslav Survey 103 (1990) (asserting that abortion is regularly used and accepted as a predominant form of birth control in the former Yugoslavia without any social stigma attached to it); Ivana Filice et al., *Bosnia-Herzegovina: Cultural Profile,* 6 Int'l J. Refugee L. 425, 435 (1994).
113. *See* WCC Report, *supra* note 83, at 20.
114. *See id.* at 20, 23.

tragically offended and to their families, in order to help them transform the act of violence into an act of love and acceptance."[115] The terms "rape" and "abortion" are noticeably absent from this document. For rape, the Pope substituted phrases such as "mothers, wives and young women who have been subjected to violence because of an outburst of racial hatred and brutal lust;" for abortion he used the phrases "since the unborn child is in no way responsible for the disgraceful acts accomplished, he or she is innocent and therefore cannot be treated as the aggressor."[116] The omission of these terms seems somewhat curious. One could speculate that because of the political and religious tensions between the various groups in the former Yugoslavia, the Pope consciously attempted to remain diplomatic in his address and avoided terms that would highlight the atrocities committed (rape) and the potential outcome of those atrocities (abortion). Instead, he focused on the need for reconciliation. The call for support and solidarity from the community and the assertion of the sanctity of the family and its role in bringing about healing prove noteworthy. This challenge of solidarity, so key to overcoming the factions within families and the social and cultural genocide that rape causes, can also serve to remove the power and genocidal motivation from this practice. If the culture, society, and family do not react according to the Serbs' projections, but instead stand by these women and support them in solidarity, an impetus for the practice is removed. The Serbian policy of rape for the purpose of ethnic cleansing is dependent not only upon the complicity of Serbs as perpetrators, but also on the Muslims and Catholics as the victims and the anticipated cultural responses towards those victims. If met with love and acceptance instead of fear and hatred, a link in the chain of genocide is removed.

The major difference between Catholicism and Islam is the possibility of obtaining an abortion in the case of rape. While Muslim religious leaders allow abortion up to the 120 day legal limit in the case of rape, officially, the Catholic church condemns abortion even in the case of rape, and, according to some Croatian women's groups, many Catholic hospitals will not perform this operation. This claim, however, has been disputed by Croatian doctors who maintain that they will perform abortions in cases of rape unless serious medical reasons mitigate against it.[117] As mentioned above, of the 119 pregnancies from rape documented by the UN special commission, eighty-eight were terminated by abortions. Thus, while in theory the religious position may dictate against abortion, it is commonly practiced, even in Catholic Croatia.

---

115. Pope John Paul II, *Change Violence into Acceptance,* THE POPE SPEAKS, 2 Feb. 1993, at 220.
116. *Id.* at 219–20.
117. *See* Stiglmayer, *supra* note 61, at 135–36.

B. Cultural and Social Practice

Frequently a stark contrast develops between religious ideologies and the actual responses of Muslims and Catholics to rape survivors. Within Muslim, Catholic, and Serbian cultures, victims of rape tend to experience alienation in varying degrees. First of all, many women refuse to discuss the rape because of the shame and humiliation associated with it, as well as the stigmatization from family, friends, and the community. These attitudes do not facilitate an openness to sharing experiences and often hamper the ability to heal emotionally, physically, and psychologically. Also, women sometimes feel responsible in some way for the rape, and this misconception can be reinforced by attitudes and comments from peers.[118] Especially in cultures where women raped in peacetime are frequently blamed for the attack, whether because of the clothes they were wearing or being out alone in public, in a wartime situation women may internalize these speculations.[119] Often, even other women who have been raped do not encourage peers to talk about the incident for fear that they themselves will be implicated as rape victims and stigmatized and ostracized by their families, husbands, or communities. Fear of reprisals towards detained family members or other women being detained poses another very real threat to these women if they speak about the event.[120] Finally, society has developed suspicions as to whether or not women fabricate these events, especially in the Bosnian conflict where propaganda has played a major role on all sides. All of these factors tend to dissuade women from talking about their experiences with friends and family as well as seeking psychological counseling.

Research shows, however, that if supported emotionally by family and friends or peers in refugee camps, the psychological disorders of raped women do not persist as long as those who keep the rape a secret or speak only to a therapist.[121] Rape is just one of the many layers of trauma that these women have experienced. They are still attempting to cope with witnessing the torture and execution of fathers, husbands, or sons, the rape of their own

---

118. *See* Ivana Filice et al., *Women Refugees from Bosnia-Herzogovina: Developing a Culturally Sensitive Counselling Framework,* 6 Int'l J. Refugee L. 207, 213 (1994).

119. The UN Special Rapporteur for the Former Yugoslavia points out that "women's experience of rape can be intensified by cultural and religious views which often blame the victim." *Rape and Abuse of Women in the Territory of the Former Yugoslavia: Report of the Secretary-General,* U.N. ESCOR, Comm'n on Hum. Rts., 50th Sess., Agenda Item 12, at 60, U.N. Doc. E/CN.4/1994/5 (1993) [hereinafter *Rape and Abuse*].

120. *See Report on the Situation, supra* note 78, ¶ 24.

121. *See* Vera Folnegovic-Smalc, *Psychiatric Aspects of the Rapes in the War against the Republics of Croatia and Bosnia-Herzegovina, in* Mass Rape, *supra* note 21, at 174, 177.

daughters or mothers, being detained in a camp, or losing their homes and personal belongings. To heal from these traumas takes love, support, compassion, and acceptance from one's family, friends, and community. Unfortunately, this support does not always exist.

A second consideration that can aggravate the trauma and suffering of the victim is the husband's response to the event. In interviews conducted with rape survivors, one of the recurring concerns is that if their husbands found out about the rape, their husbands would not take them back, or they might be violently abused, or in some cases even killed.[122] What causes such responses from the one to whom she should be able to turn for love, comfort, support, and understanding? Although the psychological reasons are complex and beyond full comprehension by this author, some justifications are rooted in the masculine myth perpetrated by a patriarchal ideal that men are responsible for "their" women. This myth, which is not limited to a particular religion, culture, or sociological stratus, demonstrates a model of masculine-feminine relations where men possess, rather than relate with, women. According to this myth, when a "man's woman" is violated through rape, it is often very difficult for him to accept the humiliation of such an event. He has failed to live up to his masculine duty and the obligation to defend "his woman," regardless of the circumstances. Frequently, though illogically, this belief translates into alienation or violence directed toward the only one whom he can punish, the woman. Empathy and compassion for the woman sometimes become displaced by masculine self-pity, humiliation, and suffering as a result of her rape.

The cultural and social practices of alienation and expulsion all too frequently oppose the religious ideology calling for compassion, love, and acceptance of rape victims. The phenomena of secondary victimization caused by this occurrence merely prolongs the recuperation process of victims and implicitly supports the very goal of rape and forced impregnation for the sake of genocide. Not only does this violation destroy the women physically, psychologically, and emotionally, but because of the masculine images that prevail in a patriarchal society, it destroys the very fabric of that society. Although patriarchal attitudes typify the Muslim culture, frequently singling out its inability to accept raped women back into its familial and social structure, Catholic Croats and Orthodox Serbs are no less plagued by this phenomenon.[123]

---

122. *See id.* at 179 n.2; LAUREL FLETCHER ET AL., NO JUSTICE, NO PEACE: ACCOUNTABILITY FOR RAPE AND GENDER-BASED VIOLENCE IN THE FORMER YUGOSLAVIA 27 (1993); Stiglmayer, *supra* note 61, at 137; Seifert, *supra* note 41, at 61; Lance Morrow, *Unspeakable: Rape in Former Yugoslavia's Civil War,* TIME, 22 Feb. 1993, at 48.
123. *See* FLETCHER ET AL., *supra* note 122, at 23 n.38; ALLEN, *supra* note 44, at 92.

C.   Media, Propaganda, and Exploitation

The media has played a significant role in the Bosnian war. Milosević used the media for a blatant propaganda campaign to instill fear and hatred and to incite Serbian nationalism, manifested as genocide toward non-Serbs. Not so blatant is the sometimes harmful effect of the media, even by the most well intentioned humanitarian groups, on the very people whom they hope to help.[124] The WCC report on raped women in Bosnia, for example, contained as an appendix a letter issued by the Zagreb Women's Lobby entitled, "Letter of Intentions to Women's and Peace Organizations all over the World."[125] While praising the support of international women's groups and peace organizations, the involvement of some of these groups with the actual victims has caused some concerns. First, concern exists that the process of helping raped women is being taken over by governmental institutions, and that the occurrence of rape thus will be used in political propaganda to spread hatred and call for revenge against the enemy, thereby encouraging further violence against women.[126] The second concern addresses those groups who have encouraged women to share their experiences publicly with promises of help and support, yet do not provide that support to the victims in the long term. The letter criticized this "sensationalistic journalist" approach which has frightened and upset raped women, prolonging their recuperation.[127] The letter continued, "the development of serious women's support projects needs understanding of the problem, patience and time. Otherwise, the good intentions could turn out to be useless or even harmful, bringing some relief only to the conscience of the support-givers."[128] Tadeusz Mazowiecki of the United Nations and his team of investigators also voiced such concern, reporting that some of the women "felt exploited by the media and the many missions 'studying' rape in the former Yugoslavia. . . . There have been reports of women attempting suicide after being interviewed by the media and well-meaning delegations."[129]

An employee of the United Nations High Commissioner for Refugees (UNHCR) reported that when news of the widespread, systematic rape of Muslim and Croat women and children by Serbs reached the world, women's groups flocked to Zagreb to obtain information and interviews from women who had suffered these atrocities.[130] Often, the presence of these

---

124. *See* Stiglmayer, *supra* note 61, at 162–63.
125. WCC Report, *supra* note 83, app. VI.
126. *See id.*
127. *Id.*
128. *Id.*
129. *Rape and Abuse, supra* note 119, ¶ 13.
130. Interview with Anonymous, UNHCR Headquarters, Geneva, Switzerland (15 Aug. 1996).

groups left the women feeling exploited and used, without providing extensive care to the victims themselves and without empowering them to regain a sense of human dignity. Physical rape is an atrocity in itself, but the psychological and emotional consequences can be prolonged and exacerbated through insensitivity toward the victims.[131]

The point here is not to cast blame on the media and well-intentioned humanitarian or women's groups. It is merely to sensitize them to the delicate nature of the situation and the need for prolonged support and care in the psychological and emotional recuperation of the traumatized women. This recuperation requires limiting the occurrences of secondary victimization.

While the media and propaganda have had a negative impact on women rape survivors in some respects, they also have had a positive impact by alerting the international community to the atrocities committed, and, in effect, mobilizing aid efforts from the international community on behalf of the victims to try to stop the violence and bring the perpetrators to justice.[132]

D.   No Justice? International Humanitarian Law and the War Crimes Tribunal

Not only is rape one of the most underreported crimes worldwide, but it is also one of the least punished in the aftermath of a war. Occurrences of rape are frequently considered an inevitable byproduct of war with the *non-sequitur,* "boys will be boys." As a result, rape as a gender specific war crime often has been ignored or considered under the auspices of human rights violations. In the former Yugoslavia where the woman's body was not only targeted through rape, but also through forced impregnation as a form of genocide, it is important to recognize this offense as a gender specific crime directed against women for at least two reasons. First, this practice demonstrates a novel and demented form of warfare directly targeting noncombatants on the basis of their gender and reproductive capabilities. International legislation needs to recognize this as a unique and novel weapon of war and a distinct violation of human rights that incorporates rape and genocide into a single practice.

Second, establishing laws that will specifically punish this crime may bring a sense of justice to those who have been violated. Part of the recuperation process of these women, especially to restore their faith in the moral and political order, is that the perpetrators be held accountable.[133] To

---

131. *See* ALLEN, *supra* note 44, at 92–94.
132. *See, e.g.,* GUTMAN, *supra* note 26.
133. *See* FLETCHER ET AL., *supra* note 122, at 14.

send a clear message that the systematic usurpation of the female body to further one's military objective is morally reprehensible and will not be tolerated, the international community must recognize the unique nature and severity of this crime and prosecute the perpetrators accordingly. There has been an internationally supported move to indict, try, and punish those responsible for these atrocities. The UN Security Council's establishment of a research team in 1991 and an international war crimes tribunal in February 1993 to investigate these reports and bring the perpetrators to justice, respectively, are steps to correct this void in international law and justice.

1.   Rape, forced impregnation, and international humanitarian law

Several international laws exist under which those responsible for rape in the Bosnian war can be held accountable. The Fourth Geneva Convention of 1949,[134] although it had an implicit precedent from previous codes and declarations, provided the first clearly articulated prohibition of rape as a crime against women in Article 27. While calling for the humane treatment and protection of all people against any act of violence, it specifically states that "[w]omen shall be especially protected against any attack on their honour, in particular against rape, enforced prostitution, or any form of indecent assault."[135] In Article 147, the Convention refers to the violations described within Article 27 as war crimes, though it does not specifically mention rape.[136] In addition, Protocol II of the Geneva Convention[137] contains specific legal sanctions protecting victims of internal armed conflicts while Protocol I protects victims of international armed conflicts from rape.[138]

Given the genocidal motivation of the rapes, the perpetrators are also subject to prosecution under the Genocide Convention of 1948, in particu-

---

134. Geneva Convention Relative to the Protection of Civilian Persons in Time of War (Geneva IV), *adopted* 12 Aug. 1948, 6 U.S.T. 3516, T.I.A.S. No. 3365, 75 U.N.T.S. 287 (*entered into force* 21 Oct. 1950) (*entered into force for U.S.* 2 Feb. 1956) [hereinafter Geneva IV].

135. Niarchos, *supra* note 49, at 673 (citing Geneva IV, *supra* note 134).

136. Geneva IV, *supra* note 134, art. 147, at 388. *See* Niarchos, *supra* note 49, at 672–79. *See generally* GOLDSTEIN, *supra* note 103 (describing the historical development of international humanitarian law).

137. Protocol II Additional to the Geneva Convention of 12 Aug. 1949, and Relating to the Protection of Victims of Non-International Armed Conflicts, *adopted* 8 June 1977, U.N. Doc. A/32/144, Annex II, art. 4, 1125 U.N.T.S. No. 17513 (*entered into force* 7 Dec. 1978), *reprinted in* 16 I.L.M. 1442 (1977).

138. Protocol I Additional to the Geneva Convention of 12 Aug. 1949, and Relating to the Protection of Victims of International Armed Conflicts, *adopted* 8 June 1977, U.N. Doc. A/32/144, Annex 1, art. 76, 1125 U.N.T.S. No. 17 (*entered into force* 7 Dec. 1978), *reprinted in* 16 I.L.M. 1391 (1977).

lar, Article II: "Killing members of a [national, ethnical, racial or religious] group; [c]ausing serious bodily or mental harm to members of the group; [d]eliberately inflicting on the group conditions of life calculated to bring about its physical destruction in whole or in part; [i]mposing measures intended to prevent births within the group; [and] [f]orcibly transferring children of the group to another group"[139] are all considered forms of genocide and are punishable under international law. The psychological trauma and physical torture of rape, which sometimes has included foreign objects such as gun barrels, constitute aspects of genocide as well.

Further genocidal consequences of the rapes arise through the reduction of birth rates in non-Serbian societies. For example, the cultural response to women who have been raped could result in the prevention of births: unmarried women will not be married within the community, or those who are married may be rejected by their husbands. In either case, reproduction is impaired within a specific community. In cases where women have suffered physical damage and are thus incapable of reproducing, the genocidal objective is clearly accomplished. Where forced impregnation was the goal, children have been considered by both Serbs and non-Serbs to carry the father's genealogy, thus allowing the Serbs to transfer what they perceive as "their children" to the Muslim or Catholic group. Cultural genocide therefore results because the presence of these children and the knowledge of the circumstances under which they were conceived causes strife and resentment within the community and serves as a constant reminder of Serbian oppression and violence. Reports that pregnant Muslim and Catholic women were released from detention camps and sent to Serbia to give birth to "Serbian children" further helps to propagate the Serbian population, as the "Serbian child" is not considered tarnished by the mother's genes in Serbia as it is with the father's genes in Catholic or Muslim Croatia. Although international law has clear guidelines for prosecuting those guilty of rape, the intention to rape for the purpose of impregnation, though implicit under genocide, is not explicitly stated as a separate crime under international law. This is a gap that requires an amendment given the atrocities in Bosnia: rape, forced impregnation, and genocide.[140]

Finally, rape also constitutes a crime against humanity that entails the intention to systematically persecute a particular group. Even though there

---

139. Genocide Convention, *supra* note 36, art. II.

140. *See* GOLDSTEIN, *supra* note 103, at 13 n.32 (noting that a Task Force of the American Bar Association has recently recommended that Article 5(g) of the International Tribunal's statute on rape should read: "rape *including enforced prostitution and enforced pregnancy, and other forms of sexual assault*") (addition in italics). *See also* AMERICAN BAR ASSOCIATION SPECIAL TASK FORCE OF THE SECTION OF INTERNATIONAL LAW AND PRACTICE, REPORT ON THE INTERNATIONAL TRIBUNAL TO ADJUDICATE WAR CRIMES COMMITTED IN THE FORMER YUGOSLAVIA 15 (1993).

are numerous stipulations under international humanitarian law to prosecute those responsible for rape and even rape for the purpose of impregnation,[141] the question is whether or not such prosecutions will come to
fruition.

2. Rape and the International Criminal Tribunal

To insure that perpetrators are brought to trial and prosecuted, the UN
Security Council passed Resolution 808[142] in February 1993, establishing the
International Criminal Tribunal for the former Yugoslavia. The Tribunal's mandate is to prosecute those people responsible for serious humanitarian law
violations committed in the former Yugoslavia since January 1991. Articles 2
through 5 stipulate prosecution for sexual assault, including rape.[143]
However, the Tribunal has no specific statute condemning forced impregnation, despite the fact that the UN Commission of Experts documented five
patterns of rape, one of which explicitly addresses this practice, and several
of the women victims interviewed recounted the perpetrators' intent to
impregnate them.[144] Notwithstanding any clear prohibition of forced impregnation in international law, the UN Commission of Experts responsible for
analyzing the data and considering human rights violations of the Geneva
Conventions and other humanitarian laws in the former Yugoslavia concluded that:

> [T]here is no doubt about the prohibition of rape and sexual assault in the
> Geneva Conventions and other applicable sources of the international human-
> itarian law. Furthermore, the Commission finds that the relevant provisions of
> the statute of the International Tribunal adequately and correctly state the appli-
> cable law to this crime.[145]

Thus, the Commission did not see a need to amend the law to include
forced impregnation as a particular violation distinct from rape.

In an address to the New England School of Law on 14 January 1998,
David Scheffer, Ambassador at Large for War Crimes Issues, gave an update
on the proceedings of the War Crimes Tribunal.[146] As of mid-January 1998,

---

141. See GOLDSTEIN, supra note 103, at 14–28 (discussing extensively the categorization of
     forced impregnation under numerous violations of international law).
142. See Resolution 808, supra note 49.
143. Statute of the International Tribunal, arts. 2–5, available on <http://www.un.org/icty/i-b-
     ens.htm#2>.
144. See Final Report, supra note 32, ¶ 248; supra text sec. II.B.3.c.
145. Final Report, supra note 32, ¶ 109.
146. As of May 1995, three indictments had been issued by the Tribunal. Of these, two were
     charged with sexual assault. See Rape and Abuse of Women in the Areas of Armed
     Conflict in the Former Yugoslavia: Report of the Secretary General, U.N. General

seventy-nine individuals have been publicly indicted by the Tribunal: fifty-seven are ethnic Serb, nineteen are ethnic Croat, and three are ethnic Bosniak. Three indictees have died, meaning that there are currently seventy-six known indictees now living. Fifty-four remain at large, and nineteen are in custody at The Hague. The indictments against three ethnic Croats were withdrawn last month and they were released from custody. Of those indictees at large, fifty-two are ethnic Serbs and two are ethnic Croats. Furthermore, only three ethnic Serbs, thirteen ethnic Croats, and three ethnic Bosniaks remain in custody.[147]

From the number of indictments, it is impossible to ascertain the indictees accused of rape for the purpose of forced impregnation, as this is not a specific violation under international humanitarian law. Consequently, the numbers of those who committed this crime will probably never be known. Nonetheless, given the prevalence of reported rapes and the United Nations' own task force that interviewed victims, collected data and testimonies from eyewitnesses and medical professionals, and identified nearly 800 victims and 600 alleged perpetrators by name, one could question the seriousness of the international effort to bring the perpetrators to justice. No wonder many women have an attitude of "what's the use?" and refuse to come forward to testify. The fear of exposing themselves and reliving the nightmare as well as the risk of reprisals, given the slim possibility of an indictment, let alone the prosecution of the perpetrator, is cause for despair. Not only does this hinder the recuperation process of rape victims, but it also sends a message to the world that women are second class citizens, and sexual crimes against them are not taken seriously by the international justice system. Although the War Crimes Tribunal conducted in The Hague thus far has not given much cause for hope that justice will be served, it is certainly a step forward in recognizing the severity of the crime.

Assembly, 50th Sess., Agenda Item 114(c) of the Provisional Agenda, at ¶ 28, U.N. Doc. A/50/329 (1995).

147. See David J. Scheffer, Challenges Confronting International Justice, Address at the New England School of Law (14 Jan. 1998) (on file with author). From these numbers, it is clear that ethnic Serbs, while having the greatest number of indictments, have been the least cooperative with the International War Crimes Tribunal. Scheffer notes that what has bedeviled the Tribunal from its creation is "state cooperation." "The worst offenders are Republika Srpska and Serbia-Montenegro. Neither has apprehended or orchestrated the voluntary surrender of a single indictee." Id. Thus, while the Tribunal has improved on its number of indictments, as the number of known perpetrators of rape indicates, it still has a long way to go before there is any semblance of justice for the women who suffered atrocities during the conflict in the former Yugoslavia. This task is especially difficult given the lack of cooperation among the states harboring these suspected criminals. For information on those indicted and the specific indictments against them, visit the website: <http://www.un.org/icty/i-b-ens.htm#2>.

IV.　CONCLUSION

The war in the former Yugoslavia has provided documented evidence of rape and forced impregnation used as a weapon of war for achieving ethnic cleansing, and has raised international awareness concerning the usurpation of the female body and her reproductive capacities to fulfill political and military objectives. This evidence proves that not only were women caught up in a circle of violence waged and executed by men in power, but that they were specifically targeted as a means of attaining a military end. This frightening occurrence in war tactics and military strategy has caused the international community grave concern, but much remains to be accomplished to put an end to present violations, to punish the perpetrators, and to prevent these acts from occurring in future conflicts. Man's inhumanity to man and woman knows no bounds. To remain passive in light of such injustice is a moral abomination and betrays those who have suffered, and will suffer, from this treatment. Protection against rape and rape for the purpose of impregnation must be insured under international humanitarian law as well as guarantees providing for swift punishment of the perpetrators.

In addition, to reduce the disparity between religious ideology and cultural practice, communities should be sensitized to receive rape victims and their children in love, compassion, and empathy to foster healing not only among the women, but within the community as a whole. The success of genocide in the form of rape and forced impregnation is dependent upon the patriarchal myth that supports its very practice. As is evident from the responses towards many of the women who have suffered this tragedy, this myth is still very much alive.

Chapter 12

Surfacing Children: Limitations of Genocidal Rape Discourse

R. Charli Carpenter

> Thus from a Mixture of all Kinds began,
> That Het'rogenous Thing, *An Englishman:*
> In eager Rapes and furious Lust begot,
> Betwixt a Painted *Britton* and a *Scot:* . . .
> In whose hot Veins new Mixtures quickly ran,
> Infus'd betwixt a *Saxon* and a *Dane.*
> While their Rank Daughters, to their Parents just,
> Receiv'd all Nations with Promiscuous Lust. . . .[1]

From Daniel Defoe, *The True-Born Englishman*

I. INTRODUCTION

The ethnic conflict in the former Yugoslavia put war crimes against women on the international human rights agenda for the first time in history.[2] In response to reports of tens of thousands of women being raped, mutilated, and executed in concentration camps as part of a systematic policy of ethnic cleansing, the international community took action against genocide for

---

1. DANIEL DEFOE, THE TRUE-BORN ENGLISHMAN 20 (1700).
2. This statement must be qualified. A legal precedent does exist for protection of civilians—particularly women—during war, which goes at least as far back as the 14th century. For a historical overview, see Catherine N. Niarchos, *Women, War, and Rape: Challenges Facing the International Tribunal for the Former Yugoslavia,* 17 HUM. RTS. Q. 649 (1995). Medieval prohibitions against rape, however, were couched in terms of male honor and female chastity, rather than as war crimes (torture or willful harm) specifically. As recently as the Nuremberg Trials, rape was never explicitly addressed. The response of the Western media and feminist legal scholars to the systematic rape in Bosnia-Herzegovina has resulted in rape being codified for the first time as a war crime and as a crime of gender.

the first time since Nuremberg.[3] In the process of addressing both rape and genocide, feminist legal scholars began to discuss rape *as* genocide, and their arguments hinged in large part on the evidence of a policy of forced impregnation.[4] Evidence of forced impregnation helped excite moral sentiment because rape-induced pregnancy was presented as a worse crime against women than rape itself, and it helped frame rape as genocidal because of pregnancy's unique role in corroding the victimized culture.

A discussion of the children born of the rapes was missing in the debate about the atrocities against women and culture. This is surprising in two respects. First, the issue of forced impregnation was inextricably linked to the genocide and because forced impregnation by definition implies the birth of children, the children of the rapes were clearly a party within the genocidal equation. Nevertheless, the particular status of the children of rapes (as rights-bearers, victims of genocide or other crimes, or refugees of war) was addressed only peripherally and never in the context of forced impregnation itself.

Failing to connect the fate of rape victims and the fate of their children in legal discourse was doubly surprising because of the widespread public awareness of the children's plight in the early 1990s. A series of news articles on the children of war-rape filled the Western press as the abandoned children filled orphanages in 1992.[5] Indicating a public sensitivity to their fate and an awareness of their existence, Western families mobilized to retrieve the stigmatized children from the war zone, but the Bosnian and Croatian governments refused to permit the children to leave the

---

3. Again, this statement deserves qualification. The response of the international community has been belated, paralyzed, and indecisive. Nonetheless, the establishment of an International War Crimes Tribunal and a subsequent consensus on an International Criminal Court are unprecedented events in the international system. Thus, the war in Bosnia provided a crucial impetus for a recognition of the need for such instruments.

4. *See generally* MASS RAPE: THE WAR AGAINST WOMEN IN BOSNIA-HERZEGOVINA (Alexandra Stiglmayer ed., 1994) [hereinafter MASS RAPE]; BEVERLY ALLEN, RAPE WARFARE: THE HIDDEN GENOCIDE IN BOSNIA-HERZEGOVINA AND CROATIA (1996); Dorean Marguerite Koenig, *Women and Rape in Ethnic Conflict and War*, 5 HASTINGS WOMEN'S L.J. 129 (1994); Jennifer Green et al., *Affecting the Rules for the Prosecution of Rape and Other Gender-Based Violence Before the International Criminal Tribunal for the Former Yugoslavia: A Feminist Proposal and Critique*, 5 HASTINGS WOMEN'S L.J. 171 (1994).

5. *See* Michael J. Jordan, *Born of Rape, Abandoned Bosnian Babies Face Uncertain Future*, MIAMI HERALD, 1 July 1995, at 20A; Stacy Sullivan & Joshua Hammer, *Born Under a Bad Sign? (Children Born of Rape During War)*, NEWSWEEK, 23 Sept. 1996, at 49; Carol J. Williams, *Bosnia's Orphans of Rape: Innocent Legacy of Hatred*, L.A. TIMES, 24 July 1993, at 1; Laura Eggertson, *Children of Rape: The War Produces a New Generation of Victims*, MACLEAN'S, 24 May 1993, at 22; Daniela Horvath, *The Children of the Rapes: Young Victims of 'Ethnic Cleansing,'* WORLD PRESS REV., June 1993, at 11.

region.[6] By the time the War Crimes Tribunal and the International Criminal Court debated genocidal rape and forced impregnation as crimes against *women,* the war-rape orphans had dropped out of the sight of human rights scholars and advocates.[7]

The purpose of this paper is twofold. The first task is to unpack the discursive politics that lay behind the marginalization of children as victims of human rights abuses in the former Yugoslavia. To this end, this paper will begin by examining the literature in which forced impregnation was articulated as a distinct crime and next attempt to identify the discursive devices through which forced impregnation was presented as a gender issue only. It will then argue that the plight of war-rape orphans escaped notice because the legal discourse that articulated forced impregnation as a distinct crime was framed in such a way as to: 1) marginalize the children as subjects of human rights law and 2) identify them with the perpetrators, rather than the victims, of genocide.

Secondly, this paper will attempt to bring to light the situation of war-rape orphans and the legal framework in which to assess their plight and to suggest redress. This subsequent section represents an attempt to carve out thinking space in which to address the particular case of war-rape orphans vis-à-vis other war crimes victims in Bosnia. It is important to emphasize that this paper is calling for a discussion rather than issuing definitive arguments. Some of the important questions yet to be raised include the following: Does international law govern children victims of the ethnic violence in the former Yugoslavia? If so, who are the perpetrators? What form of redress is necessary or appropriate? What specific rights are violated, if any, when a child is forcibly and intentionally conceived in a context that precludes her from acceptance by her family, identity with a community, or access to resources?

What emerges from an examination of these questions is that the prevailing framework of international law is capable of supplying only partial answers. This problem is in part a reflection of the general inadequacy of international law to address children's rights in general. But even within the scope of available approaches to children's rights in international law, articulating the rights of these *particular* children constitutes a unique challenge because it complicates several of the givens in international legal theory including the concept of genocide itself.

------

6. *See* Julia Elliott, *Chance to Adopt Orphans from Bosnia Won't Happen Soon; Health and Welfare Getting Many Inquiries,* Ottawa Citizen, 8 Aug. 1992, at A5; Williams, *supra* note 5, at 1.

7. On the International Tribunal for the Former Yugoslavia, see Niarchos, *supra* note 2. On the International Criminal Court Treaty, see Fanny Benedetti & John L. Washburn, *Drafting the International Criminal Court Treaty: Two Years to Rome and an Afterword on the Rome Diplomatic Conference,* 5 Global Governance, Jan.–Mar. 1999, at 1.

II. DISCOURSES OF FORCED IMPREGNATION

A. The Construction of Forced Impregnation as a Crime

Securing indictments for mass rapes became a political goal after reports of widespread atrocities filtered out of Bosnia and Croatia in the early 1990s.[8] An awareness of the rapes was decisive in galvanizing international will to establish the International Tribunal for the Prosecution of Persons Responsible for Serious Violations of International Humanitarian Law Committed in the Territory of the Former Yugoslavia Since 1991 (Tribunal) in 1993.[9] The campaign to place gender crimes high on the agenda at the Tribunal was led by US feminist legal scholars who fought to highlight the mass rapes among other crimes in the conflict and who identified forced impregnation as a specific crime.[10] The crusade was fueled by statistics issued by the Bosnian government in October 1992 indicating that 50,000 Muslim women had been raped.[11] A subsequent study conducted under the auspices of the European Community put the estimate at 20,000.[12] Additionally, estimates of the number of Muslim women killed at that point ran as high as 100,000.[13] The sheer numbers, coupled with the graphic stories of many victims, were enough to mobilize considerable attention toward the situation of Bosnian and Croatian women. Aryeh Neier stated that, "[p]rior to Bosnia, there was never an issue involving women in other countries that preoccupied American women. Overnight, it seemed that the plight of Bosnian women had become a domestic issue to American feminists."[14]

---

8. *See* Aryeh Neier, War Crimes: Brutality, Genocide, Terror and the Struggle for Justice (1998).

9. *See generally* Niarchos, *supra* note 2. On 22 Feb. 1993, the UN Security Council, acting under Chapter VII of the United Nations Charter, decided to establish the Tribunal. Its rules of procedure and evidence entered into force on 14 Mar. 1994 and have been amended three times—on 5 May 1994, 4 Oct. 1994, and 30 Jan. 1995. *International Tribunal for the Prosecution of Persons Responsible for Serious Violations of International Humanitarian Law Committed in the Territory of the Former Yugoslavia Since 1991: Rules of Procedure and Evidence,* U.N. Doc. IT/32 (1994), *reprinted in* 33 I.L.M. 484 (1994), *amendments in* 33 I.L.M. 838 (1994) & 33 I.L.M. 1619 (1994).

10. *See generally* 5 Hastings Women's L.J., Summer 1994.

11. *See* Aryeh Neier, *Watching Rights: Rapes in Bosnia-Herzegovina,* The Nation, 1 Mar. 1993, at 259.

12. Aryeh Neier, who has written articles and a book on human rights abuses in Bosnia, argues that these numbers are unsubstantiated and likely inflated and claims that the European Community does not explain in its report how it arrived at the number. *See id.;* Neier, *supra* note 8; Laurel Fletcher, *Rape as a Weapon of War in the Former Yugoslavia,* 5 Hastings Women's L.J. 69, 77 (1994).

13. Neier, *supra* note 8, at 176.

14. *Id.* at 178. On the impact of the rapes on Western feminism and feminist influence in challenging the treatment of war-rape based on these accounts, see Cynthia Enloe, *Have the Bosnian Rapes Opened a New Era of Feminist Consciousness?, in* Mass Rape, *supra* note 4, at 219.

Within the legal scholarship and activism that culminated in the recognition of gender crimes at the Tribunal, two varieties of argument highlighted the use of forced impregnation in the conflict. First, forced impregnation was seen as a part of the broader context of the mass rapes in Bosnia. Forced impregnation became an exclamation point to arguments that *rape* should be treated as a war crime and a crime against humanity. Furthermore, it was fundamental to claims that rape could also be an act of genocide. Second, forced impregnation was addressed directly as a war crime and crime of genocide in and of itself, because of its specific heinousness and distinctness from rape. The two frameworks deserve detailed comment here because they articulate core assumptions about the scope of forced impregnation in international law. Despite the differences between the approaches as well as the diversity of views within the literature, the writings uniformly treat forced impregnation as a gender issue *only*. In this sense, this paper claims, these arguments are groundbreaking but incomplete, insofar as forced impregnation potentially brings into being a child of rape whose rights may also be violated as a result of her conception.

1.   Forced impregnation as incidental to rape

The extent to which rape has been sanctioned in international law has varied over time despite the fact that rape has always occurred during armed conflict, often on a mass and systematic scale. Ancient scholars openly argued that rape was a fundamental aspect of conflict and was to be expected by the women of the conquered.[15] By the Middle Ages, women acquired some legal protection under the Ordinances of War, promulgated by Richard II at Durham in 1385 and by Henry V at Mantes in 1419, which made rape during war a capital offense.[16] However, the ordinance did not

---

15. *See* Niarchos, *supra* note 2, at 660.

> The Trojan War, described in the *Iliad,* demonstrated that women could expect rape and enslavement from warfare. The Old Testament reported that Hebrew tribes invading Canaan seized the following spoils of war, in this order, "sheep, cattle, asses, and thirty-two thousand girls who had had no intercourse with a man." The Book of Deuteronomy sanctioned the seizure of women as legitimate booty, although captors were obliged after a period of mourning to marry their stolen treasures. Hugo Grotius, writing in the seventeenth century, described classical admonitions to respect the "chastity of the women and girls," as well as frequent violations of those admonitions; although Grotius frowned upon rape during warfare, he apparently found the practice of seizing women for purposes of marriage more acceptable.

> *Id.* (footnotes omitted).

16. *See* Theodor Meron, *Rape as a Crime Under International Humanitarian Law,* 87 Am J. Int'l L. 424, 425 (1993).

apply to cities taken by siege and was seldom enforced.[17] In 1863, the
Lieber Code, a military code for the Union Army, prohibited rape on penalty
of death.[18] "The Hague and Geneva Conventions provide[] explicit or
implicit protection against rape."[19] Susan Brownmiller notes that the nineteenth and twentieth centuries saw a massive increase in the scale of rape
in armed conflict (as well as other atrocities against civilians) and the presence of legal sanctions for rape was not translated into international legal
action.[20] Despite well-documented and publicized atrocities against women
during World War I and World War II, the International Military Tribunals in
Nuremberg (IMT) and in the Far East (IMTFE) never addressed rape explicitly. Rather, the tribunals subsumed rape under the general category of "ill
treatment of the civilian population."[21]

Moreover, the basis for criminalizing rape in these contexts reflected the
very attitude that gave war-rape its salutary effect and made it inevitable.
Specifically, rape was generally proscribed on the basis of men's property
rights; it was a crime against "honor, dignity or family rights" and the rape of
women was associated with carrying off (men's) property. Such a conceptualization "obfuscates the fact that rape is fundamentally violence against
women. . . . This failure to recognize rape as violence is critical to the traditionally lesser or ambiguous status of rape in humanitarian law."[22] At the
insistence of feminist scholars, rape has been recognized as torture and as a
grave breach only very recently.[23]

---

17. THEODOR MERON, HENRY'S WARS AND SHAKESPEARE'S LAWS: PERSPECTIVES ON THE LAW OF WAR IN THE LATER
    MIDDLE AGES 111 (1993).
18. Francis Lieber, *Instructions for the Government of Armies of the United States in the Field*,
    promulgated as U.S. War Dept., Adjutant General's Office, General Orders No. 100, art.
    44 (24 Apr. 1863), *reprinted in* 1 THE LAW OF WAR: A DOCUMENTARY HISTORY 158, 167 (Leon
    Friedman ed., 1972).
19. Niarchos, *supra* note 2, at 662.
20. *See generally* SUSAN BROWNMILLER, AGAINST OUR WILL: MEN, WOMEN AND RAPE (1975).
21. *See United States v. Göring*, 22 Trial of the Major War Criminals Before the International
    Military Tribunal 411, 475 (1948).
22. Rhonda Copelon, *Surfacing Gender: Reconceptualizing Crimes Against Women in Time
    of War*, *in* MASS RAPE, *supra* note 4, at 197, 200–01.

    Where rape is treated as a crime against honor, the honor of women is called into ques-
    tion and virginity or chastity is often a precondition. . . . And while the concept of dig-
    nity potentially embraces more profound concerns, standing alone it obfuscates the
    fact that rape is fundamentally violence against women—violence against a woman's
    body, autonomy, integrity, selfhood, security, and self-esteem as well as her standing in
    the community.

    Id. at 200 (endnote omitted).

23. The State Department stated that: "In our reports to the United Nations on human rights
    violations in the former Yugoslavia, we have reported sexual assaults as grave breaches.
    We will continue to do so and will continue to press the international community to
    respond to the terrible sexual atrocities in the former Yugoslavia." Letter from Robert A.

The task for feminist scholars during the inception of the International Tribunal was to emphasize rape as violence against women, rape as torture, and rape as a crime of gender.[24] Rape, it was argued, had been used in the Bosnian conflict as a war crime and a crime against humanity.[25] Lastly, the legal innovation of rape as genocide was articulated.[26] Evidence of a systematic policy of forced impregnation punctuated and supported these claims.

Rape was initially mentioned (once) in the UN Statute for War Crimes Committed in the Former Yugoslavia (ICTY Statute). However, it was mentioned only as a "crime against humanity,"[27] which, as Dorean Koenig points out, would require "proof that the act was part of a widespread or systematic attack against a civilian population on national, political, ethnic, racial or religious grounds."[28] In the context of Bosnia, rape certainly could be seen as a crime against humanity on these grounds.[29] It was suggested that the definition of crimes against humanity be expanded to include attacks based on gender as a category.[30] Yet, due to the desire to address specific

---

Bradtke, Acting Assistant Secretary for Legislative Affairs, to Senator Arlen Specter (27 Jan. 1993), *reprinted in* Meron, *supra* note 16, at 427 n.22. *See also* Diane F. Orentlicher, *Settling Accounts: The Duty to Prosecute Human Rights Violations of a Prior Regime,* 100 YALE L.J. 2537 (1991) (discussing the interpretation of the Nuremberg Charter in Control Council Law No. 10 to include rape). *See generally* Deborah Blatt, *Recognizing Rape as a Method of Torture,* 19 N.Y.U. REV. L. & SOC. CHANGE 821 (1992).

24. *See generally* Niarchos, *supra* note 2; Green et al., *supra* note 4.
25. *See* Niarchos, *supra* note 2, at 678, 681–82; Green et al., *supra* note 4, at 186–89.
26. *See* Niarchos, *supra* note 2, at 658, 682; Green et al., *supra* note 4, at 188.
27. Article 6(c) of the Nuremberg Charter defined crimes against humanity as

> murder, extermination, enslavement, deportation, and other inhumane acts committed against any civilian population, before or during the war, or persecutions on political, racial or religious grounds in execution of or in connection with any crime within the jurisdiction of the Tribunal, whether or not in violation of the domestic law of the country where perpetrated.

Agreement for the Prosecution and Punishment of the Major War Criminals of the European Axis, *signed* 8 Aug. 1945, Charter of the International Military Tribunal, art. 6(c), 59 Stat. 1546, 1547, 82 U.N.T.S. 284, 288 [hereinafter Nuremberg Charter].

28. Koenig, *supra* note 4, at 132.
29. *See* Copelon, *supra* note 22, at 204; Koenig, *supra* note 4, at 137; Green et al., *supra* note 4.
30. *See* Niarchos, *supra* note 2, at 679 ("[I]t now would be insensible to fail to recognize rape, in war or in peace, as an extreme form of gender discrimination. . . . Either by amendment to the current conventions or by declaration, IHL [international humanitarian law] should be revised to reflect this concept."). *See also* Copelon, *supra* note 22, at 207 (stating that "[t]he expansion of the concept of crimes against humanity to include gender is thus part of the broader movement to end the historical invisibility of gender violence as a humanitarian and human rights violation."). Both Niarchos and Copelon note that this lacunae is analogous to a similar problem in asylum law, which does not recognize gender as a source of persecution. Copelon *supra* note 22, at 207; Niarchos *supra* note 2, at 679 n.184.

acts of rape in addition to the systematic policy, rape was framed as a war crime within the conflict as well as a crime against humanity.[31]

To qualify as a war crime, or "grave breach" of the Geneva Conventions, an act must be committed in the course of an armed conflict, and it need not be systematic or widespread.[32] "[R]ape on a wide scale would be prosecuted as a crime against humanity; a single case would be prosecuted as a war crime."[33] Rape, it is argued, is a grave breach on several accounts. Although rape is not listed explicitly among the crimes considered grave breaches, it is encompassed under Article 2 of the Geneva Conventions as "inhumane treatment" and "willfully causing great suffering or serious injury to body or health."[34] Additionally, scholars insisted rape be viewed as a form of torture,[35] and Koenig includes "unlawful confinement of a civilian" as applicable in the context of the rape camps in Bosnia.[36]

The pregnancies that resulted from the mass rapes were seen as exacerbating the grievousness of rape and were thus capitalized upon in constructing rape as a war crime and crime against humanity. This was the case regardless of whether forced impregnation was seen as an intentional policy or a by-product of rape. Vera Folnegovic-Smalc, writing about the psychiatric consequences of the rapes, emphasized the particular psychological damage to those women who were impregnated: "Suicidal thoughts are evident above all in women who have become pregnant as the result of rape."[37] Rhonda Copelon writes that "the fact of pregnancy, whether aborted or not, continues the initial torture in a most intimate and invasive form; and bearing the child of rape, whether placed for adoption or not, has a poten-

---

31. See Copelon, *supra* note 22, at 203 (discussing the different implications of treating rape as either a war crime or a crime against humanity).
32. Grave breaches of the Geneva Conventions of 1949 include:

> wilful killing, torture or inhuman treatment, including biological experiments, wilfully causing great suffering or serious injury to body or health, unlawful deportation or transfer or unlawful confinement of a protected person, compelling a protected person to serve in the forces of a hostile Power, or wilfully depriving a protected person of the right of fair and regular trial . . . , taking of hostages and extensive destruction and appropriation of property not justified by military necessity and carried out unlawfully and wantonly.

Geneva Convention (IV) Relative to the Protection of Civilian Persons in Time of War, art. 147, 12 Aug. 1949, 6 U.S.T. 3516, 75 U.N.T.S. 287, (*entered into force* 21 Oct. 1950) (*entered into force for U.S.* 2 Feb. 1956) [hereinafter Fourth Geneva Convention].

33. Niarchos, *supra* note 2, at 678.
34. See Green et al., *supra* note 4, at 58, 186–87.
35. See Copelon, *supra* note 22, at 201; Green et al., *supra* note 4, at 186; Koenig, *supra* note 4, at 138.
36. Koenig, *supra* note 4, at 138.
37. Vera Folnegovic-Smalc, *Psychiatric Aspects of the Rapes in the War Against the Republics of Croatia and Bosnia-Herzegovina, in* Mass Rape, *supra* note 4, at 174, 177.

tially lifelong impact on the woman and her place in the community."[38] Pregnancy may worsen the long-term impact of the rape on the victim by eliminating any chance of maintaining acceptance by a husband or family through silence about her victimization.[39] Forced impregnation "maximizes the pain of rape" because:

> [I]ike rape, but to a greater degree . . . it increases and prolongs their physical and emotional pain and makes it more difficult for them to resume any semblance of normal life. . . . Like rape, but to a greater degree, [it] is a means of demoralizing the victim and depriving her of personal dignity and family privacy.[40]

Because rape had been recognized in parts of the Geneva Conventions, such arguments only enunciated what was already accepted in international law.[41] However, treating rape as *genocidal* was something new, which fundamentally hinged on the existence of forced impregnation.

The articulation of rape as genocide was not an immediate assertion nor an uncontested one. Initially, scholarship on the human rights situation in Bosnia addressed both rape *as well as* genocide, but as distinct issues. Brownmiller, in emphasizing that mass rape in warfare is nothing new or unprecedented, appeared to be arguing against the idea held by some scholars that this *particular* situation deserved special attention.[42] The implications of this tendency to separate rape and genocide was roundly criticized by Catharine A. MacKinnon in her writings on rape *as* genocide:

> If all men do this all the time, especially in war, how can one pick a side in this one? And since all men do this all the time, war or no war, why do anything special about this now? This war becomes just a form of business as usual. But genocide is not business as usual.[43]

---

38. Copelon, *supra* note 22, at 203.
39. *See id.* at 207 ("Forced impregnation expresses the desire to mark the rape and rapist upon the woman's body and upon the woman's life."). *See also* Rachel N. Pine, *Pregnancy as Evidence of Crime*, 16 Nat'l L.J., 24 Jan. 1994, at 15.
40. Anne Tierney Goldstein, Ctr. For Reprod. Law & Policy, Recognizing Forced Impregnation as a War Crime Under International Law: A Special Report of the International Program 14–15 (1993). Additionally, Beverly Allen argues that women forcibly impregnated are victims of a crime against humanity on a basis more specific than gender, because "being a female is a necessary . . . but insufficient condition for receiving this kind of treatment. Genocidal rape . . . aimed at enforced reproduction, demands that its victims be capable of gestating a pregnancy." Allen, *supra* note 4, at 121.
41. This is not to understate the significance of explicitly addressing rape. As noted, even when rape has been addressed previously in international humanitarian law, it has usually been treated as peripheral to other crimes.
42. *See* Susan Brownmiller, *Making Female Bodies the Battlefield, in* Mass Rape, *supra* note 4, at 180. Brownmiller points out that, in fact, every historical instance of well-publicized mass rape has been described by commentators as "unprecedented." *Id.* For a concise historical summary of instances and explanations of war-rape, see Ruth Seifert, *War and Rape: A Preliminary Analysis, in* Mass Rape, *supra* note 4, at 54.
43. Catharine A. MacKinnon, *Rape, Genocide, and Women's Human Rights, in* Mass Rape, *supra* note 4, at 183, 189–90.

Yet Brownmiller and MacKinnon appear to be talking past one another because it is not necessary to argue that genocidal rape is *unprecedented* in order to argue that it should be addressed in international law. Rather, it is legal attention to genocidal rape—on women's terms—that is unprecedented and long overdue.[44] Copelon expresses reservations to both views. Even more than Brownmiller, she recognizes the importance of addressing *these* rapes as genocide. Yet, she argues that conflating genocide and rape in general is dangerous because it obscures the horror of "common" rape.[45] Moreover, Copelon stresses that articulating forced impregnation as a crime *only* in a genocidal context puts the risk of pregnancy in *all* rape on the periphery.[46] Copelon appears to support claims that the situation in Bosnia is distinct but wishes to avoid the trap of viewing "mere" rape as less atrocious than "genocidal" rape: "From the standpoint of *these* women, [rape and genocide] are inseparable. But to emphasize as unparalleled the horror of genocidal rape is factually dubious and risks rendering rape invisible once again."[47]

At its most fundamental level, genocide encompasses acts carried out with intent to destroy a national, ethnic, racial, or religious group.[48] Based on this definition, many authors writing about war-rape articulate the geno-

---

44. *See* Enloe, *supra* note 14, at 220. The rhetorical need to assert that a particular act is somehow new or unprecedented in order to justify human rights legislation is an interesting theme elsewhere in this literature. Beverly Allen makes this point in regards to forced impregnation, again in her response to Brownmiller: "there may be 'nothing unprecedented about mass rape in war', but this [forced impregnation] is something new." ALLEN, *supra* note 4, at 91. Allen is wrong, however. Forced impregnation has been used repeatedly throughout history, both as a tool of genocide (for example, in Bangladesh in 1971, (*see* BROWNMILLER, *supra* note 20, at 78–80), and for other purposes, such as against German women in Nazi Germany and in the American South during slavery. *See generally* CLAUDIA KOONZ, MOTHERS IN THE FATHERLAND: WOMEN, THE FAMILY AND NAZI POLITICS (1987); Wing & Merchán, *infra* note 81. Treating forced impregnation in Bosnia as unique particularly serves to marginalize the genocidal rapes occurring practically simultaneously in Rwanda. *See* Sullivan & Hammer, *supra* note 5, at 49–50 (discussing Rwanda).
45. Copelon, *supra* note 22, at 205.
46. *See id.* at 207.
47. *Id.* at 198 (emphasis added).
48. The legal definition of genocide is

   any of the following acts committed with intent to destroy, in whole or in part, a national, ethnic, racial or religious group, as such:

   (a) Killing members of the group;

   (b) Causing serious bodily or mental harm to members of the group;

   (c) Deliberately inflicting on the group conditions of life calculated to bring about its physical destruction in whole or in part;

   (d) Imposing measures intended to prevent births within the group;

   (e) Forcibly transferring children of the group to another group.

cidal component even without using the term "genocide." Brownmiller's influential work emphasizes the use of war-rape to attack an enemy's culture: "Rape is considered by the people of a defeated nation to be part of the enemy's conscious effort to destroy them . . . men appropriate the rape of, 'their women' as part of their own male anguish of defeat."[49] According to Ruth Seifert, "[i]f the aim is to destroy a culture, [women] are prime targets because of their cultural position and their importance in the family structure. In 'dirty wars' it is not necessarily the conquest of the foreign army, but rather the deconstruction of a culture than can be seen as a central objective of war actions."[50] Such remarks indicate an understanding of the impact of mass rape on a victimized nation but are couched in terms of armed conflict between two sides. Mass rape with the intent to destroy an opposing nation, though conceptually transferable to a genocidal situation, is not necessarily genocidal unless it comports with the definition of genocide in the Genocide Convention.[51]

Because the situation in Bosnia was certainly genocidal,[52] mass-rapes used to strike at the victimized culture were correctly articulated as *tools* of genocide. "Rapes spread fear and induce the flight of refugees; rapes humiliate, demoralize, and destroy not only the victim but also her family and community; and rapes stifle any wish to return."[53] The United Nations Commission of Experts that investigated the rapes concluded that "rape has been used as an instrument of ethnic cleansing."[54] MacKinnon described rape as genocide on three counts: 1) "the war is an instrument of the genocide; the rapes are an instrument of the war,"[55] 2) "rape as genocide [as in] rape directed toward women because they are Muslim or Croatian,"[56] and 3) "rape as ethnic expansion through forced reproduction."[57] Beverly Allen concurs with MacKinnon both in the use of the term "genocidal rape" and

---

Convention on the Prevention and Punishment of the Crime of Genocide, art. 2, *adopted* 9 Dec. 1948, 78 U.N.T.S. 277 (*entered into force* 12 Jan. 1951) (*entered into force for U.S.* 23 Feb. 1989) [hereinafter Genocide Convention].

49. BROWNMILLER, *supra* note 20, at 38.
50. Seifert, *supra* note 42, at 62.
51. Genocide Convention, *supra* note 48, art. 2.
52. *See* NORMAN CIGAR, GENOCIDE IN BOSNIA: THE POLICY OF "ETHNIC CLEANSING" 59–60 (1995). *See also* Thomas Cushman & Stjepan G. Mestrovic, *Introduction* to THIS TIME WE KNEW: WESTERN RESPONSES TO GENOCIDE IN BOSNIA 1, 13–20 (Thomas Cushman & Stjepan G. Mestrovic eds., 1996).
53. Alexandra Stiglmayer, *The Rapes in Bosnia-Herzegovina, in* MASS RAPE, *supra* note 4, at 82, 85.
54. *Report of the Team of Experts on Their Mission to Investigate Allegations of Rape in the Territory of the Former Yugoslavia from 12 to 23 January 1993,* U.N. GAOR, 48th Sess., Annex II, ¶ 62, U.N. Doc. A/48/92-S/25341 (1993) [hereinafter *Expert Report*].
55. MacKinnon, *supra* note 43, at 187.
56. *Id.* at 188.
57. *Id.* at 191.

with her description of different patterns of rape that function as genocide in multiple ways.[58] However, although it seems possible to argue that rape is genocidal without referring to the intent to destroy a culture through forced impregnation,[59] Allen concludes that it is *primarily* forced impregnation that makes rape genocidal.[60] The view that rape as genocide hinges *solely* on evidence of a policy of forced impregnation is shared by several scholars. For example, Neier argues that short of forced impregnation it was "inappropriate to single out one element, rape, and assert that it, by itself, constituted genocide."[61]

Thus, forced impregnation served first to exacerbate the perceived atrocity of rape as a war crime and a crime against humanity. Secondly, it was relied upon to construct rape as genocidal. But several writers went a step further and addressed forced impregnation as a crime that is *distinct* from, rather than a mere addendum to, rape.

2.   Forced impregnation as a specific crime

In striving for analytical clarity, Copelon emphasized in her previously noted piece that "forced pregnancy must be seen as a separate offense."[62] According to Copelon, it is necessary to separate rape and forced impregnation because using forced impregnation merely to articulate rape as genocidal obscures the extent to which it may occur in non-genocidal contexts.[63] Anne Goldstein and Siobhan Fisher respectively take up Copelon's call to deal with forced impregnation explicitly and make further distinctions between rape and forced impregnation. For Goldstein, forced impregnation may, *but need not be*, the result of rape.[64] Additionally, Goldstein recog-

---

58. Allen describes three different "types" of rape in Bosnia: 1) public rape of women, children, and men in front of members of a community, 2) abduction, rape, and murder of women, and 3) detention and repeated rape with the intent to impregnate, then detention until abortions were impossible. ALLEN, *supra* note 4, at 62–63. *See also Final Report of the Commission of Experts Established Pursuant to Security Council Resolution 780 (1992)*, U.N. SCOR, U.N. Doc S/1994/674 (1994) (describing distinct patterns of rape in Bosnia).

59. Mass rape deals a significant blow to a victimized cultural entity by breaking up families, robbing raped women of access to marriage and reproduction in the future, condemning them to refugee life, and otherwise intimidating the community into fleeing. In a strongly patriarchal society, rape alone is powerful enough to interfere with the reproduction of the group because it marks the rape victims as unmarriageable.

60. ALLEN, *supra* note 4, at 91 (stating that "the *pregnancies*, and not the rapes alone, are a major weapon of the genocide") (emphasis in original).

61. NEIER, *supra* note 8, at 186. *See also* Siobhan Fisher, *Occupation of the Womb: Forced Impregnation as Genocide*, 46 DUKE L.J. 91, 125 (1996).

62. Copelon, *supra* note 22, at 203.

63. *Id.* at 203–08.

64. GOLDSTEIN, *supra* note 40, at 4. For example, in her note 7, Goldstein argues that forced insemination could be used: "It is easy to imagine, for example, an army that desires to

nizes that forced impregnation may be covered by parts of the Geneva Conventions that do not include rape, specifically, "compelling a [civilian] to serve in the forces of a hostile Power."[65] Drawing on Goldstein's ground-breaking piece, Fisher articulates the specific and distinct barbarity of forced impregnation and particularly the extent to which it is genocidal.[66] Beverly Allen also devotes a chapter of her book to forced impregnation specifically. Allen argues that forced impregnation should be conceptualized not under the umbrella of "mere" war crimes or genocide per se but as a form of biological warfare that is prohibited under Article 3 of the International Tribunal as a violation of the laws or customs of war.[67]

As a war crime, forced impregnation—either through its association with rape or by extension—can be encompassed under several grave breaches. It is a *form* of sexual assault;[68] it is an inhumane act;[69] it is an "indecent assault" under Article 76(1) and a "humiliating [and] degrading assault," under the Additional Protocols.[70] Also, forced impregnation "wilfully caus[es] great suffering or serious injury to body or health" because

---

impregnate women while protecting its soldiers from the possibility of HIV infection, and which therefore resorts to artificial insemination or other modern alternative methods of fertilizing eggs." *Id.* at 14 n.7. Indeed, Nazi medical experiments made use of what were then high-technology means of reproductive control, as Nazi doctors experimented with surgical and nonsurgical means of sterilizing concentration camp inmates. *See also* Telford Taylor, *Opening Statement of the Prosecution, December 9, 1946, in* The Nazi Doctors and the Nuremberg Code: Human Rights in Human Experimentation 67, 79–81 (George J. Annas & Michael A. Grodin eds., 1992); Koonz, *supra* note 44.

65. Goldstein, *supra* note 40, at 15 (quoting Fourth Geneva Convention, *supra* note 32, art. 147).
66. *See* Fisher, *supra* note 61.
67. *See* Allen, *supra* note 4, at 103–32.
68. Goldstein, *supra* note 40, at 15 ("[T]he proposed Statute for the International Tribunal, does not identify forced impregnation by name as a crime to be prosecuted (though 'enforced prostitution' and 'other forms of sexual assault' are identified in the Secretary General's Report as 'inhumane acts').").
69. *Id.*
70. *See* Fisher, *supra* note 61, at 100. Article 75(2) of the Protocol (I) Additional states:

The following acts are and shall remain prohibited at any time and in any place whatsoever, whether committed by civilian or by military agents:

(a) violence to the life, health, or physical or mental well-being of persons, in particular:

   (i) murder;

   (ii) torture of all kinds, whether physical or mental;

   (iii) corporal punishment; and

   (iv) mutilation;

(b) outrages upon personal dignity, in particular humiliating and degrading treatment, enforced prostitution and any form of indecent assault;

(c) the taking of hostages;

pregnancy and childbirth are potentially injurious or fatal.[71] In addition, great suffering may encompass moral as well as physical suffering, of which forced impregnation can be considered an example.[72] Furthermore, forced impregnation constitutes "compelling a civilian to serve in the forces of a hostile power" (Article 2(e))[73] and it is a violation of honor and family rights, which Goldstein reconceptualizes in terms of a woman's self-determination and personal dignity rather than male property rights.[74] Most fundamentally, it is an act of torture under Article 1 of the Torture Convention[75] because childbirth, even when not forced, is physically painful and the emotional impact of impregnation maximizes the trauma of rape.[76]

As a crime against humanity, forced impregnation must be shown to be widespread *or* systematic. It was certainly widespread in Bosnia; to be understood as a crime against humanity, evidence of an intentional policy is not necessary.[77] In a widespread context torture is a crime against humanity.[78] Fisher incorporates forced impregnation under "other inhumane acts."[79] In addition, Goldstein characterizes forced impregnation as a potential form of "enslavement" prohibited under Article 5(c) of the Nuremberg Charter on the basis that it entails the exercise of a power "attaching to the right of ownership."[80]

Constructing forced impregnation as genocide involved a number of components. If rape were genocidal without forced impregnation, in terms of reducing the marriageability of victims and the cohesiveness of the victimized community, forced impregnation made rape more visible and explicit, symbolically branding victims and precluding silence or denials.[81] Additionally, insofar as rape victims are members of the victimized

---

(d) collective punishments; and

(e) threats to commit any of the foregoing acts.

Protocol (I) Additional to the Geneva Conventions of 12 August 1949, and Relating to the Protection of Victims of International Armed Conflicts (Protocol 1), 8 June 1977, art. 75, ¶ 2, 1125 U.N.T.S. 3 (*entered into force* 7 Dec. 1978), *reprinted in* 16 I.L.M. 1391 (1977).

71. GOLDSTEIN, *supra* note 40, at 15.
72. *See* Fisher, *supra* note 61, at 99.
73. GOLDSTEIN, *supra* note 40, at 15.
74. *Id.* at 22.
75. Convention Against Torture and Other Cruel, Inhuman or Degrading Treatment or Punishment, *adopted* 10 Dec. 1984, G.A. Res. 39/46, U.N. GAOR, 39th Sess., Supp. No. 51, art. 1, U.N. Doc. A/39/51 (1985) (*entered into force* 26 June 1987), *reprinted in* 23 I.L.M. 1027 (1984), *substantive changes noted in* 24 I.L.M. 535 (1985).
76. GOLDSTEIN, *supra* note 40, at 17. *See generally id.* app. A.
77. *See* Copelon, *supra* note 22, at 203.
78. *See* GOLDSTEIN, *supra* note 40, at 16.
79. Fisher, *supra* note 61, at 102 (quoting Nuremberg Charter, *supra* note 27, art. 6(c)).
80. GOLDSTEIN, *supra* note 40, at 15, 25.
81. *See* GOLDSTEIN, *supra* note 40, at 23 ("[I]n a culture where rape is perceived as staining its victims, making single women unmarriageable and married women subject to rejection

group, the pregnancies as serious bodily [or] mental harm to them are genocidal.[82]

According to Fisher, the pregnancies themselves also serve directly in a genocidal capacity because they interfere with the reproduction of the victimized group. "When reproduction is used to proliferate members of one group and simultaneously to prevent the reproduction of members of another, it is a form of destruction."[83] Insofar as the pregnancies deliberately interfere with a group's reproduction, they are covered by the Genocide Convention under "prevent[ing] births within the group," a claim echoed by Jennifer Green and her colleagues.[84] They go even further, also arguing—paradoxically—that forced impregnation *additionally* constitutes "forcible removal of children from the group."[85] (The contradiction is glaring. To be forcibly removed *from* the victimized group, the children must be members *of* the group, but if they are members of the group then births within the group have been facilitated, not prevented.)

Unlike crimes against humanity, allegations of genocide require proof of intent to destroy a group.[86] Fisher is quick to distinguish between genocidal forced impregnation, which requires an intentional policy, and "mere" impregnation resulting from repeated rape.[87] Copelon cautions against equating forced impregnation with genocide because forced impregnation can also happen without explicit intent, in non-genocidal contexts, and should still be recognized as a crime.[88] But since evidence of intent *is* a pre-

---

by their husbands, like rape but to a greater degree, forced impregnation '[d]eliberately inflict[s] on the group conditions of life calculated to bring about its physical destruction.'"). *Id. See also* Pine, *supra* note 39; MacKinnon, *supra* note 44, at 190. Additionally, Wing and Merchán give a detailed analysis of the impact of mass rape on the Bosnian Muslim culture, although it should be noted that the rejection of raped women is a product of patriarchy in general, not merely of Muslim tradition. *See* Adrien Katherine Wing & Sylke Merchán, *Rape, Ethnicity, and Culture: Spirit Injury from Bosnia to Black America,* 25 Colum. Hum. Rts. L. Rev. 1 (1993).

82. Fisher, *supra* note 61, at 122–23; Goldstein, *supra* note 40, at 23; MacKinnon, *supra* note 43, at 188; Green et al., *supra* note 4, at 194; Koenig, *supra* note 4, at 137.

83. Fisher, *supra* note 61, at 120–21. According to Fisher, forced impregnation interferes with group reproduction in three ways:

First, women may be psychologically traumatized by the pregnancy and unable to have normal sexual or childbearing experiences with members of their own group. Second, women who are raped and bear the children of the aggressors may no longer be marriageable in their society. Third, the women, simply because they are pregnant with the children of the aggressors, cannot bear their own children during this time—their wombs are "occupied."

Id. at 93.

84. Green et al., *supra* note 4, at 194.

85. *Id. See also* Wing & Merchán, *supra* note 81, at 19–20.

86. *See* Genocide Convention, *supra* note 48, art. 2.

87. Fisher, *supra* note 61, at 125.

88. *See* Copelon, *supra* note 22, at 207.

requisite for genocidal acts, efforts to construct forced impregnation as genocide relied on evidence of intent. Hence, much fact-finding analysis was in fact focused on determining whether the rapes and/or the pregnancies were systematic or peripheral. Although controversy still exists,[89] ample evidence exists to support the argument that forced impregnation in Bosnia was intentional.[90]

Explaining the policy is trickier because, as Allen points out, the logic behind such a policy, as extrapolated by witnesses' accounts and Serb reports, is completely irrational.[91] Even if cultural identity were genetic (in the case of ethnicity in Bosnia, *only* religion matters, *unlike* elsewhere where race may be more important)[92] the baby would presumably get half its genes from its mother. How could Serbs believe that "making more babies with a people equals killing that people off"?[93] Allen argues that the act of rape is constructed so as to erase the victim's identity and leave her merely as a symbolic vessel of reproduction, so that the child will be born "fully" Serb.[94] An entrenched notion of patrilineal descent, coupled with Serb nationalist ideology, accounts for the apparent Serb belief that children of the rapes would grow up within the Muslim community while retaining allegiance to the Serb nation. In MacKinnon's analysis: "The babies made with Muslim and Croatian women are regarded as Serbian babies. The idea seems to be to create a fifth column within Muslim and Croatian society of children—all sons?—who will rise up and join their fathers. . . . This one is the ultimate achievement of the Nazi ideology that culture is genetic."[95]

---

89. *See* Neier, *supra* note 11, at 186 ("It is more likely that the talk of little Chetniks was a boast of their masculine triumph over their victims by claiming the potency to impregnate them."). The Serb authorities themselves have staunchly denied such allegations. For examples of Serb denials of rape, *see* Lance Morrow, *Unspeakable (Rape in Former Yugoslavia's Civil War)*, TIME, 22 Feb. 1993, at 48. *See also* Fisher, *supra* note 61, at 94 (for additional sources). Fisher adds that according to her sources, "captured Serb soldiers admitted that [forced impregnation] had taken place." *Id.* at 94 n.12.

90. For accounts of ethnic slurs uttered by rapists and their intent to impregnate their victims with "Serbian" children, see Stiglmayer, *supra* note 53, at 116–17, 131–37. Forced impregnation was one allegation by victims who brought suit against Radavan Karadzic under the Alien Tort Claims Act in the United States. *See* Fisher, *supra* note 61, at 127. Moreover, evidence that raped women were given pregnancy tests and prevented from gaining access to abortions also shows that the pregnancies were intentional. *See* Niarchos, *supra* note 2, at 657. Some women were cross-examined and accused of using birth control if they did not become pregnant. *See* Pine, *supra* note 40, at 15.

91. ALLEN, *supra* note 4, at 87.

92. *See* Diana Kapidzic & Aida Daidzic, *BISER: A Conversation with Bosnian Women Living in Exile*, 5 HASTINGS WOMEN'S L.J. 53, 56 (1994). For an analysis of how and why Bosnian Muslims (a confessional group linked to a broader transnational Muslim community) came to be conceptualized as a distinct ethnic group, see TONE BRINGA, BEING MUSLIM THE BOSNIAN WAY: IDENTITY AND COMMUNITY IN A CENTRAL BOSNIAN VILLAGE (1995).

93. ALLEN, *supra* note 4, at 87.

94. *See id.*

95. MacKinnon, *supra* note 43, at 191–92.

Fisher addresses the question of where such a policy could be logically founded by examining the history of Bosnia and the relationship of the Serbs to Croats and Muslims. She concludes that because these groups are racially identical and the only differentiating factors are religion and sense of identity, the Serbs are capable of believing precisely such illogic: "A Bosnian Muslim woman may be looked upon as perhaps inferior, but not as ethnically different. Children from her womb would be regarded as South Slavs— either Serb, Croat or some mix thereof. Hence, a Serb policy of forced impregnation could logically exist."[96]

All of these authors, however, miss the crucial point. It is not necessary for the *Serbs* to believe that the children will grow up Serb in order for them to plan a policy of forced impregnation. The success of the policy, and therefore its rationality as a tool of genocide, would hinge not on what identity *Serbs* ascribe to the children of the rapes but on how the *victimized* culture views the children. To function as genocide, the children (and the mothers who bore children "of the enemy") must be seen *by the group* as alien to the group. It is the rejection of raped mothers and their children that destabilizes and destroys the group, be it in Rwanda, Bangladesh, or Bosnia. In fact, there is clear evidence that this was the case in Bosnia.

3.   Recap

Forced impregnation was thus constructed as a component of rape-as-crime and as a specific crime itself, under the rubric of war crimes, crimes against humanity, and genocide. Despite the disagreements or conceptual ambiguities within these legal arguments, taken together, they played an important role in placing gender crimes on the agenda of the War Crimes Tribunal. Feminists gained leverage when the attention given to violence against women was reflected in the 1993 Vienna Declaration of the World Conference on Human Rights, which included references to "forced pregnancy" as well as rape and other crimes of gender.[97] In the debates over the wording of an incipient International Criminal Court, feminist leaders figured prominently and the issue of forced impregnation was a critical topic, no longer marginalized by male-oriented concerns. Although rape was not defined as genocide in the International Tribunal for the Former Yugoslavia,

---

96. Fisher, *supra* note 61, at 119–20.
97. The Conference agreed: "Violations of the human rights of women in situations of armed conflict are violations of the fundamental principles of international human rights and humanitarian law. All violations of this kind, including in particular murder, systematic rape, sexual slavery, and forced pregnancy, require a particularly effective response." *Report of the Drafting Committee, Addendum, Final Outcome of the World Conference on Human Rights,* U.N. GAOR, World Conf. on Hum. Rts., Agenda Item 13, at 23, U.N. Doc. A/CONF.157/DC/1/Add.1 (1993).

its counterpart in Rwanda recently issued the first international legal definition of rape, including its genocidal aspects.[98]

But despite the strengths and successes of these arguments, an important gap leaves them incomplete in addressing forced impregnation as a human rights abuse. The common thread in all of the legal arguments is that forced impregnation is a crime against women only. The following section addresses the linguistic devices through which *children* of the rapes were excluded, unconsciously or intentionally, from consideration.

B. The Children in the Discourse

Forced impregnation was described as a conscious policy to force women to conceive *and bear* children:

> [W]omen are raped frequently, perhaps numerous times each day. . . . Some captors say their *intention is to impregnate* the women, to make "Chetnik babies". . . . [T]he women were examined by gynecologists. If found to be pregnant, they were segregated, given special privileges, and *held* until their seventh month when it was *too late to obtain an abortion;* at that point, they were released.[99]

Clearly, in this instance, forced impregnation means the conception of a child as well as the birth of a child. Yet, in constructing forced impregnation as a crime, children were never addressed as victims. The literature marginalized their existence or contributed to their status as non-beings in a number of different ways. First, the literature defined forced impregnation carelessly, thus making a focus on more than one victim problematic. Secondly, human rights violations against children born of the rape were ignored or put to the side in descriptions of the atrocity of forced impregnation. Third, children were identified as non-Muslim, a social construction that placed them outside of the group against which genocide was being committed. By implication some authors explicitly categorized them as Serb children, thus placing them not only outside the victimized group, but in the perpetrating group. Therefore, children could be seen not just as non-victims but somehow as perpetrators. The legal discourse below will detail each of

---

98. The International Criminal Tribunal in Arusha, Tanzania, stated that "sexual violence, which includes rape, is not limited to physical invasion of the human body and may include acts which do not involve penetration or even physical contact" and explicitly stated that rape and sexual violence were "integral weapons in the intended destruction of the Tutsi ethnic group." *See* Heather Sokoloff, *A New Rape Definition Brings Justice to Survivors,* Ms., Apr./May 1999, at 18.

99. Niarchos, *supra* note 2, at 657. All italics in this section have been added by the author unless otherwise noted.

these patterns before proceeding to address forced impregnation through the lens of children's rights.

1.   (Non-)definitions of forced impregnation

The legal literature on "forced impregnation" contains diverse meanings. In fact, a number of analytically distinct concepts are embedded within the single term "forced impregnation." The first component of "forced impregnation," as discussed in the legal arguments, is the act of the rape/conception itself. Second, is the prevention of access to an abortion. Third, is the actual birth of a child. These are distinct events because different perpetrators and different victims may be involved at various stages. For example, it is the Serb rapist who is guilty of impregnation, but it may be either the same rapist or a third party, such as the Croatian government, who prevents abortion access. Additionally, these factors are not necessarily inclusive of one another, prevention of abortion results logically in a live birth, but rape/conception may not result in an impregnation. Further, the three concepts are distinct because the particular pain for a specific woman may depend on how many of these factors she experienced. The pain of childbirth and subsequent emotional trauma of abandoning or raising a child of rape[100] are specific to bearing a child, whereas other factors may apply to the process of gestating a pregnancy. Rape/conception, prevention of abortion access, and actual childbirth need to be considered distinctly for all these reasons.

To add to the analytical confusion, a number of different labels besides "forced impregnation" are scattered throughout the literature. Among these are "enforced pregnancy," "forced pregnancy," "compelled pregnancy," "forced maternity," and "forced birthing." However the various labels were never systematically attached to distinct concepts, either within specific articles or throughout the literature, in order to bring about the sort of linguistic clarity that is especially needed to distinguish between women's and children's rights. The lack of a clear distinction between different components of "forced impregnation" explains some of the semantic contradictions in the writings as well as the tendency for feminists and the papacy to talk past one another on whether to treat it as a crime.[101] To elucidate this problem while avoiding directly addressing it, I will henceforth bracket "forced impregnation" with quotations when referring to the way it was used in the literature. My own definition of forced impregnation, sans quote marks, will be limited to rape with conception. For prevention of abortion access, I suggest "enforced pregnancy" as a concept distinct from "forced

---

100. See GOLDSTEIN, *supra* note 40, at 18.
101. See *infra* notes 112 and accompanying text.

impregnation." In addition, for the unique trauma of forced childbirth, I suggest "forced maternity." Although these distinctions may in fact be overly meticulous in regards to gender crimes, they become highly salient when considering forced impregnation as a crime against a child.

Consider, for example, the following description of "forced impregnation," "Croatian and Muslim women are being *raped, and then denied abortions,* to help make a Serbian state by making Serbian babies."[102] Two concepts are listed here; (1) the act of rape with intent to impregnate, and (2) the denial of abortions. I assert that MacKinnon places both acts under the same label in order to argue that "forced impregnation" is genocidal. Goldstein, at first, attempts a more careful definition: "'Forced impregnation' can be defined as an impregnation that results from an assault or series of assaults on a woman perpetrated with the intent that she become pregnant."[103] But later, in arguing why "forced impregnation" should be seen as torture, she writes: "The woman who is *forced to carry a rapist's* child *to term* is . . . humiliated and violated."[104] Again, the author is conflating all three concepts under the umbrella term of "forced impregnation."[105]

However, where abortion is available, the crime of rape with intent to impregnate is distinct from the crime of preventing access to an abortion. This becomes crucial when asking whether the child of rape is a victim. Because the right-to-life for unborn children is still contested in international law,[106] the argument that the child of rape is a victim of human rights violations only makes legal sense for born children. Although it seems that many born children resulted from these rapes, the majority of possible pregnancies most likely resulted in abortions.[107] In this context then, collapsing both cases into one legal term is confusing. In regards to children's rights,

---

102. MacKinnon, *supra* note 43, at 191 (emphasis added).
103. GOLDSTEIN, *supra* note 40, at 4.
104. *Id.* at 17.
105. A similar pattern is evident in most of the literature. *See, e.g.,* Niarchos, *supra* note 2, at 657. Niarchos stated that

> women are *raped* frequently, perhaps numerous times each day. . . . Some captors say their *intention is to impregnate* the women. . . . [T]he women were examined by gynecologists. If found to be pregnant, they were segregated, given special privileges, and *held* until . . . it was *too late to obtain an abortion;* at that point, they were released.

> *Id.* (footnotes omitted) (emphasis added).

106. Though some may argue that, by distinguishing between born and unborn children, I am negating potential fetal rights to life, it is not my intent to take a side in the abortion debate here. Whether or not fetuses should or will have rights in the future, it is still important to distinguish between children who are born and those unborn because their specific rights and relationships to all parties are different in the two cases. I focus on born children because the debate over the unborn is already well underway and does not require a digression here.
107. *See* Sullivan & Hammer, *supra* note 5, at 50 (discussing Bosnia).

some distinction must be made between forced impregnations that result in live births and those that do not.

Several authors seemed to recognize this confusion and provided more careful analytical labels for the various elements of the crime. Under the auspices of the International Women's Human Rights Clinic of City University of New York, Green and her colleagues jointly presented a proposal to the judges of the International Criminal Tribunal in which they distinguished between rape, "forced impregnation," and forced maternity:

> Rape, forced impregnation and forced maternity should be explicitly recognized as "grave breaches" under Article 2 [of the Geneva Convention] . . . [and] as violations of the laws and customs of war under Article 3.[108]

This distinction is helpful here because it separates impregnation (the conception of an embryo) and maternity (birth of a child). The former precludes an analysis of children's rights under existing international law, whereas the latter does not. Nonetheless, the language of "maternity" is clearly applicable to the mother, not to the child. Whether these interpretations of the law also apply to the children of the rape cannot be determined unless more explicitly specified, even when they are not explicitly denied. Moreover, beyond this one sentence, the authors are not clear about the analytical or legal distinctions between these crimes. Later in the same piece, the specific definitions of the various offenses do not include a definition of forced maternity as a specific crime, though rape and "forced impregnation" are clearly defined.[109]

Even if the terms had remained analytically distinct within the scope of that one paper, the term "forced maternity" (or any other term specifically denoting childbirth after rape) was never appropriated by other authors (or by the Tribunal). The term "forced impregnation" remained dominant and was vicariously used by scholars to describe conception, pregnancy, and childbirth. Other terms (compelled pregnancy, forced pregnancy, enforced pregnancy) were scattered interchangeably throughout the literature. "Forced pregnancy" was the synonymous term appropriated by human rights advocates and international bodies. In the Vienna Declaration condemning the atrocities in Bosnia, it is "forced pregnancy" that is condemned.[110] "Forced pregnancy" was also used by MacKinnon when she invoked the Alien Tort Claims Act and sued Radovan Karadivic, then traveling to the United States on diplomatic business, on behalf of several rape

---

108. Green et al., *supra* note 4, at 186–87.
109. *Id.* at 192–93.
110. Vienna Declaration and Programme of Action, U.N. GAOR, World Conf. on Hum. Rts., 48th Sess., 22d plen. mtg., part I, U.N. Doc. A/CONF.157/24 (1993), *reprinted in* 32 I.L.M. 1661 (1993).

victims now residing in the United States.[111] "Enforced pregnancy" also appears occasionally in early writings on genocidal rape. The term was used exclusively by Allen in her description of "forced impregnation" as genocide. "Enforced pregnancy" became the major term of contention in debates over the wording of the Rome Statute of the International Criminal Court in 1998.[112]

At the Rome Conference the idea of "forced impregnation" (as rape, prevention of abortion, and childbirth) became conflated with the international abortion debate (concerning the prevention of abortion, if understood as a distinct crime). In response, the random and interchangeable use of these terms throughout the literature resulted in born children's rights being confused with alleged rights of unborn children. At the Rome Conference, the Women's Caucus and the Interfaith Caucus went head to head for several months over whether to consider "enforced pregnancy" a crime. The term, which had previously been used interchangeably with "forced impregnation," became the feminist symbol for rape with intent to impregnate. They argued that the term would not necessarily imply that abortion restriction was a human rights violation. But for the interfaith network, led by the papacy, the term symbolized primarily restricted abortion access, which it was unwilling to consider as a crime even in order to prevent rape. Distinguishing between the two acts, rather than conflating them, might have mitigated this standoff.[113]

Yet, it can be argued that the equation of forced impregnation, enforced pregnancy, and forced maternity under the blanket concept of "forced impregnation" is unproblematic in regards to women. After all, one might argue, enforced pregnancy was a result of many forced impregnations; and enforced pregnancy implies forced maternity; so forced impregnation also potentially results in forced maternity. In terms of defining "forced impregnation" as a crime against women, perhaps these distinctions are not required. This certainly appears to be the consensus among legal scholars framing "forced impregnation" as a crime. However, because the distinctions are *absolutely* required for framing "forced impregnation" as a crime against children, the conflation of these various concepts serves to preclude an analysis of children's rights altogether, defining the act as a crime against only one person.

---

111. *See* Yolanda S. Wu, *Genocidal Rape in Bosnia: Redress in United States Courts Under the Alien Tort Claims Act,* 4 UCLA Women's L.J. 101, 107, 109 n.46 (1993).

112. On the evolution of this debate, see Fax Archives of the Catholic Family and Human Rights Institute, *available at* <http://cafhri.org/FAX/current_fax.html> (visited 3 Feb. 2000), especially those faxes dated 6 Apr., 19 June, 26 June, & 10 July 1998 (hereinafter Fax Archives). On the International Criminal Court generally, see <http://www.un.org/icc/index.htm> (updated 1 Feb. 2000).

113. *See* Fax Archives, *supra* note 112.

In order to extricate the rights of the children from the abortion debate one must distinguish between impregnations resulting in abortion and those resulting in live births. "Forced impregnation" was equated in one context with rape and in the other with abortion rights. The language of abortion rights applied to a situation in which both women and *born* children are involved focuses attention onto women's reproductive freedom and *unborn* children's rights, and away from the born child—she is reduced to a fetus whether she was in fact born or not. Dealing with the nuanced aspects of forced impregnation, enforced pregnancy, and forced maternity under the umbrella term "forced impregnation" or, by use of a variety of interchangeable terms, inhibited analytical clarity. This approach also obfuscated the presence of the child as a subject because addressing the child as a subject would necessitate more careful definitions than were ever used.

2. Obscuring children

In addition to defining "forced impregnation" in such a way as to preclude consideration of the children, scholars who constructed "forced impregnation" as a crime further marginalized war-rape orphans as victims by simply failing to address them.

Systematic neglect of children's rights in accounts of rape was clearly the case in treatments of "forced impregnation" as a war crime. As noted above, war crimes are those acts that are considered "grave breaches" of the Geneva Conventions. Rape is interpreted as being covered under the proscriptions of torture, ill-treatment, or willfully causing serious injury to body or health.[114] Fisher and Goldstein both address "forced impregnation" under the same headings.[115] "Forced impregnation" is torture because it maximizes the pain of rape.[116] It is additionally a grave breach under the rubric of "inhuman treatment" or "wilfully causing great suffering or serious injury to body or health."[117] "Forced impregnation" is also a "humiliating, degrading and indecent assault" and thus falls under the Additional Protocols I and II to the Geneva Conventions.[118] But the extent to which "forced impregnation" may culminate in humiliating, degrading, or inhuman treatment of a born child is not considered. Though it may be a legal stretch to consider a child's rights under grave breaches, when Goldstein describes "forced impregnation" as a war crime in older terms of "family rights,"[119] the elision of children's rights from the equation becomes more glaring.

---

114. *See* Green et al., *supra* note 4, at 186.
115. *See* Goldstein, *supra* note 40, at 16; Fisher, *supra* note 61, at 99.
116. *See* Goldstein, *supra* note 40, at 17.
117. *Id.* at 18–19.
118. Fisher, *supra* note 61, at 99.
119. *See* Goldstein, *supra* note 40, at 19–22 (for a fascinating reinterpretation of Article 27 of

Crimes against humanity differ from war crimes in that they can take place during peacetime as well as conflict, and they must be widespread and systematic. Populations, not individuals, must be victimized and government intent is necessary. In terms of intent and scope, "forced impregnation" certainly seems to fit the bill. "Forced impregnation" has been labeled a crime against humanity under the rubric of enslavement, as it "entails the exercise of a power viewed by the captor as attaching to the right or fact of ownership."[120] Additionally feminists have asked the International Tribunal to prosecute crimes based on gender as crimes against humanity.[121] This request is in keeping with the feminist position that gender is a category that should be recognized in human rights law in terms of specific crimes; "rape, forced prostitution and forced pregnancy constitute war crimes and crimes against humanity because they are crimes of gender hatred, violence, discrimination, and dehumanization perpetrated against women as a class."[122] Although this is an indisputable argument, the same argument can certainly be, but has not been, applied to children-born-of-rape as a group (or illegitimate children more generally).

It is not true that writers never mentioned the children, but it is illustrative to take note of the context and extent of the writing that did take into account their existence or plight (exactly three instances by my count):

> What would happen to [the Serb rapists] years from now, when the generation of babies created by this mass rape were adults? Would there not be a tidal wave of revenge? It all depends . . . on how the societies in which these children are raised represent the situation that produced them. And, from the point of view of the children, everything depends on whether their home societies accept the Serb ideology and consider them Serbs, and thus enemies, or whether they treat them as the innocent results of a policy for which they cannot be held responsible.[123]

Allen addresses this as part of constructing "forced impregnation" as biological warfare. Allen questions whether, like other forms of biological warfare, "forced impregnation" contains any possibility of a "blowback" effect.[124] At first, she writes no because "by definition, [Serb rapists] can

---

the Fourth Geneva Convention, which provides that "[p]rotected persons are entitled, in all circumstances, to respect for their persons, their honour, [and] their family rights. . . ." Fourth Geneva Convention, *supra* note 32, art. 27).

120. GOLDSTEIN, *supra* note 40, at 26.
121. *See* Kapidzic & Daidzic, *supra* note 92, at 67.
122. Memorandum from the International Women's Human Rights Clinic of CUNY Law School, *Gender Justice and the Constitution of the War Crimes Tribunal Pursuant to Security Council Resolution 808* (n.d.), *reprinted in* 5 HASTINGS WOMEN'S L.J. 235, 236 (1994).
123. ALLEN, *supra* note 4, at 132.
124. *See id.*

never get pregnant themselves."[125] She then considers the possibility of
vengeful war-rape orphans. Allen's point about the manner in which the
children are treated by the societies in which they are embedded goes to the
fundamental issue regarding the children, but she declines to address that
point in depth.

Adrien Wing and Sylke Merchán also wonder about the fate of the
children:

> One can only speculate as to how a generation of such children will fare, liv-
> ing among people who have just concluded a "brutal war in which the purity,
> and indeed the very survival, of nationalities has been held so consciously in
> the fore."[126]

Wing and Merchán, more than some scholars whose approach is strictly
legality-oriented, appear to be thinking harder about the use of identity in
conflict and the manner in which identity politics are manipulated to wound
or destroy the "spirit" of a cultural group. They provide a salient context
for addressing both the tenuous status of war-rape orphans within the context of the ethnic conflict and the impact of their existence as variables
in an ongoing relocation of ethnic and civic identity in post-war Bosnia. But,
beyond these lines, they fail to discuss war-rape orphans as ontological
beings directly or place their speculations in the context of human rights
law.

Taking momentary notice of children's plight and subsequently turning
back to the "more pressing" concerns of gender crimes seems to represent a
conscious subordination of children's to women's issues. Children may be
tacitly acknowledged as victims, but their rights are never articulated directly
within any legal framework. Instead, they are footnoted and marginalized,
their fate is reduced to an interesting issue to ponder rather than as a set of
crimes to observe and address.

This approach seems analogous to treating rape as a grievance against
male property rights, spelling out in detail the trauma to the man, and then
noting as an aside whether the raped women herself is not additionally traumatized as a result of the rape.[127] Such antiquated sexist hubris, which fem-

---

125. *Id.*
126. Wing & Merchán, *supra* note 81, at 20 (footnote omitted).
127. It might be said that this is a false analogy precisely because the male trauma of a property offense (vis-à-vis the rape victim) is insignificant compared to the real trauma of a
raped woman (vis-à-vis a child of rape). The author believes that this analogy holds, however, because there are many analyses that suggest that the trauma to a male of having a
female family member raped is a very real humiliation against male pride and esteem
even when situated as "merely" a property crime. *See* Seifert, *supra* note 42, at 59 (discussing the function of rape as a communication of humiliation between men). Beyond
the idea of ruined property, Folnegovic-Smalc discusses emotional trauma of male family members under the broader category of "indirect victimization." Folnegovic-Smalc,
supra note 37, at 177. Goldstein writes,

inist human rights scholars have so adeptly challenged,[128] is replicated in reference to children. They are first, as fetuses, understood only in terms of their mother's sovereignty over "her" body;[129] once born, their existence is noted primarily in order to enunciate the plight of the mothers:

> The woman . . . is placed in the unique position of either abandoning a child that is half hers or raising a child that is half her rapist's. All of her options entail anguish; the more one considers her situation; the more difficult it becomes. On the one hand, the baby was conceived in violence and hatred. On the other hand, it has grown inside her for nine months and is itself innocent of wrong-doing. A woman may have mixed feelings about the baby, and find that she is unable either to wholly love it or wholly despise it. Once it is born, the woman must either try to repress her loathing and revulsion and raise the child with love, perhaps with every feature of her assailant imprinted on the child's face as a constant reminder of her violation, or else she must give in to her revulsion and part with an innocent child that is her own flesh and blood. If her culture has now branded her unmarriagable because of the rape, she may also be giving up the only child she will ever have.[130]

While these are certainly legitimate points, and the mother's anguish in regards to the child is rightly part of constructing "forced impregnation" as a crime against her, the fact that such paragraphs are the *only* mention of the children in this legal discourse is disturbing.

3.   The children as Serbian/non-Muslim/perpetrator

Constructing "forced impregnation" as *genocide* required linking "forced impregnation" to any or all of the following genocidal acts: 1) intent to destroy, in whole or part, a national, religious, or ethnic group; 2) killing,

---

men, too, are injured by the sexual assault of women for reasons untainted by offensive, antiquated notions of chastity and ownership. To watch helplessly as someone you love is tortured may be as bad or worse than being tortured yourself, and international law should be able to reach and punish such harms.

GOLDSTEIN, *supra* note 40, at 22.

128. *See, e.g.,* V. Spike Peterson, *Whose Rights? A Critique of the Givens in Human Rights Discourse,* 15 ALTERNATIVES: SOC. TRANSFORMATION & HUMANE GOVERNANCE 303 (1990); Nancy Kim, *Toward a Feminist Theory of Human Rights: Straddling the Fence Between Western Imperialism and Uncritical Absolutism,* 25 COLUM. HUM. RTS. L. REV. 49 (1993); Marysia Zalewski, 'Well, What Is the Feminist Perspective on Bosnia?,' 71 INT'L AFF. 339 (1995). On applying feminist theory to children's rights, see Anne McGillivray, *Reconstructing Child Abuse: Western Definition and Non-Western Experience, in* THE IDEOLOGIES OF CHILDREN'S RIGHTS 213 (Michael Freeman & Philip Veerman eds., 1992).
129. *See* Jean-Bethke Elshtain, *Rethinking Sovereignty, in* POST-REALISM: THE RHETORICAL TURN IN INTERNATIONAL RELATIONS 171 (Francis A. Beer & Robert Hariman eds., 1996).
130. GOLDSTEIN, supra note 40, at 17–18. This pattern is also indicative of news reports regarding the war-rape orphans. For example, Daniela Horvath's article titled *The Children of the Rapes: Young Victims of 'Ethnic Cleansing,' supra* note 5, is composed *primarily* of references to the mothers' psychological trauma and victimization.

causing serious harm, or inflicting conditions calculated to bring about the group's destruction; 3) imposing measures to prevent births within the group; or 4) forcibly transferring children of the group to another group.[131] Whereas children were ignored in detailing "forced impregnation" as a war crime and crime against humanity, overt references to the child of rape were made throughout the arguments on "forced impregnation" as genocide. But by placing the child outside of the group against which genocide was being committed, these references distanced the idea of the war-rape orphan from the image of victim and categorized the orphans instead with the ethnic group perpetuating the genocide.

In most of the writing on "forced impregnation," the babies are referred to in some way as non-Muslim: "Croatian and Muslim women are being raped . . . to help make a Serbian state by making *Serbian* babies;"[132] "a woman who is forcibly impregnated must perform . . . the gestation of *her captor's* child;"[133] "impregnat[ing] women with children *of another ethnicity* . . . [is a] measure 'intended to prevent births within the group.' "[134]

This placing of the child into her father's ethnic category reifies the highly contradictory Serb logic that led to the policy of "forced impregnation," a mistake that Beverly Allen notices. "The Serb policy of genocidal rape aimed at pregnancy offers the specter that making more babies with a people equal killing that people off. This illogic is possible only because the policy's authors erase all identity characteristics of the mother other than that as a sexual container."[135] Allen goes on to argue that many feminist analyses have reified this mistake by failing to recognize it and have thus "also erased all the victims' identities but the sexual."[136] But in her critique, Allen explicitly identifies the victims as the mothers and the mothers' bodies alone as the battlefield on which the war of identities is fought. What is equally true is that the logic of Serb ethnicity for the baby also erases half of *her* identity and precludes her inclusion in the group against which genocide is being committed.

By extension, identifying the war-rape orphan as Serb categorizes her as a member of the perpetrating group. Perhaps this explains Allen's subsequent logic of reducing the child of rape to a tool of biological warfare: the fetus "attacks" womens' reproductive systems, causes "atrocious physical pain, mental suffering and often death."[137] While Allen describes impregna-

131. Genocide Convention, *supra* note 48, art. 2.
132. MacKinnon, *supra* note 43, at 191.
133. GOLDSTEIN, supra note 40, at 27.
134. Green et al., *supra* note 4, at 194.
135. ALLEN, *supra* note 4, at 87.
136. *Id.* at 88.
137. *Id.* at 131.

tion as biological warfare, and no doubt recognizes the innocence of the actual children, she reduces them to weapons of war and precludes their membership in the victimized group, even though she seems to believe they will indeed remain in the group. Instead, they remain in the group not as members and victims of genocide but as parasites, "unplanned children . . . taxing the target population for years, if not generations, to come."[138]

Allen is not alone in treating the war-rape orphan as one of the enemy. Fisher writes, "The forced carrying of a child *of the enemy* can certainly be interpreted as an injury to human dignity."[139] The papacy, which ironically opposed feminists on whether "forced impregnation" should be a crime, at least concurred on this point, saying, "The women should transform these acts of violence into acts of love by accepting *the enemy* within them."[140] Of course, although they are misleading, these statements are not obviously false; after all, the child is ethnically her father's as well as her mother's. But Fisher continues, for example, in her reasons for considering "forced impregnation" genocidal, "the women, simply because they are pregnant with the children of the aggressors, *cannot bear their own children* during this time— their wombs are 'occupied.'"[141] Here, the child is not just Serbian; she is explicitly *not* Muslim; she is not her mother's own child. According to Goldstein, a forcibly impregnated woman "is incapable of conceiving and bearing a child *of her own ethnicity.*"[142] The manipulation of the child's identity in feminist discourse on forced impregnation exactly echoes the given cultural schema. It reifies both the false logic of genetics that brought about the rapes and the patriarchal attitude that labels any child born of rape as automatically "other," rejected, stigmatized, and unwanted by the culture that claims the mother's reproductive identity.

For Wing and Merchán, assigning a Serb identity to the child is not necessary for denying them inclusion in the Muslim group. They refer to the children as non-Muslim but not necessarily Serb; they are in a "ethnic/religious limbo . . . some unrecognized 'mixed' ethnicity that is not likely to be accepted among Muslims or Serbs."[143] To these authors' credit, they are careful to point out that they are describing the Bosnian Muslims' beliefs that the children are non-Muslim, and not imposing their own construction of the child's identity.[144] However, they base their assertion that the children will be seen by Bosnian Muslims as non-Muslim on some very strange

---

138. *Id.*
139. Fisher, *supra* note 61, at 99.
140. Horvath, *supra* note 5, at 12.
141. Fisher, *supra* note 61, at 93.
142. GOLDSTEIN, *supra* note 40, at 24.
143. Wing & Merchán, *supra* note 81, at 20.
144. *See id.* at 11 n.56.

sources. For example, they write that "[u]nder Islamic law and Muslim culture, the ethnicity of Muslim children is determined by the ethnicity of the father."[145] At least three things are wrong with this statement. First, any Muslim scholar will explain that Islamic law and Muslim culture seldom coincide.[146] Second, there is not a single interpretation of Islamic law or a monolithic Muslim culture.[147] Though Wing and Merchán cite some Islamic legal sources, these sources represent a very narrow view of Islam (they are primarily authored by Western scholars).[148] Third, this statement suggests that Muslim identity is an ethnic category, one that Islamic scholars believe is genetic in the same sense as in the Judaic tradition. This is not the case. Although Bosnian Muslims have been constructed by Western, Serb, and local sources as an ethnic group, they are in fact a religious group of the same pan-Slavic ethnicity as Bosnian Orthodox Christians (whom we call Bosnian Serbs) and Bosnian Catholics (whom we call Bosnian Croats).[149]

But the logic of Wing and Merchán's statement, however sloppily supported, ultimately does not rest on Islamic legal texts or some amorphous "Muslim" culture; it is a question of whether the Bosnian Muslims as a distinct group will accept the children. This question has nothing to do with whether the children are raised in the Islamic faith, so "non-Muslim" is an erroneous label. It has everything to do with notions (wholly baseless in terms of genetic difference) of ethnic purity and of patriarchal control over reproduction within a group. I will return to an analysis of the social construction of the children's identity (in Bosnia) in the final section; here I am focusing on the scholarly construction of their identity within the legal texts on "forced impregnation." Within this context, it is surprising to see numerous feminist scholars reify, rather than question, the patriarchal and nationalist agenda that is manifested in a rejection by Muslims of children born to genocidal rape victims.

Or *is* it surprising? Some light can be shed on the issue by recalling the context in which these arguments were made. Scholars were trying to situ-

---

145. *Id.* at 18.
146. For general information on Islam and Muslims, see THE MUSLIM ALMANAC: A REFERENCE WORK ON THE HISTORY, FAITH, CULTURE AND PEOPLES OF ISLAM (Azim Nanji ed., 1996).
147. Wing and Merchán apparently believe that a Muslim community is a Muslim community, because they support their statement about Muslim culture (in reference to Bosnia) with a citation titled "Law and Religion in the Muslim Middle East." *See* Wing & Merchán, *supra* note 81, at 18. It is surprising to me that they instead did not refer to ethnographic studies of the Bosnian Muslims in particular, such as Tone Bringa's *Being Muslim the Bosnian Way*. BRINGA, *supra* note 92. This suggests a misunderstanding of the nature of Muslim collective identity and the tension between a transnational "Islamic" community and particularistic, local Muslim communities.
148. Some less stereotypical interpretations of Islamic doctrine, written by actual Muslim scholars, can be found in LIBERAL ISLAM: A SOURCEBOOK (Charles Kurzman ed., 1998).
149. According to Bringa, there are in fact layered and contradictory identities among the Bosnian Muslims, which manifest themselves in official discourse as well as in rural life.

ate "forced impregnation" as genocide.[150] Their two bases for doing so were: 1) prevention of births within the group and 2) forcible transfer of children from one group to another.[151] No scholar considered that there is no clear agreement as to which group these children belong. Instead, a blanket identity was assigned to the child of rape according to whichever linguistic strategy would fit the requirements of the Genocide Convention.

To prove that forced impregnation prevented births within the group, a writer would have to prove that the child born was not a member "of the group." On a genetic basis this required delegitimizing a maternal genetic link, which reifies the patriarchal notion of patrilineal descent. The child could only be Bosnian Muslim if the father was Bosnian Muslim; the father was Serb, so the child was Serb or, at least, "non-Muslim." This appears to be Goldstein's argument; births are prevented because "[f]or at least the nine months it takes to carry the rapist's child to term, a woman is incapable of conceiving and bearing a child of her own ethnicity."[152] For those scholars who admitted the contingency of a child's cultural identity, the prevention-of-births argument required an assumption that the child be rejected by the group, something much easier to argue based on the evidence. This seems to be Wing and Merchán's argument, although it would have been better supported by evidence of systematic cultural stigma rather than appeals to historical Islamic doctrine.

But if the child is not a member of the group, having never been accepted by it, how could the child also be "forcibly transferred from the group to another?" Goldstein and Fisher both make one argument but not the other, which is at least logically consistent. Nevertheless, making both arguments at once apparently posed no problem for some scholars. Green and her colleagues uncritically argue that forced impregnation is genocidal on both accounts within the same sentence.[153] Wing and Merchán employ feats of semantic inconsistency, claiming first that the "resulting child will never be considered an ethnic Muslim, thereby preventing the birth of a Muslim child" and then that "the event of the birth of such a non-Muslim child resulting from rape transfers that child *from* the Muslim population *to* the non-Muslim population."[154] The reader may ponder the logic of these statements.

The linguistic confusion comes from translating Serbo-Croat terms for both religious and ethnic identity (*muslimani* and *Muslimani* respectively) into the same interchangeable English term, "Bosnian Muslim." See Bringa, *supra* note 92, at 10.

150. *See, e.g.,* Fisher, *supra* note 61; Allen, *supra* note 4; Goldstein, *supra* note 40, at 22–24.
151. *See* Fisher, *supra* note 61, at 121 (quoting Genocide Convention, *supra* note 48, art. 2; Goldstein, *supra* note 40, at 23–24).
152. Goldstein, *supra* note 40, at 24.
153. *See* Green et al., *supra* note 4, at 194.
154. Wing & Merchán, *supra* note 81, at 19.

4.   Recap

Constructions of forced impregnation as a war crime, and as a crime against humanity, remained silent about children and in doing so marginalized them. Women were seen as the victims; children of rape were seen as irrelevant. Constructions of forced impregnation as genocide acknowledged and depended on the child's presence but treated the child not as a member of the victimized group but as either a non-victim or a member of the perpetrating group. Here, the group is the victim, the child is the perpetrator.

Consequently, scholars have failed to address forced impregnation as an abuse against children as well as women. Such a discourse precludes the child of rape from being conceptualized as a victim of genocide on behalf of membership in the victimized group. It underscores and treats as natural the unwantedness of the child on the part of the receiving culture, rather than questioning the patriarchal agenda behind it.[155] This combination of "natural" hate for the child and identification of the child with the enemy also produces indifference toward the fate of the children. This indifference has been expressed as lack of attention to widespread abandonment, neglect, or abuse, as well as outright justifications of infanticide such as in Allen's remark: "Many attempt to kill their babies at birth in a reaction that, speaking in terms of the mother's psychological well-being, *might even be considered healthy.*"[156]

III.   SURFACING CHILDREN: TOWARDS REDRESS FOR CHILDREN OF RAPE

I will henceforth be breaking with the previous literature on "forced impregnation" in two key respects. First, as mentioned above, a discussion of children's rights will require a careful redefinition of "forced impregnation," including distinctions between its various components and the addition of a new legal term that captures the situation of a child of rape, as opposed to

---

155. In fact not all of the children were abandoned by their mothers or the Muslim community, though certainly the majority were. The focus of feminist writing is on the ideal-type raped woman who hates her child, not on those who choose to raise their children. This is in keeping with the mainstream (and statistically inaccurate) notion in Western abortion-rights discourse that a raped woman never wants to raise her child. On abortion discourse, see CELESTE-MICHELLE CONDIT, DECODING ABORTION RHETORIC (1990); JAMES D. HUNTER, BEFORE THE SHOOTING BEGINS: SEARCHING FOR DEMOCRACY IN AMERICA'S CULTURE WARS (1994). On abortion preference among raped women, see Sandra Makhorn, *Pregnancy and Sexual Assault, in* THE PSYCHOLOGICAL ASPECTS OF ABORTION 55 (David Mall & Walter Watts eds., 1979).

156. ALLEN, *supra* note 4, at 99.

a rape victim. Second, I will use the Serbo-Croat, rather than English labels, to refer to the Bosnian Muslims, this will distinguish between Bosnian Muslims as an ethnic group (*Bosjnaks*), Bosnian Muslims as members of a multi-ethnic Bosnian civic nationality (*Bosanacs*), and Bosnian Muslims as Muslims (*muslimani*), in the sense of being members of a universalist, transnational, multi-ethnic religious community.[157] When I use the term "Muslim community" I am *not* refering to Bosnian Muslims (*muslimani*) but to the transnational Muslim *ummah* as represented by Islamic scholars in international legal bodies and non-governmental organizations. These distinctions are necessary because all of the various ways of relating war-rape orphans to the *ethnic* group "Bosnian Muslim" contradict one another.

A. Toward a Children's Rights View of Forced Impregnation

1. Reconceptualizing definitions of forced impregnation

Though several scholars have claimed that systematic forced impregnation is an unprecedented aspect of contemporary world politics,[158] this is untrue.[159] It should also be emphasized that orphans of genocidal war-rape are not the only children in the international arena to lose their identity by virtue of geopolitical events surrounding their birth.[160] Widespread literature on the use of women's reproductive capacity as an ethnomarker implies this

---

157. For a detailed analysis of the evolving meaning and importance attached to these terms, see Bringa, *supra* note 92, at 32–35.

158. See Allen, *supra* note 4, at 91. See also Silva Meznaric, *Gender as an Ethno-Marker: Rape, War, and Identity Politics in the Former Yugoslavia, in* Identity Politics & Women: Cultural Reassertions and Feminisms in International Perspective 76 (Valentine M. Moghadam ed., 1994).

159. Forced impregnation as a tool of genocide is not unprecedented. As recently as 1971, thousands of outcast children were born as a result of genocidal rapes of Bengali women by the West Pakistani army. See Brownmiller, *supra* note 20, at 79–83. The case of these children may have been more dismal than in Bosnia because, due to the greater racial stratification between the victimized and perpetrator groups, the children were visibly, as well as socially, marked for exclusion. Forced impregnation was also used in the American South to breed slave children and lighten the African race. See Wing & Merchán, *supra* note 81, at 25–38. Defoe's poem, quoted at the beginning of this paper, captures the use of forced impregnation in the development of an early British national identity. See also Goldstein, *supra* note 40, at 21 (discussing British use of rape to break the Scottish clan system). Stating that forced impregnation in Bosnia is unprecedented is especially odd because genocide was happening *simultaneously* in Rwanda and has produced several thousand children of genocidal rape. See James C. McKinley, Jr., *Legacy of Rwanda Violence: The Thousands Born of Rape,* N.Y. Times, 23 Sept. 1996, at A1.

160. For example, the breakup of Czechoslovakia left 1,200 Slovak babies living in Czech institutions systematically neglected and discriminated against, with no claims on

fact, but substantive research on the actual fate of such children, or their impact on the communities in which they are embedded, is nowhere to be found.[161] The plight of such children is not specific to ethnic conflicts, although it may take on a heightened meaning in international law when it involves such conflicts. A child of rape is stigmatized in most societies, regardless of the ethnic context in which the rape occurred. The willingness of many anti-abortion activists in the United States to concede to the right of abortion for victims of rape is an example of this.[162] More broadly, illegitimacy—whether by consensual sex or not—also brands children into a specific caste across historical and temporal space. In many cases, this results in conditions affecting these children that are wholly incompatible with advances in children's human rights and very different from the advantages enjoyed by "legitimate" children.[163] However, such a broad plight of children is difficult to treat as a matter of international law and only in certain cases does it result in such heightened public outrage as to warrant any sort of intervention or redress.

A precedent is clearer when the issue pertains directly to international affairs, and citizens of one state can make a claim against another.[164] The moral imperative to treat the child as a victim of crime may be easier to establish not when the state of illegitimacy is rooted in a specific cultural context, but when it results from an act of inter-ethnic violence designed to destabilize culture by manipulating a child's identity vis-à-vis his community. In other words, a denial of a child's right that is untouchable by international law in a domestic context may become salient where the surrounding context is already treated as within the reach of war crimes tribunals.

---

citizenship rights. *See* Timea Spitkova, *Slovakia Is Accused of Handpicking the 'White' Children for Repatriation,* Prague Post, 18 Apr. 1995 at 1.

161. Much attention was given to the Bengali rapes, for example, but the author has been unable to find any studies tracking the fate or well-being of the children born of those rapes.

162. It is interesting to note that the idea of "forced impregnation" as a crime distinct from rape has never been applied in any domestic context. For example, whereas a woman can prosecute her attacker for rape in the United States, there is no additional redress if she is impregnated as a result. Judging from the framing of forced impregnation discourse in international law, we may assume that were there such a legal mechanism, the redress would be for the woman and not framed in terms of the child's rights (financial support, for example, would be mitigated by the rapist father's imprisonment, unless the state were to provide a stipend). An entire debate can be imagined regarding whether forced impregnation can result in forced maternity even where pregnancy is not enforced by the state. The ramifications for "forced impregnation" discourse go beyond genocidal rape, and, taken to the level of children's rights, it may involve—in a domestic context—changes in the civil and criminal law and in cultural attitudes toward children of rape victims.

163. *See, e.g.,* Marnia Lazreg, The Eloquence of Silence 178 (1994).

164. *See* Karen Parker & Jennifer F. Chew, *Compensation for Japan's World War II War-Rape Victims,* 17 Hastings Int'l & Comp. L. Rev. 497 (1994).

Who is to be held accountable, how redress is to be allocated, or how the interests of these children are to be calculated are trickier matters. Crucial is the recognition that "forced impregnation" is a different crime from the perspective of the child conceived than it is from the perspective of the female rape victim. This requires detachment from the discourse of women's violation and engagement with the standpoint of the child vis-à-vis state and international law. Redefining the interests, and therefore the applicable rights of an involved group, reconceptualizes the treatment of a crime that may have been distorted by the dominant discourse's focus on particular groups. This was precisely the task of feminists in defining rape as a human rights abuse; feminists saw themselves as reacting to and destabilizing the dominant patriarchal discourse. In regards to rape as genocide, however, illuminating the perspective of the children situates feminist discourse itself as hegemonic and exclusionary, thus necessitating a further reconceptualization.

Let us begin by defining the term. As indicated above, the various labels, "forced impregnation," "forced maternity," "enforced pregnancy," "forced pregnancy," and "compelled pregnancy," all focus attention away from the child and are not defined well enough to admit children's rights into the discourse.

As to a definition of *forced impregnation* we can begin, though we cannot end, with Goldstein's:

> 'Forced impregnation' can be defined as an impregnation that results from an assault or series of assaults on a woman perpetrated with the intent that she become pregnant. The assault will generally take the form of rape, although it could take other forms.[165]

The key elements in the definition are that pregnancy occurs, that rape is only one possible method, and that intent to impregnate is crucial. The definition is helpful in separating forced impregnation as a crime from the crime of rape, which is important because some have claimed forced impregnation is not a crime in itself but merely a byproduct of rape.[166] But the focus on intent is simultaneously helpful and limiting. On the one hand, it enables Goldstein to suggest that an "assault should be punishable as attempted forced impregnation even if it does not result in a pregnancy, so long as the intent to impregnate can be established."[167] What it also means however is that pregnancies resulting from rape in which there was no

---

165. Goldstein, *supra* note 40, at 4. Indeed, Nazi medical experiments made use of what were then high technology means of reproductive control, as Nazi doctors experimented with surgical and nonsurgical means of sterilizing concentration camp inmates. *See* Taylor, *supra* note 64, at 79–81.

166. Neier, *supra* note 11, at 182.

167. Goldstein, *supra* note 40, at 4.

explicit intent are not included in the definition of the crime, regardless of how obviously they have been "forced" upon the woman. It means that many women who were raped and *not* impregnated may be victims of "forced impregnation," but that many women who *were* impregnated were in fact "merely" raped. According to Copelon, "As a result, the risk of pregnancy in all rape is treated not as an offense, but as a sequela."[168]

A child born of rape cannot be classified as a victim of *rape* by any scope of imagination. The child can only be classified as a victim of the rapist by virtue of forced impregnation or some similar concept. Therefore making intent so crucial to the definition of forced impregnation automatically negates a child's status as rights-bearer because it includes not all children born of rape but only those whose fathers intended them to be born. From the child's perspective, this may or may not have anything to do with the treatment it receives after it is born. The idea of intent only becomes pertinent when linking forced impregnation to genocide—on the basis of the intent clause in the Genocide Convention. It should not be understood as a necessary part of the definition of forced impregnation itself.

Hence I will borrow only portions of Goldstein's definition. *I describe forced impregnation as an impregnation that results from an assault or series of assaults on a woman, generally but not necessarily taking the form of rape.*

This definition is not intended to be a catch-all for the scope of victimization involved. Other elements of the crime deserve their own definitions and labels, particularly if one intends to bring the rights of a born child into the picture. Forced impregnation need not result in the birth of a child. Whether it does or not is dependent on a) the mother's willingness to carry the child to term and b) the availability of abortion if she is not willing. I will use the label *enforced pregnancy* to describe the act, undertaken by governments or individuals, of forcing a woman who has been forcibly impregnated to carry her child to term.[169]

Enforced pregnancy, occurring subsequent to forced impregnation, is likely to—though may not—result in a live birth. In terms of the distinctiveness of this crime from a woman's perspective, giving birth as a result of forced impregnation shall be called *forced maternity*. This definition seems to capture what Green and her colleagues meant by the term, although, oddly, they neglected to define it themselves. Forced maternity is distinct

---

168. Copelon, *supra* note 22, at 207.
169. I am not necessarily making the argument here that enforced pregnancy is or is not a violation of anyone's human rights. What I have done here is given an analytical label to a specific concept that has not, until now, been clearly distinguished from forced impregnation but has very different implications in terms of human rights law.

from forced impregnation and enforced pregnancy because it does not necessarily result from them, and because when it does it involves additional
and unique difficulties for the mother. Childbirth itself is painful and risky;
when forced it can be viewed as a form of torture. It can even result in
death. If the mother survives and the delivery was complicated she may
never be able to have other children. Regardless of physical complications,
forced maternity presents emotional torment to a rape victim.

But the definition of forced maternity says nothing of the human rights
of the child born of rape. It is self-consciously focused on the mother. This
is perfectly appropriate because the event of childbirth is different for a
mother than for a child and implies violations of different rights. The two
should not be conflated. Yet, what term would suffice to capture the extent
to which a child's rights are violated by forced impregnation?

"Forced birthing," coined by Wing and Merchán, seems plausible, in so
far as "childbirth" implies the child's presence and status as a born human
being.[170] But this label is problematic as well because it implies that the
crime is in allowing the child to be born at all. The idea of wrongful birth in
US law makes a similar claim, but leaving aside the moral tenuousness of
such legal devices, wrongful birth in US litigation concerns children who are
severely physically or mentally disadvantaged.[171] To argue that a child should
not have been born because of disadvantages that *the society imposes on her
culturally* is to further impede her empowerment and dignity as a human
being.

While forced maternity is a crime against the mother, birth of a child
can never be a crime against the child, for this is the event that brings about
her status as an ontological being and rights-bearer. The war-rape orphan is
victimized not directly through her existence, but *through her mother's victimization.* The child's status cannot be conceptually separated from her
mother's status as a victim, even though the form that her pain may take will
be different.

I suggest the term "birth-by-forced-maternity" for children born of rape.
This term is broad enough to cover all children born of rape, not merely
those in genocidal conflicts or those in which the rapist intended to conceive a child. It encompasses both forced impregnation and enforced pregnancy together (but not forced impregnation that results in an abortion). It is
through forced maternity, not forced impregnation directly, that the child
comes into being as a rights-bearer and has claims to make on the commu-

---

170. *See* Wing & Merchán, *supra* note 81, at 20.
171. *See* Jeffrey R. Botkin & Maxwell J. Mehlman, *Wrongful Birth: Medical, Legal, and
    Philosophical Issues,* 22 J.L., Med. & Ethics 21 (1994) (discussing the implications of the
    wrongful birth concept).

nity. Yet it is the aspect of force in relation to the *conception* that matters, not the question of whether the child should never have been born or the availability of abortion access.[172]

Beginning with this analytical innovation, how does birth-by-forced-maternity look as a war crime distinct from "forced impregnation?" Within the "dominant" discourse, "forced impregnation" involved a rape with intent to impregnate and prevention of abortion, either by the rapist or a third party. It was a war crime in terms of torture, a crime against humanity on the basis of gender, and it was genocidal because it aimed at destroying a cultural group by occupying the wombs of its victims and removing their cultural identity. The victims were women; the aggressors were rapists, officers, and policymakers who intended the pregnancies, and later states were implicated in enforcing the pregnancies.

The oppression of the war orphans took a very different form and resulted from different factors. I will argue that birth-by-forced-maternity is a war crime when committed in the course of an armed conflict, insofar as it ensures violations of fundamental rights unique to children including the right to resources and to membership in a community. Though it is the perpetrators of the initial rape who have committed a war crime, some human rights violations may also be perpetrated by later parties against the child as part of a policy of discrimination. In this context, the violations are not war crimes but nonetheless should be treated as human rights abuses in accordance with the Convention on the Rights of the Child and other existing human rights conventions.[173] Birth-by-forced-maternity is additionally a crime against humanity when carried out on a widespread and systematic basis, as was certainly the case in Bosnia. Moreover, when conducted with the intent to destroy the group of whom the mother is a member, birth-by-forced-maternity can also be seen as a genocidal act, because it constitutes forcible removal of children from the group.

2.   Children of the rapes

There is no way of knowing precisely how many pregnancies resulted in live births or, of these, how many children were killed, abandoned, kept by their mothers, institutionalized, or adopted by Muslims, Serbs, or foreigners.

---

172. As noted above, this conceptualization will certainly be contested by advocates of rights for unborn children. I have chosen not to broaden the scope of this definition to the unborn because fetal rights are still contested in international law, whereas the right to life for born children is not. I make no moral claims on whether or not this should change in the future; if it did, one might logically argue that the term "conception by forced impregnation" be substituted for "birth-by-forced-maternity."

173. *See, e.g.,* Convention on the Rights of the Child, *adopted* 20 Nov. 1989, G.A. Res. 44/25, U.N. GAOR, 44th Sess., Supp. No. 49, U.N. Doc. A/44/49 (1989) (*entered into force* 2 Sept. 1990), *reprinted in* 28 I.L.M. 1448 (1989) [hereinafter CRC].

These facts have not been established because these questions have not been asked. However, from a spate of brief news articles on the children and an analysis of the dynamic political context, we can suggest a continuum of possible outcomes for a given child born of rape.

Estimates of the number of existing war-rape orphans conflict. An investigation under the auspices of the United Nations found only nine unwanted births by 1993.[174] This finding seems to reflect an incredibly small number; two doctors at two separate hospitals could account for having seen that many women personally, to say nothing of those in other hospitals or without hospitalization.[175] Zvonimir Separovic, a former foreign minister of Croatia who as of 1993 was head of the Documentation Center for Genocide and War Crimes in Zagreb, was quoted in World Press Review as saying, "[t]here are certainly hundreds of them."[176] If one takes the European Community's moderate estimate of 20,000 raped at face value, then a statistic of several hundred children born of the rapes intuitively makes sense.[177] If we can believe the Bosnian government's 1993 estimate of 35,000 *pregnancies*,[178] even though the majority would have resulted in abortions, we might suppose that the number of war-rape orphans could range into the thousands. There is simply no way to be certain. But perhaps the most credible estimate comes from Ahmed Zin, who directed the Egyptian aid agency largely responsible for institutionalizing the rape orphans in 1993. (His estimate of course would have been limited to those orphans who came under his care and not those killed or abandoned by their mothers.) Zin's estimate, quoted in the Los Angeles Times, was that 500 to 600 children had been born in the space of a few months in 1993, and he speculated that "many more are probably trapped with their mothers in the 70 percent of Bosnia now under Serbian control."[179]

What precisely was the fate of children born-by-forced-maternity in the Balkans?[180] Those least lucky were probably born outside a hospital, with-

---

174. *See Expert Report, supra* note 54, at 64.
175. *See* Fisher, *supra* note 61, at 112 n.117.

> Dr. Veseljko Grizelj, director of the Petrova Hospital in Zagreb, knew of five women pregnant consequent to rape who had been treated at his hospital. . . . Dr. Miomir Krstic, director of the family planning and childbirth division of the GAK Clinical Center in Belgrade, stated he knew of four women pregnant consequent to rape in Bosnia.

> *Id.*

176. Horvath, *supra* note 5, at 11.
177. *See Expert Report, supra* note 54, ¶ 30.
178. Slavenka Drakulic, *Women Hide Behind A Wall of Silence,* THE NATION, 1 Mar. 1993, at 270.
179. Williams, *supra* note 5, at 1.
180. By the time of their birth, the children were scattered over the boundaries of several states. Many pregnant refugees apparently escaped to Croatia and gave birth in Zagreb.

out medical care, intervention, or anyone to whom their mothers could give them. In these cases it is likely that children were either strangled or drowned by their mothers. Many interviewed rape victims claimed that they would kill their children upon birth.[181] Most children who were lucky enough to be born in hospitals were simply abandoned by their mothers and turned over to the hospital authorities.[182] What seems almost certain is that they were hated by their mothers.[183] Even if certain women wished to raise their children they likely would have been ostracized by their relatives,[184] leaving the mother in the same dilemma and the child with the same outcome: death or abandonment.

Turned over to the care of hospital nurses, the war-rape orphans were likely, though not certain, to have faced systematic neglect. Overburdened with the overwhelming number of war casualties, hospitals in Croatia and Bosnia lacked staff required to provide sustained attention and affection to growing numbers of war-rape orphans.[185] If lucky, infants were fed and cared for until they could be placed in an institution.

Levels of care and access to resources in orphanages are again impossible to assess without systematic research. It is likely that they would be extremely varied. Reports of certain orphanages indicate that they were well-funded by overseas charities, particularly from Muslim countries, and that they had "everything the babies need, with the exception of parents."[186] Hospitals, run by the floundering Bosnian government or under the auspices of hospital maternity wards, may have had much worse conditions. What is documented about the conditions in some East European institutions[187] sug-

---

Other children were likely born in Bosnia. An interviewee quoted by Stiglmayer claimed that many pregnant women were taken by their captors to Serbia to give birth. *See* Stiglmayer, *supra* note 53, at 119. *See also* Eggerston, *supra* note 5, at 22. Others were relocated to Germany. *See* Jordan, *supra* note 5, at 20A.

181. "I will strangle it with my own hands," a woman is quoted as saying in Drakulic, *supra* note 178, at 270. Other (unverified) rumors of infanticide are found throughout the literature. *See, e.g.,* Niarchos, *supra* note 2, at 659; Horvath, *supra* note 5, at 11–12.

182. *See* Horvath, *supra* note 5, at 12.

183. *See, e.g.,* Stiglmayer, *supra* note 53, at 137. Uniform loathing for the children by their mothers is mentioned in nearly every news article regarding the babies. For example, "We had to put blindfolds on [the women] for the deliveries," said Dr. Asim Kurjak at Zagreb's Holy Spirit Hospital. Williams, *supra* note 5, at 1.

184. "Many women want to abort their children or give them up because their families threaten them: don't bring home any chetnik babies, or there won't be any place for you here, either." Horvath, *supra* note 5, at 12. One woman was quoted as stating, "Where I come from, everybody . . . would think of the kid as filth." Stiglmayer, *supra* note 53, at 137.

185. *See generally* Sullivan & Hammer, *supra* note 5.

186. Williams, *supra* note 5, at 1.

187. *See* Margaret Ralph, *Realizing the Educational Rights of Institutionalized Romanian Children, in* CHILDREN IN OUR CHARGE: THE CHILD'S RIGHT TO RESOURCES 112 (Mary John ed., 1996).

gests that conditions of economic impoverishment and lack of infrastructure can hit orphaned children harder than other members of society. Whether this is the case in Bosnia would likely depend on the extent that it was off-set by foreign intervention, and this is yet to be assessed.[188]

However, even those children living under the best institutional condi-tions that orphanages have to offer faced obstacles if they were born of war-rape. For instance, many could lack a nationality; children born in Croatia to Bosnian refugees (the Bosnian government estimated that 420 orphans were in Croatia)[189] were denied Croatian citizenship until 1996 and were not given access to the Croatian educational system when they came of age. Like all orphans, they faced barriers to placement with families; during the war there was no bureaucratic framework for processing adoptions. However, even after the war, they had a lesser chance of being adopted than children who were not born-by-forced-maternity.[190] The Bosnian and Croatian governments wanted to keep them in the custody of the state in the hopes of eventually placing them with their biological mothers, despite the belief of most social workers and lawyers that the mothers would not and should not be pressured into accepting the children.[191] Bosnian authorities would not release them for international adoption, and few Bosnian families were in a financial position to adopt children.[192] For all these reasons their access to family life was slim and chances of knowing their biological par-ents were practically nonexistent.[193]

But some war-rape orphans were adopted by Bosnian families.[194] Here too there was variation in each child's fate. Some orphanages made a con-scious effort not to identify children who were born of rape.[195] However for others their origin was common knowledge in the community in which they were adopted. In regards to children adopted by families who knew of their origins, would they be better off in Serb or Muslim homes? It is hard to rec-oncile because there is little data on which to draw. One news story

---

188. A number of aid groups are mentioned in news reports, including Defense for Children International, Human Relief International, and the Egyptian Aid Agency. It is impossible to assess their impact in proportion to the need without knowing what percent of war-rape orphans they were able to account for.
189. *See* Jordan, *supra* note 5, at 20A.
190. *See* Sullivan & Hammer, *supra* note 5, at 50 (discussing Bosnia).
191. *See* Williams, *supra* note 5, at 1.
192. *See generally* Elliott, *supra* note 6; Sullivan & Hammer, *supra* note 5.
193. The author located two references to women who, with the support of their husbands, had decided to keep the children. *See* Carol Williams, *Keeping a Baby Born of Violence,* L.A. Times, Oct. 24, 1993, at A1; Allen, *supra* note 4, at 107. It is possible that many women did this, but if so, their experiences were not generally noted in Western descrip-tions of "forced impregnation."
194. *See generally* Williams, *supra* note 193.
195. *See generally* Jordan, *supra* note 5; Eggertson, *supra* note 5.

described the stigma placed by a community on a war-rape orphan adopted by a Muslim family. He was well treated by the family but ostracized and labeled "chetnik" by the neighbors.[196] In a Serb community, we can only speculate whether the child would also be seen as partially "other," or whether, like the rejecting mother, the adopting Serbs would see the child as fully Serb.

The war-rape orphan thus faces a series of obstacles and a fate contingent on diverse variables. The war-rape orphan may be killed at birth; if she is "simply" abandoned she may be neglected or suffer from lack of basic resources. Also, if she is institutionalized her basic needs may be met, but she has only a small chance of being placed with a family and may never be given citizenship in the state where she was born. Furthermore, if she is lucky enough to be adopted she may then be stigmatized as being of the wrong ethnicity.

B.   Birth-by-Forced-Maternity as a Crime: Towards Thinking Space

In many respects the situation of the war orphan is morally deplorable, but does it really differ from the situation of other children in the world? How reprehensible is it in regards to the ethnic conflict from which she originated? Which human rights are being violated by her treatment in this context, and to what extent should those violations be understood in the context of international crimes rather than domestic culture?

First and foremost, the culpability of perpetrators other than aggressors in the conflict should not be overlooked. In addition to human rights as conceptualized for all humans in international law, the unique rights of children to membership in a community, to resources, and to protection are incumbent upon their state and community as well as aggressor nations. When a mother kills her child it should be understood as murder regardless of the context. If the state takes no steps to protect children in danger of infanticide or to provide resources for the mothers and children involved, it can be seen as complicit in the crime. When a state denies nationality to a child on the basis of its ethnic heritage and thus proscribes rights to resources, education, or civic identity, it is in violation of the Convention on the Rights of the Child (CRC).[197] Although I am unaware of any human rights legislation in which such acts are proscribed, when a community ostracizes a child based on its presumed ethnicity it should be understood as an outrage against justice. Given the assumption that stigma and hatred toward such a

---

196. *See* Sullivan & Hammer, *supra* note 5, at 50 (discussing Bosnia).
197. *See* CRC, *supra* note 173, arts. 7, 29.

child will prevent her full empowerment as a citizen and human being, a state in which a child has been placed is in violation of the CRC if it compels the child to remain in such a situation without relief, when alternatives such as international adoption are available and more conducive to the procurement of the child's rights and future.

That said, let us return to the question of the ethnic conflict from which the children were created. It may be clear that the Bosnian state, the *Bosnjaks*, or the children's mothers have somehow abused the children, but how can the Serb crime of genocidal rape be linked to these secondary abuses of the war-rape orphans, if at all? That is, even if we can speak of the war-rape orphans' human rights violations, can we consider birth-by-forced-maternity a war crime? As a crime against humanity? As genocide?

The following sections will first address the rights of war-rape orphans in the context of the CRC. Membership rights, resource rights, and empowerment rights are to be provided by the state (in this case, Bosnia, Croatia, or Serbia) and therefore will be analyzed in a category distinct from war crimes or genocide. A careful examination of the CRC in view of these particular children is necessary because the document was not designed to capture the needs of children of war-rape. The final section will specifically address war crimes, crimes against humanity, and genocide in order to determine whether it can be argued that these children are victims not just of discrimination at the hands of the states in which they are embedded but also of prior crimes committed by Serbs during the war. Asking these questions illustrates, in particular, difficulty with the concept of genocide as currently understood in international law.

1. The convention on the rights of the child: problems and prospects

As should be evident from the previous section, much fact-finding will be necessary to discern the nature and scope of alleged abuses against war-rape orphans in the former Yugoslavia. Little information is available and the speculations contained in this section, drawn from what is known about the conflict in general, should be seen as serving to provide thinking space and not cited as proof of mass abuse.

But let us assume, based on the information cited in this article, that at least many of these children have in fact suffered from their mother's victimization. The problem remains how to redress these abuses and whom to hold responsible.[198] The CRC, to which Yugoslavia was a signatory, outlines

---

198. On children's rights in international law, see generally Hans-Joachim Heintze, *The U.N. Convention and the Network of International Human Rights Protection by the United Nations, in* The Ideologies of Children's Rights, *supra* note 128, at 71.

a number of rights that, after a careful analysis, may be found to have been violated.[199] But it may not be as simple as just looking for the right facts. We need to carefully consider the CRC itself and try to extract the meanings and context in which these rights were articulated by the signatory nations. Doing so may suggest that the prevailing legal instruments on children's rights are not fully adequate to address Bosnia's war-rape orphans.

Lawrence LeBlanc's comprehensive book on the CRC categorizes the children's rights contained therein under "survival rights," "empowerment rights," "protection rights," and "membership rights."[200] I will not deal with protection rights, which have primarily to do with protecting children from sexual exploitation. The other types of rights do have a bearing on the present topic.

Survival rights, which charge states with "ensuring the survival and development of the child," include an adequate standard of living, social security, and health care.[201] Those babies who were allegedly killed by their mothers were deprived of their survival rights. Those children who were allegedly languishing in orphanages and hospitals while the Bosnian and Croatian governments impeded adoptions may have been deprived of adequate standards of living.[202] But the question remains: who is to blame for the lack of resources for such children in the midst of a genocidal conflict? All children in the conflict fared badly, and for much of the period there was not a functioning central Bosnian government. The CRC, like other international documents, is based on the assumption that the state party to the convention is intact. In such a circumstance, it may be necessary to fall back on treating these deprivations as consequences of the war. Can they then be called war crimes?

Empowerment rights include freedom of religion, freedom of expression, the right to assembly, and other civil rights guaranteed to adults.[203] They also include the right to an education. Reports of governments denying citizenship to war-rape orphans, and thus preventing them from entering public schools, may be in violation of that right. Whether this denial constitutes a violation of the right to education may depend on whether any other form of education is substituted.

---

199. On implementation of the CRC in other countries, see THE BEST INTERESTS OF THE CHILD: RECONCILING CULTURE AND HUMAN RIGHTS (Philip Alston ed., 1994).
200. LAWRENCE J. LEBLANC, THE CONVENTION ON THE RIGHTS OF THE CHILD: UNITED NATIONS LAWMAKING ON HUMAN RIGHTS (1995).
201. CRC, *supra* note 173, art. 6(2). See LEBLANC, *supra* note 200, at 78–81.
202. A similar argument is made, regarding the child's "right not to be in care." MICHAEL FREEMAN, THE RIGHTS AND WRONGS OF CHILDREN 150 (1985).
203. See LEBLANC, *supra* note 200, at 157.

The most important (and problematic) category of rights in the CRC is what LeBlanc calls "membership rights."[204] He states that "[i]ndividuals exist as part of a larger community, so survival rights alone will not fulfill all their needs."[205] An aspect of membership rights is nondiscrimination, which is based on the essential equality of all human beings and is stressed in all the major human rights instruments.[206] It is my opinion that little fact-finding research will be necessary to argue that war-rape orphans have experienced systematic discrimination. But discrimination on what grounds? The scope of the CRC is limited. In some respects, the CRC expands the definition of discrimination in previous instruments to include discrimination on the grounds of disability and discrimination against a child on the grounds of "'his or her parent's' or legal guardian's' race, color, gender, language, etc.[207] Moreover, according to Article 2(2), the state's parties are to take appropriate measures to ensure that children are not . . . punished because of the 'status, activities, expressed opinions, or beliefs of the child's parents, legal guardians, or family members.' "[208]

Despite advances in the conceptualization of nondiscrimination, however, Article 2 does not ban discrimination against children born out of wedlock. At first, this may seem to pose a problem for applying the CRC to discrimination against war-rape orphans. The question that may require empirical analysis is: are the children stigmatized because they were born of rape (out of wedlock) or because they were born of genocidal rape (because they are "little Chetniks")? Discrimination on the former grounds is not banned by the CRC, but the latter would constitute discrimination against a child based on ethnic or national origins, which is banned not only

---

204. *Id.* at 94.
205. *Id.*
206. *See generally* Universal Declaration of Human Rights, *adopted* 10 Dec. 1948, G.A. Res. 217A (III), U.N. GAOR, 3d Sess., Resolutions, pt. 1, at 71, U.N. Doc. A/810 (1948), *reprinted in* 43 Am. J. Int'l L. 127 (Supp. 1949); International Covenant on Civil and Political Rights, *adopted* 16 Dec. 1966, G.A. Res. 2200 (XXI), U.N. GAOR, 21st Sess., Supp. No. 16, U.N. Doc. A/6316 (1966), 999 U.N.T.S. 171 (*entered into force* 23 Mar. 1976); International Covenant on Economic, Social and Cultural Rights, *adopted* 16 Dec. 1966, G.A. Res. 2200 (XXI), U.N. GAOR, 21st Sess., Supp. No. 16, U.N. Doc. A/6316 (1966), 993 U.N.T.S. 3 (*entered into force* 3 Jan. 1976).
207. CRC, *supra* note 173, art. 2(1).
208. LeBlanc, *supra* note 200, at 97. According to LeBlanc, this is a significant step:

> Children have often become victims of serious human rights violations, including arbitrary imprisonment and even torture, because of actions that their parents or family members have engaged in or have been accused of engaging in. Article 2(2) was designed to provide an additional, and very important, measure of protection to children who might find themselves in such circumstances.

Id.

by the CRC (Article 2(1)) but by the earlier Declaration on the Rights of the Child (1959, Principle 1).[209]

But again, what is the child's ethnic and religious background? We are back to the same confusion implicit in genocidal rape arguments. And, in fact, the ethnic background of the children was and probably still is highly contested. *Bosnjak* communities may view the children as Serb and therefore they may be discriminating on that basis.

The question becomes whether the states responsible for the children committed these acts or failed to take reasonable measures to avoid stigmatization by other parties. The fact that *people* in Bosnia, including the children's biological families, discriminated against them is not a crime for which a signatory state can be held accountable, though it should be recognized as an injustice.[210] However, the international Muslim community has *not* rejected the children and in fact claims they are Muslims.[211] This assertion had an impact on their fate as well: it meant that the children should not be adopted by any of the Western families who would prefer to move them from the war zone. Some Serbian families have adopted the children and are raising them, presumably as Orthodox.[212] How can this be reconciled with the claims of the Muslim community? Is there similar discrimination on the part of these families because the children are "half-Muslim" or do the Serbs see them as Serb based on their patrilineage? Have Serb families in Bosnia also adopted war-rape orphans? Do *they* see them as *Bosnjak* or Serb? Or are they merely *Bosanac,* symbols of a new, multi-ethnic Bosnian state? How are outside observers to decide, so that they can judge whether "ethnic" or "religious" discrimination is occurring?

Beyond non-discrimination, the CRC and the previous Declaration entitle children to a name and a nationality.[213] In this case, Croatia may be held accountable for denying a child born in its borders national citizenship on the basis of its presumed ethnic identity. In Bosnia the situation is murkier. The children *have* been claimed as citizens of the state; they have not been denied nationality in the sense of citizenship. This treatment is in line with the construction of a *Bosanac* civic national identity. Bosnia, which had legitimized various ethnically rooted parties just before the outbreak of eth-

---

209. Declaration on the Rights of the Child, *adopted* 20 Nov. 1959, G.A. Res. 1386 (XIV), U.N. GAOR, 14th Sess., 841st plen. mtg., Supp. No. 16, at 19, U.N. Doc. A/4354 (1959).
210. It is probably not a "fact" that the children were uniformly discriminated against by *all Bosnjaks;* this assumption is based on indirect reports and requires empirical study.
211. *See* Ruth Gledhill, *Muslims Give Adoption Warning; Bosnian Orphans,* Times (London), 5 Jan. 1993, *available in* 1993 WL 10547320.
212. *See* Eggerston, *supra* note 5, at 22.
213. *See* CRC, *supra* note 173, art. 7(1).

nic conflict,[214] tried to self-consciously define itself along civic rather than
ethnic lines after the war.[215] Yet, given the context of a recent ethnic conflict,
membership in groups is clearly demarcated along ethnic lines to a more
heightened degree than before the breakup of Yugoslavia.[216]

It is unclear whether children's membership rights are satisfied when
they are merely given a civic nationality, if it is ethnic nationality that
defines group membership in a given cultural context. And yet if Bosnia
allowed the children to be adopted by foreigners, would this in some way
constitute a denial of Bosnian civic nationality?[217] Advocates of foreign
adoption for these children might argue, using the language of the International Covenant, that the right to *acquire* a meaningful nationality should
take precedent over the right *to* a Bosnian nationality that may not fully
satisfy membership rights for the children if all ethnic groups stigmatize
them.[218] Drawing this distinction reveals that the approach to conceptualizing and translating "membership rights" into rights for actual children—
particularly those whose identities are contested—is unclear and demands
careful attention.

2. War crimes, crimes against humanity, genocide?

Whether or not abuses of children have occurred indirectly as a result of
their origins, in what sense can the Serb crime of genocidal rape be linked
to these secondary abuses? Can we conceptualize birth-by-forced-maternity
as a war crime? As a crime against humanity? As genocide? The answer is a
tentative yes. Yes, because rights that clearly have been violated could fit
under the rubric of each category. Tentative, because it is equally clear
that these categories were not conceptualized with war-rape orphans in
mind.

Birth-by-forced-maternity can be considered a *war crime* when imposed
by aggressors during an armed conflict because it brings about all of the
above violations of young children's fundamental human rights. In the case
of an infant, these violations can be conceived as torture or inhuman treatment. For an older child, the discrimination and stigma they will face as a

---

214. *See* ED VULLIAMY, SEASONS IN HELL: UNDERSTANDING BOSNIA'S WAR 41 (1994).
215. On the tension between civic (related to citizenship) and primordial (ethnic) ideas of
    nationality, see Craig Calhoun, *Nationalism and Ethnicity, in* 19 ANN. REV. SOCIOLOGY 29
    (1993).
216. Bringa argues, however, that the ethnic conflict has further entrenched ethnic particular-
    ism, even among *Bosnjaks* for whom a sense of blood-based identity was weakest before
    the conflict. *See* BRINGA, *supra* note 92, at 36.
217. If so, important implications exist for intercountry adoption in general.
218. On the distinction, see LEBLANC, *supra* note 200, at 108.

result of their mother's victimization can be understood as great suffering. Moreover, if we accept the legal literature regarding the child's status as a tool of war against her mother's community, we may also view the child as a war crimes victim on the basis of having been compelled to serve in the forces of a hostile power.

Beyond war crimes, birth-by-forced-maternity can be considered a *crime against humanity* when not committed during an armed conflict; this is an important point because there is some debate as to whether the war in Bosnia was actually an armed conflict at all. To qualify as a crime against humanity, birth-by-forced-maternity must be widespread and systematic; not only must there be many children born who then incur the requisite pain and suffering, but a policy to bring about their birth must be systematically employed. Again, the case has been well made that not only were hundreds of children born of the rapes in Bosnia, but that forced impregnation was an intentional and conscious policy on the part of the Serbian authorities. Although the circumstances of the war-rape orphans fit the prerequisites of a crime against humanity, it is not as clear how birth-by-forced-maternity correlates with the specific crimes included under the term. Murder, extermination, enslavement, and deportation do not seem to apply. Inhuman acts could apply but the argument would need to be very carefully laid out. The more likely argument is that these children are victims of persecution on political, racial, or religious grounds: *their births were brought about in such a manner as to ensure that this would be the outcome for them.* In regards to intent, causing suffering and rejection and thus splintering a group was the fundamental purpose for which the children were born.

Still, the language of crimes against humanity was not designed to describe the phenomenon of birth-by-forced-maternity. Although to some degree birth-by-forced-maternity may be incorporated under the language defining crimes against humanity, some inconsistencies arise in trying to fit this crime to existing law. For example, though the terrible outcome for the children was premeditated by the rapists, and therefore the rapists should be held accountable, the persecution involved was not to happen at the hands of the Serbs themselves. How we are to conceptualize this crime, and whether it fits under the rubric of crimes against humanity, are certainly issues around which much contestation can and should arise.

As *genocide,* the issue of birth-by-forced-maternity illuminates further limitations of existing international law. On the surface, there are at least two ways that we can understand war-rape orphans as victims of genocide and, hence, birth-by-forced-maternity as a genocide act (when intent to commit genocide can be established as it has been in regards to rape and forced impregnation). As a member of the victimized group (that is, as her mother's child) the child of rape is a victim of genocide because she is forcibly transferred from her mother's group to another. In other words, the Serb rapists understand that both the mothers and the Muslim community will reject the children and that they will end up either in the Serbian community or in a liminal category within institutions or in the custody of the state. The children will not, presumably, grow up Muslim; in this sense they have been removed from "their" group.

Of course, making this argument implies essentializing a Muslim identity for the child, but it does not require it. Understanding her as even half Muslim, as a partial or potential member of the victimized community, suggests she has lost something by being forced out of it.[219] The only way to avoid the conceptualization as victim of genocide is to erase her Muslim identity entirely and label her fully Serb. This is what has been done by the literature so far. What I am doing is re-introducing the relationship between the child of war rape and the mother's ethnic standing; thus the child emerges as a victim of genocide as well by virtue of her forced expulsion from her mother's community.

There are notable difficulties with situating children of war-rape as victims within the legal apparatus of genocide. The concept of genocide is one way of promoting the discourse of nationalism, which is in turn the cause of the genocide. This conceptualization also suggests that a community is a unit and obscures the struggles within the community over how membership is defined. When a majority ethnic group eradicates a minority community it is genocide. When a community eradicates or expels certain of its own members this is not genocide (against women for example, or against children in this case); this is part of the process of defining itself that makes that community unique, and which is protected by the legal and social discourse of genocide.[220] As this article illustrates, defining the community in particular ways may involve negating the rights of certain individuals who in concrete terms (by virtue of biological relationships, for example) would be considered members.

---

219. This conceptualization focuses on the loss to the *child* of identity rather than the loss to the group of the child, the latter argument being problematic when it is unclear whether the child was even considered to be a member of the group. It may help to think of it as forcible removal of the *group* from the *child*.

220. Examples of groups or "nations" rejecting children to define themselves abound. The case of the Slovak babies trapped in Czech orphanages is an example. *See* Spitkova, *supra* note 160. More famously, ancient Spartans had a practice of leaving newborn male infants considered unwarriorlike in appearance exposed to the elements, thus reproducing the martial identity of the nation. *See* Charles Kegley & Gregory Raymond, How Nations Make Peace 52 (1999). On sacrificial aspects of nationhood from a feminist perspective, see Jean Bethke Elshtain, Real Politics: At the Center of Everyday Life 126 (1997).

By making this negation of rights a crime, or even by problematizing it, do we run the risk of denying a victimized group the right to their own cultural authenticity and self-determination? Moreover, does the logic of group cohesion that is the basis for the concept of genocide legitimize the very acts that the Serbs *indirectly* masterminded: the expulsion of rape victims from their communities and subsequent shattering of the victimized group?

The feminist argument is that Serbian mass rapes were genocidal because of the calculated effect on the *Bosnjak* culture—the resulting rejection of the raped women and of the children. But this construction of genocide—and indeed the entire logic of the Serbian rape policy—was dependent upon the complicity of the *Bosnjaks* in rejecting the women and children.[221]

This complicity in no way excuses or lessens the severity of the Serbian crime. What it does is challenge the current understanding of the process of genocide when it involves reproductive and identity politics. The portions of the Genocide Conventions that refer to forcible transfer of children certainly anticipated that children would clearly be in the victimized group or not; that the group was made up in part of certain children.[222] The convention did not account for the extent to which groups reproduce themselves by receiving children and can easily define themselves by rejecting children that are biologically theirs. In the case of birth-by-forced-maternity in Bosnia, many children were forcibly removed from the group, but it was the *Bosnjaks* who had the task of forcibly removing them. The Serb policy foresaw and intended that outcome, and so it was genocidal; but the Serbs alone were not responsible for the actual outcome.

Thus, strictly in terms of existing genocidal literature, we can treat Bosnian war-rape orphans as victims of not only war crimes, crimes against humanity, and human rights abuses—but also of genocide. Yet such a conceptualization challenges the very idea of genocide as it is characterized in the international discourse.[223] Though children of rape can be viewed as victims of genocide in the existing framework, the framework nonetheless fails to capture the full process of genocide in which the children play a part. In this case, the extent to which forced impregnation and birth-by-forced-

---

221. This pattern was not necessarily uniform. As Allen points out, the *Bosnjak* communities may not get the chance to reject certain victims because the communities themselves no longer exist. Reports of certain *Bosnjak* families adopting war-rape orphans or supporting the rape victims and their children also suggest that the pattern of rejection was not absolute. *See* ALLEN, *supra* note 4, at 100.

222. *See* Genocide Convention, *supra* note 48, at art. 2(e).

223. The legal definition of genocide is under continual contestation. For an interesting discussion of the implications stemming from the legal definition, see FRANK CHALK & KURT JONASSOHN, THE HISTORY AND SOCIOLOGY OF GENOCIDE (1990).

maternity are genocidal acts depends upon the compliance of the group against which genocide is being committed. The degree to which the notion of genocide becomes a reality further depends on the institutional fate of orphans and their subsequent identity formation after they have been claimed by the state. Perhaps no category exists to capture the plight of war-rape orphans, and thus children's rights theorists will have to produce an alternative framework of rights capable of doing so. So far, while commentators and social workers have remarked on the misery and injustice of their situation, children of genocidal rape have yet to penetrate legal discourses on the rights of civilians in war.

IV. CONCLUSIONS

Genocidal rape is one of the most horrendous acts imaginable in an ethnic conflict; thankfully, international law finally recognizes it as such. This article has argued that the current understanding of forced impregnation as genocide is too limited in scope. It has attempted to recognize the limited treatment of forced impregnation as genocide, which had been framed as exclusively a women's issue in human rights.

Strictly speaking, I would concur that forced impregnation and forced maternity are crimes solely against rape victims. But defining rape as genocidal primarily on the basis of forced impregnation conflates this violation of women's rights with ethnic genocide, a complex manipulation of identity and group cohesion that involves many affirmative acts beyond that of the rape and conception itself. Moreover, the act of forced impregnation potentially brings to bear at least two victimized parties with specific and at times inconsistent claims to rights. This article has argued that children of war rape have not been rightfully identified as human rights victims or even as variables in an ongoing relocation of ethnic identity in the former Yugoslavia.

Instead, "forced impregnation" was framed as a crime against women only through careless definition, through failing to account for children, and through identifying the children of the rapes with the perpetrators rather than the victimized group. To reverse this trend I have attempted to situate war-rape orphans in the existing framework of the Geneva and Genocide Conventions. They emerge as victims of human rights abuses and war crimes. It seems possible as well to identify them as victims of crimes against humanity and genocide, but so doing complicates the framework being used to address their situation.

Prevailing international law was not constructed to deal with the rights or needs of children. Nor was it constructed to grapple with the intricate political struggles through which group identity is forged and contested using manipulation of reproductive politics—a term that has also been used only in regards to women and gender, but under which, by definition, the birth and care of children into and by communities is also involved. Feminists insisted that male political leaders reconceptualize human rights and war crimes in light of the needs of women; similarly we may need to develop new ways of conceptualizing crimes against children in armed conflict if we accept that children too are victims of genocidal rape. The very inadequacy of existing legal and theoretical approaches may prove the biggest barrier to addressing and redressing children's human rights in genocidal conflicts.

Chapter 13

Rights Talk and the Experience of Law: Implementing Women's Human Rights to Protection from Violence

Sally Engle Merry

I. INTRODUCTION

From civil rights to human rights, rights talk remains a dominant framework for contemporary social justice movements. But seeing oneself as a rights-bearing subject whose problems are violations of these rights is far from universal. How does a person come to understand his or her problems in terms of rights? It is the contention of this article that the adoption of a rights consciousness requires experiences with the legal system that reinforce this subjectivity. Adoption of rights-defined selves depends on encounters with police, prosecutors, judges, and probation officers that reflect back this identity. Indications that the problem is trivial, that the victim does not really have these rights, or that the offender does not deserve punishment undermine this subjectivity. How to persuade victims to take on a rights-defined self is a critical problem for the battered women's movement, which relies heavily on rights talk to encourage abused women to seek help from the law.[1] It is also fundamental to a range of other rights-based social reform movements that depend on victim activism and rights claiming in order to promote change such as disability rights and employment rights. The human rights movement depends both on government compliance with international treaties and victim advocacy for these rights. Thus, examining how vulnerable populations come to see their difficulties as human rights violations is a fundamental question for human rights activists. This empirical study shows how victims of violence against women come to take on rights

---

1. *See* Elizabeth M. Schneider, Battered Women and Feminist Lawmaking (2000).

consciousness. It describes an interaction between consciousness, experience, and institutional receptivity that is critical to human rights practice.

The battered women's movement has always relied on a criminal justice component to its activism, which encourages victims to see their violation as a crime and to turn to the legal system for help.[2] As the global movement expands in the wake of the Vienna conference in 1993 and Beijing in 1995, a rights approach is increasingly important. The 1993 conference in Vienna focused on human rights and articulated the principle of women's rights as human rights, while the Beijing Fourth World Conference on Women in 1995 emphasized women's rights and reinforced the idea that women's rights are human rights. Yet, despite considerable emphasis on rights by shelter staff and court advocates, battered women are often slow to take on rights. Even after calling the police for help and filing for temporary restraining orders, battered women are likely to refuse to testify or to drop the restraining order. They clearly fear retaliation by the batterer, but they also resist the shift in subjectivity required by the law. This resistance often stems from a sense of self that is deeply at odds with other senses that are rooted in family, religion, and community. Taking on a rights-defined self in relation to a partner requires a substantial identity change both for the woman and for the man she is accusing. Instead of seeing herself defined by family, kin, and work relationships, she takes on a more autonomous self protected by the state. At the same time, her actions allow the law to define her husband/partner as a criminal under the surveillance and control of the state. A battered woman may be pressured by kin to feel she is a bad wife, while her partner may claim she is taking away his masculinity. The only way she can rescue him from this loss is to deflect the very legal sanctions she has called down upon him. It is hardly surprising that abused women will ask for help from the law, back away, and then ask again. Such women appear to be difficult or "bad" victims since they typically file charges then try to drop them or fail to appear for restraining order hearings. Yet, these women are tracking back and forth across a significant line of identity transformation.

A substantial body of literature in the law and society field has explored the contribution of rights talk to social movement activism.[3] From pay equity

---

2. *See id.* In her recent comprehensive discussion of law and the battered women's movement, Schneider asks about the implications of using a rights approach for this problem. As she points out, early activists saw the problem as the product of larger structural forces but also relied on the law as a way to define the problem and to intervene in it. The structural analysis of gender violence has persisted in the global human rights movement but is increasingly missing from the US movement. *Id. See also* SUSAN SCHECHTER, WOMEN AND MALE VIOLENCE: THE VISIONS AND STRUGGLES OF THE BATTERED WOMEN'S MOVEMENT (1982).

3. *See* SCHNEIDER, *supra* note 1; STUART A. SCHEINGOLD, THE POLITICS OF RIGHTS: LAWYERS, PUBLIC POLICY, AND POLITICAL CHANGE (1974); JOHN GILLIOM, OVERSEERS OF THE POOR: SURVEILLANCE, RESISTANCE, AND THE LIMITS OF PRIVACY (2001).

movements,[4] to mental health patients' rights movements,[5] to the contemporary expansion in the human rights movement, the mobilization of a rights language has proved critical for activists.[6] The literature on rights consciousness in social movements tends to focus on activists.[7] While activists turn to rights talk, however, vulnerable populations seem less inclined to do so. For example, Gilliom's research on welfare mothers in the United States suggests that this vulnerable population does not respond to their experience of extensive surveillance by asserting privacy rights.[8] Yet, many rights-based social movements, including human rights ones, depend upon individuals defining their problems in rights terms and taking action on that basis. The battered women's movement is one example of such a movement, while the international violence against women movement within the human rights framework is another. Without victim participation in the identification of violence in rights terms, movement activists are unable to further their social reforms. Thus, understanding under what conditions an individual victim comes to redefine her problem as an offense that violates her rights, rather than as a burden of everyday married life, is critical for the study of rights in social movements.

Despite a rich literature on rights in social movements, we know relatively little about why and when a person adopts rights talk. Michael McCann's study of the pay equity movement shows that rights talk is a powerful reform discourse in the USA, but he focuses on activists who become leaders in the movement rather than on the followers who come to understand their problems in terms of rights.[9] He suggests that features of personal history and orientation toward activism are important, but that winning some legal victories is also critical.[10] The use of rights in the pay equity movement was encouraged by significant victories in the courts in the early 1980s,[11] but as the tide of legal judgments turned against the movement in the late 1980s, legal decisions were less effective in mobilizing media attention and support. Neal Milner observed a similar pattern in mental health cases.[12] Yet, the definition of the pay equity problem in rights terms remained a powerful tool for local and state-level activists. Activists saw

---

4. Michael W. McCann, Rights at Work: Pay Equity Reform and the Politics of Legal Mobilization 5 (1994).
5. See Neal Milner, The Right to Refuse Treatment: Four Case Studies in Legal Mobilization, 21 Law & Soc'y Rev. 447 (1987).
6. See Margaret Keck & Kathryn Sikkink, Activists Without Borders (1998).
7. See McCann, supra note 4.
8. Gilliom, supra note 3.
9. McCann, supra note 4, at 100; see also Scheingold, supra note 3.
10. McCann, supra note 4, at 53–58.
11. Id. at 277.
12. Milner, supra note 5.

rights talk both as a social ideal and as an effective tactic for the movement because of its widespread resonance with underpaid female workers.[13] But it is not as clear that rights talk is as powerful with victims, as Gilliom's study of welfare mothers indicates.[14] These women talk about the importance of caring for their families and express anger and frustration at the high degree of surveillance they experience, but they very rarely assert a right to privacy. Ewick and Silbey's study of varieties of legal consciousness suggests several different ways individuals relate to law, many of which are not based on rights consciousness.[15]

In this article, I argue that the adoption of a rights-defined identity under identity-shifting circumstances such as battering depends on the individual's experience with the law. One of the powerful consequences of bringing gender violence cases to the attention of the legal system is the victim's and perpetrator's encounters with the new subjectivity defined within the discourses and practices of the law. Interactions with police officers, prosecutors, probation officers, judges, shelter workers, feminist advocates and even bailiffs affect the extent to which an individual victim is willing to take on this new identity. Do the police make an arrest or tell him to take a walk? Does the prosecutor press charges or *nolle prosequi* the case? Does the judge impose prison time or dismiss the case? Does she offer a stern lecture or mumble the charge and penalty? These are all indications of how seriously the legal system takes her rights. If the police are friendly to the man and fail to arrest him, if the judge suggests that battering is not a serious offense, and if the court imposes no prison sentence, this experience undermines the woman's rights subjectivity. If police act as if battered women do not have the right to complain about the violence of their husbands, then these women are discouraged from seeing themselves as having such a right. If their partners, relatives, friends, and neighbors tell battered women that a "good wife" does not take her husband to court and that she provoked him, she may also be deterred. Thus, an individual's willingness to take on rights depends on her experience trying to assert them. The more this experience reflects a serious belief that she is a person with a right not to be battered, the more willing she will be to take on this identity. On the other hand, if these rights are treated as insignificant, she may choose to give up and no longer think about her grievances in terms of rights.

To explore subjectivities produced by the encounter with the legal system, my research assistants and I interviewed thirty women and twenty-one men about their experiences with the legal system, and their reactions to the

---

13. *See* McCann, *supra* note 4, at 236.
14. Gilliom, *supra* note 3.
15. Patricia Ewick & Susan S. Silbey, The Common Place of Law (1998).

experience. This research was conducted in a small town in Hawai'i, a place typical of rural agricultural regions of the US, but different in its colonial and plantation past and contemporary diversity of ethnicity.[16] All of those interviewed had experiences with the family court and/or the district court, as well as participating in a court-mandated batterer intervention program or women's support group. The interviews were supplemented by an analysis of the discussions within women's support groups and men's batterers groups.[17]

The town of Hilo is a small port city of about 45,000 that serves a sprawling agricultural region and provides a hub for governmental, educational, medical, and retail services, as well as some tourism. Local feminists started a shelter in Hilo in 1978,[18] and in 1986, by working with an active and committed local judiciary, developed a violence control program that offered training for batterers and a women's support group. The dominant ethnic groups in the town are Japanese-Americans, whites, Native Hawaiians, Filipino-Americans, Portuguese, and a wide variety of combinations of people with ancestries from these regions, as well as from Korea, China, Puerto Rico, South Pacific Islands, and Mexico.

In this town, the number of cases involving violence against women in the courts has expanded dramatically over the last twenty-five years, particularly during the period of the early 1990s. While the population of the county surrounding this town has doubled over the last twenty-five years, the number of calls to the police for help has grown eight times, the number of requests for protective orders has jumped from one or two a year to 710 in 1998, and the number of arrests for abuse of a family or household member has increased from none to over 1,200 reports to the police and 855 cases in the courts in 1998. This dramatic increase in the number of cases of wife beating in the courts may reflect an increase in battering, but it also shows a

---

16. SALLY ENGLE MERRY, COLONIZING HAWAI'I: THE CULTURAL POWER OF LAW (2000).

17. Each of these interviews was done in person and lasted between one and two and a half hours. I did twelve of the interviews and my research assistants did the rest. Fourteen of the women's interviews were conducted by Leilani Miller, six by Marilyn Brown, seven by Madelaine Adelman, and three by me. Leilani Miller's method was to read to the person interviewed what she had written to verify that she had written it in their words while Madelaine taped the interviews. I interviewed nine men, Leilani Miller interviewed six, Linda Andres talked to three, Marilyn Brown two, and Joy Adapon one, all of whom were research assistants on the project. These interviews were conducted between 1991 and 1994, the years of the greatest expansion of gender violence cases in the courts. The interviews included both partners in six couples, although each member was interviewed separately. Interviews were solicited by researchers who attended the men's and women's groups and invited participants to volunteer in exchange for a small stipend. Although interviewees were told that the research was an independent project, it is very likely that they saw the project as closely connected to the ATV program itself.

18. See Noelie Maria Rodriguez, A Successful Feminist Shelter: A Case Study of the Family Crisis Shelter in Hawaii, 24 J. APPLIED BEHAV. SCI. 235–50 (1988).

major increase in help-seeking from the law. In most cases, the victim has taken the initiative to call the police for help or to ask the family court for a restraining order. Those who call on the legal system for help have taken a step toward seeing themselves as defined by the promises and protections of rights, even in the domain of the family. At the same time, there have been substantial changes in law, the police, and especially the courts that have encouraged women to use the law. And, most important, a strong battered women's movement in Hilo has developed a shelter, a women's support group, and batterer's intervention program in the town, along with engaging in substantial community education.[19]

II.   SHIFTING SUBJECTIVITIES

The post-structuralist concept of the self as the location of multiple and potentially contradictory subjectivities, each established within discourses and discursive practices, provides a helpful way to conceptualize the complex positioning of women who turn to the law in crises of violence. In Henrietta Moore's description of the post-structuralist gendered subject, each individual takes up multiple subject positions within a range of discourses and social practices, so that a single subject is not the same as a single individual.[20] What holds these multiple subjectivities together are the experience of identity, the physical grounding of the subject in a body, and the historical continuity of the subject.[21]

"If subjectivity is seen as singular, fixed, and coherent, it becomes very difficult to explain how it is that individuals constitute their sense of self— their self-representations as subjects—through several, often mutually contradictory subject positions, rather than through one singular subject position."[22] Instead of seeing gender as a single gender system, anthropology has moved toward an understanding of gender by examining how "individuals come to take up gendered subject positions through engagement with multiple discourses on gender."[23] Although this framework appears to emphasize choice, Moore emphasizes that there are dominant and subdom-

---

19. I have been doing ethnographic research on the legal management of gender violence in Hilo since 1991 and have compiled the information about Hilo through interviews, court records, police reports, and extensive discussions with officials and activists working on domestic violence in Hilo.

20. Henrietta Moore, *The Problem of Explaining Violence in the Social Sciences, in* Sex and Violence: Issues in Representation and Experience 141 (Penelope Harvey & Peter Gow eds., 1994).

21. *See id.*

22. *Id.* at 141.

23. *Id.* at 142.

inant discourses that are both reproduced and in some ways resisted.[24] This model opens up the possibility of multiple femininities and masculinities within the same context, onto which gender differences are again inscribed, so that some masculinities appear more feminine and others more masculine, with the hierarchical relationship between the genders reinscribed on these variations within a gender in a particular social context.[25] Moore notes that this theory of gender as consisting of multiple, possibly contradictory competing discourses enables the question, how do people take up a position in one discourse rather than another?[26]

This framework provides a way of thinking about battered women's experience with the law. In going to the law, a woman takes on a new subject position, defined in the discourses and social practices of the law. She tries it on, not abandoning her other subject positions as partner or wife, member of a kinship network that usually includes her partner's family as well as her own, along with other subject positions such as "local," Christian, and poor. She is, in a sense, seeing how it goes. The experimental subject position includes assertiveness, claims to autonomy, and mobilization of the power of the law. The encounter with the courts is an exploration of the dimensions of this position, the experience of taking it on, of seeing how it conforms with or contradicts other subject positions she occupies. There are risks: going to court typically precipitates an angry and hostile response from the partner. Indeed, her assumption of this new legally constituted subject position may be interpreted as a direct challenge to his masculinity. Insofar as women are required to confirm a man's masculinity by their adoption of a feminine subject position, "[t]he inability to maintain the fantasy of power triggers a crisis in the fantasy of identity, and violence is a means of resolving this crisis because it acts to reconfirm the nature of a masculinity otherwise denied."[27] Violence is then a sign of the struggle for the maintenance of certain fantasies of identity and power. Violence emerges, in this analysis, as deeply gendered and sexualized and as a consequence of her turning to the law for help.

The woman calling the police and pressing charges is thwarting the fantasy of power and identity of masculinity in dominant discourses. As her partner struggles to reassert his masculinity through reestablishing his control over her, she may find the new subject position within the law an alienating and empty one. It may disrupt her relations with her kin and her partner as she receives pressures to leave him and turn to a new source of support in social services and legal officials. This is a subject position

---

24. *Id.*
25. *Id.* at 146–47.
26. *Id.* at 149.
27. *Id.* at 154.

shaped by the discourses of autonomy, choice, and reasonable behavior, not by love, anger, hurt, and ambivalence. The move into this subject position initiates a period of tension, a continual questioning if it is worth it. Those who press on, who continue to take on this subjectivity, are people for whom this new position has something to offer. Perhaps they have less to lose from others who oppose them.

Although there has clearly been a substantial increase in the number of women willing to turn to the courts, many try this position and discard it, returning to a subjectivity less challenging to their partners and perhaps to their kin. Such discarding can be temporary or permanent; individuals frequently proceed through a long sequence of putting on and taking off this subject position, perhaps holding it a little longer each time, depending on what the discursively constituted position of battered woman has to offer and the extent of contradiction with other subject positions. Indeed, women are choosing between two incompatible subject positions, one the rights-bearing subject, the other the good wife. Each represents a vision of the self that produces self-esteem, but the battered woman cannot simultaneously enact both. Choosing either one represents a failure of the other. The practices of the legal system are thus of critical significance to the woman's decision as she ambivalently moves in and out of this subjectivity. Fragmentary evidence around the country of an explosion of cases in the late 1980s followed by a leveling off in the mid-1990s suggests some deep and enduring ambivalence about the legally defined subject position for situations of battering.

Law is particularly important to the redefinition of subjectivity. Hirsch and Lazarus-Black note "the productivity of the law—mobilized by the state and by individual actors—yields new subjectivities and thereby refigures relations of power."[28] Indeed, the making of subjectivity through law "is a particularly intimate locus for the operation of hegemony and resistance."[29] Judith Butler's performative conception of gender provides one way of thinking about the contribution of law. There is no "natural" or pre-social sex: it

---

28. Susan F. Hirsch & Mindie Lazarus-Black, Contested States: Law, Hegemony, and Resistance 13 (Mindie Lazarus-Black & Susan F. Hirsch eds., 1994).

29. *Id.* This example shows the connection between the techniques of productive power Foucault describes—normalization, the production of personhood, the discipline of the body—and the law. *See* Michel Foucault, Discipline and Punish: The Birth of the Prison (1979). These techniques are fundamental to the array of social services attached to the criminal processes of modern law. Tracing these linkages shows how the disciplines gain power from the law and how the law is brought into the micro-technologies of power of everyday life. Through its productive engagement with the objects of its surveillance as well as the subjects of its intervention, legal conceptions and institutions reshape the way individuals think of themselves and their relationships to their intimate social worlds and the state. And in doing so, they redefine law itself, which exists only as it is interpreted and understood within the wider society.

is the doing of gender that creates it. Gender is an identity which is "per-formatively constituted by the very 'expressions' that are said to be its results."[30] Among the regulatory practices that generate the identities of gender is law: following Foucault, Butler argues that juridical power pro-duces what it claims only to represent. "In effect, the law produces and then conceals the notion of a 'subject before the law' in order to invoke that dis-cursive formation as a naturalized foundational premise that subsequently legitimates that law's own regulatory hegemony."[31] Thus, gender is continu-ally transformed through its performance in legally regulated contexts. It is constituted and reconstituted through regulatory practices such as the law that shift the conditions for performing gender. A change in legal practices for handling violence in intimate gendered relationships has produced a new doing of gender[32] within a changing system of regulatory constraints.

Gendered subjectivity is redefined by doing legal activities: through act-ing as a legally entitled subject in the context of these injuries. As women victimized by violence call the police, walk into courtrooms, fill out forms requesting restraining orders, tell their stories of violence and victimization in forms and in response to official queries, they enact a different self. Such performances reshape the way these women think about themselves and the relationship between their intimate social worlds and the law. Turning to the courts for help in incidents of violence by partners represents a disembed-ding of the individual in the structure of kin, neighbors, friends, and churches in favor of a new relationship to the state. That one is a subject of the state in paying taxes may be a recognized aspect of the way the law defines the self; the state's obligation to protect a wife from her husband's violence in the home, or even his overbearing and critical manner in the absence of physi-cal violence, has until recently not been a recognized aspect of selves even in the legally constituted American society. Categories such as the private domain of the family, insulated from state supervision by the patriarchal authority of the husband, although at the same time fully constituted by the state in its capacity to marry and divorce, may exist at the level of the unrec-ognized, the taken for granted, the hegemonic. It is these categories that are challenged by contemporary feminist movements about violence against women.

The promise of rights and the penetration of law into the patriarchal sphere of the family represent a radical transformation in gender and the family. The rapid movement of gender violence cases into the courts reveals

---

30. Judith Butler, Gender Trouble: Feminism and the Subversion of Identity 25 (1990).
31. Id. at 2.
32. The phrase "a new doing of gender" refers to performative theories of gender, which argue that gender is not an innate characteristic of a person, but a set of actions and presenta-tions of self that announce and display gender and that fall along a continuum rather than falling into dichotomous categories.

this new awareness of a definition of the self as protected by law from violence even within the sphere of intimate, romantic relationships. It is not that the right to protection from assault has changed, but that the meaning of the sphere of the family as a private domain secluded from legal scrutiny has changed to one more porous.

Yet as women approach the legal system, their new subjectivity is mediated by their experiences with the law. They encounter widespread leniency concerning these cases. When police fail to arrest, prosecutors fail to push a case forward, or probation officers fail to compel an offender to attend the battering program, the rights-bearing endowed self is compromised. As women confront the demand to testify against an offender in open court, unsure of the penalty that will follow, but certain of the anger he feels as a result of her testimony, the nature of the new subjectivity offered to her by the law appears ambiguous and unclear. When women find that their batterers are not punished but sent to violence control programs, they hope for reform.

Women encounter conditional help. Becoming an entitled person in this situation depends on being the rational person who follows through, leaves the batterer, cooperates with prosecuting the case, and does not provoke violence, take drugs or drink, or abuse children. A woman's ability to perform such a self is conditional upon conforming to the law's definitions of rational and autonomous reactions to violence. The victim of violence encounters this conditional definition of the legally protected self offered to her as she endeavors to assume the proffered identity. She acquires a new self, now no longer enclosed in the private sphere of the family but constituted by the law even within that family, but it is a self wrapped in expectations of a continued commitment to prosecution and severing the relationship with the violent man.

It is not surprising, given the significance of this cultural change for concepts of privacy, that there are significant class differences in the extent to which women have participated in the opening of the family to legal surveillance. One of the consequences of opening the family to legal surveillance is a loss of control. The law takes over the case and imposes penalties on the perpetrator, whether or not the victim wishes them. There may also be a public announcement of the problem, at least in court if not, as in the town studied in this article, in the local newspaper. In Hilo, the town paper prominently publishes the names of all men arrested for abuse of a family and household member or violation of a protective order, listing them by name, age, and place of residence.

Thus, turning to the legal system for help is a difficult decision, in which the practices of the legal system itself are critically important. Even when a new law specifically criminalizing gender violence was passed in 1973 in Hawai'i, very few women filed cases. It was only after substantial changes in police practice, the elimination of the requirement to use an attorney to get a TRO, and greater attention to these cases by prosecutors and judges, that women began to turn to the law in larger numbers. The impact of an active feminist movement in the town, as well as increasing media attention, clearly affected women's willingness to complain. The law has constituted women as legal subjects no longer mediated by their embeddedness in family relationships, but now standing alone in relation to the state. At the same time, it has reduced the patriarchal privileges of males within the domain of the family. For poor families, such an opening to state surveillance was already well established by regulations governing welfare, child abuse, and housing allowances, and in earlier periods, vagrancy and alcoholism.

Thus, the new terrain is ambiguous, both offering a new legal self protected from violence by men, but providing in practice a far more limited and nuanced legal self whose protection is never fully guaranteed nor experienced. It is through experience, through encounters with the multiple responses of the police, prosecutors, courts, and probation officers, that a new legal subjectivity about gender violence is made, along with a new sense of marriage, family, community, and the place of the law. The law claims for itself the definition of gendered relationships within the family as well as outside the family, but ambivalently and uncertainly, creating areas of leniency and inaction that characterize this sphere of the law. Even as the law restricts men from using violence to control their partners, it does so in a contingent and variable fashion, incorporating the possibility of unmaking, as well as making, this change. There is a tension between the construction of new discourses of rights and the practices through which these promises are disclosed, which mediate the reconstitution of both male and female subjectivity.

One of the tensions is produced by the insistence of the legal system that the women it helps are "good victims."[33] Social movements that advocate the expansion of law into new domains represent the problem as requiring legal sanctions. Stories of innocent victims injured by malicious offenders are clearly the most powerful. These are the stories that have encouraged the law to engage in protecting women from intimate violence. The battered women's movement has always insisted on a broader and more complex analysis of the dynamics of battering,[34] but the law looks for innocent victims, labeling those who fight back as trouble and their problems as garbage cases.[35] The good victim in the law is not a woman who fights back,

---

33. The idea of a "good victim" emerged from my ethnographic research with individuals working with battered women in the courts and women's centers.
34. See SCHECHTER, *supra* note 2.
35. See SALLY ENGLE MERRY, GETTING JUSTICE AND GETTING EVEN: LEGAL CONSCIOUSNESS AMONG WORKING CLASS AMERICANS (1990).

drinks or takes drugs along with the men, or abuses her children. When women act in violent and provocative ways or refuse to press charges or testify, legal officials are often frustrated. Women who do not fit the image of the good victim become redefined as troublesome and difficult and are likely to receive less assistance. Good victims are also those who follow through with their cases. To begin a legal case, then to drop it, then to go back for another TRO or to call the police again but not to testify in court, earns a woman the label of difficult and "bad" victim. Thus, the very hesitancy and ambivalence about making this identity change that women experience, as well as their desire to defend themselves, conspire to define them as "bad" victims. Obviously, representatives of the legal system, and even some feminist shelter workers, are likely to be less supportive of the rights of those who are not "good" victims. And they are less likely to take on rights.

A new "good victim" is being constructed at this point, the battered child.[36] The child preserves an innocence that women seem not always to have. But this frame sometimes reveals the mother as abuser. Abusive mothers are sent to anger management programs as well as their partners, and those who refuse to leave their batterers face having their children removed by the state. Women now experience the expanded surveillance of the law, the demand to produce and analyze experiences with violence in order to have their children returned. And they must choose between staying with a violent man and giving up their children or keeping the children and giving up the man. Thus, the changing cultural construction of the good victim defines the privileged subject of legal assistance and excludes others as unworthy of help.

III.   GENDERING THE TURN TO THE LAW

The interviews that my research assistants and I conducted, which are described in the introduction section of this article, indicate that the encounter with the law affects the way these people think about themselves in fundamental ways, but that there are enormous differences in its impact on men and women. While women respond by trying on and sometimes discarding what they usually see as a more powerful self, but also one whose adoption is scary, men resist and reject a diminished self that is not heard, is sometimes humiliated and ignored, and is subject to penalties both restrictive and expensive. The women talk about gaining courage and appreciating the help of the law, while the men talk about shock, anger, surprise, and a sense of betrayal by the women who have accused them. In an

---

36. *See* Barbara J. Nelson, Making an Issue of Child Abuse (1984).

excruciating turn, the women typically feel some concern and even love for the men they have helped to humiliate while the men find solace in moments when the women drop charges or switch from a no-contact to a contact TRO. A woman's willingness to join with her partner in opposing or subverting the law recuperates some of his damaged identity as a man and allows him to confront the legal system, not as a diminished man whose wife no longer submits, but as a stronger man who still controls his wife and can count on her support. Thus, the woman assaults his masculinity by turning to the law, adopting its definition of her autonomous personhood and protection from violence, while gaining for herself greater control over his violence and domination in her relationship with him.

Insofar as gender hierarchies are mapped onto these new subjectivities, the woman could be said to become masculinized and the man feminized in this encounter. Concepts of masculinity and femininity are of course cultural products, culturally variable and the product of particular histories, but within a social space there is some level of shared understandings. I am referring to these concepts as they are located within the dominant American framework of masculinity and femininity, recognizing that there are regional, ethnic, class, and other variations within this general pattern. In the shape that gender takes within this community, the woman who gives in and withdraws from the legal process returns to a more feminized self and allows her male partner to recuperate his masculinity. Because gender is produced by such performances, the way that women and men chart courses through the tensions of violence and its legal regulation shapes their gendered selves. As they do law, they also do gender.

It is not surprising that women would adopt a tentative stance toward this transformation—trying it on, dropping it, trying it again—given the significance of the change and the mutually constitutive nature of gender. The way she plays gender affects the way the man with whom she is in a relationship can play gender. The move back to the more familiar femininity in which the man can oppositionally be a man is undeniably seductive, while the stance of refusing femininity opens her to his sense of betrayal, to the extent to which he is diminished both by the performances of the court and by her very rejection of feminine submissiveness. It is hardly surprising that this position seems scary to women and that they enter and leave it many times before finally seizing it more or less permanently as a new identity. Those women who have taken on this subject position, however, no longer express a sense of scariness and anxiety about court hearings and instead eagerly pursue their assailants in court. Such women may no longer be those most seriously victimized, leading some critics to argue that trivial incidents are coming under the scrutiny of the court. They are, however, the women who have moved through a series of experiments and reinforcements from others into a new subjectivity within the law. This probably accounts for what Judith Wittner finds is the court's central problem and "most baffling contradiction": women with the genuine and serious complaints of the type the court was designed to help frequently drop out, while women with the most minor and trivial complaints were often those who were most energetic about prosecuting, eager to see the perpetrator punished, and willing to return to court many times.[37] As Ferraro and Pope observe, at the point of arrest there is a dramatic and irreconcilable clash between the culture of power embodied in the law and the relational culture within which battered women live.[38]

Women's ability and willingness to move into this subjectivity depends, of course, on how the law treats them. As the interviews indicate, the police play a critical role in either taking them seriously or telling them the bruises are insignificant or the assault minor. Women notice if the police chat and joke with the batterer. Both men and women attend closely to the demeanor of the judge, the things she says, and the extent to which penalties are actually imposed. As they move into this subjectivity, the support or opposition of kin and friends, including the man's kin, friends, and other women in the support group, are extremely important. One woman said that when she consulted with her friends, for example, she discovered that they were all in the same boat with her. Yet when they talked about their problems and hers, they did not urge her to leave the man. The staff of the feminist advocacy program, Alternatives to Violence (ATV) and the Shelter staff play critical roles in fostering this transformation of self. One woman, for example, said that the support of the ATV advocates in court was very helpful. "They really changed my life around." With the support of others in the women's support group, this woman said she was able to "tell off" her batterer, letting him know that he was "playing with her mind" and that she wanted him to leave her alone. She said in an interview that in the group she learned that despite her boyfriend's constant insults, she had nothing to be ashamed of. She was proud of the certificate she received from attending the support group, and commented that she and others framed them and put them on the wall. Taking on this new identity requires a social shift of some magnitude. For many abused women, their most important relationship is with the man. Taking on this subjectivity inevitably excludes him from her life unless he is willing to adopt the new identity the law offers him. Her ability to make this change depends on the social support she receives for the new identity offered to her by the law.

---

37. Judith Wittner, *Reconceptualizing Agency in Domestic Violence Court, in* Community Activism and Feminist Politics: Organizing Across Race, Class, and Gender 88–89 (Nancy A. Naples ed., 1998).
38. Kathleen J. Ferraro & Lucille Pope, *Irreconcilable Differences: Battered Women, Police, and the Law, in* Legal Responses to Wife Assault 96–127 (N. Zoe Hilton ed., 1993).

Difficult as the change is for women, the transformation for men into a new subjectivity that seems less masculine within dominant cultural frameworks is far more challenging. This new subjectivity represents the masculinity of a different social class, one to which few of these men have the education, income, or job skills to aspire. In effect, through the ATV program, the men are offered a masculinity developed by men of wealth and education, in which authority over women depends on resources and allows some negotiation of power, an authority constructed by dominant whites, in place of that grounded in strength, physical competence, sexual prowess, and control over women favored by the working-class men in Hilo. As a Native Hawaiian man in the program said, "ATV teaches the haole way of handling conflicts." As Connell's work indicates, masculinities are multiple and developed within particular class and cultural contexts.[39]

The women are also offered a more middle class vision of family and gender relations. One woman, for example, a twenty-three-year-old unmarried mother of three, said that she has learned to communicate in ATV and she and her partner are now more aware of each other's feelings. "I feel like we can have the American Dream—now we can grow. I want it all too. I want the two-door garage, the house, and the big dog." Thus, the new subjectivity for women promises more control over her life, a new relationship to courts and the law, and the prospect of a more orderly and less chaotic life. Men, on the other hand, are encouraged to control their emotions and to see the legal system not as support for their gendered authority in the family, but as a source of surveillance and critique. The new subjectivity for men offers a masculinity dependant on a more negotiative relationship with a partner, even in such fundamental arenas as sexual privilege. Authority is displaced from control over women to control over property. It is not surprising that poor men often reject this identity, as the resistant conversation in the treatment groups reveals.

Within these general patterns, there is an important difference between those who are new to the law and those who have previous experience as the subjects of legal concern. Two of the men who were interviewed had long histories of court involvement for crimes dating back to their juvenile years. These men expressed none of the sense of outrage or humiliation of the other men; instead they appreciated the contributions of the program to their understanding of how to keep their partners. Some women, on the

---

39. R.W. Connell, Masculinities (1995); *see also* Matthew C. Gutmann, The Meanings of Macho: Being a Man in Mexico City (1996); Matthew C. Gutmann, *The Ethnographic (G)ambit: Women and the Negotiation of Masculinity in Mexico City,* 24 American Ethnologist 833–55 (1997); Matthew C. Gutmann, *Trafficking in Men: The Anthropology of Masculinity,* 26 Annual Rev. Anthropology 385–409 (1997); David Gilmore, Manhood in the Making: Cultural Concepts of Masculinity (1990).

other hand, who have histories of involvement with the child protective services and thus have been in the position of receiving legal and social service scrutiny and control in order to get their children back, felt little of the sense of awe and scariness inherent in their new subjectivity in the law. They took a far more instrumental view toward what the law could do for them. Similarly, women who had toyed with this new subjectivity for some time and developed a more enduring commitment to it were more deliberate, strategic, and committed to legal remedies and more willing to press forward even when the law let them down.

The adoption or rejection of new subjectivities is not only about the discursive construction of the self in relationship to others, however. Identities cannot be simply assumed and discarded like clothes, although like clothes they are subject to constraint in choice and in the resources available to acquire them. These identities are linked to institutional systems that locate individuals within productive relationships that allow them to acquire skills and secure jobs or deny them these opportunities. For example, batterers' economic marginality means that they cannot adopt the proffered resource-rich expression of masculinity in which power depends on economic providing rather than on violence. Gendered identities are also located within historically created and regionally specific class and ethnic structures. In Hilo, this includes colonialism and the plantation system. The cultural meanings of masculinity and femininity are pulled out of the matrix of opportunities and disabilities provided by these class and ethnic structures, including Native Hawaiian warrior symbolism, sexual prowess among groups which immigrated largely as single males, such as Filipinos, and hard drinking and risk-taking, often sources of masculine pride among whites. These are historically produced subject positions, shaped by larger institutional structures and adopted or discarded only within the constraints of wealth, color, and class. They provide repertoires of gendered subjectivities, and the law does as well.

A.   Women and Subjectivity in the Law

Interviews with thirty women between 1991 and 1994 reveal their gradual adoption of a new rights subjectivity in the early years of the movement against domestic violence in this town. This was a time of intense activism by a feminist organization that created a shelter and batterer treatment program and support group, called Alternatives to Violence (ATV), and by a very supportive judiciary.[40] At the same time, the idea of intervening strongly in

40. See Sally Engle Merry, *Rights, Religion, and Community: Approaches to Violence Against Women in the Context of Globalization,* 35 Law & Soc'y Rev. 1301–50 (2001).

domestic violence incidents was new to the police and one that contradicted their previous practices. By 2000, police were more supportive of victims.

Four women who were interviewed reported fears and anxieties about turning to the courts for the first time, but found that at least some parts of it supported their new subjectivity. It is clear in these accounts that the role of the advocates and shelter workers from ATV is critically important, while the police tend to trivialize the problem. In 1992, Dora (a pseudonym) turned to the courts for help after years of violence from her husband, the father of her young child. Her story is typical of battered women's experiences in that she hesitated for a long time to do something about an ongoing pattern of violence and then, when she finally did act, found the court scary and her partner's angry reaction terrifying. She even helped him escape legal penalties for his violence against her. In her interview, she said that she found the legal system powerful and supportive at some times and overly lenient and slow at others. She describes the violence in a document she wrote requesting compensation for her abuse as a crime victim:

> Sam and I have been together for almost five years. There has been abuse on and off for the first few years. This past year has been the worst, it got to the point where he would beat me at least once a day and for about four weeks he beat me two or three times a day. It was so hard living with him. I have no family out here, only myself and our son. I lived in constant fear of Sam, never knowing of his coming here, afraid of what he was going to be like. Sam has threatened me with guns, spear guns, knife on one occasion. He would drag me down the hill by my hair, rip my clothes off of me, smash pans over my head. We had to replace or fix all but two doors in our house because he threw me through the other doors.
>
> There was so much constant abuse it seemed like it would never end. Many times I thought that when I died it would be because my husband killed me. I was afraid to have him arrested because I knew he wouldn't stay in that long and I thought that he would kill me when he got out. Finally, on May 31, 1992, I couldn't deal with it. We were driving home from Hilo, my husband was sitting in the back of our truck. I was driving because Sam was too drunk. We were driving down the road and he reached through the back window and grabbed my face, scratching my face, then he tried to choke me and I felt that if he got open the door he would kill me. I looked over at my son in his car seat. He was frightened, screaming, crying and I knew I couldn't put up with this terror any more. I managed to drive away when he got out of the back to open my door. I just wanted the hell that my life had become to end. Since that time Sam has started ATV classes and is making much improvement. He knows that he needs to change to keep his family, and that abusing me is wrong. I feel that calling the police was the hardest, and best thing I ever did.

They had been together five years, married for three of them, and he had abused her most of the time. Dora explained his violence in terms of his cultural background, saying that in Samoa it is the man's responsibility to keep the woman in line. After this incident, Dora called the police to help her get her things and go to the shelter, but the police let him follow her alone into the bedroom, which frightened her. Then the police started "talking story" with him, discussing where to go fishing. They took him away, but only to his sister's house which was four houses away. Ten minutes later he was back. The next day he was still there and she called the police, discovering that she had a 24-hour restraining order against him. This meant that he got arrested for violating the order of the court. Dora said that she always thought that if he were arrested, he would kill her, so his sister went down and posted bail. Using the law clearly represented a powerful challenge to him.

Dora got a no-contact restraining order against Sam, but he came to visit her at the house anyway. Two weeks after the incident they went together to family court, which required both of them to attend ATV. "It was scary going to court. I didn't know if they would send him to jail. But I was also glad because he had to go to classes now." Both attended meetings at the ATV program. She was pleased that the court required him to attend ATV because otherwise he would not have gone. Her mother had sent her a ticket from the mainland to come home, but she decided not to go.

By September, three months later, Dora said that things had gotten a lot better. He had not been violent to her since July. She has learned a lot more about his controlling actions towards her. Before it felt like she was in prison, forced to go places with his family who didn't like her because she was white, but now she is better able to gauge what is happening to him. Dora thought the family court judge was concerned about her safety, while the police were overly lenient, telling her that there was hardly a scratch on her and that they couldn't arrest him. Dora is in her early twenties, a mainland white woman from a middle class family with two years of college and an adequate family income. She said, "I had the stereotype that it doesn't happen to people like me with a house and education. I thought it just happened to welfare people." This was her first experience with bringing an abuse charge to court and she knew no one else who had done so.

Thus, turning to the legal system was scary and difficult for Dora, something she hesitated to do for a long time, yet when she did so, at least some of those she encountered took her and her problems seriously as rights claims. Although the police treated the problem as relatively unimportant, the combined effect of the stern family court judge and the feminist ATV program moved her toward a new position of seeing herself as a person who was battered and had rights not to put up with it.

Darlene went to the shelter after her husband Bill, whose story is described below, hit her when he was drunk.[41] With the help of advocates

---

41. She is a thirty-nine-year-old white woman with a high school education.

at the shelter, she filed for a no-contact TRO which she later modified to a contact TRO while her husband was prosecuted for the charge of assault. This was the first time she had taken a violence problem to the courts, and she knew no one else who had. She found the law helpful and supportive but she got a "major reaction" from his family. They said to her, "but he only hit you once." In an intake form, she expressed some concern for him: "There is a really angry little boy inside of Bill. The boy does not come out too often. He is usually a good person and tries to stay that way, but he also feels violence can solve problems." Similarly, another woman who had experienced a series of abusive relationships said that these happened because the men were not happy with themselves. With reference to one, she said: "He didn't have a job, he didn't have nothing to do, he didn't have no friends, and the kinds of friends he did have that he finally did meet aren't the right kind."

Darlene was glad of the law. She said, "I'm anti-abuse, and I'm glad that the law has gotten involved. I wanted to give him a chance and let him know it's not going to happen again." Both Darlene and Bill were sent to ATV, Darlene to the support group, Bill to the violence control program. Although she felt the police officer was a "total jerk" and kept hassling her about the charges with no empathy or respect for what she was going through, she says she is glad she found a way to be backed up by the courts and to let Bill know he was wrong. (Bill's view, below, is that one of the police sided with him.) "I had to rely on my instincts through this whole thing." At the shelter she says she learned that there are laws now and places to go. The family court judge gave her husband a speech that she thought was quite helpful. Yet, she was disappointed by the criminal court and the jail experience. She thought jail should be a punishment and stigma, but for Bill it was like going to summer camp. He enjoyed it. He found others to collaborate with him in making himself look right. Through her participation in the courts and ATV, she now has a lot of awareness of power and control and understands that abuse is happening around the world and that women are starting to gain back their dignity. She would like to be involved with changing things, but she needs to take care of herself now.

Darlene is characteristic of many of the women we interviewed who were in the ATV support group. This was her first time in court and she had mixed experiences with the law. The police were not very supportive of her rights not to be battered and the jail failed to provide an atmosphere critical of male battering. She faced opposition from Bill's family and had no family of her own to support her. On the other hand, the family court judge gave a good lecture. The personnel of the shelter and the ATV program were very important in encouraging her and showing her how to use the system. Although she requested a contact TRO and moved back in with him, she has tried on the new self offered by the law: one which sets limits to violence and punishes those who violate these limits. Bill, however, resisted the new identity the law offered him as batterer. He found support for this resistance from his comrades in jail, the police, and his family's opposition to her actions.

Beatrice[42] filed for a TRO against her husband Sam who had been abusing her emotionally and physically for thirteen years. His perspective is included below as Sam's story. She was also a relative newcomer to the law. Once she went to a police station with abuse charges against him, but she dropped the charges. In her version of the story, Sam went drinking and did not come home. She found him at his sister's, where he told her he was a hit man and had killed someone. Frightened, she took her children to the shelter to get a TRO. The day he was supposed to be served the TRO, he tried to commit suicide. At the hospital he told her it was a hoax, that he had never killed anyone but just wanted to see how she would react. At the court hearing, the judge mandated him to ATV, as she requested. But the initial no-contact TRO was converted to a contact order at the first hearing and then dropped at her request after six months. Sam strongly resisted Beatrice's move into the legal arena, threatening to commit suicide. She persisted out of fear for her children's safety. She had never gone to court before and knew no one else who had, but she appreciated the court's willingness to condemn his violence. The court was scary: "It was my first time, I didn't know what to say. I also felt relieved because these things were mandated. I know he would not have come on his own." Beatrice says Sam has learned a lot at ATV. Yet under pressure from him she backed away from legal remedies.

Jane had a far more rights-supportive experience with the police than many other women at this time. When Jane's boyfriend of seven years started pushing her and smashing her into the garage wall, she called his friend who called the police. In front of the police, her boyfriend denied the blows, but she said she wanted to charge him with everything and the police took him away. The next day she went to the shelter and got a no-contact TRO. When he appeared at her house to pick up some things, the police came and told him that he could not stay because of the TRO. This was Jane's first time in court with a violence charge. In family court she asked for a contact TRO and to have him receive counseling and ATV. The judge sent them both to ATV and extended the no-contact order for two weeks but later, at her request, changed it to a contact order. She said the court was scary. "Really scary. I think it was more scary than being beat up." But ATV has really helped her boyfriend to break down his pattern of violence and helped him to identify his "emotional being." "He's changed so

---

42. She is a thirty-three-year-old Japanese-American woman married with three children, an eleventh grade education, and a life-long Hilo resident currently supported by welfare.

much, much more for the better." She was very pleased with the concern the police expressed to her, the information and help they provided, and their resistance to accepting his story.

All four of these women tried the court for the first time and found some strength in its support although they also found the experience mixed and the assertiveness it required frightening. The actions of the particular police and judges they encountered profoundly affected how each felt about the law and their willingness to follow through. Each of these women also backed away from the legal process at some point, usually because they got what they needed and the pressure on them from their partners and their families to give in was great. Each had, in a sense, tried on this new self, made some headway, then retreated, but with some change in their sense of personhood.

Other women interviewed told similar stories of the scariness of the court and the support offered by the law. Judy was threatened with a gun by her husband who she had dated since 6th grade. He had been abusive since she was 17. He had demanded sex from her and she refused. Although a staff member helped her write a TRO, "I was scared, I doubted myself, I was talking to God." Her husband was also scared because he already had charges. "I didn't want to punish him, just set him straight." The judge ordered counseling and ATV for both of them, but he didn't like it—he didn't want to be controlled. She says, "I felt weird being in court. Who would have ever dreamed of being in the courtroom doing this with someone I love?" But things had changed. She remembers that in 1979 when her mother called the police several times they were "real COLD, not compassionate." Now the family court judge was cold but fair. Her husband was not arrested but was already on five years' probation for sexual assault and has served one month in prison. She still loves him, although not as a spouse should. But she sees her children sad and asking for their father. Thus, she is caught between protecting herself and denying her children access to their father, another kind of pressure on her to drop legal sanctions. Both were mandated to ATV, first with a no-contact TRO and subsequently a contact TRO.

Jane is a thirty-three-year-old white woman from the mainland with two children who works as a chef and gets child support and welfare. She had no previous court experience when her partner assaulted her and smashed her furniture. The police persuaded her not to press charges and had her sign a paper to that effect. Even though he hit her, she was reluctant to file for a TRO because she thought the courts did not favor women. Police think she's the "crazy one." She has felt embarrassed and degraded by the police attitude in this and previous abusive relationships. Such humiliating experiences clearly deter a woman from calling the police again. However, when she went for a TRO, the judge had a great impact on her partner. When her husband complained that she was not being nice to him, the judge cut him off, saying "Did you punch her in the head?" He had to say, "Yes I did." In court she "found out she has rights." It seemed that he went through a big shift in his attitudes. However, she noticed that it was the judge he respected, not her. After the court hearing Jane was surprised to find she felt like a citizen for the first time and that someone really cared. Her husband had eroded her self-esteem but she says now she feels empowered. This experience has changed her life; now she sees how violence permeates society. Jane's advice to women is, "Have self-love. A lot of us don't go through with it because the man might get angry. The woman should believe she shouldn't be hit no matter what. Sometimes the women think they deserve it." Jane has clearly reformulated her battering experience as larger than her own relationship and as a site for the creation of the rights-bearing subject. Despite her bad experience with police, she felt that the court cared about her problems and she learned she had rights. Several other women also described feeling stronger and more empowered after their encounters with the courts and ATV.[43]

Women with extensive experience in court respond very differently to the new subjectivity it offers. If they have been through a series of encounters with the law, they have built up a rights subjectivity through experience. Those who have left their partners typically feel less frightened by the legal process and are less afraid of the effects of their actions on their partners. A thirty-year-old mother of four who has spent at least four years in and out of court with charges of abuse against her and her children is now separated from her husband and getting divorced. She said that she is more relaxed now. She is not in an abusive situation "and I have the court to back me up now." Some of the police were good, she said, but some knew him and were

---

43. A twenty-eight-year-old Japanese woman born and raised in Hawai'i says, after she got a TRO, that she felt stronger and more informed. She first asked for a contact order and then shifted to a no-contact. She was down on herself and believed the bad things he said about her. Now she feels happy and confident. "I don't need a man." Her advice to women is to get a TRO the first time. "Go on intuition so you can see how it is." Again, she emphasizes that moving into the legal arena is hard, scary, and uncertain. One woman was helped to fill out forms by a shelter advocate and said that it is "Giving me courage." A twenty-nine-year-old Hawaiian/Chinese/Caucasian married mother of two with a little college, a native of Hilo, found the court scary because "she didn't know what to expect after that." Her husband Keo (see below) was furious. A thirty-eight-year-old Mexican housewife on welfare said that the ATV classes "have helped me to be strong." She felt that she had more power and control inside herself to control the anger and the outbursts so that hopefully the police won't have to come. She said "I was shame. I don't want the cops to come anymore. The same cop keeps coming over and over calling you by name already." Her husband threatened to give their children "dirty lickins" if they called the police. A twenty-five-year-old single Portuguese/Puerto Rican mother of three living at home on welfare said that she had never gone to court before, and it was scary: "I felt weird telling the judge that I still wanted contact even though I was still getting lickins."

not helpful. The shelter taught her that she was a person who had feelings and did not have to be his servant and jump when he said jump. She mostly learned that she "did not have to put up with his shit." The court was effective because "it shook up his ass." She thought that for her the court was fair because she knows how to dress, look presentable, speak clearly, and she understands how the legal system works. She has mastered the ATV program's perspective through years of experience with abuse and in ATV. She uses the feminist language of ATV to describe her experiences: "In the past . . . it has mostly been emotional abuse, threatening to leave me, to send me back to my mom. He used male privilege and said I had to do all the work in the house. He tried to keep me isolated by not letting me use the car. He used economic abuse by saying I couldn't/shouldn't get a job so that I became dependent on his income alone." She has had three supportive judges and the encouragement of ATV has increased her willingness to turn to the courts and helped her to adopt a rights consciousness.

Among the thirty women interviewed, twelve were in court for the first time. Five of these women mentioned without prompting that the experience was scary, one that it was very tense, and several that it was in various ways stressful. Only two first-timers suggested that they were not scared. Those with more experience never said that the court was scary but instead described annoyance, frustration, anger, and support. For example, a thirty-five-year-old Hawaiian/Chinese woman said that when she dropped her TRO, the judge told her that if she needed it again, he would be there. Yet the same woman recognized that members of the legal system were disappointed and that they did not understand the emotional side of why women drop TROs and get back together with their batterers.

Facilitators of the women's support groups at the ATV program emphasize rights and the importance of using the courts. My research assistants and I observed at least forty women's support groups between 1991 and 2000. The facilitators commonly provide information and advice about how to file TROs, what will happen in court, and how important it is to use the courts. Even though facilitators emphasize rights, the women are more likely to talk in terms of empowerment, courage, and surviving. Some claim they are learning to stand up for their rights but more describe themselves as survivors. By 2000, many more described positive experiences with police than had in the early 1990s. One talked about a police officer who called her regularly for days afterwards to check on her safety. In 2000, a police officer in a special domestic violence unit acknowledged that the police often fail to intervene strongly in battering situations for several reasons: they know the man, they are trying to avoid the paperwork of an arrest, they do not take the problem seriously, or their supervisor does not care. In contrast to the police, most of the judges in town viewed battering as a serious problem throughout the 1990s. For about five years during the 1990s, the prosecutor's office had a special domestic violence unit with a prosecutor who cared about these problems, but in the late 1990s attention was shifting to other areas such as child abuse.

Clearly, the engagement in the legal system, including the act of initiating that engagement, changes the way women feel about themselves. For many using the courts for the first time, this is a scary endeavor requiring courage but provides the comforting realization that members of the legal system care. This realization is tempered by experience, however, particularly with the ambivalence of the police, the protracted criminal court process with its plea-bargained outcomes, and the man's occasional escape from ATV despite mandated participation. The program talks about rights, but the women talk about finding themselves, about following their intuitions, about having courage, and about surviving. Advocates at the shelter and at ATV, who also go to court with the women, are critically important supporters for the kinds of transformations the women experience. Victims constantly describe the support they receive from these advocates, most of whom are previously battered women. They provide support as advocates in both criminal court and family court, as people who help them file TRO petitions, and as facilitators of support groups. They help the victims try on this new identity to see how it feels. This is clearly an iterative process, tried over and over in front of different audiences, only some of which are sympathetic and supportive. There are some women who take it on with intensity and commitment, sometimes working for a program such as ATV or pursuing men through whatever legal channels they can, while others get discouraged and back away.

Women caught up in the child protective services (CPS) system express a different kind of subjectivity, one closer to what the men feel; they are now subject to surveillance and questioning about a fundamental feature of their own gender identity: their capacity to raise children. Just as the CPS workers' critique of their parenting and the removal of children from their homes strike at the heart of their identities as mothers, so women's refusal to play the submissive wife assaults men's identities as husbands. Several of the women we interviewed described long, painful efforts to get their children back through attendance at parenting classes, drug-treatment programs, and anger management classes.

There is a class dimension to the new self offered through the law. Such a person is less dependent on a man, but also capable of a more orderly life, a new family form, a house, garage and a big dog. Several women said they felt shamed or humiliated by the police intervention into their families and looked for the day when they wouldn't need to call the police any more. Similarly, men found the intervention of the law against them as batterers a degrading experience. Yet this seemed less humiliating to those men with extensive experience in the legal system.

Despite their gradual adoption of a new subjectivity, women commonly felt dissatisfied with the effectiveness of the system itself. They complained about the lack of jail time for perpetrators, the slowness of the criminal court, and the mixed response of the police, particularly when they knew the defendant. Most have maintained their relationships with their partners and have young children, so they are torn between protecting their children from the man's violence and trying to maintain the connection between the children and their father. Yet, the need to protect children seems an important reason for turning to the law, allowing the woman to take on the subjectivity of protective mother rather than non-submissive wife. Finally, it is quite striking that virtually all of the women report long histories of abuse dating from the beginnings of the relationship with their abusers, so that their mobilization of law is a response to a history of difficulties.

There is little sense that distinctive cultural patterns justify violence among the ethnic groups in Hilo in these women's stories, although some use ethnic factors to explain its source. Men typically defend their violence as justified by the woman's sexual activities or her failure to care for their children, but more often they simply deny that the blow was significant. It appears that money problems frequently trigger the fights. Both the women and the men who attend ATV have very low incomes and limited education.[44] Many are on welfare or working only intermittently. In sum, legal intervention offers a new subjectivity to women that requires asserting rights. Such assertions are scary and risk disrupting important relationships

---

44. Program intake forms for 1,574 people served between 1990 and 1998, two-thirds men and one-third women, provide demographic data on who is referred. About three-quarters of the men (77 percent) and women (70 percent) earned under $11,000. Over half earned under $8,000 a year, a low income even in a place where housing costs for substandard housing are low and hunting and fishing routinely supplement incomes. Only 6 percent earned above $25,000 a year. In contrast, the 1990 Census found that only 19 percent of the town's residents earned under $10,000 in household income while 53 percent earned over $25,000, an income level reached by only 4 percent of the ATV women participants. Men and women in the men's violence control program and women's support groups frequently talked about welfare, survival by fishing, hunting, and odd construction jobs, and the pressures of poverty. Their discussions suggested that many did not have steady jobs. These clients are also substantially less educated than town residents, with the men even less educated than the women. Half are high school graduates (46 percent) and one quarter started college (25 percent), but only 3 percent have a college degree. In contrast, 29 percent of Hilo's population has an associate's, bachelor's, or higher degree, while only 5 percent of the ATV population does. Thus, the men sent to the violence control program as well as the women they batter are significantly poorer and less educated than the town overall. Many are on welfare or living with partners who are; many camp in forests or beaches; many are embittered by a colonial past and present poverty; many suffer from emotional scars of childhood physical and sexual abuse. Two thirds of both the male and female participants in the feminist program said that they had either witnessed or experienced violence as children. Almost half the men in the feminist batterer program have been arrested for something in addition to battering.

with partners and kin. Women's willingness to take the risk depends on the extent to which ATV and shelter staff, police, judges and prosecutors, as well as their own friends and family, support them.

B.   Men and New Subjectivities in the Law

The male experience in this situation is predominantly one of betrayal. Overall, men express anger, humiliation, and dismay. They describe feeling that no one is listening to them and that the court is on the woman's side. Some complain that the criminal court drags on and hangs over their heads. A few say that they have been treating their wives this way for many years, and cannot understand why their wives are now objecting. Many claim that their behavior is not so serious. Those whose partners recant find deep comfort in their change of heart, seeing them as an ally in their now mutual opposition to the legal system. None defend the right to batter their wives, but many argue that the penalty is too severe, the program too long, the offense not so serious, or their violence less than that of others. Some complain that they did not know about the length or cost of the ATV program when they agreed to plead guilty and attend ATV in order to avoid jail.

For those for whom this is the first encounter with legal scrutiny, this is a humiliating and degrading experience. The identity of the batterer as it is defined within legal discourse is energetically resisted. Most find ways of rejecting or refusing this new subjectivity by blaming their partners or by observing that such things happened in their own families when they were children and elicited no public reaction. Many said that their violence was not serious like that of other men. One man insisted "I don't batter nobody." He acknowledged slapping his partner on the side of the head, but not punching her in the mouth. A Native Hawaiian claimed that the courts were not relevant to him because he was governed under native rights and the Hawai'i courts did not exercise control over him.

For those men with more extensive experience in the law, the edge of anger and outrage is muted. Some emphasize the contribution the ATV program has made in helping them keep in touch with wives and children. Many commented positively about ATV, although this must be assessed against the method of obtaining interviews and the participants' assumptions of connections between the research and the program. Thus, these statements may be biased since only those at least somewhat positive toward the program may have agreed to be interviewed.

Men often describe their experiences in court, particularly those for whom this was a new experience, as frightening and infuriating. Joe, a thirty-six-year-old Hawaiian/Chinese man who had a TRO issued against him, and then was referred to ATV, and subsequently appeared in Family Court for the full hearing on the TRO application, was very angry, his wife said, because he had hoped his wife would drop the TRO. But she did not. The ATV advocates had encouraged her not to drop it. She describes the waiting as a tense hour and a half. In his interview, he said it was a very tense three hours. He says she had an attorney; she says she was accompanied by an ATV advocate. Although Joe had previous troubles in court, he described these as only "small mischief"—drinking, fights—apparently fairly acceptable offenses. At this Family Court hearing, however, he felt very alone. He felt that he received little advice in advance. He had not seen his wife since the incident. He felt hurt and awkward because of all the other people waiting outside the court, including some he recognized from the ATV classes. He sat by himself while his wife sat and waited with her attorney (probably an ATV advocate). No one told him what was going to happen, and he had no idea of his rights. The process seemed very impersonal, he said: the woman has all the support and the resources and the man is left alone.

However, he found the judge calm and understanding and listened when the judge said he needed to change his violent behavior. In ATV, Joe has learned to distinguish between anger and violence. He feels he now understands himself better and can use this knowledge in other relationships and to better himself. As he put it, the experience with the law led him to "a pot of gold," consisting of ATV, his desire to change, and the support of his wife. He says that he obeyed the TRO because his wife and children believed in him, not because he was afraid of the courts.

Bill, discussed above as Darlene's husband, said that he was only defending his wife against her co-workers at a party when he landed in both Family Court and District Court. He was very "pissed off" when he found out that she had requested a no-contact TRO. "I felt like she was being brainwashed and that our relationship was not important to her." The judge sent him to ATV and told him the penalty for failure to attend was a "messed-up relationship." The criminal court sentenced him to ten days in jail, of which eight were suspended and two served. Darlene said he did not seem to find jail stressful. As a result of his experiences, including ATV, he says that they communicate "way better." He has learned, he says, that just because you are married this does not mean that you should take anything for granted, nor that your wife should stay home and cook. Bill is thirty-two, a high school graduate who works as a carpenter and is of Hawaiian/Chinese/Portuguese/Irish ancestry.

A thirty-five-year-old Hawaiian/Chinese man, Keo, had a fight with his wife that led him to move out onto the beach. When she filed for a TRO, he was furious: it was the first time he had a TRO issued against him "and I never did nothing, I mean, we fight but it's my right; she's my wife. I never hit her, ever, that's rare, you know, for one Hawaiian." He felt the judge, who he described as Japanese, never listened to him but cut him off all the time.

He kept explaining that he was not violent and should not be there. His wife had an elderly haole lawyer who kept giving him "stink eye." Although sentenced to attend ATV in June, as of September he had still not started and insisted that he did not have a problem with violence. According to his wife, this man grew up in an abusive home and spent several years in both juvenile and adult prison, as well as some years living on the streets as a teenager. He did not finish high school and is currently spending his time caring for his children.

Sam, the husband of Beatrice, tells the story of their conflict somewhat differently than she does. He says that he drank, had a fight with his wife, told her a story about killing someone, and when she failed to return home, took pills to commit suicide. When he woke up in the hospital, she came home and changed the no-contact TRO to a contact TRO. He was "pissed" that she had applied for a TRO and found the experience in court "kind of shocking." It was his first time, and he just had to listen. He was sent to ATV, which he now thinks was fair, but at the time he did not think he had done anything wrong. He has learned a lot in ATV and now thinks they can communicate better with less yelling and screaming. He says he is almost finished ATV and is scared to leave the program because he can share things with the guys that would make his wife angry if he talked to her about them. Sam is thirty-three, a high school graduate of Japanese/Chinese/Hawaiian/Caucasian ancestry who is on welfare. He is an unemployed laborer who has spent his life in Hilo. Like many of the other men interviewed, Sam has little or no income and a habit of drinking and drug consumption. Here, it appears that he used his suicide attempt as a way to force Beatrice to stay with him.

Some men had different reactions to the court. A forty-three-year-old Hawaiian/Chinese man with no income said he was glad when his girlfriend took out a TRO on him and charged him with abuse because she was fooling around and he wanted her to leave. He was afraid of the woman judge and went to ATV as mandated. Here he felt that they were too negative: as he put it, if you tell a person over and over that they are stupid, they will be stupid. He resisted attending: although the incident and referral took place in November, by February he had missed enough sessions to have his case referred back to the court by the ATV program. The court held a hearing in March, imposed a 90-day suspended sentence, and sent him back to ATV. By July, he had completed only half the ATV program.

George, a forty-nine-year-old man of Puerto Rican ancestry, had a fight with his teenaged children and his wife. In his account of the fight at the ATV intake, he said that at the beginning, he yelled at his daughter "You've got no respect for me." He was angry and refused to plead guilty, so the case went to trial. He was sentenced to two days in jail and ATV. George did not think the jail served any purpose nor did he learn anything. When he was growing up, things were different: "If it was back then, my parents would be in jail." But, he concludes, whatever they did when he was young, he deserved it. When he began attending ATV he was very hostile and thought his wife deserved the violence, but now he does not think so. He grew up in Hilo and works in a maintenance job and, like several of the other men interviewed, has a drinking problem.

Outrage and dismay are common responses to women's mobilization of the law. For example, Rod says he hit his wife Judy, described above, on and off for ten years because he didn't know how to express feelings and didn't know how to deal with stress. He said that whenever he got frustrated he would look for another woman. Police interviewed him under a sexual assault complaint five years ago, but he thinks that the woman he picked up was a prostitute. He would fight with Judy because when she refused sex with him, he would go out, presumably seeking sex from other women. She said if you go, that is the end of the marriage. But when she filed for a TRO and he received it from his probation officer, "I was stunned, I was shocked, couldn't believe she would do that." When they went to court he was angry, hated the police, the advocates with his wife, the judge, and the bailiff. He felt like he was being manipulated and judged and felt it was unjust, that he shouldn't have been there, "like my rights were being violated." According to the interviewer, he said "I felt like a piece of meat in the court. There's no emotions there. The feeling is that you're not human. Nobody cares about you there. It's just black and white. I felt like a reject from society." He thinks that in the eyes of the court, women are classified as the "weaker vessel" and men are the brutes. His previous sexual assault case had prepared him for this experience with the court. Rod did not think the requirement to attend ATV was fair because he was forced to do it against his wishes. But he has now learned that his wife wanted a divorce and he has to think about paying child support. In contrast to other men, he does not talk about learning about relationships and himself, although he does say that ATV taught him about his anger and how to express his feelings. One intriguing observation is that he found the program very gentle. He expected it to be run "by all these militaristic women: but it wasn't like that."

In this interview, Rod clearly expresses a loss of autonomy and rights in the vivid metaphor of feeling like a piece of meat. His sense of identity assault is dual, initiated first by his arrest for predatory sexuality, then for violence, but he has found ways of resisting both identities in his sense of anger and outrage and the violation of his rights. Rod is not as poor as many of the men interviewed, and unlike them holds a job with some skill. He works as an accountant and in conjunction with Judy's work makes a family wage. He has a high school diploma and one year of college and is thirty-two years old.

Instead of surprise and outrage, John talks about shame. In a family battle, his wife got "battered a little" but he didn't think she would go through with it. He "kind of felt ashamed" for being in court, for having all these people involved in his life. He said he was "a bit humiliated. I was resistant at first." As he became involved with the child protective services, he said that he recognized that he was up against people in power and did not try to "buck it." He experienced a loss of masculinity by the intrusion of state/social services into his family. As a forty-two-year-old white male from the mainland who works as a carpenter, he has a relatively large income for this group. His interpretation of violence is that it's "really bad in Hawai'i— that macho thing, the 'warrior trip.' It's ego and pride." In his view, if the court puts you on probation, it's like a watchdog on you. In another intriguing reference to the power of the professional arena of law, he says that it would be good to simplify legal jargon. "The language is above everyone." Thus, he points to embedded class power in the language of the law. The experience of intrusion, powerlessness, and subjection to the language of an elite class reinforces his sense of class vulnerability.

Similarly, Clay was angry when the TRO arrived, although this was his third encounter with TROs. When I asked what he learned in ATV, he responded, "Don't do it again. I served time already. Eight months too long." Has he learned anything new at ATV? "Some stuffs. They don't listen. They have their own set theory." He says he really did not do anything, only talked mean, and there is no proof. He is angry. The courts are not fair because they don't listen to him. "They only hear one side. Try to say something, brush you off." The court is one-sided: "They think only of the girls." Clay has been in and out of juvenile court for many years and is currently twenty-eight, married, and although a carpenter, is not working, but surviving by hunting.

Fred, in court for the first time, claims his violence was only a few backhands. He feels unfairly treated. The police didn't want to arrest him, he says, and his wife filed charges because she didn't know much about the system. Then she wanted to drop the charges, but couldn't and regretted that he was charged. She thought the case would be dropped, but even though her paper was filed to drop the charge, it was not. The case is not settled yet and he has been going to ATV for six and a half months. Now he knows nobody deserves to be beaten up. He promises it will not happen again, that he would just walk out. They are still together and things are now better for him since he can cool his temper down. He had to get his own lawyer for $400 since he did not qualify for a public defender. He thinks that in the Family Court the man is always wrong, already guilty, but he thinks this is right. But in the criminal court there were all kind of cases and he wondered, "What am I doing here?" Criminal court was fair because he was not arrested, finger printed or photographed and there was no bail. Thus, the criminal court's apparent leniency confirmed his view that this was not so serious. But Fred also complained that the criminal court was confusing, that there were a lot of new words. He emphasized that he came from a "good family" with "church connections" and the police knew him and his family. He just got a little intoxicated, and his wife told the police not to arrest him.

Thus, he recuperates a masculine and respectable sense of self by emphasizing his wife's lack of desire to pursue the charges and his insistence that he does not belong in criminal court. The leniency of the court and the police are interpreted as tolerance for his behavior, minimized as trivial and undeserving of punishment and done while he was "a little intoxicated." Notice that he does not argue that his violence was acceptable or admirable, only that it was trivial and excusable. Fred is 25, white, and a long-term Hawai'i resident who speaks pidgin. He is married with two children and, like so many of the men interviewed, works in a variety of relatively low-paid jobs including bartender and security guard.

Bob claims he is a pacifist who served in Vietnam in 1968 and is furious that he was persuaded to plead guilty to an abuse charge and has been sent to ATV for eight months. Two days after the arrest, his wife said she would drop the charges, but it was too late. He was really "pissed" because he knew she attacked him. The ATV homework makes him sick because he doesn't batter. "I get uptight having to think of myself as the kind of person who batters women." This is his third wife, and he is angry that the second left him and took the house he built. He voices a common complaint that he is not like the other men in the program, and that there should be different kinds of counseling for different kinds of people. For the average person, he thinks, it would be fair to send them to ATV for 2 months, then reevaluate; only repeat offenders should have to go all eight months. And not everyone should be sent to one program where all are treated like the "worst guys." As he approaches 44, he says he is turning harder in his heart and having trouble trusting women. He came from a working-class blue-collar family on the mainland but has lived most of his adult life in Hawai'i. He is a carpenter who works on and off. Bob resists taking on the legally constituted subjectivity as batterer, even admitting that it makes him "uptight." As women adopt their new subjectivity with both trepidation and eagerness, men resist this self with anger, shame, and denial.

A twenty-three-year-old Portuguese man complained that he feels as if he is behind bars at ATV and thinks that the courts treat all the men as if they are the same. His partner does not know how to stop when she gets angry, but the court never listened to his side of the story. Another man, despite six previous visits to court, thought his partner's charge of abuse was not necessary. He was "shocked. Never thought I would get arrested. Not the type. I've heard about domestic violence—didn't think it would be me. I went to the police station, posted $250 bail, went to Mom's." In court he was not frightened, but confused. The public defender did not talk to him. He has learned from court that "Violence is a crime." Before, he didn't think that what he did was a crime. At 29, this man is unmarried but the father of two children, a lifelong Hilo resident, Filipino/Japanese in ancestry, and a draftsman but currently unemployed. He is eager to deny that he is the "kind of person who does this."

Kalae, a thirty-three-year-old almost full Hawaiian man arrested on an abuse charge, expresses most vividly the sense of humiliation in the legal process. Because he was unable to make bail, he spent the night in jail and arrived in court in chains wearing an orange jump suit along with all the other arrested people. He said he looked like a criminal and was automatically looked down on as a criminal. It was the first time he had been arrested like that. He also emphasizes that this is a new world: he and his wife used to fight when they were younger, but he was never arrested before. "It was your pilikia [trouble]—no one called the police if you raised your voice." In those days, when they were 16 or so, people just ignored fights like that. [This is the beginning of the same fifteen-year time span mentioned by others.] But now, he says, times have changed and the laws have changed. "They treated me like a criminal. I didn't think it was that serious. I did slap her." He takes comfort in her resistance to the law. Although he was required to stay away from her for eight weeks, he only stayed one week. His wife and he both wanted him home. His wife had to come forward and request it, but then the judge canceled the restraining order. He is needed at home because he has children. He complained that the system is unfair and the judge is like God. "She didn't listen to me when I said I have children. Eight weeks is too long. It was like my word didn't matter. Made it like it was the only thing I do. In an orange suit, I was very ashamed; I was a criminal." Clearly the prison uniform added to his sense of degradation and humiliation, to which he responded by asserting the identity of responsible father to his children. In Family Court he thought the judge was rude and took for granted that it was all his fault no matter what he said. "She mentioned I drink beer; I don't think it's a problem. So what's wrong with my having a few beers?"

There is in these legal arenas a struggle for identity, for defining who one is within this powerful discursive space. And in this space, men experience not being heard and losing voice. This is an experience more common for women. The men are in a sense feminized in the process, moved into the cultural space typically defined as appropriate for women.

But, as men deal with this feminization, they turn to their wives as allies in combating it. In Kalae's case, his wife joined with him in resisting the law, thus restoring some of his masculinity. They were both sneaking to be together. She was protecting him from the law. She was also afraid of the system and of getting arrested. "They have everybody scared. I'm not afraid. I know how they work. I'm not afraid of what they put on paper." He portrays himself again as courageous in juxtaposition to a timid fearful wife, taking risks to restore himself to his rightful place in the home. He uses one further strategy to recuperate a masculine self by appealing to his Native Hawaiian identity. He says he does not have to obey the court because he is Hawaiian and falls under "native rights." He belongs to an important Hawaiian sovereignty organization and comes from a people who were warriors a century ago. He notes that there are many differences between Hawaiian and British/English ways of doing things, and that there are many reasons for Native Hawaiians to be angry about past treatment by the US. He grew up learning from his grandparents how the US took Hawaiian lands and sovereignty and realizes that wrongs have happened to his people and that the government is not good. He connects this history to the fact that "most of my people are in jail." He observes that 90 percent of prison inmates are Hawaiians. "A lot of Hawaiians are in jail because they are angry at the government and the foreigners for the way they are living now." Thus, along with many other Native Hawaiians, he expresses the anger of Native Hawaiian people, now largely poor and politically marginalized, and invokes the historic takeover of Hawai'i as a way of diminishing the authority of the current legal system over him. He emphasizes its alien roots. He traces his own ancestry to the Hawaiian chiefs and their warrior traditions, and his present poverty to the state's seizure of his lands. The sovereignty movement has exposed some of this history and given him more knowledge and grounds for protest.

Thus, Kalae both shares other men's experiences in the legal system and asserts a different kind of masculine identity rooted in Hawaiian tradition. He undermines the authority of the law through a critique of the law in the context of the history of American colonialism in the islands. His wife apparently shares some ambivalence in deploying this alien legality against him, and is persuaded to subvert it and rejoin him despite the episode of violence. It is clear that there are multiple identities at play here in addition to those defined by gender. It is through such skirmishes with the legal system that new subjectivities emerge, but such identities are obviously gendered, raced, and classed as well. Such constructions depend not only on the texts of the laws, but also on men's interpretation of the relevance of the law to their lives. This depends both on how the legal system treats them and on their historic and cultural relationship to its authority.

In contrast to these angry, surprised, and entitled men, Peter, a Samoan man born in Hawai'i who has been in court and attended ATV before, says he knows that his present violence is wrong. He is worried that he will lose his children. The police told him to control his temper, leave his wife alone, and get counseling. He is now doing so with his pastor. He talks more to his wife about doing household things and is trying to lead a normal life and build trust. ATV made him look at power and control strategies, which he was not aware of using with his wife. He thinks it is good that the court stops the problem in its early stages and was relieved that "at least it did not appear in newspaper." Men arrested for abusing their spouses are listed by name in the local newspaper. Even though the judge was on the wife's side and treated him like he was nothing, he thought the judge was fair. Peter expresses a desire for "normalcy" in the cultural terms of the ATV program and does not express the same resentment against legal intrusion as many of the other men interviewed. Instead, he sees court and ATV as a way to achieve social class mobility with the help of the law.

But the number of men who enter willingly into the subjectivity offered to them by this regime of scrutiny and correction is very small. Anger is a far more common response. Out of the twenty-one men interviewed, twenty were defendants and one was a plaintiff. Sixteen of the twenty defendants said they were angry, while three of the four who said they were not angry had previous court experience.[45] Virtually all were seeking ways of reframing their experiences to diminish the extent to which they were defined as criminals. Most were humiliated and degraded by their court treatment and took comfort in their wives' resistance and in signs that the legal system was not taking their offense seriously. Yet, of the twenty referred to ATV, only four denied that they had learned helpful new things and only one failed to attend. As I said in the beginning of the article, however, it is possible that this positive assessment is skewed by the fact that interviewees were people who volunteered to talk to a person perceived as having some connection to the program. On the other hand, several of the interviewees did complain about ATV, despite the fact that they were approached for interviews by researchers in the ATV offices. Interviewers did stress that this project was not connected to the ATV program.

The new identity offered to batterers by the law is not only one of legal subjugation; it is also one of lower social class status. Men developed a variety of ways of distancing themselves from this status, either by claiming that they did not belong in the program, they came from good families, they were Native Hawaiians and part of a warrior tradition confronting an alien and illegitimate law, they were following common cultural practices in Hawai'i with its "macho thing," or that they were acting in accustomed ways acceptable in the past. Men of more subordinate class status tended to find this aspect of the legal encounter less infuriating than those with higher aspirations.

It is notable, however, that within this ethnically diverse population ranging in age from their twenties to their forties, a dominant characteristic is economic marginality. A few have steady jobs but only moderate incomes,

---

45. Eleven of the twenty defendants had previous experience in court.

but the majority is unemployed, on welfare, or occupying marginal and transitory jobs. Indeed, one of the interviewees observed that stress at work leads to violence at home. As Connell points out in his study of masculinities in Australia, men unable to perform the core task of breadwinning face great difficulties in constructing a masculine identity and frequently adopt violent patterns of behavior. In Connell's study as in this one, prestige accrues to success in fights with peers and in responding to provocation, but there is little pride in hitting women, although it happens frequently.[46] Most of the men we interviewed in Hilo were not proud of their violence against women, although some justified it by her provocative behavior or "fooling around." Instead, as they struggled to build a fragile masculinity unsupported by the core functions of breadwinning and sometimes even marriage, they searched for glimmerings within the legal system that this was not really such a serious offense, that the police or judges really did not care, and that the system was designed for people different from themselves. This was not an assertion of the right to batter but a resistance to the new criminalized identity the law was constructing for behavior that had in the past been normalized.

IV. CONCLUSIONS

For men, the law offers a new identity as a batterer, with a loss of class status and self-respect along with humiliating appearances before the police, the judge, and the ATV program, settings in which a man is either refused the opportunity to speak or not heard if he does. His wife or partner is ultimately the source of this humiliation; it is she who holds the key to supporting and even constructing his masculinity. It is then a great source of solace if she tries to undermine the process, drop the charges, change the TRO from a no-contact to a contact order, or even sneak visits with him despite the legal prohibition. Her return to the more feminine, submissive role seems to provide solace, to mitigate the pain of a damaged masculinity.

There is an important class interpretation to these encounters with the law as well. The intervention of the law into the inner workings of the family—the police at the door, the judge reading the description of the blows—is generally experienced as a humiliating experience, even by women. This opening of the family appears to be both a sign of a subordinate social status and, in many ways, an effect of that status. A lack of resources renders families open to a variety of legal interventions from welfare supervision to child protective investigations. The closing off of family relationships from such legal scrutiny is both a mark and an effect of higher social status.

---

46. *See* Connell, *supra* note 39, at 99–100.

Men resist the new masculinities constructed within law by joking and
sexual innuendo in the meetings, by failing to appear for court and ATV
meetings, by denying the construction of their violence as inappropriate battering, and by pressuring their partners to withdraw charges. The joking,
back talk to the facilitators, and talk about sex in the group meetings asserts
a different kind of masculinity, a kind of potency and power that escapes the
new model of masculinity defined within the parameters of the law and the
feminist program, both of which are based on an elite, white identity which
appears feminized in contrast to that which they have adopted.[47]

Although these subjectivities are open to some negotiation and choice,
it is a negotiation clearly constrained by a wide range of institutional factors,
such as the legal system's sympathy for battered women and the resources
available to men to live a more middle-class, contained life outside the
scrutiny of the law. It seems clear that the inability of many of these men to
perform the breadwinner or father tasks impinges on their own sense of
masculinity and their ability to assert control over their wives. At the same
time, women seeking help acquire a more autonomous subjectivity defined
by rights, but also one which denigrates their own feminine identities as
wives and subjects them to the kinds of intrusions characteristic of lower
class lives. It is not surprising that their entrance into this subject position is
ambivalent, hesitant, and intermittent.

Women's greater willingness to use the law to deal with gender violence is a response to a powerful feminist movement to redefine the meaning of battering from an inevitable feature of everyday life—an inescapable
risk—to a domain of behavior subject to prevention and change. But it is
also a response to the law's greater willingness to treat complainants with
respect and to take their problems seriously. A more complex set of penalties for batterers has developed both within and outside the law. Of particular importance is the development of new forms of governance that focus
on self-management and a redefinition of masculinity. These interventions
represent a dramatic shift away from earlier ideas of deterrence through
punishment. Instead of changing behavior by imposing punishment, the law
now channels offenders into group environments in which their use of violence in work as well as family settings and their ideas about gender relationships come under scrutiny and critique. New images of egalitarian
gender relations based on negotiation and responsibility for naming and
knowing feelings are taught to men named as batterers. Batterers meet in
quasi-therapeutic settings in which they are encouraged to share their experiences and their feelings and learn to name and understand those feelings.
At the same time, women are advised that they have rights and encouraged

---

47. *See* CONNELL, *supra* note 39.

to use the courts to assert these rights. Contemporary systems of governance focus on providing safety for the woman and on retraining batterers, helping them to name and anticipate their feelings, to see new dimensions of choice for their actions, to value themselves, and to change their beliefs about masculinity and marriage.

The new regime affects men differently from women. It has emancipated women from the governance of their husbands and partners and provided them a more autonomous subjectivity defined by a feminist interpretation of the law as providing them the right not to be battered, no matter what they have done. At the same time, it has reduced men's rights to discipline and control their wives. Men sometimes report surprise, dismay, and anger that things that they could do in the past with impunity now earn them prison sentences and the requirement to attend batterers intervention programs. There is no increase in autonomy or freedom experienced by these men; instead they feel more strongly the effect of new forms of governance, directed not only at punishing them but reforming them, training them in new practices of masculinity and performing gender roles in the family. For many of the women, the entitlement to rights from the law is a new experience, as is the support for their autonomy offered by shelter and program staff and the judiciary. For some of the men, state supervision and control is a familiar experience. Almost a third of the men interviewed had previous arrests and some have long histories with the juvenile and adult courts. Almost half the men in the feminist batterer program have been arrested for something in addition to battering according to intake interviews. Thus, the men brought into the court and the violence control program have experienced the criminal justice system in other areas.

These changes do not fall equally on all social classes or races. Working class and poor women are more likely to use the law for help because they lack expensive alternatives such as private counseling or moving to a new house. Poor men are more likely to end up in the courts and treatment programs. Men with race and class privilege have typically escaped the criminalization of their violence in the home, while psychological and economic violence have not been defined as crimes. Men of higher social classes often escape the feminist training program. In the earlier years, a few were sent to the treatment program and protested loudly about the infringement on their rights. More recently, men with greater means are buying their way out of the violence control program through recourse to private counseling services, counseling through their churches, or perhaps changing their patterns of battering from physical to more emotional and verbal strategies. They are more likely to hire an attorney. It is not that only poor men batter, but only poor batterers end up in court and ATV. It is impossible to know how much battering remains hidden behind window shades and unreported to the police. There has been a strong challenge to patriarchal authority in this movement, but it is, in effect, predominantly lower class men who feel this challenge.

The right not to be battered and the capacity to make choices are important extensions of the definition of the autonomous self to a relatively poor and marginalized group of women. Those who arrive in court accused of battering are those whose partners or neighbors were willing to complain. Yet, the right of women to complain about violence has come at a cost: women are encouraged or forced to testify against their partners in court, a dangerous and often undesirable form of participation. As the battered women's movement has come to depend on the legal system for support and for funding, it has had to compromise its support for women, to tone down its rhetoric of patriarchy, and to move toward a service delivery system in which its emancipatory potential is compromised by the need to service cases and to get women to testify. In order for women to adopt this new sense of rights, however, their initial forays into the legal arena require experiences of support from participants in that arena as they struggle to redefine a self between the obligations of the good wife and the entitlements of the autonomous self not to be hit. This is a difficult journey that inevitably means hesitation and vacillation.

This analysis suggests that the adoption of a rights consciousness about a particular form of behavior requires a shift in subjectivity, one that depends on wider cultural understandings and individual experience. It is in the particular interactions and encounters of an individual that this subjectivity shift takes place. That the adoption of rights depends on individual experiences in the social world has significance for a range of rights-based social movements from pay equity and mental health rights to human rights. Such adoptions depend not only on educating people about the availability of rights, but also putting into place practices within legal systems that will reinforce the experience of these rights. This reinforcement depends on social encounters in which those endeavoring to exercise rights, and thus redefining their previous relationships, find positive reinforcement for this change. Human rights are difficult for individuals to adopt as a self-definition in the absence of institutions that will take these rights seriously when they are claimed by individuals. Rights cannot precede concerns about implementation. This analysis suggests that implementation is fundamental to establishing human rights consciousness.

Chapter 14

Used, Abused, Arrested, and Deported: Extending Immigration Benefits to Protect the Victims of Trafficking and to Secure the Prosecution of Traffickers

Dina Francesca Haynes

PROLOGUE

Madeleina was a slight, delicate-looking sixteen-year-old girl from Moldova. She left Moldova in 1998, when her sister's husband convinced her and another girl to go with his friend who promised to find them hostess jobs in Italy. She was given a fake passport, and after about a week of traveling, found herself locked in a brothel in what she later discovered was the Republika Srpska, Bosnia and Herzegovina (Bosnia).[1] A woman interpreting for the brothel owner told her that she had been sold to him to be his "wife." The brothel owner forced Madeleina to have sex with him and his friends and told her that she could begin working off her debt to him immediately. He told her that she already owed him more than $2,000 for her purchase price and working papers.

Madeleina had no money and no friends. She could not speak the local language and the owner threatened her regularly, beating her and telling her that police would arrest her if she tried to leave. There were at least eleven other girls and women at this brothel, all foreigners. Most of them were from Moldova or Romania, and the brothel owner tried to keep them separated as much as possible to prevent their collusion and escape. The owner sometimes forced them to take drugs to keep them more compliant, the cost of which was added to their debt. The brothel owner kept Madeleina for about five months, forcing her to have sex with as many as twenty men a day. She

---

1. Bosnia is currently divided into two entities and a district: the Republika Srpska, the Federation, and Brcko District.

thought that some of the customers at the brothel were local police. She also knew that Russian and either American, Canadian, or British men, and she thinks Italian, had visited her and had sex with her, in addition to local men.

When police raided that brothel, she was taken by car to Arizona Market, near Brcko, where cars, goods, and women are sold. Two foreign men purchased her; she thinks they were Swiss and American peacekeepers. These two men put her in a car and took her to an apartment in Tuzla where they kept her locked up and came to visit her every day or two, often with friends, and forced her to have sex with them. Over the course of these months, Madeleina had begun to teach herself some of the Serbian language.

One day, after no one had visited her for several days and she was running out of food, the landlord of the apartment opened the door and told her to get out. It was winter, and with no warm clothes Madeleina went out to find the local police, not because she believed the police would help her, but because she knew she would freeze to death with no place to go.

The local police promptly jailed her for prostitution. A Human Rights Officer with the Organization for Security and Co-operation in Europe (OSCE) intervened, and Madeleina was transported to a makeshift shelter in Sarajevo.[2] International and local nongovernmental organizations were then just establishing the shelter.

I. INTRODUCTION

Trafficking in human beings is an extremely lucrative business, with profits estimated at $7 billion per year[3] and a seemingly endless supply of persons to traffic, estimated at between 700,000 and four million new victims per

---

2. As related to the author during her work with the OSCE in Bosnia. For similar stories, *see* HUMAN RIGHTS WATCH, HOPES BETRAYED: TRAFFICKING OF WOMEN AND GIRLS TO POST-CONFLICT BOSNIA AND HERZEGOVINA FOR FORCED PROSTITUTION (2002) [hereinafter HRW REPORT]; John McGhie, *Bosnia—Arizona Market: Women for Sale* (UK Channel 4 News television broadcast, 8 June 2000), *available at* fpmail.friends-partners.org/pipermail/stop-traffic/2000-August/000113; William J. Kole & Aida Cerkez-Robinson, *U.N. Police Accused of Involvement in Prostitution in Bosnia,* ASSOC. PRESS, 28 June 2001; Colum Lynch, *U.N. Halted Probe of Officers' Alleged Role in Sex Trafficking,* WASH. POST, 27 Dec. 2001, at A17, *available at* www.washingtonpost.com/wp-dyn/articles/A28267–2001Dec26.

3. UNITED NATIONS CHILDREN'S FUND (UNICEF) ET AL., TRAFFICKING IN HUMAN BEINGS IN SOUTHEASTERN EUROPE xiii (2002) [hereinafter JOINT REPORT ON TRAFFICKING] (stating that trafficking in human beings is the third most lucrative organized crime activity after, and often conjoined with, trafficking in arms and drugs). *See also* GILLIAN CALDWELL ET AL., CRIME AND SERVITUDE: AN EXPOSÉ OF THE TRAFFIC IN WOMEN FOR PROSTITUTION FROM THE NEWLY INDEPENDENT STATES 14 (1997), *available at* www.qweb.kvinnoforum.se/misc/crimeru.rtf (citing 1988 German police estimates that "traffickers earned US $35–50 million annually in interest on loans to foreign women and girls entering Germany to work as prostitutes").

year.[4] Trafficked persons, typically women and children, can be sold and resold, and even forced to pay back their purchasers for the costs incurred in their transport and purchase.[5] In fact, the United States Central Intelligence Agency estimates that traffickers earn $250,000 for each trafficked woman.[6] Economic instability, social dislocation, and gender inequality in transitioning countries foster conditions ripe for trafficking.

Trafficking in human beings involves moving persons for any type of forced or coerced labor, for the profit of the trafficker.[7] Several countries are finally adopting domestic legislation to criminalize trafficking in human beings, although many continue to punish the victims of trafficking, charging them with prostitution, possession of fraudulent documents, or working without authorization.[8] Many international organizations and consortiums of grassroots anti-trafficking organizations have also put forward models for combating trafficking.

None of these models is yet terribly effective, for a variety of reasons. At the forefront of these reasons is the fact that several countries have yet to

---

4. U.S. Dep't of State Office to Monitor and Combat Trafficking in Persons, Trafficking in Persons Report 1 (2002).

5. *The Sex Trade: Trafficking of Women and Children in Europe and the United States: Hearing before the Commission on Security and Cooperation in Europe,* 106th Cong., 1st Sess. 22 (1999) (testimony of Laura Lederer) [hereinafter, The Lederer Report] (stating that women trafficked into North America are sold for as much as $16,000 to each new brothel owner, and have to pay or work off a debt of $20,000 to $40,000); *see also,* Jennifer Lord, *EU Expansion Could Fuel Human Trafficking,* United Press Int'l, 9 Nov. 2002, *available at* caymannetnews.com/Archive/Archive%20Articles/November%202002/Issue%20286%20Wed/EU%20Expansion.html.

6. Caldwell, *supra* note 3, at 10.

7. While there are a multitude of definitions of trafficking, the most widely used definition derives from the current legal standard bearer, the Protocol to Prevent, Suppress and Punish Trafficking in Persons, Especially Women and Children, Supplementing the United Nations Convention Against Transnational Organized Crime, *adopted* 15 Nov. 2000, G.A. Res. A/55/25, Annex II, 55 U.N. GAOR Supp. (No. 49), at 60, U.N. Doc. A/45/49 (Vol. I) (2001) (*entered into force* 25 Dec. 2003) [hereinafter Trafficking Protocol]. Article 3 of The Protocol defines trafficking as:

> the recruitment, transportation, transfer, harbouring or receipt of persons, by means of the threat or use of force or other forms of coercion, of abduction, of fraud, of deception, of the abuse of power or of a position of vulnerability or of the giving or receiving of payments or benefits to achieve the consent of a person having control over another person, for the purpose of exploitation.

> See United Nations, Office of Drugs and Crime *available at* www.unodc.org/unodc/en/trafficking_human_beings. Solely for the purposes of narrowing discussion, this article will emphasize trafficking for sex work. This narrow focus should not be viewed as support for a definition of trafficking that bifurcates trafficking that results in sex work from other forms of trafficking (such as indentured domestic service, forced labor, forced marriage, subjugation in making pornography, etc.). All trafficking in human beings is a violation of human rights in that it involves affronts to human dignity and arguably constitutes a form of slavery.

8. *See infra* text and accompanying notes pt. IV(A).

adopt anti-trafficking laws.[9] Second, of those that have, many completely fail to implement those laws even after undertaking domestic and international obligations.[10] A third major reason is that some governments have failed to incorporate the advice of grassroots and international anti-trafficking organizations that have worked for years drafting recommended legislation based upon their observations in the field.[11]

A particular contemporary problem is trafficking for the sexual exploitation of women[12] in and from Central and Southeastern Europe.[13] Currently, Central and Southeastern Europe are the primary sources from which women are drawn into global sex traffic through Europe,[14] and some countries in this region are actively engaged in developing anti-trafficking initiatives pursuant to their obligations as signatories to the 2000 Protocols to the UN Convention on Transnational Organized Crime.[15] In addition, some countries in the Balkans have the added presence of international peace-

---

9. In South Eastern Europe, for instance, Croatia, Serbia, and Montenegro, have no distinct criminal offense for trafficking, despite being known countries of origin, transit, or destination, although a law is under consideration in Serbia. For review of laws related to trafficking in these countries, see KRISTI SEVERANCE, ABA: CENTRAL EUROPEAN AND EURASIAN LAW INITIATIVE SURVEY OF LEGISLATIVE FRAMEWORKS FOR COMBATING TRAFFICKING IN PERSONS (2003) [hereinafter ABA CEELI REPORT] available at www.abanet.org/ceeli/publications/concept papers/humantrafficking/home. See infra note 109. In March 2003, the Office of the High Representative imposed a law criminalizing trafficking as a distinct offense, as the Bosnian authorities had failed to do. As yet, however, no traffickers have been charged under this new law.

10. See infra text pt. III(B)(1).

11. See infra text pt. IV(B)(1)(b).

12. For the purposes of simplicity, the paper will refer to women in particular, and use the feminine pronouns when referring to victims of trafficking, as the majority of victims of trafficking for sexual exploitation are women and girls.

13. Since the early 1990s countries in political and economic transition in Central, Eastern, and South Eastern Europe and the Former Soviet Union have not only become main countries of origin for trafficked persons, but also of transit and destination. See OFFICE FOR DEMOCRATIC INSTITUTIONS AND HUMAN RIGHTS, ORGANIZATION FOR SECURITY AND CO-OPERATION IN EUROPE, REFERENCE GUIDE FOR ANTI-TRAFFICKING LEGISLATIVE REVIEW 20 (2001) [hereinafter OSCE REFERENCE GUIDE]. South Eastern European countries offer the unique combination of being countries deeply mired in trafficking, and simultaneously interested in entering the European Union (EU). As such, they are in the process of bringing their legislation and administrative bodies into compliance with European standards, and are particularly useful for viewing the process of developing anti-trafficking initiatives. Cyprus, the Czech Republic, Estonia, Hungary, Latvia, Lithuania, Malta, Poland, the Slovak Republic, and Slovenia, are set to join the EU in 2004, while Romania, Bulgaria, and Turkey all have active applications for EU membership. See EUROPEAN UNION WEBSITE, CANDIDATE COUNTRIES, available at europa.eu.int/comm/enlargement/candidate.

14. Central and Eastern Europe have surpassed Asia and Latin America as countries of origin since the breakdown of the Soviet Union in 1989. See OSCE REFERENCE GUIDE, supra note 13, at 7.

15. U.N. Convention Against Transnational Organized Crime, G.A. Res. 55/25, Annex I, U.N. GAOR 55th Sess., Supp. No. 49, at 44, U.N. Doc. A/45/49 (Vol. 1) (2000), entered into force 29 Sept. 2003 [hereinafter Organized Crime Convention]. Serbia, Montenegro, and

keepers and humanitarian workers, which in many respects exacerbates the problem.[16]

This paper will, in Part II, discuss the recent increase in trafficking. Part II will explore how and why governments have failed to effectively address the problem, despite being aware of its existence for decades. Part IV illustrates that two dominant anti-trafficking models have emerged in recent years, one of which is oriented towards prosecution of traffickers while the other emphasizes victim protection. Part V proposes a specific combination of the best of the two models, recommending several additional elements to create a new model that will more effectively combat trafficking, highlighting immigration benefits, and responds to anticipated arguments against such an expansion.

The principal recommendation of this article is that the best of the "jail the offender" and "protect the victim" models should be combined. The new model should incorporate advice from grassroots organizations that work directly with trafficked persons, in order to craft anti-trafficking programs that promote protection of victims. This new model should include immigration protection, should hit traffickers where it hurts, and should prioritize full implementation.

II.   THE RECENT RISE OF TRAFFICKING IN HUMAN BEINGS

The horrific practice of trafficking in human beings has long been a serious problem throughout the world, but in the last fifteen years trafficking from European countries has been on the rise. Trafficking in Europe has been fueled by the social dislocations, increasing pockets of poverty, gender imbalance, bureaucratic chaos, and legislative vacuums resulting from the collapse of communism.[17]

Bosnia have ratified the Organized Crime Convention, and its Protocols. All other South Eastern European countries are parties and it remains unclear as to how they will implement their commitments.

16. *See infra* text pt. III(B)(2). International Administration is still in effect in Kosovo (through the U.N. Mission in Kosovo, pursuant to U.N. Resolution 1244 (S.C. Res 1244, U.N. SCOR, 4011th mtg., S/RES/1244 (1999)), and partially in Bosnia and Herzegovina.

17. *See* Jenna Shearer Demir, The Trafficking of Women for Sexual Exploitation: A Gender-based and Well-founded Fear of Persecution? 4–5 (2003), *available at* www.unhcr.ch/cgi-bin/texis/vtx/home/opendoc.pdf?tbl=RESEARCH&id=3e71f84c4&page=publ (arguing that women disproportionately suffer the effects of an economic upheaval); Sergei Blagov, *Equal Opportunities Remain a Pipedream*, Asia Times Online, 10 Mar. 2000, *available at* www.atimes.com/c-asia/BC10Ag01.html (stating that "[s]ome 70 percent of Russian unemployed with college degrees are women. In some regions, women make up almost 90 percent of the unemployed.")

Women already disenfranchised within their communities are most often those who fall prey to traffickers: ostracized minorities, women without employment or future economic prospects, and girls without family members to look out for them or who have fallen outside of the educational system.[18] These girls and women are lured by traffickers into leaving their countries, believing that they will work in the West as dancers, hostesses, or nannies, and instead find themselves forced to have sex for the profit of the men and women who purchased them.[19]

In order to secure their silence and compliance, traffickers threaten, beat, rape, drug, and deprive their victims of legitimate immigration or work documents. Women are forced to sell themselves in brothels, often receiving several clients per day.[20] They rarely see any wages for their work; in fact, most victims are kept in indentured servitude and told that they owe their traffickers or the brothel owners for their own purchase price and for the price of procuring working papers and travel documents.[21]

The rings of traffickers are often vast, extremely well connected to police and government officials, well hidden, and reach across borders and continents.[22] Traffickers in human beings are also known to traffic in weapons and drugs, and to use trafficking in human beings to bring in initial cash flow to support the riskier traffic in drugs and arms.[23] Human beings, being reusable commodities that can be sold and resold, are both more lucrative[24] and less risky to traffic than drugs and arms, in that traffickers of human beings are rarely prosecuted for this particular offense.[25]

While between 700,000 and four million women are trafficked each year,[26] only a fraction of those are known to have received assistance in

---

18. Based on the author's discussion with anti-trafficking NGOs and UN officials in Bosnia and Serbia, and on direct discussion with trafficking victims.
19. *Id.*
20. HRW Report, *supra* note 2, at 18.
21. *Id.* at 4, 11.
22. *Report of the Special Rapporteur on Violence Against Women, its Causes and Consequences, Ms. Radhika Coomaraswamy,* U.N. ESCOR, Comm'n on Hum. Rts., 53rd Sess., U.N. Doc. E/CN.4/1997/47 (1997) § IV (expressing concern about government complicity in trafficking).
23. *See* Amy O'Neill Richard, U.S. Dep't of State Center for the Study of Intelligence: International Trafficking in Women to the United States: A Contemporary Manifestation of Slavery and Organized Crime 1 (1999), *available at* www.odci.gov/csi/monograph/women/trafficking. pdf [hereinafter CSI Report]. *See also* IOM, Applied Research and Data Collection on A Study of Trafficking in Women and Children For Sexual Exploitation To, Through and From the Balkan Region 7 (2001) [hereinafter IOM Report]
24. *See* CSI Report, *supra* note 23, at 19–20.
25. *See infra* text pt. IV (C)(2)(a).
26. U.S. Dep't of State, Office to Monitor and Combat Trafficking in Persons, Trafficking in Persons Report 1, *supra* note 4, at 1. The numbers for South Eastern Europe in particular are difficult to specify. For example, one Swedish NGO estimates that "500,000 women . . . are trafficked each year into Western Europe alone. A large proportion of these come from

order to escape trafficking.[27] Many are re-victimized by being deported from the countries in which they are found,[28] sanctioned by law when attempting to return to their countries of origin,[29] and ostracized within their communities and families.[30]

Governments appear to have recognized the importance of the issue, many having ratified international instruments established to eradicate trafficking in human beings. Nevertheless, trafficking is neither slowing, nor is the prosecution of traffickers or the protection of their victims becoming any more certain.

III.   GOVERNMENTAL FAILURES TO CONFRONT THE ISSUE

As early as 1904, concern over "white slavery," in which European women were exported to the colonies, prompted the adoption of the International Agreement for the Suppression of White Slave Traffic, addressing the fraudulent or abusive recruitment of women for prostitution in another country.[31] The issue was addressed again in 1933 with the International Convention on the Suppression of the Traffic in Women of Full Age, by which parties agreed to punish those who procured prostitutes or ran brothels.[32] In 1949, the United Nations adopted the Convention for the Suppression of the Traffic in

---

the former Soviet Union countries." JOINT REPORT ON TRAFFICKING, *supra* note 3, at 4. IOM estimates that in 1997, "175,000 women and girls were trafficked from Central and Eastern Europe and the Newly Independent States." *Id.* As of 2002, IOM estimates that 120,000 women and children are trafficked into the EU each year, mostly through the Balkans, and that 10,000 are working in Bosnia alone, mostly from Moldova, Romania and the Ukraine. *Id.*

27. JOINT REPORT ON TRAFFICKING, *supra* note 3, at xv (only 7 percent of the foreign migrant sex workers known to be victims of trafficking receive any long term assistance and support).

28. HRW REPORT, *supra* note 2, at 38.

29. GLOBAL ALLIANCE AGAINST TRAFFIC IN WOMEN ET AL., HUMAN RIGHTS STANDARDS FOR THE TREATMENT OF TRAFFICKED PERSONS 13, 15 (1999), *available at* www.hrlawgroup.org/resources/content/ IHRLGTraffickin_tsStandards.pdf. Countries from which trafficked persons originate are referred to as countries of origin. Countries through which victims are trafficked are called countries of transit, and destination countries are those in which victims ultimately find themselves engaged in sex work.

30. *Id.* at 13.

31. International Agreement for the Suppression of White Slave Traffic, 1 U.N.T.S. 83 (*signed* 18 May 1904) (*entered into force* 18 July 1905) (amended by the Protocol signed at Lake Success, New York, 4 May 1949). The Agreement was ratified by Belgium, Denmark, France, Germany, Italy, the Netherlands, Portugal, Russia, Spain, Sweden, and Norway, Switzerland, and the United Kingdom and consented to by their respective colonies, and dealt with European women being exported to the colonies for prostitution, sometimes forcibly.

32. International Convention for the Suppression of the Traffic in Women of Full Age, Concluded at Geneva 11 Oct. 1933, as amended by the Protocol signed at Lake Success, New York, on 12 Nov. 1947, *registered* 24 Apr. 1950, No. 772.

Persons and of the Exploitation of the Prostitution of Others.[33] Until 2000, the only other international treaty to address trafficking was the 1979 UN Convention on the Elimination of All Forms of Discrimination Against Women (CEDAW), which required states to take all measures to suppress both trafficking and "exploitation of prostitution," meaning forced prostitution.[34]

Beginning in the late 1980s, the European Union and the United Nations began addressing the issue repeatedly, yet little progress was made and the collapse of communism flooded trafficked persons throughout Europe. With trafficking recognized as a distinct problem since 1903, with the ratification of four treaties by many nations, and with trafficking recently and dramatically on the rise, why has so little progress been made?

A. Some Politicians Use Trafficking to Direct Attention to Unrelated Political Agendas

Trafficking is a low priority for many governments who pay lip service to solving the problem only to harness more support for other political objectives. Because of the visceral reaction trafficking elicits with the public, it has recently been used by politicians and governments to bolster other political agendas, such as curtailing illegal migration, fighting prostitution, and even combating terrorism.

Some governments pretend to care about trafficking when the real objective is controlling unwanted migration.[35] Trafficking in human beings is a very serious topic in its own right, but the gravity and emotional impact of the topic unfortunately render it vulnerable to political manipulation. With illegal migration, smuggling, terrorism, and prostitution now on many political agendas, the pledge to combat trafficking is misused as justification for "clamping down" on these other threats that also have immigration

---

33. Convention for the Suppression of the Traffic in Persons and of the Exploitation of the Prostitution of Others, *opened for signature* 21 Mar. 1950, 96 U.N.T.S. 271 (*entered into force* 25 July 1951). Parties agreed to "punish any person who, to gratify the passions of another: (1) Procures, entices or leads away, for purposes of prostitution, another person, even with the consent of that person; (2) Exploits the prostitution of another person, even with the consent of that person." *Id.* art. 1.
34. Convention on the Elimination of All Forms of Discrimination Against Women, *adopted* 18 Dec. 1979, G.A. Res. 34/180, U.N. GAOR, 34th Sess., Supp. No. 46, U.N. Doc. A/34/46 (1980) (*entered into force* 3 Sept. 1981), 1249 U.N.T.S. 13, *reprinted in* 19 I.L.M. 33 (1980).
35. *See* CSI Report, *supra* note 23, at 31 (stating that "[d]efinitional difficulties still persist regarding trafficking in women.... Distinctions regarding trafficking in women, alien smuggling, and irregular migration are sometimes blurred with INS [former US immigration department] predisposed to jump to the conclusion that most cases involving illegal workers are alien smuggling instead of trafficking cases").

implications.[36] Authorities have remained cynical and hardened to the plight of victims who are easier to treat as prostitutes or illegal immigrants.[37]

In fact, some countries seem to view the existence of trafficked women within their sovereign borders as evidence of a breach of security or the failure of their domestic immigration mechanisms, and accordingly attempt to address trafficking through simple reconfiguration of their border control mechanisms.[38] Traffickers are often extremely savvy transnational organized criminals, while their victims are most often women and children already victimized by economic, political, or social conditions in their home countries. Viewing trafficking as an immigration issue overly simplifies the complexity of preparing effective anti-trafficking measures.

As this section will demonstrate, politicians and governments have blurred the distinctions between illegal migration, trafficking, and smuggling, taking advantage of the current world fear of terrorism committed by legal and illegal immigrants, to restrict immigration and freedom of movement further. They have purposely co-mingled anti-trafficking initiatives with anti-prostitution initiatives. They have tried to further curtail migration by blurring the distinction between trafficking and smuggling. Finally, it is my opinion that some governments are motivated not by a keen belief in the necessity of curtailing trafficking, but by a desire to secure international financial assistance or enter the European Union.

1. Prostitution

Prostitution and trafficking are not one and the same, yet some would treat them as such.[39] Prostitution involves persons willingly engaging in sex work. Although there may be a gray area involving different degrees of consent,

---

36. *See, e.g.,* Richard Monk, Organization for Security and Co-operation in Europe Mission to the FRY: Study on Policing in the Federal Republic of Yugoslavia 21 (2001), *available at* www.osce.org/yugoslavia/documents/reports/files/report-policing-e.pdf [hereinafter Monk Report] (Commenting: "Additionally, these statistics [on successful anti-trafficking ventures] are used for various political purposes—for example, prevention of trafficking is used as an argument for refusing young women entry to a country or for refusing to issue them a visa, and then, in the police statistics, these cases are relabeled as successful cases of rescuing 'victims of trafficking.'").

37. *See, e.g.,* CSI Report, *supra* note 23, at 35 (US government officials cited as holding the opinion that trafficking victims are part of the conspiracy and therefore view them as accomplices).

38. "More often than not, anti-trafficking laws, be it domestic or international, tend to be conceived and are employed as border-control and immigration mechanisms," Agnes Khoo, *Trafficking and Human Rights: Some Observations and Questions,* 12 Asia Pacific Forum on Law, Women and Development 3 (Dec. 1999), *available at* www.apwld.org/vol 123–02.htm.

39. In explaining its priorities for 2003, the Stability Pact of South-Eastern Europe stated: "Attention will be drawn to maintain the differentiation between victims of human traf-

choice, and free will, trafficking goes well outside of this gray area. While a valid argument could be made that gender imbalances in economic or social factors drive a woman to consent to such labor as her chosen profession, thus effectively removing her "will,"[40] trafficking involves clear deprivation of choice at some stage, either through fraud, deception, force, coercion, or threats.

Whether a trafficked woman was initially willing or unwilling when she entered into sex work should make no legal difference when the outcome is enslavement or forced servitude; a person cannot consent to enslavement or forced labor of any kind.[41] While some trafficked persons may be willing to work in the sex industry, they do not anticipate being forced to pay off large forcibly imposed debts, being kept against their will, having their travel documents taken from them, or being raped, beaten, and sold like chattel.[42]

Nevertheless, within the community of NGOs, international organizations, governments, and working groups laboring to define and combat trafficking, the issue of prostitution regularly enters the deliberation. As recently as 2001, for example, some persons working for the United Nations Mission in Bosnia and Herzegovina (UNMIBH) and partner organizations tasked with assisting the Bosnian government to eradicate trafficking refused to provide trafficking protection assistance to women who at any point willingly engaged in prostitution.[43]

The Organized Crime Convention has encouraged countries to focus on coercion and use of force in identifying whether a woman is a victim of trafficking, rather than on whether she has ever engaged in prostitution. Never-

---

ficking and prostitutes, which is currently becoming blurred, to the detriment of effective and targeted victim protection." SPECIAL CO-ORDINATOR OF THE STABILITY PACT FOR SOUTH EASTERN EUROPE TASK FORCE ON TRAFFICKING IN HUMAN BEINGS, ANTI-TRAFFICKING POLICY OUTLINE FOR 2003 [hereinafter SP Trafficking Task Force Priorities], *available at* www.stabilitypact.org/trafficking/info.html#four. For more discussion on the Stability Pact, *see* discussion *infra* pt. IV(D)(3).

40. NGO Consultation with the UN/IGO's on Trafficking in Persons, Prostitution and the Global Sex Industry, Trafficking and the Global Sex Industry: The Need for a Human Rights Framework, 21–22 (1999), Room XII Palais des Nations, Geneva, Switzerland [Panel A and Panel B] (some IGO's arguing that all prostitution is forced prostitution and calling for its abolition, with others arguing for a distinction between voluntary and forced prostitution in order to focus on preventing the worst forms of exploitation of prostitutes).

41. *See, e.g.,* CSI REPORT, *supra* note 23, at vi ("The Thirteenth Amendment outlawing slavery prohibits an individual from selling himself or herself into bondage, and Western legal tradition prohibits contracts consenting in advance to assaults and other criminal wrongs."). This argument is further developed in pt. V(A)(1).

42. *See* HRW REPORT, *supra* note 2, at 15–20 (detailing common treatment and expectations of trafficked women).

43. *Id.* at 13. This practice of excluding prostitutes from victim protection results from criteria set by donor agencies rather than international law; *see e.g., infra* note 44 and accompanying text.

theless, the US government agency tasked with distributing funding to international trafficking initiatives recently determined that it would refuse to fight trafficking where doing so might appear to treat prostitution as a legitimate activity.[44] Thus, trafficking is politicized, a volatile topic easily used to affix other political agendas. Even while most experts working in anti-trafficking initiatives agree that trafficking and prostitution are separate issues, to be handled separately as a matter of law, the United States took a step backwards in attempting to tackle prostitution under the guise of combating trafficking.

2. Smuggling

Politicians have also attempted to link smuggling and trafficking in order to achieve tightened border controls. While most governments acknowledge that smuggling and trafficking are two distinct crimes, they nonetheless use trafficking statistics and horrific trafficking stories to justify tightened border controls when the primary goal is not the elimination of trafficking, but the reduction of illegal migration, some of which occurs via smugglers, and perhaps preventing terrorism.

The United States Department of State, for instance, opened the Migrant Smuggling *and* Trafficking in Persons Coordination Center in December 2000, even while acknowledging, "at their core . . . these related problems are distinct."[45] The US government nevertheless justified combining the two issues by pointing out that "these related problems result in massive human tragedy and affect our national security, primarily with respect to crime, health and welfare, and border control."[46] By way of another example, the Canadian government supported a study jointly reviewing both smuggling and trafficking, even while pointing out the legal distinctions between the two.[47] The study was justified under the premise that "as human smuggling and trafficking are increasing, the tightening of border controls has taken on

---

44. In its report entitled "Trafficking in Persons, The USAID Strategy for Response," designed to implement several provisions within the Trafficking Victim's Protection Act (TVPA), the US Agency for International Development (USAID) states that it will only work with [e.g. fund] local NGOs "committed . . . to combat trafficking *and prostitution,*" [emphasis added], explaining that: "organizations advocating prostitution as an employment choice or which advocate or support the legalization of prostitution are not appropriate partners," US Agency for International Development, Trafficking in Persons: The USAID Strategy for Response (Feb. 2003), *available at* www.usaid.gov/wid/pubs/pd-abx-358-final.pdf.

45. U.S. Dep't of State International Information Programs, Fact Sheet: Migrant Smuggling and Trafficking in Persons (2000), *available at* www.usembassy.it/file2000_12/alia/a0121523.htm.

46. *Id.*

47. *See* Jacqueline Oxman-Martinez, Human Smuggling and Trafficking: Achieving the Goals of the UN Protocols? 1 (2003), *available at* www.maxwell.syr.edu/campbell/XBorder/Oxman Martinez%20oped.pdf.

a new urgency from the fear of terrorism in the West, as well as restrictive measures placed on irregular migratory movements."[48]

Smuggling involves delivering persons to the country they wish to enter, initiated by the potential migrant. Smuggling often takes place under horrible and possibly life threatening conditions, but smuggled persons are left to their own devices upon delivery. Smuggling is not as lucrative for the perpetrators, as smugglers usually make only a short-term profit on the act of moving a person, while traffickers regard people as highly profitable, reusable, re-sellable, and expendable commodities.[49]

In order for anti-trafficking initiatives to be effective, politicians must make the eradication of trafficking and the protection of trafficked persons into a prioritized goal, distinct from the elimination of smuggling or the tightening of border controls.

3.   *Some governments are motivated by a desire to meet EU entrance requirements or to obtain financial assistance*

Not surprisingly, the European Union and the United States, among other institutions and governments, are conditioning financial assistance[50] and entry into the European Union on the country's willingness to develop legislation curtailing trafficking within and across its borders[51]. Countries set to enter the European Union in 2004[52] are eager to pass legislation recommended by the European Union and the Council of Europe (CoE), and join working groups that address stemming the flow of trafficking and smuggling.[53]

---

48. *Id.* at 1.
49. In the last decade, Southeast Asia alone has produced nearly three times as many victims of trafficking than produced during the entire history of slavery from Africa. Melanie Nezer, *Trafficking in Women and Children: "A Contemporary Manifestation of Slavery,"* 21 REFUGEE REPORTS 1, 3 (2000) (400 years of slavery from Africa produced 11.5 million victims; victims of trafficking in the 1990s within and from Southeast Asia are estimated to be more than 30 million).
50. The United States Trafficking Victims Protection Act of 2000, Pub. L. No. 106-386, 114 Stat. 1464 (2000) [hereinafter TVPA], for instance, requires an annual submission to Congress by the Department of State on the status of trafficking in each country. Financial assistance is tied directly to the level of each country's compliance with US directives. U.S. DEP'T OF STATE OFFICE TO MONITOR AND COMBAT TRAFFICKING IN PERSONS, TRAFFICKING IN PERSONS REPORT 10 (2002). (Beginning in 2003, those countries ranked lowest in this report "will be subject to certain sanctions, principally termination of non-humanitarian, non-trade-related assistance. Consistent with the Act, such countries also would face U.S. opposition to assistance . . . from international financial institutions.")
51. In the case of the European Union, entry into the Union is conditioned upon compliance with general respect for human rights and compliance with human rights standards.
52. For list of applicant countries to the European, *see supra* note 13.
53. In the author's experience working with ministries of justice, interior, and human rights in Bosnia, Croatia, and Serbia and Montenegro, high level government authorities were

Passing recommended legislation and making real efforts to stem the flow of trafficking, however, are often two different things. When countries simply adopt legislation in order to secure entry into the European Union or to meet financial assistance requirements, there is no real ownership or commitment to eradicating trafficking. The legislation, no matter how meticulously in conformity with international standards, will not be fully or adequately implemented at the local level without serious political will.

B. Governments Ignore Obvious Problems with Anti-Trafficking Initiatives

Many countries have now finally adopted some domestic legislation addressing trafficking, and most have eradicated earlier laws that punished trafficked persons for immigration or prostitution offenses.[54] This section points out reasons no current laws are very effective in the fight to eradicate trafficking.

By no means, however, have all countries adopted laws to specifically target trafficking.[55]

1.   Government fail to prioritize the implementation of anti-trafficking laws

A piece of legislation is useful to trafficked persons and threatening to violators only if it is implemented and known by the traffickers to be fully in force. No matter how great the economic or political pressure applied by the European Union or the United States to encourage countries to introduce legislation to prosecute traffickers, no incentive can create the politi-

---

typically keen to attend high level working groups addressing the drafting of trafficking legislation, but were much harder to pin down when it came to establishing work plans to train field level government authorities.

54. See infra text pt. IV(A). For example, in Israel as recently as 1998, a victim's best hope was to have the brothel or massage parlor she worked in raided by police. She would then be taken to prison, not a shelter or detention center, and offered two options: be deported and have criminal prostitution charges dropped, or file a complaint against her trafficker or those holding her in involuntary servitude. If she chose to file charges, however, she would remain in prison until a trial was held. Not surprisingly, no women between 1994 and 1998 chose to testify against their traffickers in Israel. Most traffickers were well aware that the laws favored them, if only because the women they trafficked were illegally in the country and were engaging in criminal activity. Michael Specter, Traffickers' New Cargo: Naïve Slavic Women, N.Y. Times, 11 Jan. 1998, at A1.

55. Serbia, Montenegro, and Croatia, for example, have no distinct criminal offense for trafficking. See generally ABA CEELI Report, supra note 9, for updates on domestic trafficking legislation. Although Bosnia's law criminalizing trafficking was imposed in March 2003, it has yet to yield a prosecution. See infra note 109.

cal will to *implement* legislation if such will or ability does not exist or is not prioritized.[56]

In Bosnia, for example, UNMIBH reported that of sixty-three cases brought against traffickers in 2000, only three were successfully prosecuted.[57] Of those three, the defendants were *all* tried on charges related to prostitution, not trafficking. According to the HRW Report, all of the thirty-six cases brought involved charges related to prostitution and not trafficking—not just the three successful ones.[58] In one of the three cases, three trafficked women and two brothel owners were arrested in a raid. Although the defendants admitted that they had purchased the women for prices ranging between $592 and $1,162, the court convicted the three women for prostitution and dropped the charges against the male defendants.[59]

Coordination among responsible agencies to implement the law is often flawed in the best of circumstances, further obstructing implementation.[60] Meetings are held at the highest levels and those in attendance come away full of self-congratulations that plans are being made and laws adopted. Yet out in the community, brothels are raided and no screening is done for victims of trafficking; victims identify themselves to police and face prosecu-

---

56. One way to encourage implementation of anti-trafficking laws is for the European Union and United States to condition their assistance on implementation, rather than on simple passage of anti-trafficking laws, a recommendation made in this paper, and finally acknowledged in the 2003 Trafficking in Persons Report, U.S. Dep't of State Office to Monitor and Combat Trafficking in Persons, Trafficking in Persons Report 2 (2003) [hereinafter 2003 Trafficking in Persons Report], *available at* www.state.gov/documents/organization/21555.pdf.

57. HRW Report, *supra* note 2, at 36.

58. *Id.*

59. *Id.*

60. CSI Report, *supra* note 23, at 31. Questions about whether the United States can be considered an example of the "best of circumstances" aside, the CSI Report states that at least in 1999, prior to passage of the TVPA, "information sharing among the various entities remain[ed] imperfect. Several Department of Justice [DOJ] offices look at the trafficking issue through the prism of their particular offices' interest, be it eliminating civil rights violations, tackling organized crime, or protecting minors. Even within the [DOJ], information is not always shared." *See also* Monk Report, *supra* note 36, at 76. Although Serbia and Montenegro are actively participating in high level working groups to combat trafficking, including suggesting progressive programs for victim protection, the police force is incapable of coping with the scale of the phenomenon:

   Apart from within the border police departments, there is poor awareness and interest generally on the part of police and the public about the subject [of trafficking], and the prevailing disregard for gender equality contributes to indifference about the plight of victims. . . . Because of the lack of reciprocal agreements with neighboring States, the incompatibility of laws, the absence of [domestic] laws which enable successful prosecutions to be brought against the traffickers and pimps and the lack of [domestic] legal authority to produce evidence obtained by the internal use of technical and surveillance aids, victims' cases are generally viewed as time and energy consuming and inevitably unproductive. The very fact that victims' statements, both verbal and written, will be in a foreign language further reduces responsiveness.

tion;[61] traffickers supply false passports to border police,[62] and the girls and traffickers are waived through.

For example, during the author's tenure in Belgrade, Serbia, and Montenegro, a brothel was raided and trafficked women were placed in jail, rather than the new shelter for trafficked persons, on the very same day that a high-level regional meeting took place in Belgrade between ministries and Stability Pact, UN, and OSCE officials to discuss follow up victim protection mechanisms for the new shelter. There seemed to be no communication between those making the decisions to adopt new laws and practices and those carrying them out in the field, and there was an inability or unwillingness to train these low-level government employees.

2. *Governments fail to penalize or even acknowledge the complicity of peacekeepers and international workers in trafficking*

Despite a growing awareness that peacekeeping forces and humanitarian workers regularly and knowingly obtain the services of trafficked women and sometimes even engage in or aid and abet trafficking, governments have failed to publicly address this issue. Trafficked women in Bosnia, for instance, report that approximately 30 percent of their clients are internationals.[63] Countries that had never before been countries of destination began receiving trafficked women when peacekeepers and international aid workers moved into Bosnia, Croatia, and Kosovo.[64] Neighboring countries quickly became countries of transit and origin. While the use of trafficked women by international workers might constitute only a fraction of the total number of trafficked women and the fraction of those trafficked by international workers is even less, the participation of international humanitarian workers and peacekeeping forces in trafficking conveys a powerful symbolic message to local authorities and traffickers. The message is this: governments working to "democratize" developing countries do not really care about eradicating trafficking.

For years international organizations operating in the Balkans have been unwilling to determine how they can best prevent their employees from frequenting brothels known to harbor trafficked women. In recent years, when

---

61. HRW Report, *supra* note 2, at 61.
62. *See id.* at 16.
63. *Id.* at 11. *See also,* 2003 Trafficking in Persons Report, *supra* note 56, at 35 (acknowledging that the international civilian and military personnel have contributed to trafficking in Bosnia).
64. *See, e.g.,* HRW Report, *supra* note 2, at 4, 11. ("According to [IGOs and NGOs] trafficking first began to appear [in Bosnia] in 1995," and "[l]ocal NGOs believe that the presence of thousands of expatriate civilians and soldiers has been a significant motivating factor for traffickers to Bosnia and Herzegovina.")

it has become clear that most brothels in the Balkans, for instance, do contain trafficked women,[65] these international organizations have still failed to enforce internal rules or laws against frequenting brothels.[66]

Ninety percent of foreign sex workers in the Balkans are estimated to be trafficked, although less than 35 percent are identified and deemed eligible to receive protection assistance, and less than 7 percent actually do receive long-term support.[67] It is therefore well known among those charged with teaching Bosnians how to better enforce their laws, e.g. peacekeepers, the International Police Task Force [IPTF][68], and international humanitarian workers, that by visiting a prostitute, one stands a good chance of visiting a trafficked woman.[69] One would think, therefore, that workers paid by the foreign ministries whose goals are combating trafficking and promoting safety and democracy would be strictly forbidden to visit brothels, but they are not. In fact, sometimes they receive no punishment whatsoever even when caught engaging in such activity.[70] How can a victim of trafficking be expected to escape her captor and seek safety with the very men paying her captors for her services?

Some international organizations such as the OSCE and some branches of the United Nations have recently developed "Codes of Conduct" which implicitly forbid their personnel from seeing prostitutes by exhorting that they not "engage in any activity unbecoming of a mission member," subsequent to widely-publicized scandals involving international troops engaged in trafficking.[71] Nevertheless, several recent articles indicate that local police, international peacekeepers, and humanitarian aid workers continue to be major users of brothels in the Balkans in particular.[72] Developing and enforcing prohibitions against this practice are crucial, because the international police, peacekeepers, and humanitarian workers are the very persons

---

65. *See id.* at 4 (227 of the nightclubs in Bosnia are suspected of harboring trafficked women).
66. *Id.* at 46–60.
67. *See* JOINT REPORT ON TRAFFICKING, *supra* note 3, at xv.
68. In January 2003, the duties of the IPTF were assumed by the European Union, and are now referred to as "European Union Police Mission."
69. In Serbia for example, of 600 women questioned by police during brothel raids between January 2000 and July 2001, 300 were determined to be victims of trafficking. *See id.,* at 78.
70. HRW REPORT, *supra* note 2, at 62–67.
71. The author, a member of the OSCE Mission to Bosnia, signed such a Code of Conduct.
72. *See, e.g.,* McGhie, *supra* note 2; Kole, *supra* note 2; Lynch, *supra* note 2; Daniel McGrory, *Woman Sacked for Revealing UN Links with Sex Trade,* THE TIMES ONLINE (LONDON), 7 Aug. 2002; Robert Capps, *Crime Without Punishment,* SALON.COM, 27 Jun. 2002, *available at* www.salon.com/news/feature/2002/06/27/military; Robert Capps, *Outside the* Law, SALON.COM, 26 June 2002, *available at* www.salon.com/news/feature/2002/06/26/bosnia/index_np; *US Scandal, Prostitution, Pimping and Trafficking,* BOSNIA DAILY, Daily e-newspaper, 25 Jul. 2001, No. 42, at 1 (on file with author).

whose duty it is to work with local authorities to eradicate trafficking in this part of the world, and the victims are supposed to be looking to international police and peacekeepers for protection.[73]

IV. MODELS OF ANTI-TRAFFICKING LEGISLATION

In recent years, two main anti-trafficking models have emerged. Some countries and international institutions, such as the United States and the European Union, promote anti-trafficking programs that emphasize the prosecution of traffickers. Other countries and institutions such as the United Nations High Commissioner for Human Rights (UNHCHR) and United Nations High Commissioner for Refugees (UNHCR) are pressing for a victim-oriented or "human rights" approach to fighting trafficking.

Both models offer vast improvements over virtually any model used as recently as the late 1980s, when horror stories were emerging and statistics were first being gathered to identify the problem.[74] These two dominant models have come about through a series of legislative drafts and counter-proposals made by various governments, international institutions (IOs), and consortiums of interested international organizations and NGOs.

Both models contain provisions touching on enforcement and protection, but vary in their emphasis according to their motivations. Governments and institutions interested primarily in curtailing organized crime or illegal migration craft prosecution-oriented models, while those interested primarily in human rights develop victim-protection models. Because these models cover, to varying degrees, everything from witness protection to victim restitution and minimum sentencing guidelines for traffickers, the following sections will focus on one aspect touched upon, but not satisfactorily covered in either model—immigration benefits for trafficked persons. Immigration solutions should be viewed as *both* a victim protection measure *and* a mechanism for enhancing prosecution of traffickers.

---

73. UNHCHR recently addressed this issue openly in its guideline covering "Obligations of peacekeepers, civilian police and humanitarian and diplomatic personnel," asking states to consider "[e]nsuring that staff employed in the context of peacekeeping, peace-building, civilian policing, humanitarian and diplomatic missions do not engage in trafficking and related exploitation or use the services of persons in relation to which there are reasonable grounds to suspect that they may have been trafficked." *Recommended Principles and Guidelines on Human Rights and Human Trafficking, U.N. High Commissioner for Human Rights*, E/2002/68/Add.1, Guideline 10, ¶ 3 [hereinafter *Recommended Principles and Guidelines*]. *See infra* text pt. IV(C)(2).

74. For example, "in Milan [Italy] a week before Christmas [in 1987], the police broke up a ring that was holding auctions in which women abducted from the countries of the former Soviet Union were put on blocks, partially naked, and sold at an average price of just under $1,000." Specter, *supra* note 54.

A. "Arrest and Deport the Victim"

As recently as the late 1980s government authorities in virtually all countries tended to treat trafficked persons as criminals, rather than victims of both a crime and of human rights violations.[75] Governments were regularly jailing trafficked persons for violations of immigration status, unauthorized employment, or prostitution, and deporting them.[76] Some countries, such as Bosnia, Serbia, and Montenegro still arrest and deport, as a matter of practice,[77] even when it contravenes newly adopted laws or international obligations.

Grassroots anti-trafficking workers state that prosecutors do not want to tackle the difficult charge of prosecuting a trafficker when they can win the easier charges of prosecuting the victim for prostitution, document fraud, or immigration or labor violations.[78] The deplorable treatment of trafficked persons by police, prosecutors, and judges,[79] who are themselves sometimes complicit in the trafficking, serves only to discourage victims from agreeing to cooperate with prosecution. In one case in Bosnia, a woman had been accepted into an International Organization for Migration (IOM) program as a trafficked person and agreed to testify against her "owner." On the stand as a witness, the judge turned her into a defendant, charging her with use of false documents, despite the fact that she had just testified that her owner had purchased and provided her with a false passport, beaten her regularly, and forced her to work in a brothel for a year without a salary.[80]

B. "Jail the Offender"

1. Model examples

This model emphasizes prosecution of the trafficker, and all examples of this model have certain elements in common, with different degrees of emphasis. They use illegal migration and the combat against organized crime, in this instance trafficking, as their starting point and focus on prosecuting

---

75. OSCE Reference Guide, *supra* note 13, at 8.

76. *Id.*

77. HRW Report, *supra* note 2, at 19.

78. *Id.*

79. In one case, two fifteen- and sixteen-year-old girls found locked in a room during a raid on a Bosnian nightclub were asked by an investigative judge and the prosecutor whether they derived any pleasure from their sex work. This was only after the judge and prosecutor were pressured by the United Nations to take testimony from the girls at all. *Id.* at 36.

80. *Id.* at 39.

traffickers. They use strong language when referring to law enforcement mechanisms for prosecuting traffickers, and weak language when discussing victim protection measures; and they condition those protection measures on the willingness or ability of a victim to aid the prosecution of traffickers.

a. Convention and protocol developed by United Nations Commission on Crime Prevention and Criminal Justice

The current legal standard-bearers for anti-trafficking initiatives, the Organized Crime Convention[81] and the Trafficking Protocol,[82] are both whole-hearted instruments that emphasize the prosecution of traffickers.[83] Developed by a law enforcement body, the United Nations Commission on Crime Prevention and Criminal Justice (UN Crime Commission), the Organized Crime Convention, and the Trafficking Protocol respond to the international battle against transnational crime.[84] While the Trafficking Protocol takes steps in the direction of victim protection, it does not go far enough.

The Organized Crime Convention and Trafficking Protocol provide a reference point for countries without domestic legislation to begin preparing anti-trafficking initiatives, but provide curiously broad and vague guidance on how to implement measures related to protection. For instance, on the one hand, the Trafficking Protocol broadly requires states to "take or strengthen measures . . . to alleviate the factors that make . . . women and children [especially] vulnerable to trafficking, such as poverty, underdevelopment, and lack of equal opportunities."[85] On the other hand, the protection measures they do require are limited generally to assistance that will render the victim able to serve as a witness against a trafficker.[86] Reflecting this prosecution emphasis, the Protocol only asks states to "consider" adopt-

---

81. Organized Crime Convention, *supra* note 15.
82. Trafficking Protocol, *supra* note 7.
83. For an analysis of both the Organized Crime Convention and the Trafficking Protocol and how they relate to each other, see Ann Jordan, International Human Rights Law Group: Annotated Guide to The Complete UN Trafficking Protocol (2002), *available at* www.hrlawgroup.org/initiatives/trafficking_persons/. During negotiations for the Trafficking Protocol, NGOs argued for recognition of the rights of trafficked persons. However, as reported by Ann Jordan of the International Human Rights Law Group, "[g]overnment delegates concentrated on creating a strong law enforcement instrument and many of them did not believe that human rights are appropriate in the Trafficking Protocol. Consequently . . . enforcement provisions in the Trafficking Protocol contain mandatory language, such as 'states parties shall,' while the protections and assistance provisions . . . contain weaker terms, such as 'in appropriate cases,' and 'to the extent possible.'" *Id.* at 3 (*citing* Trafficking Protocol arts. 6, 7; Organized Crime Convention, arts. 24, 25).
84. Forty-four countries have ratified the Protocol, which entered into force on 25 Dec. 2003.
85. Trafficking Protocol, *supra* note 7, art. 9, ¶ 4.
86. These include witness protection, the right to have her identity kept confidential, provision of shelter, and other protections. *Id.* art. 6.

ing measures that would permit trafficked persons to remain in the destination country, failing to overtly acknowledge, as will be argued within, that assisting with immigration solutions would also improve the availability of trafficked persons as witnesses.[87]

b.   United States Trafficking Victims Protection Act

The Trafficking Victims Protection Act [TVPA], another prosecution-oriented piece of anti-trafficking legislation, does include provisions for the care of victims.[88] It even allows the provision of temporary visas for victims, so-called T-visas, and further allows for the possibility of permanent residency. The TVPA conditions the permanent residency, however; it "permits victims to remain in the US if it is determined that the victim is 'a potential witness to such traffickings.'"[89] It also limits the number of T-visas granted to 5,000 (regardless of how many trafficked persons might qualify),[90] and limits T-visas to victims of "severe forms of trafficking."[91] Finally, it relies heavily on economic sanctions to punish countries of origin or transit for failing to effectively prosecute traffickers.[92] While the concept of imposing economic sanctions for human rights violations is arguably sound, a country in political, administrative, and economic transition is not likely to be able or willing to rally its resources to effectively combat trafficking even with loss of aid as an incentive.[93]

Despite its heavy emphasis on prosecution, in 2001 and 2002, the Department of Justice successfully prosecuted only thirty-six cases, although the Department of State projects that more than 50,000 persons are trafficked into the United States each year.[94] As of February 2003, two years after the TVPA went into effect, only twenty-three T-visas had been granted.[95]

---

87. *Id.* art. 7, ¶ 1.
88. TVPA, *supra* note 50, § 107.
89. *Id.* § 107(c)(3).
90. *Id.* § 107(e)(2).
91. *Id.* § 107(c)(3). "Severe" is defined as "trafficking involving force, fraud, or coercion or any trafficking involving a minor." *Id.* § 103 8 (A) & (B).
92. *Id.* § 110(d)(1)–(5).
93. The agency responsible for distributing aid pursuant to the TVPA, USAID, currently spends $10 million annually in "programs specifically aimed at trafficking." *See* THE HONORABLE ANDREW NATSIOS, U.S. AGENCY FOR INT'L DEV.: PATHBREAKING STRATEGIES IN THE GLOBAL FIGHT AGAINST TRAFFICKING 55 (2003), *available at* www.state.gov/documents/organization/20942.pdf.
94. *Id.* at 47.
95. *See* DEP'T OF JUSTICE, FACT SHEET: ACCOMPLISHMENTS IN THE FIGHT TO PREVENT TRAFFICKING IN PERSONS (25 Feb. 2003), *available at* www.usdoj.gov/opa/pr/2003/February103-crt-110. If the statistics cited by the United States government, CSI REPORT, *supra* note 23, at 1, are correct and 45,000 to 50,000 women and children are trafficked into the United States annually, while only twenty-three T-visas had been granted as of February 2003, there exists a seri-

On the whole, and particularly in comparison with other anti-trafficking legislation, the TVPA is quite comprehensive. However, the legislation focuses too much on funding annual reports criticizing countries for failures to enact or adopt legislation, and too little on ensuring that anti-trafficking legislation and initiatives are actually *implemented* and that US-funded programs are held accountable for producing results at a grassroots level.[96]

c.   *European Union's directives and resolutions*

In late 2001, the European Union, following up its Resolutions on trafficking in human beings and trade in persons and the 2000 Organized Crime Convention and its Trafficking Protocol, discussed above, issued a "Proposal for an EU Council Framework Decision on Combating Trafficking in Human Beings."[97] The proposal was drafted after pleas from the NGO and international community to address victims in the context of transnational anti-trafficking measures.

Nevertheless, the European Union has specifically emphasized the prosecution of traffickers as its primary objective. The amended EU proposal changed little, offering only temporary immigration protections to victims when and if they cooperated with prosecution endeavors. If trafficked persons did not have anything to offer prosecutors, they could be deported. In fact, the European Union took great pains to point out that temporary residence permits were *not to be granted for the benefit of the victim*, but rather

---

ous problem either with information regarding the existence of T-visas reaching actual victims or with requirements being too stringent to allow victims to obtain T-visas.

96. The US Department of State has also released a *Model Law to Combat Trafficking in Persons,* directed at those countries that have yet to adopt anti-trafficking laws. The model law does contain some victim protection measures, but many are conditioned upon furtherance of prosecution efforts. U.S. DEP'T OF STATE, OFFICE TO MONITOR AND COMBAT TRAFFICKING IN PERSONS: MODEL LAW TO COMBAT TRAFFICKING IN PERSONS § 300–12 (2003). Notably, the Model Law, unlike the TVPA, explicitly directs that victims shall have immunity from prosecution for any criminal offense related to trafficking. *Id.* § 208. Furthermore, on 23–26 Feb. 2003, the US Dept. of State hosted a conference called *Pathbreaking Strategies in the Global Fight Against Sex Trafficking* attended by grassroots organizations as well as members of foreign governments involved in combating trafficking, in which it finally listed "victim protection" ahead of prosecution, but noted that the recommendations "were not endorsed by the conference as a whole nor do they necessarily represent the policies of the United States government." U.S. DEP'T OF STATE, PATHBREAKING STRATEGIES IN THE GLOBAL FIGHT AGAINST SEX TRAFFICKING: CONFERENCE RECOMMENDATIONS (2003), *available at* www.state.gov/g/tip/rls/rpt/20834.

97. This Proposal also attempted to correct an earlier gaff, in which the EU Commission introduced yet another definition of trafficking into the debate, mere weeks after the UN Trafficking Protocol had been opened for signatures. The EU, recognizing that this approach did little to add to the necessary harmonization of laws and definitions, agreed to use a definition modeled after the UN Protocol in its current draft. *Council Proposal for a Council Framework Decision on Combating Trafficking in Human Beings,* art. 1, 2002 O.J. (L 203) 1, 2.

for the sole purpose of facilitating prosecution of traffickers.[98] States were not obliged to develop any programs or immigration measures to assist trafficked persons.

The Council Framework Decision on Combating Trafficking in Human Beings requires that by August 2004, member states must pass "effective, proportionate and dissuasive" legislation to penalize traffickers.[99] The Framework Decision is generally very skeletal, leaving much to states to decide in some respects, yet oddly specific when it comes to certain provisions such as setting the maximum penalty for trafficking at "no less than eight years," but not setting a minimum penalty.[100] The Decision further elaborates on jurisdiction, granting each member state the right to prosecute trafficking when 1) the offense is committed on its territory, 2) the offender is its national, or 3) the offense is committed for the benefit of a person "established" in the territory of that member state.[101] Although anti-trafficking NGOs and IOs have been pushing EU institutions for six years to strengthen protection measures, most decisions regarding the prosecution of traffickers have been left to individual member states and no victim protection requirements have been established.

2.   Advantages to "jail the offender" models

If implemented well, prosecution-oriented models have the potential to deter traffickers by setting forth requirements, for example, to pass laws "dissua-

---

98. *Proposal for a Council Directive on the short-term residence permit issued to victims of action to facilitate illegal immigration or trafficking in human beings who cooperate with the competent authorities,* Council of Europe, Commission of the European Communities, COM/2002/0071, 2002/0043 (CNS) (2002) at § 2.3, *available at* http://europa.eu.int/eur-lex/pri/en/lip/latest/doc/2002/com2002_0071en01.doc. The title of Section 2.3 is, "Not a victim protection or witness protection or witness protection measure," should anyone miss the point:

> This proposal for a Directive is concerned with a residence permit and defines the conditions for its issue. In this sense . . . *the proposal may appear to serve to protect victims. This is not however, the case: the proposed Directive introduces a residence permit and is not concerned with protection of either witnesses or victims. This is neither its aim nor its legal basis.* Victim protection and witness protection are matters of ordinary national or European law. [Emphasis added.]

Id.

99. *Council Framework Decision of 19 July 2002 on Combating Trafficking in Human Beings,* Council of Europe, 2002/629/JHA (L 203) art. 3(1), *available at* www.europa.eu.int/eur-lex/pri/en/oj/dat/2002/l_203/l_20320320020801en00010004.pdf. Member states are: Austria, Belgium, Denmark, Finland, France, Germany, Greece, Ireland, Italy, the Netherlands, Portugal, Spain, Sweden, and the United Kingdom. Candidate countries are: Bulgaria, Cyprus, the Czech Republic, Estonia, Hungary, Latvia, Lithuania, Malta, Poland, Romania, Slovakia, Slovenia, and Turkey.

100. *Id.* art. 3(2).

101. *Id.* art. 6(1).

sive" to traffickers. To date, however, even supposedly dissuasive laws have not been implemented and applied in such a way as to actually dissuade traffickers.[102]

Furthermore, if it were established that prosecution-oriented models increased the likelihood of prosecution of traffickers, these models could be considered advantageous. At present, however, the only certainty is that victims of traffickers who do not agree to cooperate with prosecutors are not offered protection.[103] In essence, they are re-victimized by the government in their country of destination. Good prosecution-oriented anti-trafficking models could begin to provide a deterrent effect; at present, however, with trafficking on the rise, it does not appear that any laws yet serve as a deterrent.

3. Drawbacks of "jail the offender" models

Where restriction of migration or combating organized crime is the primary policy concern, states will naturally focus on law enforcement, and they may accordingly limit their protective responsibilities. They will not focus on extending immigration protections to trafficked persons, because the emphasis is on the state's sovereign gatekeeping role. They even forgo extending non-immigration related protections unless the trafficked person agrees to testify or assist with prosecution.

A prosecution-oriented approach that fails to place any premium on protection may contravene existing international law.[104] Prosecution models may also simply be ineffective in the face of the multitudinous pitfalls to successful prosecution in countries where trafficking is most prolific: corrupt or inefficient police and border guards; lack of an administrative structure to support the complex task of investigating, arresting, prosecuting, and convicting traffickers; lack of communication between various agencies involved; failures or ineptitude within the judicial process; the preference of police to go for the easier arrest of the victim rather than of the trafficker; the preference of the prosecutors to go for the easier charges of "prostitution," illegal immigration, unauthorized labor, or fraudulent documents (charging the victim), rather than to prosecute for the trafficking; the difficulty of reaching across borders to find the perpetrators (particularly between unfriendly neighboring nations); and the reluctance or inability of national

---

102. *See infra* text pt. IV(C)(2)(i).
103. Except in the rare instances in which asylum has been granted "on account of membership in a particular social group." *See infra* text pt. V(A)(5)(c)(ii)(b).
104. It is arguable that the ICCPR alone entitles trafficked persons to assistance and protection by virtue of their status as victims of crime whose human rights have been violated. International Covenant on Civil and Political Rights, *adopted* 16 Dec. 1966, G.A. Res. 2200 (XXI), U.N. GAOR, 21st Sess., Supp. No. 16, arts. 2, 7, 8, U.N. Doc. A/6316 (1966), 999 U.N.T.S. 171 (*entered into force* 23 Mar. 1976).

police to cooperate internationally to effectively attack organized crime.[105] Prosecution models barely begin to address any of these less legal and more systemic administrative hurdles to prosecution.

Convictions are difficult to come by even in the best of circumstances. The list of hurdles is seemingly endless,[106] and the number of prosecutions, as compared to the reported numbers of trafficked persons, is infinitesimal.[107]

a. Weak actual prosecutions and short sentences

While most countries currently have some legislation on the books that could be used to prosecute traffickers, typically having to do with illegally procuring persons for prostitution, these laws have had little impact on restricting traffickers or protecting trafficked persons, and are rarely, if ever, enforced. Bosnia, for instance, has successfully prosecuted only eleven traffickers to date, with the traffickers sentenced to between only one and three years, and the testimony of over 190 victim-witnesses was necessary to secure even these short sentences.[108] In Moldova, only fifteen cases were

---

105. *See, e.g.,* Monk Report, *supra* note 36, at 6.

> [The police force's] [d]ealing with sexual crime and domestic violence is impaired by poor perception of the seriousness and extent of each. Both require re-modelling and co-operation with non-government organisations, to provide for the rights of the victims. The investigation of trafficking in females for the purpose of prostitution, in drugs and other commodities, require strengthening not just by policing expertise but also by regional arrangements and co-ordinated assistance by regional organizations. There is no consistent co-ordination of the crime detection effort and [police] require advice on maximising local and national effort.

> These hurdles are not limited to countries in transition.

106. In Serbia and Montenegro for example, trafficked women arrive from and pass through Russia, Romania, Ukraine, and Moldova. They work in Montenegro and then pass on to Albania, Italy, or gravitate to the international military communities in Kosovo or Bosnia. *See* Monk Report, *supra* note 36, at 77.

> Girls are provided with passports and visas and enter through Serbia. Club owners are seldom prosecuted on the grounds that the women choose prostitution of their own free will. Victims that are removed by police have few safe refuges. In Belgrade, the IOM recently created a Shelter with funding obtained from Austria. Police within both Serbia and Montenegro encounter the frustration of victims' unwillingness to give evidence. More women police investigators are needed and the disclosure by victims, needs to be dealt with as part of a criminal continuum that should be maintained and added to as part of an intelligence picture.

107. *See* Joint Report on Trafficking, *supra* note 3, at 146. "At this moment, prosecution is the weakest part of the whole anti-trafficking system in SEE. Even if, in some countries, there are many people arrested and charged with trafficking, very few are prosecuted and sentenced."

108. *Id.* at 67 ("repatriation of the victims prior to trial is one of the most significant impediments to successful prosecution").

brought against traffickers as of 2002, and all were amnestied.[109] In 2002, forty-two cases were initiated in Moldova, eight of which were brought to court, while nineteen are still pending, two were suspended, and thirteen dismissed.[110] Until 2003, in Serbia only one person had been charged,[111] but as of 2003, 104 persons had been charged with trafficking-related offenses, although all cases are still pending.[112]

Even in the best of situations, when strong prosecution-oriented anti-trafficking laws are in place and the judicial system sound, the criminal sanctions that are applied are not a strong deterrent. In Austria, for instance, a trafficker found guilty of not only trafficking, but also bodily injury, rape, forced abortion, forgery, and damage to property, and who had two trafficked persons testifying against him, was *still* only sentenced to eight years in prison.[113] In the United States, albeit prior to the passage of the TVPA, three defendants were allowed to plead guilty to conspiracy to violate anti-slavery laws, extortion, and transportation for illegal sexual purposes (rather than to more serious but harder to prove kidnapping and trafficking-related offenses) and were sentenced to only two to eight years.[114] By way of comparison, those convicted of certain drug trafficking offenses were ordered to serve life sentences.[115]

If states with strong anti-trafficking laws are unable or unwilling to prosecute and sentence traffickers for a number of years sufficient to cause traffickers to reconsider the benefits of trafficking, then it is quite unlikely that states without sophisticated legal systems and laws will be able to do so. As this is a multi-billion dollar business, with a seemingly endless supply of traffickable persons and users, prosecution which threatens only a short prison sentence or small fine is unlikely to have an impact on traffickers who stand to make vast sums of money with little risk.

---

109. *Id.* at 29. *See* UNICEF, TRAFFICKING IN HUMAN BEINGS IN SOUTHEASTERN EUROPE (2003), *available at* http://www.osce.org/documents/odihr/2003/12/1645_en.pdf [hereinafter 2003 JOINT REPORT]. "In the first four months of 2003, there were 41 trafficking cases investigated by police, 36 cases before the court and 8 persons convicted of trafficking." *Id.* at 14. It must be noted, however, that no prosecutions have yet been made under the 2003 Criminal Code imposed by OHR, which makes trafficking an offense. No convictions in Bosnia have yet been made for the specific offense of trafficking. *Id.*
110. HRW REPORT, *supra* note 2, at 107.
111. JOINT REPORT ON TRAFFICKING, *supra* note 3, at 80.
112. HRW REPORT *supra* note 2, at 132.
113. OSCE REFERENCE GUIDE, *supra* note 13, at 49–50.
114. CSI REPORT, *supra* note 23, at 48.
115. *Id.* at 33 (stating that in 1999, the statutory maximum sentence in the United States for dealing ten grams of LSD or distributing a kilo of heroin was life, while the statutory maximum for sale of a person into involuntary servitude was only ten years per count).

b. Weak victim protection

Weak protection hurts trafficked persons, adding further insecurity to their future prospects, but it also hinders the prosecution of traffickers. A trafficked person who does not feel that the police, prosecutors, and judiciary are on her side is unlikely to come forward.[116] States that emphasize prosecution of traffickers typically do not make victim protection a priority, until and unless the testimony of the trafficked person is necessary to effectively prosecute the trafficker. Even then, such protection is offered only if the trafficked person is willing to testify, and often only for a limited duration determined by the length of the prosecution. This sort of conditional protection is too little, too late. Such an approach offers little incentive for trafficked persons to come forward, to remain and testify, and fails to sufficiently protect persons who have already been seriously harmed.[117]

Add to this the possibility of a corrupt, ineffective, or transitioning judicial system, obstacles with which many countries of destination, origin, and transit are burdened, and trafficked persons can expect to be guaranteed neither a fair nor a secure trial, either as witnesses or if prosecuted for labor or immigration violations.[118] Even in countries with effective judicial systems, serious prejudices still exist against people who have been trafficked, which may also enhance victims' feelings of insecurity and inhibit them from coming forward.[119] Thus, the women are victimized again and again as they pass out of the hands of traffickers and into the hands of authorities. While modern prosecution models offer a vast improvement when they eliminate the prosecution of victims for immigration or prostitution offenses, they still leave much to be desired.

---

116. *Report of the Special Rapporteur, supra* note 22, ¶¶ 213–15; 255 (commenting that obstacles to relying on victims to provide testimony against traffickers include fear of arrest, legal sanctions, and reprisals by trafficking rings).

117. *See* Human Rights Watch, Commentary on the European Commission Proposal for a Council Directive "On the Short Term Residence Permits Issued to Victims of Action to Facilitate Illegal Immigration or Trafficking in Human Beings Who Cooperate with the Competent Authorities" 4 (2002), *available at* www.hrw.org/campaigns/migrants/docs/recidence-permit.pdf (noting that "no other victims of human rights violations are required to cooperate with authorities in criminal investigations or proceedings in order to enjoy the protection of the state") [hereinafter HRW Briefing Paper].

118. Monk Report, *supra* note 36 (commenting that "[i]nternal reform of the police will only proceed as far as budget and political will, will allow. At present all three Ministers of the Internal Affairs [Federal, Montenegrin and Serbian] are supportive but face constant constraints on funding and distractions as a result of continuing political instability").

119. *See, e.g.,* CSI Report, *supra* note 23, at 31. Police officers, too, are believed to hold the opinion that "trafficking victims [are] part of the conspiracy and consequently . . . accomplices." *Id.* at 35. Other INS agents believe that these cases are closer to "alien smuggling for prostitution" than trafficking, which would simply ignore the fact that force or coercion was involved. *Id.* at 36.

C.   "Protect the Victim"

Broadly stated, examples of victim-protection models have certain elements in common, with different degrees of emphasis. They start from a human rights perspective and have protection of the victim as their primary aim. They promote prosecution of traffickers, but do not condition victim protection (excluding immigration protections, as discussed above) on the willingness or ability of the victim to assist with the prosecution.

Intergovernmental organizations (IGOs), NGOs, and some UN bodies are pushing countries to adopt a victim-oriented approach to trafficking, also referred to as a "human rights" approach, which would emphasize protection of the victim.

1.   Model examples

Provisions common to victim-protection models are extending rights to victims and insisting that protection not be conditioned upon a victim's ability or willingness to assist with prosecution. Victim-protection measures include assistance with psychological and social services, temporary employment and legal services, the provision of safe houses, protection during the prosecution of their traffickers, and perhaps sustainable alternative employment programs. While no organizations have yet ventured to propose all those attributes in the form of draft legislation, a victim-oriented approach should also promote the extension of residence, asylum, or third country hosting for trafficking victims, when repatriation to the country of origin or settlement in the country of destination would jeopardize the safety of the victim.

a.   GAATW and its partners

The Global Alliance Against Traffic in Women (GAATW), an organization working to develop effective anti-trafficking measures produced a definition of trafficking in 1997. Frustrated by what it deemed to be an irrelevant and irresponsible linking of prostitution to the issue of trafficking, to the detriment of protection for victims of trafficking, the GAATW and its partners developed the Human Rights Standards for the Treatment of Trafficked Persons (Human Rights Standards) in 1999.[120] The Human Rights Standards require first and foremost that states recognize that victims of trafficking are not simply unwilling workers, but are victims of serious human rights abuses who should be protected by states not only from prosecution for immigra-

---

120. GLOBAL ALLIANCE AGAINST TRAFFICKING IN WOMEN (GAATW), HUMAN RIGHTS STANDARDS FOR THE TREATMENT OF TRAFFICKED PERSONS (Jan. 1999), *available at* www.thai.net/gaatw/GAATW_BODY_HRS_ENGLISH.

tion violations, labor violations, and prostitution, but also from reprisals and other harm.[121] Specifically, the Human Rights Standards require that states provide victims access to justice, the ability to bring private actions and to seek reparations from their victimizers, health care, and other services. In so doing, the Human Rights Standards made the first attempt to place the emphasis in anti-trafficking on victim protection.

In its contemplation of immigration protections, however, the Human Rights Standards only go so far as to suggest that temporary visas be granted to victims while criminal or civil actions are pending, that victims also be granted the right to seek asylum,[122] and that states repatriate victims who are willing and able to return to their countries of origin.[123]

b.   United Nations High Commissioner for Human Rights

UNHCHR's *Recommended Principles and Guidelines on Human Rights and Human Trafficking: Report of the UN High Commissioner for Human Rights to the Economic and Social Council*[124] (UNHCHR Recommended Principles), released May 2002, came in response to the European Union's "Council Directive on the short-term residence permit issued to victims . . . who cooperate with the competent authorities."[125] Like the Human Rights Standards, the UNHCHR Recommended Principles attempt to place victim protection squarely at the foundation of all anti-trafficking measures. The first paragraph states that "[t]he human rights of trafficked persons shall be at the center of all efforts to prevent and combat trafficking and to protect, assist and provide redress to victims."[126]

The UNHCHR formally asks that states not detain victims for illegal entry or unlawful activity,[127] that protection and care not be conditioned upon willingness to cooperate in legal proceedings against the traffickers,[128] that states

---

121. *Id.* art. II, ¶ ¶ 3–7.
122. With consideration being given to the risk of retaliation victims might reasonably fear. *Id.* art. II, ¶ ¶ 17–20.
123. *Id.*
124. Recommended Principles and Guidelines on Human Rights and Human Trafficking: Report of the U.N. High Commissioner for Human Rights to the Economic and Social Council, E/2002/68/Add.1 (2002).
125. *See Commission Proposal for a Council Directive, supra* note 98.
126. *Recommended Principles and Guidelines on Human Rights and Human Trafficking, supra* note 124, ¶ 1.
127. *Id.* ¶ 7.
128. States shall ensure that trafficked persons are protected from further exploitation and harm and have access to adequate physical and psychological care. *Such protection and care shall not be made conditional upon the capacity or willingness of the trafficked person to cooperate in legal proceedings.* (Emphasis added.)
     Id. ¶ 8.

provide protection and temporary residence during legal proceedings, and that they make available "legal alternatives to repatriation in cases where it is reasonable to conclude that such repatriation would pose a serious risk to their safety and/or to the safety of their families."[129] However, while insisting that non-immigration assistance (shelter, medical treatment, legal services, etc.) not be conditioned upon willingness to testify,[130] the UNHCHR Recommended Principles still allow states to condition *immigration* protection, in this case residency permits, on willingness to testify.[131]

It is unclear why UNHCHR demanded so little and offered such minimal guidance regarding immigration protections in its Recommended Principles. Instead of requiring any immigration solutions, they ask states "to consider" some measures which "may include some or all of the following elements [shelter, legal counsel, protected identity and] identification of options for continued stay, resettlement or repatriation"[132] and to "explor[e] the option of . . . third country resettlement."[133] Most likely the UNHCHR Recommended Principles were watered down in order to make them politically palatable.

c. *Stability Pact of South Eastern Europe*[134]

The Stability Pact for South Eastern Europe (Stability Pact) was adopted in 1999 after the war in Bosnia, at the European Union's initiative, as an attempt to replace reactive crisis intervention with long-term conflict prevention strategies. More than forty partner countries and organizations undertook to strengthen the countries of South Eastern Europe "in their efforts to foster peace, democracy, respect for human rights and economic prosperity in order to achieve stability in the whole region." At a summit meeting in Sarajevo, Bosnia on 30 July 1999, the Stability Pact was reaffirmed, and priorities were established on which the member countries would work together. One such priority was combating trafficking.

---

129. *Id.* ¶ 11.
130. *Id.* ¶ 8.
131. *Id.* ¶ 9; Guideline 4, ¶ 7.
132. *Id.* Guideline 5, ¶ 8.
133. *Id.* Guideline 6, ¶ 7.
134. The so-called "Stability Pact countries" include the South Eastern European countries of Albania, Bosnia, Bulgaria, Croatia, Serbia, and Montenegro (and the region of Kosovo in an autonomous capacity, pursuant to UN Resolution 1244), Macedonia, Moldova, Romania, Slovenia, and Turkey. Information concerning the Stability Pact is *available at* www.stabilitypact.org/trafficking/031210-sofia. Pursuant to the Stability Pact South Eastern European Anti-Trafficking Ministerial Declaration of 13 Dec. 2000, these countries play a particularly important role, as all are countries of origin, transit or destination for trafficking and sometimes all three.

In December 2000, at a Regional Ministerial Forum of the Stability Pact, eleven countries and one region signed the Palermo Declaration, undertaking the responsibility to address trafficking in human beings by implementing effective programs of prevention, victim assistance and protection, legislative reform, law enforcement, and prosecution of traffickers.[135] As part of its multi-year strategy, victim protection was identified as *the* priority for 2001, "because it is recognized as the most urgent need to be addressed and one that truly requires a response coordinated at the regional level." The Stability Pact Task Force on Trafficking in Human Beings (SP Trafficking Task Force) placed emphasis on a core group of activities that they believe promote victim protection: 1) establishing regional "clearing points" for information on transnational trafficking (one person or place that would serve as a receptacle for information and statistics on regional trafficking issues); 2) establishing National Referral Systems for victims (mechanisms by which victims would be identified and referred to shelters and follow up assistance); 3) creating a network of shelters and safe houses; and 4) promoting the return and reintegration of victims.[136] The first three points the author would endorse; the last is too narrow and potentially harmful to victims for several reasons that will be discussed below.

The SP Trafficking Task Force determined that in order to be successful, it must not only coordinate anti-trafficking activities, but also advocate for governments in the region to make anti-trafficking issues a priority. As such, the SP Trafficking Task Force identified individuals whose primary responsibility is to promote the political will necessary to prioritize and combat trafficking within each member country. This is an excellent and necessary initiative.

One significant weakness with the Stability Pact framework is the emphasis on return and reintegration, most likely due to the fact that the IOM, as a member of the SP Trafficking Task Force, has undertaken responsibility to coordinate the physical movement of trafficked persons and fund their temporary shelter. The immigration solutions envisaged by the Stability

---

135. The Palermo Declaration was signed by Albania, Bulgaria, Croatia, the Federal Republic of Yugoslavia, the former Yugoslav Republic of Macedonia, Moldova, Romania, Slovenia, Turkey, Montenegro, and Kosovo. *Anti-Trafficking Declaration of SEE,* Task Force on Trafficking in Human Beings, Stability Pact for South Eastern Europe, Palermo, Italy (13 Dec. 2000) *available at* www.stabilitypact.org/trafficking/001213-palermodeclaration. doc.
136. SP Trafficking Task Force Priorities, *supra* note 39. The 2003 priorities include witness protection and encouraging more countries to offer temporary residence to victims, as well as branching out to identify and target root causes of trafficking, including targeting users. *Id.*

Pact are therefore in part limited to those within the IOM mandate—the temporary protection, return, and reintegration of trafficked persons. The Stability Pact is silent on alternative immigration solutions as a means of victim protection. The Stability Pact plan would provide much stronger protection (and better possibilities for prosecution) if it did not limit immigration solutions to repatriation and reintegration.

2.   Advantages to the "protect the victim" model

a.   Protects victims and promotes witness testimony in prosecution of traffickers

The benefit to the victim-oriented approach is that it not only protects trafficked persons, but also allows them to become better potential witnesses simply by virtue of securing their safety and physical presence and promoting their psychological capacity to testify. A victim-oriented or human rights approach "empowers" trafficked persons, not only to leave the cycle of trafficking, but also to become witnesses against their abusers by providing them with safety during the hearing and offering justice.

b.   Discourages repeat trafficking

A victim-oriented approach "enables former victims to regain control over their lives in a safe manner."[137] In order to begin to achieve this objective, victim-oriented approaches include scores of subsidiary programs to be conducted in countries of origin, transit, and destination.

Unless the underlying causes, including social mores and economic and cultural practices that foster trafficking, are exposed and uprooted, women are likely to remain available to feed the trafficking machine, as social and economic marginalization only increases the susceptibility to trafficking. Furthermore, the social stigma attached to sex activities, even if undertaken by unwilling victims of traffickers, can be so great that women return to the sex trade even if repatriated, believing that they are "ruined" for marriage or any legitimate place in the society.[138]

A risk of failing to attack trafficking from the victim-protection perspective is that women who do manage to escape trafficking as victims then become recruiters of other women, either to pay off their debt bondage, or

---

137. JORDAN, *supra* note 83, at 4.
138. HUMAN RIGHTS WATCH, A MODERN FORM OF SLAVERY: TRAFFICKING OF BURMESE WOMEN AND GIRLS INTO BROTHELS IN THAILAND (1993), *available at* www.hrw.org/reports/1993/thailand.

to establish their own brothels, as they consider themselves already ruined, "marked" as prostitutes.[139] Anti-trafficking measures that include alternative job assistance and educate societies about trafficking, demonstrating that those who fall prey to traffickers are victims, have a chance of preventing the sort of marginalization that contributes to trafficking and re-trafficking.

c.   Easier to protect victim than prosecute trafficker

It does not require as much legal definition to identify a trafficked person and provide assistance as it does to identify and prosecute a trafficker. A cynical, but unfortunately accurate, view in support of a victim-oriented approach is this: if neither the victim-oriented nor the prosecution-oriented approaches have been successful to date in reducing trafficking in human beings, at least the victim-oriented approach offers the opportunity to remove the victim from her current situation and protect her from future harm and victimization.

3.   Drawbacks to "protect the victim" model

One drawback to the victim-oriented approach is that it fails to get to the root of organized crime. As pointed out in earlier portions of this article, however, organized criminals involved in trafficking are often also involved in trafficking weapons and drugs, as well as smuggling humans. A prosecution-oriented approach to combating trafficking, therefore, is similarly unlikely to reach the organized crime elements engaged in such a wide array of activities.

For all of the reasons highlighted in drawbacks to prosecution-oriented models, protection measures are similarly afflicted with implementation difficulties in countries with underdeveloped judicial systems and administrative structures. Finally, and central to the thesis of this article, none of the victim-oriented models thus far boldly endorse immigration solutions as a means of protection. This is particularly notable, as most examples of victim protection models emphasize the need for immigration solutions as a mode of victim protection, then fail to fully or adequately promote or provide for them.

---

139. Fanny Polania Molina, *Japan, the Mecca for Trafficking in Columbian Women,* www.DECEMBER18.NET, 2, *available at* www.december18.net/paper30ColumbiaJapan.pdf (stating "women who recruit . . . in most cases were women who were trafficked and engaged in prostitution"); Iowa State University Women's Studies 201 Homepage, Prostitution and the Trafficking of Women, *available at* www.public.iastate.edu/~womenstu/ws201student/prostitution/homepage.html (stating that "some of these women end up working for the people who enslaved them in the sex trade by recruiting more women to join them. They do this by telling the same lies that convinced them in the first place.").

V.   RECOMMENDATIONS

A.   The Best Way to Combat Trafficking is to Take the Best from the Two Models and Add the Missing Elements

The two anti-trafficking approaches can be combined in order to effectively combat trafficking. Victims must be protected from traffickers, protected from prosecution for illegal immigration, labor violations, or prostitution, and empowered to step out of the cycle of victimization. Traffickers must be identified and aggressively prosecuted, with alternatives to relying solely on the testimony of trafficked persons to prove the crime.

1.   Alter perception of what constitutes a "trafficking victim"

Anti-trafficking laws and the persons determining who is eligible for "victim" protection measures must acknowledge that women can, and more and more often do, consent to engage in commercial sex work, yet still do not consent to working in debt-bondage or slave-like conditions. When considering whether or not a woman qualifies as a "victim" of trafficking, a better approach would be to look at her situation at each stage, and grant her status as a "trafficking victim" (or a woman in need of and qualified to receive the benefit of any available protection) if she were unable to exercise control over her own destiny at *any* point after entering into the flow of trafficking in human beings. This would, in fact, also be considered a human rights approach, in that it would focus on the violation of a woman's rights at any stage in the process, rather than on her initial mind set. It would allow protection to be extended to the woman who, for example, took affirmative steps to migrate illegally, but did so because she thought that she was going to be working illegally as a waitress and instead found herself forced into the sex trade. But, and significantly, it might also allow protection to be extended to a person who was coerced into being trafficked, but then willingly remained in the sex trade or returned to work in the sex trade once repatriated. Expanding protection to cover those persons who consent to illegal migration or to sex work does not offer a negative outcome, particularly if one goal is to ultimately curtail trafficking and re-trafficking through offers of assistance and alternatives to all trafficked persons.

Why extend the victim-protection eligibility determination process to look at the mind set of the person at any stage in the trafficking process? Because it could help more people, would harm no one, and would not require significantly more state resources. Many government officials and even NGO staff whose duty it is to provide protection to trafficking victims believe that they should or are required by law to preclude from protection women who have ever willingly engaged in sex work, even if they were also enslaved or forced into labor.[140] The author's proposal does give latitude to those who argue that dire economic or social conditions that disproportionately impact women also deprive her of her ability to give effective consent, or that trafficking is a form of slavery to which a woman cannot consent. It might be deemed paternalistic, in that it would allow one to argue that a woman who has consented to remain in or return to the commercial sex trade could still be considered a "victim" of trafficking for the purposes of offering her protection, but at least the option of seeking and receiving protection is open to her.

2.   Start with a human rights perspective

Combining elements that promote the prosecution of traffickers with elements that protect and empower victims, anti-trafficking programs could more effectively: 1) protect victims by providing immediate shelter as well as psychological and medical care; 2) pursue prosecution of traffickers by providing a safe space for victims to recuperate while freely deciding whether to aid prosecutors; 3) increase the feasibility of prosecuting traffickers by looking at the intent of the trafficker to profit from moving people; 4) empower trafficked persons by creating labor training programs to mitigate gender-based economic inequity;[141] and 5) increase both the likelihood of victims providing testimony and the level of protection offered to victims by offering them permanent residency or asylum in the country of destination or in a third country.

a.   Protect, don't prosecute the victim

Traffickers must rejoice when the odd trafficked person is arrested or deported, as the inconvenience of losing the income from the one victim is offset by highlighting the threat of arrest and deportation, which serves to deter other victims from attempting to escape.

At a minimum, modern anti-trafficking programs must first ensure that victims of trafficking are not prosecuted as criminals. Second, they must protect victims by providing shelter with all necessary medical and psychological follow up care, including investing in programs that develop economic alternatives for trafficked women.[142] Third, they must create

---

140. Based on the author's experience while working in Bosnia.
141. This huge task, however, might rightfully be deemed too large an agenda to tackle within an anti-trafficking initiative.
142. TVPA, *supra* note 50, § 106(a)(5) (offering grants to NGOs in countries with trafficking problems to "advance the political, economic, social, and educational roles and capacities of women in these countries" under the Prevention of Trafficking heading).

education campaigns that individually target the potential victim audience, the potential user audience, and the actual victims. The education campaigns should inform potential trafficked persons and families about specific schemes known to be used by traffickers, educate potential victims regarding the known risks of accompanying smugglers, invest in programs that develop economic alternatives for potential trafficked persons, offer information about shelters and assistance to actual victims, and develop media campaigns to deter users of brothels and provide information about how to report the presence of trafficked persons. Finally, public awareness campaigns should be directed particularly at women refugees and potential immigration applicants, a plan endorsed by the CoE's Committee of Ministers, providing these groups with information about legal migration options, however few, in order to make them aware of legal routes to obtaining visas and residence permits.[143]

b. Address the social and economic reasons for vulnerability to trafficking

Trafficking in women is fueled by poverty, and women in transitioning and developing countries are exceptionally vulnerable.[144] Poverty conditions in these countries tend to impact women in particular, as their economic status vis-à-vis men is usually even lower in these countries. While the eradication of gender-based poverty is too large of an agenda to be tackled within an anti-trafficking scheme, the conditions that foster a vulnerability to trafficking must at least be addressed at some point.

In both the smuggling and trafficking scenarios, it is crucial to look at the reasons why a person would feel the need to leave her home country and travel abroad in search of work or escape from a violent or unsuitable life, but also to remember that some simply leave home in search of adventure or a better life and find themselves held against their will or forced into labor. Fully understanding the reasons women fall prey to traffickers can help legislators determine how best to draft and implement anti-trafficking legislation. Without pretending to tackle wholesale economic and social reform, anti-trafficking initiatives could realistically include fact-finding to

---

143. *Recommendation No. R (2000) 11 of the Committee of Ministers to Member States on Action Against Trafficking in Human Beings for the Purpose of Sexual Exploitation,* Council of Europe, Comm. of Ministers, Rec. No. R (2000) 11, 710th meeting, § IV (Prevention), subsection IV, ¶ 25, *available at* cm.coe.int/ta/rec/2000/2000r11.htm.
144. HRW Report, *supra* note 2, at 15 (from interviews with trafficking victims: "Due to the fact that the living conditions in [Moldova] are very hard and that I lost my job, I met a person . . . and she told me that . . . I could get a lot of money [in Italy] by working in the shop or as the cleaning lady in some hotel." "I want to buy a ticket to go back home and take some money back to feed my child. In the Ukraine we have nothing to eat.").

investigate precisely why women are leaving, education campaigns targeting potential victims and their families about the perils of accepting promises of foreign employment, information about legitimate options for migration, and extensive work with the governments and local NGOs to create alternatives to departure.

c. Address migration and immigration factors that sustain trafficking

A lack of viable and legal migration options leads people into trafficking; fear of deportation often keeps them there. Some countries have already acknowledged these migration routes and have begun instituting programs to allow legal migration of potential victims of trafficking. Italy, for instance, has granted 5,000 work visas annually to Albanians, acknowledging that Albania is its largest source country for trafficking and smuggling.[145] Although only limited visas are offered, if persons understand that they may legally be able to migrate, they may not believe that traffickers offer their only choice for migration.

3. Prosecute traffickers and those who aid and abet traffickers

Corruption is rampant among police, border police, and other government officials responsible variously for perfecting immigration status, regulating the presence of foreigners, and enforcing the laws in countries with major trafficking problems. In Bosnia, for instance, trafficked persons regularly identify local police as clients and friends of "nightclub" owners.[146] Police are known to tip off club owners before raids of those nightclubs suspected of harboring trafficked women in order to give owners time to hide women or supply false working papers.[147] Police and administrative officials are also known to accept bribes, supply false papers, or to turn a blind eye to the presence of undocumented foreigners.[148] The presence of police as guests in the nightclubs makes it highly unlikely that victims will ever turn themselves

---

145. *See* OSCE Reference Guide, *supra* note 13, at 37. Although intended to curtail trafficking, this in fact reaches primarily persons who would be smuggled, not necessarily those trafficked, as evidenced by the fact that the vast majority of those granted visas were men, although they might have otherwise fallen into indentured servitude schemes. *Id.*

146. HRW Report, *supra* note 2, at 18–19; OSCE Reference Guide, *supra* note 13, at 28 (quoting an IOM trafficking expert as stating that: "The local police is one of the main user groups—we proved that through interviews [with victims]. There are close connections to the bar owners and the traffickers. The women have nowhere to turn, and . . . I don't know of a single case of a police officer who was [prosecuted].").

147. *Id.* at 18–19, 28, 31.

148. *Id.* at 18–19, 26–33.

over to the police, if given the opportunity. It also makes it very unlikely that trafficked persons will have any desire to remain in the country of destination in order to supply testimony against their traffickers, assuming they are given the opportunity.

Even with trafficking on the agenda of so many countries, traffickers are still rarely prosecuted and the rare conviction almost never reflects the severity of the crime. Even in a country like Bosnia, in which the criminal code prohibits sale of human beings, rape, physical assault, kidnapping, slavery, and labor violations,[149] traffickers know that they are unlikely to be charged with anything more severe than promoting or procuring persons for prostitution, if they are charged at all. Police blame this on the courts, claiming that if courts were more efficient and less corrupt, traffickers would be punished.[150] Judges and prosecutors blame this on the fact that the victims leave before trial and are unwilling to return to the country to testify during the hearing.[151] Neither side mentions lack of victim protection or even the deportation of victim-witnesses as a factor in failing to secure convictions against traffickers.

a. Make it a punishable offense for international workers to visit brothels

In countries in which international humanitarian workers and peacekeepers are present and trafficking is a known problem, these organizations should establish more effective internal investigation mechanisms and policies by which their employees will be subject to dismissal and prosecution in their home countries should they contribute to the trafficking problem. As it stands, buying another human being or having sex with women known to be trafficked is not an offense punishable by law (though it could be deemed rape), nor do culpable employees fear sanction in the form of being fired, even those hired through their foreign ministries.[152]

Formally and publicly addressing the involvement of international and local military, police, and government officials would send a powerful message that silence regarding use of trafficked women will no longer be toler-

---

149. ABA CEELI Report, *supra* note 9, at 39–42. In March 2003, a new Criminal Code came into effect in Bosnia, criminalizing trafficking. *See also*, 2003 TRAFFICKING IN PERSONS REPORT, *supra* note 56, at 35.

150. HRW REPORT, *supra* note 2, at 35.

151. *Id.*

152. *Id.* at 46. "Jurisdictional gaps, lack of political will, and indifference toward the crime of trafficking ensure that the small number of SFOR and military contractors and IPTF monitors who participate in trafficking-related offenses do so with nearly complete impunity." *See also* the entire report, and specifically 41–68, dealing with the fact that no international employees are tried or sanctioned by their governments or employers.

ated. Publicly acknowledging that those tasked to combat trafficking can also be deeply embroiled in perpetuating it openly addresses corruption in the combat against trafficking, acknowledging that the use of trafficked women by international workers is an appalling symptom of the scant attention given to trafficking.

b. Make trafficking less economically appealing to traffickers

Trafficking is a lucrative business: because men seek out women with whom to have sex and are willing to pay for it; because there are few, if any, negative consequences to paying for sex even when the sex workers are likely to have been trafficked; because human beings can be sold and resold; because traffickers are not facing punishment; and because trafficking is still quite easy. Some argue that legalizing prostitution would reduce the amount of money traffickers make buying and selling human beings, so that sex work would come out into the open and not have the premium price tag attached to it that "illicit" work does. The author does not support legalization of prostitution as a means of eradicating trafficking, as many brothels host both trafficked women and willing commercial sex workers and consumers do not seem to differentiate between the two. Nor is criminalizing prostitution the means to eradicate trafficking. Prostitution should not be tied to anti-trafficking measures. One way to reduce economic incentives for traffickers would be to sharply increase the penalties for engaging in trafficking, including forfeiture of assets and restitution to victims, and to enforce these penalties.

4. Implement the laws

Practically speaking, the primary problem with both prosecution and victim-oriented anti-trafficking legislation as they currently stand, particularly in many South Eastern European countries, is that the legislation is only as good as its implementation. Whatever law is passed domestically, it must be fully implemented at every level. Police and border police must be trained; prosecutors and judges must be trained; NGOs skilled in victim protection must be engaged; funds must be made available; shelter, repatriation, and integration procedures and options must be known by each official likely to come in contact with a trafficked person; and victims must be educated about their rights and potential assistance. After years of experience arresting prostitutes or illegal migrants, it takes painstaking, regular, well-funded, and technically proficient training to teach a police officer and border policeman how to recognize and what to do with a trafficked person, in order to comply with new laws and obligations. Unless all persons who might come into contact with a trafficker or a victim understand the law and every procedure attached to the law, little changes.[153] As much emphasis should be placed on making the laws work as on adopting them.

Countries such as the United States and international organizations such as the European Union, which have expressed an interest in funding programs to quash trafficking, should shift their efforts from funding high-level ministerial meetings and working groups regarding adoption of recommendations. Instead, they should devote at least 50 percent of their anti-trafficking budgets to the massive job of disseminating information about new laws, procedures, regulations, and policies at the grassroots level in countries of origin, transit, destination, and in their own countries, to ensure that those who are most likely to encounter a trafficked woman know how to recognize her, are sensitive to her needs, and can direct her to the appropriate shelter or protection organization.

5. Extend legal solutions

a. Promote international cooperation

A necessary element for improving prosecution would be extraterritorial jurisdiction, or the ability of a state to prosecute a perpetrator for offenses that did not occur within its borders.[154] Currently, the Organized Crime Convention allows a state party to establish jurisdiction when a crime is committed against a national of that state, when it is committed by a national of that state, or when it entails a serious crime involving organized criminal groups.[155] The European Union has also recommended extraterritorial jurisdiction to secure prosecution.[156] In order to become truly effective, all countries trying to combat trafficking must adopt such provisions.

b. Target users of brothels

No laws currently penalize users of brothels known to contain trafficked women. In this day, when it is becoming widely known in certain countries

---

153. *See* Declaration of Basic Principles of Justice for Victims of Crime and Abuse of Power, G.A. Res. 40/34, *adopted* 29 Nov. 1985, U.N. GAOR, 40th Sess., Annex, art. 16, U.N. Doc. A/Res/40/34/Annex (1985) (recommending enhanced education and awareness of the applicable laws and procedures as a tool for positive change).

154. Universal jurisdiction has not been applied to trafficking at this point, although it could be argued that as an extension of slavery, it should.

155. Organized Crime Convention, *supra* note 7, art. 15. Austria, Belgium, and Cyprus, for instance, have all adopted legislation allowing them to prosecute if the act violated national interests, if the person cannot be extradited or, in the case of Belgium and Cyprus, if they have simply been caught in the country. OSCE REFERENCE GUIDE, *supra* note 13, at 52.

156. *See Council Proposal for a Council Framework Decision on Combating Trafficking in Human Beings, supra* note 97 at 3, ¶ 10.

that most brothels and nightclubs contain or have contained trafficked women,[157] countries will be considering whether to criminalize the use of these brothels, not only because users "assist" in the violation of prostitution laws, if such exist, but for using establishments known to harbor trafficked women. This could be particularly appropriate in regions in which international peacekeepers and humanitarian workers frequent brothels, knowing that they are filled with trafficked women.[158]

Nevertheless, the author would not endorse such a deterrent law at this time. Some countries have legalized prostitution and an obvious question would be: who has the burden of demonstrating that a particular brothel harbored trafficked women rather than willing sex workers. As most states agree upon the necessity to distinguish prostitution from trafficking, as well as guaranteeing due process for defendants, such a law would be too difficult to enact without jeopardizing other rights. The author would, however, strongly endorse education campaigns aimed at deterring users of brothels. These campaigns should be included in anti-trafficking legislation, containing information such as the fact that at least one trafficker in the US admitted purchasing HIV-positive women because he found them to be cheaper labor, having convinced himself and the women he trafficked that they had nothing left to live for.[159]

c. Create immigration solutions for trafficked persons

Failing to extend immigration benefits to victims hinders both prosecution and victim protection. Trafficked persons are reluctant to seek help in countries of destination or transit, even in the rare instance when they are able to escape confinement or after a brothel has been raided, for fear of being arrested for engaging in prostitution or deported for violating immigration laws.

More importantly, the restrictive immigration laws themselves are contributing to the growth of trafficking, a fact of which traffickers take advantage. In its Reference Guide for Anti-Trafficking Legislative Review, the OSCE states that

> Persons willing to migrate and work abroad in order to look for a better life, but who have no legal possibility to do so, tend to rely on persons who provide them with false documents, arrange the journey and find them employment. As restrictive immigration policies do not allow for enough legal immigration to fill the jobs that exist, migrants are forced to use illegal means to get to those avail-

---

157. *See supra* text accompanying notes 41–53.
158. *Id.*
159. *See* CSI Report, *supra* note 23, at 1.

able jobs. Once they arrive, migrants might find themselves forced to work and live under slavery-like conditions.[160]

As discussed earlier, some countries have already begun acknowledging the well-known routes of illegal migration into their countries and have tried to regulate migration in part by providing legal means to immigrate and work.[161]

i. Repatriation is an insufficient solution

Repatriation to the country of origin, the most common "immigration solution" employed by most countries encountering trafficked persons, is often an even worse solution. Upon return, trafficked persons face real threats of retaliation from traffickers,[162] as well as a host of problems stemming from social and economic exclusion.[163]

Internationally devised and run programs that promote repatriation only partially remedy these problems. While an IGO can assist with travel documents and provide some small "repatriation allowance," assistance by an IGO can also be the basis for even worse stigmatization. Police in Serbia, for instance, state that trafficked women refuse to participate in the repatriation program run by the IOM, not only because they do not wish to return

---

160. OSCE Reference Guide, *supra* note 13, at 36–37.
161. *See id.* at 38; OSCE Reference Guide, *supra* note 13, at 33. While the OSCE concludes that "such agreements . . . are likely to contribute to the prevention of trafficking in human beings," it is difficult to see in either case that granting such a low number of migrant worker visas will reduce the flow of illegal migration or trafficked persons into the countries, save for reducing it by the number of visas granted. *Id.* at 37 (citing IOM press release of 13 July 2001, *available at* www.iom.int). Furthermore, the OSCE Report acknowledges that most applicants from Albania to Italy were men with secondary education. *Id.* While there exists such high unemployment in transitioning countries, those most heavily economically impacted—the women—are unlikely to benefit from the grant of such a small number of work visas. The OSCE Reference Guide does recommend that such initiatives be revamped to allow equal participation of women. *Id.* at 37–38.
162. Demir, *supra* note 17, at ii (stating that it is common for victims to face violence or threat of violence by organized crime groups in the country of origin upon repatriation). *See also* HRW Briefing Paper, *supra* note 117, at 7 (HRW research in Bosnia and Herzegovina and Greece also indicated deportees or unaccompanied persons being "repatriated" are likely to face further human rights violations in the form of reprisals or reintegration into the trafficking network).
163. OSCE Reference Guide, *supra* note 13, at 87–88.

  Many trafficking victims are heavily traumatized because they were subjected to physical, psychological and/or sexual violence and are in need of medical treatment and psychological counseling. Especially women who worked in the sex industry in particular fear stigmatization and rejection by their families and social environment. Furthermore, in order to enable trafficked persons to integrate or re-integrate into the labor market, education and vocational training programmes, as well as assistance with finding employment are essential.

home, but because they are afraid that returning home with IOM will stig-matize them as prostitutes. The Moldovan press had run articles about IOM activities, identifying them as a "prostitute support" agency.[164]

A trafficked person who knows that repatriation is her only immigration option may not believe that law enforcement officials in her own country will be able to protect her should she testify against her traffickers (some of whom were in her country of origin).[165] Countries that still address traffick-ing as an illegal immigration issue, with deportation and repatriation being the only remedy, fail to acknowledge that they not only further victimize the victim of a crime, but also sabotage their own attempts to quash trafficking. A victim who has been repatriated to her country of origin will not be pres-ent in the country of destination to testify against her trafficker. Furthermore, women who fear arrest and deportation are unlikely to come forward. And finally, of course, women who are repatriated may have a legitimate fear of being approached again by traffickers and pressured either to pay more bribes or to be trafficked again. As one victim from Moldova stated, "I am afraid that my brother's friend [the person who sold me], will come and demand money from me. The police are corrupt there. They'll say that I was a prostitute and then the police won't help. He'll find out that I am home and demand more money."[166]

Finally, the author argues that state parties expelling trafficked victims are in contravention of International Covenant on Civil and Political Rights (ICCPR) Article 7 if the victim is at risk of being subjected to torture or inhu-man or degrading treatment in the country of origin.[167] ICCPR protection should be triggered when a victim is subjected to social ostracism rising to the level of degrading treatment upon return to her country of origin.

ii. Temporary and permanent immigration solutions for victims

As a starting point, if temporary residence permits are not extended to vic-tims, victims will not be available to testify against traffickers. The United States and several member states in the European Union have adopted leg-islation that extends the opportunity for victims of trafficking to gain tempo-rary visas. However, each state makes the provision of such visas contingent upon victims "cooperating" with or providing witness statements for the prosecution of traffickers.

---

164. JOINT REPORT ON TRAFFICKING, *supra* note 3, at 79.
165. HRW REPORT, *supra* note 2, at 26–34. (Victims are aware that police and local authorities are complicit in trafficking and will be reluctant to seek assistance.)
166. *Id.* at 20.
167. International Covenant on Civil and Political Rights, *supra* note 104, art. 7. Albania, Bosnia, Bulgaria, Croatia, Macedonia, Moldova, Romania, Serbia and Montenegro, and Slovenia are all parties to the ICCPR.

No countries in South Eastern Europe currently have legislation granting residency permits or other immigration protections to victims of trafficking. In Germany, trafficking victims have four weeks to consider whether to press charges against traffickers and are granted a stay of deportation only if they decide to do so and then only for the length of criminal proceedings.[168] The United States limits the total number of T-visas to 5,000 visas per year and offers residence permits only to victims of "severe forms of trafficking," although it does allow those who are awarded T-visas to apply for permanent residency.[169] In the Netherlands, victims have three months to consider whether to press charges and are entitled to remain during the length of criminal proceedings if they do; if they do not, they are deported.[170] Belgium grants longer permits to victims, depending on how useful their testimony is in serving the prosecution. It grants forty-five days to persons identified as "true" victims of trafficking to consider whether to press charges and allows them a three month residence permit if they decide to cooperate with prosecution, which can then be extended by another six months and is renewable. If the information given by the victim was significant in bringing a case to court, the victim may be granted permanent residence.[171] These flawed conditions turn temporary and permanent residence opportunities into a sort of lottery in which the winner is the victim who happens to provide the best evidence for prosecution. They would also seem to increase the risk of false testimony by victims against traffickers in order to secure a longer stay in the country.

Italy has a novel approach, granting residence permits based upon: 1) the need of the victim; 2) whether her life is in danger; or 3) whether she risks further exploitation.[172] Additionally, if a victim is employed at the end of the residence permit, the permit will be extended to the duration of the labor contract.

---

168. *See* OSCE Reference Guide, *supra* note 13, at 64 (during the stay, if they are accepted on a recommendation made by police, victims are able to work or participate in vocational programs, receive victim support, accommodation, counseling, and medical treatment).

169. TVPA, *supra* note 50, § 107.

170. OSCE Reference Guide, *supra* note 13 at 64 (during the stay, victims are offered financial, legal, and psychological assistance).

171. *Id.* at 64–65.

172. Nevertheless, Italy's anti-trafficking program has been criticized for a racist application of victim protection, in which African victims, who are the majority of victims in Italy, are offered protection less often than other victims, or are perceived more often as "prostitutes," rather than victims of a crime. *See* Marian Douglas, *International Trafficking in Black Women "La Africana" and "La Mulata" Out in the World: African Women and Women of African Descent,* Lola Press (2001), *available at* www.lolapress.org/elec2/artenglish/doug_e. For instance, Italy cites that 45,000 women are *trafficked* out of Nigeria annually, but then states that 80 percent of its 18,000 *prostitutes* are Nigerian, seemingly failing to observe the distinction when it comes to women from Africa. *See* IOM Migration Information Programme, Trafficking in Women to Italy for Sexual Exploitation

When countries offer only temporary residence permits to women who testify against their traffickers, they do little to help prevent trafficking and the further exploitation of women. At a minimum, states should implement short-term residency permits during which time humanitarian assistance is provided and victims can recover and decide whether they wish to cooperate with prosecutors. This option does not provide much incentive, however. Women are unlikely to come forward in exchange for an offer of a temporary residence permit, conditioned upon willingness to testify, followed by deportation. More importantly, the alleged justification for offering any type of residency *conditioned* upon testifying can backfire at trial. On cross-examination, the witness can be impeached with the question "isn't it true that you are testifying *in order to* secure an immigrant benefit?" When immigration solutions are offered to protect victims, rather than to secure prosecution, the witness cannot be thus impeached. Finally, unless she is allowed to remain in the country of destination, a victim will also be deprived of availing herself of any civil legal remedy, which the author recommends be adopted, in which she might seek restitution for lost wages or other claims against her trafficker.[173]

a. Temporary protection at a minimum

Starting from a human rights approach, acknowledging that victims of trafficking should be offered protection and accepting that immigration solutions of some sort are necessary in order to prevent deportation or unwanted repatriation, it is clear that immigration solutions should not be conditioned upon ability or willingness to cooperate with prosecution.

At a minimum, temporary residence permits or visas should be offered to victims, regardless of their willingness to assist in prosecution, in order to enable them to access the kind of health care, psycho social support, and shelter assistance they will need upon escaping a trafficking situation. Women offered humanitarian grants of temporary protection might be less likely to immediately re-enter the trafficking flow, a valuable outcome for countries intent on combating trafficking. Legal residence would also

---

(1996), *available at* www.globalmarch.org/child-trafficking/virtual-library/italy_traff_eng. Even so, the IOM contends that any disparity between the way African and non-African victims are treated is a result of the more entrenched African organized crime rings in Italy, making it more difficult to find victims. *Id.*

173. In the United States, for example, criminal courts may order convicted traffickers to pay restitution to the victim, including the value of the victim's labor. Because prostitution is illegal and therefore has no "market rate," restitution is equal to the value gained by the trafficker for the victim's services. OSCE Reference Guide, *supra* note 13, at 89–90 (stating that in Germany, trafficked persons granted a stay of deportation are entitled to compensation under the Act on Compensation of Victims of Violent Crimes).

enable victims to access legal assistance, not only helping to ensure that their rights are protected, but also serving the states' interests in prosecuting the traffickers.

There is currently a movement underway to set a European standard "reflective period," in which victims can remain in the destination country while contemplating whether or not to become witnesses to a prosecution.[174] While this could improve the situation in countries that currently do not have even a temporary visa regime for victims, attempts such as these to "harmonize" laws among European nations risk serving only to divert energy away from implementation of existing laws.

b. Asylum is a better solution

Although the European Parliament did recommend to EU member states that they should extend asylum eligibility to victims of trafficking, no states have explicitly offered asylum in their trafficking legislation, though some do not exclude the possibility for victims to make the argument that they do qualify for asylum.[175] The most serious obstacle to extending asylum to victims of trafficking lies in a state's fundamental right to preserve its own gate-keeping power.[176] A state that promotes combating trafficking in order to reach another ultimate goal—the fight against illegal migration and organized transnational crime—is not likely to expand the definition of asylum to include victims.[177] However, some parties have already acknowledged that repatriation may endanger the victim, and that local integration in the country of destination may be both warranted and desirable.

In its April 2002 issue of "Refugee Women," UNHCR stated for the first time that:

> Some trafficked women may be able to claim refugee status under the 1951 Convention. . . . In individual cases, *being trafficked could therefore be the basis for a refugee claim where the State has been unable or unwilling to provide protection against such harm or threats of harm.* It is crucial to the protection of

---

174. *See, e.g., Recommendation No. R (2000) 11, supra* note 143. Italy, Belgium, the Netherlands, and Spain grant temporary residence permits to trafficking victims who are willing to cooperate with prosecution of traffickers.

175. *See* OSCE REFERENCE GUIDE, *supra* note 13, at 62–64.

176. For discussion of states that have accepted the possibility of allowing trafficking victims to claim asylum, *see Id.,* at 66–69.

177. To qualify for asylum, a person must establish that he or she has a "well-founded fear of being persecuted for reasons of race, religion, nationality, membership in a particular social group or political opinion." Convention Relating to the Status of Refugees, *adopted* 28 July 1951, U.N. Doc. A/CONF.2/108 (1951), 189 U.N.T.S. 150, art. 1 ¶ 4 (*entered into force* 22 Apr. 1954), *reprinted in* 3 WESTON III.G.4. [Hereinafter Refugee Convention]. A victim of trafficking would most likely argue that she qualified as a member of a particular social group.

individual women for States to ensure that trafficked women and girls who wish to seek asylum also have access to asylum procedures.[178] [Emphasis added]

While mild on its face, the comment packs substantial force in that the argument could be made that most countries from which trafficked women originate are currently unable or unwilling to provide protection against trafficking.[179] It may also either force the hand of the European Union or send a message to member states, and perhaps more importantly, states hoping to enter the European Union, that in order to effectively combat trafficking, they may need to extend asylum, visas, or permanent residence options to victims retrieved within their borders. The flip side, of course, is that the European Union may use this as an excuse to insist that countries further tighten asylum regulations and illegal migration, if trafficking victims are a newly-eligible pool of asylum applicants.

As this author sees it, the grounds upon which asylum could arguably be extended to victims of trafficking, as members of a particular social group, are: 1) past persecution (by a group the government is unable or unwilling to control); 2) well-founded fear of being re-trafficked or suffering retaliation from traffickers (whom the government is unable or unwilling to control); and 3) well-founded fear of serious social or economic ostracization based upon status as trafficking victim.[180]

A few countries have already granted asylum to a very few victims of trafficking, as members of a particular social group.[181] Canada granted asylum to a Ukrainian woman trafficked into prostitution, finding that she was a member of a particular social group consisting of "impoverished young women from the former Soviet Union recruited for exploitation in the international sex trade," that upon return to the Ukraine, there was a "reasonable possibility that she would be subjected to abuse amounting to persecution

---

178. John Morrison & Beth Crossland, *The trafficking and smuggling of refugees: the end game in European asylum policy?*, WORKING PAPER No. 39 (UNHCR), Apr. 2001, at 54 (2001), *available at* www.unhcr.ch/cgi-bin/texisvtxhome+iwwBmeFiT89wwwwnwwwwwwwh Fqo20l0E2gltFqoGn5nwGqrAFqo20l0E2glcFqfnDmatwMnaoDa01GdpnwDaw5 Oc1MapdcoqODzmxwwwwwww/opendoc.pdf. UNHCR did, however, condition its promotion for extension of asylum to victims, stating that status as a victim of trafficking should not in and of itself allow access to refugee status determination. *Guidelines on International Protection: Gender-Related Persecution within the context of Article 1A(2) of the 1951 Convention and/or its 1967 Protocol relating to the Status of Refugees*, UNHCR, U.N. Doc. HCR/GIP/02/01 (2002).
179. *See, e.g.,* a typical government reaction as recent as 1998, made by Gennadi Lepenko, then-chief of Kiev's branch of Interpol, who stated, "[w]omen's groups want to blow this all out of proportion. Perhaps this was a problem a few years ago. But it's under control now." Specter, *supra* note 55.
180. Refugee Convention, *supra* note 177.
181. Denmark, Germany, Ireland, Norway, Sweden, the United Kingdom, and Australia have recognized gender-based persecution claims, a category into which most assume trafficking cases would fall.

at the hands of organized criminals," and that she would not be able to seek protection from local authorities, given the links between organized crime and the government, as well as the government's inability to combat trafficking.[182]

The United Kingdom granted asylum to a Ukrainian woman promised employment as a nurse in Hungary, who was instead raped, assaulted, and forced to work as a prostitute upon her arrival in Hungary. Even though she first returned to the Ukraine before fleeing to the United Kingdom, the court found that she qualified for asylum because organized criminals were looking for her upon her escape and return to the Ukraine, because the Ukrainian authorities rarely prosecute men for exploiting women (citing to a US Department of State Report on the Ukraine),[183] and because she belonged to a "particular social group that consists of women in Ukraine who are forced into prostitution against her [sic] will."[184]

In the United States, a Chinese woman forced into prostitution in China was granted asylum. The court found that she belonged to a "particular social group of women in China who oppose coerced involvement in government sanctioned prostitution."[185] The court looked to the US Department of State's Country Reports, which indicate that local officials are often complicit in organized, coerced prostitution, and determined that the applicant was "unable to avail herself of the protection of the authorities."[186]

The US government has granted asylum to trafficking victims, and gives high praise under the TVPA criteria to countries that "provide victims with legal alternatives to their removal to countries *where they would face retribution or hardship.*"[187] Nevertheless, when it comes to determining how to provide those legal alternatives to victims found in the United States, the TVPA suspends deportation only for victims willing to cooperate with prosecution, not to those who would face retribution or hardship upon repatriation.[188] Women who willingly entered the trafficking flow, but found themselves trapped in slave-like conditions in the United States, therefore, would receive no special protection.

UNHCR's willingness to recommend expanding the definition of "membership in a particular social group" to include victims of trafficking, com-

---

182. OSCE Reference Guide, *supra* note 13, at 67.
183. Immigration and Appeal Tribunal, CC-50627-99 (00TH00728), 17 May 2000.
184. *Id.*
185. OSCE Reference Guide, *supra* note 13, at 67. *See also* Tala Hartsough, *Asylum for Trafficked Women: Escape Strategies Beyond the T Visa*, 13 Hastings Women's L.J. 77, 115 (2002). (Makes the important observation that the applicant in this case was not trafficked *into* the United States, but rather was trafficked in China and used this as a ground to apply for asylum.)
186. OSCE Reference Guide, *supra* note 13, at 67 [emphasis added].
187. TVPA, *supra* note 50, § 108 (b)(2).
188. *Id.* § 106 (c)(3).

bined with the fact that several countries have, in fact, granted asylum to victims of trafficking on a case-by-case basis, makes a compelling argument for allowing victims to apply for asylum in the country of destination or in a third country.

c.   Third-country hosting

The concept of third-country hosting of victims has just begun to surface in Europe. While a victim of trafficking may not be repatriated to her home country, for fear of retaliation from traffickers, persecution, or stigmatization, she may also be unwilling or unable to seek asylum or temporary refuge in the country where she is found, most likely the country of transit or destination, for similar reasons. Third-country hosting may, in fact, be a better approach, if a more challenging option to execute, than asylum, in that victims of trafficking have different needs than refugees, even refugees who have suffered severe forms of torture. A further argument in favor of third-country hosting is that many countries of destination have not developed protection or even reception mechanisms for victims of trafficking (or refugees) and trafficking victims would be better off in a third country.

Some asylum cases are, in essence, already promoting the concept of third-country hosting. As described earlier, the extension of asylum by the United Kingdom to a Ukrainian national who was trafficked to Hungary comes close to the concept of a third country offering asylum to a victim of trafficking. In this case, however, the victim had to make her own way to the third country, entering illegally or under alternative justification, and then seek asylum. A bona fide third-country host should assist the victim with travel documents, travel to the third country, and assistance upon arrival.

In its Recommended Principles and Guidelines, UNHCHR's guideline addressing "ensuring an adequate law enforcement response," does urge states to consider "identification of options for continued stay, *resettlement* or repatriation," with resettlement being to a third country.[189] In its guideline covering "protection and support for trafficked persons," UNHCHR also asks states to "explor[e] the option of . . . third country resettlement in specific circumstances (e.g. to prevent reprisals or in cases where retrafficking is considered likely)."[190]

Countries that already operate under a quota system, offering permanent residence to a certain number of trafficking victims or migrants per year, would not overly burden themselves by designating that a certain portion of that quota be filled by trafficking victims.

---

189. UNHCHR Recommendations and Guidelines, *supra* note 73, Guideline 5, ¶ 8 (emphasis added).
190. *Id.* at Guideline 6, ¶ 7.

B. Response to Arguments Against Extending Immigration Benefits

The most likely argument against granting immigration benefits to victims of trafficking is that it will open up the floodgates, encouraging women to seek out opportunities to be trafficked, hoping to ultimately be granted permanent residency in a Western country. This argument does not have substantial merit for several reasons, as suggested in this section:

a) A woman who is trafficked for sex work will be forced to have sex with strangers, will be deprived of her liberty, will retain little or no profit from her work, and is likely to be threatened, raped repeatedly, isolated from friends and family, sold from person to person like chattel, and beaten on a regular basis. It is highly unlikely that many women would willingly put themselves into the flow of trafficking if they have knowledge of the potential consequences.

b) Traffickers already lure women into trafficking with promises of jobs abroad. Perhaps the trafficker tells the victim that the nanny position she will have in Italy will be legal, but he is lying. Most likely the victim knows that she will be engaging in some form of illegal migration or illegal employment, but she is unaware that she will be trafficked into sex work. Since most victims already have the intention of migrating illegally, the outcome of being trafficked does not increase the total number of persons migrating illegally.

c) Only a fraction of women have been granted visas or residency permits based on trafficking.[191] Those who are must still come forward and establish their eligibility for such a benefit, the numbers are not likely to increase drastically.

d) Even if they do increase drastically, countries could simply designate that a certain percentage of visas or residency grants already reserved for immigrants could be reserved for a subgroup of trafficking victims.

e) Even if this would reduce the number of visas or immigration benefits that, for instance, family members of immigrants would be eligible to obtain, it would not be by much.

f) Furthermore, countries could enlarge the total number of preferential visas in order to accept victims of trafficking without harming other candidates.

---

191. *E.g.* twenty-three over the course of two years, and estimated 50,000 per year in the United States. *See* Dep't of Justice, Fact Sheet, *supra* note 95. If the statistics cited by the United States government, CSI Report, *supra* note 23, at 1, are correct and 45,000 to 50,000 women and children are trafficked into the United States annually, while only twenty-three T-visas had been granted as of February 2003, there exists a serious problem either with information regarding the existence of T-visas reaching actual victims or with requirements being too stringent to allow victims to obtain T-visas.

g)   Finally, countries could simply adopt a libertarian viewpoint and endorse open immigration, deeming trafficking victims in particular to be "invitees."[192]

VI.   CONCLUSION

As it stands, the victim-protection model discussed above currently offers more than the prosecution-oriented model, which has numerous drawbacks. However, even the victim-protection model, of which several examples are highlighted, does not currently offer solid immigration solutions for victims as a victim-protection measure. The correct approach would be to take the best elements from the prosecution model and the best from the victim-protection model and add the missing components, such as durable immigration solutions for victims, an emphasis on implementation of the laws, a look at the users of trafficked women, and improved international cooperation in prosecution of traffickers.

At a minimum, trafficked persons should not be arrested for illegal migration or labor violations. Merely preventing the arrest of victims, however, does not go far enough. These are not merely "victims," they are also persons whose human rights have been violated and who are entitled to call upon the state for support and protection. Countries should adopt laws that emphasize protection, recognizing that the rights of trafficked persons to seek durable immigration solutions should improve the prospects of bringing solid cases against traffickers. Extending legal rights and protection to victims empowers them, rendering them less vulnerable to further economic and social exploitation, and perhaps ultimately limiting both their willingness to re-enter sex work and their desirability as sex workers. Empowered women are less desirable in the sex trafficking industry, in which women are valued for their silence, their timidity, their vulnerability, their inability to communicate, and their unwillingness to oppose or fight with their traffickers.

Most importantly, countries should then actively *implement* these laws, concentrating on training each and every person likely to come into contact with victims of trafficking. Governments must take the eradication of trafficking seriously, by adopting and implementing domestic legislation and

---

192. While the libertarian model would open borders, it would cut off welfare benefits, so that countries would need to permit immigrants to work upon arrival. For more on libertarian perspectives on immigration *see* Kent Van Cleave, *Settling the Libertarian Immigration Debate*, THE LIBERTARIAN ENTERPRISE, ONLINE EDITION, No. 162, 25 Feb. 2002, *available at* www.webleyweb.com/tle/libe162-20020225-03; Michael Tanner, *Libertarian Solutions: The benefits of open immigration*, LIBERTARIAN PARTY NEWS ARCHIVE, June 1998, *available at* www.lp.org/lpn/9806-immigration.

honoring their international obligations. Traffickers should be harshly punished, but a premium should be put on the protection of the victims of trafficking, to avoid what is currently the common practice of government complicity in the re-victimization of women who have already had their human rights so sorely violated.

EPILOGUE

Madeleina was returned to Moldova by an international organization. Her testimony was not used to prosecute her traffickers or the brothel owners. The international organization that repatriated her is unaware of her present circumstances.

PART IV

Economic Rights

Chapter 15

Measuring Women's Economic and Social Rights Achievement

Clair Apodaca

I. INTRODUCTION

In recent years empirical research in the field of human rights produced several different measures along with volumes of literature.[1] This scientifically oriented research has, for the most part, concerned itself with civil and political rights. Economic and social rights, due to the lack of sufficiently valid and reliable measures, have received far less academic attention. Similarly, although women's rights have been the focus of scholarly concern, scant consideration has been paid to empirical, cross-national studies on women's economic and social rights. Yet, the Committee on the Elimination of Discrimination Against Women (Committee)[2] recently noted the importance, and relative absence, of disaggregated and precise indicators on the situation of women.[3] The Committee remarked that "statistical information is

---

1. *See* Michael Cain et al., *A Guide to Human Rights Data Sources, in* Human Rights and Statistics: Getting the Record Straight (Thomas Jabine & Richard Claude eds., 1992) (registering human rights data sources). *Compare* Mark Gibney & Matthew Dalton, *The Political Terror Scale, in* Human Rights and Developing Countries (David Cingranelli ed., 1996) (describing the Purdue Political Terror Scale (PTS) which is derived from the US State Department country reports and Amnesty International reports—focusing on violations of physical integrity—to rate countries on their human rights conditions), *with* Freedom House, Freedom in the World: Political Rights and Civil Liberties 1–98 (1987) (using data from English language media reports, the Freedom House data set is created to score countries on their perceived adherence to civil and political human rights standards), *and* Charles Humana, *World Human Rights Guide, in* Economist (1986) (publishing the Humana Ratings, which scores countries on each of forty human rights, according to a four point scale).
2. Convention on the Elimination of All Forms of Discrimination Against Women, *adopted* 18 Dec. 1979, G.A. Res. 34/180, U.N. GAOR, 34th Sess., Supp. No. 46, U.N. Doc. A/34/36 (1980) (*entered into force* 3 Sept. 1981), *reprinted in* 19 I.L.M. 33 (1980) (creating the Committee on the Elimination of All Forms of Discrimination Against Women in Article 17) [hereinafter CEDAW].
3. *Report of the Committee on the Elimination of Discrimination Against Women: General*

absolutely necessary in order to understand the real situation of women in each of the States parties to the Convention."[4]

Although data analysis is important in evaluating the status of women's rights, aggregated data masks portentous differences in the realization of economic and social rights between males and females. Some examples will illustrate this point. In 1985, 60 percent of the developing world's adult population was literate; but disaggregating the numbers reveals that 70 percent of the males were literate while only 49 percent of the females were literate.[5] In 1990, 52 percent of all adults (fifteen years of age and older) were economically active; close inspection of the data indicates that while 67 percent of the males were gainfully employed, only 36 percent of the women held jobs that paid a wage.[6] Consequently, the Committee's General Recommendation No. 9 requests that states make every effort to collect and provide appropriate data on the situation of women.[7] Recommendation No. 9 confirms that sex differentiated data is extremely useful in assessing compliance with clauses found in both the International Covenant on Economic, Social and Cultural Rights (ICESCR)[8] and in the Convention on the Elimina-

---

Recommendation No. 9 (8th Sess. 1989), adopted 3 Mar. 1989, U.N. GAOR, 44th Sess., Supp. No. 38, ¶ 392, U.N. Doc. A/44/38 (1990) [hereinafter *General Recommendation No. 9*].

4. *Id.*

5. See United Nations Development Programme, Human Development Report 1991, at 166 (1991) (referring to Table 5).

6. *See* International Labour Organization, Yearbook of Labour Statistics (1990). The right to gainful employment, found in the International Covenant on Economic, Social and Cultural Rights, is the most contentious of the specified subsistence rights. The argument is that the right to work outside the home is an equality goal set by Western feminists that is not shared by women who wish to stay at home and rear their children. *See* Vandana Shiva & Mira Shiva, *Was Cairo a Step Forward for Third World Women?* (5–13 Sept. 1994) (unpublished position paper presented at the United Nations International Conference on Population and Development in Cairo) (on file with author). This argument ignores the reality of many women's lives and presupposes two conditions. The first is that there is a second adult in the household, generally male, who is the breadwinner. This presumption is plainly at odds with the reality that in Africa, Latin America, and the developed world, women are the heads in more than one-third of the households and that many more households require two paychecks to provide subsistence to the family. The second presumption is that of social affluence and technology. Only when women have access to time saving household gadgets (dishwashers, clothes washers, plumbing, modern stoves) can they turn their full attention to the rearing of children. Women who have to walk miles for fresh water, forage for hours for a supply of wood for cooking fuel, stand in line for hours for a loaf of bread, or do the washing by hand are not "choosing to stay at home and rear the children." Gainful employment is the most prevalent, stable, and acceptable method of securing the means of survival. Remunerative work is often the right to exist; the right to feed, cloth, and shelter oneself and one's children.

7. *General Recommendation No. 9, supra* note 3.

8. International Covenant on Economic, Social and Cultural Rights, *adopted* 16 Dec. 1966, 993 U.N.T.S. 3, G.A. Res. 2200 (XXI), U.N. GAOR, 21st Sess., Supp. No. 16, U.N. Doc. A/6316 (1966) (*entered into force* 3 Jan. 1976) [hereinafter ICESCR]. As of June 1994, 129 nation states have signed and ratified the ICESCR, accepting their responsibility to pro-

tion of All Forms of Discrimination Against Women[9] that mandate nondiscrimination and equality of treatment.

This study is a beginning step in the long process of understanding women's situations in regard to the realization of economic and social human rights. Steven Poe, Karl Ho, and Dierdre Wendel-Blunt also have taken up the inquiry into cross-cultural variations in the realization of women's rights, by originating a coding scheme (Poe measure) that uses the US State Department's country reports to classify the economic and political situation of women in each nation.[10] This project, still in its initial stages, constructs the groundwork for the evaluation of women's situations throughout the world by establishing the validity and reliability of rights measures.[11] An additional tool to evaluate and analyze women's human rights status is the 1995 publication of the *Human Development Report*.[12] Subtitled "The Revolution for Gender Equality," the report is dedicated to the problem of women's political, economic, and social inequality.[13] The 1995 report introduces two new measures to capture sex disparities in the achievement of human rights: the gender-related development index (GDI) that measures achievement in the human development index (HDI) with regard to sex disparity, and the gender empowerment measure (GEM) that assesses women's participation in economic and political life.[14] The Poe measure and the new human development indexes are impressive scholarly endeavors on women's inequality, yet lack the time component of the Women's Economic and Social Human Rights (WESHR) achievement index introduced in this article. With the time extension (inclusion of 1995 data), the WESHR achievement index can be used in conjunction with the Poe measure, the GDI, and the GEM to reach a more conclusive understanding of women's human rights situations worldwide.

II. CONSTRUCTION OF WOMEN'S EQUITABLE HUMAN RIGHTS ACHIEVEMENT INDEX

Despite the emerging recognition of the importance of economic and social rights, and the need to enhance women's enjoyment of these rights on a

---

tect and provide for the population. The United States has not ratified ICESCR. *See United Nations Human Rights International Instruments: Chart of Ratifications as of 30 June 1994*, at 10, U.N. Doc. ST/HR/5, U.N. Sales No. E.87.XIV.2 (1994).

9. CEDAW, *supra* note 2.
10. Steven C. Poe et al., *Global Patterns in the Achievement of Women's Human Rights to Equality*, 19 Hum. Rts. Q. 813 (1997).
11. *See id.*
12. United Nations Development Programme, Human Development Report 1995 (1995).
13. *Id.*
14. *Id.* at 72.

level comparable to men's, scholars have yet to develop empirical strategies to define, operationalize, and measure these rights. As a result of the ICESCR's identification of numerous rights, researchers face the task of reducing a long and complicated list of rights into a manageable set for research purposes.[15] The task of reducing a complex list of rights into a manageable number of variables is daunting. Yet, there are a few rights that some have identified as so basic for human welfare and survival that these rights are considered to be of the highest priority. Henry Shue identifies these rights as subsistence rights: the rights to adequate food, clothing, shelter, unpolluted water, and basic health care.[16] David Trubek refers to these core rights as welfare rights because they evoke "what is most basic and universal."[17] United Nations agencies (UNRISD, UNICEF, and the World Bank) have also classified certain rights as basic, fundamental, core rights.[18] Among these rights are the right to health and well-being, the right to a basic education, the right to work and fair remuneration, and the right to an adequate standard of living.[19]

In order to capture the substance and spirit of the ICESCR, an index was built using those rights generally accepted as essential for human dignity and the satisfaction of which is necessary for human subsistence. The index includes:

1) the Right to Work, measured by rates of economic activity disaggregated by sex;
2) the Right to an Adequate Standard of Living, as indicated by the ratio of anemia rates of women and the total daily caloric intake per country;
3) the Right to Health and Well-being, measured by sex-differentiated mortality rates, sex ratios, and child mortality rates; and
4) the Right to an Education, evidenced by literacy rates and rates of primary school enrollment disaggregated by sex.

---

15. ICESCR, *supra* note 8.
16. HENRY SHUE, BASIC RIGHTS: SUBSISTENCE, AFFLUENCE, AND U.S. FOREIGN POLICY 23 (1980).
17. David Trubek, *Economic, Social, and Cultural Rights in the Third World: Human Rights Law and Human Needs Programs, in* 1 HUMAN RIGHTS IN INTERNATIONAL LAW: LEGAL AND POLICY ISSUES 205 (Theodor Meron ed., 1984).
18. *See, e.g.,* DONALD MCGRANAHAN ET AL., MEASUREMENT AND ANALYSIS OF SOCIO-ECONOMIC DEVELOPMENT: AN ENQUIRY INTO INTERNATIONAL INDICATORS OF DEVELOPMENT AND QUANTITATIVE INTERRELATIONS OF SOCIAL AND ECONOMIC COMPONENTS OF DEVELOPMENT (1985); WORLD HEALTH ORGANIZATION, WORLD HEALTH STATISTICS ANNUAL vi-vii (1988); UNICEF, THE STATE OF THE WORLD'S CHILDREN 12 (1989).
19. *See* INTERNATIONAL LABOUR OFFICE, TARGET SETTING FOR BASIC NEEDS (1982) (providing a thorough discussion of economic and social rights); *see also Report of the Secretariat: Report of the Seminar on Appropriate Indicators to Measure Achievement in the Progressive Realization of Economic, Social and Cultural Rights,* U.N. GAOR, World Conf. on Hum. Rts., Prep. Comm., 4th Sess., Agenda Item 6, U.N. Doc. A/CONF.157/PC/73 (1993) (discussing economic and social rights).

All items are regarded as equal because each item represents a basic, fundamental, core right. Therefore any question of weighing indicators on importance is moot. Appendix A contains a more detailed outline of the indicators
and data sources used to construct the WESHR achievement index.

The WESHR achievement index measures any disparity between male/
female rates in these specified economic and social rights.[20] A ratio for each
indicator (female rate/male rate) is made because the indicators have different units of measure. The ratio depicts the level of female achievement as a
percentage of the male level for each indicator. After calculation, the seven
ratios can be readily added together for a composite score that is the
WESHR index. In theory the range of the index can extend from 0 (total
advantage given to men), through 14 (where women have every advantage).
A score of 7 indicates parity between the sexes. In reality the index ranges
from a low of 3.18 through a high of 6.04 (world mean of 5.79, standard
deviation of .66).

III. THE CORNERSTONE OF HUMAN RIGHTS: NONDISCRIMINATION

The ICESCR affirms and describes the rights of all individuals, without discrimination of any kind, to: food; education; medical assistance; work; adequate shelter; and clothing.[21] Article 2(2) of the ICESCR requires states to
guarantee equal enjoyment of economic rights to all people regardless of,
among other categories, sex.[22] The ICESCR is unique in its repeated
acknowledgement of and attempt to alleviate the injustice and inequality

---

20. *See generally* GEORGE W. BOHRNSTEDT & DAVID KNOKE, STATISTICS FOR SOCIAL DATA ANALYSIS 384 (2d
    ed. 1988) (providing a detailed analysis of the function of the Cronbach's alpha). A
    Cronbach's alpha reliability test was applied to the WESHR achievement index resulting
    in a score of .74 for the seven items. The Cronbach's alpha measures the internal consis-
    tency of the index; that is, the reliability that the index is capturing an underlying con-
    struct. When a set of indicators is posited to simulate the underlying construct, the
    variables should be significantly correlated with one another. The larger the intercorrela-
    tion between variables, the more confident we are that the variables are measuring the
    same phenomenon. Our confidence in an index also increases with the number of indi-
    cators that comprise it. A Cronbach's alpha of .7 or higher is considered, by convention,
    good. *Id.*
21. ICESCR, *supra* note 8.
22. *Id.* art. 2, § 2. The exact language reads:

    The State Parties to the present Covenant undertake to guarantee that the rights enun-
    ciated in the present Covenant will be exercised *without discrimination of any kind* as
    to race, colour, *sex,* language, religion, political or other opinion, national or social ori-
    gin, property, birth or other status.

    Id. (emphasis added).

suffered by women. In what many would call a superfluous or redundant gesture, the drafters of the ICESCR unanimously voted to include Article 3, which requires states to ensure that women enjoy their economic and social rights at levels comparable to men.[23]

Yvonne Klerk concludes that after an analysis of the preparatory work, the delegates' realization that women were systematically denied their rights, even in the developed world, resulted in the decision to add Article 3.[24] Thus, in an attempt to abolish discrimination against women, the delegates decided that the principle of equality in rights fulfillment warranted specific clarification.[25] Of further note, the Committee on Economic, Social and Cultural Rights' General Comment No. 3 declares that, despite the fact that some states have claimed that financial constraints prevent them from immediately implementing policies to fulfill their obligations under the ICESCR so that instead they must take a gradual approach to those obligations, nondiscrimination in the enjoyment of economic, social, and cultural rights can be obtained.[26] Therefore, budgetary limitations do not eliminate the state's immediate obligation of nondiscrimination in the improvement of the economic and social condition of its citizens.[27]

IV.   THE PRINCIPLE OF PROGRESSIVE REALIZATION

The principle of progressive realization means the continuous improvement of rights. The ICESCR places an obligation on states to take steps to achieve full realization of these recognized rights without discrimination.[28] The vaguely defined duties articulated in Article 2 of the ICESCR call for a state to undertake "steps . . . to the maximum of its available resources, with a view to achieving progressively the full realization of the rights recognized in the present Covenant."[29] Article 2 has been used to claim that states are under no immediate obligation to realize economic, social and cultural

---

23. *Id.* art. 3 ("The State Parties to the present Covenant *undertake to ensure the equal right of men and women* to the enjoyment of all economic, social and cultural rights set forth in the present Covenant.") (emphasis added).

24. Yvonne Klerk, *Working Paper on Article 2(2) and Article 3 of the International Covenant on Economic, Social and Cultural Rights,* 9 Hum. Rts. Q. 250 (1987) (discussing the principle of nondiscrimination in the ICESCR).

25. *See id.* at 253.

26. *The Nature of States Parties Obligations,* General Comment No. 3, *adopted* 13–14 Dec. 1990, U.N. ESCOR, Comm. on Econ., Soc. & Cult. Rts., 5th Sess., 49th & 50th mtgs., at ¶ 9, U.N. Doc. E/C.12/1990/8 (1990) [hereinafter General Comment No. 3].

27. *See id.* ¶ 8.

28. ICESCR, *supra* note 8, art. 2, §§ 1–2.

29. *Id.* art. 2, § 1.

rights.[30] The Limburg Principles, created by an international body to clarify the duty of the states under the ICESCR, clearly refute such a claim.[31] The Limburg Principles interpret Article 2 of the ICESCR thus:

> The obligation "to achieve progressively the full realization of the rights" requires States parties to move as expeditiously as possible towards the realization of the rights. Under no circumstances shall this be interpreted as implying for States the right to defer indefinitely efforts to ensure full realization. On the contrary all States parties have the obligation to begin immediately to take steps to fulfill their obligations under the Covenant.[32]

In addition, the Committee on Economic, Social and Cultural Rights explicitly outlined the basic obligations imposed by the ICESCR with the adoption of General Comment No. 3, entitled "The Nature of States Parties Obligations."[33] According to this, a state's obligations under the ICESCR require the undertaking of immediate steps to effectively realize the rights guaranteed to all.[34] The wording "progressive realization" signifies the express duty of states to "move as expeditiously and effectively as possible" to guarantee right satisfaction.[35] The Committee further stated that "a State party in which any significant number of individuals is deprived of essential foodstuffs, of essential primary health care, of basic shelter and housing, or of the most basic forms of education is, *prima facie,* failing to discharge its obligations under the Covenant."[36]

The only defense against a charge of noncompliance is insufficient resources. If such a defense is invoked, the burden of proof falls to the signatory state to demonstrate that resources were so inadequate that it was impossible for the state to fulfill its obligations. However, the state still maintains its obligation to use its meager resources to protect and provide for the

---

30. *See* Philip Alston & Gerard Quinn, *The Nature and Scope of States Parties' Obligations under the International Covenant on Economic, Social and Cultural Rights,* 9 Hum. Rts. Q. 156, 177–81 (1987).

31. *The Limburg Principles on the Implementation of the International Covenant on Economic, Social and Cultural Rights,* U.N. ESCOR, Comm'n on Hum. Rts., 43rd Sess., Agenda Item 8, U.N. Doc. E/CN.4/1987/17/Appendix (1987). The Limburg Principles were drafted by a group of scholars, international lawyers, and human rights practitioners gathered by the International Commission of Jurists to clarify the duties of states outlined by the International Covenant on Economic, Social and Cultural Rights. This international body met in Maastricht, the Netherlands, on 2–6 June 1986.

32. *Id.* ¶ 21; *see also Symposium: The Implementation of the International Covenant on Economic, Social and Cultural Rights,* 9 Hum. Rts. Q. 121 (1987) (providing background on the Limburg Conference).

33. General Comment No. 3, *supra* note 26.

34. *Id.* ¶ 2.

35. *Id.* ¶ 9.

36. *Id.* ¶ 10.

greatest number of people in a nondiscriminatory manner.[37] As was indicated in the introduction, progressive realization in the enjoyment of economic and social rights often hides the persistent disparities between the sexes. The *Human Development Report* 1994 concludes, after adjusting its human development index for gender disparity, that "[a]ll countries treat women worse than men . . . but some countries do [so] less badly than others."[38] The disparities in the progressive realization of economic and social rights between females and males are still widespread, even though, by many accounts, the gap between male and female rates of rights enjoyment is diminishing.[39]

V.   TO THE MAXIMUM OF ITS AVAILABLE RESOURCES

The inclusion of the statement to the "maximum of its available resources" in the ICESCR clearly requires states parties to use their available resources to realize their citizens' economic and social rights.[40] David Trubek argues that the clause "maximum of its available resources" imposes an obligation upon the state to give social welfare priority in resource allocation, both in domestic allocation and in international aid.[41] In contrast, Philip Alston and Gerard Quinn argue that many of the rights specified in the ICESCR depend upon the availability of resources. Analyzing the *travaux preparatoires,* Alston and Quinn find that the framers of the ICESCR intended the concept of progressive realization to simply reflect "a necessary accommodation to the vagaries of economic circumstances."[42]

Economic development has traditionally been considered the dominant force in improving human rights. The liberal view of development holds that the elevation of human welfare is an automatic response to economic development and progress, and that economic development presumably does more than increase a nation's wealth. This view assumes that economic development will also modify customs, societal preferences, and cultural patterns that encourage the victimization of women. This modification occurs by transforming traditional values and beliefs into modern concepts of tolerance, diversity, and social status, based upon achievement rather than ascription. Economic development is believed to be a precursor of political,

37. See ICESCR, *supra* note 8, art. 2, § 1.
38. United Nations Development Programme, Human Development Report 1994, at 97 (1994).
39. See United Nations Development Programme, *supra* note 12, at 3; United Nations, The World's Women 1995: Trends and Statistics (1995).
40. ICESCR, *supra* note 8, art. 2, § 1.
41. Trubeck, *supra* note 17, at 215.
42. Alston & Quinn, *supra* note 30, at 175.

social, and cultural changes that will benefit the status of women.[43] Furthermore, economic development is thought to free women from the authority of fathers, brothers, or husbands by opening opportunities in employment and education.

In contrast, the literature on women in development suggests that economic development does not necessarily have the beneficial effects that proponents claim.[44] Development projects commonly regard the male as head of household, and therefore all services, training, and credits are in his name. More devastating for female farmers, title to land is routinely given to the male, denying women the right to cultivate their own or communal lands, or to obtain seed, or to sell their produce. Gita Sen and Caren Grown contend that economic development strategies often reinforce gender, class, and race privileges.[45] Part of their argument is that development strategies use women to reconstruct the economy.[46] Women provide cheap industrial labor that subsidizes profits while making domestic markets internationally competitive.[47] Nuket Kardam asserts that, overall, women's situation declined because development planners failed to recognize women's role in production.[48] Women, identified as housewives and mothers, were denied access to credit, technology, and land.[49] Susan Marshall's study of gender inequality found that economic development failed to "have [a] positive effect on gender equality in the modern employment sectors."[50] She found that the growth of the economy systematically favors male workers, who are recruited for managerial or skilled positions, while leaving women to labor as subsistence farmers, low status poorly paid clerical workers, service workers, petty traders, or temporary labor.[51]

The strength of the state's economy is the yardstick by which the state's compliance with its duty to protect and provide for the well-being of its citizens is measured. By grouping states at similar economic levels, a comparison can be made with regard to the fulfillment of economic and social rights. This comparison enables the determination of whether states with different economic levels, measured by GNP per capita,[52] experience statis-

---

43. See Janet Chafetz, Sex and Advantage: A Comparative, Macrostructural Theory of Sex Stratification (1984); Jean Lipman-Blumen, Gender Roles and Power (1984).
44. See Troth Wells & Foo Gaik Sim, Till They Have Faces: Women as Consumers (1987).
45. Gita Sen & Caren Grown, Development, Crises, and Alternative Visions: Third World Women's Perspectives (1987).
46. See id.
47. See id.
48. Nuket Kardam, Bringing Women In 11 (1991).
49. See id.
50. Susan E. Marshall, Development, Dependence, and Gender Inequality in the Third World, 29 Int'l Stud. Q. 217, 230 (1985).
51. Id. at 223–26.
52. See Robert E. Robertson, Measuring State Compliance with the Obligation to Devote the

tically significant differences in their level of fulfillment of women's economic and social rights.

VI. THE METHOD

The method chosen to investigate the possibility of sex discrimination in the realization of economic and social rights is quantitative analysis. Herbert Spirer and Louise Spirer contend that the use of statistics in human rights research fulfills many functions.[53] Statistics allows the researcher to "[a]ssess the magnitude and scope of human rights violations," that is, how many violations are encountered and their severity.[54] Statistics aid in determining patterns or trends of human rights violations—who is being targeted or which regions are being targeted—that anecdotal evidence cannot detect.[55] Statistics also provide visibility, credibility, and understanding.[56] A variety of statistical procedures will be performed in order to evaluate the hypotheses presented in this chapter (each procedure will be discussed as it is submitted, all statistical work was performed with the use of SPSS (Statistical Package for Social Science)).

Although a comprehensive study was attempted, several states were necessarily excluded due to a deficiency of data. The proliferation of countries due to the breakup of the Soviet Union and Yugoslavia are not included because the analysis ends at 1990. The unit of analysis is the country/year (a country at a particular point in time). The time points are every five years from 1975 through 1990. Missing data proved to be a significant problem, greatly reducing the number of valid cases. An attempt was made to collect data on every country, but if data were missing on one of the seven index indicators, the country was dropped for that year. A total of 114 countries remained, enough data for at least one time point, and this resulted in 315 cases. For a detailed examination of the origin of the information used,

---

"Maximum Available Resources" to Realizing Economic, Social and Cultural Rights, 16 HUM. RTS. Q. 693 (1994) (urging that the state's available resources should include more than just GNP). Robertson argues for incorporation of a measure of the availability of human resources, technological resources, information resources, natural resources, and financial resources. Id. at 695–97. However, as Robertson realizes, the resources (in terms of time, money, and methodology) needed to broaden our measure of resource allocation are restrictive. Id. at 713–14. Until we can develop standards for defining and measuring what the maximum of a state's available resources is, GNP per capita will have to do. See id.

53. HERBERT F. SPIRER & LOUISE SPIRER, DATA ANALYSIS FOR MONITORING HUMAN RIGHTS (1993).
54. Id. at 1.
55. See id.
56. See id.

please see Appendix A for a discussion of the adjustments and compromises required to build a workable data set and Appendix B for a list of the countries, by year, included in the study and their index scores.[57]

VII. FINDINGS

A. Is Progressive Realization a Reality?

This research will determine if economic and social rights have been, however limited, progressively and equitably realized. First, the levels of economic and social rights from 1976, the date the ICESCR took effect, through late 1990 are compared in order to discern trends (e.g., progressive growth, stagnation, or deterioration) in the realization of women's economic and social rights.

As indicated in the introduction, progressive realization in the enjoyment of economic and social rights often hides the persistent disparities between the genders. Presentation of the data disaggregated by sex clearly shows that significant differences exist. Overall, the measures of economic and social enjoyment show improvement even though the disparities in the progressive realization of economic and social rights between females and males are still widespread.

As Figure 1 indicates, life expectancy, for both males and females, increases in a staircase fashion. The graphed values of the other selected variables (economically active, literacy rates, and primary school enrollment) also show a steady increase for both women and men. Of course in absolute terms, women's levels of rights achievement are much lower than men's. As shown in Figure 1, states appear to be fulfilling their legal obligation, under the terms of the ICESCR, because economic and social rights for both males and females are progressively improving. However, because the ICESCR sets neither achievement standards nor a time frame, any improvement at all constitutes a fulfillment of a state's treaty obligations. Nonetheless, given the reality of severe resource limitations coupled with a growing population, the measurable improvement in rights satisfaction, worldwide, is impressive.

---

57. Please note that due to the problem of missing data, the samples, region, and time are not strictly comparable. For example, for the year 1975, region Middle East, there are twelve countries in the sample whereas in 1980 there are thirteen countries; in 1985 there are ten; and in 1990, seventeen countries had enough data to be included in the sample. Thus countries drop in and out of the sample, depending on the data available. Countries, due to administrative procedure, budgetary concerns, or other reasons, collect and publish data either yearly, every five years, once a decade, or never. See Appendix B for the countries by year that are included in the data set.

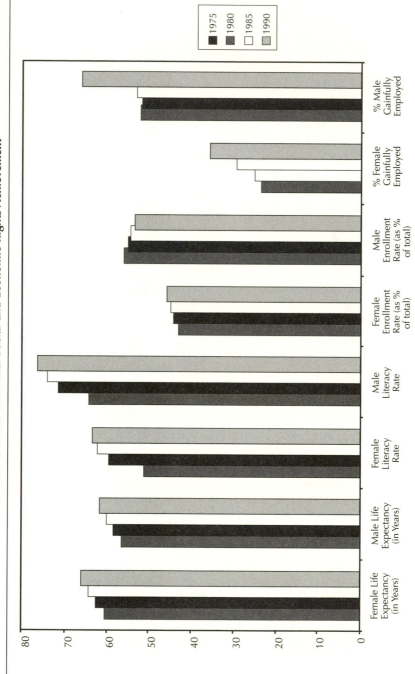

FIGURE 1

World Mean of Select Individual Social and Economic Rights Achievement

The data shows that the gender gap in rights achievement is slowly closing for many of the individual rights examined.

Figure 2 presents the worldwide mean ratio scores of each of the seven economic and social rights indicators. The ratio of gainful employment, as measured by the ratio of women to men gainfully employed, increased from 1975 through 1985, indicating progressive realization of women's economic rights. However, the ratio experienced a slight decrease from the 1985 high of 56 percent to the 1990 ratio of 55 percent. It should be noted that although women's economic activity is slowly increasing with time, women's levels of employment average only about half that of men.

The chart in Figure 2 also illustrates that both the ratio of literacy and the ratio of enrollment in primary school progressively increase throughout the period studied. The absolute number of women who are literate, and the ratio of women to men who are literate, continues to increase, although the rate of progress slows after 1980. This increase is more impressive when considered in conjunction with Figure 1, indicating a worldwide, 12 percent increase in all literate persons (58 percent in 1975 compared to 70 percent in 1990, which is an extra 1 billion, 4 hundred thousand people). Furthermore, women's enrollment in primary school has been continually progressive improvement, revealing a closing of the gender gap in primary school enrollment.

However, Figure 1 also shows the decrease in the measure of poverty (standard of living ratio), thus signifying the deterioration of the already precarious economic situation of the world's women. Women suffered greater levels of poverty, relative to men, in 1990 than in 1975.

Figure 2 also reveals that, worldwide, the ratio of child mortality is a phenomenon that is suffered by male children at greater rates than female children. Improvements in health care, nutrition, and environmental safety appear to have greatly improved female childhood survival. The ratio of life expectancy worldwide is consistent at 1.01, while the gender ratio is 1.00.

To conclude, as Figures 1 and 2 indicate, the absolute levels of economic and social rights have risen, but women lag behind men in every indicator of economic and social human rights. Yet, this discrepancy in enjoyment of rights has not increased but rather has very modestly decreased. Therefore, one can conclude that women's economic and social rights have been progressively realized, albeit slowly. Simultaneously, one must also conclude that the degree of discrimination against women in the enjoyment of their rights has not significantly improved.

A study by Susan Marshall demonstrates that gender inequality is often identified with geographic/cultural regions.[58] It is believed that due to geo-

---

58. Marshall, *supra* note 50.

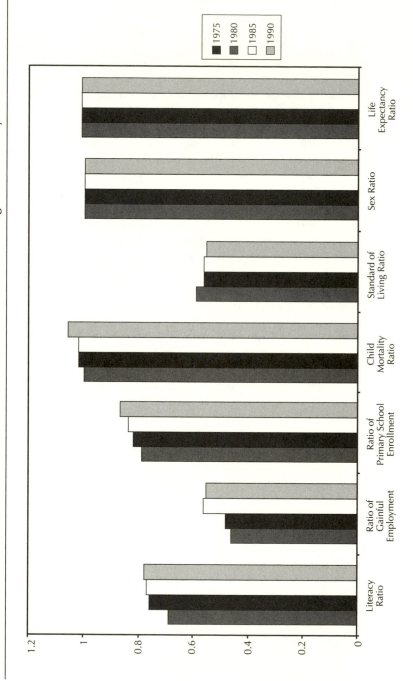

FIGURE 2

Ratio between Male-Female Achievement on Economic and Social Rights Indicators by Year

graphic clustering, states possess similar cultural and religious norms.[59] Marshall found that the region in which a woman lives (subdivided here into Latin America, Africa, the Middle East, and Asia) "appears to be the strongest predictor of female rates of educational and economic participation."[60]

In Table 1, the WESHR index is separated into the individual indicators to compare the average mean performance of geographic regions. The UN categorization of country/region was relied upon to determine a country's regional classification.[61] Analysis of variance was used to determine whether region is a predictor of women's status.

Analysis of variance (ANOVA), is a statistical procedure for determining how much of the variation in the dependent variable (individual indicators of the WESHR index) can be explained by the categorical independent variable (regions). ANOVA evaluates the difference of means for two or more groups; the greater the difference in mean scores between categories, the greater the variation explained by the categories, and the greater the likelihood the differences do not result from chance.[62] Thus, ANOVA uses the F statistic to test the relationship between regions and the WESHR indicators.[63] If the ratio is close to one then the different regions are not significantly different, and the variation in mean score is merely chance fluctuations.

By examining the regional scores in rights achievement in Table 1, it is apparent that there are strong divergent patterns of female inequality. All F statistics are very large and therefore statistically significant. Regional differences are attributed to the variations seen in the group means on all WESHR indicators. In the West, Latin America, Eastern Europe, and sub-Saharan Africa, women's life expectancies are slightly higher than the anticipated pattern outlined by the United Nations Population Fund.[64] That is, women's life expectancy is approximately one-fifth higher than that of men. Life expectancy in the Middle East and Asia is slightly lower than the United Nations calculated rate.

---

59. *See id.* at 226–29.

60. *Id.* at 229.

61. United Nations Development Programme, *supra* note 12, at 229. The table "Countries in the Regional Aggregates" divides countries into sub-Saharan Africa, Asia, Arab states, Latin America, and Europe. My study's time period was prior to the end of the Cold War, thus I subdivided Europe into Europe and Eastern Europe/Soviet Union.

62. *See* Joan W. DiLeonardi & Patrick Almond Curtis, What to Do When the Numbers Are In 131 (1988).

63. *See id.* at 136. The F statistic is calculated by dividing the between-group mean square by the within-group mean square. Within-group variability is a measure of how much the observations (index scores) within each region vary. Between-group variability measures how much the group mean score varies between regions.

64. United Nations Populations Fund, *Sex Differentials in Survivorship in the Developing World: Levels, Regional Patterns and Demographic Determinants,* 25 Population Bull. of the U.N. 51, 51–72 (1989).

TABLE 1
Analysis of Variance: Group Mean of Individual Economic and Social Rights By Region

WESHR Indicators	West	Latin America	Eastern Europe	Middle East	Asia	Africa	F stat
Life Expectancy	1.03	1.02	1.04	.99	.99	1.01	52.83**
Sex Ratio	1.04	1.00	1.05	.91	.98	1.03	43.73**
Literacy Ratio	.98	.93	.94	.60	.67	.56	104.61***
Economic Ratio	.60	.40	.77	.21	.55	.60	67.49**
Primary School Enrollment Ratio	.95	.94	.95	.76	.76	.72	46.60**
Child Mortality Ratio	1.10	.99	1.13	.98	.97	1.01	19.42**
Standard of Living Ratio	.66	.57	.63	.48	.47	.57	17.45**
Women's Economics and social Human Rights Index	6.35 n=88	5.85 n=72	6.54 n=20	5.04 n=52	5.30 n=38	5.53 n=46	85.71**

*** = p < .0001　　** = p < .001　　* = p < .01　　SPSS

In Table 1, the sex ratio results follow the pattern identified by the demographers: in most regions, women outnumber men.[65] The sex ratio reveals an alarming asymmetry to the disadvantage of women in the Middle East and, to a lesser extent, Asia. This, in part, can be attributed to the below-parity scores in life expectancy and child mortality ratios. In addition, several scholars note that the Middle East experiences high rates of male labor emigration, both from intraregional movements (Egyptian, Yemeni, and Sudanese workers), and from influxes of interstate migration (primarily Indians, Pakistanis, Thais, Chinese, and Filipinos).[66] This represents an estimated 4 to 4.5 million foreign workers, with the vast majority of these emigrants being male.[67] While the loss of 4 million mostly male, emigrants will

65. *See* Scott Smith & Kathrine Trent, *Sex Ratios and Women's Roles: A Cross-National Analysis,* 93 Am. J. Soc. 1096 (1988). Sex ratios are determined by the sex ratio at birth, sex differentials in mortality, the overall mortality rate, and migration rates. Worldwide, women outnumber men by a ratio of 103.5 to 100. *See* Shushum Bhatia, *Traditional Practices Affecting Female Health and Survival: Evidence from Countries of South Asia, in* Sex Differentials in Mortality 165 (Alan D. Lopez & Lado T. Ruzicka eds., 1981); Ansely Coale & Judith Banister, *Five Decades of Missing Females in China,* 31 Demography 459 (1994); Ingrid Waldron, *What Do We Know About Causes of Sex Differences in Mortality? A Review of the Literature,* 18 Population Bull. of the U.N. 59 (1986).
66. *See* Nazli Choucri, *Asians in the Arab World: Labor Migration and Public Policy,* 22 Middle E. Stud. 252 (1986); Nazli Choucri, *The Hidden Economy: A New View of Remittances in the Arab World,* 14 World Dev. 697 (1986); Ismail Serageldin et al., *Some Issues Related to Labor Migration in the Middle East and North Africa,* 38 Middle E.J. 615 (1984).
67. *See* Serageldin et al., *supra* note 66, at 616–19.

not skew the sex ratio of the densely populated Asian region, the loss does have an impact on the sex ratios of the more sparsely populated Middle East. The poor and often famine ridden sub-Saharan African region does not suffer a deficit of the number of women: the sex ratio of 1.03 is similar to that of more developed regions.

In every region, the score of women's equitable realization of their economic and social rights, as compared to men's, is reduced by the indicator of economic activity (*i.e.*, gainful employment). Women perform the majority of the world's labor but they are not counted as economically active because their work often does not receive economic remuneration. Unfortunately, much of the work performed by women (housework, child bearing and rearing) is not valued because it is not viewed as economically productive. In the case of the Middle East, Table 1 dramatically illustrates the situation: only twenty-one women for every 100 men are gainfully employed (*i.e.*, working for compensation).

Women in Latin America endure inordinately low rates of gainful employment (.39) but have experienced high levels of achievement on the other indicators of economic and social rights. In Eastern Europe, where women have the highest levels of out-of-home employment (.77), women still suffer inequality in the standard of living ratio, literacy rates, and primary school enrollments. In the West, women's inequality is revealed in their lower rates of gainful employment relative to men's.

Literacy rates and primary school enrollment ratios, as shown in Table 1, appear to be associated with economic development. Ratios are higher in the West, Eastern Europe, and Latin America than they are in the Middle East, Asia, and sub-Saharan Africa. Yet, even in the developed, more prosperous West and in Eastern Europe, women suffer a slight discrepancy in primary school enrollments and literacy rates. Given that females, on average, outnumber males by 104.5 to 100, this slight discrimination is alarming.

Child mortality ratios provide an unforeseen finding. Child mortality ratios expose a severe disadvantage to male children in the West and in Eastern Europe, while other regions show virtual parity in the deaths of male and female children. A close examination of the raw data indicates that the gender discrepancy in child mortality rates in the West can be attributed to a few small European countries with extensive health programs and few child deaths. For example, Denmark, Finland, and Norway suffer less than 100 child deaths per year and Iceland less than ten.[68] Under such circumstances, the mortality ratio is easily skewed if only one or two more male, than female, children perish.

---

68. *See* UNITED NATIONS, DEMOGRAPHIC YEARBOOK (1987).

Standard of living ratios from Table 1 show that women worldwide live in greater poverty than men. This finding substantiates Jodi Jacobson's conclusion that malnutrition "has more to do with gender than geography."[69] There are more poor women than poor men in the West. There are more impoverished women than men in Asia and sub-Saharan Africa, and more destitute women than men in Latin America. There are also more indigent women than men in Latin America. There are also more indigent women than men in the Middle East and there are more poor women than men in Eastern Europe. Yet the gap in the standard of living, between men and women, is smaller for sub-Saharan African women than their GNP per capita would indicate. Although poor, the poverty experienced by African women is mitigated by their high (by world comparison) ratio of gainful employment.

The geographic/cultural component appears to be an important factor in gender inequality. Women in the regions typically considered less developed do suffer from serious inequality between men and women. But these levels of equality vary by right and region. Furthermore, women in the developed regions have not gained parity with men in the fulfillment of their basic subsistence rights.

B. To the Maximum of its Available Resources?

The inclusion of the statement to the "maximum of its available resources" in the ICESCR clearly requires states to use their available resources to realize their citizens' economic and social rights. By grouping states at similar economic levels a comparison can be made with regard to the fulfillment of economic and social rights. Thus, it can be determined if states at different economic levels, as measured by GNP per capita, experience statistically significant differences in their level of economic and social rights fulfillment. The hypothesis advanced here is a significant positive relationship between economic development and the realization of women's human rights: higher levels of economic development are associated with greater fulfillment of economic and social rights for women.

Correlation analysis helps to determine whether the WESHR index and economic development covary (whether the two variables vary or change together). Correlation coefficients summarize the strength and direction of a linear relationship. Correlating economic development, measured by the

---

69. Jodi Jacobson, *Women's Health: The Price of Poverty, in* THE HEALTH OF WOMEN: A GLOBAL PERSPECTIVE 19 (Marge Koblinsky et al. eds., 1993).

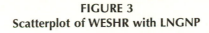

FIGURE 3
Scatterplot of WESHR with LNGNP

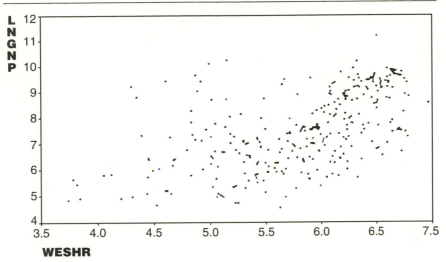

log of GNP per capita,[70] with the WESHR index produces a correlation coefficient of r=.56 p<.01. This result indicates that a substantial, significant relationship exists between economic development and the WESHR index. The positive coefficient indicates a positive relationship between economic development and the WESHR index. Therefore, as economic development increases, women's enjoyment of economic and social rights increases.

The shape of the scatterplot is an important indication of both the presence of a relationship between two variables and the nature of that relationship (positive or negative). Figure 3 indicates that the realization of women's economic and social rights is significantly correlated with economic development, as measured by GNP per capita. This lends some support to the hypothesis that higher levels of economic development are more likely to guarantee women's economic and social rights.

70. *See* Bohrnstedt & Knoke, *supra* note 20, at 271; *see also* The World Bank, The World Bank Annual Report (1977); The World Bank, The World Bank Annual Report (1982); The World Bank, The World Bank Annual Report (1987); The World Bank, The World Bank Annual Report (1992) (source of GNP per capita). One of the basic assumptions of multiple regression procedures is that of normalcy in distribution. Unfortunately, GNP per capita does not fall into a normal distribution curve. To overcome the inherent skewness of GNP per capita, it is necessary to transform the data into a loglinear relationship. Logs permit a simple, straightforward, and useful interpretation: the change in log Y approximates the relative change in Y itself. Therefore the scale of the measure is manipulated into useful form without damage to its integrity.

TABLE 2
Crosstabulation Analysis GNP With WESHR

Count Row Percent Column Percent		Low GNP	Med-Low GNP	Med- High	High GNP
	Bad 1	**32**	24	13	8
		41.6%	31.2%	16.9%	10.4
Women's		56.1%	8.6%	15.5%	9.5%
		18	**30**	21	4
		24.7%	41.1%	28.8%	5.5%
Human		31.6%	35.7%		4.8%
				25.0%	
		6	23	**34**	18
Rights		7.4%	28.4%	42.0%	22.2
		10.5%	27.4%	40.5%	21.4
	Good 4	1	7	16	**54**
Index		1.3%	9.0%	20.5%	69.2
		1.8%	8.3%		64.3
				19.0%	

Chi-sq. = 139.81   Tau-b = .50   p = .00001   n = 309   *SPSS*

The following crosstabulation tables present the relationship between the WESHR achievement index and economic development. Crosstabulation can explain the variation in joint frequency distributions of two variables, providing a way to determine whether a bivariate relationship exists. Economic development, based on the United Nations World Development Reports, is divided into four classifications: low-income economies; low-medium income economies; upper-medium income economies; and high-income economies.[71] The WESHR index was divided into quarters: low through 25 percent; 25.1 percent through 50 percent; 50.1 percent through 75 percent; and 75.1 percent through 100 percent. The range of WESHR is 1 through 4, with 1 considered bad and 4 labelled good.

As Table 2 reveals, some 87.7 percent of low income nations have poor WESHR ratings of 1 or 2. The majority of low income countries (51.1 percent) have a dismal record with regards to protecting and providing for women's equitable realization of economic and social rights. For high income nations the opposite is true, 85.7 percent of high income nations have a WESHR of 3 or 4, with 64.3 percent realizing women's rights at the highest world levels. Remember that in no country do women gain parity with men in the realization of economic and social rights. The majority of

---

71. World Bank, World Development Reports 1993: Investing In Health X (1993).

TABLE 3
Analysis of Variance: Group Mean of Individual Rights By Level of GNP Per Capita

	Low GNP	Medium— Low	Medium— High	High GNP	F stat
Life Expectancy	1.00	1.01	1.02	1.03	22.73**
Gender Ratio	1.01	1.00	1.05	.99	2.63#
Literacy Ratio	.52	.76	.88	.93	104.96***
Economic Ratio	.56	.47	.47	.56	6.01***
Primary School Enrollment Ratio	.67	.86	.91	.94	82.56**
Child Mortality Ratio	.97	.99	1.05	1.09	17.99***
Wage Ratio	.80	.74	.68	.77	4.39**
Standard of Living Ratio	.53	.55	.57	.63	7.58***
Women's Economic and Social Human Rights Index (WESHR)	5.16 n=57	5.64 n=84	5.90 n=84	6.24 n=84	46.03**

*** = $p < .0001$ ** = $p < .001$ * = $p < .01$ # = $p < .05$ SPSS

medium-low income nations also rate poorly in their WESHR ratings. Over 64 percent of medium-low income nations have low levels of WESHR, while 59.5 percent of medium-high income countries rate 3 or 4 on the WESHR index. The association between economic development and rising levels of rights attainment can be seen clearly through the diagonal (which has been highlighted for clarity). Each box of the diagonal contains the greatest number of cases for that row. This indicates that, as a state's economy grows, women's economic and social rights are being progressively realized. It appears that in countries with higher levels of economic development, women experience higher levels of economic and social rights. This finding tends to support the theory that economic development leads to higher status for women.

In Table 3 the WESHR index is separated into the individual rights indicators, and an ANOVA was run to compare the average performance of economic development on each indicator.

By inspecting WESHR indicators' mean scores, divided into the four economic categories, the variation in female inequality is clearly visible. The large and statistically significant F statistic indicates that the variations in each of the group means are attributable to the economic category.

As expected, Table 3 indicates that the low income countries' group means tend to average lower on many of the individual indicators that make up the WESHR index. As GNP per capita increases, the ratio of women's equitable achievement of economic and social rights increases in a stairstep fashion. An exception is for the economically active, where the low income countries slightly outperform the medium-low and high-medium income countries.

All statistical tests support the conclusion that economic development has a positive effect on women's equality in the enjoyment of economic and social rights. As the GNP per capita in a country increases, the levels of WESHR also rise. This supports the theory that economic development leads to reducing women's inferior educational, social, and economic status.

To further explore the question of how economic development affects women's realization of their economic and social rights, regression analysis was used. Regression analysis allows the researcher to measure the relative importance of a predictor or independent variable on one criterion or dependent variable. Furthermore, this type of analysis allows, based upon the measured value of the independent variable, for the prediction of the value of the dependent variable. The regression equation is as follows:

$$WESHR = \alpha + \beta \text{ lagged WESHR} + \beta \text{ LNCNP} + \beta \text{ Eastern Europe} + \beta \text{ Latin} \\ \text{America} + \beta \text{ Middle East} + \beta \text{ Asia} + \beta \text{ Africa} + e$$

To estimate the model, the data are stacked or pooled (country, by year) and a Least Squares Dummy Variable (LSDV) covariance procedure is used.[72] When analyzing a data set that has marked heteroskedasticity[73] and is cross-sectionally dominant (there are a large number of cases and only a few time points), a LSDV model is appropriate. The model can correct for problems of heteroskedasticity and serial correlation[74] by allowing the intercept to vary by time and across sections. Thus, the intercept manifests the effects unique to the cross sections.[75]

---

72. See Lois W. Sayrs, *Pooled Time Series Analysis,* 07–070 SAGE U. PAPER SERIES ON QUANTITATIVE APPLICATIONS IN THE SOC. SCI. 26 (1989); James Stimson, *Regression in Space and Time: A Statistical Essay,* 29 AM. J. POL. SCI. 914, 921 (1985).
73. See William D. Berry & Stanley Feldman, *Multiple Regression in Practice,* 07–050 SAGE U. PAPER SERIES ON QUANTITATIVE APPLICATIONS IN THE SOC. SCI. (1985). Homoskedasticity means consistent variance in the error term, and is one of the assumptions underlying the use of multiple regression analysis. *Id.* at 73. Violation of this inconstant variance resulting in heteroskedasticity, makes ordinary least squares regression inappropriate. *Id.*
74. See Charles W. Ostrom, Jr., *Time Series Analysis: Regression Techniques (2d ed.),* 07–069 SAGE U. PAPER SERIES ON QUANTITATIVE APPLICATIONS IN THE SOC. SCI. (1990). Serial correlation (also know as autocorrelation) refers to the correlation, or nonindependence, of terms across time. In time series, error terms tend to be similar to the previous one rather than independent white noise. The independence of error terms is a basic assumption or Ordinary Least Squares Regression. *Id.*
75. See Sayrs, *supra* note 72, at 26 ("One of the best ways to manage nonconstant variance in a pool is by introducing a fixed value that represents the variance unique to the cross-section and conditional on the sample.... A simple way to condition the variance is accomplished in least squares by using a dummy variable."); Berry & Feldman, *supra* note 73, at 77; John Fox, *Regression Diagnostics,* 07–079 SAGE U. PAPER SERIES ON QUANTITATIVE APPLICATIONS IN THE SOC. SCI. 88 (1991). The presence of heteroskedasticity or autocorrela-

There are, of course, some general drawbacks in using a LSDV model. First, the introduction of dummy variables reduces the degrees of freedom needed for statistical tests. Because this study involves 114 countries, there is ample degrees of freedom to ensure statistical power. Including an adequate number of cases enables the study to make a more convincing argument for the linkage between economic development and human rights achievement, with regional differences.

A second weakness of LSDV modelling is the interpretation of dummy variables. The coefficients of the dummy variables can only be interpreted as how each category differs from the reference category. In this study, the reference category is the West region and the LSDV estimates reflect how each region deviates from the coefficient calculated for the West. The West region was chosen as the referent for the sake of clarity (assuming that the majority of readers will be more familiar with the condition of women in the West). Without some sort of gauge, however general, it would be impossible to evaluate rights achievement.

A further benefit of pooling cross-sectional data with a time element is that such pooling allows researchers to test hypotheses over space and time simultaneously. Lagging the dependent variable (WESHR) by one time point allows us to examine the change in WESHR while controlling for the impact of previous years of WESHR scores on present WESHR scores. It is logical to presume that the previously attained level of WESHR is a principal determinant of current achievement on the WESHR index. Women's human rights are not disjunctive, independent events. For example, chances are that if a woman was literate at a previous time point, she is still literate in the current time point. If a woman was alive five years ago, she is likely to still be alive, given the statistical average of life expectancy.

As Table 4 indicates, regression analysis shows that advancements in economic development are associated with the achievement of economic and social human rights for women. This model accounts for 80 percent of the variance in WESHR, as indicated by the adjusted Rsq. .80. Furthermore, the accuracy was confirmed by a visual examination of the residual plot and the highly significant F statistic ($p < .0000$).

A regression coefficient measures the amount of increase in the dependent variable (WESHR) for each one-unit difference in the independent variables (Lagged WESHR, LNGNP, and Region). Economic development, the history of women's rights fulfillment, and region explain a considerable portion of the variance in a country's human rights performance. These findings support the hypothesis that posits a causal relationship between a nation's economic development and the level of women's realization of their economic and social rights. The coefficient for economic development is positive and very significant, and remains so through time. As the GNP per capita in a country increases, the levels of WESHR also rise. A one unit

TABLE 4
The Effects of Economic Development on Women's Equitable Attainment of their Economic and Social Rights: Utilizing Lagged Dependent Variable and Dummies for Region

	Dependent variable: WESHR			
	B	SE B	Beta	sig.T
Lagged WESHR (t-1)	.39	.04	.39	.0000
Logged GNP per capita (LNGNP)	.12	.02	.27	.0000
Regions				
Asia	−.54	.10	−.29	.0000
Eastern Europe	.02	.09	.01	.8255
Latin America	−.31	.08	−.17	.0004
Middle East	−1.02	.08	−.56	.0000
Sub. Africa	−.42	.10	−.29	.0000
Constant (West)	3.10	.27		.0000

adj. Rsq. .80
Rsq.
SE .29
n = 226

SPSS

increase in log of GNP per capita adds .12 points to the WESHR index. This analysis provides support for the theory that economic development provides the resources necessary for women to attain comparable economic and social rights with men.

In Table 4, the WESHR rating of the previous time period has a strong, statistically significant positive effect on the current WESHR rating (b = .39). Given the evolutionary nature of women's status, the finding that the previous WESHR rating is a powerful predictor of the current WESHR rating is not unexpected. For every point on the seven point WESHR scale received in the previous time frame, there is over one-third of a point added to the current WESHR. The improvement of women's rights is a continuing, building process.

Regionally, there are widely divergent patterns of women's achievement of economic and social rights. Each region, with the exception of Eastern Europe, has a large, negative, and highly significant coefficient. As was

---

tion does not make OLS beta coefficients or the intercept estimators biased but does make standard error estimators inefficient and biased, thus invalidating the tests of significance.

reported earlier, the interpretation of dummy variables is problematic in that the coefficients can only be understood by how each region differs from the reference region. The West, the reference region used here, has a coefficient of 3.10. As Table 4 indicates: Asia differs significantly from the West's 3.10 coefficient by over one-half of an index point ($-.54$); Middle Eastern nations have significantly lower rates of equitable rights achievement than the West (-1.02); the often famine ridden sub-Saharan African nations differ from the West by only $-.42$; and Latin America differs from the West by $-.31$. Since the West scores high on the WESHR scale, negative regional coefficients are to be expected. In rights fulfillment Eastern Europe is not statistically different from the West. This analysis clearly indicates that the Eastern Europe region is indeed a very strong predictor of women's equality in the achievement of economic and social rights.

Because geographical regions are dummy variables, coded as either 0 or 1 (the presence or absence of a phenomenon), while the log of GNP per capita and the previous level of WESHR are continuous variables, it is necessary to examine the standardized beta coefficients to compare the magnitude of influence each independent variable has on the WESHR index. Standardized beta coefficients are transformed to correspond to a single scale.

Economic development, although important, is not the decisive factor in explaining gender inequality in the achievement of economic and social rights. Indeed, regional coefficients (Asia $-.29$, Middle East $-.56$, sub-Saharan Africa $-.29$) play a larger role than GNP in rights achievement. The poorer regions of Asia and sub-Saharan Africa have smaller coefficients, in terms of absolute value, than do the oil rich Middle East. Such numbers indicate that gender equality in the realization of economic and social rights is not solely dependent upon having a large GNP.

VIII.   CONCLUSION

Despite the emerging recognition of the importance of economic and social rights and the need to enhance women's enjoyment of these rights on a level comparable to men's, scholars have yet to develop empirical strategies to define, operationalize, and measure these rights. This study is an attempt to quantify the pervasive and persistent inequality between men and women. The construction of an index measuring gender inequality allows a comparative and longitudinal analysis of women's realization of those human rights cataloged in the ICESCR. The use of an index is particularly serviceable with regard to the concept of nondiscrimination, and the obligation to progressively realize these rights over time.

Furthermore, this study has explored the relationship between economic development and women's status. The findings lead to the conclusion that economic development increases women's realization of their economic and social rights and that women benefit from the economic development of their country. The findings in this study suggest that women not only benefit from a larger economic pie but that their share of that pie increases as the pie enlarges. As the GNP per capita in a country increases, the levels of WESHR also rise. Yet, in no country do women reach parity with men in the realization of economic and social rights. Although the general levels of economic and social rights increase, women's levels of economic and social rights still lag behind the levels enjoyed by men.

Of importance is a state's tradition of securing women's economic and social rights. Lagging the dependent variable by one time period, it was found that previous WESHR scores portend current achievements, as measured by the WESHR index. Gender equality is thus a building process.

Geographical regions determine, in large part, gender inequality in the attainment of economic and social human rights. Cultural factors appear to be very important in explaining variations in the realization of women's human rights. Each region has its specific shortcomings. The interpretation of the effect of region on the WESHR index is problematic in that "region" moves one from general ignorance (what variables influence WESHR) to specific ignorance (the opaque variable "region" is a significant predictor of WESHR). Yet the question of why geographic region, a proxy for religious/cultural groupings, significantly affects women's human rights is not answered. Most cross-cultural human rights researchers simply accept region as an obvious category in no need of explanation.[76] These researchers concentrate on how the various differences between regions affect women's situation and standing. In contrast, Susan Marshall, determining that gender inequality is deeply embedded in cultural norms and religious structures, recounts several anthropological theories for why region (cultural/religious clustering) makes a difference.[77] Nevertheless even she concludes that: "We have discovered the importance of cultural region for explaining national

---

76. See ALAKA MALWADE BASU, CULTURE, THE STATUS OF WOMEN AND DEMOGRAPHIC BEHAVIOR (1992) (explaining how regional or cultural differences in women's status in India influence women's employment opportunities, fertility, and educational attainment; but not explaining why regional differences are important); Alaka Malwade Basu, The Status of Women and the Quality of Life Among the Poor, 16 CAMBRIDGE J. ECON. 249 (1992); UNITED NATIONS, THE WORLD'S WOMEN 1970–1990: TRENDS AND STATISTICS (series K, #8) (1991) [hereinafter THE WORLD'S WOMEN] (describing regional trends and comparing women's situations across regions, but without attempting to explain why region is an important factor in women's equality).

77. Marshall, supra note 50, at 229–33.

variations in women's status and gender inequality, but have yet to specify how this dynamic operates or to identify its sources by region."[78]

In an attempt to answer the question "what factors explain the cultural variation in women's status," Valentine Moghadam has reviewed the sociological literature on women's inequality.[79] Moghadam concludes that women's "access to economic resources, participation in the labour force, and control over income" determine, in large part, women's status and empowerment.[80] She is, unfortunately, unable to explain why women in different regions have differing access to those factors. Culturally specific attitudes towards women's status, developed under differing historical and economic conditions, are probably the key.

Researchers interested in economic and social human rights bemoan their dependence on the deficient, fragmentary character of rights indicators. The data set presented in this article, albeit crude, undeveloped, and incomplete, is critical to advancing our understanding of governmental performance in securing social and economic rights. The problems of measurement and collection are exacerbated when the researcher adds the dimension of gender. The primary purpose of this article is the building of an index with which to measure and evaluate women's equitable realization of their economic and social rights. Statistical information is essential to furthering our understanding and assessment of the life situation of women, and of furthering governmental compliance with those nondiscrimination and equality of treatment clauses found in the ICESCR.

APPENDIX A

This appendix outlines the indicators and data sources used to construct the index on women's economic and social rights (WESHR achievement index). I wish to emphasize the difficulty in obtaining accurate and comparable economic and social data generally, and to reiterate the added challenge of locating and collecting economic and social data disaggregated by sex. Due to the obstacles presented by missing data, and the scarcity of data sets disaggregated by sex, certain concessions were made.

I originally planned to collect data at orderly five year intervals (1975, 1980, 1985, and 1990). This proved to be impossible as the available data was collected in random years, thereby forcing me to make a new collection rule—the rule of two years. For example, if data could not be collected

---

78. *Id.* at 232–33.
79. Valentine Moghadam, *Women in Societies,* 46 INT'L SOC. SCI. J. 95 (1994).
80. *Id.* at 101.

on a variable for the year 1985, but was available for 1987, it was used as 1985 data. If the data were listed as 1988, the said data were unacceptable and not used as 1985 data.

Furthermore, complete data for a variable often could not be collected from a single source. Hence, I was required to piece together data from several sources. Every attempt was made to evaluate the data source in order to make the data congruous and uniform. The obstacles presented by missing data indicate the necessity of compiling an accurate, reliable, and complete data set of women's concerns and issues. The following provides explanatory information about how the rights indicators were constructed for use in the WESHR's measure of women's economic and social rights.

I.   THE RIGHT TO WORK AND FAIR REMUNERATION

Identifying work and compensation as vital concerns for survival, the drafters of the ICESCR wanted to ensure fair and equal remuneration for women. Article 6 of the International Covenant on Economic, Social and Cultural Rights recognizes the "right to work."[81]

II.   SEX DIFFERENTIALS IN THE RATES OF GAINFUL EMPLOYMENT

The International Labour Organization (ILO) defines economically active (gainful employment) to be all persons of either sex who work for pay or profit, furnishing the supply of labor for the production of goods and services during the time reference chosen for the investigation.[82] This definition includes the unemployed who are actively seeking employment and those persons engaged in the production of primary products for their own consumption.[83] It is not necessary that work be full time for inclusion as economically active.[84] The data are compiled by the ILO and presented in the United Nations *Yearbook of Labour Statistics*.[85] The data on economic activity is supplemented by data found in *The World's Women 1970–1990*.[86]

---

81. ICESCR, *supra* note 8, art. 6, § 1.
82. *See* International Labour Organization, *supra* note 6 (paraphrasing the working definition of economically active).
83. *See id.*
84. *See id.*
85. *Id.*
86. The World's Women, *supra* note 76, at 81–111.

III.   THE RIGHT TO AN ADEQUATE STANDARD OF LIVING

Article 11 of the ICESCR acknowledges everyone's right to an "adequate standard of living ... including adequate food, clothing and housing."[87] Yet, the United Nations has estimated that 1.2 billion people live in absolute poverty.[88] Absolute poverty is defined as the income level below which a minimum nutritionally adequate diet, plus essential non-food requirements, is unaffordable.[89]

Unfortunately, traditional measures of nutrition adequacy, estimated supplies of energy (calories), and protein for human consumption, are unsuitable for this study because they are not disaggregated by gender. To overcome this obstacle the World Health Organization's data on anemia was used. Anemia is a malady where the hemoglobin content of the blood is lower than normal because of a deficiency of one or more essential nutrients. The most common cause of anemia is malnutrition. The prevalence of anemia is therefore a good indicator of inadequate nutrition. To determine the differential between male and female nutritional standards, I created a ratio between anemia rates and the percent of the average caloric consumption of a nation's population.

The data on the percentage of women who suffer from nutritional anemia was taken from the World Health Organization's data as reported in the *Compendium of Social Statistics and Indicators,*[90] the *Human Development Report,*[91] and UNICEF's *The State of the World's Children.*[92] The first two sources provide virtually universal data on the rates of anemia but lack the time element. In other words, a country's data on anemia is listed as covering the years 1975 through 1990. For example, the prevalence of anemia among women in country X is listed as 40 percent throughout the time frame (1975, 1980, 1985, 1990).

The amount of calories consumed as a percentage of the human minimum requirement needed for health was taken from the *Compendium of Social Statistics and Indicators,*[93] *The Human Development Report,*[94] and *The State of the World's Children.*[95] The daily calorie consumption per

---

87. ICESCR, *supra* note 8, art. 11, § 1.
88. United Nations Development Programme, *supra* note 5, at 23.
89. *See, e.g.,* United Nations Development Programme, Human Development Report 1991 (1991); World Bank, The World Bank Annual Report (1990).
90. United Nations, Compendium of Social Statistics and Indicators 1988, at 372 (Series K, No. 9 1991) [hereinafter Compendium].
91. United Nations Development Programme, *supra* note 38, at 150.
92. UNICEF, The State of the World's Children (various years).
93. Compendium, *supra* note 90, at 392.
94. United Nations Development Programme, *supra* note 38, at 132.
95. UNICEF, *supra* note 92.

capita measure is calculated by taking the estimated amount of calories and proteins in food supplies and dividing this amount by the population.

IV.   THE RIGHT TO HEALTH AND WELL-BEING

Article 12 of the ICESCR recognizes the right "of everyone to the enjoyment of the highest attainable standard of physical and mental health."[96] Life expectancy, gender ratios, and infant mortality rates are the three universal indicators of the prevalent health conditions and well-being within a country.

V.   SEX DIFFERENTIATED MORTALITY RATES

Data on population estimates and life expectancy, disaggregated by gender, were taken from the United Nations Department of International Economic and Social Affairs publication on Populations Studies No. 120, *World Population Prospects 1990*.[97]

VI.   SEX DIFFERENTIATED CHILD MORTALITY RATES

Child mortality is defined as the mortality of children before the age of five years. These measures are originally derived from registered data on births and infant deaths. Where civil registration data are deficient, the most reliable sources are demographic surveys of households and census reports. The data were compiled and published by the United Nations in its *Demographic Yearbook*,[98] and supplemented here with data from the World Bank's *World Development Report*.[99] The *Demographic Yearbook* reported child mortality in raw numbers, that is, the total number of child deaths

---

96. ICESCR, *supra* note 8, art. 12, § 1.
97. UNITED NATIONS, WORLD POPULATION PROSPECTS (1990).
98. UNITED NATIONS, DEMOGRAPHIC YEARBOOK (1976); UNITED NATIONS, DEMOGRAPHIC YEARBOOK (1977); UNITED NATIONS, DEMOGRAPHIC YEARBOOK (1981); UNITED NATIONS, DEMOGRAPHIC YEARBOOK (1982); UNITED NATIONS, DEMOGRAPHIC YEARBOOK (1986); UNITED NATIONS, DEMOGRAPHIC YEARBOOK (1987); UNITED NATIONS, DEMOGRAPHIC YEARBOOK (1991); UNITED NATIONS, DEMOGRAPHIC YEARBOOK (1992) (compiling data for the years 1975, 1980, 1985, and 1990) [hereinafter UN YEARBOOK].
99. *See* WORLD BANK, WORLD DEVELOPMENT REPORT (1976); WORLD BANK, WORLD DEVELOPMENT REPORT (1977); WORLD BANK, WORLD DEVELOPMENT REPORT (1981); WORLD BANK, WORLD DEVELOPMENT REPORT (1982); WORLD BANK, WORLD DEVELOPMENT REPORT (1986); WORLD BANK, WORLD DEVELOPMENT REPORT (1987); WORLD BANK, WORLD DEVELOPMENT REPORT (1991); WORLD BANK, WORLD DEVELOPMENT REPORT (1992).

counted in a country.[100] The data taken from the *World Development Report* was reported as child mortality rates per 1,000 live births.[101]

VII. THE RIGHT TO EDUCATION

The right of everyone to an education is recognized in Article 13 of the ICESCR.[102] State parties accept the responsibility to provide free and compulsory primary education for all, while making higher education available and accessible.[103]

VIII. SEX DIFFERENTIATED LITERACY RATES

A functionally literate person is one "who can engage in all those activities in which literacy is required for effective functioning of his group and community and also for enabling him to continue to use reading, writing and calculation for his own and the community's development."[104] UNESCO's data are reported by the United Nations in its *Compendium of Social Statistics and Indicators*.[105] The data on literacy rates is supplemented by data found in *The World's Women 1970–1990*,[106] and *The World Development Report*.[107]

IX. SEX DIFFERENTIATED RATES OF PRIMARY
SCHOOL ENROLLMENT

Primary school enrollment is defined by UNESCO as the basic "[e]ducation at the first level, which usually begins between ages five to seven years."[108] This education level includes grades one through five. Data on primary school enrollment disaggregated by sex are reported by the United Nations in its *Compendium of Social Statistics and Indicators*.[109]

---

100. UN YEARBOOK, *supra* note 98.
101. WORLD BANK, *supra* note 71, at X.
102. ICESCR, *supra* note 8, art. 13, § 1.
103. *See id.* art. 13, § 2.
104. *See* COMPENDIUM, *supra* note 90.
105. *Id.* at 249.
106. THE WORLD'S WOMEN, *supra* note 76, at 45–53.
107. WORLD BANK, *supra* note 71, at 238–39.
108. COMPENDIUM, *supra* note 90, at 245.
109. *Id.* at 249.

APPENDIX B

WESHR Scores for the Years:

Country	1975	1980	1985	1990
*Afghanistan	———	3.84	———	———
*Algeria	5.04	4.96	4.83	5.04
*Angola	5.06	———	———	5.96
*Argentina	5.80	5.89	5.84	6.05
*Australia	6.49	6.63	6.54	6.75
*Austria	6.46	6.31	6.52	6.46
Bahrain	———	4.89	———	5.49
Bangladesh	3.76	4.22	4.32	5.07
*Belgium	6.57	6.11	6.28	6.43
*Benin	———	———	———	5.51
*Bolivia	5.42	———	———	5.83
Botswana	———	———	6.70	6.26
*Brazil	6.02	5.94	6.07	———
*Bulgaria	6.37	———	6.48	———
Burkina Faso	———	———	———	5.76
Burundi	———	———	———	5.98
*Cameroon	6.04	———	———	6.16
*Canada	6.48	———	6.56	6.46
*Cent. Afr. Rep.	———	———	———	5.51
Chad	———	———	———	5.10
*Chile	5.97	5.97	6.19	6.23
China	———	5.88	———	6.14
*Columbia	6.11	6.00	6.21	6.44
*Congo	———	———	———	5.63
*Costa Rica	5.80	5.96	5.91	6.15
*Cote d'Ivoire	———	———	———	5.32
Cuba	5.62	5.84	5.81	5.91

(continued)

Country	1975	1980	1985	1990
*Cyprus	5.49	6.12	6.14	6.20
*Czechoslovakia	———	———	———	6.48
*Denmark	6.36	———	6.58	6.63
*Dominican Rep.	5.35	5.92	———	5.35
*Ecuador	5.58	5.69	5.90	5.74
*Egypt	4.45	———	4.46	4.70
*El Salvador	6.53	———	6.48	———
*Finland	6.94	6.58	6.73	6.70
*France	6.60	6.45	6.45	6.70
*Gabon	———	———	———	5.70
*Germany (East)	6.72	6.76	———	6.39
*Germany (West)	6.44	6.42	6.32	6.66
Ghana	5.57	———	5.63	5.95
*Greece	5.95	5.99	5.91	6.02
*Guatemala	5.30	5.31	5.44	5.51
*Guinea	———	———	———	4.94
*Guinea Bissau	4.61	———	———	4.63
*Guyana	5.82	———	5.52	———
*Hondruas	5.65	———	———	6.11
*Hungary	6.63	6.70	6.67	6.61
*Iceland	6.30	———	———	———
*India	4.45	———	———	4.83
Haiti	———	———	———	5.81
Indonesia	5.31	———	5.41	5.67
*Iran	4.87	5.13	4.83	5.18
*Iraq	4.40	———	5.45	5.27
*Ireland	6.26	6.16	6.06	6.06
*Israel	6.07	6.11	6.05	6.07
*Italy	6.24	6.22	6.32	6.39
*Japan	6.48	6.52	6.52	6.58

(continued)

Country	1975	1980	1985	1990
*Jordan	5.01	5.01	————	5.21
*Kenya	5.23	————	————	6.09
*Rep. of Korea	6.22	5.98	6.22	6.32
Kuwait	4.92	4.99	5.65	5.63
*Lebanon	————	5.41	————	————
#Liberia	4.50	————	————	————
*Libya	4.36	4.31	————	5.01
*Luxembourg	5.77	5.89	6.16	————
*Malawi	5.22	5.49	————	————
Malaysia	5.62	5.71	5.91	5.89
*Mali	5.25	————	5.12	5.02
*Mexico	5.61	5.76	5.82	5.71
*Morocco	4.68	————	4.68	5.11
Mozambique	————	————	5.62	————
Myanmar	————	————	————	5.73
*Nepal	4.53	————	————	4.66
*Netherlands	6.20	6.09	6.34	6.23
*New Zealand	6.12	6.18	6.20	6.28
*Nicaragua	5.69	5.88	6.18	————
*Niger	————	————	————	5.41
*Nigeria	————	5.45	————	5.47
*Norway	6.08	6.40	6.68	6.63
Pakistan	3.86	3.80	4.07	4.13
*Panama	5.75	5.68	5.93	5.91
*Paraguay	5.49	5.42	5.33	5.91
*Peru	5.23	5.45	5.86	————
*Philippines	————	5.77	6.07	5.91
*Poland	6.62	6.76	6.68	6.74
*Portugal	6.04	6.36	6.22	6.20
Qatar	————	5.14	4.91	————

(continued)

Country	1975	1980	1985	1990
*Romania	6.58	6.49	———	———
*Rwanda	———	———	———	6.31
Saudi Arabia	———	4.61	———	5.02
*Senegal	———	5.40	———	5.02
Sierra Leone	———	———	———	5.20
*Spain	6.19	6.16	6.26	6.19
*Sri Lanka	5.21	5.42	5.59	5.95
*Sudan	———	4.55	———	5.07
*Suriname	5.96	———	5.99	———
*Sweden	6.49	6.51	6.61	6.65
*Switzerland	6.23	6.31	6.27	6.30
*Syria	4.80	4.65	4.85	5.18
Thailand	5.87	6.16	———	6.50
*Togo	———	———	———	5.31
*Tunisia	5.01	4.92	5.18	5.29
Turkey	———	———	5.30	———
*USSR	———	———	———	6.73
United Arab Em.	———	———	———	4.87
*UK	———	6.40	6.48	6.59
*Tanzania	———	———	———	5.67
#USA	———	6.59	6.64	6.61
*Uruguay	5.86	———	6.34	6.41
*Venezuela	5.95	5.95	6.04	6.25
*Yemen	———	———	———	4.46
*Yugoslavia	6.01	6.10	———	6.27
*Zambia	5.60	5.82	———	5.88
*Zimbabwe	5.43	6.09	6.34	6.16

Of the 114 countries included in the study, ninety (denoted by *) have ratified, accessed, approved, or accepted by signature the ICESCR; two (denoted by #) have signed but not yet ratified; and twenty-two have yet to sign or begin domestic ratification procedures.

Chapter 16

The Impact of Structural Adjustment on Women: A Governance and Human Rights Agenda

Bharati Sadasivam

I. INTRODUCTION

It is now well-established that structural adjustment and stabilization poli-cies (SAPs) undertaken in developing countries to receive condition-based loans from the World Bank and the International Monetary Fund (IMF) have exacerbated conditions of poverty and deprivation for large sections of the population.[1] Several commentators have also shown that these macroeco-nomic policies are not class-neutral or gender-neutral. The World Bank's emphasis on "safety nets" to cushion the poor from the impact of orthodox stabilization and adjustment policies is an admission that these policies do not affect all sections of the population equally.

The human and social costs of adjustment have evoked growing con-cern and unease at the United Nations, among governments, and among some donors. These concerns arise out of the institutionalization of the mar-ket model of economic growth that has made such growth synonymous with the dominant view of "development," although it does not favor equity, sus-

---

1. In this paper, the term structural adjustment refers to the economic reform policies pro-moted by the Bretton Woods and other financial institutions in developing countries since the 1980s. In exchange for structural adjustment loans (SALs), recipient countries are expected to restructure their economies, chiefly by dismantling protectionist struc-tures such as tariffs, controls, and subsidies for local capitalism. The basic assumption of this reorientation is that an economy's health, efficiency, and productivity will improve if market forces are allowed to operate, without outcomes being influenced by government policies of protection, subsidization, and regulation. *See generally* WALDEN BELLO, DARK VICTORY: THE UNITED STATES, STRUCTURAL ADJUSTMENT AND GLOBAL POVERTY (1994); FIFTY YEARS IS ENOUGH; THE CASE AGAINST THE WORLD BANK AND THE INTERNATIONAL MONETARY FUND (Kevin Danaher ed., 1994); CHERYL PAYER, THE WORLD BANK: A CRITICAL ANALYSIS (1982); CHERYL PAYER, THE DEBT TRAP: THE IMF AND THE THIRD WORLD (1974).

tainability, or redistribution of wealth and resources.[2] Recent UN conferences, most notably the World Summit for Social Development in
Copenhagen in March 1995 and the Fourth World Conference on Women
in Beijing in September 1995, have highlighted the ways in which such economic policies have focused on debt repayment by developing countries at
the cost of human development.[3] Specialized UN agencies, such as the
United Nations Children's Fund (UNICEF), the United Nations Development Programme (UNDP), and the United Nations Development Fund for
Women (UNIFEM), have also pointed to the growing human and economic
inequalities caused by market driven growth and stressed the need to protect the vulnerable, women in particular, from marginalization.[4]

---

2. *See* George Martine & Marcela Villareal, *Gender, Population and Sustainability: Critical Problems and Unresolved Issues,* consultants' paper submitted to the United Nations Expert Group Meeting on Women, Population and Sustainable Development: The Road from Rio, Cairo and Beijing, Santo Domingo, 18–22 Nov. 1996 (copy on file with author).
3. Chapter 2.27a of the Copenhagen Declaration and Programme of Action of the World Summit for Social Development urges governments to combat poverty by:

> Analysing policies and programmes, including those relating to macroeconomic sta-
> bility, structural adjustment programmes . . . markets and all relevant sectors of the
> economy, with respect to their impact on poverty and inequality, assessing their impact
> on family well-being and conditions, as well as their gender implications, and adjust-
> ing them, as appropriate, to promote a more equitable distribution of productive assets,
> wealth, opportunities, income and services.

United Nations, The Copenhagen Declaration and Programme of Action: World Summit for Social Development 57, 61, U.N. Doc. A/Conf. 166/9 (1995). Paragraph 20 of the Beijing Declaration and Platform for Action of the Fourth World Conference on Women states:

> Macro and micro-economic policies and programmes, including structural adjustment,
> have not always been designed to take account of their impact on women and girl chil-
> dren, especially those living in poverty. Poverty has increased in both absolute and rel-
> ative terms, and the number of women living in poverty has increased in most regions.

Beijing Declaration and Platform for Action, *adopted by* the Fourth World Conference on Women, U.N. Doc. A/Conf. 177/20 (1995) [hereinafter Beijing Platform for Action].

4. An early and exhaustive critique of structural adjustment came from UNICEF's Adjustment with a Human Face, which called for a more "people-sensitive approach to adjustment." Giovanni Andrea Cornia et al., *Introduction, in* Adjustment with a Human Face 1, 3 (Giovanni Andrea Cornia et al., eds., 1987). In a follow-up assessment, Development with a Human Face (Santosh Mehrotra & Richard Jolly eds., forthcoming) (manuscript on file with the author), UNICEF documents the advances in human development that have occurred in ten developing countries since the latter half of the 1980s due to *inter alia* "greater attention given by the Bretton Woods institutions to education, health and human concerns, active engagement of NGOs and donors in this field and crucial low-cost, high-impact interventions." *Id.* The UNDP's Human Development Reports were conceived to highlight the need for indicators other than economic growth to measure human welfare. For example, the 1996 report characterizes the current model of market-driven growth as "jobless, ruthless, voiceless, rootless and futureless" and one that does not favor equity or redistribution, both between and within countries. UNDP, Human Development Report 2–4 (1996). It shows that the globalized market economy has, over the last fifteen years, deepened the economic polarization between developed and develop-

These criticisms and the deterioration in economic and social conditions in the majority of adjusting countries during the "lost decade" of the
1980s have occasioned much introspection at the international financial
institutions. In fact, recent World Bank evaluations of the results of SAPs
acknowledge that while macroeconomic stabilization policies are necessary
for growth, they are not sufficient in reducing poverty or income inequality
in all countries.[5]

In recent years, gender analysis and feminist economics have provided
a conceptual framework for understanding the differential impact of macroeconomic policies such as structural adjustment on men and women. There
is now a vast and growing volume of literature that not only shows how the
gender bias in neoclassical economic theory renders the effects of SAPs on
women invisible in any standard measures of policy evaluation, but that
also provides empirical evidence of the heavy transitional costs of adjustment on women.[6]

In fact, recent poverty assessments by the World Bank show that women
respond differently to the opportunities afforded by economic growth due to

---

ing nations. *Id.* at 2. Only fifteen countries registered improved growth and income during this period, while nearly 100 have shown negative rates of economic growth and per
capita income. *Id.* at 1. In seventy of these countries, average income was lower than it
had been in 1980 and in forty-three countries, lower than in 1970. *Id.* The difference in
income between the developing and industrialized world tripled from $5,700 in 1970 to
$15,400 in 1993. *Id.* at 2. The United Nations Development Fund for Women, in prepa-
ration for the Beijing Women's Conference, stressed the need for a forceful call to
action by the world's governments and international institutions to address gender
inequity and women's advancement. *See* Noeleen Heyzer, *A Women's Development
Agenda for the 21st Century, in* A Commitment to the World's Women: Perspectives on Development for Beijing and Beyond 1, 1 (Noeleen Heyzer ed., with Sushma Kapoor & Joanne
Sandler, 1995).

5. *See* Social Dimensions of Adjustment: World Bank Experience, 1980–93 at 2, 54 (A World Bank
Operations Evaluation Study, 1996) [hereinafter Social Dimensions]. The study tracks
poverty and income distribution in fifty-three adjusting countries during the period
1980–1993. *Id.* at xi. Only 60 percent of the adjusting countries that adopted the right
policies and reduced poverty also reduced inequality. *Id.* at 1. The Bank, however, refutes
charges that the 1980s were a decade of deteriorating human welfare, pointing out that
poverty declined in twenty-three out of thirty-three countries and increased in ten. *Id.* at
54.

6. *See generally* The IMF, the World Bank and the African Debt, Volume 2: The Social and Political
Impact (Bade Onimode ed., 1989); Engendering Adjustment for the 1990s: Report of a
Commonwealth Expert Group on Women and Structural Adjustment (Commonwealth Secretariat, London, 1989) [hereinafter Engendering Adjustment]; Women and Adjustment Policies in
the Third World (Haleh Afshar & Carolyne Dennis eds., 1992); Unequal Burden: Economic
Crises, Persistent Poverty, and Women's Work (Lourdes Benería & Shelley Feldman eds.,
1992) [hereinafter Unequal Burden]; Male Bias in the Development Process (Diane Elson ed.,
1991); The Strategic Silence: Gender and Economic Policy (Isabella Bakker ed., 1994) [here-
inafter The Strategic Silence]; Women Pay the Price: Structural Adjustment in Africa and the
Caribbean (Gloria Thomas-Emeagwali ed., 1995); Mortgaging Women's Lives: Feminist
Critiques of Structural Adjustment (Pamela Sparr ed., 1994) [hereinafter Mortgaging
Women's Lives].

constraints on the access to productive resources such as land and credit.[7] Some of these findings demonstrate that extreme poverty affects women differently and often more severely than men. While the gender impact of SAPs is not uniformly negative throughout the reform process and across countries and economies, it is clear that it is women who, as workers, producers, consumers, wives, and mothers, are the shock absorbers of adjustment efforts at immense cost to their well-being.[8] There is now growing awareness of these effects of adjustment within the Bank.

These findings, along with the emphasis on sustainability and equity in recent UN conferences, have led the World Bank to recognize the relevance of gender issues to poverty alleviation and economic growth. The Bank approved an operational policy on gender in 1994.[9] It also set up an external gender consultative group (EGCG) composed of fourteen members who are selected for their wide-ranging policy and research experience in gender issues and familiarity with international development.[10] Taken together,

---

7. See THE WORLD BANK, IMPLEMENTING THE WORLD BANK'S GENDER POLICIES, PROGRESS REPORT No. 1 at 5 (Mar. 1996) [hereinafter BANK PROGRESS REPORT]. However, the Bank maintains that very little quantitative data is currently available on differences between the impact of economic reform on men and women. In two countries where statistical data is available, Peru and the Philippines, the Bank cites studies that show that in the former, "female-headed households appear to have fared better on average than male-headed households during the economic reform of the 1990s," while in the latter, "welfare indicators for women during periods of economic reform seem to be at least as favorable as for men." *Id.*

8. In 1989, a Commonwealth Expert Group summarized the impact of adjustment on women as follows:

   Women are at the epicentre of the crisis and bear the brunt of the adjustment efforts: it is women who have been most severely affected by the deteriorating balance between incomes and prices, and who have desperately sought means for their families to survive. It is women who have had to find extra work to supplement family income; it is women who have rearranged family budgets . . . and it is women who have been most immediately affected by cuts in health and educational facilities, and by the rising morbidity and deaths among their children. Women are at the frontline of the crisis in the developing world—and it is they who have been most severely affected and have had the greatest responsibility for adjusting their lives to ensure survival.

   ENGENDERING ADJUSTMENT, *supra* note 7, at 31–32.

9. See JOSETTE L. MURPHY, GENDER ISSUES IN WORLD BANK LENDING 21 (A World Bank Operations Evaluation Study, 1995) [hereinafter GENDER ISSUES]. Although Bank strategies to include gender issues were formulated as early as 1967, management began to take a proactive stance only in the latter half of 1986. *Id.* at 22. The visibility of gender issues during the UN Decade for Women (1975–1985) helped in part to raise their profile in the Bank. Since 1991, more than a third of all investment projects include measures dealing with gender-related issues, although these still do not include structural adjustment and debt reduction lending. *Id.* at 21.

10. Set up by the Bank in April 1996 in response to demands made by women's organizations during the Beijing women's conference, the EGCG aims *inter alia* to provide a mechanism for implementing the Bank's gender policies, responding to the Beijing Platform for Action and providing a forum for discussing public concerns about the

these initiatives provide a promising basis for an assessment of the gender impact of adjustment policies from the economic and human development perspectives. They also lay the groundwork for closer and concerted inter-action between those who design and execute SAPs and the advocates for human development.

This article examines the disparate impact of SAPs on women and the resulting unacceptable feminization of poverty in many countries with economies in transition. It argues that the disproportionate cost of adjust-ment borne by women violates their rights to development guaranteed in national and international conventions, and makes these economic reforms unsustainable in the long run. It also argues that the Bank and IMF, as well as national governments, must bear responsibility for the erosion and/or sus-pension of the rights of large sections of the poor, of whom the great major-ity are women, over an indefinitely extended period.

The focus here is on the human rights implications of adjustment efforts and the questions they raise about the responsibilities of governance. In par-ticular, the Bank, which has initiated its own debates on the subject, is ana-lyzed. From the standpoint of policymakers as well as NGOs, a coherent policy debate on the interplay between human rights, development, and economic policies is timely given that, notwithstanding current trends within the international financial institutions toward reappraisal and open-ness, economic growth driven by liberalization of markets remains the "development" formula for the foreseeable future.[11] A focus on the human rights implications of such growth is necessary also to challenge the current trend in industrialized countries to undermine the role of the UN in human development while ceding greater power and authority to the Bretton Woods institutions (over which they possess voting control) in deciding the course of the global economy.

This article begins by providing a brief background to feminist work on structural adjustment which has introduced gender as an analytical category

---

Bank's approaches to gender. The World Bank, External Gender Consultative Group: A Report on the First Annual Meeting, April 29–30, 1996 at 1 (1997) [hereinafter Bank Gender Group Report].

11. According to the World Bank, adjustment lending commitments have increased steadily since 1980, peaking at over $7 billion in 1991, during which period twenty countries began reforms of their financial sectors. The World Bank, Third Report on Adjustment Lending: Private and Public Resources for Growth (1992), cited in Pamela Sparr, What is Structural Adjustment?, in Mortgaging Women's Lives, supra note 7, at 1, 3. In 1990–1991, the loans averaged less than $6 billion a year. Id. By 1994, structural adjustment lending constituted about 30 percent of the Bank's loan portfolio. Id. at 2.

Adjustment lending is going to remain important in the 1990s. . . . It is already a major vehicle of assistance for formerly socialist countries, it is being used for the first time in India, and there are both old and new clients in most other parts of the world.

Id. at 6.

ignored in mainstream economics. Some of the literature on feminist critiques of SAPs is reviewed, along with some illustrative examples, to show how adjustment policies especially affect women. This article argues that such effects of adjustment policies are not sustainable from either the human rights or economic development perspectives. Approaches utilizing good governance and human rights principles to achieve gender justice and equality in economic restructuring are also reviewed. Finally, consideration is given to some strategies which the international financial institutions (the Bank in particular), governments, and NGOs can use to build frameworks for equitable and gender-responsive development.

II. FEMINIST CRITIQUES OF SAPS

A. The Gender Bias in Macroeconomic Policies

SAPs are presented in language that appears to be gender-neutral, but in fact has a male bias. SAPs are analyzed in terms of gross national product, balance of trade, tradeable and nontradeable goods, and so on: all seemingly with genderless implications. "Women are not 'visible' in this analysis; but then, neither are men. It is a depersonalized analysis dealing only with abstract suppliers and consumers of resources."[12]

The typical components of an orthodox stabilization and structural adjustment program are macroeconomic policies of fiscal austerity, monetary contraction and devaluation at one level, and sectoral and microeconomic policies at a second level. The second set of policies is characterized by the deregulation of labor markets, financial markets, and agricultural prices, and by the removal of trade barriers. The policy of liberalization is aimed at using all resources in the most efficient manner to produce the maximum quantity of output. A related goal is to minimize governmental involvement in the economy, based on the rationale that the state is not the most efficient producer. Accordingly, parastatal organizations are privatized, public expenditure is scaled back through lay-offs and reductions in public sector wages, and food and health subsidies are reduced or eliminated. These moves to "streamline" the economy are important aspects of SAPs.

Feminist economists critique economic reform at this macro level on three counts. First, it focuses overwhelmingly on the "productive economy,"

---

12. Diane Elson, *From Survival Strategies to Transformation Strategies: Women's Needs and Structural Adjustment, in* UNEQUAL BURDEN, *supra* note 7, at 26, 33–34. Elson's pioneering critique of mainstream economics from the gender perspective has formed the basis of much subsequent writing on the subject. Argued within the framework of mainstream economics, it raises questions and challenges that the monetarist/neoclassical school has found difficult to ignore.

on making profits and covering costs. In the process, it takes for granted the "reproductive economy," which meets needs and sustains human beings.[13] Macro models of mainstream economics assume that the process of reproduction and the maintenance of human resources will continue regardless of the way resources are reallocated. These models conceal the large contribution to the economy provided by the production and maintenance of the labor supply through childbirth and childcare, shopping, cooking, and housework. Economic reforms such as structural adjustment policies that call for cutbacks in state services and the free play of market forces fail to consider how such changes affect the relation between the "productive economy" and the "reproductive economy."

Because the latter is sustained by unpaid nonmarket work mostly undertaken by women, macroeconomics also assumes an unlimited supply of female labor. It expects this labor to adjust to and compensate for any changes in the "reproductive economy" brought about by macroeconomic policy measures such as withdrawals in state subsidies and services as well as rises in prices and taxes. By rendering unpaid household labor visible and treating it as a produced input, feminist analysis redefines the conditions necessary for the functioning of the paid productive economy.[14] This analysis challenges the theoretical basis for women's "invisibility," demonstrating how it obscures the economic and social costs of structural adjustment in women's work and lives. The feminist critique does this in at least three ways.

In the context of SAPs, male bias that does not count women's unpaid work is reflected in terms like efficiency and productivity. A public sector unit—a hospital, for example—may become more efficient by streamlining its costs and sending patients home early. But, in the effect, the efficiency is achieved by transferring costs from the productive to the reproductive economy, where women's additional and unpaid work in caring for convalescing patients at home compensates for the shortfall in hospital care.[15]

Second, feminist analysis introduces gender as an analytical tool by making gender a category of social and economic differentiation (like race and class) that influences the distribution of work, income, and wealth as well as the productivity of work and the behavior of agents in the economy.[16] Feminist economists have argued that gender, like race, class, and

13. Diane Elson, *Micro, Meso, Macro: Gender and Economic Analysis in the Context of Policy Reform, in* THE STRATEGIC SILENCE, *supra* note 7, at 33, 41–42.
14. Nilüfer Çağatay et al., *Introduction,* 23 WORLD DEV. 1829 (Nov. 1995) (special issue).
15. Elson, *supra* note 13, at 34. Such a transfer can also affect overall economic output. For instance, a study in Zambia found that women farmers, who were especially hit by declines in health expenditure, had to spend more time tending the sick and less time farming. *Id.* at 44.
16. Çağatay et al., *supra* note 15, at 1828–29.

ethnicity, is a basis for division of labor between productive and reproductive activities in most societies. Productive or income generating activities relate to the market, while reproductive activities such as caring for the young and old, maintaining health and sanitation, and taking responsibility for food, fodder, fuel, and water are unpaid and usually female activities. Feminist economics makes a distinction between these two types of activities and argues that both have to be considered in analyzing macroeconomic outcomes.

Third, feminist economic analysis leads to an understanding of the gendered nature of the economy itself and of institutions such as households, governments, firms, and markets that contribute to macroeconomic outcomes. This analysis shows that economic institutions and processes reflect and perpetuate existing gender biases by failing to recognize the gender-based divisions of labor and of access to resources underlying economic growth rates, balance-of-payments, and budget deficits.[17]

B.   Direct and Indirect Effects of SAPs on Women

It is widely documented that adjustment policies such as currency devaluation, price deregulation, privatization, export-led growth strategies, and the removal of subsidies on food and health services leave large sections of the poor in adjusting countries poorer in the short run.[18] It follows that women, who form the great majority of the world's one billion absolute poor,[19] are overwhelmingly affected by these policies. Some features of orthodox reform packages, such as the shrinking of public enterprises, state sectors, and traditional industries that employ large numbers of women, affect women wage earners directly. Other aspects, like cutbacks in public health care, food subsidies, and social security programs, affect women indirectly.[20] Given their inferior standing in the home and family in many societies, women have even less access to these services when they are reduced.

---

17. See Diane Elson & Rosemary McGee, *Gender Equality, Bilateral Program Assistance and Structural Adjustment: Policy and Procedures*, 23 WORLD DEV. 1991 (Nov. 1995) (special issue).

18. *See, e.g.*, Madhura Swaminathan, *The Impact of Policies of Orthodox Stabilization and Structural Adjustment on Women: Some Evidence from India* (paper presented at the annual summer conference of the International Association of Feminist Economists, Tours, France, 5–7 July 1995) (on file with the author). Income, poverty, and inequality worsened in India between 1991, when structural adjustment reforms were introduced, and 1994. *Id.* The proportion of households below the official poverty line rose from 39.3 percent in 1987–1988 to 40.7 percent in 1992–1993. *Id.*

19. Beijing Platform for Action, *supra* note 4, ¶ 47.

20. See ADJUSTMENT WITH A HUMAN FACE, *supra* note 5, at 76 for a list of twenty-two adjusting countries which suffered the most severe cuts in health and education expenditure in the

The distress signals resulting from the "invisible" impact of adjustment policies can be acute, especially in the area of health and reproduction. SAPs worsen the conditions in which women have to perform their family and community tasks. In many countries, they have led to a crisis in human reproduction, made worse by shrinking public health sector spending. In Tanzania, for example, seventy-one mothers died in the first thirteen weeks of 1988, when economic reforms were in force—four times the maternal death rate of previous years.[21] The deaths were attributed to poor hospital conditions as well as a shortage of blood, drugs, and transport facilities; more tellingly, they were an indication of the deteriorating physical conditions in which women carried out their reproductive roles.[22] These indirect effects of SAPs pose the greater challenge because they are not easily measured and cannot be analyzed in purely economic terms and are therefore harder to resolve politically.

III.   GENDER DIMENSIONS OF SAPS

A.   SAPs and the Household

Macroeconomic policies view the household as a single decisionmaking unit, where the head of the household makes decisions on behalf of the entire family. The differing levels of capability and well-being within the family make this assumption unrealistic.[23] Economists, sociologists, and anthropologists have taken apart this neoclassical economic construct to reveal the household as a place of cooperation and conflict, and of very

---

1980s. Of these, Bolivia, regarded by the World Bank as a success in structural adjustment, peaked with an annual percentage cut of 77.7 percent between 1980 and 1982, followed by Guatemala (58.3 percent) between 1980 and 1984 and the Dominican Republic (46.5 percent) between 1980 and 1984. *Id.* These were also countries with high rates of decline in GDP, demonstrating the link between GDP per capita and expenditure on social sector per capita. *Id.* For the effects on child welfare of government cuts in real expenditure per capita on social services, see Giovanni Andrea Cornia, *Economic Decline and Human Welfare in the First Half of the 1980s, in* ADJUSTMENT WITH A HUMAN FACE, 11, 21–47. Expenditure on food subsidies declined in four countries studied by UNICEF: Sri Lanka, Chile, Peru, and Zimbabwe. *Id.* at 28.

21. *See* Ulla Vuorela, *The Informal Sector, Social Reproduction and the Impact of the Economic Crisis on Women, in* TANZANIA AND THE IMF: THE DYNAMICS OF LIBERALIZATION 109 (Horace Campbell & Howard Stein eds., 1992).

22. *See id.*

23. *See* Amartya Sen, *Economics and the Family, in* FAMILY, KINSHIP AND MARRIAGE IN INDIA 452, 452–63. As Sen puts it, "the family is a remarkable institution. And a complex one. Indeed so complex that much of economic theory proceeds as if no such thing exists." *Id.* at 452; *see also* Amartya Sen, *Gender and Cooperative Conflicts, in* PERSISTENT INEQUALITIES 123–49 (Irene Tinker ed., 1990).

unequal treatment along gender lines.[24] The family is rarely a collective entity making decisions based on common interest. Rather, it is controlled by the will of the head of the household, usually male.

The macroeconomic view of the household as a unified, welfare maximizing unit that pools and shares resources leads designers of SAPs to assume that this is an institution which can safely absorb the transitional costs of adjustment. In reality, however, as a number of case studies show, SAPs place additional burdens of household management on women, exacerbating their position of responsibility without power.[25] In times of poverty and inflation—both effects of adjustment—household resources decline. Evidence from several countries shows that austerity is a female responsibility: men tend to maintain their social and personal expenditures, while women are expected to make ends meet with fewer resources, by working longer hours within and outside the home.

Economic stagnation and decline exacerbate gender inequality in household nutrition as well. In societies where anti-female discrimination is endemic, as in South Asia, women usually eat the last and least, and girl children are also poorly fed.[26] In times of poverty and in subsistence crises, their already poor nutritional status is worsened because women have to reduce their share of food to maintain that of their husbands, and girls get even less food than they normally would.[27] Poverty, compounded by the reduction in or withdrawal of food subsidies under an adjustment program, thus disproportionately affects female consumption within the household.[28]

---

24. There is a growing literature on feminist critiques of the neoclassical view of the household. *See, e.g.,* Naila Kabeer, *Benevolent Dictators, Maternal Altruists and Patriarchal Contracts: Gender and Household Economics, in* REVERSED REALITIES: GENDER HIERARCHIES IN DEVELOPMENT THOUGHT 95–135 (1994) [hereinafter REVERSED REALITIES] (discussing the household as an altruistic entity and as a site of bargaining and conflict and highlighting the implications for household welfare); Nancy Folbre, *Cleaning House: New Perspectives on Households and Economic Development,* 14 WORLD DEV. 245 (1986).

25. *See* Diane Elson, *Male Bias in Macro-Economics: The Case of Structural Adjustment, in* MALE BIAS IN THE DEVELOPMENT PROCESS, *supra* note 7, at 164, 183.

26. *See* Jean Drèze & Amartya Sen, *Nutrition and Capability, in* HUNGER AND PUBLIC ACTION 51 (1989).

27. The female-male ratio (FMR) in South Asia, China, West Asia, and North Africa averages 0.93 or 0.94 to 1, in contrast to 1.05 observed in developed countries. *Id.* at 51–52. The higher mortality of women reflects serious anti-female bias in the division of food and health care. *Id.* at 51–53. Higher female mortality cannot be attributed to poverty: Sub-Saharan Africa's FMR is 1.02. *Id.* at 52. If the FMR in other developing parts of the world were the same as in Sub-Saharan Africa, the proportion of missing women would be 44 million in China and 37 million in India. *Id.* at 53.

28. Available evidence from Nigeria, for example, suggests that under the adjustment regime, it is women in poor households who bear the burden of rising prices, scarcity of essential commodities, and decreased income-generating capacity to sustain the household. *See* Carolyne Dennis, *The Limits to Women's Independent Careers: Gender in the Formal and Informal Sectors in Nigeria, in* MALE BIAS IN THE DEVELOPMENT PROCESS, *supra* note 7, at 83, 100.

The promotion of cash crops to improve the efficiency of the agricultural sector is another aspect of SAPs that accentuates intrafamily inequality. In several adjusting countries the introduction of cash crops for export, such as cocoa in Ghana and groundnuts in Senegal, has led to a new sexual division of labor, with men taking over the cash crop and women being pushed to subsistence agriculture, often on marginal and less fertile lands. Cash crops have come to be seen as "male" crops and subsistence crops as "female" crops.[29] This sexual division of labor that characterizes agricultural tasks and crop cultivation affects women within an adjustment program in at least two ways. For one, it leaves women with little or no income of their own because earnings from the cash crop go into new crop investment or general household needs.[30] Second, supportive measures such as access to inputs and credit, technological training, and supervision do not reach women. At the same time, the mechanization of farming tasks has led to a strong preference for male labor.[31] Even where the expansion of labor-intensive export crops such as fruits and vegetables has enabled women to become wage earners, there has been an accompanying deterioration in women's living and working conditions.[32] Cutbacks in public spending, changes in credit facilities, and constant migration between agricultural producers, combined with a lack of childcare support, have worsened women's health and increased their workload.[33]

Cash cropping in rural economies with patriarchal traditions can have profound gender implications. In many instances it heightens conflicts of

---

29. In the eyes of some economists and anthropologists, however, this is an "overpowerful generalization." *See* Jean Drèze & Amartya Sen, *Production, Entitlements and Nutrition, in* HUNGER AND PUBLIC ACTION, *supra* note 27, at 175; *see also* Anne Whitehead, *Rural Women and Food Production in Sub-Saharan Africa, in* THE POLITICAL ECONOMY OF HUNGER 425 (Jean Drèze & Amartya Sen eds., 1990) (discussing the issues raised by the feminization of food production in the sub-continent).

30. *See, e.g.,* Marie-Angélique Savané, *What Next for African Women, in* STRUCTURAL ADJUSTMENT AND THE CRISIS IN AFRICA: ECONOMIC AND POLITICAL PERSPECTIVES 77 (David Kennett & Tukumbi Lumumba-Kasongo eds., 1992) [hereinafter STRUCTURAL ADJUSTMENT AND THE CRISIS IN AFRICA]; *see also* Elson, *supra* note 26, at 172–75 (discussing the evidence from several case studies on the gendered impact of cash cropping).

31. One African woman affected by the male orientation in agricultural policies described it as follows:

> This one they call farmer; send in teachers to teach him to farm (while I'm out there growing the food); lend him money for tractors and tillers (while I'm out there growing the food); promise him fortunes if he'd only raise cotton (while I'm out there growing the food).

U.S. CONGRESSIONAL OFFICE OF TECHNOLOGY ASSESSMENT, AFRICA TOMORROW: ISSUES IN TECHNOLOGY, AGRICULTURE AND U.S. FOREIGN AID 71 (1985), *cited in* KATARINA TOMAŠEVSKI, WOMEN AND HUMAN RIGHTS 37 (1993).

32. *See* Antonieta Barrón, *Mexican Rural Women Wage Earners and Macro-Economic Policies, in* THE STRATEGIC SILENCE, *supra* note 7, at 137, 138.

33. *See id.*

interest within households by increasing male privileges and access to new opportunities represented by cash crop cultivation (because of male mobility), and gives men greater control of household resources as a result of the enhanced role of cash in the household economy.[34] Throughout Africa, cash cropping has also imposed a double burden on women, who bear full responsibility for food crops and help their husbands in cash crop cultivation without any share of the income. In an adjusting economy, the systematic promotion of cash crops combined with a shrinking labor market and existing gender biases in land ownership and household division of labor and consumption works to worsen women's economic, family, and nutritional status.[35]

B.   SAPs and the Export-Manufacturing Sector

The shift from import substitution to export-led growth strategies, which is a central feature of SAPs, presents new opportunities and new challenges for women workers. In Europe and Central Asia, the transition from a command economy to a market system has had, by the Bank's own admission, debilitating effects for women, who have suffered disproportionately from rising unemployment, poor pay, and reduced childcare services.[36]

In many adjusting countries, however, women have gained new employment opportunities in the large export-processing zones (EPZs) that have developed in response to the globalization of production and the reconfiguration of the international labor market. From a policy perspective, the EPZs represent a commitment to employment generation in urban areas to meet the needs of the rural and urban skilled and semi-skilled underemployed and unemployed workers.

The primary goal of the EPZs, however, is to increase foreign currency earnings and help governments in adjusting countries meet debt service payments. To do this, governments have to respond to the needs of multinational corporations and their subcontractors for cheap labor, primarily in the garment, textile, and electronics industries. Currency devaluation makes investment in the EPZs attractive for the firms by reducing capital and labor costs. This collusion between state and commercial interests has resulted in

---

34. See Drèze & Sen, *supra* note 30, at 175.
35. In Zimbabwe, for example, structural adjustment policies instituted in 1991 have exacerbated iniquities in gender relations and the distribution of resources. Maternal mortality and access to education improved with increases in farming output but declined since 1991. Although it is difficult to gauge the extent to which SAPs and/or the drought of 1991–92 influenced this decline, structural adjustment had an adverse impact on health and education which suffered budgetary cuts as the government tried to service its debt. See Bank Gender Group Report, *supra* note 11, at 13.
36. See *id.* at 12.

a gross exploitation of workers in many countries.[37] In the Dominican Republic, the EPZs are characterized by strict discipline, sexual harassment, low pay, occupational health hazards, excessive and forced overtime, and arbitrary suspension and dismissal for protesting or organizing.[38] The gender, human rights, and economic implications of the role of EPZs in an adjusting country are well summed up in the following analysis:

> These extraterritorial industrial estates offer the foreign investor infrastructure and utilities . . . large tax exemptions . . . and *exemption from labour regulations in force in the host country, amounting to the suspension of the most of the rights of workers.* In exchange, these countries get employment, remunerated at only 10–20 percent [of] the level of comparable work in the developed countries, *chiefly for teenage girls who are cheaper and considered more docile workers. Because of this preference for a category of worker that has not previously been employed for wages there is no overall impact on the level of unemployment. There is no creation of transferable skills or transfer of technology.* Because of the low level of wages and salaries, foreign currency receipts are low, and must be set against the expenses incurred by the host government in providing the facilities; because of tax exemptions, income from this source is negligible. Competition among countries to attract foreign investment ensures that they will not be able to raise their share of benefits over time.[39]

The high rates of female employment in the export sector in adjusting economies are often interpreted as a positive outcome of SAPs. However, the fact is that the international and local demand has been for cheap female labor to perform repetitive tasks and dead-end jobs. This gendered demand for labor arises from the vulnerability, docility, and dispensability of young single women, who are made to work without security or safety of employment. In Sri Lanka, where literacy and education attainment levels are among the highest in developing countries, the nature of employment in the EPZs has led to considerable loss of skills among women workers, many of whom have ten to twelve years of education.[40] In fact, the high rates of female employment in the punishing conditions of the export manufactur-

---

37. *See, e.g.,* Swarna Jayaweera, *Structural Adjustment Policies, Industrial Development and Women in Sri Lanka, in* Mortgaging Women's Lives, *supra* note 7, at 96. In 1987, 91 percent of employees in garments factories, 92 percent in food processing, and 83 percent in non-metallic mineral factories were women. *Id.* at 106. Although Sri Lanka had high male unemployment, the transnational corporations preferred to employ unmarried women between eighteen and twenty-five years old. *Id.* at 107. *See also* Nilüfer Çağatay & Süle Özler, *Feminization of the Labor Force: The Effects of Long-Term Development and Structural Adjustment,* 23 World Dev. 1829, 1883–94 (examining how structural adjustment policies have led to an increase in the feminization of the labor force through worsening income distribution and increasing openness).

38. *See* Helen I. Safa & Peggy Antrobus, *Women and the Economic Crisis in the Caribbean, in* Unequal Burden, *supra* note 7, at 49, 63.

39. Payer, The World Bank: A Critical Analysis, *supra* note 2, at 156 (emphasis added).

40. *See* Jayaweera, *supra* note 38, at 111.

ing sector are distress signals from the economy. They indicate increasing male unemployment and a shrinking of women's employment opportunities in the public sector and traditional industries.

In summary, several features of the adjustment process, such as trade liberalization, agricultural reform, and privatization have exacerbated social, economic, and gender inequalities. While SAPs have opened new avenues of employment for women in the informal sector and in export processing, this feminization of employment has come about mainly because of employers' preference for low-cost and docile female labor that can be used in repetitive jobs without minimum guarantees. The cutbacks in food subsidies and in public expenditures on education and health have hit women the hardest in adjusting countries that must strive to meet fiscal austerity requirements. The integration of women in the global economy attributed to SAPs has occurred on unequal terms, worsening the working and living conditions of millions of women and deepening gender oppression and subordination.

IV. THE WORLD BANK

A. The World Bank's Response Analyzed

In the face of sustained and continuing criticism of the social and gender impact of SAPs, the Bank has in several recent statements focused attention on the various programs it has initiated since the late 1980s to mitigate the adverse effects of SAPs. Despite its assertion that structural adjustment remains the cornerstone of economic development and poverty alleviation, the Bank has taken note of the exclusionary nature of such development in many adjusting countries. Further, it has acknowledged the need to protect the poor, not by treating them as targets of add-on policies and programs in the short run, but by integrating them in the long-run growth process as active agents of growth.[41] Bank lending for "investments in people" has risen in adjustment years,[42] reflecting an awareness that SAPs do not automatically promote human and social development.

---

41. *See* SOCIAL DIMENSIONS, *supra* note 6, at 55. However, the Bank has emphasized, as have some independent analysts, that the deterioration in social conditions and declines in social sector spending cannot be directly attributed to structural adjustment, without a counterfactual analysis of what would have happened in the absence of adjustment. *Id.* at 86.
42. The Bank's lending for population, health, nutrition (PHN), and education has gone up in absolute terms and as a proportion of total lending over the last decade. BANK PROGRESS REPORT, *supra* note 8, at 9–10. Lending for PHN projects went up from $200.7 million in 1985 to over $1,152.5 million in 1995. *Id.* at 10. Educational lending went up from

Additionally, the Bank has targeted many of these investments specifically at women and girls and stressed gender related programs in its operations, although it maintains that, so far, there is little quantitative evidence
of the effects of SAPs disaggregated by gender.[43] Thus, while the Bank
acknowledges the negative impact of adjustment policies on education, for
example, by providing education sector adjustment loans and setting education targets as part of loan conditionality, the Bank does not provide conclusive evidence that gender parity has been protected.[44]

In recent assessments of the social impact of SAPs, the Bank points to
two particularly disquieting trends: "the continuous decline in infrastructure
spending, and the fall in per capita social spending."[45] It notes that public
expenditure reform, a critical part of adjustment programs, did not result in
a real location of public expenditure geared to longterm poverty reduction.[46] Although social spending (as a percentage of gross domestic product)
fell less than other discretionary expenditure, per-capita social spending fell
in real terms in almost two-thirds of the countries studied.[47] This was especially so in African countries where, the Bank states, the per-capita cuts
were felt sharply because of population growth.[48] In particular, the composition of social spending on primary (as opposed to tertiary) education, and
preventive (as opposed to curative) health worsened in many countries.[49]

To some extent, social adjustment initiatives, like the Social Dimensions
of Adjustment (SDA) Project, initiated in 1986 with the goal of undertaking
activities in ten African countries, and Ghana's Programme of Actions to
Mitigate Social Costs of Adjustment (PAMSCAD), represent attempts by the

---

$936.8 million to $2,150.7 million over the same period. *Id.* at 9. A significant proportion of projects in both sectors have a specific gender focus. *Id.* at 10. Bank lending for
human capital development went up from 5 percent a year in the 1980s to 18 percent of
all Bank lending in fiscal 1992–1996. WORLD BANK ANNUAL REPORT 47 (1996).

43. Independent studies have, however, provided some of this evidence. *See, e.g.,* Pauline
Rose, *Female Education and Adjustment Programs: A Cross-Country Statistical Analysis,*
in 23 WORLD DEV. 1931, 1931–49 (Nov. 1995) (special issue) (providing an examination
of the data on female school enrollment rates in adjusting and non-adjusting countries).
The study shows that, while the gender gap in school enrollment rates has narrowed in
both groups of countries, this is due to the average male enrollment rate falling to the
lower average female enrollment rate in adjusting countries. *Id.* at 1939–40. In contrast,
the gap has narrowed in non-adjusting countries because of increases in both male and
female enrollment rates. *Id.* at 1940.
44. *See id.* at 1932.
45. SOCIAL DIMENSIONS, *supra* note 6, at 78; *see also* THE WORLD BANK, ADJUSTMENT IN AFRICA:
REFORMS, RESULTS, AND THE ROAD AHEAD (1994) (providing a review of policy reforms in the
second half of the 1980s).
46. *See* SOCIAL DIMENSIONS, *supra* note 6, at 79.
47. *See id.* at 78.
48. *See id.* at 79.
49. *See id.*

Bank to address some of the criticisms directed at structural adjustment.[50] In 1990–1992, the Bank's share of adjustment lending for social concerns increased to 50 percent; this was up from 5 percent in 1984–1986.[51] But the theoretical and conceptual bases underlying the programs have generated much controversy, pointing to the shortcomings of the approach as applied in Africa and elsewhere.

B.   Limitations of the World Bank's "Social Safety Net" Approach

A primary problem of the safety net approach is that it addresses social dimensions as a postscript to structural adjustment. The SDA project, for example, prescribes a set of policy interventions, such as employment generation, retraining, and credit schemes that are aimed at alleviating what are seen as adverse but short-run social consequences of structural adjustment policies (SAPs).[52] Given the reality of longterm social deterioration and poverty consequences of SAPs, there is now increasing concern with the need to integrate social variables into policy analysis at the time loans are negotiated.

However, both in its compensatory and transformative strategies, the Bank's social safety measures are premised on the assumption that structural adjustment will increase output. In reality, it is not possible to enable the poor to participate in the growth process if the economy is stagnant; nor can temporary employment be justified if there are no prospects of increasing employment as a result of adjustment policies. The SDA project thus leaves unquestioned the efficacy of the price mechanism[53] in bringing about

---

50. *See* Sheila Smith, *The Social Dimensions of Structural Adjustment: A Change of Direction or a Figleaf?, in* Structural Adjustment and the Crisis in Africa, *supra* note 31, at 120. Ms. Smith is a senior economist at UNDP who was associated with the project. The World Bank is the executing agency for the project; the UNDP and the African Development Bank are the two other co-sponsoring agencies. As of 1992, thirty-two countries had asked to participate in the project, indicating the extent of the impact of adverse social repercussions of orthodox reforms, although activities had not begun in many of them. *Id.* at 123. PAMSCAD was discontinued in 1993. According to the Bank, the Program's unwieldy portfolio, complex bureaucratic procedures, and limited transparency and participatory procedures made it difficult to administer. Social Dimensions, *supra* note 6, at 110. With resources of more than $80 million, it reached only 50,000 people (0.3 percent of population), of whom only 3,000 got jobs. *Id.* at 110. Further, as women's advocates have pointed out, although PAMSCAD was often cited as a model program to mitigate the social costs of adjustment, the program hardly mentioned women. *See* Engendering Adjustment, *supra* note 7, at 89.
51. *See* World Bank Annual Report 38 (1993).
52. *See* Smith, *supra* note 51, at 122.
53. *See* discussion *infra* Part VI.A.

equitable economic and social changes.[54] Furthermore, by focusing on protecting only certain core public sector expenditures, such as in health or education, the SDA project ignores the question of the centrality of a viable and efficient public sector in the development and recovery process. For example, while food is typically purchased in the market (even when influenced by rationing or subsidies), it is public institutions that usually provide medical, education, or related facilities. The role of the state is even more direct and immediate, even in industrialized countries, in ensuring general health, eliminating infectious diseases, and providing clean water.[55]

A final contradiction in the SDA project is the centrality of the World Bank's role in it, which precludes a more fundamental critique of structural adjustment. In the eyes of some senior economists involved in it, this makes the project a figleaf that enables the Bank to deflect criticism while basically continuing with the same approach.[56]

C.   From WID to GAD

The social impact of SAPs on women cannot be softened by safety net measures that tend to be ad-hoc, piecemeal, and compensatory in nature. Such measures aim at protecting the vulnerable by trying to avoid excessive costs to poor households through supplementary programs that can be added on to existing SAPs. Because these programs do not confront the structural causes of inequity and oppression which have placed the poor in a position of disadvantages in the first place, they cannot result in genuine empowerment. Many supposedly ameliorative schemes for women, such as income generation, fail to address the sexual divisions of labor and ignore the economic value of women's unpaid work, instead imposing on women the additional burden of generating income.

In fact, structural adjustment programs run counter to the Bank's own sectoral policies aimed at social development. Its programs on reproductive health and nutrition, for example, are undermined by macroeconomic policies that erode investments in public health and education. These contradictions cannot be addressed through tack-on projects.[57]

---

54. See Smith, *supra* note 51, at 130.
55. See Jean Drèze & Amartya Sen, *The Economy, the State and the Public, in* HUNGER AND PUBLIC ACTION, *supra* note 27, at 258.
56. See Smith, *supra* note 51, at 120.
57. The Bank has approved $425 million for 1997 for a primary education project in India, targeting districts with low female literacy rates. BANK PROGRESS REPORT, *supra* note 8, at 10. However, the magnitude of the task of universal education calls for sustained state action and financial commitment, not merely through Bank loans that need to be repaid. According to a UNICEF estimate of 1991, India will need an additional 50,000 primary

The Bank's Women in Development (WID) projects, initiated in 1987, signaled official recognition of the special needs and concerns of women during the reform process. The proportion of projects with specific WID recommendations rose from 11 percent in 1988 to 45 percent in 1993.[58] But overall, the WID dimension is a disappointing tack-on to projects rather than a basic rethinking of macroeconomic and development policy.[59] Critiques of WID strategies contend that WID projects retained the fundamental neoclassical economics worldview with its failure to evaluate women's traditional roles in society. WID projects have tended to reinforce pre-existing values that restricted women's roles to domestic and childbearing activities.[60] These constraints are becoming apparent within the Bank, which has moved from a WID to a Gender and Development (GAD) approach to identify the reasons for differences in access to resources, services, and opportunities between men and women, and their consequences on the household, the community, and economic development in general.[61]

Following the Beijing women's conference, the Bank has, often with the direct involvement of its President, James Wolfensohn, instituted various measures to "mainstream" gender issues in its operations. It seeks to do this by building women's economic capacity by investing in their human capital, helping improve their economic conditions and opportunities, and improving institutional capacity to advance women's welfare and status.[62] The rhetorical commitment to gender equality and participatory processes with NGOs notwithstanding, serious concerns remain about the Bank's willingness to put these principles into practice.[63]

---

schools and 440,000 middle schools if each village is to have at least one school. Swaminathan, *supra* note 19, at 17. Central government outlays on education, however, fell in real terms in the early 1990s. *Id.*

58. *See* World Bank Annual Report, *supra* note 52, at 44–45.
59. *See* Pamela Sparr, *Feminist Critiques of Structural Adjustment, in* Mortgaging Women's Lives, *supra* note 7, at 13, 33.
60. *See* Naila Kabeer, *Treating Cancer With Band-Aid? The Theoretical Underpinnings of WID, in* Reversed Realities, *supra* note 25, at 22.
61. *See* Gender Issues, *supra* note 10, at 23. In November 1995, a plenary meeting of the Bank's Special Program of Assistance in Africa endorsed a proposal to systematically integrate gender concerns into the design, implementation, and monitoring of structural adjustment operations in Africa. Three pilot countries chosen for this exercise, as part of the Structural Adjustment and Gender in Africa Initiative, are Mali, Burkina Faso, and Mozambique. *See* Bank Progress Report, *supra* note 8, at 5.
62. These goals in gender equity are set out in several recent Bank publications. *See, e.g.,* The World Bank, Enhancing Women's Participation in Economic Development: A World Bank Policy Paper (1994); World Bank Annual Report 50–51 (1996) (providing an overview of the Bank's efforts at mainstreaming gender issues in policymaking).
63. In a letter to Bank President James Wolfensohn dated 13 December 1996, the Women's Eyes on the World Bank, *infra* note 110, expressed concern about the failure of the Mexican Country Assistance Strategy (CAS) to demonstrate how the Bank plans to address gender inequity in Mexico. By not including gender equity issues in the Mexican CAS,

V.   TRANSFORMATIONAL REMEDIES

A.   Gender and the Governance Approach

Through the 1970s and 1980s, the Bank tended to maintain a cautious and hands-off stance on gender issues, labeling them complex, sensitive, and culturally defined.[64] Both the Bank and the IMF argue that they are bound by their Articles of Agreement to be nonpolitical in their approach.[65] However, such a position is not sustainable on three counts.

First, in order to create market oriented economies, SAPs redistribute wealth and power in society by fixing prices through the removal of economic distortions.[66] By acknowledging the need for protection of the vulnerable, Bank officials admit that their prescription for economic transition creates winners and losers, which is a political act. Women constitute a disproportionate section of the losers because of the additional burdens imposed on them as a result of decline in real wages, rising unemployment, dramatic increases in prices of household goods, and changes in the level and composition of public expenditure. Macroeconomic policies, especially SAPs that seek far-reaching changes, are not conducted in a political and social vacuum.

Second, through the tool of conditionality, structural adjustment permits the Bank to function as a lawmaker in countries that seek loans, a role that Bank officials themselves acknowledge goes beyond the realm of macroeconomics.[67] In the process of adjustment, Bank officials and consultants

---

the letter said, the Bank failed to comply with its own operational principle 4.20 which states that the "Bank aims to reduce gender disparities and enhance women's participation in the economic development of their countries by integrating gender considerations in its country assistance program." Abid Aslam, *Mexico Finance: New World Bank Strategy Seen to Fail Poor, Women*, TERRA VIVA, INTERPRESS SERVICE DAILY JOURNAL, 27 Dec. 1996.

64. *See* GENDER ISSUES, *supra* note 10, at 3.

65. Article IV, section 10 of the Bank's Articles of Agreement states that:

> The Bank and its officers shall not interfere in the political affairs of any member; nor shall they be influenced in their decisions by the political character of the member or members concerned. Only economic considerations shall be relevant to their decisions, and these considerations shall be weighed impartially in order to achieve the purposes stated in Article 1.

THE WORLD BANK, ARTICLES OF AGREEMENT 12–13.

66. *See* Pamela Sparr, *Banking on Women: Where Do We Go From Here?, in* MORTGAGING WOMEN'S LIVES, *supra* note 7, at 183, 193–94.

67. *See* Jonathan Cahn, *Challenging the New Imperial Authority: The World Bank and the Democratization of Development,* 6 HARVARD HUM. RTS. J. 159 (1993). Ibrahim Shihata, the Bank's Vice-President and General Counsel has said that "conditionality has thus evolved from macroeconomic measures to detailed reforms affecting the public administration itself." Ann Crittenden, *World Bank in Shift, Lending for Trade Debts,* N.Y. TIMES, 26 May 1980, *cited in* PAYER, THE WORLD BANK: A CRITICAL ANALYSIS, *supra* note 2, at 154. According

often redraft not just the fiscal policy of a country, but its labor laws, health and educational expenditures, energy and environmental regulations, and civil service rules.[68] Through these activities, the Bank far exceeds its role as a lending institution, operating on the rationale that such legal, structural, and institutional changes will influence the outcomes of its economic policies.

Third, the integration of gender analysis in the formulation of adjustment policies can be supported as an economic proposition. The Bank's policy papers and guidelines over the years have recognized the importance of women's roles in economic development. Of particular value is girls' education, which the Bank sees as an investment that yields the highest rate of return in a developing country. Gender differences are critical to planning imperatives in alleviating poverty, increasing agricultural productivity, changing trade patterns, decreasing demographic growth, and preserving the environment.[69] The Bank's cautious stance on addressing the gender dimensions of SAPs at the policy and planning stages is therefore untenable both on political and economic grounds. Nor is it justifiable in the context of its evolving role as a governance institution or as a self-defined development agency, the largest in the world.[70]

B. Gender and the Human Rights Approach

Any attempt to deal with the social impact of adjustment in a transformative agenda must address the human rights that are implicated in the conduct of SAPs. Although according to international law, the fulfillment of human rights obligations is primarily the responsibility of individual state governments that have accepted these obligations, other institutions cannot entirely escape their share of the responsibility. This is especially so in the current economic and political context of globalization that has made for an interrelated and interdependent world. As powerful development actors

---

to another regional vice-president, S. Shahid Husain, "[t]hese loans do go to the heart of the political management of an economy. We will have to approach them with humility." *Id.*

68. *See* Cahn, *supra* note 68, at 159.
69. *See* GENDER ISSUES, *supra* note 10, at 22–23.
70. The purposes of the Bank, according to the Articles of Agreement, are:

To assist in the reconstruction and development of territories of members by facilitating the investment of capital for productive purposes, including the restoration of economies destroyed or disrupted by war, the reconversion of productive facilities to peacetime needs and the encouragement of the development of productive facilities and resources in less developed countries.

THE WORLD BANK, ARTICLES OF AGREEMENT 1.

deciding the fate of millions, the World Bank and IMF have governance obligations; as specialized UN agencies, they are international legal personalities bound by international law and human rights obligations.[71] Moreover, human rights are not restricted to the domestic domain. Under international human rights doctrine, both agencies come under the ambit of international law.

Regarding the sociopolitical and human rights implications of its policies, the Bank has again tended to seek cover under its Articles of Agreement which prohibit it from intervention in any areas that are the domain of national actors.[72] While stating that human rights concerns fall beyond its mandate, the Bank has also said that economic and social rights are addressed through its poverty alleviation programs, in provisions which address health and sanitation services and water supply.[73] But as with its WID schemes, most such programs are flawed in that they are compensatory and palliative in nature rather than transformative.

In recent years, the Bank has to some extent responded to sustained criticism of the social impact of adjustment policies by emphasizing good governance, even if only as a factor related to economic performance.[74] It has also constituted internal monitoring bodies such as the inspection panel to review allegations of failures to observe its own rules and regulations.

---

71. The Bank became a specialized agency of the UN through a relationship agreement that came into force on 15 April 1948. Article 1(2) of the agreement states that the

    Bank is a specialized agency established by agreement among its member Governments and having wide international responsibilities, as defined in its Articles of Agreement, in economic and related fields within the meaning of Article 57 of the Charter of the United Nations. By reason of the nature of its international responsibilities and the terms of its Articles of Agreement, the Bank is, and is required to function as an independent international organization.

    Id. art. 1(2), cited in PAYER, THE WORLD BANK: A CRITICAL ANALYSIS, supra note 2, at 16. Critics have described the agreement of liaison as "more a declaration of independence from than cooperation with the United Nations." Id. The Bank was fearful of political controls and insisted on a number of privileges that would enable it to keep the central UN bodies at arm's length. Id.

72. See THE WORLD BANK, ARTICLES OF AGREEMENT 12–13.
73. See THE LAWYER'S COMMITTEE FOR HUMAN RIGHTS, THE WORLD BANK: GOVERNANCE AND HUMAN RIGHTS 65 (1995) [hereinafter BANK GOVERNANCE].
74. In 1990, Bank Vice-President and General Counsel Ibrahim Shihata issued a memorandum reiterating that the Bank's Articles of Agreement required that only economic considerations be taken into account in its dealings with recipient countries. Memorandum of the Vice-President and General Counsel, Issues of Governance in Borrowing Members—The Extent of Their Relevance Under the Bank's Articles of Agreement, cited in BANK GOVERNANCE, supra note 74, at 44–45. The memorandum, however, did acknowledge that "internal or external political events may have significant direct economic effects which, due to their economic nature, may properly be taken into consideration in the Bank's decisions." Id. at 44. The violation of political rights could become a Bank concern due to significant direct economic effects. Id. at 44–45.

However, the restrictive nature of the procedures followed in the panel's operation, the panel's narrow jurisdiction, its lack of transparency, and the fact that the Bank's board of directors remain the final arbiters raise questions about its independence and credibility.[75] The pervasive human rights dimensions of structural adjustment have received critical comment from the UN Special Rapporteur on the Realization of Economic, Social and Cultural Rights, who also identified income and debt as having an impact on the realization of these rights.[76]

> Structural adjustment programs continue to have a significant impact upon the overall realization of economic, social and cultural rights, both in terms of the ability of people to exercise these rights, and of the capability of governments to fulfil and implement them. While significant and positive changes have taken place concerning the design and nature of adjustment, these have yet to result in a marked shift sufficient not only to fully protect the rights of the most vulnerable, but also actually to decrease levels of impoverishment. Human rights concerns continue to be conspicuously underestimated in the adjustment process.[77]

From the standpoint of human rights and economic development, the Bank's hands-off approach to the human and political dimensions of its policies can be countered on three grounds. First, structural adjustment results in a shift in the distribution of wealth and power in a nation. Adjustment programs, in the short and medium term, have worked to increase the economic opportunities and welfare of the few at the expense of the majority. By the Bank's own admission, SAPs have worsened inequalities even where they have promoted economic growth.[78] These inequalities of wealth and power endanger, even nullify, the entitlements guaranteed under the concept of rights, especially economic and social rights.

Second, through its policy of structural adjustment, the Bank imposes a suspension of the rights of large sections of people on the basis of pain now, gain later. The Bank has presented the economic and social costs of its pro-

---

75. *See id.* at 96–98. The report notes that although the Bank has in recent years included important human rights concerns through its consideration of governance and other rights-related issues, it avoids the use of human rights terminology. *Id.* at 99. Hence its use of terms like governance, participation, public sector management, and transparency. *Id.*

76. *See The Realization of Economic, Social and Cultural Rights: Final report submitted by Mr. Danilo Türk, Special Rapporteur,* Commission on Human Rights, Sub-Commission on Prevention of Discrimination and Protection of Minorities, 49th Sess., at 11 U.N. Doc. E/CN.4/Sub.2/1992/16 (1992).

77. *Id.*

78. In a discussion on sustainable growth and poverty reduction, the Bank states that: "Except for a few East Asian [adjusting] countries, growth has been insufficient for sustained reduction in poverty—and high levels of income inequality persist." SOCIAL DIMENSIONS, *supra* note 6, at 54.

grams of orthodox reforms as necessary features of a period of difficult but temporary transition, as a short time of hardship before overall prosperity.[79] However, the promise has not been fulfilled after a decade of structural adjustment, and the temporary suspension of fundamental economic and social rights has become a permanent deferral. Nowhere do international covenants or national laws on these rights sanction such an abrogation on grounds of economic growth or any other societal goals.

The deterioration in social conditions cannot of course be attributed entirely to Bank policies of structural adjustment: many developing countries have had poor records in health and educational sectors before SAPs were instituted. During adjustment, recipient countries that have ratified the relevant conventions and covenants have pleaded lack of resources for their failure to implement them. The International Covenant on Economic, Social and Cultural Rights (ICESCR) grants that the full implementation of affirmative rights may take time, particularly in the case of developing countries that lack the human and financial resources to implement them.[80] Enshrined in the ICESCR and the Universal Declaration of Human Rights, these affirmative rights include the rights to food and nutrition, health, education, and employment.[81] To this can be added the rights against discrimination, the

---

79. But see THE WORLD BANK, THE SOCIAL DIMENSIONS OF ADJUSTMENT IN AFRICA: A POLICY AGENDA (1990), where the Bank itself has recognized that:

> Once it was seen that the transition could well take longer than initially anticipated, public policy began to explore ways to assist the poor and vulnerable groups affected by the adjustment process. African governments and donors recognized that vulnerable groups could not wait for benefits of the adjustment process to accrue to them and that they would need various kinds of assistance during the process.

Id. at 4 (emphasis added).

80. Article 2 of the ICESCR, adopted by the U.N. General Assembly in December 1966, states:

> Each State Party to the present Covenant undertakes to take steps, individually and through international assistance and co-operation, especially economic and technical, to the maximum of its available resources, with a view to achieving progressively the full realization of the rights recognized in the present Covenant by all appropriate means, including particularly the adoption of legislative measures.

International Convention on Economic, Social, and Cultural Rights, art. 2, adopted 16 Dec. 1966, 993 U.N.T.S. 3 (entered into force 3 Jan. 1976), G.A. Res. 2200 (XXI), 21 U.N. GAOR Supp. (No. 16) at 49, U.N. Doc. A/6316 (1966) [hereinafter ICESCR] (emphasis added).

81. See, for example, Article 11(2) of the ICESCR, which states:

> States parties to the present Covenant, recognizing the fundamental right of everyone to be free from hunger, shall take, individually and through international cooperation, the measures, including specific programmes, which are needed [to improve methods of production, conservation and distribution of food].

Id. art. 11(2).

right to organize, and the right to participation.[82] The right to organize, which can be interpreted as both a civil and social right, has been explicitly curtailed by national governments seeking to meet adjustment requirements of export strategies.[83]

Insofar as Bank-supported adjustment affects a country's ability to meet its obligations under domestic and international law, both the Bank and the individual government are responsible. The UN Committee on Economic, Social and Cultural Rights has emphasized that the effort must always be to hasten, and not lengthen, the process towards achieving the goal of full realization of the relevant rights.

> [S]teps towards the goal must be taken within a reasonably short time after the Covenant's entry into force for the States concerned. . . . [T]he fact that realization over time, or in other words progressively, is foreseen under the Covenant should not be misinterpreted as depriving the obligation of all meaningful content. It is on the one hand a necessary flexible device, reflecting the realities of the real world and the difficulties involved for any country in ensuring full realization of economic, social and cultural rights. On the other hand, the phrase must be read in the light of the overall objective, indeed the *raison d'etre,* of the Covenant which is to establish clear obligations for States parties in respect of the full realization of the rights in question. It thus imposes an obligation to move as expeditiously and effectively as possible towards the goal.[84]

The Committee also interprets the phrase "to the maximum of its available resources" as those belonging to a State, as well as to the international financial assistance available to it.[85] By implication, structural adjustment loans

---

82. Under Article 2(e) of the Convention on the Elimination of All Forms of Discrimination Against Women (CEDAW), states parties agree "[t]o take all appropriate measures to eliminate discrimination against women by any person, organization or enterprise." Convention on the Elimination of All Forms of Discrimination Against Women, *adopted* 18 Dec. 1979, G.A. Res. 34/180, 34 U.N. GAOR Supp. (No. 46) at 193, U.N. Doc. A/34/36 (1980), *reprinted in* 19 I.L.M. 33 (1980) (*entered into force* 3 Sept. 1981).

83. Under SAPs, the abrogation of labor rights, especially in EPZs, has led to a legalization of sweatshops to benefit corporations. For example, Sri Lanka withdrew from the ILO's Convention on Night Work, which it had ratified earlier, to make cheap female labor readily available to investors. *See* Jayaweera, *supra* note 38, at 107. In the Philippines, certain export industries have been exempted from the minimum wage law. Women exploited by transnational corporations receive no support from their governments in their efforts for better wages and working conditions, and have no recourse to predominantly male trade unions who are not sympathetic to their concerns. *See* Sparr, *supra* note 67, at 192. A US Agency for International Development study in Jamaica revealed that American firms see unions as a major obstacle to investment. *See* Safa & Antrobus, *supra* note 39, at 62.

84. *The Nature of States Parties Obligations,* Committee on Economic, Social and Cultural Rights, General Comment No. 3, 5th Sess., ¶¶ 2, 9 (1990) (Compilation of General Comments and General Recommendations adopted by Human Rights Treaty Bodies, U.N. Doc. HRI\GEN\1\Rev.1, at 45 (1994)).

85. *Id.*

from the Bank cannot be used by the State or by the institution to curtail these rights.

Third, one cannot rely on economic growth alone to generate the rise in income among the poor necessary for the achievement of basic needs. In many poor economies, economic growth, with its presumed trickle-down effect, has been set as a precondition for achieving basic needs in the belief that no amount of redistribution of resources will secure minimum basic needs consumption. This has served as justification for not pursuing, or even dismantling, egalitarian policies in the interests of economic growth. In Nigeria, to cite just one example, such an approach has entailed an immediate setback in the fulfillment of basic needs to below the critical minimum in consumption levels.[86] The slowness or absence of the so-called trickle-down makes growth an unreliable means of general advance of a community. High growth rates do not necessarily ensure economic and social equality and quality of life, as the oft-quoted example of Brazil shows.[87]

In the context of gender and SAPs, policies that affect the economic and social rights of the poor affect women disproportionately, for the reasons discussed above. While it is easy enough to define the rights undermined in the implementation of SAPs, it is difficult to implement remedial measures. There is now enough theoretical basis and empirical evidence to support the argument that all human rights are interdependent and indivisible and that it is not possible to realize one set of rights, whether civil and political (CP), or economic, social, and cultural (ECOSOC), in the absence of the other.[88] However, the traditional neglect of economic and social rights is embedded in the fact that few states, both in the North and South, have incorporated socioeconomic rights in their constitutions or domestic legislation. This has rendered this set of rights nonjusticiable at the level of state policy.

Furthermore, the ambiguous nature of ECOSOC rights and the fact that they are aspirational and not legally binding in character make it hard to determine legal standards of minimum requirements. Some human rights

---

86. *See* Frances Stewart, Basic Needs in Developing Countries 45, 106, 118 (1985).

87. *See* Jean Drèze & Amartya Sen, *Economic Growth and Public Support, in* Hunger and Public Action 180, 189 (1989). The authors report that Brazil's gross national product per head in the 1980s was $1,640, and its infant mortality rate was 67 per 1,000 live births and life expectancy sixty-five years. *Id.* at 180. In contrast, China, with a GNP per capita of $310, had an IMR of 35/1,000 and life expectancy of sixty-nine years, while Sri Lanka, with a GNP per capita of $380, had an IMR of 36/1,000 and life expectancy of seventy years. *Id.*

88. The Vienna Declaration and Programme of Action, *adopted* June 24, 1993, Sess. 5, U.N. GAOR, World Conference on Human Rights, U.N. Doc. A/Conf.157/24, adopted by the World Conference on Human Rights, Vienna, 14–15 June 1993, adopted by 171 States at the World Conference on Human Rights, affirms that "[a]ll human rights are universal, indivisible and interdependent and interrelated." *Id.* ¶ 5. It calls for, *inter alia,* equal opportunities for participation in political and economic decision making and elimination of discrimination by gender and violence against women. *Id.* ¶¶ 8, 18.

experts have suggested that indicators of human development and social opportunity could play a useful role in their realization.[89] But given the difficulties in collection, interpretation, analysis, and sources of data, indicators are not a wholly reliable measure of the fulfillment of ECOSOC rights. Indeed, in the context of women and SAPs, the use of indicators could in fact be misleading and misrepresenting. For example, women's high labor force participation rates in the export manufacturing sector in adjusting economies could be presented as a positive indicator of their right to employment, without conveying the appalling conditions of work that violate their rights to health, organization, and equal pay for equal work.[90] Indicators can be a useful measure only after the content of the various rights has been clarified, on the basis of principles such as non-discrimination, the right to information, equality in land rights, gender equality, and democratic participation.

Another difficulty in the realization of ECOSOC rights lies in the fact that enforcement mechanisms remain embryonic. The Committee on Economic, Social and Cultural Rights was established only in 1987 and is hampered by the lack of an optional protocol to the ICESCR that prevents individuals making direct complaints. Although states parties to the Covenant are required to comply with reporting obligations, they have not taken such obligations seriously, with some failing to submit even a single report.[91]

Finally, the concern with socioeconomic rights is emerging at a time when some staunch supporters of these rights, who are also supporters of a strong state, such as India, Indonesia, and Malaysia, have given in to the

89. See The New International Economic Order and the Promotion of Human Rights: Realization of Economic, Social and Cultural Rights, First Progress Report Prepared by the Special Rapporteur to the Sub-Commission on Prevention of Discrimination and Protection of Minorities, U.N. ESCOR Comm'n on Human Rights, 42nd Sess., Prov. Agenda Item 7, U.N. Doc. E/CN.4/Sub.2/1990/19 (1990), cited in Mario Gomez, Social Economic Rights and Commissions, 17 Hum. Rts. Q. 155, 164–65 (1995).

90. A recent study of adjustment policies in Latin America and Africa provides an example of how analysis based on indicators can become a disingenuous exercise in getting certain sums right. See ELLIOT BERG ET AL., STRUCTURAL ADJUSTMENT AND THE POOR IN THE 1980S: TRENDS IN SOCIAL CONDITIONS IN LATIN AMERICA AND AFRICA (1994). The study contrasts Latin America's economic decline in the 1980s, when real wages and consumption fell and the ranks of the poor rose, with the fact that social indicators improved, signalling lower infant mortality and higher life expectancy. Id. This selective use of indicators glosses over the general deterioration in living conditions as a result of SAPs in Latin America. Moreover, indicators like child mortality have improved in many poor countries largely because of direct interventions by international agencies like UNICEF and WHO. Significantly, maternal mortality rates, which are a more accurate indicator of the far-reaching social impact of SAPs, have not shown an appreciable decline in some of the largest Latin American debtor nations. For the period 1980–1992, Brazil and Colombia registered a high maternal mortality rate (deaths per 100,000 live births) of 200, and Mexico and Argentina 110, although female life expectancy improved considerably. UNDP, HUMAN DEVELOPMENT REPORT 54–55 (1995).

91. ICESCR, supra note 81, art. 21.

dominant ideology of the market. These countries now emphasize ECOSOC over CP rights only at international forums (usually in response to Western or Amnesty International/Human Rights Watch–sponsored criticism of their political conduct), while systematically undermining ECOSOC rights at home by policies of omission and commission. The dominance of the market and the lure of foreign investment and capital have also caused the governments of many developing countries to be influenced and controlled by transnational corporations.

Apart from ICESCR and CEDAW, the human right to development also embodies norms that are violated in the context of SAPs' impact on women.[92] But a conceptual difficulty arises here in that the public/private distinction of macroeconomic policies is mirrored in the formulation of this right. Feminist critics have pointed out that although the right obliges states to ensure equal opportunities, fair distribution of income, and an active role for women in the development process, it is still written from a male perspective. Sex discrimination finds no place in it, whereas apartheid and ethnic discrimination do. The conceptualization of the right implicitly assigns women to the private sphere, which is categorized as unproductive, unoccupied, and economically inactive. This invisibility of women retards their right to development.[93]

Overall, in adopting a human rights approach in the gender context of SAPs, it cannot be assumed that women's rights are automatically recognized or subsumed in the rights of men. This is especially the case with property rights. Access to land and land tenure is crucial to both development and human rights, more so when adjustment policies in agriculture work to deprive women of access to productive resources. However, binding human rights documents do not address land rights. Furthermore, statutory matrimonial conditions in many countries are incompatible with equal rights in inheritance. Women are doubly jeopardized in property rights, as women and as married women.[94]

For all of these hurdles, however, there are good political and economic reasons for using human rights standards not only to improve the general human situation, but also to positively alter patterns of economic development. Statutes are of little worth unless people put pressure on courts, gov-

---

92. Article 1 of the Declaration on the Right to Development, adopted by the UN General Assembly in December 1986, states that by virtue of this right, the individual is "entitled to participate in, contribute to, and enjoy economic, social, cultural and political development, in which all human rights and fundamental freedoms can be fully realized." *Declaration on the Right to Development*, U.N. GAOR, 51st Sess., Annex, Agenda Item 101, at 3, U.N. Doc. A/RES/41/128 (1986).

93. *See* Hilary Charlesworth, *The Public/Private Distinction and the Right to Development in International Law*, 12 Aust. Y.B. Int'l L. 190, 199 (1992).

94. *See* Tomaševski, *supra* note 32, at 37.

ernments, and international organizations to realize them. The use of these standards to address the social dimension of SAPs would increase accountability on the part of the international financial institutions and national governments, enable participation by the intended beneficiaries of adjustment, and redirect these policies toward humane and sustainable development.[95]

VI.   STRATEGIES AND RECOMMENDATIONS

The institutionalization of the market model of growth, the gender-blind nature of international laws and economic policies, and the multitude of national and international actors in economic development make the task of formulating a meaningful approach to the social dimension of SAPs a daunting one. The call for international standards and for an adherence to the principles of cooperation, sustainability, equity, and community is everywhere, as was strikingly evident at the Beijing Women's Conference. Unfortunately, there is far less clarity concerning the means to achieve these principles as well as on devising monitoring mechanisms (especially benchmarks to measure change), and on the paths toward alternative economic frameworks.

One of the first questions facing those working to transform economic structures is where they should focus their energies: on policymaking bodies such as the World Bank and IMF, or on implementing bodies such as national governments. Whether in the international or domestic arenas, it is imperative to increase women's opportunities for economic and political decision making. Although women constitute roughly half the populations of nations, they are practically invisible in public decision-making positions in government.[96] Despite this handicap, the directions for change within the

---

95. The Bank has recently made its most promising move to date in this direction by launching the Structural Adjustment Participatory Review Initiative (SAPRI). The initiative, to be conducted jointly with NGOs, labor unions, and women's organizations in at least six countries during 1997, will focus on specific issues such as trade liberalization and its impact on the informal sector, labor market deregulation, and the different ways in which SAPs affect men and women. *See* Abid Aslam, *World Bank Faces Self-Honesty Test,* TERRA VIVA, INTERPRESS SERVICE DAILY JOURNAL, 22 Dec. 1996. The Bank and NGO teams have agreed that a common goal of the initiative is to bring into the policy making process, along with the Bank and governments, those previously excluded segments of civil society that work with and represent local populations and that can provide in each country critically important input regarding the "real economy." *See Wolfensohn Accepts NGO Challenge to Re-Examine Adjustment Operations,* BANKCHECK, Sept. 1996, at 14.

96. Women still occupy only 10 percent of parliamentary seats worldwide and only 6 percent of cabinet positions. In fifty-five countries ranging from very poor to reasonably affluent, there are either no women in parliament, or fewer than 5 percent. *See, e.g.,* UNDP, HUMAN DEVELOPMENT REPORT 1995 (1995). Women in power and decision making was one of the twelve critical areas of concern in the Beijing Platform for Action.

international financial institutions (IFIs) and the growing role of NGOs as partners in development suggest several areas for action. Some of these areas follow.

A.   Reform by the Bank/IMF

1.   Institute staff training programs in gender sensitization. However, training staff to inform them of gender-based differences and stereotypes does not automatically translate into gender-aware policy. What is needed is not only incentives to change behavior but institutional reform in recipient countries to enable agencies to better respond to the differentiated needs and priorities of men and women, to empower women to demand institutional accountability, and to include gender as a key variable in information systems to enable the production of gender-disaggregated data.[97]

2.   Build on the acceptance of social responsibility by incorporating participatory and consultative aspects to lending.

3.   Integrate gender analysis at the level of planning and design of policies and programs. One way of making economic reform programs gender-aware is to make them specific as to whose rights they change and how, and their differential impact on the rights of men and women.[98]

4.   Ensure the participation of women in the planning of Bank assisted projects. If the government does not comply, the Bank can refuse renewal of the loan.[99]

Women's equal participation in decision-making is not only a demand for simple justice or democracy but can also be seen as a necessary condition for women's interest to be taken into account. Without the active participation of women and incorporation of women's perspectives at all levels of decision-making, the goals of equality, development and peace cannot be achieved.

Beijing Platform for Action, *supra* note 4, ¶ 181. The Platform for Action continues that: "The low proportion of women among economic and political decision-makers at the local, national, regional and international levels reflects structural and attitudinal barriers that need to be addressed through positive measures." *Id.* ¶ 186.

97. *See* Bank Gender Group Report, *supra* note 11, at 15–16. In the area of agriculture, for example, the Bank argues that often, it is at the preliminary stage of overcoming governmental resistance and/or indifference to treating women as a constituency. In Central America and Mexico, the Bank has found that an institutional development approach that stresses the need to determine agricultural roles by gender as governments modernize their institutions is more acceptable than an equity approach, which can be threatening to cultural sensitivities. *Id.* at 15.

98. *See* Elson, *supra* note 14, at 43.

99. On the question of how far the Bank can influence a government's allocation of expenditures in the social sector, NGOs and women's groups have pointed out that when the

5. Uphold the commitments agreed upon by IFIs in the Beijing Platform for Action to minimize the adverse impact of lending programs on women.[100]

6. Make lending proposals public, with debates and seminars, to enable public participation.

7. Engender poverty assessments through greater utilization of time use studies and case studies on how women respond to adjustment efforts.[101]

8. Set conditionalities in the social sector, including time lines for governments to increase spending on health and education.

9. Improve monitoring and feedback mechanisms to include the welfare of women and children and the status of women in the household as some of the primary criteria by which the success and failure of policies will be judged.

10. Enable women's groups to bring complaints to the inspection panel.[102]

11. Given the differential and disproportionate adverse effect of development projects on the lives of women, the inspection panel should have at least one woman member on it. The panel's composition should also reflect a regional balance and diversity of individual expertise.[103]

12. Commit in principle and in practice to engage the bottom half of the population in growth by funding organizations, such as Women's World Banking, which have demonstrated the strength and viability of poor women's choices when it comes to control over economic resources. Micro enterprise lending gives the poor purchasing power, access to information on finance, business and legal services, and helps them build income, assets, and a voice

---

Bank is already interventionist, it should not be timid in intervening in favor of women. If structural adjustment is aimed at economic health and well-being, the health and education of women are critical elements that are not expendable. See BANK GENDER GROUP REPORT, *supra* note 11, at 16.

100. Paragraph 59(f) of the Beijing Platform for Action calls upon international financial institutions to "[r]eview the impact of structural adjustment programmes on social development by means of gender sensitive social impact assessments and other relevant methods, in order to develop policies to reduce their negative effects and improve their positive impact, ensuring that women do not bear a disproportionate burden of transition costs; [and] complement adjustment lending with enhanced, targeted social development lending." Beijing Platform for Action, *supra* note 4, ¶ 59(f).

101. *Recommendations of the External Gender Consultative Group* (Letter to World Bank President James D. Wolfensohn, 28 Aug. 1996); *see also* BANK GENDER GROUP REPORT, *supra* note 11, at 41–48.

102. *See also* Sparr, *supra* note 67, at 185–201.

103. THE WORLD BANK, THE WORLD BANK INSPECTION PANEL: ANALYSIS AND RECOMMENDATIONS FOR REVIEW: EXTENDED PAPER (Oxfam, Feb. 1996) (copy on file with author).

in decision making.[104] Despite clear evidence that low-income women are excellent borrowers and creditors, and that such initiatives promote bottom-up growth and genuine empowerment of women, there is little backing for them from the IFIs.

B.   Mobilizing Governments

1.   Governments must be held to their commitment in the Beijing Platform for Action. They must analyze their policies and programs from a gender perspective, especially those related to macroeconomic stability and structural adjustment with respect to the impact of these policies and programs on the poverty and inequality of women.[105] A policy, rather than a compensatory approach is essential because, despite the new orientation towards social measures within governments and international agencies, there is still all too little attention given to women's special needs and concerns.[106]

2.   Poverty alleviation remains the ultimate responsibility of the state and must be recognized as such by policymakers and NGOs who are increasingly being enlisted as vehicles of development. The growing role of NGOs in social development cannot be allowed to legitimize a reduction in the role of the state. As one experienced development scientist has put it:

> NGOs can act as pilots. The creative efforts of women can serve as a beacon light. However, it is the state and society which have to have the will to make room for the poor, to help them escape from the cycle of poverty through the use of their own capabilities and creativity.[107]

---

104. In India, for example, innovative and sustained lending to the Self-Employed Women's Association (SEWA) has enabled women to see themselves as economic actors and agents of change. *The Missing Links: Financial Systems that Work for the Majority,* Women's World Banking, Global Policy Forum, April 1995; *see also* Ela Bhatt, *Toward Empowerment,* 17 WORLD DEV. (1989).

105. Beijing Platform for Action, *supra* note 4, ¶ 58(b).

106. As the Commonwealth Expert Group noted:

> Any benefits women have attained from compensatory measures have been only incidental. They have not prevented devastating setbacks in crucial areas such as maternal and child health services, basic education and training, childcare, and the provision of credit, extension and other support services to help women as producers.

ENGENDERING ADJUSTMENT, *supra* note 7, at 8.

107. *See* Devaki Jain, *Letting the Worm Turn: A Comment on Innovative Poverty Alleviation, in* ASSESSING PARTICIPATORY DEVELOPMENT: RHETORIC VERSUS REALITY 80 (William P. Lineberry ed., 1989).

3. Poverty alleviation through income generating activities for women must take into account gender divisions of labor to ensure that they do not increase women's workload by making them responsible for household work as well as generating market income.

4. Make visible women's unpaid labor of reproduction and maintenance of human resources.[108] Women's domestic work should be included in the gross national product to evaluate the burden of women's unpaid work and to measure the impact of public policy on the gender divisions of labor and resources within the family.[109]

5. Re-examine and restructure public expenditure both between and within sectors to move basic services from high-cost areas to low-cost areas by improving targeting and cost effectiveness.[110] For example, eliminate user fees in public hospitals in poor urban and rural areas which affect women disproportionately.

6. Monitor health, nutrition, and income levels of poor men and women during the adjustment process to gauge the comparative effect of policies on human development.[111]

7. Generate gender disaggregated data in all categories of analysis. For example, it is not enough to count households as being male-headed or female-headed. In addition, it is necessary to examine gender asymmetries that affect decision making processes and distribution of resources within the household.[112]

8. Set up gender desks in all government ministries to enable the mainstreaming of gender concerns in the policy process. Women's ministries and bureaus not only tend to lack the resources, expertise, and political power to influence policymaking, but perpetuate compartmentalized approaches by treating women as a separate category.

---

108. *See* Diane Elson, *Overcoming Male Bias, in* MALE BIAS IN THE DEVELOPMENT PROCESS, *supra* note 7, at 191, 199.

109. Governments at the Beijing Women's Conference agreed to "conduct regular time-use studies to measure, in quantitative terms, unremunerated work . . . that is outside national accounts . . . and [to] accurately reflect its value in satellite or other official accounts." Beijing Platform for Action, *supra* note 4, ¶ 206(g)(i)–(ii). The consensus, in far more precise language than that achieved during the Women's Decade or the UN Social Summit in Copenhagen, broke through a deadlock of more than two years on the issue of measuring and valuing unwaged work. Since then, some countries, notably Denmark, Canada, New Zealand, and the United States, have made initial progress towards constructing satellite accounts to the gross national product. *See* WOMEN'S ENVIRONMENT AND DEVELOPMENT ORGANIZATION, BEYOND PROMISES: GOVERNMENTS IN MOTION ONE YEAR AFTER THE BEIJING WOMEN'S CONFERENCE (Sept. 1996).

110. *See* ADJUSTMENT WITH A HUMAN FACE, *supra* note 5, at 291.

111. *See id.*

112. *See* Elson, *supra* note 109, at 198.

C.   NGO Initiatives

1.   Enlist the principles of CEDAW and the ICESCR in particular, to lobby governments and IFIs to address the gender dimensions of economic reform.

2.   Work to bring about changes in gender-biased inheritance laws and property rights to increase women's access to productive resources.

3.   Oppose the deregulation of the labor market by states and transnational corporations who are abridging or abolishing labor laws and workers' industrial rights, especially the rights of women in free trade zones.[113]

4.   Establish collaborative accountability mechanisms, with NGOs in the North working with those in the South to identify major concerns and human rights violations arising out of SAPs so as to mobilize public opinion and lobby their governments, which are the chief donors to the IFIs.

5.   Set up agencies to monitor the extent to which the allocation of resources and funding priorities reflect gender-aware policies by governments and IFIs.[114]

6.   Organize public education and mobilization campaigns against the discriminatory and unfair labor practices employed by transnational corporations in developing countries. Challenge the failure of these non-state actors to observe human rights commitments made by their governments in treaties and declarations in domestic and international courts.

7.   Broaden the public ownership of gender initiatives by taking them out of the "women's arena." This is important not only to prevent gender advocates from being co-opted by politicians and vested interests, but also to demonstrate that greater integration of gender

---

113. A code of conduct for national, multinational, and transnational corporations to ensure workers' rights, comprehensive land reform to ensure equitable distribution of good land, and a global gender-equity social development fund financed by taxing international speculative financial flows were among the proposals submitted by the NGO, Development Alternatives with Women for a New Era (DAWN), at the Copenhagen Social Summit in 1995. *Rethinking Social Development: DAWN's Vision*, 23 WORLD DEV. 2003, 2003–04 (Nov. 1995) (special issue).

114. For example, the Women's Eyes on the World Bank Campaign, which arose out of a petition to the Bank president signed by nearly a thousand women during the Beijing Women's Conference, aims to hold the Bank accountable on gender equity by educating NGOs about the Bank's record in this area and mobilizing them to advocate for gender sensitive policies. At the national level, women's activists, researchers, and economists in South Africa have launched a women's budget initiative to examine the national budget through gendered eyes, comparing defense spending with that on health, education, and women's employment.

concerns in the policy process can lead to overall sustainable human development.

VII. CONCLUSIONS

The experiences of women as producers and reproducers, workers in industry and agriculture, wives, consumers, mothers, and crisis managers during adjustment programs show the unequal distribution of costs and benefits of SAPs. The gender-blind nature of neoclassical economic theory and gender biases inherent in societies and cultures have served to obscure the increased burdens imposed on women, which manifest themselves as deteriorating health and well-being in adjusting economies.

The differential impact of structural adjustment on women has just started to come to the attention of those who design and implement economic reform programs. This awareness is due in large part to the sustained work of feminist economists at both theoretical and empirical levels over the last two decades. Together with the focus on issues of gender and development in the international women's movement since the 1980s, this has led to a greater visibility accorded to these subjects in international forums, especially at the United Nations.

As a result, references to gender bias, gender neutrality, and gender responsiveness are now commonplace in Bank parlance and government statements on structural adjustment. However, there is still a tendency to conflate "gender" with "women," to view gender analysis as the categorizing of society into men and women. This limited understanding, combined with the pervasive faith in market driven growth as a solution to all inequities, has led to a set of add-on responses such as safety nets and poverty alleviation schemes.

While such measures are clearly necessary to offset the devastating impact of SAPs on the poor and women in the short term, they do not go to the root of the problem. The goal of gender advocacy is therefore to transform economic policymaking so that the human rights dimensions of SAPs are considered at the design stage of the programs and not as a postscript. Insofar as economic reform policies change the rights of women, the international financial institutions and governments are accountable to the human rights standards enshrined in various international and domestic covenants. As feminist economists and rights advocates have shown, SAPs do this by transferring burdens from the paid economy to the unpaid economy, exacerbating existing gender inequities in the household and the workplace, and worsening conditions of poverty and deprivation for women.

Gender advocacy in structural adjustment emphasizes that both human rights and sustainability are at stake in the economic reform process, which must aim not only at economic efficiency but economic justice. The overall negative social impact of adjustment in most countries is proof that policies that work to disenfranchise and marginalize one half of humanity cannot be sustainable in the long run. Having laid the ground for such debate, women's advocates must now build on the recent willingness shown by international financial institutions and some governments to address the gender dimensions of structural adjustment through greater involvement of women's representatives and other concerned sections of civil society. The emerging governance and human rights approaches at the lending institutions present real opportunities for policy reform and democratization of development through the principles of transparency, accountability, and participation. Today, there is a rhetorical consensus in all of these institutions about the need for equitable and gender-aware policies. The challenge lies in putting these principles into practice in order to realize the possibility of shared economic development for all.

In the final analysis, it is women's collective strength and creativity that remains the basis for transformative politics and development. Despite the severe setbacks and crises of the 1980s, women the world over have demonstrated their resilience and resourcefulness through a myriad of networks of grassroots movements as well as formal and informal lobbies. The emergence of this global coalition of women's NGOs who have created a significant political space and voice for themselves has been a positive outcome of the Women's Decade. Together and individually, these groups constitute a vibrant force that has grown in strength and sophistication during the 1990s. Through sustained feminist scholarship and unflagging activism, women's advocates have gained the authority and credibility to influence UN documents, and thereby some national governments and international financial institutions, to reflect gender and poverty concerns in economic policymaking. For the choice can no longer be between the state and the market: women have to organize to transform both patriarchal entities to be responsive to their needs.

PART V

Reproductive Rights

Chapter 17

Human Rights Dynamics
of Abortion Law Reform

Rebecca J. Cook and Bernard M. Dickens

I. INTRODUCTION

The purpose of this article is to address the modern human rights dynamics
of abortion law reform. The inspiration for reform varies among countries,
and often depends upon contextual factors peculiar to individual countries.
In some, abortion law reform is a function of respect for women's autonomy
and self-determination, while in others it is a response to demonstrated
public health dysfunctions of restrictive laws and health services. In yet
other countries, reform is addressed at the level of social justice and equality, or at the political level of rights of citizenship and democracy. Mounting
resistance to colonization and dictatorships, whether military, political, or
religious, is leading to increasingly widespread resistance to colonization
and dictatorship over women's bodies and reproductive choices. Respect
is growing for women's claims to reproductive rights as a necessary part of
citizenship.

The dynamics of reform have been aided, and occasionally triggered, by
richer varieties of pragmatic research in the social and public health sciences, and by the growing influence of feminist theories or explanations,
about law, social organization, and politics. The statistical and related data
have interacted with feminist explanations of the gendered nature of restrictive abortion laws and practices, to reveal the devastating impact on
women's lives of unsafe and unplanned pregnancy, and denial of access to
legal abortion services. In many countries of the world, women's alternative
to unsafe abortion is not safe pregnancy and childbirth, but predictable
complications during pregnancy resulting in maternal death or disability,
precluding or compromising women's ability to care for their dependent
children, and to live as full citizens.

The historical fashioning of restrictive abortion laws in Western countries, and their transmission and retention in other regions through patterns of European colonization, have resulted in an imbalance in their impact between economically developed and still developing countries. The World Health Organization (WHO) estimates that worldwide, approximately 20 million unsafe abortions occur every year, resulting in 78,000 deaths. Of these, an estimated 77,500 occur in developing countries.[1] While there has been a definite liberalization of abortion laws since 1950 in the developed world, this has not been the case in the developing world.[2] Unsafe abortion is particularly common in many countries with restrictive abortion laws, such as in Latin America.[3] It is estimated that every year approximately four million Latin American women undergo unsafe abortion, most of which are illegal.[4] In particular countries, hospital-based studies have specified the health impact of unsafe abortion, showing how urgent demands for treatment for abortion complications compromise routine maternity care where resources are scarce.[5]

The International Inter-agency Safe Motherhood Initiative,[6] beginning in the late 1980s and reinforced in the late 1990s,[7] has triggered growing international sensitivity to the burden in many countries, and to the universal injustice, of preventable pregnancy-related death, scientifically referred to as maternal mortality. The concept of reproductive health has emerged in relation to this Initiative, as a specific application of the concept of health itself. Health is described in the WHO Constitution as "a state of . . . physical, mental and social well-being." The concept of reproductive health has been internationally endorsed and legitimized through UN conferences, particularly the 1994 International Conference on Population and Development, held in Cairo,[8] and the 1995 Fourth World Conference on

1. World Health Organization (WHO), Unsafe Abortion: Global and Regional Estimates of Incidence of and Mortality Due to Unsafe Abortion with a Listing of Available Country Data 8 (1998).
2. The Allan Guttmacher Institute, Sharing Responsibility: Women Society & Abortion Worldwide 23 (1999).
3. John M. Paxman et al., The Clandestine Epidemic: The Practice of Unsafe Abortion in Latin America, 24 Stud. Fam. Plan. 205 (1994).
4. The Alan Guttmacher Institute, Clandestine Abortion: A Latin American Reality (1994) at 53, supra note 2.
5. See, e.g., Susan Checa & Martha I. Rosenberg, Aborto Hospitalizado: Un Problema de Salud Publica, Una Cuestion de Derechos Reproductiva (Hospitalized Abortion: A Public Health Problem, A Question of Reproductive Rights) (1996).
6. These agencies are of the World Health Organization, UNICEF, UNFPA, Population Council, International Planned Parenthood Federation, and Family Care International.
7. Anne Starrs, The Safe Motherhood Action Agenda: Priorities for the Next Decade: Report on the Safe Motherhood Technical Consultation 18–23 (1998).
8. Report of the International Conference on Population and Development, U.N. Doc. A/ Conf. 171/13 (1994) at ¶ 7.2 [hereinafter the Cairo Programme].

Women, held in Beijing.[9] This reproductive health concept was strengthened in subsequent five-year review conferences in 1999[10] and 2000[11] respectively. Both original and review conferences recognized the individual misfortune of unplanned pregnancy, and the aggravation of risks due to women's obstructed access to safe reproductive health care services, and women's common resort to abortions that are unsafe because of restrictions on procedures that can be undertaken in lawful, safe conditions.

Through the 1995 Beijing Conference and resulting Platform, 187 UN member states have gone beyond recognition of the individual risks of unsafe abortion, and adopted the commitment to "deal with the health impact of unsafe abortion as a major public health concern."[12] This article explains the history of abortion regulation through criminal law, and how such law has proven dysfunctional to the protection of reproductive health at the levels of both clinical and public health services. It addresses the significance of the concept of reproductive health, and how this fits into the wider framework of human rights to promotion of health and other interests that are the concern of the transcending human rights movement. The dynamic compelling consideration of abortion law reform is that criminalization of a practice that each year worldwide an estimated 20 million women seek in unsafe conditions denies their right to reproductive health in particular, and to respect for their human rights in general. The focus of concern arises, however, not just from the cumulative impact of 20 million cases, but from the risk posed to each individual woman.

Abortion laws have evolved through courts and human rights tribunals around the world interpreting human rights to recognize, and sometimes to deny, women's rights of access to abortion services and information. Courts and human rights tribunals among themselves often reflect different views on the legitimate use of law. One view is that law is an acceptable instrument to express and enforce the moral prohibition of abortion, by including criminal sanctions. Another view is that the demonstrable consequences of attempting to restrict abortion by the application of criminal sanctions are detrimental to women. They often compel continuation of pregnancies that

---

9. *Fourth World Conference on Women: Action for Equality, Development, and Peace, Beijing Declaration and Platform for Action,* U.N. Doc. A/CONF. 177/20 (1995) at ¶ 94 [hereinafter the *Beijing Platform*].

10. *Report of the Ad Hoc Committee of the Whole of the Twenty-first Special Session of the General Assembly-Overall review and appraisal of the implementation of the Programme of Action of the International Conference on Population and Development,* U.N. Doc. A/S-21/5/Add.1 (1999) [hereinafter *Cairo+5*].

11. *Report of the Ad Hoc Committee of the Whole of the Twenty-third Special Session of the General Assembly-Further Actions and Initiatives to Implement the Beijing Declaration and the Platform for Action,* U.N. Doc. A/S-23/10/Rev.1 (2000) [hereinafter *Beijing+5*].

12. *Beijing Platform, supra* note 9, ¶ 8.25.

cost women their lives or health, or lead to unskilled interventions in pregnancy that bear the same costs. Criminal sanctions are therefore rejected, on grounds of their dysfunctions.

Yet another view places abortion within a spectrum of services to which women should have safe access as a matter of human rights and of social justice in recognizing women as competent and conscientious decision-makers in their own lives.[13] Reproductive rights require that attention and respect be afforded the decisions of the approximately 20 million women each year who feel the need to resort to abortion even in unsafe circumstances.

Within the context of human rights, there are additional new ways beyond the framework of reproductive health of conceptualizing the problem of abortion. For example, the Committee on the Elimination of Discrimination against Women (CEDAW),[14] characterizes the refusal of medical procedures that only women require, such as abortion, as sex discrimination.[15] The growth of modern human rights law is founded on the claim that states are not sovereign to exercise unfettered intervention in their citizens' lives, but are accountable to transcending principles of human dignity that require their respect for individuals' rights. Accordingly, this assessment of evolving human rights dimensions of abortion laws and policies will consider human rights related to clinical abortion services, governmental responsibility for delivery and non-delivery of services, including preventive family planning services, and such related issues as the right to receive and impart information with regard to abortion.

Modern evolution of abortion law associates enforcement of repressive legislation with non-democratic governments and authoritarian religious institutions that are scornful of egalitarian "rights talk." They are fearful that women's achievement of their reproductive choices would subvert governmental and institutional pro-natalist policies, and are indifferent to the harmful impact of punitive measures on the lives of women and families. Legal approaches concerned to minimize harms to health from unplanned pregnancies accommodate abortion, but recognize how resourceful programs of sex education and family planning can reduce its incidence.

---

13. Rebecca J. Cook, Bernard M. Dickens & Laura E. Bliss, *International Developments in Abortion Law from 1988 to 1998,* 89 Am. J. Pub. Health 579 (1999).
14. The Convention on the Elimination of All Forms of Discrimination Against Women established the Committee as the treaty monitoring body to monitor state compliance with the treaty. The Convention on the Elimination of All Forms of Discrimination Against Women, *adopted* 18 Dec. 1979, G.A. Res. 34/180, U.N. GAOR 34th Sess., Supp. No. 44 at 193, U.N. Doc. A/34/36 (1980) *(entered into force* 3 Sept. 1981), *reprinted in* 19 I.L.M. 33 (1980) [hereinafter the Women's Convention].
15. Committee on the Elimination of Racial Discrimination, (CERD) Gen. Rec. 24: Women and Health, ¶¶ 11, 14, U.N. GAOR, 1999, U.N. Doc. A/54/38/Rev 1, 3–7.

Countries such as South Africa that have newly come to democracy based on an enfranchised electorate, where those who employ political power are accountable to the electorate, are taking initiatives to situate their abortion legislation within frameworks that implement principles of respect for women's human rights that are internationally recognized.

There are, of course, some modern democracies whose abortion laws remain expressed primarily in restrictive, criminally focused terms. Movement towards legal reform is not universal, and remains resisted within some democratic political establishments, particularly when leading members of their ruling elites and judiciaries are in thrall to religious authorities that have no commitment to democratic reform of conservative laws. However, experience over the last three decades shows an emerging trend of liberalization, although over the most recent decade this has been at a slower rate, and in some countries the trend is facing a backlash in restrictive legislation and court decisions,[16] and funding policies.

The backlash in funding policies is exemplified by US foreign aid policy conducted through the United States Agency for International Development. The policy restricts overseas non-governmental organizations that receive US aid from using their own private money to provide abortion services, to advocate for liberalizing change in their domestic law on abortion, or even to offer full and accurate medical information about legal abortion services to their patients. This policy, known as the Global Gag Rule, initially instituted under the Reagan administration,[17] and reinstated by President George W. Bush in January 2001,[18] undermines the ability of recipients to exercise free speech[19] and to participate in their own civil societies and democracies.

Legislatures and judiciaries respectful of women's views, including those that hear women's voices from within their own memberships, are progressively molding legislation and its interpretation sympathetically to

---

16. Rebecca J. Cook & Bernard M. Dickens, *A Decade of International Change in Abortion Law: 1967–1977*, 68 Am. J. Pub. Health, 637–44 (1978); Rebecca J. Cook & Bernard M. Dickens, *International Developments in Abortion Law: 1977–88*, 78 Am. J. Pub. Health 1305–11 (1988); Cook, Dickens & Bliss, *International Developments in Abortion Law from 1988 to 1998, supra* note 13.

17. Standard Provisions for US Grantees and US Subgrantees, *reprinted in* US Agency for International Development, 13 AID Handbook, 4C–45–50 (1985). This policy was announced by the Reagan administration at the 1984 Conference on Population and Development in Mexico City, and thus became known as the Mexico City Policy.

18. See 22 Jan. 2001 Presidential Memorandum and its implementing Memorandum, of 28 Mar. 2001-Restoration of the Mexico City Policy, 66 Fed. Reg. 61, at 17303 (29 Mar. 2001).

19. Center for Reproductive Law and Policy v. Bush, No. CIV.A.01-6168, 2002 WL 31045183 (D.NY.Sept. 13, 2002). U.S. Court of Appeals for the Second Circuit did not find this argument convincing.

women's interests in health, and in observance of human rights.[20] As women become equal citizens with men in their societies, it is anticipated that abortion concerns will evolve from placement within criminal or penal codes, to placement within health or public health legislation, and eventually to submergence within laws serving goals of human rights, social justice, and the individual dignity of control over one's own body.

II. CRIMINAL LAW

A. Abortion as a Crime

Historical systems of Western customary law, such as the Anglo-Saxon Common law, derived many offenses from religious concepts of sin, and treated deliberate termination of pregnancy as an offense. However, Common law considered pregnancy to begin only when it was first evidenced, through 'quickening'.[21] Evidence of quickening became available at a time that coincides in general with the end of the first trimester and beginning of the second trimester of pregnancy, that is at about the twelfth or thirteenth week of gestation.[22] Accordingly, absence of a single menstrual period or two consecutive periods was not legal evidence of pregnancy notwithstanding any medical practice to measure the length of gestation from the last menstrual period.

In the customary or Common law tradition, practices are legally permissible unless they violate a prohibitive provision of the law declared by a court or enacted by a legislature. Accordingly, abortion is permissible unless expressly prohibited. When English law changed in 1803 with legislation intended to protect women from "procuring a miscarriage" by seeking or self-administering any potentially harmful procedure, it made abortion both before and after quickening a crime, but only when undertaken "unlawfully." Following statutory amendments in 1828 and 1837, the offense was incorporated into the Offences Against the Person Act, 1861, section 58 of which remains the foundation of the abortion prohibition in many jurisdictions of the common law world and beyond. The section provides that:

---

20. European Parliament (Committee on Women's Rights and Equal Opportunities), Report on Sexual and Reproductive Health and Rights (6 June 2002).
21. Bernard M. Dickens, Abortion and the Law 20–28 (1966).
22. In 1973 the United States Supreme Court, in *Roe v. Wade,* 410 U.S. 113 (1973), looked to the law that existed at the time the United States Constitution was drafted at the end of the eighteenth century, and held that later legislation restricting abortion before the second trimester, that is before the historical time of quickening, violated women's constitutional rights, and that prohibition of second and third trimester abortion was subject to judicial scrutiny.

Every woman, being with child, who, with intent to procure her own miscarriage, shall unlawfully administer to herself any poison or other noxious thing, or shall unlawfully use any instrument or other means whatsoever with the like intent and whosoever, with intent to procure the miscarriage of any woman whether she be or be not with child, shall unlawfully administer to her or cause to be taken by her any poison or other noxious thing, or shall unlawfully use any instrument or other means whatsoever with the like intent, shall be guilty of felony.

Two developments in the understanding of this law warrant special attention. First, in 1869, the Roman Catholic Church redefined the mortal sin of abortion in its tradition to apply not simply from quickening, as before, but from conception. This reinforced the secular criminal law with religious support, and made defense of the criminal law a matter of concern to religious interests and institutions. Second, in 1938 in the widely influential *Bourne* case,[23] it was judicially determined that, under section 58 of the 1861 Act, there remained a category of lawful abortion. In *Bourne,* the judge directed the jury that a person would not act "unlawfully" for terminating a pregnancy in order to preserve a woman's life or her physical or mental health. The jury acquitted the defendant physician for terminating the pregnancy of a 15-year-old rape victim he feared would become "a mental wreck" by continuation of pregnancy and childbirth.

In systems of European codified law following the system of the Code Napoléon, where all rights must be contained within the framework of the Code, abortion has similarly tended to be addressed through penal or criminal provisions that reflect a religious sense of sin. Such codes tended not to address such issues as access to health services, and not to define rights of medical practice. Colonizing European countries in which the Roman Catholic Church was influential, such as France, Spain, and Portugal, have left a legacy of criminal prohibition of abortion in the laws of the countries they once dominated, such as in Africa and in Latin America. Thus, the modern history of abortion law has emphasized the criminal nature of the practice and the punishment of those who request and perform it. Criminal provisions have been invoked to support spiritual values inherent in unborn life, rather than to give explicit recognition to women's countervailing rights to protect their own lives or health endangered by continuation of pregnancy.

B. Evidence of Crime

Human reproduction is often viewed through a gendered lens that blames women both for a couple's infertility and for unplanned pregnancy. The

---

23. R. v. Bourne, 1 King's Bench 687 (Central Criminal Court, London, 1938).

punitive approach that mandates continuation of pregnancy a woman has voluntarily risked through sexual intercourse has persisted, despite its common cruelty and ignorance of the many circumstances in which women's capacity to resist spousal or other intercourse is so compromised as not to constitute their genuine choice. Nevertheless, many criminal laws that hold to this view recognize that rape, to which incest is often allied, is an exception that justifies abortion.

The gendered view remains, however, that womankind is disposed to seduction and deception of men, and that an allegation of rape is easily made and difficult to defend. Many claims remain legally inadmissible where courts deny that forced intercourse by a husband can in law constitute rape. Where rape can be claimed, demanding evidentiary standards have arisen to determine whether the admitted intercourse was rape, rather than sinful fornication or adultery. Standards of criminal evidence of rape have historically required the subject's contemporaneous complaint and signs of violent sexual penetration, forceful resistance, and even ejaculation. The justification of prompt invasive forensic testing of women alleging rape, which many have described as the second rape,[24] has been that the exception that justifies abortion must be applied only narrowly and strictly. The proportion of women who falsely allege that their pregnancy is due to rape is contentious, and depends in part on the credibility that societies attach to women's statements. Studies have identified that many women do not complain of rape, out of a sense of shame or future disadvantage to marriage prospects, or, for instance, fear of further violence. Similarly, women are often aware of the futility of contemporaneous complaint, such as when rape is perpetrated by men in positions of power or authority, such as police officers, jail guards, and priests.[25] They disclose the rape only later, upon evidence of pregnancy. As a matter of justice, however, no complaint justifies rejection for weakness of legally admissible evidence; that is, even a willfully deceptive complainant does not deserve corporal punishment by continued pregnancy and childbirth. A system of criminal law would fulfill its purposes by allowing prompt abortion on a woman's complaint, and applying its regular sanctions for deliberate falsehood. Sanctions include punishment for the offenses of knowingly making false reports to police or other officers, and of perjury in making false statements on oath. Offenses of making false claims in requests for abortion are analogous to obtaining an advantage by fraud or false pretenses.

---

24. Kathleen Kelly et al., *Insult to Injury? The Medical Investigation of Rape in England and Wales,* 20 (4) J. Soc. Welfare & Fam. L. 409, 410 (1998).
25. *See* Susan Estrich, Real Rape (1987) *quoted in* Lee Madigan & Nancy C. Gamble, The Second Rape: Society's Continued Betrayal of the Victim 3 (1991).

C. The Human Rights Violation of Forced Pregnancy

Criminal and penal law systems are becoming progressively enlightened by developments in human rights law. One expression is the recognition of domestic violence, and that women can suffer rape by nonconsensual intercourse committed by their husbands. Another is the admission of victim impact statements at criminal sentencing, when the trauma a rape victim suffered, including pregnancy and its termination, is relevant to a convicted offender's sentence. A further human rights development is in the human rights requirement of victim rehabilitation, by which legal systems must make efforts to restore victims of crimes and human rights violations to the status they would have enjoyed but for the violation they have been forced to endure. This is the principle according to which many prohibitive criminal abortion laws recognize rape as an exception. It is also the principle that recognizes the human rights violation constituted by criminal abortion laws that refuse or fail to accommodate a rape exception, and perpetuate women's victimization by compelling involuntary continuation of pregnancy. The *Beijing Platform* declares that:

> The human rights of women include their right to have control over and decide freely and responsibly on matters related to their sexuality, including sexual and reproductive health, free of coercion, discrimination and violence.[26]

It is accordingly a human rights infringement when women who have suffered the violation of rape are compelled to endure pregnancy against their will by the coercion of criminal sanctions. The Platform further condemns "torture...sexual slavery, rape, sexual abuse and forced pregnancy."[27] Forced pregnancy describes both forced initiation of pregnancy, and forced continuation of pregnancy. The Treaty of Rome constituting the jurisdiction of the International Criminal Court similarly recognizes forced pregnancy as a crime against humanity.[28] This was in reaction to preceding evidence, presented before tribunals addressing humanitarian outrages in conflicts in the former Yugoslavia and Rwanda, of systematic rape as part of "ethnic cleansing," when women pregnant by rape were denied abortion due to religious influence. Countries with criminal laws that do not permit abortion for rape recognized their vulnerability to condemnation for perpetrating forced pregnancy, and joined the Treaty only upon the acceptance of Treaty language providing that their legislation does not violate the Treaty. Nevertheless, human rights treaty monitoring bodies have identified the

---

26. *Beijing Platform, supra* note 9, ¶ 96.
27. *Beijing Platform, supra* note 9, ¶ 135.
28. Rome Statute on the International Criminal Court, U.N. Doc. A/Conf. 183/9 (1998), *reprinted in* 37 I.L.M. 999 (1998), art. 7(1)(g).

inconsistency between human rights principles and criminal abortion laws that have no explicit exception that allows lawful abortion on complaints of rape.

Recognition of forced pregnancy, however initiated, exposes the coercion women suffer to continue pregnancies against their will, by criminal laws and other means, as a human rights violation.[29] This is analogous to rape and sexual abuse. The Chief Justice of Canada, in a majority judgment holding Canada's restrictive criminal abortion law unconstitutional and inoperative, observed in 1988 that:

> Forcing a woman, by threat of criminal sanction, to carry a foetus to term unless she meets certain criteria unrelated to her own priorities and aspirations, is a profound interference with a woman's body and thus a violation of security of the person.[30]

This re-conceptualization of criminal abortion laws as human rights violations when they deny women's choice shows that restrictive laws and governmental policies can be as disrespectful of women's wishes, interests, health, and bodily integrity as are rapists. Those who support and enforce such laws and policies similarly enforce their will upon women by their power of domination, in order to advance their own social, spiritual, or other purposes.

III. HEALTH AND WELFARE

A. The Comprehensive Reproductive Health Framework

Modern thinking on abortion law directs policy and legislation away from the historical preoccupation with criminalization and punishment, towards the protection and promotion of women's health and prevention of unsafe abortion. Particularly significant is the comprehensive framework of reproductive health that was endorsed and legitimized in 1994, through the *Cairo Programme*'s adoption by 184 UN Member States. The Programme recognizes the importance of human rights in protection and promotion of reproductive health.[31] Building on the World Health Organization's definition of health, the *Cairo Programme* explains that reproductive health is

> [A] state of complete physical, mental and social well-being and is not merely the absence of disease or infirmity, in all matters relating to the reproductive system and to its functions and processes. Reproductive health therefore implies

---

29. Jed Rubenfeld, *The Right of Privacy,* 102 HARV L. REV. 737 (Feb. 1989).
30. R. v. Morgentaler v. The Queen 44 D.L.R.(4th) 385, at 402 (1998).
31. *Cairo Programme, supra* note 8, ¶ 7.2 (1994).

that people are able to have a satisfying and safe sex life and that they have the capability to reproduce and the freedom to decide if, when and how often to do so. Implicit in this last condition are the right of men and women to be informed and to have access to safe, effective, affordable and acceptable methods of family planning of their choice, as well as other methods of their choice for regulation of fertility which are not against the law, and the right of access to appropriate health-care services that will enable women to go safely through pregnancy and childbirth and provide couples with the best chance of having a healthy infant.[32]

At Cairo, governments agreed to take steps to

[M]ake it easier for couples and individuals to take responsibility for their own reproductive health by removing unnecessary legal, medical, clinical and regulatory barriers to information and to access to family-planning services and methods.[33]

Some governments took steps to reform their restrictive abortion legislation with little delay, to serve these wider reproductive health interests. For instance, Guyana enacted the Medical Termination of Pregnancy Act 1995, which is expressly based on women's needs for safe health services. The long title of the Act describes it as:

An Act to reform the law relating to medical terminations of pregnancies, to enhance the dignity and sanctity of life by reducing the incidence of induced abortion, [and] to enhance the attainment of safe motherhood by eliminating deaths and complications due to unsafe abortion.

Similarly, the Preamble to South Africa's Choice on Termination of Pregnancy Act, 1997 recognizes the constitutional right of persons "to make decisions concerning reproduction and to security in and control over their bodies" (¶ 2), and that:

[T]he decision to have children is fundamental to women's physical, psychological and social health and that universal access to reproductive health care services includes family planning and contraception, termination of pregnancy, as well as sexuality education and counseling programs and services. (¶ 4)

The *Cairo Programme* emphasizes that:

In no case should abortion be promoted as a method of family planning. All governments and relevant intergovernmental and non-governmental organizations are urged to strengthen their commitment to women's health ... to reduce the recourse to abortion through expanded and improved family-planning services. Prevention of unwanted pregnancies must always be given

---

32. *Id.* ¶ 7.2.
33. *Cairo Programme, supra* note 8, ¶ 7.20.

the highest priority and every attempt should be made to eliminate the need for abortion.[34]

Despite the unanimity of agreement that prevention of unwanted pregnancy should "be given the highest priority," approximately one in six women of reproductive age throughout the world, nearly 230 million women, lack the means to achieve their child bearing goals.[35] The gap between the number of children women want and actually have remains sizeable. The proportion of births that are actually wanted ranges from 60 percent in Egypt and 50 percent in Mexico, to 40 percent in Kenya.[36] Of the estimated 190 million pregnancies that occur worldwide each year, 51 million end in abortion, including 21 million in countries where abortion is legally restricted.

Where laws accommodate abortion but countries' lack of resources leave them dependent on overseas support for services, restrictive funding policies can also be sources of avoidable harm. For instance, the executive director of the UN Population Fund (UNFPA) has estimated that the July 2002 decision of the US government to withhold UNFPA funding would be detrimental, if not made up from other sources, since the

> US$34 million [withheld] for reproductive health and family planning would be enough to prevent: 2 million unwanted pregnancies, nearly 800,000 induced abortions, 4,700 maternal deaths, nearly 60,000 cases of serious maternal illness, and over 77,000 infant and child deaths.[37]

B.   Legal Reproductive Health Care

The primary thrusts of reproductive health care are prevention of unwanted pregnancy and promotion of wanted pregnancy and safe childbirth, such as by methods of family planning and prevention of infertility respectively. The goal of safe lawful termination of pregnancy is only complementary to avoidance of unwanted pregnancy, arising for instance on failure of the preferred family planning alternative. However, where local law addresses abortion only through its criminal provisions, many health care providers,

34. *Id.* ¶ 8.25. The *Cairo+5* Conference reiterated that "[g]overnments should take appropriate steps to help women avoid abortion, which in no case should be promoted as a method of family planning." *Cairo+5, supra* note 10, ¶ 63.
35. ALAN GUTTMACHER INSTITUTE (AGI), HOPES AND REALITIES: CLOSING THE GAP BETWEEN WOMEN'S ASPIRATIONS AND THEIR REPRODUCTIVE REALITIES 39 (1995).
36. AGI, *id.* at 24.
37. Michael McCarthy, *USA Bars Funds Slated for UN Population Fund,* 360 THE LANCET 313 (2002).

including obstetricians/gynecologists and other medically qualified practitioners, often presume that every abortion is axiomatically unlawful.
Further, some medically unqualified health care providers confuse family
planning with abortion services. The confusion may be influenced by reac-
tionary groups and institutions, many of which are as opposed to contraception and sterilization as to abortion. They deliberately conflate family
planning services with abortion for the purpose of attaching the stigma they
perceive in abortion to family planning methods in general. Conflation and
stigmatization have been successful in the U.S. where President Reagan's
restrictive 1985 "Mexico City Policy," restored in January, 2001 and now
known as the Global Gag Rule, prohibited funding the provision of "advice
that abortion is an available option in the event *other* methods of family
planning are not used or are not successful."[38]

Many countries have deliberately liberalized their abortion laws in
recent decades,[39] so that women and health care providers approach these
procedures according to their personal ethical judgment, not in the context
of potential crime. Nevertheless, where there are no explicit legal provisions
for conduct of abortion, many women and health care providers presume
illegality. The lack of clarity in many laws is a serious dysfunction, because
too often it results in preventable death. Health care providers' apprehen-
sions cause them to decline involvement, so that women resort to illegal and
unsafe practices in cases where the law actually allows procedures by
skilled, qualified providers. No law precludes abortion undertaken in the
honest belief that it is necessary to save a woman's life. Further, where legislation prohibits abortion undertaken "unlawfully," courts widely acknowledge that a procedure to preserve a woman's physical or mental health
against serious threat is lawful.[40] A contribution that lawyers can make to
reproductive health is to clarify the scope of abortion that is lawful within
their jurisdictions, and inform governments, health care providers, and the
general public of services that can be lawfully provided.

Even where women resort to abortion illegally, their right to health care
entitles them to proper post-abortion treatment. The 1999 *Cairo+5*
Conference does not distinguish legal from illegal abortion in providing that
"[g]overnments should . . . in all cases provide for the humane treatment
and counseling of women who have had recourse to abortion."[41]

---

38. Standard Provisions, *supra* note 17, at 4C–46 (d) (1) A II (emphasis added).
39. Cook, Dickens & Bliss, *International Developments in Abortion Law from 1988 to 1998,*
    supra note 13; Cook & Dickens, *A Decade of International Change in Abortion Law:*
    1977–88, supra note 16.
40. R. v. Bourne, 1 King's Bench 687 (Central Criminal Court, London, 1938).
41. *Cairo+5, supra* note 10, ¶ 63 (ii).

C.　Safe and Accessible Abortion Services

By Article 12 (1) of the International Covenant on Economic, Social and Cultural Rights[42] (the Economic Covenant), member states recognize "the right of everyone to the enjoyment of the highest attainable standard of physical and mental health." In monitoring the Covenant, the Committee on Economic, Social and Cultural Rights has developed General Comment 14 on the Right to Health, which explains that the right requires the following interrelated features of health care services, namely their:

— availability (health care services have to be available in sufficient quantity);
— accessibility (services, including information, have to be physically and economically accessible to everyone without discrimination);
— acceptability (services have to be culturally appropriate, that is, respectful of the cultures of individuals, minorities and communities, and sensitive to gender and life-cycle requirements); and
— adequate quality (services have to be scientifically appropriate and of sufficient quality).[43]

Laws and policies that unreasonably restrict safe abortion services would not comply with this performance standard. For instance, a law or policy requiring unnecessarily high qualifications for health service providers will limit the availability of safe abortion services. Such policies may be proposed in good faith in order to ensure excellence in health care. However, it is poor public health policy, and may be a human rights violation, to jeopardize health care by requiring standards that prevent delivery of medically indicated services.

Recognizing the right to health services, governments agreed through the *Cairo Programme* that:

> In circumstances where abortion is not against the law, such abortion should be safe. In all cases women should have access to quality services for the management of complications arising from abortion. Post-abortion counseling, education and family-planning services should be offered promptly, which will also help to avoid repeat abortions.[44]

The *Cairo Programme*'s promotion of reproductive health endorsed only "methods . . . for the regulation of fertility which are not against the law,"

---

42. The International Covenant on Economic, Social and Cultural Rights, *adopted* 16 Dec. 1966, G.A. Res. 2200 (XXI), U.N. GAOR 21st Sess. Supp. No. 16, at 49, U.N. Doc A/ 6316 (1966), 993 U.N.T.S. 3 *(entered into force* 3 Jan. 1976) [hereinafter the Economic Covenant].

43. *General Comment on Article 12,* General Comment No. 14 UN CEDSCR Comm. Econ., Soc. & Cultural Rts., 22d Sess., at ¶ 12, UN Doc. E/C.12/2000/4 (2000).

44. *Cairo Programme, supra* note 8, ¶ 8.25.

since a UN Conference would not endorse an act that is criminal under a country's law, including criminal abortion. Abortions that are lawful to preserve women's lives, or to preserve their physical or mental health against serious risks should, however, be available. The *Cairo Programme* provides that "in circumstances where abortion is not against the law, health systems should train and equip health-service providers . . . to ensure that such abortion is safe and accessible. Additional measures should be taken to safeguard women's health."[45]

Governments should therefore require health service providers to be adequately trained and equipped to deliver safe services. The World Health Organization is working to provide technical and policy guidance to governments to ensure safe and accessible abortion services.[46]

Laws and policies designed to limit information about safe abortion techniques and training of non-physicians in their use, in order to preserve the deterrent effect on women of the dangers of unlawful abortion, offend legal and humanitarian provisions against cruel and unusual punishment. Further, there is a denial of human rights when post-abortion care to avoid repeat abortions is obstructed. This can be due to unavailability or inaccessibility of lawful services, so that women can avail themselves only of clandestine, unskilled abortion services that are delivered without their education for future avoidance.

D.   Unsafe Abortion and Maternal Mortality

The World Health Organization (WHO) defines "unsafe abortion" as: "a procedure for terminating an unwanted pregnancy either by persons lacking the necessary skills or in an environment lacking the minimal medical standards, or both."[47]

An "unwanted pregnancy" can be unwanted at its outset, such as when due to inaccessible or failed family planning or rape, or can become unwanted when a woman finds that it presents an unacceptable risk to her life or health. Opponents of abortion choice sometimes claim that pregnancy is never "unwanted," because, even though a woman may not want her pregnancy, her family, society, or government does. The claim that women should be compelled against their will to serve the wants of others is an instrumental denial of their human dignity and an abuse of their reproductive capacities.

Maternal mortality, perhaps better understood in non-medical language as pregnancy-related death, includes deaths due to unsafe abortion, as well

---

45. *Cairo+5, supra* note 10, ¶ 63 (iii).
46. WHO, Safe Abortion: Technical and Policy Guidance for Health Systems (forthcoming 2002).
47. *Id.* at 3.

as death to women in and following childbirth. WHO defines maternal death as:

> [T]he death of a woman while pregnant or within 42 days of termination of pregnancy, irrespective of the duration and site of the pregnancy, from any cause related to or aggravated by the pregnancy but not from accidental or incidental causes or its management.[48]

Accordingly, death to "a woman while pregnant . . . irrespective of the duration . . . of the pregnancy" caused by an unskilled abortion is classified as a maternal death, as is death within forty-two days following abortion due to related complications.

Estimates of maternal deaths vary, depending on the sophistication of calculation, the time period of measurement, and classification practices. Calculation is difficult in countries that have no official registration of numbers or causes of deaths. However, an authoritative estimate of 1995 figures is that the annual toll was 515,000 maternal deaths worldwide, an average rate of over 1,400 deaths each day.[49] In 1994, WHO estimated that worldwide, about 13 percent of the 515,000 pregnancy-related deaths, almost 67,000, were due to unsafe abortion.[50] A 1997 WHO report estimating unsafe abortion presented a total of about 78,000 resulting deaths.[51] The percentage of maternal deaths due to unsafe abortion will vary according to the circumstances in each country. Beyond the deaths due to unsafe abortion are the incalculable health consequences and disabilities, such as infertility resulting from unskilled abortion.

A high-risk pregnancy may be attributable to a predisposing risk factor, such as a woman's physical condition or disease. A predisposing risk factor, for example, may be an adolescent's pelvic underdevelopment due to malnutrition. Medical research has shown that pregnancy aggravates and is aggravated by diseases such as malaria, hepatitis, sexually transmitted infections including HIV/AIDS, anemia including sickle cell anemia, jaundice, tuberculosis, and heart disease. Sickle cell anemia, for example, makes pregnancy and childbirth very risky, painful, and difficult. If a pregnant woman dies of such a disease or condition, the death is classified as an indirect maternal death. The risk of death during pregnancy, aggravated by these indirect medical causes, can be greatly reduced by safe abortion even though abortion will not reduce the more general risks associated with these diseases. If proper abortion care fails to save the life of a woman suffering a predisposing risk factor, the death is not due to "unsafe abortion."

---

48. WHO, The Tenth Revision of the International Classification of Diseases (ICD–10) (1992).
49. Id.
50. WHO, United Nations Children's Fund and United Nations Population Fund, Maternal Mortality in 1995: Estimates Developed by WHO, UNICEF and UNFPA (2001).
51. WHO, Unsafe Abortion Report, supra note 1 at 8.

In developing country settings, studies indicate that 20 percent or more of all maternal deaths are due to indirect causes.[52] The percentage varies among countries, depending upon the prevalence and severity of the diseases that are the indirect medical causes. Moreover, these diseases and conditions are more prevalent in some subgroups of women than others. For example, sickle cell anemia is common in Black women.[53] As a result, the rates at which therapeutic abortion is medically justified will vary according to the prevalence and severity of such diseases and risk factors.

E. The Public Health Setting

Each instance of a woman's death or disability due to unsafe abortion is lamentable and represents a failure, whether of prevention and control of unplanned pregnancy, access to medical care or, for instance, human rights protection. The *Beijing Platform* placed unsafe abortion on an additional plane, however, in requiring that governments "deal with the health impact of unsafe abortion as a major public health concern."[54] The public health approach opens a middle path between clinical health care based particularly on human reproductive physiology, and refined philosophical speculation that addresses such historical issues as the moral and spiritual status of human embryos and modern issues in feminist scholarship and analysis. The new approach opens a way, which parallels the growth of evidence-based clinical medicine, towards evidence-based social policy founded on public health sciences. These include epidemiology, which addresses the study of epidemics not limited to diseases, but including such phenomena as unplanned pregnancy and resort to abortion, and sociological studies of communal impacts, attitudes, behaviors, and motivations.

For instance, public health studies can identify the impact on a community hospital of coping with the needs of women suffering complications from unsafe abortion. Such studies can also show the negative impact on other women's access to public hospital services for routine prenatal care and management of mothers and children at and following complicated deliveries, and other patients' access to general emergency care. Studies can also test whether restrictive laws prevent abortions or simply direct women to unskilled providers and women's self-administered interventions, and whether liberalized laws induce couples to be casual regarding use of family planning alternatives, or reduce the communal incidence of pregnancy-related mortality and morbidity.

---

52. *Id.* at 119.

53. Mahmoud F. Fathalia, From Obstetrics and Gynecology to Women's Health, 93 (1997).

54. *Beijing Platform, supra* note 9, ¶ 106 (j).

International experience discloses several public health and social science studies that illuminate how the operation of laws has affected the incidence of abortion and access to safe services. For instance, the health
consequences of liberalized abortion laws, and the health costs to women
of repressive abortion laws, are most clearly demonstrated in data from
Romania. Legislation that took effect in 1990 reversed the severely repressive law that the former administration introduced in 1966. During the quar-
ter century of pro-natalist policies, abortion-related maternal deaths per
100,000 live births rose from under 20 in 1965 to between 120 and 150
each year between 1982 and 1989. As a percentage of maternal deaths from
all causes, abortion-related deaths rose from about 20 percent to nearly 90
percent over that period. The rate of maternal mortality, which in 1966 was
comparable to that of most other Eastern European countries, was at least
ten times higher than in any other European country by 1989. In contrast, in
the year following legalization of abortion, the maternal mortality rate fell
almost 50 percent.[55] The statistics show how restrictive abortion laws can
cost countless women their right to life.

In 1988, the Supreme Court of Canada reviewed a social science study
commissioned by the government on the operation of the prevailing abortion law.[56] The government initiated this law in 1969, claiming that its provisions would serve women's needs for safe access to therapeutic services.
The provisions introduced in 1969, which were in the Criminal Code, identified hospitals that were eligible to perform lawful procedures, on condition
of approval by hospital therapeutic abortion committees composed of at
least three doctors. On review of the actual availability of services between
1969 and 1977, the Court observed that no eligible hospital or health facility in the country had any legal duty to establish such a committee. One
province has no hospital with a committee, and 40 percent of Canadian
women lived outside areas whose hospitals were eligible to establish committees. The Court reviewed evidence that many eligible hospitals with
committees refused to treat women who resided outside their catchment
areas, and some maintained restrictive quotas for those who lived inside.
These included the larger university-affiliated teaching hospitals in major
population centers, which felt obliged to offer students a full variety of different exposures to gynecological practice. Several hospitals with committees included non-physician members opposed to abortion, such as hospital
chaplains, and approved few if any applications.

---

55. Charlotte Hord et al., *Reproductive Health in Romania: Reversing the Ceausescu Legacy*,
    22 STUD. FAM. PLAN. 231 (1991).
56. CANADA, REPORT OF THE COMMITTEE ON THE OPERATION OF THE ABORTION LAW (chaired by Robin F.
    Badgley) (1997) [hereinafter the Badgley Report].

The Court found that overall, abortion services indicated on health grounds were inequitably restricted, and often harmfully delayed into the second trimester of pregnancy, so obstructing women's right to timely health services and therefore to security of the person guaranteed by the constitution. The Court struck down the Criminal Code abortion provisions as deceptive in their claim to protect women's health, and unconstitutional.[57] They have not been replaced, in deference to women's right to health care and for apprehension that public health studies would again demonstrate the dysfunction and injustice of approaching therapeutic health care through exemptions from criminal laws.

IV. HUMAN RIGHTS, HUMAN DIGNITY, AND SOCIAL JUSTICE

The most recent stage in evaluation of abortion laws, motivated by human rights considerations, has been implicit in the concept of reproductive health, because the right to the highest attainable standard of health, of which reproductive health is part, is central to the protection and promotion of human rights. In practice, human rights are interrelated and interdependent, since a violation of any one is frequently a violation of another. Indeed, the very conventions that express these rights are themselves interrelated. Not only individual rights but also the national constitutions and international conventions that express them may be permeable. Human rights tribunals hearing complaints of discrimination under one human rights convention may consider whether there has been discrimination with respect to rights protected in other conventions.[58]

Particularly relevant to reproductive health and self-determination are rights relating to: life, liberty, and dignity; non-discrimination and due respect for difference; and citizenship. These rights are progressively being applied to the special circumstances of women, who for obvious physiological reasons bear the overwhelming burden of unplanned pregnancy and who, in protection of their lives and health in many parts of the world, most directly confront restrictive abortion laws and policies. The development of the content and meaning of these rights in the context of abortion can vary, especially given the distinct cultural and political approaches to sex and gender.[59]

---

57. R. v. Morgentaler v. The Queen 44 D.L.R. (4th) 385, at 402 (1998).
58. Broeks v. The Netherlands, Communications No. 172/1984, U.N. GAOR, 42nd Sess., Supp. No. 40 at 139, U.N. Doc. A/42/40 (1987).
59. Antoinette Sedillo Lopez, *Comparative Analysis of Women's Issues: Toward a Contextualized Methodology, in* Global Critical Race Feminism 67–80 (Adrien K. Wing ed., 2000).

A.   Life, Liberty, and Dignity

1.   Life and survival

The right to life has been invoked to support opposing claims, some on behalf of embryos and fetuses and others on behalf of women, although these rights are not necessarily in opposition, and usually coincide in the case of planned pregnancy. In controversies over abortion, courts often distinguish moral and spiritual claims made on behalf of unborn children from the legal claims they uphold on behalf of pregnant women, but some legislation explicitly recognizes legal claims made on behalf of prenatal life. Moreover, some courts recognize interests of the state itself in prenatal life, and some consider these interests potentially superior to the interests of a pregnant woman. However, courts invariably interpret laws to provide that women's interests prevail when continuation of pregnancy endangers their lives. In 1992, for instance, the Irish Supreme Court held that the equal rights to life of a pregnant woman and her fetus, set out in the Irish Constitution, must be balanced to permit abortion when necessary to protect the woman's life.[60]

a.   Legal protection of life from conception or birth

Everyone may legitimately claim respect for and protection of their human rights between complete live birth and death. Strongly contested, however, is whether the same claim may be made on behalf of a fertilized ovum from conception. In parts of the world, the contest has been particularly animated since 1869, when the Roman Catholic Church adopted the view that human life warrants full protection from conception.[61] Historical law has not recognized this claim.

The highest courts in many countries have declared that legal protection of human beings originates at live birth. In the Anglo-Saxon common law tradition, a child does not become a human "in being" (that is, a "human being" or "person") until it has completely proceeded in a living state from the body of its mother.[62] International human rights tribunals also generally adhere to the "born alive" rule, according to which a claim may be pursued for prenatal injury only on condition that the fetus is born alive.

Several national courts have held that their permissive abortion laws are compatible with the right to life provisions of either the European

---

60. The Attorney General v. X and Others, [1992] 1 IR 1 (Ir.S.C.) 54–55.
61. J. Kenyon Mason, Medico-Legal Aspects of Reproduction and Parenthood, 2 ed. 1998 at 109.
62. Rebecca J. Cook, *International Protection of Women's Reproductive Rights,* J. of Int'l Law and Politics 24(2) 645, 688–96 (1992).

Convention on Human Rights[63] (the European Convention) or the International Covenant on Civil and Political Rights[64] (the Political Covenant), and sometimes both. The French Conseil d'État held that France's liberal abortion law, which permits therapeutic abortion in broadly defined terms including a woman's distress, is compatible with the right to life articles of the European Convention (Article 2) and the Political Covenant (Article 6).[65] A Dutch court has also upheld the similar Dutch abortion law on the same grounds.[66] The Constitutional Court of Austria, in upholding the Austrian Penal Code provision permitting abortion on request during the first trimester of pregnancy and on specified grounds thereafter, interpreted Article 2 of the European Convention not to recognize a right to life before live birth.[67]

The European Commission respected this interpretation in upholding the British Abortion Act, 1967,[68] as have subsequent courts in several European countries.[69] The Commission found it contrary to the object and purpose of the European Convention that the right to life of the person already born would be considered subject to limitation in favor of the unborn. The British Abortion Act, 1967 accommodates abortion on grounds of the woman's life or health, and when continuance of pregnancy would injure the physical or mental health of the pregnant woman's existing children. The Commission did not find it necessary to decide whether Article 2 of the European Convention recognizes a "right to life" of a fetus, although subject to limitations.

The question remains, however, whether a pregnant woman's rights can be limited by the interest of the state itself in unborn human life. Attorneys General, Ministers of Justice, and other state officers, such as police officers, may initiate legal proceedings, for judicial declarations or against women and those who perform abortion, to defend the public or state interest they claim exists in human life *in utero*.

It is generally recognized that international human rights conventions are not applicable before birth of a human being. During the preparatory

---

63. European Convention for the Protection of Human Rights and Fundamental Freedoms *(opened for signature* 4 Nov. 1950), 213 U.N.T.S. 221 *(entered into force* 3 Sept. 1953) [hereinafter the European Convention].
64. International Covenant on Civil and Political Rights, G.A. Res. 2200 (XXI), 21 U.N. GAOR Supp. (No. 16) at 52, U.N. Doc. A/6316 (1966), 999 U.N.T.S. 171 *(entered into force* 23 Mar. 1976) [hereinafter the Political Covenant].
65. Judgment of 21 Dec. 1990, 7 Revue Francaise de Droit Administratif 208 (1991).
66. Juristenvereniging Pro Vita v. De Staat der Nederlanden *(Ministerie van Welzijn, Voldsgezondheid en Cultuur)* [1990] NJ 2986 (8 Feb. 1990) (The Court, The Hague).
67. Judgment of 11 Oct. 1974, Erklrungen des Verfassungsgerichtshofs 221 (Constitutional Court of Austria).
68. Paton v. United Kingdom, 3 E.H.R.R. 408 (1980) (Eur. Comm'n Hum. Rts.).
69. Principles of Medical Law 643–44 (Ian Kennedy & Andrew Grubb eds., 1998).

debates on the Political Covenant, for instance, amendments that were proposed to protect the right to life from the moment of conception were
rejected,[70] and Article 6 (1), addressing the right of every "human being," is
understood in this light. When the Convention on the Rights of the Child[71]
(the Children's Convention) was being drafted, the same question was
debated. The outcome appears in the Preamble to the Convention, which
invokes language in the Declaration that preceded the Convention.[72] The
Preamble "[Bears] in mind that, as indicated in the Declaration of the Rights
of the Child, 'the child, by reason of his physical and mental immaturity,
needs special safeguards and care, including appropriate legal protection,
before as well as after birth.' "[73]

However, Article 1 provides that, for purposes of the Convention, "a
child means every human being below the age of eighteen years unless,
under the law applicable to the child, majority is attained earlier."
Accordingly, the enforceable provisions of the Convention are widely
understood to retain the historical understanding that legally protected status as a human being begins at live birth.

The Convention gives no guidance to what the Preamble means by
"appropriate legal protection, before as well as after birth." Such protection
might include provision of reasonable prenatal care, nutrition and essential
obstetric care to ensure safety in delivery and care for the newborn.[74]
However, not all states whose laws require protection of human life from
conception accept their own legal obligation to provide resources for these
purposes.

The American Convention on Human Rights[75] (the American
Convention) provides that the right to respect for life "shall be protected by
law and, in general, from the moment of conception."[76] The words "in general" indicate that the Convention does not necessarily give priority to
unborn life over the life or health of born persons, since protection of prenatal life does not clearly withdraw protections from born persons. The pro-

---

70. Maxime Tardu, *Relationship Between Human Rights and Population Issues in United
    Nations, in* UNITED NATIONS, POPULATION AND HUMAN RIGHTS 54, 61 (1990).
71. Convention on the Rights of the Child *(adopted* 20 Nov. 1989), G.A. Res. 44/25 U.N.
    GAOR, 44th Sess., Supp. No. 49 at 167, U.N. Doc. A/44/49 (1989) *(entered into force* 2
    Sept. 1990) [hereinafter the Children's Convention].
72. Declaration of the Rights of the Child, G.A. res. 1386 (XIV), 14 U.N. GAOR Supp. (No.
    16) at 19, U.N. Doc. A/4354 (1989).
73. Children's Convention, *supra* note 71, at Preambular ¶ 9.
74. SAVE THE CHILDREN, STATE OF THE WORLD'S NEWBORNS (2001).
75. American Convention on Human Rights, *signed* 22 Nov. 1969, O.A.S. T.S. No. 36, O.A.S.
    Off. Rec. OEA/Ser.LV/II.23 doc.21 rev. 6 at 25 (1979) *(entered into force* 18 July 1978),
    reprinted in Basic Documents Pertaining to Human Rights in the Inter-American System
    (1992) [hereinafter the American Convention].
76. *Id.* art. 4 (emphasis added).

vision in the Convention may require protection of unborn life against injuries, for instance, that would impair the life of a human being, but not necessarily limit abortion to preserve the life or health of a woman, or indeed of other children in her family.

In contrast, the American Declaration on the Rights and Duties of Man[77] does not address unborn life. It recognizes the right to life of every "human being." The Declaration begins its Preamble with the observation that "All men are born free and equal," suggesting that freedom and equality are conditional on live birth. In 1981, the Inter-American Commission on Human Rights held the American Declaration inapplicable to the unborn, and determined that the 1973 US Supreme Court decision in *Roe v. Wade*,[78] which recognized women's constitutional right to abortion before fetal viability, was compatible with the Declaration.[79]

Courts often observe that their task is to interpret the law in accordance with their legal traditions, and not to engage in moral or spiritual discourse. For instance in 1997, finding that its state Civil Code, which gives rights to a "person," awards no legal personality to a fetus, the Louisiana Supreme Court observed that this refusal

> constitutes no moral or philosophical judgment on the value of the fetus, nor any comment on its essential humanity. Rather, the classification of "person" is made solely for the purpose of facilitating determinations about the attachment of legal rights and duties. "Person" is a term of art.[80]

In South Africa, the 1996 Constitution provides in section 11 that "everyone has the right to life," but a year later, the country enacted the liberal Choice on Termination of Pregnancy Act. The Minister of Health was sued for declarations that the Act is unconstitutional, on grounds that a fetus is included in the expression "everyone," and that the life of a human being starts at conception. The judge refused the declarations on the ground that "everyone" is a legal alternative expression to "every person," and on historical grounds legal personhood commences only at live birth.[81] The judge did not rule on the claim regarding the beginning of human life, explaining that even if the claim was biologically correct, it did not justify the conclusion that the human life that had begun was that of a legal person. He adopted the observation that: "the question is not whether the conceptus is

---

77. American Declaration on the Rights and Duties of Man, *signed* 2 May 1948, OEA/Ser.L./ V/II 71, at 71 (1988).
78. Roe v. Wade, 410 U.S. 113 (1973).
79. Case 2141, Inter-Am. C.H.R. 25, OEA/ser. L/V/1154, Doc. 9 rev. 1 (1981) (Inter-American Commission of Human Rights).
80. Wartelle v. Women's and Children's Hosp., Inc., 705 So. 2d 778, 780 (1997).
81. Christian Lawyers Association of South Africa v. The Minister of Health, 1998 (11) BCLR 1434 (T).

human but whether it should be given the same legal protection as you and me."[82]

The judge echoed many other courts that have addressed abortion interests by observing that the judicial task is not to resolve conflicts about biological facts or moral or spiritual values, but to make determinations of law, according to legal traditions and contexts, guided but not governed by social effects.

Legal indications of the status of human life at an early stage following conception come from the area of medically assisted reproduction. Modern techniques include *in vitro* fertilization and storage (cryopreservation) of embryos. In the United Kingdom, the Human Fertilisation and Embryology Act 1990[83] requires that embryos must usually be let perish not later than five years after their creation. In mid-1996, under the direction of the Human Fertilisation and Embryology Authority, about 3,300 stored embryos were caused to perish in accordance with the 1990 Act.[84] This public mandate for discarding embryos is consistent with the view that, whether they are located in storage or *in utero,* they warrant some degree of respect, but not that due to "human beings" as conventionally understood in law.

In several countries, however, the intention to give effect to religious faith as understood in the Roman Catholic tradition is expressed in constitutional provisions or legislation that declare the protection of human life from conception. For example, the Constitutions of Ireland,[85] the Philippines[86] and the Mexican state of Chihuahua[87] acknowledge the right to life from the moment of conception. The Czech Charter of Fundamental Rights and Freedoms contains a provision that human life is "worthy of protection already before birth."[88]

In 1994, the Constitutional Court of Colombia recognized that the right to decide the number and spacing of one's children is protected by the 1991 Constitution.[89] However, acting in the Roman Catholic tradition, it held that the right was not infringed by the criminalization of abortion, because this right can be exercised only until the moment of conception.[90] In 1997, the

---

82. *Id.* ¶ 8, *quoted in* Williams, *supra* note 61, at 78.
83. United Kingdom, Human Fertilisation and Embryology Act, 1990, Statutes, ch. 37, at 1930.
84. Micheal D. Lemonick, *Sorry, Your Time is Up,* 148 TIME MAG., 12 Aug. 1996, at 41.
85. CONSTITUTIONS OF THE COUNTRIES OF THE WORLD vol. IX (CONSTITUTIONS OF THE WORLD), Const. of Ireland, art. 40(3)(3) (Albert P. Blaustein & Gisbert H. Flanz eds., 1997).
86. CONSTITUTIONS OF THE WORLD, *supra* note 85, Const. of Philippines, art. II, § 12, at Vol XV.
87. Political Constitution of the Mexican State of Chihuahua, art. 5 (1994).
88. CONSTITUTIONS OF THE WORLD, *supra* note 85, Charter of Fundamental Rights and Freedoms, art. 6, vol. V.
89. CONSTITUTIONS OF THE WORLD, *supra* note 85, Constitution of Colombia, Title II, Ch. 2, art. 42, vol. IV.
90. Decision C-133/94 of the Constitutional Court, 17 Mar. 1994 (Colombia).

Polish Constitutional Tribunal rejected national legislation enacted in 1996 to deal with family planning, human embryo protection, and legal conditions for abortion, holding that constitutional provisions protect human life in every phase of its development.[91] The Tribunal accepted rights of abortion when women's lives are endangered, but considered the 1996 permission of economic and social grounds for abortion, such as difficult life conditions or personal situations, too vague to justify sacrifice of prenatal life.

The Constitutional Courts of Germany and Hungary have experienced similar struggles between the protection of prenatal life and of women's human rights. In 1975, the German Constitutional Court held that a fetus is not the equivalent of a person, but that it enjoys some limited constitutional protection because its life has an independent legal value.[92] In 1993, the Court upheld this approach, but gave express recognition to the constitutional protection of women's human rights to dignity, physical integrity, and personal development.[93] The outcome of the Court's struggle was to uphold legislation allowing availability of abortion on restricted grounds. In 1998, the Hungarian Constitutional Court addressed the balance between women's human dignity and interests in prenatal life[94] in Hungary's 1992 legislation allowing abortion on request in the first trimester.[95] The Court required the national parliament to clarify the legal test of "grave crisis" that justifies abortion.[96] In 2000, legislation provided that grave crisis means the presence of factors liable to cause profound physical or mental distress, or unacceptable social circumstances.[97]

b. Positive obligations to protect life

The history of the right to life in the development of national and international law[98] has been to ensure the right to fair legal proceedings before imposition of capital punishment.[99] However, the right to life is emerging

---

91. Ruling K 26/96 of the Constitutional Tribunal, 28 May 1997 (Poland).
92. Judgment of 25 Feb. 1975, Bundesverfassungshericht (Constitutional Court) 39 BverfGE 1 (W. Germany).
93. Judgment of 28 May 1993, 88 BverfGE (Second Senate) (Germany).
94. Judgment 48/1998 (IX.23) AB Hatarozat Official Legal Gazette (Magyar Kozlony 1998/105). 6654–6673 (Const. Court of Hungary). *See generally* Center for Reproductive Law and Policy, Women of the World: Laws and Policies Affecting Their Reproductive Lives—East Central Europe, 2000, 60–61.
95. Act LXXIX of 1992, "Protection of Fetal Life."
96. Judit Sandor, *From Ministry Orders towards the Constitutional Debate: Lessons Drawn from the Past 50 Years of Abortion Laws in Hungary,* 18 Med. & the Law 389 (1999).
97. Act LXXXVII of 2000, "Law on the Protection of the Life of the Fetus."
98. Manfred Nowak, U.N. Covenant on Civil and Political Rights: CCPR Commentary 103–22 (1993).
99. It is commonly observed that anti-abortion advocates who invoke the Right to Life tend to favor capital punishment, and that "many States in which religion has a powerful voice

from this narrow historical origin to require states to take positive steps to promote life and survival and to advance safe motherhood.[100] The European Commission of Human Rights, for instance, has considered a complaint alleging that a governmental vaccination program that resulted in the deaths of some vaccinated babies violated their right to life. Article 2 of the European Convention provides that "everyone's right to life shall be protected by law." On the merits of this case, the Commission found that appropriate measures to protect life had in fact been taken. Had it found otherwise, however, the defendant state would have been found in breach of its duty to safeguard the right to life.[101]

The Commission has also addressed a complaint concerning a woman who died in childbirth. Although the case was held inadmissible on technical grounds, the Commission nevertheless emphasized that the right to life has to be interpreted to require states to take steps not only to prevent intentional killing, but also to protect life against unintentional loss.[102] In monitoring the Political Covenant, the UN Human Rights Committee has explained that "the expression 'inherent right to life' cannot properly be understood in a restrictive manner, and the protection of this right requires that states adopt positive measures."[103]

The Inter-American Court of Human Rights, holding the government of Guatemala responsible for tolerating inhuman treatment and deaths of street children, explained that:

> In essence, the fundamental right to life includes, not only the right of every human being not to be deprived of his life arbitrarily, but also the right that he will not be prevented from having access to the conditions that guarantee a dignified existence. States have the obligation to guarantee the creation of the conditions required in order that violations of this basic right do not occur and, in particular, the duty to prevent its agents from violating it.[104]

Where states neglect to provide the means necessary to prevent women from dying of pregnancy-related causes, such as treatment for unsafe abortion or provision of skilled attendance at childbirth, they are failing in their

---

in governmental policy-making retain the judicial death penalty"; JOHN K. MASON, HUMAN LIFE AND MEDICAL PRACTICE 5 (1988).

100. REBECCA J. COOK & BERNARD M. DICKENS, ADVANCING SAFE MOTHERHOOD THROUGH HUMAN RIGHTS 27-29 (2001).

101. Association X. v. United Kingdom, Application No. 7154, Decision 12 July 1978, in 14 DECISIONS AND REPORTS 31 (June 1979) (European Commission of Human Rights).

102. Tavares v. France, Application No. 16593/90, Decision 12 Sept. 1991 (European Commission of Human Rights) (unreported).

103. Human Rights Committee General Comment 6: The Right to Life (art. 6), CCPR 16th Sess. (1982).

104. Villagran Morales v. Guatemala, Series C No. 63, 19 Nov. 1999, ¶ 144 (Inter-American Court of Human Rights).

obligation to ensure women's "access to the conditions that guarantee a dignified existence."

2. Liberty and security

Many national constitutions and human rights conventions protect individuals' "liberty and security" of the person. A constitution may explicitly address the security of the person in the context of reproductive integrity. For example, the 1997 South African Constitution provides in section 12(2) that

> Everyone has the right to bodily and psychological integrity, which includes the right
>
> (a)   to make decisions concerning reproduction;
> (b)   to security in and control over their body.[105]

Some courts distinguish rights to personal liberty from rights to security,[106] considering rights to security to be narrower. Security interests relate to denial of health care services that leaves individuals at risk of their lives or of grave impairment to their health. The Supreme Court of Canada held that impaired access to therapeutically indicated abortion violates women's rights to security of their person.[107] Several constitutional courts, including those of Austria,[108] France,[109] Italy,[110] and the Netherlands,[111] have gone beyond recognition of security interests, however, to find that accommodating abortion laws serve women's right to liberty. These courts recognize that women seek to control their fertility not simply to secure their lives and health, but because lack of control incapacitates them from pursuing the personal, social, spiritual, economic, and other opportunities in life that they value.

Some courts are importing notions of health into the meaning of the right to security of the person. For example, the Supreme Court of Canada heard evidence that the requirement of prior approval by a hospital abortion committee caused an average delay of eight weeks between a pregnant woman's first contact with a physician and her therapeutic abortion.[112]

---

105. Constitutions of the world, *supra* note 85, S. Afr. Const. § 12(2).
106. R. v. Morgentaler v. The Queen 44 D.L.R. (4th) 385, at 402 (1998).
107. *Id.* at 417, 420, 461, 482, 500 (Dickson, C.J.C. & Beetz, Estey, Lamer, and Wilson, J.J., respectively).
108. Constitutional Court of Austria, *supra* note 67.
109. Decision 74–54 DC, Judgment of 15 Jan 1975, Loi sur l'interruption volontaire de grossesse (Constitutional Convention of France) [law relating to the termination of pregnancy].
110. Judgment No. 108/81 of 25 June 1981, Corte Costituzionale, 57 Raccolta Ufficiale della Corte Costituzionale 823 (1981).
111. Juristenvereniging Pro Vita v. De Staat der Nederlanden, *supra* note 66.
112. R. v. Morgentaler v. The Queen 44 D.L.R.(4th) 385, at 402 (1998); Thornburgh v. American College of Obstetricians and Gynecologists, 106 S.Ct. 2196 (1986).

Although the constitutional Charter of Rights and Freedoms does not have an explicit right to health care, the Court found that the harmful physical and emotional health impact of the delay was a denial of the right to security of the person, so that the law requiring committee approval for abortion was unconstitutional.[113]

In countries with liberal laws, courts are beginning to address the lack of provision of abortion services particularly when they are necessary for therapeutic reasons. In the United States, for instance, since the "Hyde Amendment" of 1976,[114] Congress has passed legislation every year excluding abortion from health care funding for low-income women, except in limited cases. Federal funding of abortion is limited to instances where the woman's life is at stake or where pregnancy is the result of rape or incest.[115]

However, several state courts have struck down statutes restricting abortion funding for low-income women.[116] President Clinton twice vetoed bills passed by Congress banning what they called "partial birth" or late term abortions, because the bills lacked an exception for preservation of women's health. The Supreme Court has found similar state laws unconstitutional for the same reason.[117]

Negative rights to liberty or security by resort to health care services restrain police and other governmental obstruction of abortion procedures of which women can avail themselves, but positive rights require governments to provide women with reasonable access to safe services. Since abortion is a medical procedure, there is no violation of negative rights by legal limitation of services to those performed by, or under the direction of, medically qualified practitioners. The contrast between negative and positive rights is evident in the United States, where the Supreme Court has found the negative right to be constitutionally protected,[118] but has upheld limitations on governmental provision and funding of services.[119]

A more blatant threat to liberty, and often security, arises from imprisonment. Through the *Beijing Platform,* governments agree to "consider reviewing laws containing punitive measures against women who have

---

113. *R. v. Morgentaler,* at 404.
114. Public Law 94–439, § 209 (1976).
115. Departments of Labor, Health and Human Services, Education and Related Agencies Appropriations Act, Public Law 105-78 (1998).
116. Linda M. Vanzi, *Freedom at Home: State Constitutions and Medicaid Funding for Abortions,* 26 New Mexico L. Rev. 433 (1996).
117. Stenberg v. Carhart, 530 U.S. 914 120 S. Ct. 2597 (2000) (Nebraska statute that bans a particular abortion procedure, and is similar to statute in thirty other states, violates a woman's constitutional right to end a pregnancy).
118. Roe v. Wade, 410 U.S. 113 (1973).
119. Harris v. McRae, 448 U.S. 297 (1980); Webster v. Reproductive Health Servs., 492 U.S. 490 (1989); Planned Parenthood of Southeastern Pennsylvania v. Casey, 505 U.S. 833 (1992) (US Supreme Court).

undergone illegal abortions."[120] Review requires countries that imprison women for undergoing or attempting their own abortion, such as Chile[121] and Nepal,[122] to reform their penal laws. Prosecution under such laws is clearly influenced by governmental philosophies and policies. For instance, in Chile in the early 1980's under the Pinochet regime, an estimated 1,000 prosecutions each year were reported against women having abortions, many following reports to police from hospitals to which women had gone for treatment for abortion-related complications. Many of these women were young, poor, unmarried, rural immigrants to larger cities and pregnant following rape. In 1983, fifteen out of 230 women sentenced to imprisonment (6 percent) were convicted on abortion charges. However, the subsequent administration was more hesitant to press charges and seek imprisonment. In 1993, only ten of 423 women sent to prison (2.4 percent) were convicted on abortion charges.[123] Nevertheless, by reference to most other countries, Chilean statistics of prosecutions of women for abortion remain unusually high.

In Nepal, a rough 2002 estimate is that 100 women are in prison for abortion.[124] However, a 15-year-old girl sentenced to 20 years' imprisonment following an abortion, compelled by her family when she became pregnant following rape by a family member, was released at an appeal hearing in 2000 following international pressure.[125] Perhaps due to recognition of the injustice Nepalese women have suffered, the legislature subsequently liberalized the law to allow abortion on extended grounds, and to repeal provisions penalizing women for undergoing legal abortions.[126] France has also eliminated penalties against women who induce their own abortions,[127] thus ensuring the legality of self-administration of abortifacient drugs approved for prescription in France in 1988.[128]

---

120. *Beijing Platform, supra* note 9, ¶ 106(k).
121. Center for Reproductive Law and Policy & The Open Forum on Reproductive Health and Rights, Santiago, Women Behind Bars: Chile's Abortion Laws—A Human Rights Analysis (1998); Lydia Casas-Becerra, *Women Prosecuted and Imprisoned for Abortion in Chile,* 9 Reproductive Health Matters 29, 30 (May 1997).
122. Geeta Ramaseshan, *Women imprisoned for abortion in Nepal: Report of a Forum Asia Fact-Finding Mission,* 10 Reproductive Health Matters 133 (1997); Center for Reproductive Law and Policy and the Forum for Women, Law and Development, Abortion in Nepal: Women Imprisoned (2002).
123. Casas-Becerra, *supra* note 121.
124. Ramaseshan, *supra* note 122.
125. The Story of Min Min Lama, *available at* http://www.tribute.nl/wpf/uk/content/special. html (visited 1 Feb. 2000); *see also* IPPF Annual Report 1999 at 13, *available at* http:// www.ippf.org/annualreport1999/safety.htm.
126. The 11th revision of Muluki Ain 2059 B.S. (the Law of the Land 2002 AD).
127. Law No. 93-121 of 27 Jan. 1993, 20 Annual Rev. Population L. 15 (1993) (codified as Law No. 93-121 of 27 Jan 1993, J.O., 30 Jan. 1993, p. 1576–88).
128. Order of 28 Dec. 1988, 1 Journal Officiel de la Republique Francaise 465 (12 Jan. 1989) summarized in 40 Int'l Digest Health Legis. 430 (1989).

Evidence of abuses of women's physical security due to restrictive abortion laws can influence democratic law reform. In Ireland, for instance, public reaction against judicial obstruction of access to abortion services by abused young girls in highly publicized cases triggered intense political action for legislative liberalization, resulting in a referendum that approved constitutional reform.[129] Similarly, public outrage in Bolivia against judicial denial of abortion for an 11-year-old rape victim resulted in a legislative bill to ease the restrictive Penal Code, on grounds of promotion of human rights.[130]

3.   Human dignity and freedom from inhuman and degrading treatment

Related to the human right to liberty and security of the person is the right to freedom from torture and from inhuman and degrading treatment. The *Beijing Platform* recognizes that women are vulnerable to torture in sexual and other ways because of their low status in almost every society,[131] and requires governments to take preventive action.[132] Rape and domestic violence account for about 5 percent of the disease burden in women ages 15–44 in developing countries, and about 19 percent in industrial countries.[133] Violations of human dignity result in many injuries, including to self-confidence and self-esteem, that are not quantifiable as disease burdens.

The *Beijing Platform* condemns "sexual slavery, rape, sexual abuse and forced pregnancy."[134] Forced pregnancy includes denial and obstruction of abortion following pregnancy by rape. The *Cairo Programme* urges governments:

> [T]o identify and condemn the systematic practice of rape and other forms of inhuman and degrading treatment of women as a deliberate instrument of war and ethnic cleansing and take steps to assure that full assistance is provided to the victims of such abuse for their physical and mental rehabilitation.[135]

It should be remembered that Nazi governments in Europe before 1945 forced abortion of mixed-race and other "impure pregnancies," and forced continuation of "racially pure" pregnancy by prohibition of abortion. This was part of their policies to promote racial purification. The wishes of the pregnant women were legally irrelevant, since abortion, both compelled

---

129. Medb Ruane, The Irish Referendum: The End of Roman Rule, Conscience 23(1) 9–10 (2002).
130. Teresa L. Monje & Anna M. DeNicola, *Ignoring the Anguish,* 3 Conscience 21, 24 (1999).
131. *Beijing Platform, supra* note 9, ¶ 135.
132. *Id.* ¶ 107(q).
133. World Bank, World Development Report 1993: Investing in Health (1993).
134. *Beijing Platform, supra* note 9, ¶ 135.
135. *Cairo Programme, supra* note 8, ¶ 4.10.

and prohibited, was an instrument of state policy.[136] The inhumanity of forced continuation of pregnancy was addressed in the 1996 response of the UN Human Rights Committee to the Report of the Government of Peru, submitted under the Political Covenant, which the Committee monitors. In its Concluding Observations, the Committee expressed concern "that abortion gives rise to a criminal penalty even if a woman is pregnant as a result of rape and that clandestine abortions are the main cause of maternal mortality."[137] The Committee found that the criminal law subjected women to inhumane treatment contrary to Article 7 of the Covenant, and was possibly also incompatible with Article 3 on equal entitlement of men and women to the enjoyment of rights, and Article 6 on the right to life. The Committee recommended that "the provisions of the Civil and Penal Codes [of Peru] should be revised in the light of the obligations laid down in the Covenant."[138] Nevertheless, no evidence has appeared that Peru has amended this inhuman treatment of women.

An instance that occurred on Germany's border with the Netherlands also demonstrates women's continuing liability to be subjected to inhuman and degrading treatment directly by governmental officers.[139] A returning German woman was interrogated by German border guards, and subjected to physical examination to determine whether she had recently received an abortion in the Netherlands that would have been unlawful under German law due to her evasion of mandatory pre-abortion counseling requirements. This humiliating enforcement of administrative conditions shows the ease, oversight, and indifference with which women's human rights to be treated with dignity are disregarded where abortion is concerned.

Many women who are subjected to inhuman or degrading treatment and to discrimination on account of their race or ethnicity do not have access to redress through courts of law or human rights tribunals, and cannot obtain legal remedies for such human rights violations. However, media exposure of such abuses can lead to improved treatment. For example in Canada in 1992, the media exposed hospital practice in the Northwest Territories of denying anesthesia for pain relief to Inuit, Indian, Metis, and other women undergoing abortions.[140] As a result of this exposure, the Minister of Health for the Northwest Territories established an independent

---

136. *Trial of Ulrich Greifelt and Others,* 8 L. Reps of Trials of War Crims. 1 (1949).
137. United Nations, Report of the Human Rights Committee, Doc. CCPR/C/79/Add.72 (1996), ¶ 15.
138. *Id.* ¶ 22.
139. Karlhans Liebl, Ermittlungsverfahren, Strafverfolgungs-und Sanktionspraxis beim Schwangerschaftsabbruch (The Practice of Criminal Prosecution and Punishment in the Case of Abortion) (1990).
140. Miro Cernetig, *NWT Orders Abortion Inquiry: Hospital Used No Anaesthetics,* Globe & Mail (Toronto), 2 Apr. 1992.

review that resulted in changes in medical practice.[141] Comparable to reactions to the cases above of violations of women's human rights to security and liberty of the person by courts in Ireland and Bolivia, this shows growing democratic distaste of inhumane abortion laws and practices.

B. Non-discrimination and Due Respect for Difference

The right to non-discrimination has evolved to require that we treat the same interests without discrimination, for example in ensuring that all people have access to basic health care. Non-discrimination also entails treating significantly different cases according to those differences. For example, the European Court of Human Rights explained in 2001 that it:

> [H]as so far considered that the right under Article 14 [of the European Convention on Human Rights] not to be discriminated against in the enjoyment of the rights guaranteed under the Convention is violated when States treat differently persons in analogous situations without providing an objective and reasonable justification . . . However, the Court considers that this is not the only facet of the prohibition of discrimination in Article 14. The right not to be discriminated against . . . is also violated when States without an objective and reasonable justification fail to treat differently persons whose situations are significantly different.[142]

Women are often discriminated against in the exercise of their reproductive rights because governments, without an objective and reasonable justification, fail to treat women according to their different reproductive function. Sex discrimination is often compounded by discrimination, on such grounds of race and ethnicity, age, health status, and disability.

1. Sexual non-discrimination

a. CEDAW general recommendation 24: women and health

States Parties to the Women's Convention accept the obligation to confront women's inequality by addressing "all forms" of discrimination that women suffer, including discrimination on grounds both of sex, which is a biological characteristic, and of gender, which is a social, cultural, and psychological construct. The Women's Convention directs primary attention to women's health and well-being through Article 12. By this Article, member

---

141. No Choice: Canadian Women Tell Their Stories of Illegal Abortion (Childbirth by Choice Trust ed., 1998).
142. Thlimmenos v. Greece (2001) 31 E.H.R.R. 15, ¶ 44.

states agree to "take all appropriate measures to eliminate discrimination against women in the field of health care in order to ensure, on a basis of equality of men and women, access to health care services, including those related to family planning."[143]

In 1999, CEDAW elaborated the content and meaning of this Article in its General Recommendation 24: Women and Health.[144] The Recommendation requires that states, when they periodically report under the Women's Convention, address distinctive features of health and life that differ between women and men, taking into account such factors as:

— biological factors including differing reproductive health needs and functions,
— socio-economic factors including unequal power relations,
— psychosocial factors such as postpartum depression, and
— health system factors such as the protection of confidentiality, especially for the treatment of stigmatizing conditions such as unwanted pregnancy and HIV/AIDS.[145]

General Recommendation 24 explains that the legal obligation of States Parties is to provide information in their periodic reports on the impact of health policies and laws on women in contrast to the impact on men.[146] This is reinforced by the Human Rights Committee, acting under the Political Covenant, which specified through its General Comment on Equality between Men and Women that states are now required to provide data on "pregnancy and childbirth-related deaths of women."[147] Governments must accordingly report on the mortality and morbidity resulting from pregnancy and childbirth, and unsafe abortion, and mortality and morbidity rates and causes among men in the same age-groups.

The General Recommendation explains states' obligations to respect, protect, and fulfill women's rights to health care. The obligation to respect rights requires the removal of barriers to access to care, including "laws that criminalize medical procedures only needed by women and that punish women who undergo these procedures."[148] Laws criminalizing medical procedures to which only women have resort would by definition include criminal abortion laws.

The obligation to protect rights relating to women's health

---

143. Women's Convention, *supra* note 14, art. 12.
144. U.N. GAOR, 1999, U.N. Doc. A/54/38/Rev. 1, 3–7.
145. CEDAW, *supra* note 15, Gen. Rec. 24, ¶ 12.
146. CEDAW, *id.,* Gen. Rec. 24, ¶ 19.
147. Hum. Rts. Comm., Gen. Comm. 28: Equality of Rights between Men and Women, *adopted* 10 Oct. 2000, U.N. GAOR 2000, U.N. Doc. A/55/40, Annex VI, at 153, ¶ 10.
148. CEDAW, *supra* note 15, Gen. Rec. 24, ¶ 14.

> [R]equires States parties, their agents and officials to take action to prevent and impose sanctions for violations of rights by private persons and organizations ... [including] [t]he enactment and effective enforcement of laws and the formulation of policies, including health care protocols and hospital procedures to address violence against women and abuse of girl children and the provision of appropriate health services.[149]

Where states rely on private clinics to provide legal abortion services, they are obligated to ensure that services are reasonably available, and are delivered in ways that are respectful of women's rights concerning dignity.

General Recommendation 24 further explains that the duty to fulfill rights places an obligation on states to: "take appropriate legislative, judicial, administrative, budgetary, economic and other measures to the maximum extent of their available resources to ensure that women realize their right to health care."[150]

For instance, where studies show high rates of maternal mortality and morbidity, they put governments on notice that they might be in breach "of their duties to ensure women's access to health care."[151]

b. National jurisprudence

Consistently with General Recommendation 24, national courts are beginning to recognize that denial of safe abortion services constitutes sex discrimination. In conditions of therapeutic need, men are not exposed to legal denial of, and criminal punishment for resort to, safe medical services, while women often face legal and practical obstacles in seeking therapeutic abortion. For example in the United States, the Supreme Court of New Mexico held in 1999 that:

> New Mexico's Equal Rights Amendment requires a searching judicial inquiry to determine whether the [Human Services] Department's rule prohibiting state funding for certain medically necessary abortions denies Medicaid-eligible women equality under law. We conclude from this inquiry that the Department's rule violates New Mexico's Equal Rights Amendment because it results in a program that does not apply the same standard of medical necessity to both men and women, and there is no compelling justification for treating men and women differently with respect to their medical needs in this instance.[152]

The rule in question, Rule 776, defines abortion as "medically necessary" when a pregnancy aggravates a pre-existing condition, makes treatment

---

149. *Id.* ¶ 15.
150. *Id.* ¶ 17.
151. *Id.*
152. New Mexico Right to Choose/NARAL v. William Johnson, Secretary of the New Mexico Human Services Department, 126 N.M. 788, 792 (1999).

of a condition impossible, interferes with or hampers a diagnosis, or has a profound negative impact upon the physical or mental health of an individual.[153]

The New Mexico Constitution guarantees that "[e]quality of rights under the law shall not be denied on account of the sex of any person."[154] The Court explained that the judges "view New Mexico's Equal Rights Amendment as the culmination of a series of state constitutional amendments that reflect an evolving concept of gender equality in this state," and concluded that

> New Mexico's Equal Rights Amendment is a specific prohibition that provides a legal remedy for the invidious consequences of the gender-based discrimination that prevailed under the common law and civil law traditions that preceded it. As such, the Equal Rights Amendment requires a searching judicial inquiry concerning state laws that employ gender-based classifications. This inquiry must begin from the premise that such classifications are presumptively unconstitutional, and it is the State's burden to rebut this presumption."[155]

The Court further observed that "[u]nder federal law, the state's interest in the potential life of the unborn is never compelling enough to outweigh the interest in the life and health of the mother."[156]

2. Racial and ethnic non-discrimination

In some countries, women of particular races and ethnic groups are often discriminated against in the exercise of their reproductive rights.[157] The values at stake are reflected in the language of the Preamble to South Africa's Choice on Termination of Pregnancy Act 1997, through which the legislature stated the values that are intended to prevail. The first paragraph of the Act's Preamble states that its provisions are enacted "[r]ecognising the values of human dignity, the achievement of equality, security of the person, non-racialism and non-sexism, and the advancement of human rights and freedoms which underlie a democratic South Africa."[158]

The significance of this language is that the modern South Africa has been shaped in reaction to an explicit history of racial discrimination,[159] but the country moved quickly to address discrimination on grounds of sex as well as on grounds of race.

---

153. *Id.* at 791.
154. Const. of the State of New Mexico (adopted 21 Jan. 1911, as amended through 1975) at art. II, § 18.
155. New Mexico Right to Choose/NARAL, *supra* note 152, at 800.
156. *Id.* at 804.
157. Dorothy Roberts, Killing the Black Body: Race, Reproduction, and the Meaning of Liberty (1997).
158. Choice on Termination of Pregnancy Act of 1997, Preamble (South Africa).
159. Jeremy Sarkin, *Patriarchy and Discrimination in Apartheid South Africa's Abortion Laws,* 4 Buffalo Hum. Rts. L. Rev. 141 (1998).

South Africa's approach to abortion law reform reflects experience in many other countries, where it has long been recognized that socioeconomic elites and women associated with influential families in their communities have been immune from restrictive abortion laws, but that such laws have prejudiced the choice, health, and very lives of powerless women who are poor, young, and marginal to the societies in which they live.[160]

Women's experiences of race and ethnic discrimination are found in court cases, individual narratives, and scholarship.[161] Evidence of discrimination is also found in reproductive health indicators, showing disparity in access to reproductive health services among different ethnic groups. Statistics on disparity in the risk of maternal death between majority and minority populations show up to ten times greater risk, for instance, in the aboriginal population as against the non-aboriginal population in Australia.[162] Differences exist even where populations live in the same cities, such as in the United States, where the Afro-American population has a relative risk of maternal death 4.3 times higher than members of the non-black population.[163] These contrasts often reflect racial and socio-economic differences. A positive response to these differences compatible with human rights entitlements might be the allocation of reproductive health care resources proportionately to need, including family planning services backed up by abortion services for high risk pregnancies in the event of failure.

Both the International Convention on the Elimination of All Forms of Racial Discrimination (the Race Convention) and the Women's Convention require member states to take temporary special measures to accelerate *de facto* equality between men and women[164] and to ensure adequate development and protection of certain racial groups.[165] Some governments have claimed to meet their legal responsibilities to satisfy international human rights conventions with regard to abortion by enacting liberalizing laws. However, many have accommodated these rights only as negative rights, leaving proposed beneficiaries dependent on their own resources alone to pursue them. Governments often fail to allocate public resources to furnish necessary services through which abortion rights can be realized, or to require health care providers or facilities to make services available and

---

160. Alice Jenkins, Law for the Rich (1960).
161. *See, e.g.,* Global Critical Race Feminism, *supra* note 59.
162. Hani K. Atrash, Sidney K. Alexander & Cynthia J. Berg, *Maternal Mortality in Developed Countries: Not Just a Concern of the Past,* 86 Obstetrics & Gynecology 700, 703 (October 1995).
163. *Id.*
164. Women's Convention, *supra* note 14, art. 4.
165. International Convention on the Elimination of All Forms of Racial Discrimination, *adopted* 21 Dec. 1965, 660 U.N.T.S. 195 (*entered into force* 4 Jan. 1969), *reprinted in* 5 I.L.M. 352, art. 2.2 (1966).

accessible. They therefore create rights for people with financial means, but not for poor people. The role of the human rights monitoring committees, acting under the various human rights treaties, is to determine whether rights legally available in theory are equitably available in practice to members of marginalized racial groups.

The Committee on the Elimination of Racial Discrimination has developed General Recommendation 25: Gender Related Dimensions of Racial Discrimination in order to assist countries reporting under the Race Convention to address the compounding forms of race and gender discrimination.[166] The Recommendation recognizes that

> [R]acial discrimination does not always affect women and men equally or in the same way. There are circumstances in which racial discrimination only or primarily affects women, or affects women in a different way, or to a different degree than men. Such racial discrimination will often escape detection if there is no explicit recognition or acknowledgment of the different life experiences of women and men, in areas of both public and private life.[167]

In considering gender-related dimensions of racial discrimination, the Committee will give "particular consideration to: the form and manifestation of racial discrimination; the circumstances in which racial discrimination occurs; the consequences of racial discrimination; and the availability and accessibility of remedies and complaint mechanisms for racial discrimination."[168]

An example of racial discrimination is a public health service that is inadequate because it fails to ensure that subgroups of women, such as Black or Mediterranean women, are treated according to their medically significant genetic predisposition, such as to sickle cell anemia. Where women with the sickle cell trait face health risks associated with unwanted pregnancies and do not have reasonable access to medically indicated abortion services,[169] the Committee might consider that the lack of reasonable access is a form of racial discrimination that a state must remedy.

It has been explained that a consequence of the excessive certification procedures of the former South African Abortion and Sterilization Act of 1975 was to confine access to lawful abortion to primarily socioeconomically advantaged women. A 1997 study of that law conducted by the South African Institute of Race Relations noted that:

---

166. Committee on the Elimination of Racial Discrimination, (CERD) Gen. Rec. 25: Gender Related Dimensions of Racial Discrimination, UN GAOR, 2000, UN Doc. A/55/18, Annex V, at 152.
167. CERD 25, *id.* ¶ 1.
168. CERD 25, *id.* ¶ 5.
169. AbouZahr, *supra* note 52.

During the period of the Act's operation, only an average of 800–1200 women per year qualified for legal abortion. Well over 66% of such women were white and from an urban middle-class background—at a time when whites constituted 16% of the general population. On the other hand, upwards of 44,000 women a year, the preponderance of them black and poor, had recourse to "backstreet" abortion. Unofficial estimates put the number of illegal abortions much higher, at 120,000 per year or more. Illegal abortions performed under unhygienic conditions exacted an inevitable toll on health. Each year about 33,000 surgical procedures were performed to treat the residue of septic abortions. The mortality rate stood at 425.[170]

In light of the consequences of the excessive South African certification procedures for Black women, a human rights treaty monitoring committee could well be vigilant in monitoring other laws with excessively bureaucratic procedures.

The new 1997 South African Act makes termination of pregnancy accessible upon racially non-discriminatory grounds. A procedure is legal upon a woman's request up to twelve weeks of pregnancy; up to twenty weeks on physical and mental health grounds, on socioeconomic grounds, and in cases of rape or incest; and after twenty weeks if the woman's life is endangered, or there is a risk that the fetus is severely deformed. The Act enables registered midwives who have completed the prescribed training course to perform abortions up to twelve weeks (sec. 2(2)). The law does not require third party authorizations for married women or minors. Medical practitioners or registered midwives shall advise pregnant minors to consult with parents, friends, or guardians, but the Act makes clear that services for termination of pregnancy cannot be denied because a minor chooses not to consult parents, guardians, or friends (sec. 5(3)). The Act accordingly excludes discrimination on grounds of age.

3.   Age non-discrimination

Discrimination on grounds of young age is comprehensively addressed through the Children's Convention, by which states agree to "strive to ensure that no child is deprived of his or her right of access to . . . health care services."[171] Intellectually mature young women's vulnerability to age discrimination is deepened when abortion services, available to adults on their own decision, are available to them only on the condition of parental authorization.[172]

---

170. Charles Ngwena, *The History and Transformation of Abortion Law in South Africa*, 30 Acta Academica 32–68 at 8–9 (footnotes omitted) (1998).
171. Children's Convention, *supra* note 71, art. 24(1).
172. Corinne A.A. Packer, *Preventing Adolescent Pregnancy: The Protection Offered by International Human Rights Law*, 5 Int'l J. Children's Rts. 46 (1997).

Mature adolescents suffer unjust discrimination when they are not able to obtain reproductive health counseling and services with the same confidentiality as adults. The Children's Convention requires that "States Parties shall respect the rights and duties of the parents and, when applicable, legal guardians, to provide direction to the child in the exercise of his or her rights in a manner consistent with the evolving capacities of the child."[173]

Courts are increasingly rejecting interpretations of laws that, on grounds of minor age alone, deny competent adolescents reproductive health services without parental consent. When minors are intellectually mature or emancipated, many courts will recognize their equal rights with adults to health care, including preventive care, and to confidentiality.[174] A sign of maturity in minors is their understanding of the need to protect their reproductive health, and their requesting contraceptive services when they are or are about to be sexually active. Denial of reproductive health care services for adolescents often sets the scene for unplanned pregnancy and abortion.

The *Cairo Programme* recognizes that the "reproductive health needs of adolescents as a group have been largely ignored to date by existing reproductive health services."[175] As a result, in many countries, high rates of adolescent unmarried pregnancy are epidemic, and in others appear endemic.[176] For example, in its Concluding Comments on the Report submitted by the government of Saint Vincent and the Grenadines, CEDAW noted the "very high rate of pre-teen and teenage pregnancy" and recommended improved reproductive health services and information for this age group.[177]

The Cairo and Beijing texts call for the removal of regulatory and social barriers to reproductive health information and care for adolescents.[178] They recommend that countries ensure that the programs and attitudes of health care providers do not restrict adolescents' access to appropriate services,[179] and that programs protect and promote the rights of adolescents to reproductive health education, information, and care in order to reduce the number of adolescent pregnancies.[180]

---

173. Children's Convention, *supra* note 71, art. 14 (2).
174. Gillick v. West Norfolk and Wisbech Area Health Authority [1986] AC 112 (House of Lords, England).
175. *Cairo Programme, supra* note 8, ¶ 7.41.
176. P. Senanayake & M. Ladjali, *Adolescent Health: Changing Needs,* 46 Int'l J. Gynecology & Obstetrics 137 (1994).
177. Report of the Committee on the Elimination of Discrimination Against Women (CEDAW), Saint Vincent and the Grenadines, 16th Sess., U.N. Doc. A/52/38/Rev. 1, ¶¶ 123–50, at ¶ 147 (1997).
178. *Cairo Programme, supra* note 8, ¶ 7.45; *Beijing Platform, supra* note 9, ¶¶ 106–08, 281.
179. *Cairo Programme, supra* note 8, ¶ 7.45; *Beijing Platform, supra* note 9, ¶¶ 106–08.
180. *Cairo Programme, supra* note 8, ¶ 7.46; *Beijing Platform, supra* note 9, ¶¶ 83(k)(l), 107(g), 281.

4.   Non-discrimination on grounds of health status/disability

Human rights conventions prohibit discrimination not only on specified grounds such as sex and race, but also on unspecified grounds. Unspecified grounds have been interpreted to include impaired health status or disability, including asymptomatic HIV positivity.[181] The stigma against women with HIV/AIDS is exacerbated when they become pregnant, but is not to be a reason to deny or obstruct rights to otherwise indicated health care.

A serious denial of the right to non-discrimination on grounds of health status occurs when women are forced to terminate pregnancies they prefer to continue. For instance, compromise of the immune system that HIV-positive women suffer is further aggravated by pregnancy, which itself reduces women's immune reaction. It is reported that some hospitals in the United States have therefore urged HIV-positive pregnant women to terminate pregnancies, and that they have done so directively.[182] They have, for instance, overstated risks of vertical (mother-to-child) transmission of HIV infection to children born of HIV-positive mothers, and been intolerant of requests by such mothers to continue their pregnancies.[183] The risks to women's liberty and security that they will be pressured to terminate pregnancies provide the threat of a human rights violation in otherwise liberating national proposals that restrictive abortion legislation be amended to allow medical termination of pregnancy on the indication of a pregnant woman's HIV-positive status.[184]

C.   Citizenship

1.   Women as equal citizens

Discrimination excludes those who are subjected to it from equality with others who are not, particularly the perpetrators of discrimination. That is, discrimination is an exercise in superiority. The abortion-related discrimination that women suffer on grounds of sex and gender, often coupled with discrimination on grounds of race, ethnicity, and, for instance, age, illustrates the pervasive violation of the right to equality that creates the subordinate status that many women occupy in their families, communities,

---

181. Bragdon v. Abbott, 524 U.S. 624 (1998).

182. Taunya L. Banks, *Legal Challenges: State Intervention, Reproduction and HIV-Infected Women,* in HIV, AIDS AND CHILD BEARING: PUBLIC POLICY AND PRIVATE LIVES 143–77 (Ruth R. Faden & Nancy E. Kass eds., 1996).

183. Mukdawan Sakboon, *Pregnant HIV Victims Denied Every Option by Hospital,* NATION (Bangkok), 31 July 1997.

184. Temsak Trisophon, *Abortion Law Faces Key Change,* BANGKOK POST, 3 Oct. 1998.

wider societies, and legal systems. The burdens of pregnancy, post-partum recovery, nursing, and care of a dependent child or children for years, deny a woman other opportunities for applications of her energy, time, and talents that she may justly forgo only voluntarily.

The power that a state claims to conscript women to give their bodies against their will to deliver children at its legal demand confirms that women are only lesser or second-class citizens. Since the end of legal feudalism and slavery, men are not forced by law to render bodily service and sacrifice at the will of social superiors, and military conscription in war almost invariably allows rights of conscientious objection. Under restrictive criminal laws, women who conscientiously object to involuntary continuation of pregnancy by termination become criminals, liable to forfeit many of the freedoms that remain to them.

Women's lack of equality and bodily integrity under laws that deny them reproductive self-determination is increasingly perceived as a violation not only of human equality, but of full citizenship. Citizens in democracies are full participants in making the laws by which they voluntarily abide, whose will can become law. Restrictive laws on abortion are products of times, many of which continue, when women lacked or lack the political power of full citizenship to overcome patriarchal governments. Such governments are often reliant on the support of authoritarian religious institutions whose leaders exercise spiritual autocracy and command obedience. The governments and religious institutions that support restrictive abortion laws include few if any women, and some deliberately exclude them.

Issues of citizenship have arisen in debates in the US concerning whether the Supreme Court's abortion decision in Roe v. Wade is better justifiable and sustainable on the basis of the Court majority's reasoning on rights of privacy, or on rights of equality,[185] or whether the reasoning centrally implicates both.[186] Denial of reproductive rights, including to abortion, is increasingly seen as a denial of women's citizenship. This vision of citizenship as possession of equal power of participation is both geographically and legally expansive. For instance, in addressing constitutional rights in the Supreme Court of Canada, Chief Justice Dickson observed that:

> The Court must be guided by the values and principles essential to a free and democratic society which I believe embody, to name but a few, respect for the inherent dignity of the human person, commitment to social justice and equality, accommodation of a wide variety of beliefs, respect for cultural and group

---

185. Anita L. Allen, *The Proposed Equal Protection Fix for Abortion Law: Reflections on Citizenship, Gender, and the Constitution*, 18 Harv. J. L. & Pub. Pol. 419 (1994–95).

186. Reva Siegel, *Reasoning from the Body: A Historical Perspective on Abortion Regulation and Questions of Equal Protection*, 44 Stanford L. Rev. 261 (1992).

identity, and faith in social and political institutions which enhance the participation of individuals and groups in society.[187]

In this spirit of enhancement of social participation or citizenship, the Chief Justice two years later led the Court's majority judgment holding the restrictive national criminal abortion law unconstitutional, invoking its denial of women's equal right with men to security of the person.[188]

Citizenship has more recently triggered wider political, philosophical, sociological, legal, and related analysis in Western Europe in the 1990s, particularly since the 1997 Maastricht treaty of the European Union established transnational European citizenship.[189] Constructions of citizenship generally and women's citizenship particularly vary according to the social, political, and legal context of a country.

In Latin America, for example, there are at least two dynamics in the construction of women's citizenship. One is the dynamic of ensuring that women have the same rights and duties as men with regard to citizenship, such as in their ability to vote and pass on citizenship to their children. The other is women's ability to engage in social and political movements to determine their destinies.[190] Feminist movements mobilizing against dictatorship and abuse of authority have been particularly strong in Latin America, and have facilitated movements through which women have translated survival strategies into political and legal demands for access to services, including reproductive health services.[191] The women's movement ties reproductive freedom into the struggle to ensure that women are subjects of the state, not objects, and engines, rather than clients, of development.[192] In this context, the right to abortion represents achievement of women's control of their destinies in society. The construction of citizenship cannot be reduced to a simple list of legal rights, but rather requires the vindication of a series of civil, political, social, economic, and cultural rights. Moreover, this view of citizenship includes a set of organizational practices that allow women to exercise their power in the public sphere.[193]

---

187. R. v. Oakes, [1986] 1 S.C.R. 103, at 136.
188. R. v. Morgentaler v. The Queen 44 D.L.R.(4th) 385, at 402 (1998).
189. Sujit Choudhry, *Citizenship and Federations: Some Preliminary Reflections; The Federal Vision: Legitimacy and Levels of Governance in the US and the EU, in* The US and the EU 377–402 (Kalypso Nicolaidis & Robert Howes eds., 2001).
190. Jane Jacquette, The Women's Movement in Latin America (1989).
191. Berengere Marques-Pereira, *Los Derechos Reproductivos como Derechos Ciudadanos (Reproductive Rights and Citizenship Rights), in* La Ciudadania a Debate (Citizenship Debated) 126 (Eugenia Hola & Ana Maria Portugal eds., 1997); Leyla de Andrade Linhares Barsted, *Ten Years of Struggle to Legalize Abortion in Brazil, in* Women Watched and Punished 223–247 (R. Vasquez ed., 1993).
192. Magdalena Leon, *Mujeres, Genero and Desarrollo (Women, Gender and Development), in* Estudos Basicos de Derechos Humanos IV (Laura Guzman & Gildo Pacheco eds., 1997).
193. Marques-Pereira, *supra* note 191, at 126; M. Barquet, Derechos Reproductivos: Muher y Socied (Reproductive Rights: Women and Society), 1992.

The effectiveness of women's policy agencies in assisting women's movements in achieving their procedural and substantive policy goals is described as state feminism.[194] Effectiveness will depend on a variety of variables, including the strength of the women's movement, the activities and characteristics of women's policy agencies, characteristics of the communal women's movement, and the policy environment.[195] The legal status of women's rights to safe abortion is often a measure or barometer of the effectiveness of state feminism and respect for women's citizenship, in that abortion is safest where women are more respected as citizens of the countries in which they live.

2. Women's speech

It is trite to observe that knowledge is power. Citizens' power to participate as they wish in the activities of their families and societies significantly depends on their access to information.[196] The United Nations Development Programme recognizes that there is an interdependency between enjoying political freedom and participation, enjoying a decent standard of living, and being knowledgeable and enjoying good health.[197] Thus, a full understanding of the concept of citizenship mandates a recognition of the importance of access to health information in the well-being of the citizen. In many cases, however, women have been deprived of the full benefits of citizenship with respect to information about health care procedures.[198] Ultimately, this builds a self-renewing cycle that continues to marginalize women's roles and rights as citizens.

Regarding reproductive health and self-determination, the Women's Convention requires that women have "specific educational information to help to ensure the health and well-being of families, including information and advice on family planning."[199] Both the *Cairo Programme* and the *Beijing Platform* require governments to remove legal, medical, clinical, and regulatory barriers to reproductive health information[200] and to improve its quality.[201]

---

194. Dorothy M. Stetson, *Conclusion: Comparative Abortion Politics and the Case for State Feminism, in* ABORTION POLITICS, WOMEN'S MOVEMENTS AND THE DEMOCRATIC STATES: A COMPARATIVE STUDY OF STATE FEMINISM 267–95 (Dorothy M. Stetson ed., 2001).

195. *Id.*

196. Noel Whitty, *The Mind, The Body, and Reproductive Health Information,* 18 HUM. RTS. Q. 224 (1996); Lynn Freedman, *Censorship and Manipulation of Reproductive Health Information, in* THE RIGHT TO KNOW: HUMAN RIGHTS AND ACCESS TO REPRODUCTIVE HEALTH INFORMATION 1–37 (Sandra Coliver ed., 1995).

197. UNITED NATIONS DEVELOPMENT PROGRAMME, HUMAN DEVELOPMENT REPORT 2002 53 (2002).

198. Freedman, *supra* note 196, at 1–37.

199. Women's Convention, *supra* note 14, art. 10(h).

200. *Cairo Programme, supra* 8, ¶ 7.20; *Beijing Platform, supra* note 9, ¶ ¶ 103, 107(e).

201. *Cairo Programme, supra* note 8, ¶ 7.23; *Beijing Platform, supra* note 9, ¶ 103.

In a number of countries, however, it is a criminal offense, sometimes still described as a crime against morality, to spread information of contraceptive methods. In countries with restrictive abortion laws, it may be an offense to publicize access to other countries where women can obtain pregnancy termination services on more accommodating grounds.[202] In 1989, for instance, the Supreme Court of Ireland upheld injunctions prohibiting Irish student unions from distributing information of abortion clinics offering lawful services in Britain.[203] In 1992, the European Court of Human Rights found these decisions to violate Ireland's international human rights commitments to allow freedom of expression.[204] The European Court found that the restraint on expression had obstructed Irish clinics from offering abortion counseling, and created a risk to the health of women who, due to lack of proper counseling, were seeking abortions at a later stage in their pregnancy. Reflecting on some women's disadvantages, the Court noted that "the injunction may have had more adverse effects on women who were not sufficiently resourceful or had not the necessary level of education to have access to alternative sources of information."[205]

There is growing public recognition of the injustices of the efforts of the Irish government to control information and access to services. Concerning access to services, for instance, a lower Irish court had prohibited parents of a fourteen-year-old girl pregnant by rape from taking her to Britain to receive legal abortion,[206] which was reversed on appeal.[207] This dissatisfaction led to an amendment of the Irish Constitution in 1992 recognizing freedom to travel[208] and to receive information of abortion services lawfully available in another country.[209] The Supreme Court of Ireland subsequently upheld the constitutionality of these amendments.[210]

Various decisions of human rights tribunals reflect indirectly on rights to give and receive information regarding reproductive health, including lawful abortion. For instance, the European Court of Human Rights found the United Kingdom in violation of freedom of expression when its legislation

---

202. THE RIGHT TO KNOW, *supra* note 196.
203. Attorney General (S.P.U.C.) v. Open Door Counseling Ltd. and Dublin Well Woman Centre Ltd. [1994], 2 IR 333 [1994], 1 ILRM 256 (Supreme Court).
204. *Open Door Counseling Ltd and Dublin Well Women Centre Ltd v. Ireland,* 15 Eur.Ct.H.R. 244 (1993).
205. *Id.* ¶ 77.
206. The Attorney General v. X and Others [1992], ILRM 401.
207. The Attorney General v. X and Others [1992], 1 IR 1 (Ir.S.C).
208. Thirteenth Amendment of the Constitution Act, 23 Dec. 1992, Release 30, IRISH CURRENT LAW STATUTES ANNOTATED 92 (Dec. 1992).
209. Fourteenth Amendment of the Constitution Act, 23 Dec. 1992, Release 30, IRISH CURRENT LAW STATUTES ANNOTATED 92 (Dec. 1992).
210. Article 26 and The Regulation of Information (Services Outside the State for Termination of Pregnancy) Bill 1995, 1 IR 1 (Ireland) (1995).

severely curtailed private expenditures on literature for circulation in election campaigns.[211] The literature in the case outlined the views on abortion of three competing candidates. The Court favored freedom of expression, including freedom of political debate, over this governmental attempt to prevent election campaigns being unduly influenced by well-funded interest groups.

In 1991, the US Supreme Court upheld a rule that prohibited health care providers in federally funded family planning clinics from counseling patients by providing them with information on their lawful abortion options.[212] In contrast, the same Court has precluded states from requiring that doctors show patients pictures of fetuses or explain fetal development graphically for the purpose of dissuading women from having abortions.[213] Governmental manipulation of information, by denying or compelling its presentation to individuals at times when they are vulnerable and dependent, is a form of authoritarian denial of individual self-determination that is at the origin of the modern international human rights of individuals to decide what information to receive free of governmental control.

An issue arises, when women have not stated or clearly shown their refusal of abortion,[214] whether they give adequately informed and free consent to medical management of particularly difficult or high-risk pregnancies when they have not been offered information of lawful options of abortion. The US Supreme Court has upheld national abortion "gag clauses" in health care providers' terms of employment or payment by government agencies.[215] Such agencies may therefore prohibit health care providers from informing patients of constitutional rights to abortion available to them.[216] However, litigation is pending claiming that the Global Gag Rule, as revived in January 2001, is unconstitutional. Overseas recipients of US funds must undertake not to contribute to abortion law liberalization in their own countries, and accordingly cannot engage with US-based nongovernmental organizations committed to world-wide abortion law reform for compliance with human rights standards. In denying staff members of US nongovernmental organizations rights to receive information and the power of discourse with overseas organizations, it is claimed that the Global Gag Rule violates their rights to receive information and free speech. The

---

211. Bowman v. United Kingdom, 141 Eur.Ct.H.R. at 1 (1996). According to this case, the freedom to travel (the Thirteenth Amendment) was upheld but was still held to be subordinated to the right to life of the unborn unless the travel for the purpose of obtaining an abortion was necessary to protect the life of the mother.
212. Rust v. Sullivan, 500 U.S. 173 (1991) at 4420.
213. City of Akron, Ohio v. Akron Center for Reproductive Health, 462 U.S. 416 (1983).
214. *See* Arndt v. Smith (1997), 148 D.L.R. (4th) 48 (Sup. Ct. Can.).
215. *Rust,* 500 U.S. at 214.
216. William J. Curran, et al., Health Care Law and Ethics 213–61 (5th ed., 1998).

US Court of Appeals for the Second Circuit did not find this argument convincing.[217]

Laws that require the offer of pre-abortion counseling are consistent with women's rights to information, provided that the offer is an opportunity for enhanced exercise of choice. Laws that compel abortion applicants to listen to counseling they do not request or approve demean women as competent decision-makers, and violate their rights of liberty[218] even when, as is not invariably the case, the counseling is non-judgmental. Legislation sometimes also requires that there be a "reflection delay" between a woman's request for lawful abortion and its performance, so that she may reflect on the moral and associated implications of her decision. These provisions also demean women as capable decision-makers, and are often applied to discourage or frustrate their choice.

3.   Women's choice: third party authorization requirements

The *Cairo Programme* and the *Beijing Platform* invoke individuals' right to private life to resist public officers' intrusions, in order to ensure that women can exercise self-determination and confidential choice in reproductive matters.[219] CEDAW General Recommendation 24 explains that:

> The obligation to respect rights requires States parties to refrain from obstructing action taken by women in pursuit of their health goals. . . . For example, States parties should not restrict women's access to health services or the clinics that provide those services on the ground that women do not have the authorization of husbands, partners, parents or health authorities, because they are unmarried or because they are women.[220]

Laws or practices that require third party authorization of women's abortion, for instance by their male partners, parents, doctors, or hospital committees, have been scrutinized for their negative impact on health and their infringement of women's rights to make decisions in their private lives. Claims by women to choice of lawful abortion over their partners' attempted

---

217. Center for Reproductive Law and Policy v. Bush, US District Court, Southern District of New York, 2001 WL 868007 (S.D.N.Y.), 2001 (31 July 2001); 2001 U.S. Dist. LEXIS 10903, The Center for Reproductive Law & Policy, Janet Benshoof, Anika Rahman, Katherine Hall Martinez, Julie Ernst, Laura Katzive, Melissa Upreti and Christina Zampas, Plaintiffs, v. George W. Bush, in his official capacity as President of the United States, Colin Powell, in his official capacity as Secretary of State, and Andrew Natsios, in his official capacity as Administrator of the United States Agency for International Development, Defendants, 01 Civ. 4986 (LAP), U.S. Dist. Ct. S.D.N.Y., 31 July 2001, Decided; 31 July 2001, filed.

218. Nanette Funk, *Abortion Counseling and the 1995 German Abortion Law*, 12 Conn. J. of Int'l L. 33 (1996).

219. *Cairo Programme, supra* note 8, ¶¶ 7.3, 7.12, 7.17–7.20; *Beijing Platform, supra* note 12, ¶¶ 103, 107(e), 108(m), 267.

220. CEDAW Gen. Rec. 24, *supra* note 15, ¶ 14.

vetoes have been consistently upheld by courts in countries of many regions of the world,[221] the European Court of Human Rights,[222] and the Commission of Human Rights.[223]

Courts have uniformly rejected claims that abortions requested by women that are otherwise lawful are unlawful without authorization of male partners. The Italian Constitutional Court, for instance, rejected a claim that Italy's abortion law was in violation of Articles 29 of the Constitution because it provided no role for the husband in a wife's determination whether to have an abortion.[224] Article 29 states that marriage is based on the moral and legal equality of a husband and wife. The Court held that the legislature had placed the burden of making an abortion decision on the wife, and that this decision was rational in light of the much greater effect that pregnancy has on a woman's physical and mental health than on those of a man. The European Court of Human Rights consistently reasoned that any interpretation of a putative father's right must first take into account the rights of the woman requesting abortion, since she is the person primarily concerned with the pregnancy and its termination or continuation.[225]

The US Supreme Court has considered a law enacted in Pennsylvania that requires a married woman not necessarily to obtain her husband's authorization, but to sign a statement that she had notified him of her intent to obtain an abortion.[226] The Court held such a provision unconstitutional as a violation of the woman's right to privacy. However, the Court upheld provisions that require the woman to receive certain information at least twenty-four hours before the abortion is performed, that mandate the informed consent of one parent of a minor seeking an abortion, and place reporting requirements on facilities providing abortion services.

4. Conscience and professional duty

Some hospitals and other health care facilities make an institutional claim to allegiance to a religious faith that condemns abortion, and to rights not to offer such procedures. The origin of human rights shows them to reside,

---

221. A v. B, 35 (iii) P.D. 57 (Supreme Court of Israel, 1981); Attorney-General (QLD) ex rel. Kerr v. T, 46 ALR 275 (High Court of Australia, 1983); C. v. S., 2 W.L.R. 1108 (Court of Appeal, England, 1987): Judgment of 15 Feb. 1978, Dec. No. 157/77, 3 Yugoslav Law 65 (Constitutional Court of Yugoslavia, 1979); Judgment of 31 Oct. 1980, Conseil d'Etat, D.S. Jur. 19,732 (Council of State of France, 1980); Kelly v. Kelly, 2 FLR 828 (Court of Session Scotland 1997); Planned Parenthood v. Danforth, 428 U.S. 52, 69 (1976); Tremblay v. Daigle, (1998) 62 D.L.R. (4th) 634, 665 (Can.).

222. H v. Norway, 73 DECISIONS AND REPORTS 155 (1992) (European Court of Human Rights).

223. Paton v. United Kingdom, 3 E.H.R.R. 408 (1980) (Eur. Comm'n Hum. Rts.).

224. Judgment No. 389 of 31 Mar. 1988, Corte Cost., Gazz. Ufficiale, 1 serie speciale, 13 April 1988, n.15 Giur. Cost e Civ. 2110 (1988).

225. H v. Norway, supra note 222, at 170.

226. Planned Parenthood of Southeastern Pennsylvania v. Casey, 505 U.S. 833 (1992).

however, only in individuals, not institutions such as legal corporations. Administrators of religiously affiliated facilities may claim the right not to become personally complicit in conduct they consider sinful. Their consciences should be accommodated to a maximum degree possible. However, when their facilities are publicly responsible for the health care of individuals of varied religious conscience, who have no access to alternative facilities, a conflict exists between the human rights of facility administrators and those whose health care and well-being are entrusted to them. Some countries have explicitly legislated that publicly funded health care facilities are required to satisfy requests for lawful health services made by members of the communities the facilities serve.[227]

Health service providers' human rights entitle them, particularly on grounds of freedom of religion, to claim conscientious objection to their performance of abortion. Accordingly, they cannot be subject to legally enforceable demands that they participate. Health care providers may also claim rights of conscientious objection to lesser forms of collaboration in abortion procedures, such as nursing preparation of abortion patients. Women who are not at imminent risk of death cannot demand physicians' and other health care providers' participation in the direct performance of abortion procedures. They can, however, require health care facilities to have appropriate staff available to render the lawful abortion and related services they require unless, as in several of the United States, facilities have received legislated immunities.

Several countries' legislation makes explicit what is usually implicit in laws governing the general delivery of health care services, namely that they accommodate the right of conscientious objection.[228] Section 4 of British Abortion Act 1967, as amended, serves as a model. Subsection 1 provides that "no person shall be under any duty, whether by contract or by any statutory or other legal requirement, to participate in any treatment . . . to which he has a conscientious objection." The burden of proof of objection rests on the person claiming it. The subsection does not affect the duty to participate in treatment necessary "to save the life or to prevent grave permanent injury to the physical or mental health of a pregnant woman."[229] In 1989, Denmark amended its abortion law to recognize rights of conscientious objection for health service providers and trainees,[230] but requires facilities to ensure

227. See, e.g., Danish Act on Abortion, Order 633 (15 Sept. 1986).
228. Emily N. Marcus, Conscientious Objection as an Emerging Human Right, 38 VA J. INT'L L. 507 (1998).
229. British Abortion Act 1967, as amended, § 4(2).
230. See supra note 227; Danish Acts. No. 350 (24 May 1989), 389 (7 June 1989) amending the 1986 Act.

women's appropriate access to services. Similarly, legislation in Guyana, for instance, reflects the general background law governing health service providers, in that it recognizes conscientious objection in principle but it precludes such objection where women's lives are at risk and no alternative services are immediately available.[231]

Conscience based on religious faith usually allows life-preserving interventions, including those that terminate pregnancies, under the doctrine of double effect.[232] Termination, for instance, of ectopic or tubal pregnancy is not regarded as direct or deliberate abortion. The scope of rights of objection is governed by features of individual national laws. For instance, some disallow refusals to deliver post-operative care to abortion patients and to type referral letters for abortions.[233] It is often the role of courts to balance various interests at stake in the performance of abortions. Institutions' refusal to employ staff members unless they share a common conviction, whether to object to abortions or to perform them in all circumstances, may violate human rights duties of non-discrimination in recruitment for employment on grounds of potential employees' religious or other convictions. Laws usually contain implicit provisions, which the Danish law makes explicit, that institutions responsible for health services in their region must meet their duties to make lawful abortion services available by employing adequate staff, while respecting individuals' rights of conscientious objection. Nevertheless, CEDAW has criticized countries that have allowed health care providers' conscientious objections to deny women's timely access to legal abortion services, for instance in Croatia[234] and Southern Italy.[235] States may be internationally accountable under human rights conventions for failing to ensure proper recruiting practices to serve women's health interests.

Women's human rights to liberty and to security of abortion choice are diminished when health care providers deliver services not only without respect for patients' confidentiality, but also judgmentally. Providers may, for instance, approach women as being immoral, or ignorant because they have an unplanned pregnancy. More harmful are punitive treatments of women that deny them physical pain-relief and psychological comfort during performance of abortion procedures, or that are accompanied by threats against future unplanned pregnancies, such as denial of health services. Not only

---

231. Medical Termination of Pregnancy Act, No. 7 (1995).
232. Daniel P. Sulmasy & Edmund D. Pellegrino, *The Rule of Double Effect: Clearing Up the Double Talk,* 159 Archives of Internal Med. 545 (1999).
233. Janaway v. Salford Health Authority, 3 All ER 1079 (1988) (House of Lords, England).
234. Report of the Committee on the Elimination of Discrimination against Women: Croatia (18th Sess. 1998), U.N. Doc. CEDAW/C/1998/I/L.1/Add.3. (1998) ¶ 31, 35 (1998).
235. Report of the Committee on the Elimination of Discrimination against Women: Morocco (16th & 17th Sess. 1997), U.N. Doc. A/52/38/Rev.1 ¶¶ 353, 360.

are health care providers responsible for such unethical, punitive approaches and treatments, but governments are liable when they fail to take measures to discourage, discipline, and eliminate practices that deny patients' human rights. For example, professional and institutional licensing bodies that discharge functions delegated by governments can sanction health care professionals and facilities when they violate patients' human rights.

V.   A WAY FORWARD: HUMAN RIGHTS NEEDS ASSESSMENT

Guidance on a country's legal compliance with human rights obligations to advance women's health regarding abortion can be based on an assessment of the scope, causes, and consequences of unsafe abortion at national or particular community levels. Assessment can employ available data sources, or be based on the collection of relevant new data. Assessment should identify codes of medical ethics, laws, including the language of enacted laws and decisions of courts, and policies of governments, health care facilities, and other influential agencies that facilitate or obstruct abortion services. A determination should be made of whether codes, laws, and policies that would facilitate access are actually implemented, and if they are not, of how they might be. Laws and policies that obstruct women's choice regarding their health generally and abortion specifically, and their access to services, should be identified, along with laws that facilitate and obstruct women's empowerment.

Assessment is needed of compliance with human rights at different levels, including clinical care, the operation of health systems, and the influence of underlying social, economic, and legal conditions. These levels are not necessarily distinct and often overlap. Failure to respect women's human rights at one level can cause or exacerbate failure at another level. Social science, epidemiological, and legal research can be drawn upon to conduct a human rights assessment of abortion services. In addition, Concluding Observations of human rights treaty monitoring committees and human rights fact-finding reports often indicate what more needs to be done to bring laws, policies and practices into compliance with human rights standards. Examples are explored below of information that a human rights needs assessment might include when addressing the three levels of clinical care, organization of health systems, and underlying social, economic, and legal conditions.[236]

---

236. Compare the work on developing a human rights impact assessment in the context of HIV/AIDS by Lawrence O. Gostin & Zita Lazzarini, Human Rights and Public Health in the AIDS Pandemic ch. 3 (1997).

A. Clinical Care

An approach to assessing respect for rights in clinical care is to examine treatment protocols for women seeking abortion services, or treatment for incomplete or spontaneous abortion. If such treatment protocols do not exist, inquiries should address whether steps are being taken to develop them. Where protocols exist, assessments are needed to determine the extent to which they require respect for women's decisions and the extent to which they are used in training health care providers and whether they are actually followed in the delivery of services.

An assessment should examine the ways clinical care for abortion incorporates attention to underlying diseases or conditions specific to or more prevalent among certain subgroups of pregnant women, such as malaria, sickle cell trait, hepatitis, and HIV/AIDS. Steps taken to ensure that abortion services are provided to affected women should also ensure that these underlying conditions are treated and that affected women are referred for appropriate treatment. The reproductive health problems among such women should be addressed in a nondiscriminatory, constructive way. An assessment should also examine responses to social conditions with clinical manifestations, such as domestic violence resulting in unwanted pregnancy that leads to unsafe abortion.

Emphasis should be on efforts taken to reduce the stigma of unplanned pregnancy, and whether resort to abortion in the clinical care context includes respectful treatment of all women seeking services, irrespective of their reasons, circumstances, or socio-economic status. An assessment might seek data, including anecdotal data, of whether providers show respect for women's dignity, and are non-judgmental toward abortion clients. Health care providers should be trained in the importance of maintaining confidentiality, since breaches may be violations not only of service providers' professional ethical duties, but also of laws on patient confidentiality.[237]

Resort to care for perhaps life-endangering post-abortion complications is deterred where laws permit or even compel medical practitioners to report women they believe may have had unlawful abortions to police authorities. For instance, in Argentina in 1998, the Supreme Court of the Province of Santa Fe held that a gynecologist was entitled to breach professional confidentiality to inform authorities that a patient seeking treatment for abortion complications may have initiated the procedure unlawfully.[238]

---

237. Bernard M. Dickens & Rebecca J. Cook, *Law and Ethics in Conflict Over Confidentiality*, 70 Int'l J. Gynecology & Obstetrics 385–91 (2000).
238. Case T. 148 PS. 357/428, Corte Suprema de la Provincia de Sante Fe, 2 Aug. 1998 (Supreme Court of the Province of Sante Fe, Argentina).

This type of reporting to police authorities and its judicial endorsement raise profound concerns about observance of women's human rights.

Even where induced abortion is legally restricted, women's health requires competent treatment for incomplete and spontaneous abortion, of whatever origin. Post-abortion care requires that when women suffer complications following unlawful procedures, they be treated with the care, courtesy, and compassion that health service providers are expected to apply as an aspect of their professionalism. Deliberate cruelty or indifference to suffering is no more tolerable in the case of unlawful abortion than when, for instance, surgeons treat the wounds of criminal fugitives or military opponents.[239] An assessment should consider means by which professional standards in post-abortion care are monitored and maintained.

B.   Health Systems

An assessment of the degree to which women's reproductive and wider human rights are respected throughout the health system might be approached through an examination of barriers to the availability of care and to laws, policies, and practices that deter women from seeking access to care. Where assessment at the clinical level indicates unacceptable rates of hospitalization due to unsafe abortion, the relevant ministry of health might be encouraged to evaluate how the government might respond and, for instance, better meet the need for preventive family planning services. In May 1998, for instance, the Committee on Economic, Social and Cultural Rights, monitoring the Economic Covenant, expressed its concern in its Concluding Observations on the Report of Poland that "family planning services are not provided in the public health care system so that women have no access to affordable contraception." The Committee also noted that "restrictions have recently been imposed on abortions that exclude economic and social grounds for performing legal abortions . . . because of this restriction, women in Poland are now resorting to unscrupulous abortionists and risking their health in doing so."[240]

Examination is required of barriers to availability of abortion and abortion-related services. Barriers include lack of implementation of related laws and policies that are beneficial to women's health, due to legal prohibition or restriction of procedures or, for example, abuse of conscientious objection to participation in lawful services by health personnel. Attention should

---

239. British Medical Association, Medicine Betrayed: The Participation of Doctors in Human Rights Abuses (1992).

240. *Report of the Committee on Economic, Social and Cultural Rights,* U.N. Doc. E/C.12/ 1998/28, ¶ 12, at 40–49.

be given to low priority of lawful abortion services in health facilities, or in allocation of necessary budgetary resources. Lack of services being offered at times when it is convenient for women to attend for them, including lack of facilities to care for their young children while they receive counseling and treatment, should be explored.

Deterrents to access to services a health care system claims to provide include third party authorization, such as spousal authorization requirements;[241] failure to treat adolescents according to their "evolving capacity" to exercise mature choice in abortion care;[242] and payment or co-payment requirements, particularly for adolescent girls. CEDAW has condemned as discriminatory against women the laws and policies that condition women's access to lawful abortion services upon the authorization of other persons or groups of persons, such as therapeutic abortion committees; men encounter no such obstacles to obtain the medical care they request. Addressing the Report submitted by the government of Turkey, for instance, CEDAW considered that the legal requirement that a woman obtain the authorization of her husband in order to have an abortion violated her right under the Women's Convention to equality before the law.[243]

Assessments are needed at the health systems level, of the degree to which legal grounds for abortion are actually put into operation. Some jurisdictions, such as some states in Mexico, recognize legal abortion following rape, but provide little or no facilities through which women can avail themselves of lawful procedures.[244] In one such state, governmental health care providers notoriously obstructed access of an adolescent rape victim to services to which she was legally entitled, forcing her to deliver a child.[245] In contrast, a women's health advocacy group in Brazil has developed collaborative arrangements with the police to investigate rape complaints and provide timely access to abortion services in legally justifiable cases, where the evidence of sexual aggression is persuasive.[246] Women's health advocacy

---

241. Rebecca J. Cook, *International Protection of Women's Reproductive Rights*, 24 N.Y. Univ. J. Int'l L. & Pol. 645, 697–98 (1992); Reed Boland, *Population Policies, Human Rights, and Legal Change*, 44 Am. Univ. L. Rev. 1257, 1276–68 (April 1995).

242. Rebecca J. Cook & Bernard M. Dickens, *Recognizing Adolescents' "Evolving Capacities" to Exercise Choice in Reproductive Health Care*, 70 Int'l J. Gynecology & Obstetrics 13–21 (2000).

243. Report of the Committee on the Elimination of Discrimination against Women, Turkey, 16th Sess, Doc. A/52/38/Rev 1, ¶¶ 151–206, at ¶ 196 (1997).

244. Marie Claire Acosta, *Overcoming the Discrimination of Women in Mexico: A Task for Sysiphus*, in The (Un)Rule of Law and the Underprivileged in Latin America 160–80 (Juan Mendez, Guillermo O'Donnell, Paulo S. Pinheiro eds., 1999).

245. Grupo de Informacion en Reproduccion Elegida (GIRE), Paulina: In the Name of the Law (2000).

246. Jacqueline Pitanguay & Luciana S. Garbayo, Relatorio do Seminario a Implementacao do Aborto Legal no Servico Publico de Saude (Report of a Seminar on the Implementation of Legal Abortion with the Public Health Service) (Rio de Janeiro, Brazil: Cicadania, Estudo, Pesquisa, Informacao e Acao, 1995).

groups, working together with the Brazilian Federation of Associations of Gynecologists and Obstetricians and the Brazilian Ministry of Health, developed a treatment protocol for rape victims that is now widely used to guide services in hospital emergency departments and to train health service providers. Assessments should note such collaborations.

Assessments should determine whether abortion laws and policies require excessive qualifications for health care providers to perform abortion services. Where excessive qualifications are required, so limiting the number of personnel able to provide services, options should be explored to determine whether governmental agencies might change such policies, or whether, for instance, a court declaration might clarify whether other appropriately trained personnel such as nurses are legally able to provide services. The Royal College of Nursing of the United Kingdom sought a judicial declaration leading to clarification that abortion may be conducted, under medical supervision, along extended lines of authority. Accordingly, nurses who assist, even instrumentally, in the management of abortion procedures, were ruled to be legally protected in the same way as the doctors in charge.[247]

Legislation may show how health systems can calibrate requirements for approval of abortion to levels of medical intervention, such as to simplify requirements for the more basic services. For instance, the Guyanan and South African abortion laws permit termination of pregnancy during the first trimester to be undertaken or supervised by a registered medical practitioner in, for instance, a doctor's office. However, despite widespread debate about enactment of Guyana's 1995 law, major hospitals in the country were found at its enactment to be unprepared to implement its provisions, lacking means to deliver clinical services and lacking regulations for pre- and post-abortion counseling for women and their partners.[248] This lack of ability to implement progressive laws is not unique. Research shows that women still find it necessary to resort to abortion by unskilled personnel for instance in India[249] and Zambia[250] even though their laws were liberalized in 1971 and 1972 respectively. The problem is particularly acute in India, where over 90 percent of abortions are done in illegal settings due to a combination of indirect rights infringements and the structure of the health care

247. Royal College of Nursing of the United Kingdom v. Department of Health and Social Security, 1 All ER 545 (1981) (House of Lords, England).
248. Fred E. Nunes & Yvette M. Delph, *Making Abortion Law Reform Work: Steps and Slips in Guyana,* 9 Reproductive Health Matters 66–76 (1997).
249. Bela Ganatra, *Unsafe Abortion in South and South East Asia, in* Priorities and Needs in the Prevention of Unsafe Abortion and its Consequences: Report of an International Consultation (Iqbal Shah & Ina Warriner eds., forthcoming 2002) (on file with author).
250. Winny Koster-Oyekan, *Why Resort to Illegal Abortion in Zambia? Findings of a Community-Based Study in Western Province,* 46 Soc. Sci. & Med. 1303 (1998).

system.[251] Accordingly, an assessment cannot presume that legal reform itself achieves health system reform.

C.   Social, Economic, and Legal Conditions

Barriers to improving women's reproductive health including access to safe abortion services are often rooted in social, economic, cultural, and legal conditions that infringe upon women's human rights. A human rights needs assessment might reveal that social factors, including lack of literacy and of educational or employment opportunities, deny young women alternatives to early unwanted or repeated pregnancy and deny them economic and other means of access to contraception.

Women's vulnerability to sexual and other abuses, in and out of marriage, increases their exposure to unplanned pregnancy and unsafe abortion, and has been associated with further deterioration of their health, including mental health.[252] Investigation should determine, for instance, whether laws adequately protect girls and women from sexual coercion and sexual abuse. Studies show that forced first intercourse is prevalent in many communities, affecting as many as 32 percent of girls and women.[253] Laws that inadequately protect girls and women from coercion in sexual relations undermine women's independence and ability to protect themselves from unwanted pregnancies. Assessment should focus on whether laws and policies exist and are enforced that afford women effective defense against unwanted sexual relations, so that they can control the timing and number of their births.

Gender-sensitive social science and legal research can identify how underlying socio-legal conditions relate to the incidence of unwanted pregnancy and resort to unsafe abortion. For example, a study in Dar es Salaam, Tanzania showed that 432 of 455 hospitalized young women (about 95 percent) were admitted for abortion complications. These abortions were due to unwanted pregnancies resulting from the young women's relationships with older men, who acted as so-called "sugar daddies" and paid for their food in exchange for sex.[254]

---

251. Vandana Tripathi, *Applying a Human Rights Framework to the Provision of Abortion Care and Related Reproductive Health Services in India,* 2 J. HEALTH & POP. IN DEV. COUN. 11 (1999).
252. Leyla Gulcur, *Evaluating the Role of Gender Inequalities and Rights Violations in Women's Mental Health,* 5 HEALTH & HUM. RTS. 47–66 (2000).
253. Lori Heise & Ellsberg M. Gottemoeller, *Ending Violence Against Women,* 11 POPULATION REPORTS, Series I, at 9–17 (1999).
254. Gottlieb S. Mpangile, Melkizedeck T. Leshabari, David J. Kihwele, *Induced Abortion in Dar es Salaam, Tanzania: The Plight of Adolescents, in* ABORTION IN THE DEVELOPING WORLD 387–403 (Axel I. Mundigo & Cindy Indriso eds., 1999).

Several comparative studies are available that provide information on women's status and opportunities under laws in various countries[255] and regions.[256] Legal research can show how laws advance or compromise women's interests in their personal, family, and public lives, with indirect effects on their reproductive health. Family law frequently expresses the basic cultural values of a community, such as rights to inheritance of property including land. Cultures resistant to women's equality with men have unselfconsciously perpetuated women's subordination and powerlessness as a "natural" condition of family life and social order so profoundly as often to render women's disadvantage invisible. Where women's subordination and powerlessness are perceived, they are considered not just a feature but a necessary condition of social order and stability. Family and social discipline are seen as dependent on men's authority to make decisions.

Laws that entrench women's inferior status to men and interfere with women's access to health services seriously jeopardize efforts to improve women's reproductive and wider health. These laws take a variety of forms, such as those that obstruct economic independence by impairing women's education, inheritance, employment, or acquisition of commercial loans or credit, but they all infringe on women's ability to make their own choices about their lives and health.[257] Account should be taken of criminal, family, and other laws that condone, tolerate, or neglect violence against women, and, for instance, of inequitable family, education, and employment laws that deny adolescent and adult women alternatives in life to marriage, or that condition women's self-realization on marriage and motherhood. These include laws that require or allow pregnant girls' expulsion from school, and virginity tests for admission to educational or employment training institutions.

The compatibility of abortion laws and policies with human rights entitlements may be understood through factors specific to women's circumstances. A human rights needs assessment must address how women cope with unplanned pregnancy and resort to safe and unsafe abortion services, the health care systems on which they are dependent, and the social, economic, and legal conditions that affect their reproductive health and choices.

---

255. The Anti-Abortion Law in Poland: The Functioning, Social Effects, Attitudes and Behaviors (Wanda Nowicka ed., 2000).

256. See, e.g., Violeta Bermudez, La Regulacion Judica del Abortio en America Latina Y el Caribe (1997); Center for Reproductive Law and Policy, and Demus, Estudio para la Defensa de los Derechos de la Mujer, Women of the World: Laws and Policies Affecting their Reproductive Lives—Latin America and the Caribbean (1997) and Progress Report (2000); Center for Reproductive Law and Policy and International Federation of Women Lawyers—Kenya Chapter, Women of the World: Laws and Policies Affecting their Reproductive Lives: Anglophone Africa (1997) and Progress Report (2001).

257. Center for Reproductive Law and Policy, Reproductive Rights 2000—Moving Forward (2000).

Chapter 18

Debating Reproductive Rights in Ireland

Siobhán Mullally

I. INTRODUCTION

The Programme of Action adopted at the 1994 International Conference on Population and Development (Cairo Programme of Action) defines reproductive health as "a state of complete physical, mental, and social well-being . . . in all matters relating to the reproductive system and to its functions and processes."[1] The 1995 Beijing Declaration and Platform for Action (Beijing Declaration) reiterates this definition, listing as a human right the right of a woman to control her own sexuality and reproduction.[2] This limited recognition of women's reproductive rights has been difficult to secure and is the subject of an ongoing struggle, both at national and international levels.[3] This article examines that struggle within the context of the abortion debate in Ireland.

---

1. Programme of Action of the International Conference on Population and Development, *adopted* 18 Oct. 1994, U.N. GAOR, Ch. VII, ¶ 7.2, U.N. Doc. A/CONF.171/13 (1994) [hereinafter ICPD].
2. *Report of the Fourth World Conference on Women, Beijing Declaration and Platform for Action, adopted* 17 Oct., U.N. GAOR, 50th Sess., ¶ ¶ 94–96, U.N. Doc. A/CONF.177/20 (1995); *Report of the Committee on the Elimination of Discrimination Against Women on its Twentieth Session: General Recommendation 24*, U.N. GAOR, 54th Sess., Supp. No. 38, Pt. I, ¶ 23, U.N. Doc. A/54/38/Rev.1, ch. I (1999).
3. Rebecca J. Cook & Mahmoud F. Fathalla, *Advancing Reproductive Rights Beyond Cairo and Beijing, in* Women and International Human Rights Law Vol. 3, at 73–90 (Kelly D. Askin & Dorean M. Koenig eds., 1999); Maja Kirilova Eriksson, *Abortion and Reproductive Health: Making International Law More Responsive to Women's Needs, in id.* at 71; Rishona Fleishman, *The Battle Against Reproductive Rights: The Impact of the Catholic Church on Abortion Law in Both International and Domestic Arenas,* 14 Emory Int'l L. Rev. 277 (2000); Doris Elisabeth Buss, *Going Global: Feminist Theory, International Law, and the Public/Private Divide, in* Challenging The Public/Private Divide: Feminism, Law, and Public Policy 360 (Susan B. Boyd ed., 1997); Mary Ann Glendon, Abortion and Divorce in Western Law (1987); Drucilla Cornell, The Imaginary Domain: Abortion, Pornography & Sexual Harassment 31–37 (1995).

To date, there have been five constitutional referenda on the subject of abortion in Ireland—the most recent on 6 March 2002. Despite these repeated referenda and ongoing debate at the national level, Ireland's abortion laws continue to be amongst the most restrictive in the world.[4] In recent years, these restrictions have attracted criticism from UN human rights treaty bodies. The Committee on the Elimination of Discrimination Against Women (CEDAW) has called for the full implementation and protection of women's right to reproductive health in Ireland and has expressed concern that women's human rights were being compromised by the continuing influence of the Catholic Church in official state policy.[5] The Human Rights Committee[6] has pointed out that compelling a woman to continue with a pregnancy, particularly where that pregnancy is a result of rape, may violate the prohibitions of torture and of cruel, inhuman, or degrading treatment in the International Covenant on Civil and Political Rights (ICCPR).[7]

As can be seen, Ireland is bound by several international conventions and agreements that deal either directly or indirectly with women's rights to sexual and reproductive health and freedom. Ireland has not entered a reservation to the 1979 Convention on the Elimination of All Forms of Discrimination Against Women (Women's Convention) concerning abortion.[8] Furthermore, unlike other states parties to the Convention on the

---

4. For a comprehensive discussion of Ireland's abortion laws, see JAMES KINGSTON ET AL., ABORTION AND THE LAW 52–78 (1997); Nuala Jackson, *Family Law: Fertility and Parenthood, in* GENDER AND THE LAW IN IRELAND 130 (Alpha Connolly ed., 1993); Irish Council for Civil Liberties (Women's Committee), *Submission to the UN Committee on the Elimination of All Forms of Discrimination Against Women* (1999), *available at* http://iccl.ie/women/cedaw/cedaw.htm.

5. *Report of the Committee on the Elimination of Discrimination Against Women on its Twenty-First Session,* U.N. GAOR, 54th Sess., Supp. No. 38, Pt. II, ¶ 180, U.N. Doc. A/54/38/Rev.1 (1999) (concluding observations on Ireland). The Committee has also expressed concern about the particular hardships experienced by vulnerable groups of women in Ireland. For an asylum-seeking woman, for example, an attempt to leave the state may lead to criminal prosecution. *Id.* ¶ 185.

6. *Concluding Observations of the Human Rights Committee: Ireland, adopted* 21 July 2000, U.N. ESCOR, Hum. Rts. Comm., 69th Sess., 1858th mtg., ¶ 18, U.N. Doc. CCPR/CO/69/IRL (2000). *See also General Comment No. 28, Equality of Rights Between Men and Women, adopted* 29 Mar. 2000, U.N. ESCOR, Hum. Rts. Comm., 68th Sess., 1834th mtg., ¶ 11, U.N. Doc. CCPR/C/21/Rev.1/Add.10 (2000). The Human Rights Committee has expressed similar concerns in relation to the restrictive abortion laws in Poland. *See Concluding Observations of the Human Rights Committee: Poland, adopted* 28 July 1999, U.N. ESCOR, Hum. Rts. Comm., 66th Sess., 1779th mtg., U.N. Doc. CCPR/C/79/Add.110 (1999). In particular, the Committee has noted "with concern" the strict laws on abortion "which lead to high numbers of clandestine abortions with attendant risks to life and health of women." *Id.* ¶ 11.

7. International Covenant on Civil and Political Rights, *adopted* 16 Dec. 1966, G.A. Res. 2200 (XXI), U.N. GAOR, 21st Sess., Supp. No. 16, U.N. Doc. A/6316 (1966) (*entered into force* 23 Mar. 1976), 999 U.N.T.S. 171.

8. Convention on the Elimination of All Forms of Discrimination Against Women, *adopted*

Rights of the Child (CRC),[9] Ireland's ratification of the CRC was not accompanied by a declaration or stipulation concerning the protection of the child before birth.[10] Neither has Ireland made any interpretive declarations or reservations to the Cairo Programme of Action or the Beijing Declaration. Though no such formal reservations have been made, the Irish Minister for Health emphasized the importance of recognizing that abortion policy and legislation were "a matter for each country to determine for itself" when he

---

18 Dec. 1979, G.A. Res. 34/180, U.N. GAOR, 34th Sess., Supp. No. 46, U.N. Doc. A/34/46 (1980) (*entered into force* 3 Sept. 1981), 1249 U.N.T.S. 13, *reprinted in* 19 I.L.M. 33 (1980) [hereinafter Women's Convention]. Although the Women's Convention does not include any reference to abortion, CEDAW has examined the restrictive abortion laws in many states. *See Report of the Committee on the Elimination of Discrimination Against Women on its Twenty-First Session,* U.N. GAOR, 54th Sess., Supp. No. 38, Pt. II, ¶¶ 202–35, U.N. Doc. A/54/38/Rev.1 (1999) (concluding observations on Chile). CEDAW expressed concern about the "inadequate recognition and protection of the reproductive rights of women in Chile." *Id.* ¶ 228. It was especially concerned about the laws prohibiting and punishing any form of abortion, which CEDAW said, affected women's health by increasing maternal mortality and causing further suffering when women are imprisoned for violation of the law. The Committee urged the government "to consider review of the laws relating to abortion with a view to their amendment, in particular to provide safe abortion and to permit termination of pregnancy for therapeutic reasons or because of the health, including mental health, of the woman. The Committee also urges the government to revise laws which require health professionals to report women who undergo abortions to law enforcement agencies and which impose criminal penalties on these women." *Id.* ¶ 229. *See also Report of the Committee on the Elimination of Discrimination Against Women on its Seventeenth Session,* U.N. GAOR, 52d Sess., Supp. No. 38, Pt. II, ¶¶ 273–321, U.N. Doc. A/52/38/Rev.1 (1997) (concluding observations on Argentina). The Committee expressed concern that, "despite economic and social development in Argentina, maternal mortality and morbidity due to childbirth and abortion remained high." *Id.* ¶ 304. It recommended that legislation penalizing mothers who had abortions should be reviewed. *Id.* ¶ 319. In commenting on Slovenia's initial report under the Convention, the Committee noted "with satisfaction the inclusion of the right to abortion in the Constitution of Slovenia." *Report of the Committee on the Elimination of Discrimination Against Women on its Sixteenth Session,* U.N. GAOR, 52d Sess., Supp. No. 38, Pt. I, ¶¶ 81–122, ¶ 98, U.N. Doc. A/52/38/Rev.1 (1997) (concluding observations on Slovenia).

9. Convention on the Rights of the Child, adopted *20 Nov. 1989,* G.A. Res. 44/25, U.N. GAOR, 44th Sess., Supp. No. 49, U.N. Doc. A/44/49, at 166 (1989) (*entered into force* 2 Sept. 1990), *reprinted in* 28 I.L.M. 1448 (1989).

10. *See* Philip Alston, *The Unborn Child and Abortion under the Draft Convention on the Rights of the Child,* 12 Hum. Rts. Q. 156 (1990). The ninth preambular paragraph of the CRC refers to the child's right to legal protection before as well as after birth, reiterating the third preambular paragraph to the Declaration on the Rights of the Child. The Working Group on the Convention included an interpretive statement in the *travaux preparatoires,* to the effect that the ninth preambular paragraph did not have any bearing on the definition of the child as a human being in Article 1 of the Convention. It also rejected a draft savings clause providing that nothing in the Convention should affect any provisions more conducive to the rights of the child before as well as after birth. The definition of a child continues to remain controversial. *See, e.g.,* Reservations and Declarations entered by Argentina, Ecuador, Guatemala, the Holy See, *available at* www.unhchr .ch/html/menu3/b/treaty15_asp.htm.

spoke at the Cairo + 5 review meeting.[11] Interestingly, no such concerns were expressed at the Beijing + 5 review meeting, held just one year later. Addressing the Special Session of the General Assembly, the Irish Minister for Justice, Equality and Law Reform emphasized Ireland's "full endorsement" of the Beijing Declaration[12] and agreed that there should be no renegotiation of the 1995 texts.[13] This difference in approach might be explained by the more ambiguous language in the Beijing Declaration. It might also be explained by the Irish government's growing recognition of the difficulties that any renegotiation would create. Having come through a difficult preparatory process at the national level, the Minister was all too aware of the religious-cultural claims that could be raised by states.[14]

In examining the entanglement of religious and nationalist principles with the struggle for reproductive rights in Ireland, part II of this article describes the challenges raised by international human rights law to Ireland's inherited "pro-life" and "pro-family" values. Part III examines this challenge in the context of the abortion debate and looks at the many constraints surrounding women's attempt to claim reproductive autonomy. Part IV focuses on the ill-fated attempts of abortion reform and the continuing reluctance to recognize the legitimacy of women's reproductive rights.

---

11. Brian Cowen, Address at the United Nations Special Session of the General Assembly for the Review and Appraisal of the Implementation of the Programme of Action of the International Conference on Population and Development (30 June 1999), *available at* www.un.org/popin/unpopcom/32ndsess/gass/state/ireland.pdf.

12. John O'Donoghue, Minister for Justice, Equality and Law Reform, Address to the Special Session of the UN General Assembly, "Women 2000: Gender Equality, Development and Peace for the 21st Century" (6 June 2000), *available at* www.un.org/womenwatch/daw/followup/beijing+5stat/statments/ireland6.htm.

13. In the build up to the Beijing + 5 review meeting, many feared that conservative forces would try to undermine the Beijing Declaration and Platform of Action. In the final negotiations, however, the coalition of the Holy See and G-77 states disintegrated. Led by Brazil and Peru, a new bloc emerged—known as Some Latin American Countries (SLAC). *SLAC* came under intense pressure from the Holy See and certain other members of the G-77. Its strengths grew, however. It was joined by the fourteen Caribbean CARICOM countries (thus becoming "SLACC") and in the final negotiations worked closely with India and the bloc of Southern African countries known as SADC, as well as Cameroon, Ghana, and Kenya. This fragmentation ensured that the Beijing Declaration and Platform of Action were accepted as a floor for further negotiations. Attempts to roll back the achievements of Beijing, the ICPD, and the ICPD + 5 were thwarted. However, little was achieved in the way of progress. Against a background of fragmentation and dissent between states, negotiations were largely focused on containment rather than progress. *See generally,* CENTER FOR REPRODUCTIVE RIGHTS, BEIJING + 5: ASSESSING REPRODUCTIVE RIGHTS (Nov. 2000), *available at* www.reproductiverights.org/pub_bp_beijing5.html.

14. *See* Department of Justice, Equality and Law Reform, *Report of Proceedings, UN General Assembly Special Session, Women 2000: Gender Equality, Development and Peace for the 21st Century; National Forum for Non-Governmental Organisations* (10 May 2000).

II.   IRELAND'S GENDER-DIFFERENTIATED CITIZENSHIP: RESISTING THE INTERNATIONAL STRUGGLE FOR GENDER EQUALITY

Women's reproductive rights in Ireland have long been a contested terrain. As in many postcolonial states, the demarcation of gender roles in Ireland has always been intertwined with debates on national identity.[15] In a struggling nation state, scarred by the trauma of partition and civil war, gender trouble could not be tolerated. The overwhelming push to define Ireland as "not-England" led to a search for distinguishing marks of identity. The Roman Catholic religion, adhered to by a majority of the Irish people, became one of these distinguishing identity markers.[16]

Nationalist ideologies have always tended "to define their groups in either/or terms."[17] In Ireland, the search for homogeneity and national unity transformed Irish republicanism into a "conservative . . . Catholic nationalist movement."[18] This transformation was to have a significant impact on women's citizenship. Like the Roman Catholic religion, the definition of Ireland in exclusively "pro-life" terms served as another distinguishing mark of Irish identity. Women's reproductive autonomy was sacrificed to the greater good of a postcolonial political project, and women were defined not by their equal capacity for moral agency, but by their reproductive and sexual functions. When abortion came to the forefront as a political issue in the early 1980s, it was debated less on its own terms and more in terms of the consequences that freedom of choice would have for Ireland's inherited religious-cultural traditions.[19] The Catholic Right in Ireland, concerned with preserving the conservative ethos that permeates the Irish Constitution, has portrayed feminism and human rights discourse not only as a threat to Ireland's "pro-life" and "pro-family" traditions, but also as a threat to Ireland's sovereignty.[20] Thus, debates centered on the family and reproductive rights form the bedrock of the Catholic Right's backlash.

---

15.   *See* Yvonne Scannell, *The Constitution and the Role of Women, in* DE VALERA'S CONSTITUTION AND OURS 123–36 (Brian Farrell ed., 1988); GENDER AND SEXUALITY IN MODERN IRELAND (Anthony Bradley & Maryann Gialanella Valiulis eds., 1997); IRISH WOMEN'S STUDIES READER (Ailbhe Smyth ed., 1993); Hanna Sheehy-Skeffington, *Bean na h-Éireann, in* IN THEIR OWN VOICE: WOMEN AND IRISH NATIONALISM 32–34 (Margaret Ward ed., 1995); CAROL COULTER, THE HIDDEN TRADITION: FEMINISM, WOMEN AND NATIONALISM IN IRELAND (1993).

16.   DECLAN KIBERD, INVENTING IRELAND 9 (1996).

17.   IRIS MARION YOUNG, INCLUSION AND DEMOCRACY 252 (2000).

18.   Noel Browne, *Church and State in Modern Ireland, in* IRELAND'S EVOLVING CONSTITUTION 1937–1997, 41, 48 (Tim Murphy & Patrick Twomey eds., 1998).

19.   Ruth Fletcher, *Post-colonial Fragments: Representations of Abortion in Irish Law and Politics,* 28 J. L. & SOCIETY 568, 574 (2001).

20.   *See* National Union of Mothers of Ireland, *Submission to the Forum on Europe* (3 Dec. 2001), *available at* www.forumoneurope.ie/index.asp?locID=65&docID=-1; NEART, BEIJING + 5: ALTERNATIVE REPORT FOR IRELAND (May 2000) *available at* www.nwci.ie/documents/beijing.doc; Ailbhe Smyth, *The "X" Case: Women and Abortion in the Republic of*

For women, the postcolonial moment was often a moment of exclusion. In Ireland this exclusion arrived with the enactment of 1937 Constitution, *Bunreacht na hÉireann*.[21] Traditionally, the Irish nation had been defined by mythical female figures, Yeats and Gregory's *Cathleen ni Houlihán* being one of the most well-known personifications of the nation.[22] While the nation came to be defined as feminine, the political activity came to be defined as peculiarly masculine.[23] Though many women participated in the war of independence—as fighters, messengers, and leaders—they found themselves confined to hearth and home in an independent Ireland.[24] The depiction of the self-sacrificing mother as an emblem of Irish nationalism was to limit the transformative potential of rights discourse for many years. This phenomenon, of course, is not unique to Ireland. Various studies have revealed the dominance of single unifying forms of nationalism and the silencing of those who challenge the unity of the national self.[25] In Ireland, the silencing of women's dissenting voices was to limit the transformative potential of rights discourse for many years.

The 1937 Constitution of Ireland posed a tragic dilemma for Irish feminists. It marked the transformation of the "Irish Free State," which had been in existence since the end of the war of independence in 1922 when the Anglo-Irish Treaty was signed, into the Republic of Ireland.[26] For women, however, the constitution failed to fulfill its promise of a liberal rights-based democracy. The leading female figures in the independence movement had opposed the 1921 Anglo-Irish Treaty, rejecting the oath of allegiance to the British Crown and the partition of Ireland into North and South.[27] Although

---

Ireland, 1992, 1 FEMINIST LEGAL STUD. 163 (1993); THE ABORTION PAPERS, IRELAND (Ailbhe Smyth ed., 1992).

21. Constitution of Ireland, 1937 [hereinafter IR. CONST.].

22. *See* YEATS AND WOMEN (Deirdre Toomey ed., 1997). *Cathleen Ni Houlihán* is one of W.B. Yeats' most popular poems. It is now accepted that it was in fact co-written by his patron, Lady Gregory.

23. *See* MARGARET WARD, UNMANAGEABLE REVOLUTIONARIES: WOMEN AND IRISH NATIONALISM (1983).

24. Until 1922, Ireland was under British rule. Following the war of independence, which occurred between 1919 and 1921, the Irish Republican Army, under Michael Collins, and the British government entered into the Anglo-Irish Treaty. Pursuant to this treaty, the new nation would be referred to as the "Irish Free State." The nation would remain under the British Commonwealth, but could have its own army. *See* Anglo-Irish Treaty, 6 December 1921. The Irish Free State became the Republic of Ireland in 1937 with the enactment of Bunreacht na hÉirean, the Constitution of Ireland.

25. *See generally* ANIA LOOMBA, COLONIALISM/POSTCOLONIALISM: THE NEW CRITICAL IDIOM (1998); RATNA KAPUR & BRENDA COSSMAN, SUBVERSIVE SITES: FEMINIST ENGAGEMENTS WITH LAW IN INDIA (1996); Ratna Kapur, *A Love Song to Our Mongrel Selves: Hybridity,* 8 SEXUALITY & L. 353 (1999); Valentine M. Moghadam, *Patriarchy and the Politics of Gender in Modernising Societies: Iran, Pakistan and Afghanistan,* 7 INT'L SOCIOLOGY 35 (1992).

26. *Supra* note 24 and accompanying text.

27. *See generally* LINDA CONNOLLY, THE IRISH WOMEN'S MOVEMENT: FROM REVOLUTION TO DEVOLUTION (2002); CAROL COULTER, THE HIDDEN TRADITION: FEMINISM, WOMEN AND NATIONALISM (1993).

not foreseen at the time, the partition of the state significantly impacted women's citizenship in the Irish Free State. The corollary of a Protestant Parliament for a Protestant people in the North was presumed to be a Catholic Parliament for a Catholic people in the South.[28] Catholic triumphalism was rooted in the necessity to find something to celebrate in an infant state scarred by political disappointments.[29] Adherance to the Roman Catholic teachings on issues involving the family, sexuality, and reproductive health served to distinguish "Irish laws and Irish ways" from the "polluting" forces of English law.[30]

The 1937 Constitution was drafted by the Prime Minister, De Valera, with the assistance of a few senior civil servants and the leading figures within Ireland's Catholic Church and the Vatican.[31] The influence of the Catholic Church is particularly evident in the constitutional chapter on Fundamental Rights. Although the Roman Catholic Church had supported the Anglo-Irish Treaty of 1921 and the establishment of the Irish Free State in 1922, there was a strong feeling that the 1922 Constitution was not a wholly Irish document.[32] Leaders of the Catholic Church argued that it was an imposed document, "exotic, unnatural and quite foreign to the native tradition."[33] De Valera was urged to make "a definite break with the Liberal and non-Christian type of state" that had been "forced upon [the Irish People] by a foreign, non-Catholic power."[34] The conservative Catholic ethos that permeates much of the 1937 Constitution culminates in the provisions on the family.[35] Article 41 (2)(2) leaves little room for debate as to the nature of women's citizenship under the Irish Constitution: "[t]he State shall, therefore, endeavour to ensure that mothers shall not be obliged by

---

28. *See generally* Fletcher, *supra* note 19.
29. *See* Ronan Fanning, *Mr. De Valera Drafts a Constitution, in* DE VALERA'S CONSTITUTION AND OURS, *supra* note 15, at 33, 43.
30. In Re Howley [1940] I.R. 119. In this case, Justice Gavin Duffy referred to the reformation and subsequent common law jurisprudence as "temporary pollutions" that interrupted and distorted the normal flow of "a Catholic common law."
31. The role of the Roman Catholic hierarchy in Ireland in drafting the 1937 Constitution has been the subject of much historical commentary. *See* Browne, *supra* note 18, at 41; DESMOND M. CLARKE, CHURCH AND STATE: ESSAYS IN POLITICAL PHILOSOPHY (1984); Dermot Keogh, *Church, State and Society, in* DE VALERA'S CONSTITUTION AND OURS, *supra* note 15, at 103; DERMOT KEOGH, IRELAND AND THE VATICAN: THE POLITICS AND DIPLOMACY OF CHURCH-STATE RELATIONS 1922–1960 (1995); DERMOT KEOGH, THE VATICAN, THE BISHOPS AND IRISH POLITICS 1919–1939 (1986).
32. Dermot Keogh, *Church, State and Society, in* DE VALERA'S CONSTITUTION AND OURS, *supra* note 15, at 109.
33. *Id.*
34. *Id.*
35. *See generally* Siobhán Mullally, *Equality Guarantees in the Irish Constitution: The Myth of Constitutionalism and the Neutral State, in* IRELAND'S EVOLVING CONSTITUTION, *supra* note 18, at 147; Dolores Dooley, *Gendered Citizenship in the Irish Constitution, in id.* at 121; Frank Martin, *The Family in the Constitution—Principle and Practice, in id.* at 79.

economic necessity to engage in labour to the neglect of their duties in the home."[36]

A commitment to this "separate spheres" ideology, premised on the complementarity of gender roles and the presumption of natural sex differences between women and men, is central to much Roman Catholic teaching. In his *Letter to Women*, issued prior to the Beijing Conference, Pope John Paul II reiterates the Vatican's commitment to this teaching.[37] Similarly, the "uni-duality" of women and men and the significance of "biological conditioning" is re-emphasized in the "Letter to the Bishops of the Catholic Church on the Collaboration of Men and Women in the Church and in the World."[38]

The continuing influence of the Catholic Church on Ireland's constitutional text has attracted the criticism of UN human rights treaty bodies. In its concluding observations on Ireland's combined second and third reports, CEDAW expressed particular concern at the constitutional emphasis on the role of women as mothers and care givers.[39] The UN Human Rights Committee also has expressed concern about the "traditional attitudes" toward women's roles evident in Ireland's constitutional text.[40] As a result of these comments, opposition to the liberalizing agenda of international human rights law gained momentum in Ireland. In preparation for the Beijing + 5 review process, a new umbrella body, *Neart* (meaning strength) was formed. *Neart*'s objective was to defend the constitutional recognition of women's roles within the home.[41] *Neart* prepared an alternative report for the Beijing + 5 meeting, highlighting Ireland's cultural and religious specificity.[42] *Neart* also distanced itself from Ireland's official report[43] to the meeting and from

---

36. Ir. Const. art. 41 (2)(2).

37. *See* Letter of Pope John Paul II To Women 6 (29 June 1995), *available at* Congregation for the Doctrine of the Faith, www.vatican.va/holy_father/john_paul_ii/letters/documents/hf_jp-ii_let_29061995_women_en.html.

38. Letter to the Bishops of the Catholic Church on the Collaboration of Men and Women in the Church and in the World, by Cardinal Joseph Ratzinger, approved by Pope John Paul II (31 July 2004), *available at* Congregation for the Doctrine of the Faith, www.vatican.va/roman_curia/congregations/cfaith/doc_doc_index.htm.

39. *Report of the Committee on the Elimination of Discrimination Against Women on its Twenty-First Session*, U.N. GAOR, 54th Sess., Supp. No. 38, Pt. II, ¶¶ 161–201, U.N. Doc. A/54/38/Rev.1 (1999) (concluding observations on Ireland).

40. *Concluding Observations of the Human Rights Committee: Ireland, adopted* 21 July 2000, U.N. ESCOR, Hum. Rts. Comm., 69th Sess., 1858th mtg., ¶ 16, U.N. Doc. CCPR/CO/69/IRL (2000).

41. *See* Alison Healy, *New Coalition Formed to Challenge Views of National Women's Council*, Ir. Times, 11 May 2000. (Neart comprised more than twenty affiliate groups, including Human Life International, National Union of Mothers Working at Home.)

42. Neart, *supra* note 20, at 62. *See also* Department of Justice, Equality and Law Reform, *supra* note 14.

43. Department of Justice, Equality and Law Reform, *supra* note 14.

the submission by the National Women's Council of Ireland (NWCI),[44] both of which reports *Neart* portrayed as "anti-family" and a threat to Ireland's inherited traditions. Much of *Neart's* opposition has centered on the abortion debate.

The scrutiny of Ireland's abortion laws by UN human rights treaty bodies has led *Neart* and other facets of the Catholic Right to mobilize in opposition of the UN human rights agenda. Drawing on the critiques put forth by the Holy See, these groups have rejected human rights discourse as impoverished, libertarian, and peculiarly western.[45] In doing so, they have exposed the dangers to feminism of yielding to cultural claims. In the context of the abortion debate, such claims have meant that the jurisdiction in which a woman lives determines whether her abortion is that of "a safe, legal method for terminating an unwanted pregnancy" or "a dangerous, painful and criminal act."[46]

The Catholic Right's response to women's struggle to secure reproductive freedom is not unique to Ireland. The Holy See's opposition to an expanding human rights agenda within the United Nations is well-documented.[47] At the Fourth World Conference on Women held in Beijing in 1995 (Beijing Conference), the progression of women's rights, particularly in areas relating to reproductive and sexual health, was opposed by an emerging alliance between the Holy See and conservative Catholic and Muslim states.[48] The Holy See criticized the Beijing Declaration, arguing

---

44. NATIONAL WOMEN'S COUNCIL OF IRELAND, PROMISES MADE PROMISES BROKEN: BEIJING + 5 ALTERNATIVE REPORT FOR IRELAND (2000) *available at* www.nwci.ie/documents/beijing.doc. The Council is a nongovernmental organization representing more than 300 women's groups in Ireland.

45. *See generally* MARY ANN GLENDON, RIGHTS TALK: THE IMPOVERISHMENT OF POLITICAL DISCOURSE (1991); GLENDON, ABORTION AND DIVORCE IN WESTERN LAW, *supra* note 3. Much of the Catholic Right discourse in Ireland draws on the work of US lawyer Mary Ann Glendon.

46. KAJSA SUNDSTROM, ABORTION—A REPRODUCTIVE HEALTH ISSUE 3 (1993), *quoted in* Eriksson, *supra* 3, at 6.

47. See CENTER FOR REPRODUCTIVE RIGHTS, THE HOLY SEE AT THE UNITED NATIONS: AN OBSTACLE TO WOMEN'S REPRODUCTIVE HEALTH AND RIGHTS (2000), *available at* www.crlp.org/pub_bp_holysee.html; Doris Buss, *Racing Populations, Sexing Environments: The Challenges of a Feminist Politics in International Law*, 20 LEGAL STUD. 463 (2000); Joel Richard Paul, *Cultural Resistance to Global Governance*, 22 MICHIGAN J. INT'L L. 1 (2000).

48. *See Report of the Fourth World Conference on Women, Beijing Declaration and Platform for Action, adopted* 17 Oct., U.N. GAOR, 50th Sess., at 157, U.N. Doc. A/CONF.177/20 (1995). After the draft resolution was adopted, representatives of the following states made general and interpretative statements or expressed reservations: Peru, Kuwait, Egypt, Philippines, Holy See, Malaysia, Iran (Islamic Republic of), Libyan Arab Jamahiriya, Ecuador, Indonesia, Mauritania, Oman, Malta, Argentina, Brunei, Darussalam, France, Yemen, Sudan, Dominican Republic, Costa Rica, United Arab Emirates, Venezuela, Bahrain, Lebanon, Tunisia, Mali, Benin, Guatemala, India, Algeria, Iraq, Vanuatu, Ethiopia, Morocco, Djibouti, Qatar, Nicaragua, Togo, Liberia, Syrian Arab Republic, Pakistan, Nigeria, Comoros, Bolivia, Colombia, Bangladesh, Honduras, Jordan, Ghana, Central African Republic, Cambodia, Maldives, South Africa, United Republic of Tanzania, Brazil,

that it was marked by "exaggerated individualism" and that it gave "disproportionate attention" to sexual and reproductive health while neglecting the
concept of family as a "fundamental societal unit."[49] According to the Holy
See, this neglect was further evidence that the rich discourse of universal
rights was being colonised by an "impoverished, libertarian rights dialect."[50]

In the United States, similar sentiments have been expressed by a range
of Christian Right groups who oppose the application of international
human rights law to family, reproductive health, and sexuality. Joel Richard
has described this opposition as a "displaced response to the anxiety produced by globalization."[51] Globalization has brought with it a sense of economic displacement and loss of control over the nation state's destiny.[52] In
attempting to regain that control, the Christian Right seeks protection for the
nation state's claim to a distinct cultural identity.

Recently, in Ireland, this claim clashed with the economic agenda of a
center-right government and an expanding economy. The demands of globalization and participation in the European Union's market economy have
challenged traditional gendered divisions of labor.[53] Religious-cultural arguments invoking family values and a "cult of domesticity" have threatened to
undermine the economic boom experienced in Ireland throughout the
1990s, dubbed by commentators and investment firms as the "Celtic Tiger"
project.[54] As a result, such arguments have been marginalized within political debate. Seeking to protect a distinct religious identity, the Catholic Right
has relocated its religious-cultural claims within debates on women's reproductive health.

Panama, El Salvador, Madagascar, Chad, Cameroon, Niger, Gabon, United States of
America, and Canada. The observer for Palestine also made a statement.

49. *Id.* at 159–60. In a statement that reveals a broader agenda, the Holy See criticized the
"ambiguous language" of the Declaration and Platform concerning unqualified control
over sexuality and fertility, which in its view, could be interpreted as including "societal
endorsement of abortion and homosexuality."

50. *Id.*

51. *See* Paul, *supra* note 47, at 7.

52. *Id.* at 7–8.

53. In 1971, 60 percent of women aged fifteen years and over were engaged full time in
"home duties." In 1991, this had fallen to just under 50 percent. In 1970, women
accounted for 28 percent of the labor force. In 1991, this had risen to just 32.9 percent.
Following the rapid expansion of the Irish economy in the 1990s, this figure has now
risen to approximately 46 percent. *See generally* First Commission on the Status of
Women (Ireland), *Report to Government* (1972); Second Commission on the Status of
Women (Ireland), *Report to Government* (1993); Ethel Crowley, *Making a Difference?:
Female Employment and Multinationals in the Republic of Ireland, in* Women and Irish
Society: A Sociological Reader 81 (Anne Byrne & Madeleine Leonard eds., 1997).

54. The Report of the Second Commission on the Status of Women, published in 1993, called
for tax individualization to eliminate disincentives for married women seeking to enter
into employment. Second Commission on the Status of Women, *supra* note 53, at 76.
Finally, in 1999, in response to increasing labor shortages, the government decided to
act, introducing a series of measures including individualization of the income tax system and tax incentives to encourage women to return to paid employment. This challenge

III.   THE ABORTION DEBATE: REPARTITIONING THE STATE

In 1983, the Irish Constitution was amended to recognize, under Article 40(3)(3), the "right to life of the unborn."[55] Under the 1861 Offences Against the Person Act, abortion was a criminal offense.[56] However, prior to 1983, there was no explicit constitutional prohibition on abortion. The move to introduce a constitutional amendment banning abortion followed the Supreme Court's recognition of a right to marital privacy in *McGee v. Attorney General.*[57] There, the Supreme Court of Ireland concluded that the right to have access to contraceptives was protected as part of the personal right to marital privacy.[58] Anti-abortion activists feared that a right to privacy, broadly interpreted, might be invoked by Irish courts to strike down legislation criminalizing abortion. For example, the *Roe v. Wade*[59] decision in

---

to the traditional gendered division of labor met with opposition. As one commentator noted, "old allies re-emerge[d] to criticise women who go to work." Mary Holland, *Old Allies Re-Emerge to Criticise Women Who Go to Work,* Ir. Times, 9 Dec. 1999. *See also Dáil Debates* 15 Dec. 1999 *per* Mr. John Bruton T.D., *available at* www.gov.ie/debates-99/15dec99/sect9.htm. Catholic Right groups pointed to the constitutional commitment to recognizing and protecting women's lives within the home. Citing Article 41(2) of the Constitution of Ireland, 1937, they argued that if women should not be, "forced by economic necessity to neglect their duties within the home," economic incentives should not be offered by government to encourage such neglect. Portrayed as an attack on the family, a devaluation of women's work within the home, and possibly unconstitutional, the tax individualization plan was withdrawn, to be resubmitted one year later modified to take into account the criticisms levied against it. The debate has not ended, however. Incentives to encourage greater female participation in the labor force have been given added momentum by European Union membership and Community strategies to promote gender equality. The European Community framework strategy on gender equality (2001–2005), seeks to promote gender equality in economic life and a change in gender roles and stereotypes. Communication from the Commission to the Council, the European Parliament, the Economic and Social Committee and the Committee of the Regions: Towards a Community Framework Strategy on Gender Equality (2001–2005), COM(2000)335. As a strategy, it conflicts directly with the Catholic Right's concern to protect women's roles within the home and Ireland's inherited tradition of gender-differentiated citizenship. These concerns have voiced themselves most recently in opposition to the Treaty of Nice. Neart, *Submission to the National Forum on Europe: Opposition to Nice Treaty* (1 Dec. 2001), *available at* www.forumoneurope.ie/index. asp?locID=65&docID=-1. *See generally* Siobhán Mullally, *Beyond the Limits of the Discrimination Model: Promoting Gender Equality, in* Equality in Diversity: The New Equality Directives 295 (Eilis Barry & Cathryn Costello eds., 2003).

55. Article 40(3)(3), inserted following the enactment of the Eighth Amendment to the Constitution Act, No. 8 (7 Oct. 1983), reads:

   The State acknowledges the right to life of the unborn and, with due regard to the equal right to life of the mother, guarantees in its laws to respect, and, as far as practicable, by its laws to defend and vindicate that right.

56. Offences against the Person Act §§ 58, 59 (1861), *reprinted in* 7 The Statutes 266 (3d ed. 1950). *See also* Kingston, *supra* note 4, at ch. 3.

57. McGee v. Attorney General [1974] I.R. 284.

58. *Id.*

59. Roe v. Wade, 410 U.S. 113 (1973).

the United States was preceded by *Griswold v. Connecticut,*[60] a case similar to *McGee v. Attorney General.* To guard against a comparable development in Ireland, the Pro-Life Amendment Campaign (PLAC) was launched in 1981.

PLAC was composed primarily of groups drawn from the Catholic Right. The amendment campaign and the bitter debates that ensued have been described as a "second partitioning" of the state.[61] Although *PLAC* was careful to employ secular language in its campaign, it clearly drew on a conservative Catholic ethos to support its claim of the absolute inviolability of fetal life.[62] Recognizing this, each of Ireland's Protestant Churches issued statements opposing the proposal for a "pro-life" amendment.[63] The anti-amendment campaign argued that an absolute constitutional prohibition on abortion would deny non-Catholics equal rights to citizenship in Ireland and would perpetuate politics of exclusion. *PLAC,* however, continued to represent abortion as a "violent colonial tool" threatening the integrity of the Irish nation.[64] Ultimately, the pro-life campaign prevailed. Significantly, however, the enacted amendment does recognize the need for "due regard to the equal right to life of the mother."[65] Almost a decade later, the requirement of "due regard" was to give rise to one of Ireland's most controversial constitutional debates,[66] but before this was to happen, further attempts were made to limit the scope of women's reproductive autonomy. Access to information and women's right to travel came under threat as anti-abortion campaigners sought to entrench an increasingly conservative Catholic ethos in Irish law.

In *S.P.U.C. v. Grogan and others,*[67] the Society for the Protection of the Unborn Child (SPUC) applied to the High Court for an injunction to prevent student groups from distributing information on abortion services available in the UK. The High Court requested a ruling from the European Court of Justice (ECJ) as to: (a) whether abortion was a "service" within the meaning of the Treaty of Rome[68] and; (b) whether student groups have a right under

---

60. Griswold v. Connecticut, 381 U.S. 479 (1965).
61. *See* Tom Hesketh, The Second Partitioning of Ireland: The Abortion Referendum of 1983 (1990).
62. See Kingston, *supra* note 4, at 4–6; Fletcher, *supra* note 19, at 574–75.
63. *See* Fletcher, *supra* note 19, at 576.
64. One anti-abortion slogan read: "The Abortion Mills of England Grind Irish Babies into Blood that Cries out to Heaven for Vengeance." *Id.* at 577. *See also* Emily O'Reilly, Masterminds of the Right (1992).
65. Ir. Const. art. 40(3)(3).
66. *See* Attorney General v. X [1992] 1 I.R. 1.
67. S.P.U.C. v. Grogan, 3 C.M.L.R. 849 (1991). See also Society for the Protection of Unborn Children v. Coogan [1989] I.R. 734.
68. *See* Treaty Establishing the European Community, 25 Mar. 1957, 298 U.N.T.S. 11, art. 60 (1957) (*entered into force* 1 Jan. 1958), *reprinted in* European Community Law: Selected Documents 4 (George A. Bermann et al. eds., 1993).

Community law to distribute information concerning abortion services available in other member states. At the ECJ, Advocate General Van Gerven concluded that in the absence of a uniform European conception of morals, state authorities were better placed to assess the requirements of public morals than were European institutions.[69] In his view, Ireland was entitled to claim a wide margin of appreciation in the adjudication of the conflicting rights-claims arising in this case. He went on to find that the aim pursued by prohibiting the distribution of abortion information was legitimate and refused to consider evidence that the absence of such information led to later-obtained, unsafe abortions. He thus concluded that the prohibition on distributing information satisfied the requirement of proportionality.

The ECJ departed from the Opinion presented by the Advocate General. The ECJ defined abortion, "solely in terms of the possible commerce and profit resulting from it."[70] Questions relating to fundamental rights were dismissed as raising nonjusticiable moral rather than legal arguments.[71] The ECJ concluded that the termination of a pregnancy in accordance with the law of the state in which it was carried out constituted a service within the meaning of the Treaty of Rome.[72] However, the ruling was only a partial victory. Although the Court was willing to address concerns relating to trade in services, it refused to address reproductive health as a question of human rights. Furthermore, as the student groups had no direct links with the provision of abortion services in the UK or elsewhere, they could not claim the protection of EC law.[73] Thus, EC law could not prevent Irish courts from issuing an injunction prohibiting the student's activities in distributing abortion information. The limits of the European integration project are clear in the court's judgment.[74] Lost in the debate on trade in services is a recognition of women's right to reproductive health. That right was to be the subject of further political trade-offs in the months to follow.

Although the ECJ's ruling in the *Grogan* case was limited in scope, its potentially liberalizing impact on Ireland's abortion law complicated national debates regarding European integration. As a constitutional referendum on the Treaty of the European Union (the *Maastricht* Treaty) loomed,

---

69. S.P.U.C., 3 C.M.L.R. 849, ¶¶ 30–32 of Advocate General Van Gerven's opinion.
70. Jason Coppel & Aidan O'Neill, *The European Court of Justice: Taking Rights Seriously?* 29 Common Market L. Rev. 669, 687 (1992). *See also* Diamuid Rossa Phelan, *Right to Life of the Unborn v. Promotion of Trade in Services: The European Court of Justice and the normative shaping of the European Union,* 55 Mod. L. Rev. 670 (1992).
71. S.P.U.C., 3 C.M.L.R. 849, ¶¶ 20, 21 of the judgment. Coppel & O'Neill, *supra* note 70, at 687.
72. *Id.*
73. *Id.* ¶¶ 25–27.
74. *See generally* Phelan, *supra* note 70.

the abortion debate became further entwined with debates on national sovereignty.[75] The ECJ's ruling in the *Grogan* case coincided with ongoing negotiations on the *Maastricht* Treaty. Concerned with the possibility of a
backlash from anti-abortion groups, the Irish government added a protocol
to the *Maastricht* Treaty, without consulting Parliament. The Protocol
(No. 17) sought to protect Ireland's constitutional prohibition on abortion
from any change that might be required as a result of European Union membership.[76]

Before the constitutional referendum on the *Maastricht* Treaty was to
take place, however, a young woman's body became the subject of further
contestation between pro-choice and anti-abortion groups. In *Attorney
General v. X*, the Supreme Court of Ireland recognized a limited right to
reproductive health. This case involved a fourteen-year-old girl who became
pregnant as a result of a rape. The Attorney General, acting on information
provided by the Director of Public Prosecutions secured an injunction
restraining *X* from leaving Ireland for a period of nine months.[77] Effectively,
X was imprisoned within the state. The *X* case provoked a huge outcry at
national and international levels. Weeks of media attention followed. The
international media reported Ireland to be "backward," "barbarous," "punitive," "priest-ridden"—a portrayal that did not sit well with the modernizing
image of an emerging Celtic Tiger economy.[78] Embarrassed by this potentially damaging attention, the government undertook to pay all legal
expenses arising from *X*'s appeal to the Supreme Court. The Supreme Court
lifted the injunction, reversing the High Court's ruling on the substantive
question of abortion. Pointing out the state's duty to have "due regard" for
the life of the mother, the Supreme Court concluded that abortion was lawful in Ireland where there was a "real and substantial risk" to the life, as distinct from the health, of the mother.[79] The risk to life could include a
threatened suicide. In this case, medical evidence had been submitted to
show the young woman's suicidal state of mind and the resulting threat to
her life. In the Court's view, her right to terminate her pregnancy was therefore protected by the Article 40(3)(3) as amended in the Constitution. At the

---

75. Treaty on European Union and Final Act, 7 Feb. 1992, *reprinted in* 31 I.L.M. 247 [here-
    inafter Maastricht Treaty].
76. Protocol No. 17 annexed to the Treaty on the European Union and the Treaties estab-
    lishing the European Communities. Specifically, it provided:

    Nothing in the Treaty on European Union, or in the Treaties Establishing the European
    Communities, or in the Treaties or Acts modifying or supplementing those Treaties,
    shall affect the application in Ireland of Article 40.3.3 of the Constitution of Ireland.

77. Attorney General v. X [1992] 1 I.R. 1, 7 (per Costello, J.).
78. Fletcher, *supra* note 19, at 574. *See generally*, THE ABORTION PAPERS, IRELAND, *supra* note 9.
79. Attorney General v. X [1992] 1 I.R. 1, 57–58 (per Finlay, C.J.).

time that it was adopted, supporters of this amendment intended that it would absolutely prohibit abortion in Ireland. After the Supreme Court's ruling in *Attorney General v. X,* the amendment had been turned on its head to provide equal protection to the life of the mother.

The Supreme Court's judgment on the substantive issue of abortion was welcomed by the women's movement. However, its ruling on the right to travel raised widespread concern. The High Court had ruled that the state's duty to protect the life of the unborn amounted to a public policy derogation from the freedom of movement guaranteed under EC law.[80] The Supreme Court agreed. However, in its view, the right to travel to terminate a pregnancy was protected only if the mother's right to life was in danger. In the balancing of rights, a woman's right to travel could not, *per se,* take priority over the right to life of the unborn.[81] The potential restriction on a woman's freedom of movement, and with it, the specter of anti-abortion groups seeking injunctions to restrain pregnant women from traveling abroad, provoked widespread protests.

Debates concerning the potential restriction on travel were particularly worrying for the Irish government, given the pending constitutional referendum on the *Maastricht* Treaty. Now, it seemed that the addition of Protocol No. 17 to the Treaty may have been misguided. Controversy ensued as to whether the Protocol would prevent a reversal of the Irish courts' rulings on the rights to travel and to information. Ratification of the *Maastricht* Treaty was threatened as women's groups mobilized in opposition to the Protocol. In a last ditch attempt to save the ratification process, the government sought to amend the Protocol so as to exclude any effect that it might have on issues relating to travel or the provision of information. A "Solemn Declaration" was adopted, stating that Protocol No. 17 would not have any impact on the rights to travel or information.[82] Prior to the referendum on the *Maastricht* Treaty, each of the main political parties gave assurances that a further constitutional referendum would be held to resolve the questions raised by the *X* and *Grogan* cases. The assurances succeeded in allaying

---

80. Society for the Protection of Unborn Children v. Grogan, [1994] 1 I.R. 46 (Ir. H. Ct.).
81. Justice O'Flaherty, dissenting on this point, held that restricting a woman's right to travel would interfere to an unwarranted degree with the individual's freedom of movement, the authority of the family and the protection of the dignity and freedom of the individual. Attorney General v. X [1992] 1 I.R. 1, 88 (per O'Flaherty, J.).
82. Declaration of the High Contracting Parties to the Treaty on the European Union, *adopted* 1 May 1992, in Guimaráes (Portugal). The Declaration provided, *inter alia*:

   That it was and is their intention that the Protocol [No. 17] shall not limit freedom to travel between Member States or, in accordance with conditions which may be laid down, in conformity with Community law, by Irish legislation, to obtain or make available in Ireland information relating to services lawfully available to member states.

public fears and the referendum allowing for ratification of the *Maastricht Treaty* was approved by the Irish people in June 1992.[83]

Before a further referendum on abortion could take place, European human rights law asserted its voice in the national debate. On 29 October 1992, the European Court of Human Rights (ECHR) ruled on the challenge brought against Ireland by the *Open Door Counselling & Dublin Well Woman* centres.[84] Both Centers had been forced to close their nondirective pregnancy counseling services, following injunctions taken against them by SPUC.[85] They now complained that this constraint on the provision of information violated their rights to privacy and to freedom of expression under the European Convention for the Protection of Human Rights and Fundamental Freedoms (European Convention).[86] In a judgment clearly attempting to prevent encroachment upon contracting states' margin of appreciation, the ECHR concluded that Ireland's prohibition on abortion information fell within the scope of permissible restrictions on the right to freedom of expression.[87] The ECHR found that the prohibition was prescribed by law and pursued a legitimate public aim, namely, the protection of public morals. However, the ECHR concluded that Ireland had not satisfied the requirement of proportionality. The absolute nature of the injunction against the applicants proved fatal, and the ECHR ruled that Ireland had violated Article 10 of the European Convention, protecting the right to freedom of expression.[88] Having found a violation of Article 10, the ECHR held that it was unnecessary to consider the scope of the right to privacy. The ECHR also declined to consider arguments concerning the right to life, noting that the applicants had not complained of the substantive prohibition on abortion *per se*.[89] However, in a tentative step towards recognizing women's right to reproduc-

---

83. The Eleventh Amendment to the Constitution Act, No. 11 (16 July 1992) was enacted, amending Article 29 of the Constitution and thereby permitting Ireland's ratification of the Treaty. *See* IR. CONST. Art 29(4)(4).
84. Open Door Counselling & Dublin Well Woman v. Ireland, App. Nos. 14234/88, 14235/88, 15 Eur. H.R. Rep. 244 (1993).
85. *See* Attorney General v. Open Door Counselling & Dublin Well-Woman Centre [1988] I.R. 593.
86. European Convention for the Protection of Human Rights and Fundamental Freedoms, 4 Nov. 1950, 213 U.N.T.S. 221, Europ. T.S. No. 5 (*entered into force* 3 Sept. 1953), *available at* www.echr.coe.int/Eng/BasicTexts.htm [hereinafter European Convention].
87. Open Door Counselling & Dublin Well Woman v. Ireland, App. Nos. 14234/88, 14235/88, 15 Eur. H.R. Rep. 244 (1993).
88. *Id.*
89. The European Court of Human Rights has not ruled on whether the Convention requires contracting states to permit a woman to terminate a pregnancy. From the Court's jurisprudence to date, it would seem that contracting states enjoy a very wide margin of appreciation in regulating abortion. However, the former European Commission on Human Rights has stated that placing a higher value on the "unborn life of the fetus" than on the life of a pregnant women would be contrary to the object and purpose of the Convention. X v. United Kingdom, App. No. 8416/79, 3 Eur. H.R. Rep. 408 (1980) (admissibility decision of 13 May 1980). The Commission supported this interpretation of the right to life,

tive health, the ECHR did point out that the applicants were providing information on services lawfully available in other states and that those services could be crucial to a woman's health and well-being.[90]

Less than one month after the ECHR's ruling in *Open Door Counselling and Others v. Ireland,* a further constitutional referendum on abortion was held. On 25 November 1992, the Irish people were asked to vote on three possible constitutional amendments. The first amendment proposed to roll back the Supreme Court's judgment in the *X* case and to prohibit abortion arising from a risk to a woman's life posed by a threatened suicide.[91] The second and third amendments sought to protect the right to travel and to provide and obtain information on abortion.[92] The first amendment was defeated. The second and third proposed amendments were passed, thereby providing constitutional protection for the right to travel and to information.[93] Despite this vote, however, the government was slow to act. Having secured the ratification of the *Maastricht* Treaty and fulfilled its promise of a referendum on the *X* case, the government now failed to introduce legislation clarifying the conditions under which a woman could lawfully terminate a pregnancy in Ireland. Earlier, in the *X* case, the Supreme Court had condemned as "inexcusable" the government's similar failure to enact legislation giving effect to the Eighth Amendment of the Constitution Act, which amended Article 40(3)(3).[94] The amendment, "born of public

---

as protected under Article 2 of the Convention, by pointing out that most of the contracting states allowed abortions when necessary to save the mother's life. In H v. Norway, Application No. 17004/90 (unreported 19 May 1992), the applicant argued that the Convention must grant the father of a 14-week-old foetus a minimum of rights regarding his unborn child, where the health of the mother is not endangered. The Commission found his application to be inadmissible. It concluded that any interpretation of the potential father's right under the Convention, "in connection with an abortion which the mother intends to have performed on her, must first of all take into account her rights, she being the person primarily concerned by the pregnancy and its continuation or termination." Any possible interference with the applicant's rights under the Convention was "justified as being necessary for the protection of the rights of another person."

90. Open Door Counselling & Dublin Well Woman v. Ireland, App. Nos. 14234/88, 14235/88, 15 Eur. H.R. Rep. 244, ¶ 76 (1993).

91. The proposed Twelfth Amendment of the Constitution Act (Referendum on right to life), dealing with the right to life of the unborn, was defeated. The Bill proposed to amend Article 40(3)(3) as follows:

It shall be unlawful to terminate the life of an unborn unless such termination is necessary to save the life, as distinct from the health, of the mother where there is an illness or disorder of the mother, giving rise to a real and substantial risk to her life, not being a risk of self-destruction.

92. Thirteenth Amendment of the Constitution Act, No. 13 (23 Dec. 1992) (providing that Article 40(3)(3) be amended so as not to limit freedom of travel); Fourteenth Amendment of the Constitution Act, No. 14 (23 Dec. 1992) (providing that Article 40(3)(3) be amended so as not to limit freedom of information regarding abortion services).

93. *Id.*

94. Attorney General v. X [1992] 1 I.R. 1, at 92.

disquiet, historically divisive of our people," was, the Supreme Court said, "bare of legislative direction."[95] It remained without direction for some time.

In 1995, the government finally introduced legislation allowing for the provision of abortion information.[96] Before it was finally signed into law, however, the 1995 Regulation on Information (services Outside the State for the Termination of Pregnancies) Bill (Information Bill) was the subject of a Supreme Court referral.[97] Counsel representing the rights of the unborn challenged the constitutionality of the Bill arguing *inter alia* that "the natural law is the foundation upon which the Constitution was built and ranks superior to the Constitution."[98] According to this line of argument, the constitutional amendments introduced following the *X* case could not take priority over this body of natural law. The Supreme Court rejected this claim. Invoking the pluralist nature of Irish society, Chief Justice Hamilton concluded that the religious doctrines of one particular faith could not be relied on to determine the limits and scope of fundamental rights.[99] Drawing on the preamble to the Constitution, he argued that fundamental rights must be interpreted in the light of prevailing ideas of prudence, justice, and charity.[100] The court upheld the constitutionality of the Information Bill, thereby rendering it immune from any further challenge.

The Supreme Court's recognition of the pluralist nature of Irish society was echoed by the Constitution Review Group, reporting one year later. The Group concluded that the religious references in the constitutional text no longer reflected a shared sense of national identity.[101] On the subject of abortion, the Group recommended the introduction of legislation to give effect to the Supreme Court's judgment in *Attorney General v. X*, concluding that this was the only practical possibility available at that time. Despite the Group's recommendation, the government again failed to act. In the absence of a clear legislative framework, the Irish Medical Council Guidelines continued to exclude a threat of suicide as a ground for terminating a pregnancy.[102]

---

95. *Id.*
96. Regulation of Information (Services Outside the State for Termination of Pregnancies) Act, No. 5 (1995).
97. Re Article 26 and the Regulation of Information (Services Outside the State for the Termination of Pregnancies) Bill, 1995 [1995] 1 I.R. 1.
98. *Id.* at 98.
99. *Id.* at 41.
100. *Id.* at 43.
101. Constitution Review Group (Ireland), *Report of the Constitution Review Group* 257–59 (1996).
102. See Irish Medical Council, A Guide to Ethical Conduct and Behaviour (5th ed. 1998). The Medical Council is a regulatory body established by the Medical Practitioners Act, No. 4 (1978).

In November 1997, the uncertain implications of *Attorney General v. X* resurfaced in *A. & B. v. Eastern Health Board & C.* (the *C* case).[103] This case involved a young woman ("C"), a member of the Irish Traveling Community, who was under the care of the Eastern Health Board, a statutory body charged with duties of care under the 1991 Child Care Act. C had become pregnant as a result of a rape when she was thirteen years old. Concerned about the reaction of C's parents to the rape, the Eastern Health Board obtained a care order for C and placed her with a foster mother. C had at all times expressed a wish to terminate her pregnancy. Initially, her birth parents agreed to support her decision and arrangements were made for C to travel with the assistance of her foster mother to the United Kingdom. C's birth parents subsequently changed their mind due to intensive lobbying from anti-abortion groups. Uncertain as to the precise legal consequences of this change, the Eastern Health Board applied to the District Court for a further interim care order and a direction permitting C to travel to the United Kingdom for the purposes of terminating her pregnancy. The District Court granted the order.[104]

C's birth parents immediately appealed to the High Court. The High Court accepted the psychiatric evidence showing that a real and substantial risk to C's life existed, arising from the threat of suicide. The High Court concluded, therefore, that a direction authorizing travel for the purposes of terminating the pregnancy was lawful.[105] However in a statement giving rise to much controversy, the High Court determined that the constitutional amendment protecting the right to travel prevented the issuance of injunctions against a woman seeking to travel abroad but did not introduce a new substantive right. On this reading, a court could only authorize travel for the purposes of terminating a pregnancy if the requirements set out in *Attorney General v. X* were satisfied, namely that a real and substantial risk to a woman's life existed.[106]

The High Court was clearly reluctant to recognize C's reproductive rights. A protective welfarist approach underpins the court's ruling. In deciding whether the proposed abortion would be lawful, the court's primary concern was "the welfare of an Irish child in Ireland."[107] The child, C, was firmly situated within the Irish legal system. The constraints that came with Ireland's inherited traditions were to determine the limits of her reproductive rights. Rather than taking a universal perspective, the court defined the context as involving "an Irish Child in Ireland," narrowly examining the

---

103. A. and B. v. Eastern Health Board & C. [1998] 1 I.R. 464 [hereinafter C].
104. *Id.* at 468.
105. *Id.* at 483 (per Geoghegan, J.).
106. *Id.* at 482.
107. *Id.*

child's rights. The child's human rights—as universal claims—were rendered subordinate to the particular assessment of the needs and welfare of an Irish child. The court's protectionist approach focused on the welfare of the child rather than her rights claims, in particular her right to reproductive health. The determination of whether travel should be permitted in this case was both narrow in scope and couched in protectionist language, thus marginalizing the universalist concern at stake, namely the right of a child to reproductive health. To date, the precise implications of the High Court's ruling remain uncertain, though it is clear that the ruling could have a potentially far-reaching impact on women's reproductive rights.

IV. ONE STEP FORWARD—TWO STEPS BACK: ABORTION REFORM IN IRELAND

In 1997, the center-right *Fianna Fáil, Progressive Democrats* coalition government was formed.[108] A minority government, they were dependent for support on the votes of four independent members of Parliament (TDs). The TDs' support was secured by the promise of yet another abortion referendum. Before any such referendum occurred, a gradual process of consensus-building took place. This process began with the establishment of an inter-departmental working group on abortion. In an unprecedented response to this process, the inter-departmental working group received over 10,000 written submissions from individuals and groups concerned with abortion reform. Following the conclusion of the review, the Working Group published a parliamentary Green Paper setting out a range of legislative and constitutional options available to government.[109]

The Green Paper was referred to the All-Party Oireachtas (Parliament) Committee on the Constitution. The committee continued to receive submissions, both oral and written, on the options set out in the Green Paper. The US based organization, Catholics for a Free Choice (CRFC), argued from a pro-choice Catholic perspective in favor of "Option 7," which proposed

---

108. *Fianna Fáil* is one of the oldest and largest political parties within the Irish state. Further information is *available at* www.fiannafail.ie. The Progressive Democrats were a minority party in the coalition government. They were formed as a political party in 1985 and currently hold eight seats in the Irish Parliament. Further information is *available at* www. progressivedemocrats.ie/.

109. OFFICE OF THE TAOISEACH, GREEN PAPER ON ABORTION (1999), *available at* www.taoiseach.gov.ie/ upload/publications/251.rtf. The Green Paper was prepared by an inter-departmental Working Group, charged with considering the constitutional, legal, medical, moral, social and ethical issues surrounding the question of abortion. A Cabinet Committee, composed of four men and two women oversaw the Group's work. Submissions were invited from interested members of the public.

permitting abortion on grounds beyond those specified in the X case. CRFC argued that the other options detailed in the Green Paper represented "a narrow continuum of extremely restrictive policy options that range from explicit or de facto bans on abortion to very limited availability on a case-by-case basis."[110] Ultimately, the Oireachtas Committee was unable to achieve majority support for any one of the options set out in the Green Paper.[111] Despite the absence of consensus, the government decided to hold another referendum. In March 2002, the Irish people were asked to vote on the Twenty-Fifth Amendment of the Constitution (Protection of Human Life in Pregnancy Bill).[112] The Bill proposed a prohibition on abortion except in circumstances where there was a risk to the life of the mother. In an attempt to limit the effect of *Attorney General v. X,* drafters of the bill excluded the risk arising from a threatened suicide as a ground for permitting abortion. A similar proposal had been placed before the people in the constitutional referenda of 1992. The Protection of Human Life in Pregnancy Bill differed from this earlier proposal in that it protected the fetus' right to life only following implantation in the womb, thereby allowing for the use of contraceptives such as the morning-after pill.[113] A twelve year prison sentence was proposed for any woman who performed an abortion on herself or for any person aiding and abetting a woman in performing an abortion.[114] In addition, where life-saving abortions were permitted, they could only be carried out in "approved place[s]."[115]

The referendum on the Protection of Human Life in Pregnancy Bill was held on 6 March 2002. It was defeated by the narrowest of margins, with

---

110. See CATHOLICS FOR A FREE CHOICE, SUBMISSION TO THE INTER-DEPARTMENTAL WORKING GROUP ON ABORTION, CATHOLIC OPTIONS IN THE ABORTION DEBATE: REFORMING IRISH LAW (Mar. 1998), *available at* http://flag.blackened.net/revolt/darg/sub_cont.html; Press Release, Opening Remarks by Catholics for a Free Choice to the All-Party Oireachtas Committee on The Constitution (12 July 2000) *available at* www.cath4choice.org/new/pressrelease/071200Dublin AbortionReform.htm

111. *See* ALL PARTY OIREACHTAS COMMITTEE ON THE CONSTITUTION, FIFTH REPORT: ABORTION (2000) *available at* www.taoiseach.gov.ie/attached_files/upload/publications/1434.pdf. Three options commanded support within the Committee, though not majority support. The first was to leave the legal position unchanged and to focus instead on measures to reduce crisis pregnancies. The second was to introduce legislation to give effect to the Supreme Court judgment in the X case. The third was to amend the Constitution so as to protect existing medical practice while at the same time maintaining a prohibition on abortion—in effect rolling back the options opened by the Supreme Court judgment in the X case.

112. Twenty-Fifth Amendment of the Constitution (Protection of Human Life in Pregnancy) Bill, No. 48 (2001) [hereinafter Proposed Twenty-Fifth Amendment]. The Bill draws on similar legislation introduced in Poland in 1993, the Family Planning, Protection of the Human Foetus, and Conditions Permitting Pregnancy Termination Act. Prior to 1993, abortion on social grounds was permitted in Poland.

113. *See* Proposed Twenty-Fifth Amendment, *supra* note 112, at Second Schedule § 1(1).

114. *Id.* Second Schedule § 2(3).

115. *Id.* Second Schedule § 1(2).

49.58 percent voting "Yes" and 50.42 percent voting "No."[116] Only 42.89 percent of the electorate voted in the referendum and the results displayed a strong urban rural divide, with most rural constituencies voting "Yes."[117] In an ironic twist of fate, the rapist at the center of *Attorney General v. X* was convicted and sentenced for the sexual assault of a nineteen-year-old woman on the day preceding the referendum, 5 March 2002. This grim reminder of the trauma that led to the *X* case litigation may have influenced the electorate. However, it is likely that the decisive factor in the "No" vote was the split in the anti-abortion movement. Although the Catholic church mobilized behind the government's referendum proposal, extremists in the anti-abortion movement called for a "No" vote because of the Bill's failure to protect human life prior to implantation in the womb.[118]

Despite the defeat of the referendum, the prospects of a legislative framework allowing for a limited right to abortion remain remote. The willingness of the Irish government to ignore the rights questions at the heart of these debates was evident in the Prime Minister's comments following the defeat of the referendum on 6 March 2002. He "indicated that he had no plans to legislate on the issue" and give effect to the people's decision.[119] The government was facing a referendum on the Treaty of Nice; the treaty sought to introduce further reforms in the EU and to provide for the expansion of the Union to include an additional ten member states.[120] Given the opposition of Catholic Right groups to the Treaty, the government was reluctant to risk any reforms that might alienate them further.[121] The recently agreed to draft Constitution for Europe, concluded under the Irish Presidency of the EU, is supplemented by a Protocol, providing that the application of Article 40(3)(3) would not be affected by the Constitution.[122]

---

116. Mark Brennock, *Taoiseach Rules Out Abortion Legislation Following Defeat,* IR. TIMES, 8 Mar. 2002, at 1.
117. *Id.*
118. *See, e.g.,* Press Release, S.P.U.C., International Pro-life Leaders Call for a No Vote in Irish Abortion Referendum (28 Feb. 2002), *available at* www.spuc.org.uk/releases/20020228. htm.
119. *Id.*
120. Treaty of Nice Amending the Treaty on European Union, the Treaties Establishing the European Communities and Certain Related Acts 2001/C80/01, 2001 O.J. (C80/1). The Twenty-First Amendment of the Constitution Act, No. 2 (2001) was defeated in a referendum held on 7 June 2001. A second referendum on the Treaty of Nice was held on 19 October 2002. This time the referendum was carried, with 63 percent voting "Yes."
121. Christian Democrat Party, *The Laeken Summitt: Creating an Alternative Vision of the European Union, Submission to the Forum on Europe* (19 Dec. 2001), *available at* www.forumoneurope.ie/uploadedfiles/documents/christian_dems.doc.
122. *See* Protocol on Article 40.3.3 of the Constitution of Ireland, Provisional consolidated version of the Protocols annexed to the Treaty establishing a Constitution for Europe and of Annexes I and II, 2003/2004 IGC, at 313, *available at* www.euobserver.com/nice/ nice5.html.

Ratification of the Treaty must take place within two years, during which time there will be yet another referendum in Ireland and further debate on the meaning and scope of the constitutional prohibition on abortion. Against the background of this political wrangling, more than 7,000 women will continue to travel to the United Kingdom each year to terminate their pregnancies. For unemployed women or women earning low wages, this freedom to travel remains illusory.[123]

While anti-abortion and pro-choice debates were dominating the political arena, the rights of the "unborn" were being tested again in Ireland's Supreme Court.[124] *Baby O & Another v. Minister for Justice Equality & Law Reform* involved a Nigerian woman who was seven months pregnant and subject to a deportation order from the state, following a failed application for asylum. The woman challenged the validity of the deportation order, arguing that the state's duty to defend and vindicate Baby O's right to life prevented the state from deporting her to Nigeria, where infant mortality rates were substantially higher and the standard of living substantially lower. The Attorney General, acting on behalf of the Minister for Justice, Equality and Law Reform, appealed to the common good, to the need to defend and vindicate the territorial integrity of the state, and to the Minister's right to deport failed asylum seekers.[125] The Supreme Court agreed with the submissions of the Attorney General. The threat posed by higher infant mortality rates could not invoke the protection of Article 40(3)(3).[126] The state's duty to defend and vindicate the right to life of the unborn did not extend to ensuring the health and well-being of Baby O, or even to ensuring a safe delivery. Article 40(3)(3) could not be relied on to invoke unenumerated social and economic rights, which the Court held, were not implicit within the constitutionally protected right to life.[127] The Court upheld the deportation order and also refused a final application to stay the order pending an appeal to the ECHR. If Baby O was born in Ireland, she would have been entitled to Irish citizenship by virtue of her birth, and her mother would have had a claim to residence in Ireland arising from Baby O's right to the "company, care and parentage" of her mother. The "common good" required a speedy deportation of the mother and fetus. Again, the narrative of nation was to prove exclusionary. The self-styled "pro-life" movement,

---

123. *See* IRISH COUNCIL FOR CIVIL LIBERTIES (WOMEN'S COMMITTEE), THE NEED FOR ABORTION LAW REFORM IN IRELAND: THE CASE AGAINST THE TWENTY-FIFTH AMENDMENT OF THE CONSTITUTION BILL, 2001 (2002), *available at* www.iccl.ie/women/abortion/abortion_paper2002.html.

124. Baby O v. Minister for Justice, Equality and Law Reform, Unreported Supreme Court Judgment, [2002] I.R. 169.

125. *Id.* at 173.

126. *Id.* at 182.

127. *Id.*

preoccupied with another referendum on abortion, had little to say in support of Baby O or her mother.

The exclusionary narrative of nation was evident again in recent debates on the right to citizenship by birth in Ireland. The insertion of a new Article 2 into the Irish Constitution following the 1998 Belfast Agreement[128] gave constitutional recognition to the *jus soli* principle and to birthright citizenship.[129] The coincidence of increasing immigration in Ireland with the Belfast Agreement and constitutional change, has been described by the Irish Supreme Court as an "accident of history."[130] It is an "accident" that provided the Irish government with an opportunity to develop an open and inclusive concept of citizenship. That opportunity, at least for the moment, appears to have been passed by. As immigration controls have tightened, with increasing numbers of people denied leave to enter the state, so also have citizenship laws been restricted. On 11 June 2004, a referendum was held in Ireland on the question of birthright citizenship. By a majority of four to one, the electorate voted to impose restrictions on birthright citizenship for children born to non-national parents.[131] The Irish Nationality and Citizenship Bill, currently pending before the Irish Parliament, provides that children born to non-nationals will only acquire citizenship by birth if one parent has been lawfully resident within the state for a minimum period of three years.[132]

---

128. Agreement between the Government of the United Kingdom of Great Britain and Northern Ireland and the Government of Ireland, 1998, *cited in* 37 I.L.M. 751 (1998) (hereinafter Belfast Agreement). *See also,* Colin Harvey & Stephen Livingstone, *Human Rights and the Northern Ireland Peace Process,* Eur. Hum. Rts. L. Rev. 162 (1999); Human Rights, Equality, and Democratic Renewal in Northern Ireland (Colin J. Harvey ed., 2001); Colin Harvey, *Governing After the Rights Revolution,* 27 J.L. & Soc'y 61 (2000).

129. Nineteenth Amendment of the Constitution Act, No. 19 (3 June 1998). The full text of Article 2 of the Constitution of Ireland (as amended) reads:

> It is the entitlement and birthright of every person born in the island of Ireland, which includes its islands and seas, to be part of the Irish Nation. That is also the entitlement of all persons otherwise qualified in accordance with law to be citizens of Ireland. Furthermore, the Irish nation cherishes its special affinity with people of Irish ancestry living abroad who share its cultural identity and heritage.

130. *See* L. and O. v. Minister for Justice, Equality and Law Reform, [2003] I.E.S.C. 1, ¶ 451 (per Fennelly, J.).

131. Twenty-Seventh Amendment of the Constitution Bill, No. 15 (24 June 2004). The referendum followed a period of heated debates on the rights of migrant families to remain in Ireland on the basis of having an Irish born child. In the L. and O. cases, the Supreme Court held that the right of a citizen child to the company, care and parentage of her or his parents was subject to the common good, namely the state's interest in immigration control and the integrity of the asylum process. L. and O. [2003] I.E.S.C. 1, ¶ 148 (per Murray, J.).

132. Irish Nationality and Citizenship Bill, No. 40 (2004), *available at* www.oireachtas.ie/viewdoc.asp?fn=/documents/bills28/bills/2004/4004/document1.htm.

Debates on birthright citizenship in Ireland have placed migrant women's roles in reproduction at the centre of legal and political discourse on immigration. Migrant women's bodies, their sexuality and childbearing roles, have become the subject of heightened scrutiny, with newspapers reporting daily on the numbers of migrant women availing of maternity services in Irish hospitals.[133] Introducing the proposal for a referendum on citizenship, the Minister for Justice, Equality and Law Reform highlighted the threat posed to the nation state by pregnant migrant women coming to Ireland. "How," he asked, "do we respond?"[134] To require non-national women of childbearing age to make declarations of pregnancy when arriving in the state was, he said, "clearly unworkable—especially in a common travel area."[135] That requiring a migrant woman to make a declaration of pregnancy might amount to inhuman or degrading treatment, a violation of a woman's right to privacy, or a violation of her right to bodily integrity, did not appear to be a concern.

V. CONCLUSION

In Ireland, as elsewhere, cultural claims concerning gender identities and roles have been given greater or lesser weight depending on their "fit" with state interests and the ongoing process of nation-building. Lost within these negotiations and compromises is a recognition of the universal legitimacy of women's human rights claims. In recent years, this loss has been most evident in debates surrounding women's reproductive health and the right to access abortion services. The difficulties encountered by feminist movements within Ireland mirror those encountered within the international human rights movement. Both at national and international levels, the deference paid to cultural claims reveals a gendered division between the public and the private and a willingness to shield the private sphere from public tests of justice and rights. Debates concerning reproductive health have been isolated within the boundaries of that untouchable private sphere. Allegedly falling essentially within the domestic jurisdiction of the state, the battle over women's reproductive rights has been manipulated to serve as the underpinning of the nation state's claim to a distinct cultural identity.

---

133. Eithne Luibhéid, *Globalization and Sexuality: Redrawing Racial and National Boundaries Through Discourses of Childbearing, in* WOMEN'S MOVEMENT: MIGRANT WOMEN TRANSFORMING IRELAND 77 (Ronit Lentin and Eithne Luibhéid eds., 2003), *available at* www.tcd.ie/ Sociology/mphil/dwnl/migrantwomenpapers.PDF.
134. *Proposed Citizenship Referendum,* SUNDAY INDEPENDENT, 14 Mar. 2004, at 6.
135. *Id.* at 6.

Evident within Ireland's constitutional text are the tensions that arise between, on the one hand, a liberal rights-based democracy and, on the other, a communitarian ethos that appeals to an explicitly Christian (and for the most part Roman Catholic) conception of the common good.[136] For many years, it was presumed that such tensions could be resolved by an appeal to the "ethical values, which all Christians living in the State acknowledge and accept."[137] A politics of presumed consensus prevailed. Given the dominant position of the Roman Catholic Church in the early years of independence and its role in the drafting of the Irish Constitution, this is not surprising. In more recent years, we have witnessed what Habermas might term a shift from ethnos to demos in legal discourse.[138] This shift, limited though it is, can be attributed to a number of factors. Meeting the demands of globalization required that Ireland assert itself as a modern European state, capable of feeding the appetite of the "Celtic Tiger" economy. The Northern Ireland Peace Agreement, concluded on 10 April 1998, called for a recognition of the diversity of identities and traditions on the island of Ireland.[139] Irishness could no longer be defined simply as "not English." "Reinventing Ireland"[140] to meet the changing political and economic context meant searching for an identity that would allow greater space for diversity. As yet, however, these changes have not led to greater reproductive autonomy for Irish women. In its submission to the inter-departmental working group on abortion, *Catholics for a Free Choice* argued that even in a predominantly Catholic country, laws governing abortion should be formulated on secular, plural, democratic principles.[141] Irish feminists have always sought to move beyond the constraints of particularistic, cultural discourse. Today, as in the early stages of nation-building, the challenges raised by feminist movements have been perceived not only as hostile to religious-cultural beliefs and practices, but also to the very ties that bind the nation state.

---

136. *See* G. Quinn, *Reflections on the Legitimacy of Judicial Activism in the Field of Constitutional Law,* Dᴜ 29 (1991); Gerry Whyte, *Constitutional Adjudication, Ideology and Access to the Courts, in* Lᴀᴡ ᴀɴᴅ Lɪʙᴇʀᴛʏ ɪɴ Iʀᴇʟᴀɴᴅ 149 (Anthony Whelan ed., 1993).
137. People v. Shaw [1982] I.R. 1 (per Kenny, J.).
138. Jürgen Habermas, *Multiculturalism and the Liberal State,* 47 Sᴛᴀɴ. L. Rᴇᴠ. 849 (1995).
139. *See* Belfast Agreement, *supra* note 128. *See generally* Geoff Gilbert, *The Northern Ireland Peace Agreement, Minority Rights and Self-Determination,* 47 Iɴᴛ'ʟ Cᴏᴍᴘ. L. Q. 943 (1998); Harvey & Livingstone, *supra* note 128.
140. This phrase is adapted from Kɪʙᴇʀᴅ, *supra* note 16.
141. Cᴀᴛʜᴏʟɪᴄs ғᴏʀ ᴀ Fʀᴇᴇ Cʜᴏɪᴄᴇ, *supra* note 110.

Chapter 19

China to CEDAW: An Update on Population Policy

Carmel Shalev

"Hate the sin and not the sinner. . . ." It is quite proper to resist and attack a system, but to resist and attack its author is tantamount to resisting and attacking oneself. For we are all tarred with the same brush, and are children of one and the same Creator, and as such the divine powers within us are infinite. To slight a single human being is to slight those divine powers, and thus to harm not only that being but with him the whole world.[1]

I. INTRODUCTION

In January 1999, the People's Republic of China presented its third and fourth periodic reports to the Committee on the Elimination of Discrimination Against Women (CEDAW Committee). China's population policy had raised questions at previous reportings and continued to be of particular concern, not on a substantive level, but in relation to coercion in the implementation. This article presents the information that came to light in the course of the reporting process. Information on violations of human rights is largely anecdotal, due to restrictions on freedom of association and freedom of the press. Nonetheless, the anecdotes point to consistent patterns of abuse in violation of the Convention on the Elimination of All Forms of Discrimination Against Women (CEDAW).

It appears that coercive measures, including economic sanctions and physical violence, continue to be employed by local officials, in violation of women's human rights, and are condoned by the state through its failure to take action against wrongdoers. Coercion is a response to popular resistance to the government's population policy. In rural areas, resistance is motivated by an economy dependent on family labor and traditional son preference. In ethnic minority areas (such as Tibet or Uyghur), the resistance

---

1. M.K. GANDHI, AN AUTOBIOGRAPHY OF THE STORY OF MY EXPERIMENTS WITH TRUTH 230 (1927).

is also politically motivated, in connection with freedom of religion. Coercive measures are targeted primarily at women, and thus, constitute gender discrimination. They not only violate fundamental human rights, but are arguably ineffective in achieving population goals.[2]

The birth control policy impacts other forms of systemic gender discrimination. Harmful traditional practices associated with son preference in rural areas lead to sex-selective abortion, female infanticide, and the abandonment and non-registration of girl children. The imbalance in the sex ratio at birth raises concern about "shortages" of women in marriage cohorts and about societal instability, and has been linked with an increase in bride-selling and the trafficking in women. In addition, the policy has discriminatory effects in terms of women's mental and physical health, as a result of forced reproductive health interventions, sometimes performed by unskilled workers under nonhygienic conditions.

This article illustrates the monitoring and reporting process of a UN human rights treaty body. Information sources include official reports and statements by the state party under Article 18 of the CEDAW Convention, as well as information from other independent sources, including UN agencies, nongovernmental organizations (NGOs), and academic journals. The information provided by NGOs is particularly noteworthy because restrictions on freedom of association in China prevent the kind of grass-roots organization that is critical to local human rights monitoring.

The CEDAW Committee has developed a working method for the examination of periodic reports. The official reports, together with the NGO "shadow" reports and additional information from independent sources, are considered by a pre-session working group. Its task is to present questions in writing to the representative of the reporting state party, in advance of the meeting with the Committee. The delegation of the state party meets with the Committee in "constructive dialogue" for a few hours. The representative of the government presents its responses to the questions of the pre-session working group, then CEDAW members are free to take the floor with additional questions and comments. Finally, the government representative is given the floor for closing remarks. The Committee then sums up in "Concluding Comments" that are part of its official report.

Part II of this article gives an overview of the CEDAW Convention and its underlying principles in relation to women and reproductive health. It then presents information on China's population policy officially reported by the Chinese government to the CEDAW Committee. Part III describes the details of the birth control policy in its legal framework, the discriminatory targeting of women, and the various economic sanctions that may be

---

2. Amartya Sen, *Population: Delusion and Reality,* N.Y. REV., 22 Sept. 1994, at 62.

incurred for noncompliance. Part IV looks at the dynamics of resistance and coercion, the violence used by state officials against women to force compliance, and the discriminatory effects of the policy, particularly with respect to the lives of girl children. The Concluding Comments of the CEDAW Committee are considered in Part V.

II. THE CEDAW CONVENTION

A. Women's Rights in Relation to Health: Underlying Principles

China signed and ratified the CEDAW Convention in 1980. The Convention contains several articles that relate to women's health rights.[3] In particular, Article 12(1) provides: "States Parties shall take all appropriate measures to eliminate discrimination against women in the field of health care in order to ensure, on a basis of equality of men and women, access to health care services, including those related to family planning."[4]

In addition, Article 16(1)(e) on marriage and family relations guarantees women, "on a basis of equality of men and women . . . [t]he same rights to decide freely and responsibly on the number and spacing of their children and to have access to the information, education and means to enable them to exercise these rights."[5]

The CEDAW Committee has addressed particular aspects of women's rights to health in some of its General Recommendations.[6] For example,

---

3. *See, e.g.,* Convention on the Elimination of all Forms of Discrimination Against Women (CEDAW), *adopted* 18 Dec. 1979, G.A. Res. 34/180, U.N. GAOR, 34th Sess., Supp. No. 46, at arts. 5, 10(h), 11(f), 14(h), U.N. Doc. A/34/46 (1980) (*entered into force* 3 Sept. 1981), 1249 U.N.T.S. 13, *reprinted in* 19 I.L.M. 33 (1980). Article 5 requires the state party to eliminate prejudices based on the idea of the inferiority of either of the sexes, and to ensure that family education includes a proper understanding of maternity as a social function. Article 10(h) on education guarantees the right of access to specific educational information to ensure the health and well-being of families, including information and advice on family planning. Article 11 (f) protects the right to protection of health and to safety in working conditions, including the safeguarding of the function of reproduction. Article 14(h) grants rural women the rights to adequate living conditions, including sanitation in particular.
4. *Id.* art. 12(1).
5. *Id.* art. 16(1)(e).
6. *Compilation of General Comments and General Recommendations Adopted by the Human Rights Treaty-bodies: Note by the Secretariat,* U.N. ESCOR Committee on the Elimination of Discrimination Against Women, 13th Sess., at 72, U.N. Doc. HRI/GEN/ 1/Rev.1 (1994) [hereinafter *Compilation of General Comments*]. *See, e.g.,* General Recommendation No. 14, 9th Sess., on Female Circumcision; No. 15, 9th Sess., on Avoidance of Discrimination Against Women in National Strategies for the Prevention and Control of Acquired Immunodeficiency Syndrome (AIDS); and No. 18, 10th Sess., on Disabled Women.

General Recommendation No. 19 on Violence against Women noted that "compulsory sterilization or abortion adversely affects women's physical and mental health, and infringes the right of women to decide on the number and spacing of their children."[7] It then recommended that "[s]tates parties should ensure that measures are taken to prevent coercion in regard to fertility and reproduction."[8]

Likewise, General Recommendation No. 21 on Equality in Marriage and Family Relations includes the following commentary on Article 16(1)(e):

> 21. The responsibilities that women have to bear and raise children affect their ... personal development. ... The number and spacing of their children have a similar impact on women's lives and also affect their physical and mental health, as well as that of their children. For these reasons, women are entitled to decide on the number and spacing of their children.
>
> 22. Some reports disclose coercive practices which have serious consequences for women, such as forced pregnancies, abortions or sterilization. Decisions to have children or not, while preferably made in consultation with spouse or partner, must not nevertheless be limited by spouse, parent, partner or Government. ...
>
> 23. There is general agreement that where there are freely available appropriate measures for the voluntary regulation of fertility, the health, development and well-being of all members of the family improves. Moreover, such services improve the general quality of life and health of the population, and the voluntary regulation of population growth helps preserve the environment and achieve sustainable economic and social development.[9]

The Committee's interest in reproductive health rights also found expression in its suggestions regarding the 1994 Cairo International Conference on Population and Development (ICPD). Suggestion No. 6 of the Committee reiterated that the role of women in procreation should not be a basis for discrimination.[10] It reaffirmed the right of women to decide freely and responsibly on the number and spacing of their children, and emphasized that one of the main objectives should be to eliminate discrimination against the girl child, especially with regard to health.[11] On follow-up to the ICPD, the Committee recalled, among other things, the right to equality in health services and to receive appropriate pregnancy and childbirth services. It noted

---

7. General Recommendation No. 19, 11th Sess., on Violence Against Women, ¶ 22, *in Compilation of General Comments, supra* note 6.
8. General Recommendation No. 19, 11th Sess., on Violence Against Women, ¶ 24(m), *in Compilation of General Comments, supra* note 6.
9. General Recommendation No. 21, 13th Sess., on Equality in Marriage and Family Relations, ¶¶ 21–23, *in Compilation of General Comments, supra* note 6.
10. *Report of the Committee on the Elimination of Discrimination Against Women: Suggestion No. 6 (13th Sess. 1994), adopted* 12 Apr. 1994, U.N. GAOR, 49th Sess., Supp. No. 38, ¶ 2, U.N. Doc A/49/38 (1994).
11. *Id.* ¶¶ 3, 7.

the importance of women's reproductive health as a precondition to their enjoyment of all other human rights and freedoms, including the fundamental right to life.[12]

1. Autonomy

Rights to reproductive health embrace various human rights recognized in international treaties. A right to enjoyment of the highest attainable standard of health—within maximum available resources—is guaranteed by Article 12 of the International Covenant on Economic, Social and Cultural Rights (ICESCR).[13] Certain fundamental freedoms protected under the International Covenant on Civil and Political Rights (ICCPR) are relevant to health, including *inter alia* the right to life, to bodily integrity and security of the person, and to privacy.[14] The right to liberty is central, in both its negative and positive sense.

According to Isaiah Berlin, "liberty" in the ordinary sense is a "negative" right, in that one is entitled to be free in certain areas from the interference of others.[15] "I am normally said to be free to the degree to which no man or body of men interferes with my activity."[16] But "liberty" also has a "positive" sense. It is not merely freedom "from" but freedom "to." This positive right to freedom is "autonomy," in the sense that one is entitled to recognition of one's capacity, as a human being, to exercise choice in the shaping of one's life. It derives from the wish of the individual "to be his own master" and to conceive and realize one's own goals, as a thinking, willing, active being, bearing responsibility for one's choices.[17]

Autonomy means the right of a woman to make decisions concerning her fertility and sexuality free of coercion and violence. Key to autonomy is the notion of choice. In health care contexts, rights to informed consent and confidentiality are instrumental to ensuring free decision making by the

---

12. *Report of the Committee on the Elimination of Discrimination Against Women: Suggestion No. 8 (14th Sess. 1995), adopted* 31 May 1995, U.N. GAOR, 50th Sess., Supp. No. 38, U.N. Doc A/50/38 (1995).
13. International Covenant on Economic, Social and Cultural Rights, *adopted* 16 Dec. 1966, G.A. Res. 2200 (XXI), U.N. GAOR, 21st Sess., Supp. No. 16, art. 12, U.N. Doc. A/6316 (1966), 993 U.N.T.S. 3 (*entered into force* 3 Jan. 1976).
14. International Covenant on Civil and Political Rights, *adopted* 16 Dec. 1966, G.A. Res. 2200 (XXI), U.N. GAOR, 21st Sess., Supp. No. 16, arts. 6.1, 7, 9, 17, U.N. Doc. A/6316 (1966), 999 U.N.T.S. 171 (*entered into force* 23 Mar. 1976). Article 6.1 guarantees the right to life. Article 7 guarantees the right to bodily integrity which underlies the prohibition against torture. Article 9 guarantees the right to security of person in relation to the right to liberty. Article 17 guarantees the right to privacy.
15. Isaiah Berlin, *Two Concepts of Liberty,* in Four Essays on Liberty 118, 121–22 (1969).
16. *Id.* at 122.
17. *Id.* at 131.

client. A woman's rights to equality before the law and to full legal capacity[18] include her right to make free and informed decisions about health care, medical treatment, and research. Women have the right to be fully informed of their options in health care, including likely benefits and potential adverse effects of proposed methods of treatment and available alternatives, as well as the option of refusing treatment.

These rights impose correlative duties upon health care providers and deliverers of services. They are bound to disclose information of proposed treatments and their alternatives so as to obtain the informed consent of the client, and they must respect her right to refuse treatment. Likewise, they must preserve her confidentiality, which enables her to make private decisions without the interference of others whom she has not chosen to consult, and who might not have her best interests at heart.

2. Equality

The CEDAW Convention is aimed at the elimination of discrimination against women, "for the purpose of guaranteeing them the exercise and enjoyment of human rights and fundamental freedoms on a basis of equality with men."[19] Article 1 of the Convention defines the term "discrimination against women" as any distinction, exclusion or restriction made on the basis of sex which has the *effect* or purpose of impairing the exercise by women of human rights and fundamental freedoms.[20]

The Committee has included "indirect discrimination" in this definition, meaning that discrimination is condemned even if it is not purposeful.[21] This is of particular significance in the area of health, where much of the discrimination is the result of certain patterns of behavior, sometimes described as "natural." These patterns persist by the mere inertia of habit if no intervention is undertaken to address and remove the structures of the discriminatory practice.

The area of health is particularly interesting in terms of equality theory because of supposedly "real" differences between women and men—some

---

18. *See* CEDAW, *supra* note 3, art. 15.
19. *Id.* art. 3.
20. *Id.* art. 1.
21. This is oral jurisprudence that has been expressed numerous times in the comments of expert members during the constructive dialogue with states parties reporting to the Committee. It is derived from the language of "effect or purpose" in the definition of discrimination in Article 1 of CEDAW. It is this jurisprudence that underlies the Committee's General Recommendation No. 19 on Violence Against Women, which opens with the statement: "Gender-based violence is a form of discrimination that seriously inhibits women's ability to enjoy rights and freedoms on a basis of equality with men." General Recommendation, *supra* at note 7, ¶ 1.

biological (or physiological), and some social. Women's health needs are different from men's due to both biological differences and societal factors. This is particularly true in terms of reproductive and sexual health, both because of biological differences and patriarchal stereotypes of women's sexual and reproductive roles and functions.

Contemporary feminist legal theory expounds that the principle of gender equality takes into account gender difference, and does not require women to meet standards set by a male model.[22] Equality requires that we treat the same interests without discrimination, and that we treat different interests in ways that respect those differences. Women's rights to health and health care on a basis of equality with men encompass both comparable health needs as well as sex-specific health needs. Failure to take into account the special health needs of women, so as to ensure their access to appropriate information and safe services, constitutes discrimination. Targeting women for coercive measures under a policy of population control constitutes discrimination. Equality is not merely a formal matter of guaranteeing to women the same rights as men, nor even of combating purposeful discrimination. It is rather a substantive matter of ensuring the effective enjoyment of equal outcomes in health status and well-being.

B.   The Reporting Process

1.   The initial report

The implementation of China's population policy has long been a matter of interest to the CEDAW Committee. The committee considered China's initial report in 1984.[23] Questions posed by the Committee referred to "the prevailing conditions in a family with more than one child," "the position of women's organizations . . . regarding the policy of birth control," and "genetics."[24] One expert asked "whether, in cases where the first child was a girl, the baby was hidden or made to disappear."[25] The report also noted a "difference in gynecological illnesses that affected rural women and urban women."[26]

---

22. *See, e.g.,* Ann C. Scales, *The Emergence of Feminist Jurisprudence: An Essay,* 95 YALE L. J. 1373 (1986); CATHARINE A. MACKINNON, *Difference and Dominance: On Sex Discrimination, in* FEMINISM UNMODIFIED: DISCOURSES ON LIFE AND LAW 32 (1987).

23. *Report of the Committee on the Elimination of Discrimination Against Women to the General Assembly,* 3rd Sess., Supp. No. 45, ¶¶ 125–80, U.N. Doc. A/39/45 (1984).

24. *Id.* ¶ 148.

25. *Id.* ¶ 140.

26. *Id.*

The representative of China replied that China needed to adopt an effective family planning policy, and that the main obstacles had been traditional ideas. "The Chinese had considered for centuries that to carry on the family with a line of male offspring was a matter of great importance."[27] She explained that "child-bearing was not only a family issue, but also of interest to the State and the people as a whole," and described the policy as follows: "A couple could have two children if the first-born had a nonhereditary disease or was disabled, if both husband and wife were the only children of their respective families, and if two or three consecutive generations of the family had only one child each."[28]

Answering a question regarding genetics, she stated that "the marriage law in China forbade union between ... those who had diseases which were considered by medical science as unfit for marriage."[29] Moreover, "in the case of fetal defects, abortion was encouraged."[30]

"One expert inquired whether the family planning policy did not contradict Article 16 of the Convention on equality in marriage and the family, which ensured freedom of choice in the number of children."[31] The representative replied that freedom to marry had been a breakthrough for women in China, away from the old system of prearranged marriages, and that the family planning program was not compulsory.[32]

2. The second periodic report

China reported to CEDAW again in 1992.[33] On that occasion its representative stated that China had put maternal and child "health care into the plan for primary health care with an emphasis on rural areas. ... Special attention would be paid to the training of rural medical workers in basic preventive skills."[34] Collaboration with the United Nations Population Fund Agency (UNPFA) had produced more effective modern contraceptives, and "had also enabled Chinese researchers to carry out studies to diminish the adverse effects of certain products on women's health."[35] China itself was

---

27. *Id.* ¶ 162.
28. *Id.* ¶¶ 162–63.
29. *Id.* ¶ 164.
30. *Id.*
31. *Id.* ¶ 178.
32. *Id.* ¶ 179.
33. *Report of the Committee on the Elimination of Discrimination Against Women to the General Assembly,* 11th Sess., Plenary Mtg., at ¶¶ 145–218, U.N. Doc. A/47/38 (1992).
34. *Id.* ¶ 150.
35. *Id.* ¶¶ 187–90. The response to a question concerning the mass manufacturing of Norplant subdermal contraceptive implants, without adequate follow-up to monitor health risks, was that the project referred to had not been executed.

developing similar products. In response to a question on male involvement in family planning, the representative said that "[b]irth control was the duty and obligation of both husband and wife."[36]

Another question was raised regarding whether the policy of the single child, and the preference for boys, would cause the number of women to diminish and create a sex imbalance. The representative replied that the 1979 policy had led to an increase in one-child families. He claimed "that the one-child family policy had not resulted in a sex imbalance."[37]

> He reiterated that the one-child policy had been quite successful, and it was in line with the common interest of the population. Implementation was more successful in urban areas and among the better educated groups of society. There were distinctions in the enforcement of the policy, in particular with regard to minorities and areas with lower population density.[38]

During consideration of China's second report to CEDAW, some experts had requested it to provide in its subsequent report information broken down by region, "due to the vastness of the country, to give a better picture and to make it easier for members to understand the issues involved."[39] In summing up, the chairperson also "expressed her hope" that the Committee would receive more statistical details in the next report.[40]

3. The current report

China did not, however, comply with these requests. It combined its third and fourth periodic reports in a short twenty-six page document,[41] to which it added an eleven-page addendum.[42] The Committee considered the combined periodic report at its twentieth session in February 1999. The report of the pre-session working group of the Committee stated in its introduction:

---

36. *Id.* ¶ 193.
37. *Id.* ¶ 197.
38. *Id.* ¶ 213.
39. *Id.* ¶ 212.
40. *Id.* ¶ 218.
41. See *Consideration of Reports Submitted by States Parties Under Article 18 of the Convention on the Elimination of All Forms of Discrimination Against Women: Third and Fourth Periodic Reports of States Parties, China,* U.N. Doc. CEDAW/C/CHN/3–4 (10 June 1997)[hereinafter *Third and Fourth Periodic Reports of States Parties, China*].
42. See *Consideration of Reports Submitted by States Parties Under Article 18 of the Convention on the Elimination of All Forms of Discrimination Against Women: Third and Fourth Periodic Reports of States Parties, China,* addendum. U.N. Doc. CEDAW/C/CHN/3–4/Add.1 (25 Nov. 1998). China also submitted a seven-page corrigendum, which said, "For *Act* read *Law.*" *Consideration of Reports Submitted by States Parties Under Article 18 of the Convention on the Elimination of All Forms of Discrimination Against Women: Third and Fourth Periodic Reports of States Parties, China,* corrigendum, U.N. Doc. CEDAW/C/CHN/3–4/Corr.1 (4 Feb. 1999).

2. The reports indicate serious commitment, national planning and a wide range of legal and administrative measures to promote gender equality. However, insufficient information is provided on actual implementation and results achieved. The reports also lack information about available measures in cases of non-compliance [with the Convention—CS]. The reports fail to document growing disparities between rural and urban areas in the field of education, health and social security and do not contain any reference to women and girls belonging to ethnic minority groups, who make up about eight per cent of the population. There is an absence of data disaggregated by region or province. The reports do not address the questions put by the Committee in the previous report.[43]

China's initial written report stated that, as of 1995, China had a total population of 1.2 billion, of which 48.97 percent were women.[44] One-fifth of the world's women live in China. The report covered a period of economic restructuring which had disproportionately affected women's employment.[45] Despite effective literacy campaigns, the gender ratio in illiteracy rates had remained constant, with women still comprising 70 percent of China's illiterate.[46] An increase in violence against women had also occurred, including kidnapping and trafficking in women.[47] The continuing gap between the situation of women in rural and urban areas appeared to be a major obstacle to implementation of the Convention.[48]

With respect to reproductive health, the report noted success in reducing maternal and infant mortality rates since the founding of the People's Republic in 1949. It noted also that one of the objectives of the Programme

---

43. *Committee on the Elimination of Discrimination Against Women, Report of the Pre-Session Working Group,* 20th Sess., ¶ 2, U.N. Doc. CEDAW/C/1999/I/CRP.1/Add.1 (1999).

44. *See Third and Fourth Periodic Reports of States Parties, China, supra* note 41, ¶ 3.

45. Sixty percent of all laid-off employees were women, and after one year 75 percent had not found reemployment (compared with 50 percent of laid-off men). Kasia Polanska & Karina Milosovich, *IWRAW to CEDAW Country Reports,* INT'L. WOMEN'S RTS. ACTION WATCH 33 (Jan. 1999).

46. *Third and Fourth Periodic Reports of States Parties, Addendum, China* 5, U.N. Doc. CEDAW/C/CHN/3–4/Add.1. The committee stated: "notwithstanding the government's positive efforts and achievements in reducing illiteracy, the Committee is concerned about the disproportionate persistence of illiteracy among women." *Concluding Comments on China's Third and Fourth Periodic Reports, adopted* 3 Feb. 1999, U.N. ESCOR Committee on the Elimination of Discrimination Against Women, 20th Sess., ¶ 44, U.N. Doc. CEDAW/C/1999/I/L.1/Add.7 (1999).

47. *Id.* The Addendum reported in relation to Article 6 of the Convention that China's Code of Criminal Procedural and Penal Code were amended in 1996 and 1997, and that "important amendments were made with regard to punishment for the abduction of and trafficking in women and children and forcing women to engage in prostitution"; *see also* Report of the Special Rapporteur on Violence Against Women, ¶ 88, U.N. Doc. E/CN.4/1997/47 (1997) (reporting the increase in trafficking and kidnapping since the mid-1980s).

48. *See Concluding Comments on China's Third and Fourth Periodic Reports, supra* note 46, ¶ 28.

for the Development of Chinese Women was to guarantee women's right to family planning, and to improve maternal and child care so that all urban and rural women could enjoy health care, including sound reproductive health care. Under Article 12, it focused on maternal and child health care with reference to the 1995 Maternal and Infant Health Care Law ("MIHCL"). In the entire report, however, there was no mention of the family planning policy.

More information emerged in response to the questions of the CEDAW pre-session Working Group. It had prepared a total of seventy questions for the government representatives, and five of these related directly to China's population policy. Under "General questions," the representative was asked: "5. Describe the status of the Tibetan population, particularly women, in terms of . . . access to health services, maternal and child mortality . . . What is the population policy in the Tibetan Autonomous Region?" Under Article 12 on health, the following questions were posed:

36. What social mechanisms and health measures exist to implement the 'one-child policy'?;

37. What are the reasons for the high rate of infanticide and sex-selective abortions? What measures are taken to address the problem?

38. What kind of contraceptive choices are available to couples? What percentage of men are using contraceptives as opposed to women?

39. Provide information about the discrepancy between the male and female birth ratio. What measures are being taken to correct the demographic imbalances currently faced by China?[49]

In response to these questions, the representative of China said:

The advocacy of one couple one child does not mean that all couples have only one child. China's family planning policy is actually one composed of three policies: in the urban areas it is advocated that one couple have one child; in the rural areas, those families who have practical difficulties and wish to have a second child do so with a proper spacing; couples of ethnic groups usually have two or three children. As for the people of the ethnic groups that have a very small population, there are no specific requirements in family planning.[50]

He continued to say: "The principle of combining government guidance with voluntariness of people is employed to conduct the family planning programme. . . . Vast numbers of people are encouraged to exert self-education, self-management, and self-service in their family planning practice."[51] The

---

49. *Committee on the Elimination of Discrimination Against Women, supra* note 43, ¶¶ 36–39.

50. Reply by the Chinese Delegation to the Questions of the CEDAW Pre-Session Working Group (informal translation) (1 Feb. 1999), ¶ 36 (on file with author) [hereinafter Response by the Chinese Delegation].

51. *Id.*

focus of family planning work, he continued, was in rural areas. Stress was laid on publicity and education rather than economic disincentives, on contraception rather than induced abortions, and on daily family planning work rather than irregular campaigns.

Following comments from the floor by CEDAW members, the Chinese representative stated in his final remarks to the Committee: "Coercive measures of any form are prohibited."[52] Indeed, the Committee noted in its Concluding Comments: "The Committee welcomes in particular the Government's strong and unequivocal objection to the use of coercive measures in implementation of its population policy."[53]

The Committee recognized that population growth was a genuine and severe problem and that considerable progress had been made in providing family planning services, but nevertheless, expressed concern at certain problems associated with the implementation of China's population policy.[54] Coercive measures have been employed by officials at the local level in rural and remote areas. The central government has not only failed to make clear that such violent measures are prohibited and to enforce existing criminal laws, but it also maintains a system of bureaucratic incentives that joins with traditional gender prejudice to produce patterns of grave violations of women's human rights neither addressed nor redressed by the law. These include forced abortions and forced sterilizations. In addition, the targeting of women for family planning responsibility and for noncompliance measures is discriminatory. Moreover, the policy as a whole has unintended effects on the right to life of girl children, particularly in rural areas, where practices of sex-selective abortion, female infanticide, and the abandonment of female children occur due to a discriminatory tradition of son preference.

An anecdotal illustration can be found in a 1998 report of the Special Rapporteur on Violence Against Women ("Special Rapporteur"). The case concerned the denial of a request for asylum in Canada by a Chinese national who had been employed as a birth control officer for three years in his commune.

> On four occasions he participated with other officers in seeking out women who had violated the one-child policy imposed by the Government, tying the women up with ropes and taking them to the hospital where they were forcibly aborted or sterilized. He testified that he was aware of all the methods used to

---

52. Response by the Chinese Delegation to the Questions Raised During the Consideration of China's Report by CEDAW Members (New York, 2 Feb. 1999), ¶ 21 (on file with author).

53. *Concluding Comments on China's Third and Fourth Periodic Reports, supra* note 46, ¶ 24.

54. *See Concluding Comments on China's Third and Fourth Periodic Reports, supra* note 46, ¶ 49.

implement the one-child policy in his commune, including forcible abortion on women in advanced stages of pregnancy and the killing by injection of fetuses born alive.[55]

In her 1999 report, the Special Rapporteur stated that China's one-child policy demonstrated the linkage between reproductive health policy and violence:

> Through this policy the Chinese Government restricts the number of children a married couple may have, and, at times, violently enforces this policy through forced abortions. . . . Family planning officials in China allegedly employ intimidation and violence to carry out the policy, sometimes removing women from their homes in the middle of the night to force them to have abortions. Former family planning officials reported having detained women who were pregnant with "out of plan" children in storerooms and offices for as long as necessary to "persuade" them to have an abortion. Once a woman relented, the official would escort her to the hospital and wait until the doctor could provide the official with a signed statement documenting that the abortion had been performed. Relatives of those attempting to avoid forced abortion are also subject to detention and ill-treatment.[56]

Despite assurances by the State Family Planning Commission that "coercion is not permitted," there had been no indication of sanctions being taken against officials who perpetrated such violations.[57]

III.   THE BIRTH CONTROL POLICY

A.   Background Information

The Chinese government has sponsored birth control campaigns since 1954.[58] The first campaign relied on advocating late marriage as a means of postponing rather than controlling reproduction.[59] The second campaign,

---

55. *Report of the Special Rapporteur on Violence Against Women, Its Causes and Consequences, Ms. Radhika Coomaraswamy, Submitted in Accordance with Commission on Human Rights Resolution,* U.N. ESCOR, Comm'n On Hum. Rts., 54th Sess., Agenda Item 9(a), ¶ 206, U.N. Doc. E/CN.4/1998/54 (1998).

56. *Report of the Special Rapporteur on Violence Against Women, Its Causes and Consequences, Ms. Radhika Coomaraswamy, Submitted in Accordance with Commission on Human Rights Resolution 1997/44, Policies and Practices that Impact Women's Reproductive Rights and Contribute to, Cause or Constitute Violence Against Women,* U.N. ESCOR, Comm'n on Hum. Rts., 55th Sess., Agenda Item 12(a), addendum, ¶ 50, U.N. Doc E/CN.4/1999/68/Add.4 (1999).

57. *Id.* ¶ 53.

58. *See* Deborah S. Davis, *Family Planning in China: The Social Consequences of the One Child Campaign,* 7 China Update: The Yale-China Ass'n Newsl. 1 (1987).

59. *See id.* at 1.

between 1962 and 1966, introduced voluntary sterilization and abortion in urban areas.[60] The third campaign, begun in 1969, emphasized modern methods of contraception and achieved a significant decline in total fertility rates (the average number of children born by one woman in her lifetime) from 5.8 children per woman in 1970 to 3.5 in 1975.[61] Nonetheless, crude birth rates continued to rise, due to the size of the existing population of childbearing age.[62]

The current policy, known as the "one-child" policy, was announced in 1979 out of government concern for population growth, and resulted in a sudden upsurge in the number of forced abortions and involuntary sterilizations. Public outrage led to a Communist Party directive which outlined exceptions to the one-child quota. The most important distinction allowed rural families "in hardship" to apply to have another child. This effectively equated "hardship" with the absence of a son, and promised all those whose firstborn was a girl the chance to have a second child. One-child certificates were issued to couples who had promised to have no additional children, and qualified them for cash bonuses at work and preferential treatment in housing, medical care, and daycare services. The vast majority of these couples lived in large cities, and they were almost all state employees.[63]

It should be noted that the priority given by the government of China to maternity and child health has produced successful results. China's maternal mortality rate is estimated to be 95 per 100,000, one-fifteenth of the rate before establishment of the People's Republic in 1949.[64] According to the official report to CEDAW, it now stands at 61.9 per 100,000.[65] In other respects, there has been great progress in the health status of Chinese women—female infant mortality decreased from 400 per 1,000 in some areas prior to 1949 to under fifty per 1,000 nationally in 1990, and life expectancy for women doubled.[66]

B.   Law and Policy

In terms of the law, the 1980 Marriage Law had made "family planning" an obligation of couples. The 1982 Constitution of the People's Republic of

---

60. See id.
61. See id. at 2.
62. See id. at 5.
63. See id. at 6.
64. See World Health Organization, Report to CEDAW, 20th Sess., U.N. Doc CEDAW/C/1999/1/3/Add.2, ¶ 1.1.1 (1999); Cf. M. Yu & R. Sarri, Women's Health Status and Gender Inequality in China, 45 Soc. Sci. Med. 1885, 1889 (1997).
65. Third and Fourth Periodic Reports of States Parties, China, supra note 41, at 20.
66. Yu & Sarri, supra note 64, at 1893.

China stipulated that the entire country should promote family planning, and also made it a duty of all couples to practice birth control.[67] In 1982, the Central Committee of the Communist Party and the State Council issued a joint directive, ordering the provincial governments to adopt strict methods of policy implementation.[68]

In 1991, a second joint directive urged provincial governments to tighten enforcement of birth control. The state warned that unbridled population growth retarded economic development, depressed the standard of living, kept infant mortality high, and perpetuated poverty.[69] A major change tied the evaluation of the performance of family planning personnel and other local cadres to the achievement of centrally allocated birth quotas in their area. Failure to contain the number of births within the quota for the locality entailed sanctions.[70]

In 1992, China enacted the Law on the Protection of Rights and Interests of Women (LPRIW).[71] Article 47 provides as follows:

> Women have the right to child-bearing in accordance with relevant regulations of the State as well as the freedom not to bear any child.
>
> Where a couple of child-bearing age practise family planning according to the relevant regulations of the state, the departments concerned shall provide safe and effective contraceptives and techniques, and ensure the health and safety of the woman receiving any birth-control operation.[72]

The mention of the freedom not to bear any child is rare and commendable, but the positive right to child-bearing is subject to state regulations.[73] The family planning policy as such has never been codified in legislation. It is implemented not according to the rule of law, but rather according to rule by unpublished administrative directives.[74] Local authorities are expected to

---

67. *See* X. Li, *License to Coerce: Violence Against Women, State Responsibility, and Legal Failures in China's Family-Planning Program,* 8 Yale J.L. & Feminism 145, 149 (1996).
68. *See id.*
69. *See id.* at 149–50.
70. *See* Human Rights in China, *Report on Implementation of CEDAW in the People's Republic of China* 74 (1998).
71. The Law of the People's Republic of China on the Protection of Rights and Interests of Women, *adopted at* the Fifth Session of the Seventh National People's Congress on 3 Apr. 1992, *entered into force* 1 Oct. 1992, *reprinted in* 4 Laws of the People's Republic of China, 1990–1992, 373 (1992).
72. *Id.* at 382.
73. Note, furthermore, that the right to safe birth control appears to be conditioned on compliance with state regulations. This might well be counter-effective, since it is precisely those who fail to comply who require the most education, counseling, and health services. In any event, however, it might amount to a violation of Article 12 of the Convention. Women's right of access to health services, on a basis of equality of men and women, means that they may not be penalized in relation to their access and use of safe reproductive health services.
74. Li, *supra* note 67, at 151–52.

implement the birth control policy and keep births within quotas determined by the central government. Failure to make a quota entails the risk of disciplinary sanctions, demotion, fines or the loss of bonuses.

Before taking a closer look at the system of sanctions that are in place to induce compliance, one should note a matter of some concern that arose in relation to China's 1995 Maternal and Infant Health Care Law ("MIHCL"). This law, sometimes referred to as the "eugenic law," requires medical counseling before marriage for people whose families suffer from a group of conditions, including mental illness, that the law presumes are hereditary with little or no scientific basis.[75] It requires sterilization or long-term contraception as a precondition of marriage if a person is determined by a doctor to be at risk for bearing an affected child. One response to this law was a statement by the American Society of Human Genetics in 1998, reaffirming "its commitment to the fundamental principle of reproductive freedom" and deploring "any . . . coercive effort intended to restrict reproductive freedom or to constrain freedom of choice on the basis of known or presumed genetic characteristics of potential parents."[76]

C.   The System of Administrative Sanctions

The major elements of the administrative system as currently practiced appear to be the following:

---

75. The Law of the People's Republic of China on Maternal and Infant Health Care, *adopted at* the Tenth Meeting of the Standing Committee of the Eighth National People's Congress on 27 Oct. 1994, *entered into force* 1 June 1995, *reprinted in* 6 LAWS OF THE PEOPLE'S REPUBLIC OF CHINA, 1994, 119 (1994). Article 10 of the MIHCL provides that people with serious hereditary diseases or relevant mental disorders must postpone marriage, and if either partner has such a disease, the couple may marry only if they agree "to take long-lasting contraceptive measures or give up child bearing by undergoing ligation." The world scientific community long ago rejected the assumption that mentally disabled persons will give birth to children with the same disabilities. *Id.* at 123.

76. Board of Directors of the American Society of Human Genetics, *ASHG Statement, Eugenics and the Misuse of Genetic Information to Restrict Reproductive Freedom*, 64 AM. J. HUM. GENET. 335 (1999). It is worth noting that in 1990, the Chinese government apparently indicated that there were supposedly 10,000 "inferior" Tibetans in the Tibetan Autonomous Region (TAR). International Committee of Lawyers for Tibet, Women's Commission for Refugee Women and Children & Tibetan Centre for Human Rights and Democracy, *Violence and Discrimination Against Tibetan Women* 17 (Dec. 1998) (a report submitted by the International Committee of Lawyers for Tibet, Women's Commission for Refugee Women and Children and the Tibetan Centre for Human Rights and Democracy, to the CEDAW Committee) [hereinafter International Committee of Lawyers for Tibet]. Note, too, the concern of the Committee on the Elimination of Racial Discrimination, "about the content and implementation of the law of 1995 on mother and child health care and its impact on minority nationalities." *Concluding Observations of the Committee on the Elimination of Racial Discrimination*, 49th Sess., ¶ 20, U.N. Doc. CERD/C/304/Add.15 (1996).

- married couples have to apply for birth permits before starting a pregnancy;
- out-of-wedlock pregnancies are illegal;[77]
- unauthorized pregnancies have to be terminated;
- in many rural and minority areas, couples can have two children, especially if the first-born is a daughter, but a third is forbidden;
- after giving birth to the first child, women are required to wear an IUD or use other contraceptive measures; and
- after having an out-of-plan child, one spouse must be sterilized.

As already noted, failure of family planning officials to meet quotas entails the risk of disciplinary sanctions, demotion, fines or the loss of bonuses. However, the system of administrative sanctions extends further. Persons acting in compliance with the practice include doctors performing forced medical intervention on behalf of the state. The Special Rapporteur noted that, in China, "forced sterilization has been carried out by or at the instigation of family planning officials."[78] The killing of fetuses who survive late-term induced abortion is the result of enforcement by authorities who supervise abortions of "illegal" pregnancies. Such killings are carried out virtually under official order and are often overseen by family planning officials.[79] Doctors who refuse to perform abortions and sterilizations in compliance with the policy may face sanctions, including stiff fines and dismissal from their jobs. The unauthorized removal of an IUD is also punishable, even though improperly inserted IUDs often result in pelvic infection and heavy menstruation, and more than one-third of abortions are attributed to IUD failure. Doctors may be penalized if they remove IUDs without permission from population control officials, even for medical reasons.[80]

Parents and children also suffer economic penalization. Penalties for noncompliance include economic sanctions on the adults in the form of fines, administrative demotion, loss of job or reduction in pay, and even loss of housing. Of particular concern is the discrimination of "illegal" or "out-of-plan" children, a status to which girls are particularly susceptible because of the tradition of son preference.

---

77. For further the comment in the 1999 report of the *Special Rapporteur on Violence against Women, see supra* note 56, ¶ 50: "Under the one-child policy, single women and migrant women unable to return to their home regions are subject to compulsory abortions."

78. *Id.* ¶ 53.

79. *See* Li, *supra* note 67, at 163.

80. Human Rights in China, *Caught Between Tradition and the State—Violations of the Human Rights of Chinese Women: A Report with Recommendations Marking the Fourth World Conference on Women,* 45–46 (1995).

Children born out-of-plan are not entitled to state subsidies, admission to public day care and schools, and access to public health care. These children, whose births go unreported, may not have an official identity. Until they are registered, they are not eligible for such services as immunization, public education, and medical care.[81] Their family might have been penalized by a fine, payment of "birth fees," or denial of "land use rights."[82] A 1989 State Council's Order stated: "Poor families with out-of-plan children should not be given any 'poverty assistance' until they take effective contraceptive measures . . . If they are already beneficiaries of 'poverty assistance' programs, their participation is terminated and they must pay fines for violating the birth quota."[83]

D.   Gender Discrimination

Before continuing to view the dynamics of coercion and resistance, it is important to note that women are primarily targeted for implementing this policy. Therefore, gender discrimination is an integral part of the policy. In 1992, 95 percent of all sterilizations were performed on women, despite the fact that tubal ligation is a far more complicated, intrusive, and expensive procedure than vasectomy.[84] Some reports from Tibet illustrate this point:

—   A woman who gave birth to an unauthorized child in Lhasa was forced to pay substantial penalties out of her government salary and was denied permanent status as a worker. Her husband, also a government employee, received no penalty.[85]

—   A woman from Amdo described regular birth control meetings where they instructed women to have abortions, take pills, or insert rings. Men did not have to attend birth control meetings, and officials never talked about birth control for men.[86]

—   A male health care worker reported that he was trained to perform abortions and sterilizations on women. "I was never trained in or saw any operations on men." There were house-to-house visits to monitor menstrual cycles of women, but "it was not in the training for us to distribute condoms."[87]

---

81. *See* Human Rights in China, *supra* note 70, at 75.
82. *Id.* at 80.
83. Li, *supra* note 67, at 157–58.
84. V. Pearson, *Women and Health in China: Anatomy, Destiny and Politics*, 25 J. Soc. Pol. 529, 533 (1996).
85. International Committee of Lawyers for Tibet, *supra* note 76, at 16.
86. *Id.*
87. *Id.*

IV. RESISTANCE AND VIOLENCE

A. Economic Factors of Resistance

The one-child policy has been successful in urban locations where many are state-employed and can thus enjoy the benefits. However, in rural areas, where the economy is based on male manual labor and women marry out of the family, there has been economically motivated resistance. In ethnic minority areas, such as Tibet and Uyghur, resistance has also been politically motivated by factors related to restrictions on religious expression. Quotas, as well as enforcement, vary from region to region, but where there is resistance, there is coercion.

Resistance in rural areas has stemmed from a feudal tradition of son preference. By tradition daughters marry out, belong to their husbands' families, and do not inherit family property from their fathers. Sons look after their parents in old age in shared households, and they are needed to carry on the family name. According to China's official report, "women make up 70 per cent of the workforce in crop farming and animal husbandry,"[88] yet sons are still thought necessary for some of the heavier work.[89]

In rural areas, patrilineal communities and patrilocal residence patterns mean that the elderly depend entirely upon their sons to support them in their old age. Traditional son preference is reinforced by the "family responsibility system" of rural economics, and the absence of an old-age social security system. Exceptions to the one-child policy accommodate this gender bias.[90] There are, however, strong economic incentives for parents in rural areas to make girls disappear. Rural market pressures have made conventional preference for sons a socioeconomic necessity. Parents desperate for boys may fear punishment for having more than the permitted number of children and therefore resort to female child abandonment and neglect. Thus there appears to be an abnormally high mortality rate among girls after one month.[91] Girls constitute the overwhelming majority of abandoned children[92] and of those living in orphanages throughout China.[93]

---

88. Third and Fourth Periodic Reports of States Parties, China, *supra* note 41, at 22.

89. *See* Pearson, *supra* note 84, at 532.

90. *See* Ann D. Jordan, *Women's Rights in the People's Republic of China: Patriarchal Wine Poured from a Socialist Bottle,* 8 J. Chinese L. 47 (1994).

91. *See* Human Rights in China, *supra* note 70, at 84. But note that the infant mortality rates of females was extremely high prior to 1949, particularly in rural areas. Yu & Sarri, *supra* note 64, at 1888.

92. According to one study of 237 families that had abandoned children, *reported in* 7 Reprod. Health Matters 168 (1999) (citing K. Johnson et al., *Infant abandonment in China,* 24(3) Pop. & Dev. Rev. 469 (1998)), 90 percent of the children were girls, and most were abandoned after their parents had exceeded limits imposed by birth planning authorities.

93. *See* Li, *supra* note 67, at 170.

B.   Political Factors of Resistance

In areas of ethnic minorities, resistance may be motivated by political factors. This is the case in Tibet, where human rights violations have been well
documented.[94] Thousands of people have been imprisoned for exercising
their rights to freedom of religious practice, expression, and peaceful
demonstration. Most live in rural communities under heavy tax burdens and
are unable to pay school fees for their children. Stories of coercive reproductive measures against women abound. Tibet is taken as an indicator of
what is happening elsewhere in China. Where there is the organizational
capacity to monitor the individual narratives of human rights abuse, human
rights monitors have information that alerts them to variations of the same
practice in other parts of China. Where political resistance joins with rural
economic conditions the violence of the state is particularly marked.

According to nongovernmental sources of information, the Tibetan
Autonomous Region (TAR) has a significantly higher maternal mortality rate
than the rest of China.[95] Most Tibetan women have almost no access to basic
medical care and cannot afford the costs of what is available. There is anec-

---

94.   *See, e.g., Committee Against Torture, Concluding Observations: China*, U.N. Comm.
       against Torture, 51st Sess., Supp. No. 44, ¶ 149(e), U.N. Doc A/51/44 (1996), expressing
       concern "that the special environment that exists in Tibet continues to create conditions
       that result in alleged maltreatment and even death of persons held in police custody and
       prisons"; *Committee on the Rights of the Child, Concluding Observations: China, Report
       of the Twelfth Session*, U.N. Comm. on the Rights of the Child, 12th Sess., ¶ 19, U.N.
       Doc CRC/C/15/Add.56 (1996), expressing concern "about reports that school attendance
       in minority areas, including the Tibet Autonomous Region, is lagging behind, that the
       quality of education is inferior and that insufficient efforts have been made to develop a
       bilingual education system which would include adequate teaching in Chinese"; *Report
       of the Special Rapporteur on Torture, Mr. Nigel S. Rodley, Submitted Pursuant to
       Commission on Human Rights Resolution 1997/38*, U.N. ESCOR Comm'n on Hum. Rts.,
       54th Sess., ¶ 73, U.N. Doc E/CN.4/1998/38/Add.1 (1997):

       Tsering Youdon, a 16-year-old girl, was reportedly arrested at her home in Lhuntse on
       29 February 1994, following the arrest of the headmaster of her school. While interro-
       gated at the police station as to whether the headmaster had taught her to demand
       independence for Tibet, a hot iron was allegedly placed firmly on her leg and left there
       for five minutes. She was reportedly also thrown against a desk, resulting in injuries to
       the head, and kicked in the stomach.

       Report of the Working Group on Enforced or Involuntary Disappearances, U.N. ESCOR
       Comm'n on Hum. Rts., 53rd Sess., ¶ 103, U.N. Doc E/CN.4/1997/34 (1996):

       Sixteen of the newly reported cases of disappearance are said to have occurred in Tibet
       and concerned eight monks, a church leader, an accountant, a driver, a mechanic, a
       teacher, two businessmen and one person of unknown profession. . . . One of the dis-
       appeared persons is said to have been arrested for having participated in a religious
       ceremony in which a prayer was offered for the long life of the Dalai Lama.

95.   *See* International Committee of Lawyers for Tibet, *supra* note 76, at 25 (up to 20 per
       10,000 as opposed to six per 10,000 for China).

dotal evidence of discrimination in fees-for-service.[96] There is also concern that Tibetan women might avoid medical care out of fear that the authorities will force unwanted birth control methods on them.[97]

A nongovernmental report prepared for the Fourth World Conference on Women held in Beijing in 1995 stated:

> China's current national birth control policy states that Tibetan "minority" women are allowed to have two children, while Chinese women are allowed to have only one child. In order for a Tibetan or a Chinese woman to have a child, she must be married and between the ages of 25 to 35. A Tibetan woman desiring a second child must wait four years before becoming pregnant again. Women who become pregnant outside of these parameters must have an abortion and/or be sterilized, or face severe social and economic sanctions.[98]

The number of permitted children varies by district and employment— government officials may be allowed two children, while nomads and farmers may be allowed three. Vast regions of Kham and Amdo are parts of Tibet that do not fall within the official TAR.[99] There are reports that population control is more intense in these areas; government employees are allowed only one child and others only two.

C. Coercive Measures

Accounts of violations of reproductive health rights include descriptions of late abortions, forced sterilization, and other coercive measures. Forced medical procedures, such as IUD insertion, abortion, and sterilization constitute battery of a woman. They are a violation of the human right to bodily integrity, security of the person, nonviolence, and to autonomy in making decisions about medical care. Furthermore, the methods employed to ensure compliance entail violations of privacy, personal liberty and constitute forms of collective punishment. These include public menstrual moni-

---

96. *See Id.* at 26.
97. *See Id.*
98. The Tibetan Women's Association, Tears of Silence—A Report on Tibetan Women and Population Control 12 (May 1995). The preface refers to the global attention to issues of reproductive rights and women's health in the wake of the International Conference on Population and Development held in Cairo in 1994. It explains that the report demonstrates that a coercive population control policy is being implemented by the Chinese authorities in Tibet, in violation of the CEDAW Convention. *Id.* at 4.
99. This accounts for discrepancies in population figures between the Chinese Government and the Tibetan Government in Exile. According to Chinese figures, there are approximately 2 million Tibetans and 68,000 Han Chinese in the TAR. According to Tibetan figures, there are approximately 6 million Tibetans and 7 million Chinese in the area of Tibet. This colonization is accompanied by positive economic incentives for Han settlers, leaving the Tibetans an impoverished, and disadvantaged rural minority in their own land.

toring, roundups for medical intervention, and detention of family members as hostages.

Women have their periods monitored by public officials, either at village meetings or by house-to-house visits of birth control units. They are forced to terminate unauthorized pregnancies if they are detected. Women may go into hiding to avoid abortion, but then they might be hunted by the authorities and their relatives taken hostage. Women in late stages of illegal pregnancies may be taken into custody until the abortion has been performed. They may be subject to forced sterilization if they have already had two children. All this amounts to cruel, inhuman, and degrading treatment by persons acting in official capacity,[100] if not "torture" within the definition of Article 1 of the Convention Against Torture.[101]

For example, a birth control "experiment" in the Uyghur Autonomous Region allegedly involved 846 women who were forced to undergo abortion, seventeen of whom reportedly died within three months.[102] There are numerous reports of similar campaigns in Tibet. According to one report from Amdo, women were brought from nearby villages by trucks to be sterilized. If the sterilization team did not meet their quota, they received a pay cut.[103]

Group pressure is brought through public criticism, monitoring of menstrual periods at village meetings, and periodic pregnancy tests. A thirty-one-year-old woman from Phenpo recalled weekly meetings: "If the woman was not menstruating, she was given a blue tablet to remove the child or taken to the hospital to check them [sic] and get an abortion."[104]

Mobile birth control teams carry out government policy in rural villages and nomadic areas. One thirty-seven-year-old man from Kham reportedly witnessed nomadic people rounded up for abortions. His village job required him to participate in the annual roundups where up to 200 women were aborted at a time.[105] A monk named Tashi described a mobile team that came to his village in Amdo in 1987:

---

100. Convention Against Torture and Other Curel, Inhuman or Degrading Treatment or Punishment, *adopted* 10 Dec. 1984, G.A. Res. 39/46, U.N. GAOR, 39th Sess., Supp. No. 51, at art. 16, U.N. Doc. A/39/51 (1985) (*entered into force* 26 June 1987) *reprinted in* 23 I.L.M. 1027 (1984), *substantive changes noted in* 24 I.L.M. 535 (1985).
101. *Id.* art. 1:

> For the purposes of this Convention, the term "torture" means any act by which severe pain or suffering, whether physical or mental, is intentionally inflicted on a person for such purposes as . . . intimidating or coercing him or a third person . . . when such pain or suffering is inflicted by or at the instigation of or with the consent or acquiescence of a public official or other person acting in an official capacity.

102. Amnesty International, Supplementary Information for the CEDAW Committee 6 (Jan. 1999) [hereinafter Amnesty International, Supplementary Information].
103. *See* International Committee of Lawyers for Tibet, *supra* note 76, at 14.
104. *Id.* at 15.
105. *See Id.* at 13.

> I watched a mobile birth control team set up their tent next to my monastery. First the villagers were informed that the team had arrived, and that all women had to report to the tent or there would be grave consequences, like fines of 1000 yuan ($US200) to women who did not comply. . . . The women who went peacefully received medical care. Women who resisted were rounded up by the police and taken by force. No medical care was given.[106]

Family planning officials not only detain the women themselves while forcing them to undergo medical procedures, but also take hostage the relatives of couples who flee to avoid abortion, sterilization or the payment of fines for out-of-plan births. One report concerned the death in custody of one such relative.[107] In a 1998 interview, a twenty-two-year-old female population control officer described her daily work in a city suburb in Zhejiang Province:

> Some of the people we are trying to control want to escape from us. Then we hold someone else in the family in a cell—the mother, the father . . . —for several weeks, several months, sometimes until the person in question shows up. Occasionally the whole family disappears, they go off to another region. Then we burn their house.[108]

According to testimony from a former detainee, local governments in Zhunyang County, Henan Province, maintain detention centers where they routinely hold hundreds of people. He testified that in one village of Dalian Township, "people say whenever they hear the sound of a motor vehicle, it doesn't matter if it's day or night, they think it's the Township government's birth planning Special Action Team come to grab someone. Everybody scatters and hides. Terrified children watch parents and grandparents get carted off."[109]

Indeed, the representative of China reported to CEDAW, in his final remarks to the Committee, on one such instance in which family planning officials acting in abuse of their authority had been prosecuted.

> In 1996 two staff in Liancheng County, Fujian Province, tied up, beat and detained unlawfully some persons during their work concerning family planning, violating their lawful rights and interests. They were prosecuted by the local procuratorate, and were sentenced to fixed-term imprisonment of two years and two years six months respectively.[110]

It should be noted that this was the first occasion on which China has made it known that officials have been prosecuted for such crimes.

---

106. The Tibetan Women's Association, *supra* note 98, at 24.
107. *See* Amnesty International, Supplementary Information, *supra* note 102, at 5.
108. Human Rights in China, *supra* note 70, at 77.
109. *Id.* at 78.
110. Response by the Chinese Delegation, *supra* note 52, ¶ 21.

D. Discriminatory Effects

The discriminatory effects of China's policy in terms of the girl child have been commented on above. The violence has taken a particularly heavy toll among female infants.

Sex-selective abortion is carried out, despite the fact that it is forbidden by Article 3 of the Maternal and Infant Health Care Law.[111] Ultrasound technology is available in many cities and towns. Strict birth control measures and couples' strong desire for sons has made the demand for sexscreening so overwhelming that it has become a profitable business. Besides the failure to enforce existing criminal laws, this discriminatory practice raises questions about medical ethics and human rights.

Likewise, the traditional practice of abandoning baby girls has flourished despite the explicit language of Article 35 of the Law on the Protection of Rights and Interests of Women: "Women's right of life and health shall be inviolable. Drowning, abandoning or cruel infanticide in any manner of female babies shall be prohibited."[112] It is true that child abandonment and female infanticide are an age-old practice in China, largely due to poverty, out-of-wedlock birth, and son preference, but contemporary practice is clearly related to birth control restrictions.

One indicator is the skewed sex ratio at birth. The government's response to questions by the CEDAW committee on this matter referred to the 1990 Fourth National Census, which showed that the sex ratio at birth was 111 males per 100 females.[113] "[F]or second-order births and above the ratio was dramatically imbalanced in favor of males."[114] The higher the order of birth, the higher the disparity. It should be noted that the imbalance might be even greater if unreported female births are accounted for. It has been estimated that some 12 percent of females are unaccounted for each year.[115] The nonregistration of newborn girls has been recognized as a major factor contributing to the imbalance in the sex ratio.[116]

Moreover, there is a long-term concern about the shortage of women among cohorts of marriageable age, and the threat to societal stability and public order posed by the growing number of young men unable to find

---

111. "Identification of the sex of a fetus through technological means is strictly forbidden unless it is necessary on medical grounds." Li, *supra* note 67, at 169.

112. Article 35 of the LPRIW continues *inter alia* to state: "discrimination against or maltreatment of women who gave birth to female babies" shall be prohibited. LPRIW, *supra* note 71, at 380.

113. Reply, *supra* note 50, at 38. The normal sex ratio at birth is 105 boys to 100 girls. Pearson, *supra* note 84, at 533.

114. Susan M. Rigdon, *Abortion Law and Practice in China: An Overview with Comparisons to the United States,* 42 Soc. Sci. Med. 543, 551 (1996).

115. *See* Yu & R. Sarri, *supra* note 64, at 1888.

116. *See Committee on the Rights of the Child, supra* note 94, ¶ 37.

wives. Many of these men are living in rural areas, where villages are affected not only by the skewed sex ratio but also by the desire of young women to go to towns and cities to find work, given the limited economic opportunities for women on farms. This has led to another phenomenon, the kidnapping of women for sale to farmers in remote rural areas as wives.[117]

Bride-selling, too, is an ancient tradition in rural areas of China, and China's report to CEDAW included information on the success of a "crack down" on trafficking, indicating the seriousness of the problem and its dimensions. Article 35 of the LPRIW provides that the abduction of and trafficking in, or kidnapping of women, as well as the buying of such women shall be prohibited. In 1996 and 1997, China's criminal code was amended to increase criminal penalties and strengthen administrative and economic penalties for trafficking and forcing women to engage in prostitution.[118] In response to CEDAW questions, the government of China also produced statistical figures. "In 1995, 10,531 cases of abducting and selling of people were uncovered, and 13,934 women victims were rescued,"[119] and between 1992 and 1997 the number of recorded cases had been on the decrease. "The incidence has been brought under control."[120] This is also an illustration of the capacity of the government to enforce laws if it so wishes.

Finally, it is important to note the adverse health consequences of the birth control policy for women. The medical procedures that are forced upon hundreds of women at a time are often performed by underskilled staff and under unsafe conditions. A Tibetan paramedic who had worked in a rural area of Kham in Szichuan Province reported: "because of lack of hygiene [IUD] insertions were followed by infections."[121] Complications may go untreated. Women may fear contact with health providers, especially because IUD removal requires official authorization. Women's targeting for reproductive health measures has already been noted as gender discrimination. The failure to provide safe services, with its adverse consequences on women's health, is also in violation of women's right to nondiscrimination under Article 12 of the CEDAW Convention.

Many testimonies report health problems that are adverse consequences of unsafe reproductive health services, including lower back pain and pelvic inflammatory disease. Abortion and sterilization operations

> are often carried out . . . with questionable procedures and with under-qualified medical staff, under poor conditions, and without the woman's consent. The symptoms described are remarkably consistent and include most com-

---

117. *See* Yu & Sarri, *supra* note 64, at 1888–1889.
118. *See Third and Fourth Periodic Reports of States Parties, China, supra* note 42, at 4.
119. Reply by the Chinese Delegation, *supra* note 50, at 20.
120. *Id.*
121. The Tibetan Women's Association, *supra* note 98, at 21.

monly, backache, loss of appetite with attendant gastric problems, weakness and tiredness. Some report fever and headaches. There are even reports that some women have died or suffered chronic problems as a result of such operations.[122]

Moreover, the synthesis of the birth-control policy with traditional gender prejudices may also have led to other health consequences for women. There are very clear problems in the area of mental health, where suicide statistics are of concern. China is the only country in the world where more women than men commit suicide. Moreover, China accounts for 56 percent of all female suicides worldwide.[123] Rural suicide rates are three times higher than urban rates.[124] This attests to the low value set on female lives, and also reflects on the mental health status of women living in impoverished rural China.

V. CONCLUSION

The information that came to light as a result of the CEDAW reporting process from independent reliable sources across China points to a consistent pattern of official actions which constitute systematic violations of human rights. In summing up China's third and fourth periodic reports to CEDAW, the Concluding Comments of the Committee expressed concern about the following problems associated with the implementation of China's population policy:

(a)   The Committee notes with concern that only 14 per cent of men use contraceptives, thus making contraception and family planning overwhelmingly a woman's responsibility. In the light of the fact that vasectomy is far less intrusive and costly than tubal ligation, targeting mainly women for sterilization may amount to discrimination;

(b)   Notwithstanding the Government's clear rejection of coercive measures, there are consistent reports of abuse and violence by local family planning officials. These include forced sterilizations and abortions, arbitrary detention and house demolitions, particularly in rural areas and among ethnic minorities . . .;

(c)   The Committee is concerned about the growing disparity in the male/female sex ratio at birth as an unintended consequence of the population policy, owing to the discriminatory tradition of son pref-

---

122. *Id.* at 36.
123. *See IWRAW to CEDAW Country Reports, supra* note 45, at 34.
124. *See* Human Rights in China, *supra* note 70, at 8.

erence. The shortage of females may also have long-term implications regarding trafficking in women;

(d)   The Committee is concerned about illegal practices of gender-selective abortion, female infanticide and the non-registration and abandonment of female children. The Committee expresses particular concern about the status of "out-of-plan" and unregistered children, many of them girls, who may be officially non-existent and thus not entitled to education, health care or other social benefits.[125]

The Committee concluded its comments on China's population policy by urging the Government to promote information, education, and counseling and to introduce gender-sensitivity training for family planning officials in order to underscore the principles of reproductive choice and increase male responsibility. "The Government should make clear that coercive and violent measures are prohibited and enforce such prohibition through fair legal procedures that sanction officials acting in excess of their authority."[126]

China reported to CEDAW at its twentieth session in January 1999. At the same session, the Committee also adopted its General Recommendation on Women and Health. Some of the commentary on the Convention is pertinent to the situation in China. State parties have the responsibility to ensure that executive action and policy comply with the obligations to respect, protect and fulfill women's rights to health care.[127] "Acceptable services are those which are delivered in a way that ensures that a woman gives her fully informed consent, respects her dignity, and guarantees her confidentiality."[128] Forms of coercion are not permitted. All health services must "be consistent with the human rights of women, including the rights to autonomy, privacy, confidentiality, informed consent, and choice."[129]

In Chinese thinking, birth fundamentally affects the family and the state. It is the collective right of a family unit, not the right of the individual woman, to control her reproductive organs. With the birth control policy, the state has joined with tradition and poverty, to control women's bodies and their lives. Yet coerced abortions are "one in a long list of state interventions in the lives of individuals" that fail to adhere to fundamental principles of international human rights law.[130]

---

125. *Concluding Comments on China's Third and Fourth Periodic Reports, supra* note 46, ¶ 49.
126. *Id.* ¶ 50.
127. *See* General Recommendation No. 24, UN CEDAW, 20th Sess., ¶ 13 (1999).
128. *Id.* ¶ 22.
129. *Id.* ¶ 31 (e).
130. *See* Rigdon, *supra* note 114, at 556.

In human rights discourse, the notion of human dignity implies a right to autonomy and to privacy, in the sense of a right of the individual to make decisions on intimate matters, such as reproduction and sexuality, free of state interference. They imply a kind of private jurisdiction or branch of government in which the individual is sovereign and constitutionally protected against other state organs—especially the executive branch. This human rights notion is foreign to Chinese culture.

Health and human rights advocacy is an essentially subversive activity, requiring the overturn of deeply-rooted social and political structures that produce ill health.[131] Rights are the building blocks of power relationships. They structure responsibility, trust, and obligation. They are at the root of principles of transparency and accountability. This is of particular importance in the relations of trust that should be the basis of health care.

Human rights standards define the process of decision-making, starting from the autonomy of the individual. Rights of due process, whether legal or administrative, are key to respect for human dignity. Rights empower people by making them aware of their own power and the ways in which their actions and stories impact upon the lives of others.

Human rights narratives—the stories human beings tell—reveal that structural injustice creates multiple forms of suffering and human rights abuse. Women are one vulnerable group because they are so easily reduced to bodily aspects of their selves. China is one regime that does not have any structural understanding of the concept of human rights. Tibet is one parable of human resistance in the spirit of *ahimsa*. The Dalai Lama says it well: "Fundamentally we are all the same human beings. We all seek happiness and try to avoid suffering. We have the same basic needs and concerns. Furthermore, all of us human beings want freedom and the right to determine our own destiny as individuals. That is human nature."[132]

---

131. *See* Lynn P. Freedman, *Reflections on Emerging Frameworks of Health and Human Rights,* 1 HEALTH & HUM. RTS. 314 (1995).
132. TENZIN GYATSO, FREEDOM IN EXILE—THE AUTOBIOGRAPHY OF THE DALAI LAMA 270 (1990).

Appendix

Convention on the Elimination of All Forms of Discrimination against Women

Adopted and opened for signature, ratification and accession by General Assembly resolution 34/180 of 18 December 1979

entry into force 3 September 1981, in accordance with article 27(1)

The States Parties to the present Convention,

Noting that the Charter of the United Nations reaffirms faith in fundamental human rights, in the dignity and worth of the human person and in the equal rights of men and women,

Noting that the Universal Declaration of Human Rights affirms the principle of the inadmissibility of discrimination and proclaims that all human beings are born free and equal in dignity and rights and that everyone is entitled to all the rights and freedoms set forth therein, without distinction of any kind, including distinction based on sex,

Noting that the States Parties to the International Covenants on Human Rights have the obligation to ensure the equal rights of men and women to enjoy all economic, social, cultural, civil and political rights,

Considering the international conventions concluded under the auspices of the United Nations and the specialized agencies promoting equality of rights of men and women,

Noting also the resolutions, declarations and recommendations adopted by the United Nations and the specialized agencies promoting equality of rights of men and women,

Concerned, however, that despite these various instruments extensive discrimination against women continues to exist,

Recalling that discrimination against women violates the principles of equality of rights and respect for human dignity, is an obstacle to the participation of women, on equal terms with men, in the political, social, economic and cultural life of their countries, hampers the growth of the prosperity of society and the family and makes more difficult the full development of the potentialities of women in the service of their countries and of humanity,

Concerned that in situations of poverty women have the least access to food, health, education, training and opportunities for employment and other needs,

Convinced that the establishment of the new international economic order based on equity and justice will contribute significantly towards the promotion of equality between men and women,

Emphasizing that the eradication of apartheid, all forms of racism, racial discrimination, colonialism, neo-colonialism, aggression, foreign occupation and domination and interference in the internal affairs of States is essential to the full enjoyment of the rights of men and women,

Affirming that the strengthening of international peace and security, the relaxation of international tension, mutual co-operation among all States irrespective of their social and economic systems, general and complete disarmament, in particular nuclear disarmament under strict and effective international control, the affirmation of the principles of justice, equality and mutual benefit in relations among countries and the realization of the right of peoples under alien and colonial domination and foreign occupation to self-determination and independence, as well as respect for national sovereignty and territorial integrity, will promote social progress and development and as a consequence will contribute to the attainment of full equality between men and women,

Convinced that the full and complete development of a country, the welfare of the world and the cause of peace require the maximum participation of women on equal terms with men in all fields,

Bearing in mind the great contribution of women to the welfare of the family and to the development of society, so far not fully recognized, the social significance of maternity and the role of both parents in the family and in the upbringing of children, and aware that the role of women in procreation should not be a basis for discrimination but that the upbringing of children requires a sharing of responsibility between men and women and society as a whole,

Aware that a change in the traditional role of men as well as the role of women in society and in the family is needed to achieve full equality between men and women,

Determined to implement the principles set forth in the Declaration on the Elimination of Discrimination against Women and, for that purpose, to adopt the measures required for the elimination of such discrimination in all its forms and manifestations,

Have agreed on the following:

PART I
Article 1

For the purposes of the present Convention, the term "discrimination against women" shall mean any distinction, exclusion or restriction made on the basis of sex which has the effect or purpose of impairing or nullifying the recognition, enjoyment or exercise by women, irrespective of their marital status, on a basis of equality of men and women, of human rights and fundamental freedoms in the political, economic, social, cultural, civil or any other field.

Article 2

States Parties condemn discrimination against women in all its forms, agree to pursue by all appropriate means and without delay a policy of eliminating discrimination against women and, to this end, undertake:

(a) To embody the principle of the equality of men and women in their national constitutions or other appropriate legislation if not yet incorporated therein and to ensure, through law and other appropriate means, the practical realization of this principle;

(b) To adopt appropriate legislative and other measures, including sanctions where appropriate, prohibiting all discrimination against women;

(c) To establish legal protection of the rights of women on an equal basis with men and to ensure through competent national tribunals and other public institutions the effective protection of women against any act of discrimination;

(d) To refrain from engaging in any act or practice of discrimination against women and to ensure that public authorities and institutions shall act in conformity with this obligation;

(e) To take all appropriate measures to eliminate discrimination against women by any person, organization or enterprise;

(f) To take all appropriate measures, including legislation, to modify or abolish existing laws, regulations, customs and practices which constitute discrimination against women;

(g) To repeal all national penal provisions which constitute discrimination against women.

Article 3

States Parties shall take in all fields, in particular in the political, social, economic and cultural fields, all appropriate measures, including legislation, to ensure the full development and advancement of women, for the purpose of guaranteeing them the exercise and enjoyment of human rights and fundamental freedoms on a basis of equality with men.

Article 4

1. Adoption by States Parties of temporary special measures aimed at accelerating de facto equality between men and women shall not be considered discrimination as defined in the present Convention, but shall in no way entail as a consequence the maintenance of unequal or separate standards; these measures shall be discontinued when the objectives of equality of opportunity and treatment have been achieved.

2. Adoption by States Parties of special measures, including those measures contained in the present Convention, aimed at protecting maternity shall not be considered discriminatory.

Article 5

States Parties shall take all appropriate measures:

(a) To modify the social and cultural patterns of conduct of men and women, with a view to achieving the elimination of prejudices and customary and all other practices which are based on the idea of the inferiority or the superiority of either of the sexes or on stereotyped roles for men and women;

(b) To ensure that family education includes a proper understanding of maternity as a social function and the recognition of the common responsibility of men and women in the upbringing and development of their children, it being understood that the interest of the children is the primordial consideration in all cases.

Article 6

States Parties shall take all appropriate measures, including legislation, to suppress all forms of traffic in women and exploitation of prostitution of women.

PART II
Article 7

States Parties shall take all appropriate measures to eliminate discrimination against women in the political and public life of the country and, in particular, shall ensure to women, on equal terms with men, the right:

(a) To vote in all elections and public referenda and to be eligible for election to all publicly elected bodies;

(b) To participate in the formulation of government policy and the implementation thereof and to hold public office and perform all public functions at all levels of government;

(c) To participate in non-governmental organizations and associations concerned with the public and political life of the country.

Article 8

States Parties shall take all appropriate measures to ensure to women, on equal terms with men and without any discrimination, the opportunity to represent their Governments at the international level and to participate in the work of international organizations.

Article 9

1. States Parties shall grant women equal rights with men to acquire, change or retain their nationality. They shall ensure in particular that neither marriage to an alien nor change of nationality by the husband during marriage shall automatically change the nationality of the wife, render her stateless or force upon her the nationality of the husband. 2. States Parties shall grant women equal rights with men with respect to the nationality of their children.

PART III
Article 10

States Parties shall take all appropriate measures to eliminate discrimination against women in order to ensure to them equal rights with men in the field of education and in particular to ensure, on a basis of equality of men and women:

(a) The same conditions for career and vocational guidance, for access to studies and for the achievement of diplomas in educational establishments of all categories in rural as well as in urban areas; this equality shall be ensured in pre-school, general, technical, professional and higher technical education, as well as in all types of vocational training;

(b) Access to the same curricula, the same examinations, teaching staff with qualifications of the same standard and school premises and equipment of the same quality;

(c) The elimination of any stereotyped concept of the roles of men and women at all levels and in all forms of education by encouraging coeducation and other types of education which will help to achieve this aim and, in particular, by the revision of textbooks and school programmes and the adaptation of teaching methods;

(d) The same opportunities to benefit from scholarships and other study grants;

(e) The same opportunities for access to programmes of continuing education, including adult and functional literacy programmes, particulary those aimed at reducing, at the earliest possible time, any gap in education existing between men and women;

(f) The reduction of female student drop-out rates and the organization of programmes for girls and women who have left school prematurely;

(g) The same opportunities to participate actively in sports and physical education;

(h) Access to specific educational information to help to ensure the health and well-being of families, including information and advice on family planning.

Article 11

1. States Parties shall take all appropriate measures to eliminate discrimination against women in the field of employment in order to ensure, on a basis of equality of men and women, the same rights, in particular:

(a) The right to work as an inalienable right of all human beings;

(b) The right to the same employment opportunities, including the application of the same criteria for selection in matters of employment;

(c) The right to free choice of profession and employment, the right to promotion, job security and all benefits and conditions of service and the right to receive vocational training and retraining, including apprenticeships, advanced vocational training and recurrent training;

(d) The right to equal remuneration, including benefits, and to equal treatment in respect of work of equal value, as well as equality of treatment in the evaluation of the quality of work;

(e) The right to social security, particularly in cases of retirement, unemployment, sickness, invalidity and old age and other incapacity to work, as well as the right to paid leave;

(f) The right to protection of health and to safety in working conditions, including the safeguarding of the function of reproduction.

2. In order to prevent discrimination against women on the grounds of marriage or maternity and to ensure their effective right to work, States Parties shall take appropriate measures:

(a) To prohibit, subject to the imposition of sanctions, dismissal on the grounds of pregnancy or of maternity leave and discrimination in dismissals on the basis of marital status;

(b) To introduce maternity leave with pay or with comparable social benefits without loss of former employment, seniority or social allowances;

(c) To encourage the provision of the necessary supporting social services to enable parents to combine family obligations with work responsibilities and participation in public life, in particular through promoting the establishment and development of a network of child-care facilities;

(d) To provide special protection to women during pregnancy in types of work proved to be harmful to them.

3. Protective legislation relating to matters covered in this article shall be reviewed periodically in the light of scientific and technological knowledge and shall be revised, repealed or extended as necessary.

Article 12

1. States Parties shall take all appropriate measures to eliminate discrimination against women in the field of health care in order to ensure, on a basis of equality of men and women, access to health care services, including those related to family planning.

2. Notwithstanding the provisions of paragraph I of this article, States Parties shall ensure to women appropriate services in connection with pregnancy, confinement and the post-natal period, granting free services where necessary, as well as adequate nutrition during pregnancy and lactation.

Article 13

States Parties shall take all appropriate measures to eliminate discrimination against women in other areas of economic and social life in order to ensure, on a basis of equality of men and women, the same rights, in particular:

(a) The right to family benefits;

(b) The right to bank loans, mortgages and other forms of financial credit;

(c) The right to participate in recreational activities, sports and all aspects of cultural life.

Article 14

1. States Parties shall take into account the particular problems faced by rural women and the significant roles which rural women play in the economic survival of their families, including their work in the non-monetized sectors of the economy, and shall take all appropriate measures to ensure the application of the provisions of the present Convention to women in rural areas.

2. States Parties shall take all appropriate measures to eliminate discrimination against women in rural areas in order to ensure, on a basis of equality of men and women, that they participate in and benefit from rural development and, in particular, shall ensure to such women the right:

(a) To participate in the elaboration and implementation of development planning at all levels;

(b) To have access to adequate health care facilities, including information, counselling and services in family planning;

(c) To benefit directly from social security programmes;

(d) To obtain all types of training and education, formal and non-formal, including that relating to functional literacy, as well as, *inter alia,* the benefit of all community and extension services, in order to increase their technical proficiency;

(e) To organize self-help groups and co-operatives in order to obtain equal access to economic opportunities through employment or self employment;

(f) To participate in all community activities;

(g) To have access to agricultural credit and loans, marketing facilities, appropriate technology and equal treatment in land and agrarian reform as well as in land resettlement schemes;

(h) To enjoy adequate living conditions, particularly in relation to housing, sanitation, electricity and water supply, transport and communications.

PART IV

Article 15

1. States Parties shall accord to women equality with men before the law.

2. States Parties shall accord to women, in civil matters, a legal capacity identical to that of men and the same opportunities to exercise that capacity. In particular, they shall give women equal rights to conclude contracts and to administer property and shall treat them equally in all stages of procedure in courts and tribunals.

3. States Parties agree that all contracts and all other private instruments of any kind with a legal effect which is directed at restricting the legal capacity of women shall be deemed null and void.

4. States Parties shall accord to men and women the same rights with regard to the law relating to the movement of persons and the freedom to choose their residence and domicile.

Article 16

1. States Parties shall take all appropriate measures to eliminate discrimination against women in all matters relating to marriage and family relations and in particular shall ensure, on a basis of equality of men and women:

(a) The same right to enter into marriage;

(b) The same right freely to choose a spouse and to enter into marriage only with their free and full consent;

(c) The same rights and responsibilities during marriage and at its dissolution;

(d) The same rights and responsibilities as parents, irrespective of their marital status, in matters relating to their children; in all cases the interests of the children shall be paramount;

(e) The same rights to decide freely and responsibly on the number and spacing of their children and to have access to the information, education and means to enable them to exercise these rights;

(f) The same rights and responsibilities with regard to guardianship, wardship, trusteeship and adoption of children, or similar institutions where these concepts exist in national legislation; in all cases the interests of the children shall be paramount;

(g) The same personal rights as husband and wife, including the right to choose a family name, a profession and an occupation;

(h) The same rights for both spouses in respect of the ownership, acquisition, management, administration, enjoyment and disposition of property, whether free of charge or for a valuable consideration.

2. The betrothal and the marriage of a child shall have no legal effect, and all necessary action, including legislation, shall be taken to specify a minimum age for marriage and to make the registration of marriages in an official registry compulsory.

PART V

Article 17

1. For the purpose of considering the progress made in the implementation of the present Convention, there shall be established a Committee on the Elimination of Discrimination against Women (hereinafter referred to as the Committee) consisting, at the time of entry into force of the Convention, of eighteen and, after ratification of or accession to the Convention by the thirty-fifth State Party, of twenty-three experts of high moral standing and competence in the field covered by the Convention. The experts shall be elected by States Parties from among their nationals and shall serve in their personal capacity, consideration being given to equitable geographical distribution and to the representation of the different forms of civilization as well as the principal legal systems.

2. The members of the Committee shall be elected by secret ballot from a list of persons nominated by States Parties. Each State Party may nominate one person from among its own nationals.

3. The initial election shall be held six months after the date of the entry into force of the present Convention. At least three months before the date of each election the Secretary-General of the United Nations shall address a letter to the States Parties inviting them to submit their nominations within two months. The Secretary-General shall prepare a list in alphabetical order of all persons thus nominated, indicating the States Parties which have nominated them, and shall submit it to the States Parties.

4. Elections of the members of the Committee shall be held at a meeting of States Parties convened by the Secretary-General at United Nations

Headquarters. At that meeting, for which two thirds of the States Parties shall constitute a quorum, the persons elected to the Committee shall be those nominees who obtain the largest number of votes and an absolute majority of the votes of the representatives of States Parties present and voting.

5. The members of the Committee shall be elected for a term of four years. However, the terms of nine of the members elected at the first election shall expire at the end of two years; immediately after the first election the names of these nine members shall be chosen by lot by the Chairman of the Committee.

6. The election of the five additional members of the Committee shall be held in accordance with the provisions of paragraphs 2, 3 and 4 of this article, following the thirty-fifth ratification or accession. The terms of two of the additional members elected on this occasion shall expire at the end of two years, the names of these two members having been chosen by lot by the Chairman of the Committee.

7. For the filling of casual vacancies, the State Party whose expert has ceased to function as a member of the Committee shall appoint another expert from among its nationals, subject to the approval of the Committee.

8. The members of the Committee shall, with the approval of the General Assembly, receive emoluments from United Nations resources on such terms and conditions as the Assembly may decide, having regard to the importance of the Committee's responsibilities.

9. The Secretary-General of the United Nations shall provide the necessary staff and facilities for the effective performance of the functions of the Committee under the present Convention.

Article 18

1. States Parties undertake to submit to the Secretary-General of the United Nations, for consideration by the Committee, a report on the legislative, judicial, administrative or other measures which they have adopted to give effect to the provisions of the present Convention and on the progress made in this respect:

(a) Within one year after the entry into force for the State concerned;

(b) Thereafter at least every four years and further whenever the Committee so requests.

2. Reports may indicate factors and difficulties affecting the degree of fulfilment of obligations under the present Convention.

Article 19

1. The Committee shall adopt its own rules of procedure. 2. The Committee shall elect its officers for a term of two years.

Article 20

1. The Committee shall normally meet for a period of not more than two weeks annually in order to consider the reports submitted in accordance with article 18 of the present Convention.

2. The meetings of the Committee shall normally be held at United Nations Headquarters or at any other convenient place as determined by the Committee.

Article 21

1. The Committee shall, through the Economic and Social Council, report annually to the General Assembly of the United Nations on its activities and may make suggestions and general recommendations based on the examination of reports and information received from the States Parties. Such suggestions and general recommendations shall be included in the report of the Committee together with comments, if any, from States Parties.

2. The Secretary-General of the United Nations shall transmit the reports of the Committee to the Commission on the Status of Women for its information.

Article 22

The specialized agencies shall be entitled to be represented at the consideration of the implementation of such provisions of the present Convention as fall within the scope of their activities. The Committee may invite the specialized agencies to submit reports on the implementation of the Convention in areas falling within the scope of their activities.

PART VI
Article 23

Nothing in the present Convention shall affect any provisions that are more conducive to the achievement of equality between men and women which may be contained:

(a) In the legislation of a State Party; or

(b) In any other International convention, treaty or agreement in force for that State.

Article 24

States Parties undertake to adopt all necessary measures at the national level aimed at achieving the full realization of the rights recognized in the present Convention.

Article 25

1. The present Convention shall be open for signature by all States.

2. The Secretary-General of the United Nations is designated as the depositary of the present Convention.

3. The present Convention is subject to ratification. Instruments of ratification shall be deposited with the Secretary-General of the United Nations.

4. The present Convention shall be open to accession by all States. Accession shall be effected by the deposit of an instrument of accession with the Secretary-General of the United Nations.

Article 26

1. A request for the revision of the present Convention may be made at any time by any State Party by means of a notification in writing addressed to the Secretary-General of the United Nations.

2. The General Assembly of the United Nations shall decide upon the steps, if any, to be taken in respect of such a request.

Article 27

1. The present Convention shall enter into force on the thirtieth day after the date of deposit with the Secretary-General of the United Nations of the twentieth instrument of ratification or accession.

2. For each State ratifying the present Convention or acceding to it after the deposit of the twentieth instrument of ratification or accession, the Convention shall enter into force on the thirtieth day after the date of the deposit of its own instrument of ratification or accession.

Article 28

1. The Secretary-General of the United Nations shall receive and circulate to all States the text of reservations made by States at the time of ratification or accession.

2. A reservation incompatible with the object and purpose of the present Convention shall not be permitted.

3. Reservations may be withdrawn at any time by notification to this effect addressed to the Secretary-General of the United Nations, who shall then inform all States thereof. Such notification shall take effect on the date on which it is received.

Article 29

1. Any dispute between two or more States Parties concerning the interpretation or application of the present Convention which is not settled by negotiation shall, at the request of one of them, be submitted to arbitration. If within six months from the date of the request for arbitration the parties are unable to agree on the organization of the arbitration, any one of those parties may refer the dispute to the International Court of Justice by request in conformity with the Statute of the Court.

2. Each State Party may at the time of signature or ratification of the present Convention or accession thereto declare that it does not consider itself bound by paragraph I of this article. The other States Parties shall not be bound by that paragraph with respect to any State Party which has made such a reservation.

3. Any State Party which has made a reservation in accordance with paragraph 2 of this article may at any time withdraw that reservation by notification to the Secretary-General of the United Nations.

Article 30

The present Convention, the Arabic, Chinese, English, French, Russian and Spanish texts of which are equally authentic, shall be deposited with the Secretary-General of the United Nations. IN WITNESS WHEREOF the undersigned, duly authorized, have signed the present Convention.

Contributors

Janet Afary is an associate professor of history and women's studies at Purdue University.

Clair Apodaca is an assistant professor in the Department of International Relations at Florida International University.

Gayle Binion is a professor of political science at the University of California, Santa Barbara, where she has been on the faculty since 1976.

Eva Brems is a professor of human rights law at the University of Ghent in Belgium.

Charlotte Bunch is the founder and executive director of the Center for Women's Global Leadership at Douglass College, Rutgers University.

R. Charli Carpenter is an assistant professor of international affairs at the University of Pittsburgh Graduate School of Public and International Affairs.

Hilary Charlesworth is a professor in the Regulatory Institutions Network (RegNet) and director of the Centre for International Governance and Justice at the Australian National University. She also holds an appointment as professor of international law and human rights in the Faculty of Law, ANU.

Christine Chinkin is a professor of international law at the London School of Economics and Political Science, University of London.

Rebecca J. Cook is a professor and faculty chair in international human rights and co-director of the International Programme on Reproductive and Sexual Health Law in the Faculty of Law at the University of Toronto.

Bernard M. Dickens is the Dr. William M. Scholl Professor of Health Law and Policy at the Faculty of Law and is cross-appointed to the Faculty of Medicine and Joint Centre for Bioethics at the University of Toronto.

Ustinia Dolgopol is a senior lecturer in law at The Flinders University of South Australia.

Uche U. Ewelukwa is an associate professor of law at the University of Arkansas School of Law and teaches in the areas of international law and intellectual property. She is a native of Nigeria.

Arvonne S. Fraser is a senior fellow emerita of the Humphrey Institute of Public Affairs, University of Minnesota and the former director of the International Women's Rights Action Watch (IWRAW) project.

Dina Francesca Haynes is a visiting associate professor of law at the University of Nevada at Las Vegas. Prior to joining the faculty at UNLV, she was a visitor/practitioner-in-residence in the International Human Rights Law Clinic at American University's Washington College of Law, where she also designed and taught an advanced seminar on post-conflict nation building.

Sally Engle Merry is the Marion Butler McLean Professor in the History of Ideas and a professor of anthropology at Wellesley College, where she is also co-director of the Peace and Justice Studies Program.

Siobhán Mullally lectures in human rights law at the Law Faculty, University College, Cork, Ireland.

Catherine N. Niarchos is a lawyer with the United Nations Agency for Development.

Bharati Sadasivam is program coordinator for women's rights at the Women's Environment and Development Organization in New York. She has written extensively on development, women's health, and rights issues as a journalist with *The Times of India* and other newspapers in Bombay, India.

Todd A. Salzman is an associate professor of theology at Creighton University.

Carmel Shalev is the director of the Unit for Health Rights and Ethics at the Gertner Institute for Epidemiology and Health Policy Research at the Sheba Medical Center, Israel. She is an expert member of CEDAW.

Kamala Visweswaran is an associate professor of anthropology at the University of Texas.